ISBN 978-0-265-15110-5
PIBN 10925152

# 1 MONTH OF
# FREE
# READING

## at

## www.ForgottenBooks.com

By purchasing this book you are eligible for one month membership to ForgottenBooks.com, giving you unlimited access to our entire collection of over 1,000,000 titles via our web site and mobile apps.

To claim your free month visit:

www.forgottenbooks.com/free925152

English
Français
Deutsche
Italiano
Español
Português

# www.forgottenbooks.com

**Mythology** Photography **Fiction**
Fishing Christianity **Art** Cooking
Essays Buddhism Freemasonry
Medicine **Biology** Music **Ancient
Egypt** Evolution Carpentry Physics
Dance Geology **Mathematics** Fitness
Shakespeare **Folklore** Yoga Marketing
**Confidence** Immortality Biographies
Poetry **Psychology** Witchcraft
Electronics Chemistry History **Law**
Accounting **Philosophy** Anthropology
Alchemy Drama Quantum Mechanics
Atheism Sexual Health **Ancient History**
**Entrepreneurship** Languages Sport
Paleontology Needlework Islam
**Metaphysics** Investment Archaeology
Parenting Statistics Criminology
**Motivational**

# REPORTS

OF

## CASES DECIDED

IN THE

# APPELLATE COURT

OF THE

## STATE OF INDIANA

WITH TABLES OF CASES REPORTED AND CITED, TEXT-
BOOKS CITED, STATUTES CITED AND CONSTRUED, AN
INDEX, AND NOTES TO THE REPORTED CASES

---

## WILL H. ADAMS,

OFFICIAL REPORTER

WILBUR G. CARPENTER,
CONNOR D. ROSS,
LUCY H. WILHELM,
ASSISTANTS

---

## VOL. 63

---

INDIANAPOLIS:
WM. B. BURFORD, PRINTER TO THE STATE
1918

# CASES REPORTED

# CASES REPORTED.

# CASES CITED

# STATUTES CITED AND CONSTRUED

# TEXT-BOOKS CITED

# JUDGES

# APPELLATE COURT

OF THE

## STATE OF INDIANA

WHOSE OPINIONS ARE CONTAINED IN THIS VOLUME

---

HON. FRED S. CALDWELL.*‡‡
HON. MILTON B. HOTTEL.§†¶
HON. EDWARD W. FELT.‡¶
HON. JAMES J. MORAN.**
HON. JOSEPH H. SHEA.††
HON. JOHN C. McNUTT.§§
HON. JOSEPH G. IBACH.¶
HON. IRA C. BATMAN.¶¶
HON. ETHAN A. DAUSMAN.¶¶

*Chief Judge, May Term, 1916.
§ Chief Judge, November Term, 1916.
† Presiding Judge, May Term, 1916.
‡ Presiding Judge, November Term, 1916.
** Appointed February 10, 1915.
†† Elected in 1912.
‡‡ Appointed September 1, 1913, and elected in 1914.
§§ Appointed April 28, 1916.
¶ Elected in 1910, and reëlected in 1914.
¶¶ Elected in 1916.

# OFFICERS

OF THE

# APPELLATE COURT

ATTORNEY-GENERAL,

## ELE STANSBURY

REPORTER,

## WILL H. ADAMS

CLERK,

## J. FRED FRANCE

SHERIFF,

## HARRY W. PEMBERTON

LIBRARIAN,

## RICHARD W. ERWIN

# In Memoriam

## JAMES B. BLACK

*To the Chief Judge and Members of the Appellate Court of Indiana:*

Your committee submits the following memorial of Judge James B. Black, formerly a member of this court:

James B. Black, who died in Indianapolis on Monday, December 11, 1916, was born at Morristown, New Jersey, July 21, 1838, and at an early age came with his parents to Wabash, Indiana, where his father was a minister of the Methodist Episcopal Church. He taught school when a young man to earn money with which to procure a college education, and then attended what is now DePauw University for three years; afterwards he attended Indiana University until the beginning of the Civil War, in which he enlisted as a private in 1861 and served for three years and eight months, being advanced in rank from time to time until he became a lieutenant-colonel. He also served as Judge Advocate in a number of courts-martial.

Colonel Black moved to Indianapolis in 1865 and became a law student in General Harrison's office and also attended law school. He was admitted to the bar in 1866 and formed a partnership with the late Judge Byron K. Elliott, which partnership continued until he was elected Reporter of the Supreme Court in 1868, succeeding General Harrison. He was re-elected in 1872. After retiring from office he resumed the practice of law in Indianapolis; and in 1879 he became a member of the faculty of the Central Law School. In 1882 he was appointed a member of the Supreme Court Commission where he served for three years. He was the author of Black's Indiana Digest of the Supreme Court

## JAMES B. BLACK.

decisions, which was published in 1889. During the years 1890 and 1891 he was a member of the Board of School Commissioners of Indianapolis, which position he resigned to accept an appointment as Judge of the Appellate Court. He was selected by his associates as the first Chief Judge of this court. He was several times re-elected and served as a member of this court from the time of its establishment in 1891 to January 1, 1907.

In 1875 Indiana University conferred upon Judge Black the degree of Master of Arts. He was a Mason and a member of Beta Theta Pi college fraternity and of the G. A. R. and of many social organizations. Judge Black was married in 1873 to Amelia Keith Prudden, who died in 1910.

Modesty, congeniality, kindliness and consideration for others brought to Judge Black many personal friends by whom he was greatly loved.

As a member of the Supreme Court Commission, and of this court, Judge Black made a record second to no one of his associates. He was always fair and considerate of the opinions of other members of the court, and above all, was as nearly free from bias and predjudice as it is possible for man to be; so it may, and should, be truly said of him, "Well done, good and faithful servant!"

JOHN C. McNUTT,
J. G. IBACH,
FREDERICK S. CALDWELL,
Committee.

This memorial, having been reported to the full court, is approved and adopted as the memorial of the court; and it is ordered that it be spread upon the records of the court and a copy thereof sent to the family of the deceased.

# DANIEL WEBSTER COMSTOCK

*To the Chief Judge and Members of the Appellate Court of Indiana:*

Your Committee reports the following memoriam:

Daniel Webster Comstock was born at Germantown, Ohio, December 16, 1840, and died in Washington, D. C., May 19, 1917. He was graduated from Ohio Wesleyan University when twenty years of age, receiving the degrees of A. B. and A. M. In 1861 he located at Newcastle, Indiana, and was there admitted to the bar. In 1862 he was elected district attorney for the Eleventh Common Pleas district, but shortly thereafter resigned to join the Union Army, and he served with distinction in different capacities throughout the Civil War. In 1867 he married Miss Josephine Rohrer, who with their three children survives him. In 1913 he was elected Department Commander of the G. A. R. of Indiana. At the close of the war he took up his residence at Richmond, Indiana, where he again engaged in the practice of his profession. He was city attorney for Richmond in 1866, was prosecuting attorney for Wayne county from 1872 to 1876; and he represented that county in the State Senate in 1878. He was judge of the Seventeenth Judicial Circuit for two terms, and in 1896 became a member of this court where for many years he proved himself to be both diligent and painstaking, having in mind in the performance of his judicial duties the single purpose of being just.

In 1911 Judge Comstock returned to Richmond and engaged in the practice of law until in 1916, when he was again honored by being elected to Congress from the Sixth Indiana District.

These honors and preferments, covering a long period of years, are unmistakable indications of the estimate which

## DANIEL WEBSTER COMSTOCK.

those who knew him best placed upon his character and ability as a man and a citizen. He was one of those amiable, kind-hearted men whom it is always a pleasure to meet—a true friend one never forgets and a faithful public servant, who always endeavored to do his duty faithfully and well.

JOSEPH G. IBACH,
IRA C. BATMAN,
E. A. DAUSMAN,
Committee.

This memorial, having been reported to the full court, is approved and adopted as the memorial of the court; and it is ordered that it be spread upon the records of the court and a copy thereof sent to the family of the deceased.

MILTON B. HOTTEL, C. J.

# CASES DECIDED

IN THE

# APPELLATE COURT

OF THE

## STATE OF INDIANA,

AT INDIANAPOLIS, MAY TERM, 1916, AND NOVEMBER TERM,
1916, IN THE ONE HUNDREDTH AND ONE HUNDRED
AND FIRST YEARS OF THE STATE.

---

## AMERICAN CAR FOUNDRY COMPANY *v.* WILLIAMS.

[No. 9,172. Filed June 21, 1916. Rehearing denied October 6,
1916.]

1. APPEAL.—*Waiver of Error.—Briefs.—Failure to Set Out Proposition in Points and Authorities.*—Alleged error is waived on appeal by failure to set out the proposition in appellant's brief under the points and authorities. p. 4.

2. MASTER AND SERVANT.—*Employers' Liability Act.—Constitutionality.*—The Employers' Liability Act of 1911 (Acts 1911 p. 145, §8020a *et seq.* Burns 1914) is constitutional. p. 4.

3. MASTER AND SERVANT.—*Injuries to Servant.—Action under Statute.—Complaint.—Sufficiency.*—Where the complaint in an employe's action for personal injury alleged facts to show that the defendant was a corporation employing more than five men; that at the time of the injury plaintiff was acting in the line of his employment and was, in obedience to his foreman's order, to which order he was bound to conform, about to remove certain timbers from a building to another part of defendant's yard, when he was struck by a timber which was pushed out of a window by other of defendant's employes across an alley through which plaintiff was required to pass in carrying out the foreman's order, and that at the time such order was given the foreman knew that timbers were being frequently shoved across the alley, so that it was dangerous to pass through the same, such complaint states a cause of action within the provisions of the Employers' Liability Act of 1911 (Acts 1911 p. 145, §8020 *et seq.* Burns 1914). p. 4.

American Car, etc., Co. *v.* Williams—63 Ind. App. 1.

4. APPEAL. — *Review.* — *Errors Assignable on Review.* — *When Waived.*—*Statute.*—Under §344 Burns 1914, Acts 1911 p. 415, providing that where a demurrer to a complaint is filed for want of facts, a memorandum shall be filed therewith stating wherein such pleading is insufficient and that defects not questioned in such memorandum shall be deemed waived, and under §348 Burns 1914, Acts 1911 p. 415, providing that when objection is not taken by answer or demurrer to any of the matters enumerated as grounds for demurrer, except joinder of causes, which do not appear on the face of the complaint, such objection shall be deemed waived, an assignment of error that "the complaint * * * does not state facts sufficient to constitute a cause of action against appellant" presents no question for review on appeal. p. 5.

5. MASTER AND SERVANT.—*Injuries to Servant.*—*Verdict.*—*Answers to Interrogatories.*—In an employe's action for personal injuries under a complaint stating a cause of action within the provisions of the Employers' Liability Act of 1911 (Acts 1911 p. 145, §8020a *et seq.* Burns 1914) answers to interrogatories supporting the averments of the complaint are not in irreconcilable conflict with a general verdict for plaintiff, even though such answers tend to establish plaintiff's assumption of risk and contributory negligence while obeying his superior's command, since the Employers' Liability Act eliminates the defenses of contributory negligence where the injury complained of resulted from the employe's obedience to his superior's command, and that the inherent dangers of the employment contributed to the injury. p. 5.

6. MASTER AND SERVANT.—*Employers' Liability Act.*—*Contributory Negligence of Servant.*—*Compliance with Command.*—In an employe's action for personal injuries, the foreman's order to plaintiff to carry timbers from defendant's building to the yard, obedience to such order necessitating plaintiff's passing through an alley where he was injured, was a sufficiently specific direction to bring the case within the purview of the Employers' Liability Act of 1911 (Acts 1911 p. 145, §8020 *et seq.* Burns 1914), abolishing the defense of contributory negligence where the injury complained of results from the employe's obedience to the command of a superior. p. 6.

From Marion Superior Court (91,916); *Charles J. Orbison,* Judge.

Action by Thomas H. Williams against the American Car Foundry Company. From a judgment for plaintiff, the defendant appeals. *Affirmed.*

*W. H. H. Miller, C. C. Shirley, S. D. Miller* and *W. H. Thompson*, for appellant.

*Wymond J. Beckett* and *William F. Elliott*, for appellee.

FELT, J.—Appellee recovered a judgment for $2,000 against appellant for injuries alleged to have been received by him while in its employ.

The complaint shows that appellant is a corporation and, at the time of appellee's injury, was engaged in the business of repairing cars, in which business it employed more than five men; that appellee was employed as a laborer in and about its plant to move material from one place to another as he was directed by the foreman, to whose orders he was bound to conform; that on the day in question appellant's foreman ordered him to move certain timbers from a building to another part of appellant's yard, and in order to reach such building appellee walked through an alley between two of appellant's buildings; that such was the usual, customary and only way to reach said building, which facts appellant's foreman well knew; that on one side of such alley and near thereto appellant maintained a machine for shaping and sawing material for use in said plant; that its servants, when using the machine, would run boards with great force endwise out of a window into and across the alley, which fact made it dangerous for any one to pass the machine while in operation; that the machine was in operation when the foreman ordered appellee to move the lumber and to pass said machine, which fact was known to the foreman; that the foreman also knew at the time that other servants were shoving boards with great force endwise through said window and across the alley, and that it would be dangerous to any one to walk through the alley, but he negligently failed to notify appellee that said machine was in operation and that appellant's servants were in the course of their work, at frequent intervals, shoving boards endwise out of said window; that appellee obeyed said order to pass through said alley and, while passing the window above described, was struck by one of the boards so thrown out of it and was injured.

Appellant demurred to the complaint, and the demurrer was overruled. The complaint was answered by a general denial, and the case was tried by a jury. With their general verdict, the jury returned answers to interrogatories. Appellant moved for judgment on such answers and for a new trial, and each of said motions was overruled.

The errors assigned and relied on for reversal are: The overruling of the demurrer to the second paragraph of complaint; that "the second paragraph of complaint  *  *  * does not state facts sufficient to constitute a cause of action against appellant"; error in overruling appellant's motion for judgment on the answers to interrogatories and in overruling appellant's motion for a new trial.

Appellant's objections to the sufficiency of the complaint, as stated in the memorandum accompanying the demurrer, are that the Employers' Liability Act of 1911 (Acts 1911 p. 145, §8020a *et seq.* Burns 1914) is unconstitutional, and that, such being the case, the complaint is bad for certain alleged reasons. This case was appealed to the Supreme Court, and was by that court transferred to this court for

1. want of jurisdiction. Furthermore, the question of the constitutionality of the act is waived by failure to mention the same under points and authorities in the briefs. However, the act has been held constitutional by our Supreme Court. *Vandalia R. Co.*

2. v. *Stillwell* (1913), 181 Ind. 267, 104 N. E. 289; *Nordyke-Marmon Co.* v. *Hilborg* (1916), 62 Ind. App. 196, 110 N. E. 684.

The complaint is drawn under the provisions of the Employers' Liability Act, *supra.* Under this act as construed

3. by numerous decisions, the complaint is not bad for any of the alleged reasons, and is sufficient to state a cause of action. *Vandalia R. Co.* v. *Stillwell, supra; Nordyke-Marmon Co.* v. *Hilborg, supra; Chicago,*

*etc., R. Co.* v. *Mitchell* (1915), 184 Ind. 588, 110 N. E. 680;
*Chicago, etc., R. Co.* v. *Mitchell* (1915), 184 Ind. 383, 110
N. E. 215; *Vandalia Coal Co.* v. *Alsopp* (1915), 61 Ind.
App. 649, 109 N. E. 421; *Kokomo Brass Works* v. *Doran*
(1915), 59 Ind. App. 583, 105 N. E. 167.

4.  The second assignment of error presents no question.
§§344, 348 Burns 1908; Acts 1911 p. 415. *Indiana
Life Endow. Co.* v. *Carnithan* (1915), 62 Ind. App. 567,
109 N. E. 851.

Under the third assignment of error, it is claimed that the
answers to the interrogatories show conclusively that appellant was guilty of no negligence, and that appellee
5.  was guilty of negligence which proximately contributed to his injury; that for these reasons the
answers are in irreconcilable conflict with the general verdict, and the court erred in overruling appellant's motion
for judgment on such answers.

The answers support the averments of the complaint.
They do not overcome or contradict the facts that appellee
was in the employment of appellant and that he was injured
while obeying an order of the foreman, to whose orders he
was bound to conform; that he was at the time acting in the
line of his employment and in obedience to an order to take
certain timbers from a building to another part of appellant's yard, when he was struck by a timber which was
pushed out of a window and across an alley by other employes of appellant, through which alley he was required
to pass in carrying out said order of the foreman.

The act of 1911, *supra*, provides that, in actions of this
kind brought against an employer of five or more persons,
"it shall not be a defense that the dangers or hazards inherent or apparent in the employment in which such injured
employe was engaged, contributed to such injury." The
statute also eliminates the defense of contributory negligence
"where the injury complained of resulted from such employe's obedience or conformity to any order or direction

of the employer or of any employe to whose orders or directions he was under obligation to conform or obey.'' *Vandalia R. Co.* v. *Stillwell, supra; Vandalia Coal Co.* v. *Alsopp, supra.* The order of the foreman was sufficiently spe-

6. cific to bring the case within the purview of the statute. *Vivian Collieries Co.* v. *Cahall* (1915), 184 Ind. 473, 110 N. E. 672, 678.

The court, therefore, did not err in overruling the motion for judgment on the answers of the jury to the interrogatories.' The instructions given were as favorable to appellant as the law of the case will warrant. Those refused, in so far as they state the law correctly, were covered by those given.

In the light of the statute under which the action was brought, the verdict of the jury is sustained by the evidence, and is not contrary to law. We find no reversible error. Judgment affirmed.

NOTE.—Reported in 113 N. E. 252. Workmen's compensation acts, constitutionality, Ann. Cas. 1912B 174; Ann. Cas. 1915A 247, 1916B 1286.

---

## THE BROWNSTOWN WATER AND LIGHT COMPANY ET AL. *v.* HEWITT.

### [No. 9,498.   Filed October 10, 1916.]

APPEAL.— *Transcript.— Supplemental.— Certiorari.*— Where appellants, after the filing of the original transcript, procured a *nunc pro tunc* entry correcting the finding and the judgment rendered by the trial court, and a record of all proceedings concerning such action was embodied in a document which was certified to by the clerk of the court and filed in the Appellate Court under the title of "additional transcript," such document is no part of the record and will be stricken from the files, since it was the duty of appellants to bring the *nunc pro tunc* entry, and the proceedings related thereto, before the appellate tribunal by means of a writ of *certiorari.*

From Marion Superior Court (96,936) ; *John J. Rochford,* Judge.

Action by Allen W. Hewitt against The Brownstown
Water and Light Company. Judgment for plaintiff, and
defendants appeal. Subsequent to the filing of the original
transcript appellant filed an additional transcript, and appellee moved that it be stricken from the files of the court.
*Motion sustained.*

*James M. Winters,* for appellants.
*Pliny W. Bartholomew,* for appellee.

MORAN, J.—The question presented for consideration at
this time arises upon appellee's motion to strike from the
files of this court what is designated in the record as an
"additional transcript," and which will hereafter be referred to as such. On January 4, 1916, a transcript and
an assignment of error were filed in this court and the
record shows the filing of the additional transcript on June
7, 1916.

The judgment appealed from was rendered on June 16,
1915, and on January 3, 1916, pursuant to notice, appellant filed a motion in the lower court to redocket the cause
for the purpose, as is stated in the motion, of correcting the
finding and judgment, so that the same would be a correct
entry, and for a transcript on appeal; and thereafter the
motion was granted and the correction made in the order
book as prayed. All the steps taken in reference to the
filing of the motion, the giving of the notice of its hearing,
and the action taken on the part of the court in reference
thereto were embodied in a document by the clerk and certified to, and the same was filed in this court under the title
of an "additional transcript"; and it purports to be a part
of the transcript although no steps were taken by appellants, nor by anyone acting for them, to have the same
brought to this court by a writ of *certiorari.*

"Where a trial court record is corrected or amended upon
an application there filed, the amendment or correction becomes part of the original record in legal contemplation,

and the party desiring its presentation on appeal should apply for an order to have it certified to the appellate tribunal." Elliott, App. Proc. §207; *Berkey* v. *Rensberger* (1911), 49 Ind. App. 226, 96 N. E. 32. In *Mitchell* v. *Stinson* (1881), 80 Ind. 324, the clerk of the lower court certified to the upper court a copy of an original note, and the court said in reference thereto: "We can not treat the note as in the record. The practice here adopted is not warranted by law. Papers can not be made part of the record in any such manner." After appellants procured a *nunc pro tunc* entry to be made, it became their duty, if they desired the same to reach this court, under the facts before us, to apply for a writ of *certiorari.* Elliott, App. Proc. §216; *Berkey* v. *Rensberger, supra;* Ewbank's Manual §209.

The motion must be sustained, and the document designated an "additional transcript" is hereby ordered stricken from the files of this court.

NOTE.—*Nunc pro tunc* entries, when made, note (1) 62 Ind. App. 311. Writ of *certiorari*, when denied, note, 61 Ind. App. 189.

---

## LEWIS ET AL. *v.* GUTHRIE.

### [No. 8,933. Filed October 11, 1916.]

1. TRESPASS.—*Evidence.*—*Sufficiency.*—In an action against joint tort-feasors to recover damages for trespass to timber lands and the wrongful removal of timber therefrom, evidence as to the removal and sale of timber from plaintiff's land owing to a mistake as to boundary lines and the acquiescence by two of the defendants in an estimate of the amount of timber taken is held sufficient to sustain a verdict against such defendants, but insufficient to justify a verdict against one of the defendants where it appeared that he neither participated in, directed, nor ratified the trespass complained of. p. 10.

2. TRESPASS.—*Actions.*—*Cutting and Removal of Timber.*—*Measure of Damages.*—In an action to recover damages for the wrongful removal of timber under a complaint seeking recovery for injury to the land caused thereby, the diminution in the value of the land occasioned by cutting and removing the timber for the

most part immature, rather than the value of the timber as a severed product, was the proper measure of recovery, particularly as much young and growing timber was destroyed in felling and hauling the trees which were removed. p. 13.

From Owen Circuit Court; *James B. Wilson*, Judge.

Action by William H. Guthrie against Charles Lewis and others. From a judgment for plaintiff, the defendants appeal. *Affirmed in part and reversed in part.*

*Fowler & Elliott,* for appellants.
*Willis Hickam* and *Hubert Hickam,* for appellee.

CALDWELL, C. J.—Appellee brought this action against appellants George C. Tanner, Gordon B. Tanner and Charles Lewis, and also certain other individual and corporate defendants as joint tort-feasors, to recover damages for trespass on lands. A trial resulted in a verdict and judgment against the Tanners and Lewis for $900, the cause having been dismissed as to the other defendants at the close of the evidence. The errors relied on for reversal are based on the overruling of appellants' joint and several motion for a new trial.

The substance of the first paragraph of complaint is as follows: Since 1907 appellee has been the owner of 120 acres of land in Owen county. Prior to the grievances complained of, it was covered by a growth of young timber of a number of varieties. The Tanners were the owners of timber lands adjoining appellee's land on the west and south, upon which Lewis resided as superintendent and manager for the Tanners. Lewis acted with the Tanners as coprincipal in committing the wrongs complained of. The three appellants in 1911, 1912, and 1913 wrongfully and unlawfully sold certain varieties of young and growing timber on appellee's lands to the persons and corporations originally sued also as defendants, and procured them to cut and remove the same, and in so doing to destroy certain other young timber growing on appellee's land. Prior to the trespass, appellee's lands were worth $3,500, but by reason of the trespass, such lands were not worth more than $1,500.

The second paragraph of complaint differs from the first, in that by the former it is alleged that appellants did not know the location of the line between the two tracts, and that they negligently failed to ascertain its location, and that as a result the injury was inflicted. In addition to general denials filed by each appellant, Gordon B. Tanner answered specially in effect that he sold to one Clark certain timber to be cut and removed from Gordon's lands adjoining appellee's lands; that he caused the line between the two tracts to be surveyed and ascertained; that he and Lewis, who was Gordon's employe, directed Clark not to encroach upon appellee's lands, but that Clark disregarded his instructions, and without Gordon's knowledge, cut and removed from appellee's lands about fifty-five sawlogs of the value of $95, and also certain logs from Gordon's lands, all of which were sold by Clark, the purchaser crediting Gordon and Clark with the amount of the selling price. That the purchaser paid Gordon on the account $71.29; that $40.01 of the selling price was held by the purchaser on appellee's order; that Clark left on appellee's lands logs cut by him, which were subsequently sold for $20.79, and the money was paid to and retained by appellee; that the logs cut from both tracts by Clark were of the total value of $132.09; that Gordon sold no saw timber to any one other than Clark. The answer denies all allegations of the complaint not specifically met thereby. The special answer is silent respecting the sale of timber other than saw timber.

We have very carefully examined the evidence. We regard it as insufficient as to appellant George C. Tanner.

We are unable to discover that he participated in,
1.  directed, or ratified the commission of the trespass complained of, or that he received any of the fruits thereof, either in person or by agent. Our search discloses

that, in the course of the trial, his name was mentioned but twice: Once by way of excluding him from a transaction related to the trespass, and again in an agreed stipulation to the effect that Gordon B. Tanner executed a deed to him December 4, 1909, recorded October 24, 1915. The stipulation, however, is so uncertain in language that it can not be determined therefrom whether the lands described in the deed are the lands involved in this action. The deed was not read in evidence. Assuming, however, the identity of the tract described in the deed as the Tanner lands involved here, the activity of Lewis, the occupant of the latter, in the trespass and matters relating thereto is clearly shown to have been due to the direction of Gordon B. Tanner, rather than George C. Tanner. The evidence bearing on the question of the liability of appellants Gordon B. Tanner and Charles Lewis is, in substance, as follows: Since September, 1907, appellee has been the owner of a tract of timber land consisting of eighty acres, lying north and south, and a forty-acre tract lying east of the north forty acres of the first tract. In December, 1907, Gordon B. Tanner became the owner of timber lands adjoining appellee's land on the west and south. Appellee lived in California. In June, 1913, he learned that his timber was being cut and removed. He came to Indiana and, by inspection, discovered that 213 trees, consisting of poplar, walnut, ash, oak and cherry, had been cut, the most of which had been removed, and that other timber had been destroyed in felling trees, cutting out roads for the purpose of hauling timber, etc. Lewis lived on the Tanner land. Large quantities of timber were sold to various persons and corporations, to be cut and removed from the Tanner land. In some cases, it was purchased as saw timber, and in other cases to be manufactured into excelsior and handles. In some instances Gordon personally sold the timber and in other instances Lewis, by Gordon's direction, sold it. Lewis, assisted somewhat by Gordon, supervised the cutting and removal of the timber.

It was apparently the purpose of both Gordon and Lewis
to sell only the timber on the Tanner land. Lewis, however, pointed out to purchasers and cutters the east line of
appellee's eighty-acre tract as the line between the Tanner
land and appellee's land, and directed that the timber be
taken, and it was taken, up to the line as pointed out. Gordon B. Tanner subsequently ratified the acts of Lewis in
this respect, and also personally pointed out to purchasers
and cutters, as his east line, the east line of appellee's eighty
acres. Lewis also, frequently, and Gordon, occasionally, were
present while timber was being cut on appellee's land.
After this controversy arose, both Gordon and Lewis contended that no timber had been taken from appellee's land.
Such contention was apparently based on their belief that
the east line of appellee's eighty acres was the east line of
the Tanner land. Gordon on a number of occasions stated
that he would not believe that the line was as contended by
appellee until a survey disclosed the fact. He thereupon
caused a survey to be made, which located the line as claimed
by appellee. There was no controversy at the trial respecting the correctness of the survey. While it is now conceded
that Gordon and Lewis encroached upon appellee's land and
caused timber to be cut and removed therefrom, it is contended that the evidence did not establish that appellants
were chargeable with the removal of all the timber that had
been taken from appellee's lands; that appellee in his evidence had been able to identify, as having been taken by
Gordon and Lewis, a certain number of trees, considerably
fewer than the number that formed the basis of his damage.
It may be said, however, that Gordon and Lewis, at least
impliedly, conceded that they were responsible for all the
timber that had been taken from appellee's land. They
were present when several men were going over appellee's
land for the express purpose of estimating the damages
caused by the trespass committed by them. These men
were counting the stumps and measuring their dimensions.

Neither Gordon nor Lewis, under such circumstances, claimed that any part of the timber being estimated had not been taken by their direction. On the contrary, Gordon asked one of the men to make an inventory of the timber that had been cut. No evidence was offered that any timber had been taken or cut except by persons who had purchased of Gordon and Lewis. Under the rule that controls in this court, the evidence is sufficient as against Lewis and Gordon B. Tanner.

It is urged that the damages assessed by the jury are excessive. By his complaint, appellee sought to recover damages for injury to the land caused by the cutting and

2. removal of timber and the destruction of other timber growing thereon. In its scope the complaint presents a case in the nature of trespass *quare clausum fregit*, with added matter in the nature of *de bonis asportatis*. That is, the entire injury complained of consisted in the destruction of certain growing timber, the cutting of other timber, and the removal and appropriation of the timber cut. By the complaint the entire injury is declared on as an injury to the land, and the case was tried on that theory. That is, the case was tried on the theory that diminution in the value of the land occasioned by the cutting and removing and destruction of timber, rather than the value of the timber as a severed product, was the proper measure of recovery. Under the allegations of the complaint and the facts proven, the timber being immature, and certain young timber having been merely destroyed rather than cut, damages based on the value of the severed timber would not amount to full compensation. The following cases are instructive: *Disbrow* v. *Westchester, etc., Co.* (1900), 164 N. Y. 415, 58 N. E. 519; *Doak* v. *Mammoth, etc., Co.* (1911), 192 Fed. 748; *Dwight* v. *Elmira, etc., Co.* (1892), 132 N. Y. 199, 15 L. R. A. 612, 28 Am. St. 563, 30 N. E. 398; *Cleveland School District* v. *Great Northern R. Co.* (1910), 20 N. D. 124, 126 N. W. 995; 28 L. R. A. (N. S.) 757, note; *Reynolds* v.

*Great Northern R. Co.* (1912), 119 Minn. 251, 138 N. W. 30, 52 L. R. A. (N. S.) 91, and note; *American Sand, etc., Co.* v. *Spencer* (1913), 55 Ind. App. 523, 103 N. E. 426; *Sunnyside, etc., Co.* v. *Reitz* (1896), 14 Ind. App. 478, 39 N. E. 541, 43 N. E. 46.

There was substantial evidence that the diminution in the value of appellee's lands caused by the trespass thereon, and the cutting, destroying and removing of the timber was at least equal to the amount of the verdict. The evidence disclosed, however, that when appellee intervened and stopped the cutting and removing of the timber, there remained on the land several cords of excelsior wood that had been cut by purchasers from Lewis· and Gordon, and that appellee took possession of and sold the same. It is urged by appellants that appellee realized from the sale of such excelsior timber a sum in excess of its value in the tree, and that as the evidence indicated that the trespass was unintentional and the result of mistake, appellants should have received the benefit of such excess value created by purchasers as their representatives, and that the verdict is, for this reason, excessive.

It is true, as argued by appellants, that under some circumstances, and in some forms of action, where the trespass is innocently or mistakenly committed, the value added to the severed or removed product by the labor of the trespasser, is not recoverable as a part of the damages, the rule in such cases being that full compensation limits the recovery. We do not find it necessary to determine whether such principle is applicable to any phase of the case here, but see the following and cases cited: *Sunnyside* v. *Reitz*, supra; *American Sand, etc., Co.* v. *Spencer*, supra.

Appellee by his complaint predicated the damages alleged to have been suffered upon the following elements: Entering on the land and cutting timber for the most part immature, the removal of such timber and the destruction of other young and growing timber in felling and hauling the trees cut and removed. By reason of such elements, appellee alleged facts showing the diminution in the value of his lands. All the facts were submitted to the jury, including the fact that certain timber that had been cut was left piled on the land, its value in the tree and its value after it had been cut and piled, and what appellee realized therefrom.

The court instructed the jury that the action was brought not to recover the value of timber cut and removed and sold, but rather to recover damages to the land occasioned by cutting, removing and destroying young and growing timber. It is true that damage to land occasioned by cutting timber therefrom is complete when the timber is severed and reduced to personal property. It is apparent, however, that in a case of unlawful cutting of timber, which has a value as such, and independent of its connection with the land, the landowner's damages in fact are greater where the timber is removed and appropriated by the wrongdoer than where the timber is left on the land, and the landowner possesses himself of it. In the latter case, the timber, after it is severed, may be as valuable as when it was a part of the land, in which case the landowner's damages would be merely nominal. *Decamp* v. *Wallace* (1904), 45 Misc. Rep. 436, 92 N. Y. Supp. 746.

In the case at bar, witnesses testified to all the facts about cutting and removing the timber, and that certain timber that had been cut was left on the land, and passed into the appellee's possession, and from such viewpoint were permitted to testify to the value of appellee's lands before the timber was cut and removed therefrom, and also after such cutting and removing of the timber, as a basis for the measure of damages. Thus the facts respecting the entire injury were submitted to the jury and from their consideration the verdict was returned under the guidance of comprehensive instructions given by the court. It appears to us, therefore, that the verdict accomplished substantial justice.

Other questions are presented. Such questions, however, to the extent that they might otherwise be important, are eliminated by our view that the evidence is insufficient as to George C. Tanner, and that it convicts Gordon B. Tanner of having actively participated in the trespass complained of.

The judgment is affirmed as to Gordon B. Tanner and Charles Lewis, and reversed as to George C. Tanner, with instructions to sustain the motion for a new trial as to him, costs to be taxed one-third against appellee, and two-thirds against appellants Gordon B. Tanner and Charles Lewis.

NOTE.—Reported in 113 N. E. 769. Damages, measure of, in trespass for cutting, removing or injuring timber, 1 Am. St. 497; 38 Cyc 1131; 15 Ann. Cas. 917; Ann. Cas. 1912A 920.

---

## SCOTT v. BAIRD.

[No. 9,128. Filed October 11, 1916.]

1. APPEAL.—*Waiver of Error.*—*Briefs.*—Alleged error in the ruling of the trial court on the demurrer to the complaint is waived on appeal by appellant's failure to state any point or proposition relating thereto, or to mention or discuss the same in his brief under the heading of "Points and Authorities," as required by the fifth clause of Rule 22 of the Appellate Court. p. 17.

2. APPEAL.—*Transcript.*—*Motion for a New Trial.*—No question is presented for review on appeal by an assignment of error that the trial court erred in overruling defendant's motion for a new trial, where such motion was not made part of the record by setting it out in the transcript. p. 17.

From Porter Circuit Court; *Ralph N. Smith*, Special Judge.

Action by Ervin Baird against John T. Scott. From a judgment for plaintiff, the defendant appeals. *Affirmed.*

*Daniel E. Kelly* and *Walter J. Fabing*, for appellant.

*T. H. Heard* and *Henry Clay Holt*, for appellee.

FELT, J.—This case was tried on an amended complaint in four paragraphs, for money loaned and for conversion, which was answered by a general denial, a plea of payment, and a plea of accord and satisfaction. A reply in general denial was filed to each of the special answers. The jury found for the plaintiff in the sum of $548.25, and returned answers to certain interrogatories. The motion for a new trial was overruled, judgment was rendered on the general verdict, and appellant appealed to this court.

The errors assigned are the overruling of the motion for a new trial, and error in overruling the demurrer to each paragraph of the amended complaint.

The alleged error in ruling on the demurrer to the complaint is waived by appellant's failure to state any point or proposition relating thereto or to mention or in 1. any way refer to the subject under the heading of "Points and Authorities" as required by Rule 22 of this court. *Kaufman* v. *Alexander* (1913), 180 Ind. 670, 103 N. E. 481; *German Fire Ins. Co.* v. *Zonker* (1914), 57 Ind. App. 696, 701, 108 N. E. 160; *Board, etc.* v. *State, ex rel.* (1910), 175 Ind. 147, 156, 93 N. E. 851.

Appellee insists that no question is presented by the assignment that the court erred in overruling appellant's motion for a new trial because the motion was not 2. in fact filed and is not a part of the record in the case. The record at page 96 shows the filing of such motion, and subsequent entries show that a motion was made to strike it from the files, which was overruled. The transcript also shows that the motion for a new trial was overruled and this appeal prayed and granted, but the motion is not set out any place in the transcript. The motion for a new trial not being in the record, no question relating thereto is presented or can be considered by this court. Elliott, App. Proc. §§186, 709 *et seq.; Brown* v. *State* (1895), 140 Ind. 374, 39 N. E. 701; *Hobbs* v. *Salem-Bedford Stone Co.* (1899), 22 Ind. App. 436, 53 N. E. 1063; *LaFollette* v. *Higgins* (1887), 109 Ind. 241, 9 N. E. 780; *Wurfel*

v. *State* (1906), 167 Ind. 160, 78 N. E. 635; *Vesey* v. *Day* (1910), 175 Ind. 406, 409, 94 N. E. 481; *Mesker* v. *Fitzpatrick* (1911), 48 Ind. App. 518, 94 N. E. 827; *Lawrence* v. *Oliver Typewriter Co.* (1912), 51 Ind. App. 434, 99 N. E. 809; *McCardle* v. *McGinley* (1882), 86 Ind. 538, 541, 44 Am. Rep. 343.

Judgment affirmed.

Note.—Reported in 113 N. E. 769.

# WORKINGMEN'S MUTUAL PROTECTIVE ASSOCIATION v. ROOS.

[No. 9,117. Filed October 13, 1916.]

1. APPEAL.—*Waiver of Error.—Briefs.*—Alleged error in overruling the demurrer to the complaint is waived where appellant's brief fails to address any point or proposition thereto. p. 19.

2. INSURANCE.—*Accident Insurance.—Total Disability.*—Where an accident insurance policy provided for the payment of total disability benefits in case the assured should suffer injury which should, from the date of the accident, disable him and prevent him from performing every duty pertaining to any and every kind of business or occupation, and if such injuries wholly and continuously from date of accident should disable and prevent the assured from performing one or more important duties pertaining to his occupation, or in event of like disability immediately following total loss of time, partial disability benefits should be paid, the words "total loss of time" in the provision concerning partial disability, when read in connection with the stipulation in reference to total disability, make it clear that the assured would not be entitled to recover for total disability except in event of total loss of time, during which he was prevented from performing every duty pertaining to any and every kind of business. p. 20.

3. APPEAL.—*Review.—Erroneous Instruction.—Presumption.*—In an action to recover benefits on an accident insurance policy, an instruction that, if a person was so disabled that he was disqualified and rendered unable to perform substantially and in a reasonable way his usual and ordinary work and vocation, he was totally disabled, was, in view of the stipulations in the policy, incorrect, and will be presumed to have been harmful. p. 25.

4. APPEAL.—*Excessive Verdict.*—*Erroneous Instruction.*—*Cure by Remittitur.*—Where, in an action on an accident insurance policy, defendant made no contention that plaintiff was not partially disabled so as to bring them within the stipulation of the policy in respect thereto, an instruction, which erroneously defined the insurer's liability under the total disability provision contained in the policy, could not have been prejudiced to defendant's rights except to the extent that the verdict exceeded what it would have been had the recovery been for partial disability and will be cured by a remittitur of such amount. p. 26.

From Madison Circuit Court; *Charles K. Bagot,* Judge.

Action by Leo Roos against the Workingmen's Mutual Protective Association. From a judgment for plaintiff, the defendant appeals. *Affirmed conditionally.*

*Teegarden & Kimball* and *Long, Yarlett & Souder,* for appellant.

*Walter Vermillion,* for appellee.

MORAN, J.—Appellee recovered of appellant the sum of $75 upon an insurance policy indemnifying him against loss by accident or sickness for an injury, which he alleged was sustained by him during the life of the policy. A review of the judgment is sought upon errors assigned: (1) in overruling appellant's demurrer to appellee's complaint, and (2) in overruling appellant's motion for a new trial.

The first error assigned is waived, as no point or proposition in appellant's brief is addressed to the overruling of the demurrer to the complaint. *Mutual Life Ins. Co.* v. *Finkelstein* (1914), 58 Ind. App. 27, 107 N. E. 557; *Dunton* v. *Howell* (1915), 60 Ind. App. 183, 109 N. E. 418. Therefore, nothing further need be said in reference to the complaint than that it is in the usual form of an action of this character, with a copy of the policy of insurance made a part thereof.

Within the specification that the court erred in overruling appellant's motion for a new trial, the correctness of the instructions given by the court of its own motion to the jury and the refusal to give certain instructions requested by appellant, together with the sufficiency of the evidence to sustain the verdict of the jury are presented for consideration; the main objection being that, under the stipulations of the policy and the evidence in the cause, the court erred in instructing the jury as to what constituted total disability, and, by reason thereof, a recovery was had for total disability of appellee when he was not entitled to recover on this theory.

By the provisions of the policy, appellee was indemnified against the effect of bodily injuries caused directly, solely, and independently of all causes by external, violent 2. and accidental means, and, if such injuries from the date of the accident disabled and prevented the assured from performing every duty pertaining to any and every kind of business or occupation, the association was to pay for such total disability for a period not to exceed twenty-four consecutive months at the rate of $50 per month; and if such injuries wholly and continuously from date of accident disabled and prevented the assured from performing one or more important duties pertaining to his occupation, or in the event of like disability immediately following total loss of time, the insured was to be paid $25 per month for the period of such partial disability, not to exceed six consecutive months. And further, in the event of injury or loss, fatal or otherwise, of which there were no external and visible wound or contusion on the exterior of the body, or injury, fatal or otherwise, due wholly or in part, directly or indirectly, to disease or bodily infirmity, or in the event of disability, or death, due to either accident or illness where the loss was occasioned or contributed to in any way by tuberculosis, rheumatism, paralysis, the limit of the association's liability was not to exceed one month's indemnity as provided for total disability; and that indemnity should not accrue in excess of the time the assured was by reason of the injury under the professional care and regular attendance of a legal qualified physician and surgeon.

There is evidence in the record disclosing that about the hour of 9:30 p. m. on the evening of October 5, 1913, the assured entered his real estate office located in the city of Anderson, Indiana, while the office was very dark, and, while attempting to turn on the electric lights, he struck his head violently against the corner of a high desk that stood in the room, from the effects of which he fell to the floor. The injury he received was painful and caused dizziness. The part of the head that came in contact with the desk became swollen and left a blue mark about the size of a quarter, and to relieve the pain hot applications were applied shortly thereafter; that on either the next or the second day after he received the injury he consulted a physician, who treated him continuously until December 5, 1913. The injury caused paralysis of the side of the face, so that he could not close his eye, and it interfered with his speech; likewise his rest was considerably impaired for more than a month after receiving the injury. The physician gave him electrical treatments for the fifth nerve at the side of the temple over the parietal region of the head. There is a conflict in the evidence as to whether he was able to perform any service during the period of time for which a recovery was sought. The assured testified that he was unable to transact any business during this period of time; while other witnesses testified that they saw him going about and attending in part, at least, to his real estate business. With the record disclosing the foregoing as to the nature of the injury and appellee's condition physically, the court, in construing the policy in reference to total and partial disability, informed the jury that if appellee was injured as alleged in the complaint, and by reason thereof he was immediately thereafter disabled from performing his usual vocation for any period of the time mentioned in the complaint, then for such time as he was totally disabled, he would be entitled to recover $50 per month; and if, on account of the injury, he was immediately thereafter partially disabled from performing his usual vocation to the extent of being unable to perform one or more of his duties during any part of the time mentioned in the complaint, then for such portion of the time, he would be entitled to recover $25 per month. "Total disability," as used in the policy, the jury was informed is such disability as disqualified appellee from performing his usual regular work and vocation; and that if a person was so disabled that he was disqualified and rendered unable to perform substantially and in a reasonable way his usual and ordinary work and vocation, then he was totally disabled within the meaning of the language used in the policy, even though he might be able to perform some of the minor and less important portions of such service or vocation; and, on the other hand, if his disability was such as not to render him incapable of performing the major and more important portions of his work and vocation, he was not totally disabled within the meaning of the language used in the policy.

As to what, under the law, constitutes total disability in an accident insurance policy has been before the courts for consideration upon numerous occasions, and, as disclosed by the decisions, the language covering such stipulation varies in form. In many of the decisions, the language is substantially to the effect that should the assured be disabled from prosecuting his usual employment, or from prosecuting any and every kind of business pertaining to his occupation, he would be entitled to the indemnity; and under such language or language similar in effect, Cooley, in his brief on the Law of Insurance (Vol. 4, p. 3290), after reviewing the decisions generally, says: "It must not, however, be inferred that to constitute total disability the insured must be unable to perform each and every act and duty connected with his occupation. On the contrary, the weight of authority supports the rule that even under the clause providing for indemnity for disability preventing the insured from prosecuting any and every kind of business pertaining to his occupation, it is sufficient if insured is disabled from performing the substantial and material acts connected with such occupation." While the courts are not in complete accord on this subject, the weight of authority, as was said, supports the doctrine thus announced. *Young* v. *Travelers Ins. Co.* (1888), 80 Me. 244, 13 Atl. 896; *Hohn* v. *Interstate Casualty Co.* (1897), 115 Mich. 79, 72 N. W. 1105; *Indiana Life, etc., Co.* v. *Reed* (1913), 54 Ind. App. 450, 103 N. E. 77; Kerr, Insurance 385, 386; *Commercial Travelers* v. *Barnes* (1905), 72 Kan. 293, 80 Pac. 1020, 82 Pac. 1099, 7 Ann. Cas. 814, and note 815.

The courts are, however, practically a unit in declaring that stipulations in reference to total disability, irrespective of the technical variance in the language employed, should be given a rational and practical construction; that the term "total disability" is a relative term, depending in a measure upon the character of the employment and capabilities of the person injured as well as of the circumstances of each particular case, and is usually a question of fact to be determined by the court or jury trying the cause. Fuller, Accident and Employers' Liability Ins. 296; *Indiana Life, etc., Co.* v. *Reed, supra; Industrial Mutual, etc., Co.* v. *Hawkins* (1910), 94 Ark. 417, 127 S. W. 457, 29 L. R. A. (N. S.) 635, 21 Ann. Cas. 1029, and note page 1031.

In the case of *Hooper* v. *Insurance Co.* (1860), 5 Hurl. & N. 546, apparently one of the leading English cases on the subject of accident insurance, the court, in construing a stipulation that provided that the assured should recover a certain sum per week in case he receive by accident a bodily injury "of so serious a nature as wholly to disable him from following his usual business," that he could recover indemnity for an injury that confined him to his room, although during such time he was able to receive his clients, being a solicitor.

In *Young* v. *Travelers Ins. Co., supra,* the Supreme Court of Maine said, in construing an accident insurance policy:

"A contract of insurance is to receive a reasonable construction so as to effectuate the purpose for which it was
made. In case of doubt it is to be liberally construed in
favor of the insured that in all proper cases he may receive
the indemnity contracted for."

It was held in the case of *Commercial Travelers, etc.,
Assn.* v. *Springsteen* (1899), 23 Ind. App. 657, 55 N. E.
973, that there was no error in refusing to give an instruction to the effect that, in order to recover, appellee's injury
must have been such as to wholly disable him from performing any and every kind of business pertaining to his occupation as manager of the When Clothing Store; and that there
was no error in instructing the jury that, if the assured was
disabled to the extent that he could not do any and all kinds
of business pertaining to his occupation, he could recover. The stipulation in the policy in the Springsteen case
was: " 'No claims of any character shall accrue upon this
contract unless it arises from physical bodily injury, through
external, violent and accidental means, while this contract
is in force, and then only when the injury shall, independently of all other causes, immediately and wholly disable
the insured from performing any and every kind of business
pertaining to his occupation  *  *  *.' "

The *Commercial Travelers, etc., Assn.* case, *supra,* was followed in *Pacific Mutual Life Ins. Co.* v. *Branham* (1904),
34 Ind. App. 243, 70 N. E. 174, and the principle announced
in each of these decisions finds support in *Indiana Life, etc.,
Co.* v. *Reed, supra,* which latter case provides, among other
things, that a fair and reasonable construction should be
given to all the language employed in the policy, and, in
doing so, consideration should be given the situation of the
parties when the policy was issued, and to ascertain the
meaning upon which the minds of the contracting parties
may have met.

But in the case at bar we have a policy providing for a
partial as well as total indemnity, and, as we have seen, the

stipulation in reference to total disability is that, if the injuries "shall from the date of the accident disable and prevent the assured from performing every duty pertaining to any and every kind of business or occupation, the association will pay for such total disability." And as to partial disability, it is provided that: "If such injuries shall wholly and continuously from date of accident disable and prevent the assured from performing one or more important duties pertaining to his occupation, or, in the event of like disability immediately following total loss of time, the association will pay the assured for the period of such partial disability." In this latter stipulation, the words "total loss of time," when read in connection with the stipulation in reference to total disability, make it clear and free from doubt that the assured would not be entitled to recover for total disability except in the event of a total loss of time, as he must have been prevented from performing every duty pertaining to any and every kind of business or occupation. Our attention has not been called to, nor has our research been rewarded by, the finding of a decision construing language of the import found in the policy under consideration as to the right to recover for total disability when followed in the stipulation as to partial disability by language indicating that a total loss of time was necessary in order for the insured to recover for total disability.

If the conclusion thus far reached is correct, then the instruction of the court, which informed the jury that, if a

3. person was so disabled that he was disqualified and rendered unable to perform substantially and in a reasonable way his usual and ordinary work and vocation, he was totally disabled within the meaning of the language used in the policy, is incorrect, and under the circumstances will be presumed to have been harmful. *Neely* v. *Louisville, etc., Traction Co.* (1913), 53 Ind. App. 659, 102 N. E. 455; *Cleveland, etc., R. Co.* v. *Case* (1910), 174 Ind. 369, 91 N. E. 238.

In *Fidelity and Casualty Co.* v. *Getzendanner* (1900), 93 Tex. 487, 53 S. W. 838, 55 S. W. 179, 56 S. W. 326, in construing a stipulation in an accident insurance policy that, if the injury should "wholly disable and prevent the assured from performing any and every kind of duty pertaining to his occupation, the company" should pay the assured the weekly indemnity. An instruction was held erroneous that authorized a recovery if the assured was unable to transact his business "in a manner reasonably as effective as the same would have been performed if the injury had not been sustained." However, as to whether the instruction under consideration would be erroneous under a policy that employed language less favorable to the insurer, or, in other words, similar to the language employed in the policy referred to in the case last mentioned or in the cases of *Hooper* v. *Insurance Co., supra,* and *Commercial Travelers, etc., Assn.* v. *Springsteen, supra,* we are not called upon to decide in view of the conclusion reached.

There is no contention on the part of appellant that appellee was not partially disabled so as to bring him within the stipulation of the policy in this respect from October 5 to December 5, 1913, which would entitle him to recover the sum of $50. The erroneous instruction given could not have been prejudicial to appellant's rights, except to the extent that the verdict, which was for the sum of $75, exceeds what it would have been had the recovery been for partial disability only.

Therefore, if within thirty days from the date hereof, appellee enters a remittitur of the judgment in the sum of $25, the judgment will be affirmed; otherwise, it is reversed, with instructions to the trial court to grant appellant a new trial, and for further proceedings in accordance with this opinion. In the event there is a remittitur, as aforesaid, one-third of the costs made in this court will be taxed against appellee and the two-thirds against appellant.

NOTE.—Reported in 113 N. E. 760. Total disability, what constitutes under accident insurance policy, 38 L. R. A. 529; 23 L. R. A. (N. S.) 352; 29 L. R. A. (N. S.) 635; 34 L. R. A. (N. S.) 120; 21 Ann. Cas. 1031. See under (2) 1 C. J. 402, 465; 1 Cyc 269, 272; (3, 4) 3 Cyc 436.

# GARDNER *v.* VANCE.

## [No. 9,110. Filed October 25, 1916.]

1. APPEAL.—*Instructions.—Applicability to Pleading.*—In an action for personal injuries received when plaintiff was struck by defendant's automobile, defendant cannot on appeal complain of an instruction that does not follow the averments of the complaint as to plaintiff's location at the time of the accident, where the facts referred to in such instruction are supported by uncontradicted evidence which was received without objection. p. 28.

2. NEGLIGENCE.—*Driving Automobile.—Collision on Highway.—Verdict.—Evidence.—Sufficiency.—Violation of Statute.*—In an action for personal injuries, where it appeared from the evidence that defendant was proceeding along a public highway in his automobile at a speed of twenty-five miles per hour, and, although he was signalled to stop his car or slacken its speed, failed to do so, but, in attempting to pass plaintiff's wagon and team, struck and injured plaintiff, who was walking on the road beside his horses so as to better control them, such evidence was sufficient to sustain a verdict for plaintiff, since it showed defendant guilty of actionable negligence, especially as he was so operating his motor car at the time of the accident as to violate one of the penal laws of the state. pp. 29, 30.

3. TRIAL.—*Jury Questions.—Conflicting Evidence.*—Where the evidence upon an issue is conflicting, a question of fact is presented for determination by the jury. p. 29.

4. NEGLIGENCE.—*Use of Highway.—Presumptions.*—In an action for personal injuries sustained in a collision with a motor car, plaintiff was without fault in walking on the road beside his horses so as to better control them, since one lawfully using a public highway has the right to assume that others using the highway in common with him will take notice of his presence and exercise a proper degree of care not to harm him. p. 30.

From Hendricks Circuit Court; *George W. Brill,* Judge.

Action by David W. Vance against Charles J. Gardner. From a judgment for plaintiff, the defendant appeals. *Affirmed.*

*Harvey, Harvey & Harvey.* and *Means & Buenting*, for appellant.

*Bert Winters, O. E. Gulley* and *A. J. Shelby*, for appellee.

IBACH, J.—On the day of the accident complained of, appellee charges that he was driving a team of horses attached to a wagon along one of the public highways of Boone county; that while so doing appellant approached him from the rear driving an automobile at a speed of twenty-five miles an hour; that appellee, fearing that his horses might become frightened at the approaching car, when appellant was one hundred yards to the rear, signalled him to stop his car or to slacken his speed; that he alighted from the wagon, and, while walking alongside of his wagon and horses to better control them, appellant negligently failed to stop or slacken his speed and negligently and carelessly ran his automobile against him and severely injured him. Appellee obtained a verdict and judgment for $600 in the court below, from which judgment appellant has appealed, and has assigned as error the overruling of his motion for a new trial. Under this assignment we are required to consider whether the court erred in giving to the jury instructions Nos. 2 and 5 and, whether the verdict of the jury is sustained by sufficient evidence.

Among the substantial averments of the complaint there is no specific charge that immediately before the collision occurred "appellee was riding in the vehicle of a 1. friend which was traveling immediately behind his team," yet the court added that element to his instruction wherein he attempted to inform the jury of the averments of the complaint. This is objected to.

The complaint also charges that when appellee was injured he was walking alongside of his team and wagon; but the trial court, referring to appellee's position upon the highway when injured, added in his charge to what is averred in the complaint in that connection the phrase, "or running up to his team." This is also objected to on the ground that there was no averment in the complaint which warranted the use of such language.

It is the duty of the court, when charging the jury, to correctly state the issues upon which the cause is tried and any instruction given which has no application to any issue is erroneous and in many instances may be harmful and reversible error. And while the trial court, in using the language complained of to explain the position of appellee just prior to and at the time of the collision, went beyond the specific averments of the complaint, yet we are entirely satisfied that the appellant was not harmed thereby, especially since the uncontradicted evidence supported the additional facts referred to in the instruction and that evidence went to the jury without objection. Such being the case appellant is in no position to urge the objections which he now urges to the instructions given, and it is unnecessary to give them further consideration.

The other question discussed by appellant is whether there was sufficient evidence to sustain the verdict. The proof shows that at the time of the accident appellant was

2. violating one of the penal statutes of this state; that a sufficient length of time before the collision, and while appellee was traveling upon the public highway, he indicated to appellant that his situation was such at that time as to make it necessary for appellant either to stop his car or to slacken its speed in order that a possible collision might be avoided, and yet he failed to use any precaution of any kind. In short there was evidence to sustain the charge that appellant carelessly and negligently and in violation of a penal statute of the state so operated his automobile as to inflict serious injury upon appellee. Appellant himself introduced no testimony on this branch

3. of the case, but defended solely upon the theory that he was not there, and that it was not his car that inflicted the injury. This issue upon conflicting evidence was for the jury. It is apparent that appellant did not

exercise that degree of care which the situation of appellee and the character of the agency used by him required. It is also apparent that appellee was himself without 4. fault. There was no reason for him to suppose that he would be run down by a reckless driver while he was lawfully walking beside his team traveling on a public highway. Other persons traveling upon the same highway were bound to take notice of his presence and were required to exercise a proper degree of care not to do him harm, and appellee had a right to assume that other travelers would so act. There is no excuse or justification offered for 2. the careless and negligent manner in which the automobile was operated; and appellant, like all others who insist on speeding on the public highways of the state with no regard for the safety of other travelers, must respond in damages for injuries negligently done. No good reason appears why this court should overthrow the result reached in the court below

Judgment affirmed.

NOTE.—Reported in 113 N. E. 1006. Reciprocal duties of operators of automobiles and pedestrians, care required, 51 L. R. A. (N. S.) 900; 21 Ann. Cas. 648; 37 Cyc 273, 279. Negligence of operators of automobiles under particular state of facts, 1 L. R. A. (N. S.) 228.

---

## CHICAGO AND ERIE RAILROAD COMPANY *v.* BIDDINGER.

[No. 9,122. Filed October 25, 1916.]

1. ACTIONS.—*Predicating Action on a Statute.*—Where one predicates his cause of action on a statute, he must bring himself within it. p. 38.

2. RAILROADS.—*Crossing Accidents.—Complaint.—Allegations.—Inferences.—Sufficiency.*—In an action for personal injuries sustained in a railroad crossing accident, allegations in the complaint that defendant negligently ran its train against plaintiff while running at the high and dangerous speed of fifty miles per hour, and that the engine crew carelessly and negligently failed

to sound the whistle or ring the bell of the locomotive on approaching the crossing when within 100 rods thereof, until about 150 feet therefrom, sufficiently showed, aided by reasonable inference permitted in favor of a pleading, that the train which injured plaintiff approached from a point not less than 100 rods from the crossing, and that from such point the whistle was not blown until the train was about 150 feet from the crossing, and such averments were sufficient to charge defendant with negligence in failing to give the signals required of trains by statute when approaching highway crossings. p. 38.

3. RAILROADS.—*Crossing Accidents.—Negligence.—Failure to Give Statutory Signals.*—The failure of a railroad company to ring the bell on the engine continuously as a train approaches a street crossing, being in itself a violation of the statute, constitutes negligence. p. 39.

4. RAILROADS.—*Crossing Accidents.—Failure to Give Signals.*—Independent of statute, it is the duty of those in charge of a railroad train to give reasonable and timely warning of its approach to a highway crossing, and failure to do so constitutes negligence. p. 39.

5. RAILROADS.— *Operation.— Speed.— Crossing Watchman.— Negligence.*—While running a train over a crossing at a high rate of speed, or failure to have a flagman or watchman stationed at the crossing, is not negligence *per se,* in the absence of a statute making it so, yet such operation of a train may, in fact, constitute negligence depending upon all the facts and circumstances surrounding the particular case under consideration. p. 39.

6. RAILROADS.— *Crossing Accidents.— Speed.— Negligence.— Care Required.*—The rule permitting a train to be run in the country at a high rate of speed without the imputation of negligence does not obtain as to trains when operated through populous cities and over the much-traveled crossings therein, but the railroad owes to those traveling over such crossings the duty of ordinary care. p. 39.

7. NEGLIGENCE.—*Complaint.—Necessary Averments.—Sufficiency.—* Where the duty to use ordinary care is shown by the complaint, the general averment therein that defendant carelessly and negligently did, or omitted to do, the acts necessary to the discharge of such duty, and that such negligent acts were the proximate cause of the injury complained of, renders the complaint sufficient as against a demurrer, unless the specific acts pleaded are of a character to destroy the force and effect of such general charge of negligence. p. 40.

8. RAILROADS.— *Crossing Accidents.— Complaint.— Construction.*— In an action for personal injuries sustained in a railroad crossing accident, the specific averment in the complaint that the train which injured plaintiff was running at the high and dangerous

speed of fifty miles an hour, when considered in the light of averments showing that the crossing where the accident occurred was in a city where vehicles were passing over it every two minutes, did not tend to destroy the effect of a general charge of negligent speed. p. 40.

9. RAILROADS.— *Crossing Accidents. —Complaint.— Construction.—* In an action for injuries sustained in a railroad crossing accident, an averment in the complaint as to the frequency of travel at the crossing strengthens the averment that defendant negligently and carelessly failed to maintain a watchman at such crossing. p. 41.

10. RAILROADS.—*Crossing Accidents.—Complaint.—Construction.—* Averments in a complaint alleging that defendant railroad was operating a line of railway through a county named and' was doing business therein; that Main street, or the Michigan road, which it crossed, is the principal street of the city of Rochester, and very much used by the public at the point where it crosses defendant's railway, are sufficient to show, aided by reasonable inference permitted in favor of a pleading, that the crossing referred to was located within the city of Rochester, and that the railroad was therefore subject to its ordinances. p. 41.

11. APPEAL.— *Review.— Issues.— Amendments Deemed Made.—* In an action against a railroad for injuries sustained by plaintiff when struck by a train at a street crossing, even though the averments of the second paragraph of complaint were insufficient to show that the crossing was within the corporate limits of the city of Rochester, and that the railroad was, therefore, subject to its ordinances, where the issue as to the location of such crossing was fully tried and proof thereon made under the first paragraph of complaint, the second paragraph, being in all other respects sufficient as against demurrer will be treated on appeal as having been amended in respect to such defect to conform to the proof. p. 42.

12. RAILROADS.—*Crossing Accidents.—Complaint.—Construction.—* In an action for personal injuries sustained in a railroad crossing accident, while averments in the complaint charging that plaintiff's view of the crossing was obstructed by buildings, etc., as he approached riding in a top buggy with the side curtains down, and that on account of obstructions he could not see or hear any train approaching, may tend to show, when standing alone, that plaintiff was guilty of contributory negligence in going upon the crossing, yet such averments, read in connection with others in the complaint alleging that when he approached the crossing he proceeded carefully and exercised all due care and caution to see and hear any train, may be fairly interpreted as meaning that plaintiff used all care and caution usually exercised by a man of ordinary care and prudence to see and hear an

approaching train, and that he could not, and did not, see the train. pp. 42, 43.

13. NEGLIGENCE.— *Complaint.*— *Disclosure of Defense.*— *Contributory Negligence.*—Contributory negligence is a defense, and, while it may appear from the complaint, when it does, it is the duty of the court to hold the complaint insufficient as against a demurrer predicated on such ground, yet the court can do this only when it can say, as a matter of law, that under the facts pleaded, honest and reasonable men could draw but one inference therefrom—that the plaintiff's conduct was not that of a man of ordinary care and prudence. p. 42.

14. RAILROADS.—*Crossing Accidents.*—*Duty of Traveler Approaching Crossing.*—*Pleading.*—The law requires persons traveling on the streets of a city in a vehicle, and approaching a railroad crossing, to stop before passing over a crossing only in those cases where ordinary prudence would dictate such a course, and it is only in exceptional cases that the court can say that the facts pleaded affirmatively show the necessity for such action. p. 43.

15. APPEAL.— *Review.*— *Verdict.*— *Answers to Interrogatories.*— *Presumptions.*—A general verdict for the plaintiff is a finding that every averment of the complaint essential to his cause of action is true, and to support the verdict against a motion for judgment on the answers to interrogatories, the court on appeal must assume as proven every fact provable under any supposable evidence admissible under the issues which in any way tends to support the general verdict, or which tends to reconcile it with the answers to interrogatories. p. 44.

16. RAILROADS.—*Crossing Accidents.*—*Answers to Interrogatories.* —*Construction.*—In an action against a railroad for injuries sustained in a collision at a street crossing, a finding by the jury, in answer to an interrogatory, that obstructions along and immediately east of the street, the side curtains on plaintiff's buggy and the noise from the steel tires on the buggy did not prevent him from hearing the train approaching as he traveled from a distance 200 feet south of defendant's main track toward the crossing, is not in irreconcilable conflict with a general verdict for plaintiff, since it does not mean that he heard, or could have heard, the train within the distance mentioned, but means, fairly interpreted, that the things mentioned in the interrogatory did not prevent plaintiff from hearing the train, and not that he may not have been prevented from hearing it by something else, or that he in fact heard it. p. 44.

17. RAILROADS.—*Crossing Accidents.*—*Answers to Interrogatories.* —*Construction.*—In an action for injuries in a railroad crossing accident, the jury's finding, in answer to interrogatories, that

with a box car standing east of the crossing on the elevator track, which was about twenty-one feet south of the main track, plaintiff could have heard the approach of the train which struck him without stopping his horse, and could have heard the approach of the train before he crossed such elevator track if he had stopped and listened, is not in irreconcilable conflict with the general verdict, which is a finding that plaintiff used ordinary care and that he did not hear the train, since the answer of the jury, under the interpretation most favorable to defendant, will be construed as meaning that plaintiff could have heard the approaching train either by stopping his horse and listening, or without stopping his horse, which is not the equivalent of a finding that he did hear such train, or that by the use of ordinary care he could have heard it. p. 45.

18. RAILROADS.—*Crossing Accidents.*—*Review.*—*Answers to Interrogatories.*—In an action for personal injuries sustained in a collision with defendant's train at a crossing, where the facts elicited by the jury's answers to interrogatories do not show that plaintiff failed to use ordinary care to ascertain the approach of the train before proceeding upon the crossing, or that obstructions or noises other than those mentioned in the interrogatories may not have made it difficult or impossible to hear the approach of the train except by the use of extraordinary care, such facts will not invoke the application of the principle that the law will presume, generally, that a person actually saw what he could have seen if he had looked, and heard what he could have heard if he had listened, such presumption being indulged only in cases where one fails to look or listen, or where the physical surroundings and conditions are such as to force conviction that one did see or hear, notwithstanding a statement or finding that he did not. p. 45.

19. APPEAL.— *Review.*— *Presumptions.*— *Verdict.*— *Answers to Interrogatories.*—In an action for personal injuries in a railroad crossing accident where the general verdict was for the plaintiff, it will be assumed on appeal, on consideration of the refusal of a motion for judgment on the answers to interrogatories, that the evidence showed that there was something to prevent the plaintiff from hearing the approach of the train at the time inquired about in the interrogatories, in the absence of a contrary finding. p. 46.

20. APPEAL.— *Briefs.*— *Points and Authorities.*— *Abstract Statements.*—*Instructions.*—Where appellant's brief, under its points and authorities, makes general statements concerning what is proper and required in giving the instructions, but under such heading makes no application of any of these statements nor reference to any particular instruction, the brief does not comply

with the rules of the Appellate Court, and no question on the instructions is presented for review. p. 46.

21. APPEAL.—*Briefs.—Presenting Grounds for Review.—Instructions.*—No question is presented for review by criticism of certain instructions made in the argument in appellant's brief, where the rule of the Appellate Court relating to the presentation of alleged error under the heading of points and authorities' has not been complied with. p. 47.

22. APPEAL.—*Waiver of Error.—Briefs.*—A ground for a motion for a new trial not referred to under the heading of points and authorities in appellant's brief is waived. p. 47.

23. EVIDENCE.—*Testimony of Physician.—Personal Injuries.—Examination.*—In an action for personal injuries, a physician, called to examine plaintiff to ascertain the extent of his injuries, but not to treat him, could testify as to what he saw and found in such examination. p. 48.

24. EVIDENCE.—*Self-Serving Declarations.—Physician's Examination.—Personal Injury.*—In an action for personal injuries, the testimony of a physician that he found, when examining the plaintiff to ascertain his injuries, a "slight soreness in the intercostal region," was not objectionable as being a self-serving declaration, where such statement did not purport to be what the plaintiff told the witness, but was based on what the witness found in his examination. p. 48.

From Miami Circuit Court; *Joseph N. Tillett*, Judge.

Action by Err Biddinger against the Chicago and Erie Railroad Company. From a judgment for plaintiff, the defendant appeals. *Affirmed.*

*W. O. Johnson, Bull & Johnson* and *Antrim & McClintic,* for appellant.

*Arthur Metzler,* for appellee.

HOTTEL, P. J.—This is an appeal from a judgment in appellee's favor in an action brought by him against appellant for damages alleged to have resulted from injuries received while attempting to cross appellant's railroad tracks at a public street crossing in the city of Rochester, Indiana. The complaint was in two paragraphs, each of which was challenged by a demurrer. This demurrer was overruled and exceptions were properly saved. The only answer was a general denial. There was a trial by jury and interrogatories submitted to it for answer. Upon the return of a general verdict for appellee with the answers to interrogatories, appellant moved for judgment on such answers, which motion was overruled and exceptions were properly saved. These several rulings of the trial court are assigned as error and relied on for reversal. The only objections to each paragraph of the complaint stated in the respective memoranda filed with the demurrers thereto are the same, viz.: (1) That no negligence on the part of appellant is disclosed; (2) that it is disclosed "by fair inference from the alleged facts as pleaded that the plaintiff was guilty of negligence."

The substance of that part of the complaint necessary to an understanding of said objection thereto, and our disposition thereof, is as follows: Appellant's railroad passes through the city of Rochester, Indiana, in an easterly and westerly direction and crosses almost at right angles with the main street in said city, which is the continuation through said city of the highway known as the Michigan road. Such street or road is the principal street of Rochester and is much used by the public at the point where it crosses appellant's railroad. On April 1, 1911, when appellee was injured, there were located on the west side of said street and south of and near the crossing a large number of dwelling houses and lumber sheds, and on the east side of the street and the south side of the railroad, and near thereto, there were located a number of dwelling houses, piles of tile, forest trees, an elevator, and freight cars standing on the switch south of appellant's main track. On account of these obstructions, appellee could not and did not see or hear any train or engine approaching from the east at the time he was injured as hereinafter set out. On April 1, 1911, appellee was in a buggy driving north on said street, intending to pass over said crossing, and *"as he approached and entered near and to said crossing he proceeded carefully and exercised all due care and caution to hear and see*

*any train, engine or locomotive that might be approaching
said crossing either from the east or the west;* and as plaintiff was about to pass over said crossing at the intersection of
said railway and main street appellant *carelessly and negligently ran its engine and train of cars on and against plaintiff* and his horse and buggy with great force and violence,
*which engine and train of cars were carelessly and negligently run at a high and dangerous rate of speed, to wit,
about fifty miles an hour'';* that "said defendant and its
servants, who were then operating said engine and train of
cars and controlling the same, *carelessly and negligently
failed and omitted to sound the whistle, or ring the bell on
said locomotive and train so approaching said crossing,*
when the same was within one hundred rods from said
crossing until about one hundred fifty feet therefrom, and
at that moment for the first time, a whistle on said locomotive was sounded and from the time said train first came
into view, and the time it struck plaintiff there was not
sufficient time by any human effort to escape, and plaintiff
says further that the defendant *carelessly and negligently
failed and omitted to maintain a watchman, flagman, person
or gate at said crossing* to notify plaintiff of the approach
of said engine and train of cars, notwithstanding that on
said day and previous thereto, said crossing was much used
by the public, as many as one or more vehicles passing over
the same in the interval of every two minutes, as well as
many pedestrians crossing the same; * * * that *solely
by and through the negligence of the defendant, as aforesaid,* said engine and train of cars then and there ran with
great force and violence upon and against the plaintiff and
said buggy, and the plaintiff was then and there and thereby
thrown with great force and violence from and out of said
buggy, and was thereby injured * * *.'' (Our italics.)

The second paragraph, except as hereinafter indicated, is
substantially the same as the first and contains additional
averments to the effect that the city of Rochester, on the day

in question, had in force an ordinance, duly passed by the common council, which provided as follows:

> "Section 133. No person shall run a locomotive or steam railway car faster than twenty-five miles an hour within the limits of the City of Rochester.
> "Section 134. Any person violating section 133 of this ordinance shall, upon conviction thereof, be fined in any sum not exceeding $100."

In support of its first objection, *supra*, to the first paragraph of the complaint, appellant insists that it is not alleged that appellant's train approached from a point eighty rods or more from the crossing where appellee was injured, and hence, that the duty to give the signals required by statute is not shown; *that when one predi-*
1. *cates his cause of action on a statute, he must bring himself within it.* That the italicized words, *supra,* announce a correct legal proposition may be conceded, but its applicability in this case depends on the correctness of appellant's assumption that the sufficiency of this paragraph of complaint rests alone upon the sufficiency of a charge of the violation of the statute requiring signals, and the further assumption that the averments here under consideration do not show that appellant's train approached from a point more than eighty rods from the crossing. This paragraph of complaint in fact charges several acts, any of which, if sufficiently charged, would make it good against de-
2. murrer. If, however, such other acts of negligence be entirely disregarded, the averments relating to the failure to give the said statutory signals, are sufficient in and of themselves to show that appellant was guilty of negligence: (1) Because they show, at least by *reasonable inference,* that the train which injured appellee approached from a point not less than 100 rods east thereof, and that from such point the whistle on said train was not blown until the train was about 150 feet from said crossing. We are of the opinion that said averments measure up to the requirements of the cases holding that only necessary in-

ferences can be indulged in favor of a pleading, but in any event they are sufficient under the more recent holdings which permit reasonable inferences to be drawn in favor of a pleading. *Domestic Block Coal Co.* v. *DeArmey* (1913); 179 Ind. 592, 100 N. E. 675, 102 N. E. 99. (2) Said 3. averments expressly show that the bell on such train was not rung continuously as it approached the crossing, which omission was in itself a violation of the statute, and hence negligence, and, independent of the statute, 4. "it is the duty of those in charge of a railroad train to give reasonable and timely warning of its approach to a highway crossing." *Pittsburgh, etc., R. Co.* v. *Terrell* (1911), 177 Ind. 447, 456, 95 N. E. 1109, 1113, 42 L. R. A. (N. S.) 367. What we have said disposes of appellant's first objection, *supra,* to each paragraph of the complaint. However, it is urged against the averments attempting to charge negligence on account of the speed of the train and the failure to provide a flagman, that these averments are not sufficient because there is no averment that there was any legislative or municipal requirement, either limiting the speed of trains, or providing for a gate or flagman at the crossing where appellee was injured, and, that, in the absence of such requirements, neither the running of the train at high speed over the crossing nor the failure to provide a gate or flagman thereat is negligence *per se.*

The legal proposition involved in appellant's contention is substantially correct, but while the running of a train over a crossing at high speed or without any flagman 5. or watchman stationed at the crossing is not negligence *per se,* in the absence of a statute making it so, yet such operation of a train may, in fact, constitute negligence, depending upon all the facts and circumstances surrounding the particular case. *Wabash R. Co.* v. *McNown* (1912), 53 Ind. App. 116, 123, 99 N. E. 126, 100 N. E. 383, and cases there cited. The rules as to operation of 6. trains in city and country are different. The rule

which generally obtains, permitting a train to be run
in the country at a high speed without the imputation of
negligence, does not obtain as to trains when operated
through populous cities and over the much-traveled crossings therein. *Cleveland, etc., R. Co.* v. *Lynn* (1908), 171
Ind. 589, 598, 85 N. E. 999, 86 N. E. 1017; *Pittsburgh, etc.,
R. Co.* v. *Lynch* (1908), 43 Ind. App. 177, 180-182, 87 N.
E. 40; *Wabash R. Co.* v. *McNown, supra,* 123.

The averments above indicated, show that appellee was a
traveler on said street attempting to cross appellant's tracks,
and hence show that appellant owed to appellee the duty
of ordinary care. They also show that it failed to discharge
that duty by *carelessly* and *negligently* running its train
*"at a high and dangerous rate of speed, to wit, about 50
miles an hour"*; that *"it carelessly and negligently* failed
and omitted to maintain a watchman, flagman, person or
gate at said crossing"; that said crossing "was much used
by the public, as many as one or more vehicles passing over
the same * * * every two minutes, as well as many pedestrians crossing the same." Where the duty to use
7.  ordinary care is shown, the *general averment* that
appellant *carelessly and negligently did or omitted to
do* the acts necessary to the discharge of such duty, and that
such negligent acts were the proximate cause of the injury
complained of, render the complaint sufficient as against a
demurrer, unless the specific acts pleaded are of a character
to destroy the force and effect of such general charge of
negligence. *Tippecanoe Loan, etc., Co.* v. *Cleveland, etc.,
R. Co.* (1914), 57 Ind. App. 644, 656, 657, 104 N. E. 866,
106 N. E. 739, and cases there cited; *Cleveland, etc., R. Co.*
v. *Clark* (1912), 51 Ind. App. 392, 404, 405, 97 N. E. 822;
*New York, etc., R. Co.* v. *Lind* (1913), 180 Ind. 38, 44, 45,
102 N. E. 449. We do not think it can be seriously
8.  contended that the specific averments that follow the
general charge of negligent speed, viz., that it was
at a high and dangerous rate, to wit, fifty miles an hour,

when considered in the light of the averments showing that such crossing was in a city where vehicles were passing over it every two minutes, even tend to overthrow such general averment. The averment as to the frequency of

9. the travel at the crossing also strengthens the averment that the appellant *negligently and carelessly* failed to maintain a watchman, etc. Judged by any or all of the authorities, each of said paragraphs of complaint contains facts sufficient to show actionable negligence on the part of appellant in each of the respects indicated.

In connection with this ground of the demurrer to the second paragraph, appellant suggests an additional objection, which, on account of its influence on other questions presented by the appeal, will be here considered. It is insisted by appellant that the charge of negligence in this paragraph, which is predicated on the violation of the ordinance above set out, is insufficient because of the absence of averments showing that appellant's railroad was located within the city of Rochester; and hence, that there was nothing to show that the council of the city of Rochester had jurisdiction over appellant, or that such council could enact ''a valid ordinance regulating the operation of appellant's locomotive or cars within the corporate limits of said city.''

The second paragraph, as affecting the question raised by appellant's objection, contains averments as follows, to wit:

10. That appellant was operating a line of railway in and through Fulton county, Indiana, and doing business as such railroad company, among other countries, in said county of Fulton and State aforesaid; ''that said *Main street*, or *Michigan road*, is the principal street of the city of Rochester, and very much used by the public, especially at the point where the same crosses defendant's railway. While these averments may not necessitate the inference that said crossing was within the city limits of the city of Rochester, we think such fact may be reasonably inferred there-

from, and hence meet the requirements of the later decisions of the Supreme Court. *Domestic Block Coal Co.* v. *De-Armey, supra.*

Assuming, however, without deciding, that such averments are not sufficient to show that the crossing in question was within the limits of the city of Rochester, the fact

11. remains that such second paragraph is, in any event for reasons already indicated, sufficient against demurrer and, as affecting any other question suggested by appellant, this court may and will treat said paragraph as amended in the respect indicated to conform to the proof, such issue having been fully tried and proof thereon made under the first paragraph. *Chicago, etc., R. Co.* v. *Gorman*
• (1914), 58 Ind. App. 381, 106 N. E. 897, and cases there cited.

In support of its second objection to said paragraphs of complaint, appellant insists, in effect, that because of the averments therein showing the obstruction of appel-

12. lee's view as he approached the crossing; that he was riding in a top buggy with the side curtains down; that "on account of * * * obstructions appellee *could not* * * * see or hear any train or engine approaching from the east on the day and time that he was injured," nothing short of stopping could relieve appellee from being guilty of negligence, and that, because of the absence of such averment, the court should have held that under the facts pleaded, appellee was guilty of contributory negligence. There is no doubt that some of the averments above indicated, especially when separated from those in connection with which they are pleaded, tend to show that appellee was guilty of contributory negligence. It must be remembered, however, that contributory negligence is

13. a defense, and, while it is true, as appellant contends, that such negligence may appear from the complaint, and when it does so appear it is the duty of the court to hold the complaint insufficient as against a demurrer predicated

on such ground, yet the court can do this only when it can say, as a matter of law, that under the facts pleaded, honest and reasonable men could draw but one inference therefrom, viz., that the plaintiff's conduct was not that of a man of ordinary care and prudence. *Cleveland, etc., R. Co.* v. *Clark, supra,* 412, 413; *Cole* v. *Searfoss* (1911), 49 Ind. App. 334, 338-340, 97 N. E. 345; *Wabash R. Co.* v. *McNown, supra,* 135.

The averments, *supra,* upon which appellant relies must be read in connection with and in the light of those which

12. follow them which charge that appellee, when he approached and entered near the crossing, proceeded carefully and exercised all due care and caution to see and hear any train. When these averments are so read, we think that a fair interpretation of their meaning is that appellee in approaching said crossing used all due care and caution; that is to say, all care and caution usually used by a man of ordinary care and prudence to see and hear an approaching train, and that by the use of such care he could not, and did not, see such train. The law requires

14. persons traveling on the streets of a city in a vehicle and approaching a railroad crossing to stop before passing over the crossing only in those cases where ordinary prudence would dictate such a course, and it is only in exceptional cases that the court can say that the facts pleaded affirmatively show the necessity for such action. *Lake Erie, etc., R. Co.* v. *Moore* (1912), 51 Ind. App. 110, 117, 97 N. E. 203; *Cleveland, etc., R. Co.* v. *Lynn* (1911), 177 Ind. 311, 322, 95 N. E. 577, 98 N. E. 67; *Pennsylvania Co.* v. *Horton* (1892), 132 Ind. 189, 194, 31 N. E. 45.

The particular interrogatories and answers thereto on which appellant predicates its contention that its motion for judgment on the answers to interrogatories should have been sustained are as follows: "Interrogatory No. 2. At the point near where said main track crosses Main street in

said city of Rochester, was there a spur track, also called
the elevator track, running parallel with said main track
and 21½ feet south of said main track? Answer. Yes.

"Interrogatory No. 20. Did plaintiff see or hear said
train No. 9 approaching from the east before he reachxd
the elevator track? Answer. No.

"Interrogatory No. 23. Did the obstructions along and
immediately east of Main street, the side curtains on plaintiff's buggy and the noise from the steel tires on his buggy
passing over said brick pavement prevent him from hearing
said train No. 9 approaching from the east while he traveled
from a distance two hundred feet south from the center of
defendant's main track until he reached the elevator track?
Answer. No.

"Interrogatory No. 39. With a box car standing on the
elevator track east of the crossing, could plaintiff have heard
the approach of said train without stopping his horse? Answer. Yes.

"Interrogatory No. 40. With a box car standing on the
elevator track east of the crossing could plaintiff have heard
the approach of said train before he crossed the elevator
track if he had stopped and listened? Answer. Yes."

What we have just said in our discussion of appellant's
second objection to each paragraph of the complaint, is
applicable to this question. The general verdict is a
15. finding that every averment of the complaint essential to appellee's cause of action is true, and to support such verdict against the attack under consideration,
the court must assume as proven every fact provable under
any supposable evidence admissible under the issues which
in any way tends to support such general verdict, or which
tends to reconcile it with the answers to interrogatories.

Appellant apparently attaches a meaning and importance
to interrogatory No. 23 which we cannot give it. It is our
duty to so interpret it as to reconcile it with the
16. general verdict, if its words will permit such inter-

pretation. As we interpret the answer to said interrogatory, it does not mean that appellee heard or that he could have heard said approaching train from a point 200 feet south of the center of appellant's main track. On the contrary, a fair and reasonable interpretation of such answer, and one in no way in conflict with the general verdict, is simply that the things *mentioned in the interrogatory* did not prevent appellee from hearing, etc. This does not necessarily mean that something else may not have prevented him from hearing the train, or that he in fact heard it. Neither do we attach to interrogatories Nos. 39 and 40 the

17. importance which appellant gives to them. In the first place, the interrogatories are in a sense misleading, especially when read together. The jury may have meant by their answers thereto simply that the presence of the box car on the elevator track would have had nothing to do with appellee's hearing the train either if he had or had not stopped his horse, but giving to appellant the most favorable interpretation to which the answers are susceptible, they mean that appellant *could* have heard the approaching train, either by stopping his horse and listening, or without stopping his horse. This is not a finding, nor is it the equivalent of a finding that he did hear such train, or that by the use of *ordinary care only* he could have heard such train. On the contrary, the general verdict is a finding that he did use ordinary care, and that he did not hear said train. It is not at all inconsistent to say that a thing *could be seen or heard* which one who used only ordinary care failed to see or hear. The use of ordinary care to see and hear

18. will ordinarily reveal the things which are likely to be seen, but will not ordinarily reveal those things which it is possible to see or hear only by the exercise of extraordinary care or effort to see and hear. It is true, as appellant contends, that, generally speaking, the law will presume that a person actually saw what he could have seen if he had looked, and heard what he could have heard if he

had listened, but this presumption is indulged in cases where
one fails to look or listen, and in cases where the physical
surroundings and conditions are such as to force conviction
that one did see or hear, notwithstanding a statement or
finding that he did not. *Cones, Admr., v. Cincinnati, etc.,
R. Co.* (1888), 114 Ind. 328, 16 N. E. 638; *Lake Erie, etc.,
R. Co. v. Stick* (1896), 143 Ind. 449, 41 N. E. 365; *Pittsburgh, etc., R. Co. v. Fraze* (1898), 150 Ind. 576, 50 N. E.
576, 65 Am. St. 377; *Malott v. Hawkins* (1902), 159 Ind.
127, 63 N. E. 308; *Cleveland, etc., R. Co. v. Moore* (1909),
45 Ind. App. 58, 90 N. E. 93; *Cleveland, etc., R. Co. v.
Pace* (1912), 179 Ind. 415, 101 N. E. 479; *Cleveland, etc.,
R. Co. v. Starks* (1913), 58 Ind. App. 341. The facts elicited
by the answers, *supra*, do not invoke the application of this
principle because there is no finding that appellee did not
use ordinary care, and there is no finding that some obstruction other than the box car on the elevator track or that
some noise present at the time appellee approached the crossing may not have interfered with and made the hearing of
the approach of such train difficult or impossible except by
the use of extraordinary care. The evidence may have
shown, and for the purposes of the question under
19. consideration, we must assume that it did show, that
there was something to prevent appellee from hearing
at the time inquired about in the interrogatories. We conclude, therefore, that no error resulted from the ruling on
the motion for judgment on said answers.

Appellant, in its points and authorities, makes some general statements with reference to what is proper and required in the giving of instructions, but under such
20. heading no application is made of any of these statements to any particular instruction, nor is there any
mention of, or reference to, any particular instruction. This
is not a compliance with the rules of the court, and hence no
question is presented on the instructions. *German Fire Ins.
Co. v. Zonker* (1914), 57 Ind. App. 696, 701, 703, 108 N. E.

160; *Pittsburgh, etc., R.·Co.* v. *Lightheiser* (1906), 168 Ind. 438, 460, 78 N. E. 1033; *Chicago, etc., R. Co.* v. *Dinius* (1913), 180 Ind. 596, 626, 627, 103 N. E. 652; *Kaufman* v. *Alexander* (1913), 180 Ind. 670, 671, 103 N. E. 481; *Weidenhammer* v. *State* (1913), 181 Ind. 349, 350, 103 N. E. 413, 104 N. E. 577; *Bray* v. *Tardy* (1914), 182 Ind. 98, 105 N. E. 772.

In its *argument*, appellant challenges and criticizes particular instructions, but this does not meet the requirements of said rule. *Leach* v. *State* (1912), 177 Ind: 234, 21. 239, 97 N. E. 792. We might say, however, that in our discussion of the several grounds of the objections to the complaint, we, in effect, dispose of most of said criticisms and objections. Of twenty-five instructions tendered by appellant, all but four were given, and the instructions are as favorable to it as the law would warrant.

The first, second, third and fourth grounds of appellant's motion for new trial are predicated on alleged errors in the admission of evidence. For convenience, we take up these grounds in their reverse order.

The fourth ground is not referred to in appellant's points and authorities, and hence is waived.

Dr. Homer C. Haas was asked the following question: "Now state to the Court and jury what you discovered with reference to the conditions of his body," to which 22. he answered: "I found that there is a slight enlargement of the ninth rib on the left side *with slight soreness in the inter-costal region.*" This question was objected to on the ground that the evidence was incompetent because the examination was made for the purpose of testifying at the trial. Appellant also objected to and moved to strike out the italicized portion of the answer, *supra*, on the ground that "it is a self-serving declaration on the part of the plaintiff." The second and third grounds of the motion for new trial, as set out in appellant's brief, are respectively based on the court's action in overruling the objection to said question and its motion to strike out the part of the answer indicated.

As preliminary to its objection, appellant developed, by questions put to and answered by the witness, that the examination of appellee made by the witness was 23. made the night before the trial and not for the purpose of treating appellee. It is so well settled in this State that a physician may testify to what he saw and found as a result of such an examination that citation of authorities is unnecessary. The part of the answer which the appellant sought to strike out did not purport to be what the appellee told the witness, but is a statement of 24. what the witness found from his examination, and hence was not subject to appellant's objection.

The first ground of appellant's motion for new trial is predicated on the action of the trial court in overruling appellant's objection to a similar question put to another doctor, the objection being the same as that made to the question, *supra*, put to Dr. Haas, and, hence, for the same reason does not present error.

Appellant also challenges the verdict of the jury on the ground that it is not sustained by sufficient evidence, but our examination of the record convinces us that there was evidence at least tending to support all of the elements of the complaint essential to appellee's cause of action.

Finding no error in the record, the judgment below is affirmed.

NOTE.—Reported in 113 N. E. 1027. Violation of rule as to the giving of signals as evidence of negligence, note, 8 L. R. A. (N. S.) 1063. Care required of railroad companies at crossings, 26 Am. Rep. 207. Discussion of the duty of railroad companies to maintain flagmen at crossings, in the absence of statute, 4 Ann. Cas. 294; 17 Ann. Cas. 962. See under (2) 33 Cyc 1053, 1058; (3) 33 Cyc 968; (4) 33 Cyc 958; (5) 33 Cyc 943, 971; (6) 33 Cyc 974; (7, 10) 29 Cyc 570; 33 Cyc 1054; 33 Cyc 1058; (14) 33 Cyc 1010.

## CENTRAL INDIANA RAILWAY COMPANY v. CLARK.

[No. 9,041. Filed June 1, 1916. Rehearing denied October 25, 1916.]

1. MASTER AND SERVANT.—*Injuries to Servant.—Employers' Liability Act.—Fellow-Servant Doctrine.—Instruction.*—In an action for injuries to plaintiff caused by the breaking of a drift pin, an instruction that defendant was not liable, if the boilermaker with whom plaintiff was working at the time of the injury procured the defective drift pin from the blacksmith shop instead of from the tool room where defendant kept the supply of drift pins for use in the shop, was properly refused, since it is based on the fellow-servant doctrine which was abolished by §1 of the act of 1911 (Acts 1911 p. 145, §8020a *et seq.* Burns 1914). p. 51.

2. MASTER AND SERVANT.—*Injuries to Servant.—Liability of Master.*—In an action by a boiler-shop employe for personal injuries sustained by the breaking of a defective drift pin, the act of defendant's boiler maker who had charge of the boiler repair work, in getting the drift pin from the blacksmith shop rather than from the tool room, where tools and supplies were provided for use in the shops, was the act of the defendant and he was responsible therefor. p. 51.

3. MASTER AND SERVANT.—*Injuries to Servant.—Duty to Furnish Safe Tools.—Instruction.*—In an action for personal injuries, an instruction that it was the employer's duty to furnish safe tools and appliances for its servants to work with was too broad a statement of the law. p. 52.

4. APPEAL.—*Harmless Error.—Instruction.*—In an employe's action for personal injuries sustained by the breaking of a drift pin used in the repair of a boiler, a statement in an instruction that the master was bound to furnish safe tools and appliances for his employes to work with, which was a too broad statement of the law as tending to impute that the master was the insurer of the safety of his servants, was harmless, where the jury found by answers to interrogatories, that the pin provided was not made of proper material and that it was not suitable for the purpose for which it was being used at the time of the accident. p. 52.

5. MASTER AND SERVANT.—*Injuries to Servant.—Defective Appliance.—Knowledge of Employer.—Burden of Proof.—Statute.*—Under §3 of the Employers' Liability Act of 1911 (Acts 1911 p. 145, §8020a *et seq.* Burns 1914), when an appliance furnished the complaining servant has been proved defective, the burden is on the employer to prove that it did not know of the defect. p. 52.

6. MASTER AND SERVANT.—*Injuries to Servant.—Independent Acts of Negligence.—Liability.—Instruction.*—In an action for personal injuries, a statement in an instruction that the jury should find for the plaintiff, if any of the acts of negligence charged in the complaint was established and such negligent act was the proximate cause of the injury, as it was not incumbent upon the plaintiff to prove all the acts of negligence alleged, was not erroneous, when considered in connection with other instructions given, where several distinct acts of negligence were charged in the complaint, any one of which might have been sufficient to make the defendant liable. p. 52.

7. TRIAL.—*Instruction—Withdrawing Evidence from Jury.*—Where evidence has been stricken out on motion, the giving of an instruction withdrawing such evidence from the consideration of the jury is not error. p. 53.

8. DAMAGES.—*Personal Injuries.—Diminished Earning Capacity.—Instruction.*—In an action for personal injuries, an instruction that the jury should consider, in assessing damages, plaintiff's diminished earning capacity, due to his injuries, was proper. p. 53.

9. DAMAGES.—*Personal Injuries.—Medical Expenses of Minor.*—In an action by an infant for personal injuries, where there was testimony that the physician attending plaintiff had made a certain charge for his services, but it was not in evidence to whom the charge was made, it was not improper to allow plaintiff to recover for medical expenses. p. 53.

10. DAMAGES.—*Medical Expenses of Minor.—Liability of Father.*—While a father is liable for necessaries furnished to a minor child, such as a physician's services, yet such obligation is also the debt of the minor, and he may recover for his medical expenses in an action for personal injuries. p. 53.

From Delaware Superior Court; *Robert M. VanAtta,* Judge.

Action by Samuel R. Clark, by his next friend, Eli H. Clark, against the Central Indiana Railway Company. From a judgment for plaintiff, the defendant appeals. *Affirmed.*

*U. C. Stover, Thompson & Sprague, A. N. Van Nuys* and *James L. Murray,* for appellant.

*George W. Cromer, A. C. Gadbury* and *Harry Long,* for appellee.

IBACH, J.—Appellee recovered damages for injuries alleged to have been caused by appellant's negligence. The

errors assigned and argued all arise upon the court's overruling of appellant's motion for new trial. One charge of
the complaint was that appellant furnished appellee, an in-
experienced minor, with a drift pin made from unsuitable
material and ordered him to drive it through a hole in a
boiler that he was helping to mend; and that the pin broke
when he struck it and, by reason of the faulty material, a
piece of the broken pin flew off and hit his eye, injuring his
vision. The cause is brought under the act of 1911, (Acts
1911, ch. 88, p. 145, §8020a *et seq.* Burns 1914).

Objection is first made to the refusal to give instruction
No. 15 on appellant's request. This instruction is as follows: "If you find from a preponderance of the evi-
1. dence that the defendant maintained in its shop where
the plaintiff was working a tool room in which was
kept a supply of drift pins and such other tools as were required for use in its shop, and if you further find that the
boiler makers, including the said Flannigan, were each provided with a tool box in which were two or more drift pins
for their use in said shop in patching or mending boilers,
and if the evidence shows that said Flannigan, with whom
said Clark was working at the time of the injury, a few days
prior to said injury went into the the blacksmith shop and
secured a certain pin from the defendant's blacksmith in
said shop which pin afterwards broke and thereby injured
plaintiff's eye, then I instruct you to find for the defendant."

There was no error in refusing this instruction. This instruction was based on the fellow-servant doctrine, and this is
abolished by §1 of the act of 1911, *supra*, under consideration. Further, the jury found by answer to inter-
2. rogatories that Flannigan was given charge of the
boiler mending and had authority to direct the work.
So far as appellee is concerned the act of Flannigan in getting the drift pin in question from the blacksmith shop
rather than from the tool room was the act of appellant.

Objection is also made to instruction No. 13 given of the

court's own motion by which the jury was told, among other
things, that it was the duty of appellant to furnish
3. safe tools and appliances for its servants to work with.
This portion of the instruction is too broad a statement of the law although, when considered in connection
with the other instructions on the same point, it is
4. doubtful whether the jury could have been misled
into believing that appellant was an insurer of appellee's safety as contended by appellant. However, the
complaint alleges, and it is found by the jury in answer to
interrogatories, that the drift pin furnished by appellant to
appellee to work with was made of a file, which is not proper
material, and that it was not a proper and suitable drift pin
for the purpose for which it was being used when broken,
for the reason that it was too hard. Such finding is supported by the evidence. If there was error in the giving
of the instruction, it is shown by the answers to inter-
5. rogatories that such error was harmless, since the jury
clearly found such a condition of the tool furnished
that appellant is liable. When the pin was proved defective,
the burden was on appellant to prove that it did not know of
the defect. Acts 1911 (§3), *supra*.

When considered with the other instructions given, there
was no error in that portion of the court's instruction No. 10,
which stated to the jury that if it should "find from
6. the evidence that the defendant was guilty of any of
the acts of negligence charged in the complaint, and
that such act of negligence was the proximate cause of the
plaintiff's injury, then your verdict should be for the plaintiff, if he has otherwise made his case, it is not incumbent
upon plaintiff to prove all the acts of negligence charged
in the complaint." There were several distinct acts of negligence which were charged in the complaint, any one of which
might have been sufficient to make appellant liable. Further, the jury in answer to interrogatories found appellant

had committed enough negligent acts charged to establish liability.

There was no error in the giving of instruction No. 17 whereby the consideration of certain evidence was withdrawn from the jury. The court had previously sustained 7. the motion of appellee to strike out all of the testimony which was withdrawn by the instruction, and the record shows that such motion was sustained. The action of the court in sustaining such motion is not assigned as error. There could be no error in withdrawing from the jury by an instruction evidence which had already been stricken out on motion.

Instruction No. 16 given by the court told the jury in assessing damages, if any should be found, to consider, among other things, "the plaintiff's ability to earn money 8. in the support of himself, prior to his injury, and the ability of the plaintiff to earn money since the injury, as shown by the evidence; any expense the plaintiff has incurred in and about healing or curing the injuries which he has sustained, by way of physician's bills, expenses for medicine, and necessary care bestowed upon him, if any, as disclosed by the evidence." There was no error in allowing recovery for a diminished ability to earn money.

It is objected that as appellee is a minor, the doctor 9. bill is a debt of the father and not of appellee. However, the instruction only allowed a recovery for expenses actually incurred by appellee, and though there was testimony that the doctor had charged $37 for his 10. services, it was not in evidence to whom the charge was made. Although the father is liable for necessaries furnished a minor, yet the obligation for such is also a debt of the minor, and it is not improper to allow him to recover for his medical expenses. Such recovery would cut off the right of the father to recover. *City of Columbus* v. *Strassner* (1894), 138 Ind. 301, 34 N. E. 5, 37 N. E. 719; *Board, etc.* v. *Castetter* (1893), 7 Ind. App. 309, 33 N. E.

986, 34 N. E. 687; 22 Cyc 581, 582. The evidence was sufficient to sustain the verdict.

Judgment affirmed.

NOTE.—Reported in 112 N. E. 892. Master and servant: (a) degree of care required of master in providing appliances, 1 Ann. Cas. 340; (b) master's knowledge of defective appliance, effect, 98 Am. St. 303; (c) right of recovery by infant for loss of services or diminished earning capacity during minority, 6 L. R. A. (N. S.) 552.

---

## NATIONAL LIFE INSURANCE COMPANY v. HEADRICK ET AL.

[No. 9,023. Filed May 9, 1916. Rehearing denied October 26, 1916.]

1. TRIAL.—*Verdict.*—*Construction.*—The verdict of a jury for the plaintiff is a finding for plaintiff of every fact essential to a recovery. p. 58.

2. APPEAL.—*Review.*—*Evidence.*—*Sufficiency.*—Where there is evidence from which the facts found by a verdict that are essential to a recovery may have been reasonably inferred by the jury, the evidence is sufficient on appeal, even though other and contrary inferences may be reasonably drawn therefrom. p. 58.

3. PRINCIPAL AND AGENT.—*Ratification.*—Ratification means the adoption of that which was done for and in the name of another without authority, and, when ratification takes place, the act stands as an authorized one and makes the whole act, transaction, or contract good from the beginning. p. 58.

4. PRINCIPAL AND AGENT.—*Ratification.*—*Evidence.*—Ratification is a question of fact which may ordinarily be inferred from the conduct of the parties, and the acts, words, silence, dealings and knowledge of the principal, as well as many other facts and circumstances, may be shown as evidence tending to warrant the inference or finding of the ultimate fact of ratification. p. 58.

5. PRINCIPAL AND AGENT.—*Ratification.*—*Acceptance of Benefits.*—*Estopped.*—Knowingly accepting benefits of an unauthorized employment amounts to a ratification of such contract of employment, and is in the nature of an estoppel to deny the authority to make such contract. p. 58.

6. PRINCIPAL AND AGENT.—*Ratification.*—*Corporations.*—*Acts of Officers.*—Ratification by a corporation, which can act only through its officers and agents, may be shown by conduct without any formal action by its board of directors, and may be

inferred from affirmation, from passive acquiescence, or from the receipt of benefits with knowledge. p. 58.

7. PRINCIPAL AND AGENT.—*Ratification.—Knowledge.—Evidence.*—Where it is sought to show ratification of an unauthorized act, transaction, or contract by the fact that benefits have been knowingly accepted, knowledge, like other facts, need not be proven by a particular kind or class of evidence, and may be inferred from facts and circumstances. p. 58.

8. APPEAL.— *Review.— Incomplete Instructions.—* Where the instructions given, although incomplete, were correct as far as they went, appellant, having failed to present more complete instructions on the subject, cannot on appeal object for that reason. p. 59.

From Marion Superior Court (93,009); *Charles J. Orbison*, Judge.

Action by William D. Headrick and others against the National Life Insurance Company. From a judgment for plaintiff, the defendant appeals. *Affirmed.*

*Charles W. Miller, Henry M. Dowling* and *J. B. Boyer*, for appellant.

*Headrick & Ruick*, for appellees.

FELT, P. J.—This suit originated before a justice of the peace where a judgment was rendered for $100 for legal services alleged to have been rendered appellant at its special instance and request. From the judgment an appeal was taken to the Marion Superior Court where the case was tried by a jury on an issue formed by a general denial of all the averments of the complaint. The jury returned a verdict for appellees in the sum of $95, and also answers to interrogatories. From a judgment on the verdict appellant has appealed and assigned as error the overruling of its motion for a new trial, and certain other alleged errors which are not grounds for independent assignments of error but causes for a new trial. A new trial was asked on the grounds that the court erred in giving the jury certain instructions; that the verdict is not sustained by sufficient evidence; that it is contrary to law; that the assessment of the amount of recovery is erroneous in that the verdict is too large.

In its brief appellant states that: "The theory ultimately relied on by appellees and adopted by the trial court was that the employment of appellees was not authorized by appellant, but that it ratified it. The theory, therefore, is that of ratification, and this is the theory of the case which must be adopted by the Appellate Court." This proposition is not denied by appellees but they contend that the services were rendered with the knowledge and approval of appellant under such circumstances as to show an acceptance of the benefit of the services by appellant, and a ratification of the employment. There is ample evidence to show the rendition and value of the services, but the question of ratification is sharply controverted. There is no denial of the fact that services were rendered in connection with the business of appellant under an employment or arrangement by and between appellees and one V. C. Vette, who was at the time general manager of the railroad accident department of appellant at Indianapolis, but it is contended that he held such position under a written contract which did not authorize him to bind appellant by any contract for the employment of attorneys.

The evidence tends to show that appellant's principal office was in Chicago; that Mr. A. M. Johnson was president of the company during 1911 and up to April, 1912; that Mr. Vette was acquainted with Mr. Johnson and in the summer of 1911 appellee Ruick and Mr. Vette attended a convention of insurance commissioners or state officials appointed by the governors of the several states held in Milwaukee and while there Mr. Vette introduced Mr. Ruick to Mr. Johnson, and in conversation with him in the presence of Mr. Ruick informed him that, if they consummated their contemplated arrangement for Mr. Vette to represent the company, "We will expect to have Mr. Ruick as our attorney," to which Mr. Johnson answered, "Yes, that is all right''; that during the time the services of appellees were being rendered Mr. Vette spent part of his time in his Indianapolis office and part of the time in the Chicago office of appellant; that Mr. Hallman was chief clerk in appellant's accident department and Mr. J. B. Boyer was attorney for that department; that one C. H. Boyer was general manager of appellant's casualty department which included the railroad department.  One Howard Beecham testified that he had worked for Mr. Vette and had also been employed in appellant's Chicago office and worked in the accident department from November, 1911, to the latter part of March, 1912, under Mr. C. H. Boyer and also under instructions of Mr. Vette; that Vette had charge of the railroad department at Indianapolis after January 1, 1912; that he heard the names of appellees mentioned by Mr. Hallman and Mr. J. B. Boyer in connection with the business of appellant in the Chicago office a number of times; that on one occasion Mr. Hallman told him that they were sending some proofs back to Indianapolis to be examined and discussed by Mr. Vette and appellee Ruick; that Mr. Hallman and Mr. J. B. Boyer spoke of appellee as attorneys for the railroad department.  The evidence also tends to show that in 1912 Mr. Vette traveled back and forth between Chicago and Indianapolis frequently in transacting the business of his department, and in his absence from Indianapolis Mr. Ruick attended to any business of appellant that needed attention; that Mr. J. B. Boyer and Mr. Ruick, in January, 1912, had communication about printed matter to be used by the company in its business, Mr. Boyer being at the time in Chicago and Mr. Ruick in Indianapolis; that Mr. Vette severed his connection with appellant the latter part of April, 1912.  Mr. Vette testified that the services of appellees were rendered for appellant and not for him personally; that appellees made out their bill against appellant and handed it to him with a request that he see that it be paid by the company.

The verdict of the jury is a finding for appellees of every fact essential to a recovery. If there is evidence from which such facts may have been reasonably inferred by the

1. jury, it is sufficient on appeal, even though other and contrary inferences may be reasonably drawn there-

2. from. *Abelman* v. *Haehnel* (1914), 57 Ind. App. 15, 21, 103 N. E. 869; *Parkison* v. *Thompson* (1904), 164 Ind. 609, 620, 626, 73 N. E. 109, 3 Ann. Cas. 677.

Ratification means the adoption of that which was done for and in the name of another without authority. It is in the nature of a cure for lack of authorization. When

3. ratification takes place the act stands as an authorized one and makes the whole act, transaction, or contract good from the beginning. Ratification is a question

4. of fact and ordinarily may be inferred from the conduct of the parties. The acts, words, silence, dealings and knowledge of the principal as well as many other facts and circumstances may be shown as evidence tending to warrant the inference or finding of the ultimate fact of ratification. 1 Mechem, Agency §§347-349, 430-434; *Indiana Union Traction Co.* v. *Scribner* (1910), 47 Ind. App. 621, 630, 93 N. E. 1014; *Minnich* v. *Darling* (1893), 8 Ind. App. 539, 544, 36 N. E. 173. Knowingly accepting benefits of an unauthorized employment amounts to a ratification of

5. such contract of employment, and is in the nature ot an estoppel to deny the authority to make such contract. Ratification by a corporation may be shown by conduct without any formal action of its board of directors. Corporations act only by and through their officers and

6. agents and ratification may be inferred from affirmation or from passive acquiescence, or from the receipts of benefits with knowledge. Knowledge like other facts need not be proven by any particular kind or class

7. of evidence and may be inferred from facts and circumstances. *Indiana Union Traction Co.* v. *Scribner, supra*, pp. 629, 630 and authorities cited; *Wilson* v.

*McKain* (1895), 12 Ind. App. 78, 80, 39 N. E. 886; *American Quarries Co.* v. *Lay* (1905), 37 Ind. App. 386, 392, 73 N. E. 608; *Voiles* v. *Beard* (1877), 58 Ind. 510, 511. The jury inferred from the evidence the ultimate fact of ratification by appellant of the employment on its behalf of appellees by appellant's agent, Vette. Other and different inferences might reasonably have been drawn from the evidence, but we cannot say there is a total lack of evidence warranting the inference drawn by the jury.

Some objections are urged to the instructions, but a careful reading and study of all the instructions show that they state the law substantially correctly and the jury 8. could not have been misled by them. If some of them were incomplete, they were correct as far as they went, and appellant, having failed to present more complete instructions on the subject, cannot be heard now to object for such reason. Other questions suggested are waived by failure to present them in the briefs. We find no reversible error. Judgment affirmed.

NOTE.—Reported in 112 N. E. 559. See under (3, 4) 5 Am. St. 109; 31 Cyc 1245, 1263, 1283; 2 C. J. 467, 489, 516; (5) 31 Cyc 1267; 2 C. J. 493; (6) 10 Cyc 1072, 1076, 1078; (7) 31 Cyc 1253, 1641; 2 C. J. 480, 922.

---

## COOLEY ET AL. *v.* POWERS.

[No. 9,436. Filed June 28, 1916. Rehearing denied October 26, 1916.]

1. ADOPTION.—*Power of Legislature.*—The legislature has the power to declare the legal status of an adopted child and invest him with the capacity of inheriting from his adopting parent the same as if he were the adopting parent's child born in wedlock. p. 61.

2. BASTARDS.—*Inheritance.—Adoption.— Legitimate Child.— Statutes.*—Under §§870, 871 Burns 1914, §§825, 826 R. S. 1881, providing that an adopted child shall be entitled to receive the same rights and interest in the estate of the adopting parent

by descent or otherwise that it would if the natural heir, and that the adopting parent shall occupy the same position toward such child as a natural father or mother, an adopted child, by virtue of the statute, stands in the same relation to the estate of the adopting parent as a legitimate child, and must be regarded as such, and, when such child survives, the right of an illegitimate child to inherit the estate of the father under §3000 Burns 1914, Acts 1901 p. 288, providing that where any man acknowledges an illegitimate child as his own, such child shall inherit from his estate, unless a legitimate child or descendants of legitimate children survive, is barred. p. 61.

3. BASTARDS.—*Inheritance.*—*Statute.*—*Construction.*—Section 3000 Burns 1914, Acts 1901 p. 288, provides only for a contingent right of inheritance in some instances in the illegitimate child, and cannot be construed to include the children or descendants of such illegitimate child. p. 63.

From Montgomery Circuit Court; *Jere West,* Judge.

Action by Joseph G. Cooley and another against Francis W. Powers.

From a judgment for defendant, the plaintiffs appeal. *Affirmed.*

*Williams & Murphy,* for appellants.

*Stewart, Hammond & Stuart* and *Simms & Fulwider,* for appellee.

IBACH, J.—In the year 1910, William Powers died intestate, the owner in fee simple of a tract of land in Montgomery county, Indiana. Appellants are the natural children and only heirs of Charley Cooley who was the alleged illegitimate son of said William Powers, and who died intestate before the death of his putative father. Appellee is the legally adopted child of said William Powers. The adopting father of appellee having died without children born in wedlock or their descendants, the point of contention presented by the appeal is whether the adopted child, appellee, was a legitimate child and rightfully entitled to inherit the estate of his adopting father as his heir, within the meaning of §3000 Burns 1914, Acts 1901 p. 288, which provides: "That the illegitimate child or children of any man dying intestate and having acknowledged such child or children during his lifetime as his own, shall inherit his estate, both real and personal, and shall be deemed and taken to be the heir or. heirs of such intestate in the same manner * * * as if such child or children had been legitimate. * * * The provisions of this act shall not apply where the father of the illegitimate child, at his death, had surviving legitimate children or descendants of legitimate children.'' The only error assigned is the court's action in sustaining a demurrer to a complaint by appellants seeking to establish an interest as heirs in the estate of William Powers.

It cannot be successfully contended that the legislature can by statute constitute a child a natural child of any persons other than his natural father and mother,

1. but it has the power to declare the legal status of an adopted child and make him capable of inheriting from his adopting parent the same as if he were his own child born in lawful wedlock. As it is expressed in some of the older cases: "It is competent for the legislature to place a child by adoption in the direct line of descent as it is for the common law to place a child by birth there." And this is what we believe the legislature of this state has

2. done. The statute on this subject, §868 *et seq.* Burns 1914, §823 *et seq.* R. S. 1881, provides the manner in which a child may be adopted, and by §3 of the act it is provided that from and after such adoption the adopted child shall be entitled to receive the same rights and interest in the estate of the adopting parent by descent or otherwise that it would if the natural heir of such adopting parent; and by §4 of the same act it is provided that, after such adoption, the adopting parent shall occupy the same position toward such child that he or she would if the natural father or mother, and be liable for the maintenance and education of such child, and in every way as a natural parent. This language is broad and comprehensive, and when construed in connection with the adjudicated cases

on kindred questions, and in the light of the civil law from which the principles declared in the statute are taken, we believe it to be clear that the legislature intended to create between the adopting father and the adopted child a relation like that existing between the natural father and his child, and with respect to the adopting father's estate he must be regarded as a child in the degree of a legitimate child as that term is used in §3000 Burns 1914, *supra*. He is an heir, a lineal descendant, the same as if born in lawful wedlock, not because of any natural relation existing between them as parent and child, but because he has been given that status by virtue of the statute. *Humphries* v. *Davis* (1885), 100 Ind. 274, 50 Am. Rep. 788. An adopted child, like every other child in the state, is either legitimate or illegitimate; he does not occupy a middle ground. This court in the case of *Harness* v. *Harness* (1911), 50 Ind. App. 364, 98 N. E. 357, quotes with approval this language from *Gates* v. *Seibert* (1900), 157 Mo. 254, 57 S. W. 1065, 80 Am. St. 625: "The word (legitimate) is used without qualification or restriction. There are no degrees of legitimacy, a child is either legitimate or it is illegitimate, and whether it is one or the other depends upon whether or not it comes within the requirements of the law to make it legitimate." See, also, *In re Wardell* (1881), 57 Cal. 484, 491. In the case at bar it is conceded that appellee was legally adopted. The adoptive statutes of this state have already been considered many times by the courts, and while the precise question here involved has not been determined, the conclusion we have reached is supported by the reasoning employed in all those cases where the same general principles have been involved. *Markover* v. *Krauss* (1892), 132 Ind. 294, 31 N. E. 1047, 17 L. R. A. 806, and cases there cited. The common law made no provision for the adoption of children, so that the contention of appellant that the term "legitimate children" meant at common law only those born of the blood in wedlock, and that the legislature in using this term in

§3000 Burns 1914, *supra,* used it in this sense, is erroneous, and the authorities cited by appellants have no application to the precise question under consideration. This conclusion is further supported by another line of cases in which §267 Burns 1914, §264 R. S. 1881, was considered and discussed. By virtue of this statute it has been held that a right of action is vested in the foster parent to maintain a suit for the death of an adopted child but not for the death of an illegitimate child, upon the theory that the adopted child is a legitimate child, its relation to the adopting parent differing in no substantial degree from the relation of the child born of the blood in wedlock to its natural parent. *McDonald* v. *Pittsburgh, etc., R. Co.* (1896), 144 Ind. 459, 43 N. E. 447, 32 L. R. A. 309, 55 Am. St. 185; *Citizens Street R. Co.* v. *Cooper* (1899), 22 Ind. App. 459, 53 N. E. 1092, 72 Am. St. 319; *Thornburg* v. *American Strawboard Co.* (1895), 141 Ind. 443, 40 N. E. 1062, 50 Am. St. 334; *Citizens' Street R. Co.* v. *Willoeby* (1896), 15 Ind. App. 312, 43 N E. 1058. Appellee, the adopted child, by virtue of his status must be regarded as a child in the degree of a legitimate child of his deceased adopting parent, and the effect of such adoption in view of the facts of this case was to cast succession upon him the same as if he had been a natural child.

It is proper to add in this connection that §3000, *supra,* makes provision only for a contingent right of inheritance in some instances in the illegitimate child, and in no 3. way can it be construed to include the children or descendants of such illegitimate child, who died prior to the death of the putative father, but it is unnecessary to discuss this phase of the case further, as the disposition of the proposition considered disposes of the entire case. The demurrer to the complaint was properly sustained. Judgment affirmed.

Caldwell, C. J., Moran and Felt, JJ., concur.

Hottel, P. J., and McNutt, J., concur in result.

### CONCURRING OPINION.

HOTTEL, P. J.—I concur in the conclusion reached in the majority opinion but I am unable to say that I wholly concur with the reasoning upon which it is based.

I do not question the right of the legislature "to place a child by adoption in the direct line of descent," nor do I doubt that, subject to the proviso therein, such is the effect of §870 Burns 1914, *supra*, which provides that such adopted child shall "be entitled to and receive all the rights and interest in the estate of such adopting father or mother, by descent or otherwise, that such child would if the *natural heir* of such adopting father or mother."

It is equally certain that the legislature has the right to place the illegitimate child also in the direct line of descent or do what it did do by §3000 Burns 1914, *supra*, viz.: make him an *heir* of his intestate, putative father under the conditions therein named "in the same manner as if such *child* had * * * been *legitimate*," provided such putative father at his death left surviving him no *legitimate children* or the descendants of *legitimate children*.

In my judgment the legislature had in mind, when §3000, *supra*, was enacted, children of the blood only, viz., those begotten or born in wedlock and those begotten and born out of wedlock; the intent of the legislature being to provide for the inheritance of the latter when there was a failure of the blood of the former. The word "illegitimate" as used in such act means the child of the putative father begotten and born out of wedlock and the word "legitimate" means a child begotten or born in wedlock.

By what I have said I do not desire to be understood as expressing any opinion as to the interpretation or construction that should be given to the sections of the statute, *supra*, further than as to the meaning of said words, "legitimate" and "illegitimate," as used in said §3000. Nor do I deem it necessary in this case that the court should determine or decide what would be the relative rights of the adopted child and the illegitimate child under said sections of the statute. Such question is not necessarily involved in this appeal. For the purposes of the question here presented it is sufficient to say that the right of inheritance exists only by virtue of the law which creates the right, and neither the adopted child nor the illegitimate child, nor its descendants, can inherit from the adopting father or the putative father, in the absence of a statute giving it such right.

The appellants are the children of the alleged illegitimate child of the decedent, William Powers, and as such are claiming the real estate in question under §3000, *supra*. This section does not purport to confer any right on the descendants of illegitimate children.

Section 868, *supra*, is very comprehensive and in effect makes the adopted child the legal heir of his adopting father "with all the rights of the natural child," subject only to the proviso therein which does not affect the question here presented.

It follows that appellants are not entitled to the real estate in question because of the absence of any law conferring on them any right of inheritance in the estate of said decedent and that appellee is entitled to such real estate because the law makes him the legal heir in such a case. Upon this ground and for this reason I concur in the conclusion reached in the majority opinion.

McNutt, J., concurs.

NOTE.—Reported in 113 N. E. 382. Power of legislature to give child under existing adoption right to inherit from parent or parent's relatives, note, 35 L. R. A. (N. S.) 216. Inheritance by, through or from illegitimate persons, note, 23 L. R. A. 753; Ann. Cas. 1913C 1338; 7 C. J. 965. See under (1, 2) 1 Cyc 918, 931; 1 C. J. 1372, 1395.

# FOX *v.* CLOSE.

### [No. 9,097.  Filed October 27, 1916.]

1. APPEAL.—*Assignment of Error.—Sufficiency.*—Assignments of
error that the decision of the court is contrary to the evidence
and that the decision of the court is contrary to the law and
the evidence present no cause for a new trial, as they are not
in the form provided by statute, and, since the alleged errors
relate to matters which are required to be brought into the
record by a motion for a new trial, they cannot be made the
subject of independent assignments of error on appeal. p. 68.

2. EXECUTION.—*Proceedings Supplementary to Execution.—Statutes.—Construction.*—Section 859 Burns 1914, §816 R. S. 1881,
providing that if, after issuing an execution against property, the
execution plaintiff, or other person in his behalf, shall file an
affidavit with the clerk of any court of record that the judgment
debtor has property which he unjustly refuses to apply toward
the satisfaction of the judgment, the court shall make an order
requiring the judgment debtor to appear to answer the affidavit,
and such proceeding may thereafter be had for the application
of the property of the judgment debtor toward the satisfaction
of the judgment, as provided upon the return of an execution,
and §860 Burns 1914, §817 R. S. 1881, providing that when the
plaintiff, his agent or attorney, shall at the time of applying for
the order, or at any time afterward, file an affidavit that there
is danger of the debtor leaving the state or concealing himself,
and that there is reason to believe he has property. etc., which
he unjustly refuses to apply to the judgment, with intent to
defraud the creditor, an order for arrest and bail shall issue,
must be considered together, and, when so construed, an execution against the body of a judgment debtor cannot issue, under
the provisions of such sections, while an execution against his
property is unreturned. p. 68.

3. EXECUTION.—*Proceedings Supplementary to Execution.—Complaint.—Sufficiency.*—In a proceeding supplementary to execution
based on §§859, 860 Burns 1914, §§816, 817 R. S. 1881, where the
complaint does not in direct terms aver that execution had been
returned unsatisfied and that defendant did not have property,
other than that alleged to be concealed, on which execution
might be satisfied, is insufficient, when properly attacked, to
warrant the issuance of an execution against the body of a
judgment debtor alleged to be about to leave the state. p. 69.

4. PLEADING.—*Complaint.—Attack by Motion for a New Trial.*—
Where, in a proceeding supplemental to execution, the defect in

the complaint consists of omissions of essential averments and
its sufficiency is attacked on appeal by a motion for a new
trial, such defect will be deemed cured by the verdict, the statute
of amendments, or waived by failure to demur. p. 69.

5. PLEADING.— *Complaint.*— *Omission of Material Averments.*—
*Cure by Evidence.*—Since the amendment of §348 Burns 1908,
§343 R. S. 1881, by the Act of 1911 (Acts 1911 p. 415, §348 Burns
1914), it will be assumed on appeal that any omission of a
material averment from the pleading was cured by the evidence,
if from the affirmative facts pleaded it might have been so
cured. p. 69.

From Vigo Superior Court; *John E. Cox*, Judge.

Action by Elva Close against Winfield M. Fox. From a
judgment for plaintiff, the defendant appeals. *Affirmed.*

*Edward M. White* and *Alexander G. Cavins*, for appellant.
*Walker & Blankenbaker*, for appellee.

IBACH, J.—This was a proceeding supplemental to execution in a cause wherein appellee had previously obtained a
judgment. The substance of the verified complaint, which
is the "foundation of the judgment and the order complained of" is that on March 5, 1912, the plaintiff Eva Close
recovered a judgment against appellant in the Vigo Superior
Court; that thereafter on February 6, 1913, she caused an
execution to be issued on her judgment which was delivered
to the sheriff; that he now holds the execution and the same
is unsatisfied; that there is danger of said defendant leaving
the state of Indiana, or concealing himself, and there is reason to believe and she does believe that defendant has property rights, credits, moneys and effects which he unjustly refuses to apply to the payment and satisfaction of said judgment with intent to defraud the plaintiff.

The court below found the defendant had control of $300
which was subject to execution; that he had been secreting
the same with intent to cheat and defraud the plaintiff; and
that he had unjustly refused to apply said money toward
the satisfaction of the judgment. The court ordered the defendant to deliver such money to the clerk of the court, and

further ordered his imprisonment in the county jail until he should comply with the order for the payment of the money or until otherwise ordered by the court. Appellant prosecutes his appeal from that judgment and assigns as error the overruling of his motion for a new trial.

The assignment of error that the decision of the court is contrary to the evidence presents no cause for a new trial.

1.  *Gates* v. *Baltimore, etc., R. Co.* (1899), 154 Ind. 338, 56 N. E. 722; *Bass* v. *Citizens Trust Co.* (1903), 32 Ind. App. 583, 70 N. E. 400. The same is true of the third assignment of error, ''That the decision of the court is contrary to the law and the evidence.'' Since these assignments are not in statutory form and relate to matters which are required to be brought into the record by a motion for a new trial they cannot be made independent assignments of error. *Whitinger* v. *Nelson* (1868), 29 Ind. 441.

We shall therefore proceed to consider the first specification in the motion, ''That the decision is contrary to law.'' Appellant contends that the decision is contrary to law because it is based on an insufficient complaint and for the further reason that there was no evidence to sustain it. The proceeding is based on §§859, 860 Burns 1914, §§816, 817 R. S. 1881. The filing of the affidavit under the first section gives the right to the filing of the affidavit provided for by

2.  the second. We are of the opinion that the two sections must be considered together and a complaint which omits the essential averments of either must be held to be insufficient when properly attacked. We do not believe it was the intent of the legislature to provide for an execution against the body of a judgment debtor while an execution against his property was unreturned. It was said in the case of *Baker* v. *State, ex rel.* (1887), 109 Ind. 47, 49, 9 N. E. 711: ''An execution against the body is an extraordinary remedy and is not to be resorted to if the amount due upon the judgment may be made by an ordinary execution against the property of the judgment debtor.'' The complaint does

not in direct terms aver that the execution was re-
3. turned unsatisfied by the sheriff and contains no specific averments that appellee did not have property,
other than that concealed, on which the execution might have
been satisfied. As above indicated these were essential averments. We are of the opinion, however, that as against an
attack of the kind here made such defects or omis-
4. sions will be deemed cured by the verdict, the statute of amendments, or waived by failure to demur.
Since the amendment of §348 Burns 1908, §343 R. S. 1881, by
the act of 1911 (Acts 1911 p. 415, §348 Burns 1914),
5. this court will assume that any omission of a material averment from the pleadings was cured by the
evidence, if from the affirmative facts pleaded it might have
been so cured. *Pillsbury, etc., Co.* v. *Walsh* (1915), 60 Ind.
App. 76, 110 N. E. 96.

Applying these principles and well-established rules of
giving all intendments in favor of a complaint where it is
not challenged until after verdict, the complaint will be held
to be sufficient. We need not go into all the facts and circumstances proven at the trial of this case. It is sufficient to
state that the trial court reached the right conclusion, which
is supported both by the positive testimony and the many
circumstances connected with the matter in litigation. The
only reasonable and certain inference to be drawn from the
evidence justified the judgment of the trial court. Judgment
affirmed.

NOTE.—Reported in 113 N. E. 1007. See under (2) 17 Cyc 1434,
1504, 1506; (4) 31 Cyc 763, 769.

## NATIONAL LIVE STOCK INSURANCE COMPANY v. OWENS.

### [No. 9,121.  Filed October 27, 1916.]

1. APPEAL.—*Record.—Matters Not in Record.—Bill of Exceptions.
   —Failure to File in Time.*—Under §657 Burns 1914, Acts 1897
   p. 244, concerning the use of original bills of exception on appeal, a bill of exception containing the evidence which is not
   presented to the trial judge for settlement and signing within
   the time allowed by the court is not a part of the record on
   appeal, and presents no question for consideration. p. 72.

2. APPEAL.—*Record.—Ruling on Demurrers.—Several Exceptions.*
   —A single exception to the ruling of the court sustaining demurrers to several paragraphs of answer is separate and several and presents the question of the sufficiency of each of such
   answers, where the demurrers were separate and several and
   the ruling was on each of them. p. 73.

3. APPEAL.—*Record.—Matters Not in Record.—Scope of Review.*—
   Where the evidence is not in the record, it is not available to
   determine appellee's argument that error, if any, in sustaining
   demurrers to several paragraphs of answer was harmless because evidence in support of such answers was introduced at
   the trial. p. 73.

4. INSURANCE.—*Action on Policy.—Pleading.—General Denial.—
   Evidence Admissible.*—In an action on an insurance policy, where
   it was unnecessary to make plaintiff's application a part of the
   complaint, and for plaintiffs to allege or prove, in the first instance, that the answers made in such application were true to
   entitle them to a recovery, evidence in support of a paragraph
   of answer interposing a defense that false answers in the application constituted a warranty upon which defendant relied, and
   that, when it learned that such answers were untrue the premiums paid were tendered to the assured, was inadmissible under
   an answer of general denial, since §361 Burns 1914, §356 R. S.
   1881, provides that "all defenses, except the mere denial of the
   facts alleged by the plaintiff, shall be pleaded specially," the
   scope of the general denial being merely to put in issue such
   of the averments of the complaint as the plaintiff is bound to
   prove to maintain his action. p. 74.

5. INSURANCE.—*Application.—False Answer.—Validity of Policy.*—
   The mere falsity of an answer in an application for an insurance policy is insufficient to avoid the policy, it being necessary for the insurer to avoid the policy, by reason of such false
   answer, by tendering to the assured the premiums paid. p. 75.

National Live Stock Ins. Co. *v.* Owens—63 Ind. App. 70.

6.  PLEADING.— *General Denial.— Defenses Admissible.*— Defenses admissible under the general denial are those which deny that there ever was a cause of action.  p. 76.

7.  PLEADING.—*Answer.—Pleading Conclusions.—Rights of Plaintiff.—Statute.*—Under §343a Burns 1914, Acts 1913 p. 850, relating to the construction of allegations in pleadings, the pleading of conclusions in a paragraph of answer is permissible, and, if plaintiff desires the facts pleaded which are required to sustain the conclusions, he may obtain relief by the filing of a proper motion, as provided in such statute.  p. 77.

8.  INSURANCE.—*Representations.—Effect of False Statements.— Warranty.*—A mere representation, as distinguished from a warranty, in an application for insurance on the life of an animal, although false, will not necessarily avoid the policy in the absence of bad faith, unless it is substantial and material to the risk; but if statements are warranted to be true and the policy is issued upon the agreement that such statements are warranted, the warranty must be strictly satisfied.  p. 77.

9.  INSURANCE.—*Warranties.—Construction.*—While a warranty relating to an existing fact must be literally true, or the policy does not attach, that which is promissory in its nature is not so strictly construed.  p. 77.

10.  INSURANCE.— *Policy. — Construction. — Forfeiture.*— Insurance contracts are to be strictly construed against the company whenever a strict construction is necessary to prevent the forfeiture of the policy.  p. 77.

11.  INSURANCE.—*Warranties.—Construction.*—A warranty is created only by the most unequivocal language, and, where the words used will admit of two interpretations, that which is the most favorable to the assured will be adopted.  p. 78.

12.  INSURANCE.—*Action on Policy.—Application.—Warranties.*—In an action on a live stock insurance policy, it was error for the trial court to sustain demurrers to paragraphs of answer interposing as a defense alleged false answers in an application for insurance on a horse that the assured had not lost live stock by death, accident, disease or theft within two years and that the horse insured would be cared for by the assured, where such answers were made warranties by the terms of the application, since a breach of such warranties, as pleaded, constituted a defense to the action.  p. 78.

From Johnson Circuit Court; *William E. Deupree*, Judge.

Action by Walter Owens and another against the National Live Stock Insurance Company.  From a judgment for plaintiffs, the defendant appeals.  *Reversed.*

*M. S. Meyberg, L. Ert Slack* and *Berne B. Cohen*, for appellant.

*Elba L. Branigin* and *Thomas Williams*, for appellees.

McNUTT, J.—This was an action in the court below by appellees against appellant on a live stock insurance policy, upon the life of a stallion. Appellant filed its answer in four paragraphs, the first being a general denial. Separate demurrers were filed to the other paragraphs, which were sustained as to the second and fourth paragraphs and overruled as to the third, to which appellees filed a reply in four paragraphs. There was a trial by a jury and a verdict for appellees. Appellant's motion for a new trial was overruled and this action of the court and its action in sustaining said demurrers are assigned as error in this court. The only questions presented by appellant's motion for a new trial requires an examination of the evidence. Appellees insist that this is not in the record, because the bill of exceptions containing the evidence was not filed in time.

The record discloses that appellant's motion for a new trial was overruled on May 28, 1914, and that it was
1. given sixty days in which to file a bill of exceptions. The record further shows that the bill of exceptions was not presented to the trial judge for settlement and signing until August 8, 1914, on which day it was signed and filed. Under the statute and the many decisions of this court, we must hold that the bill of exceptions containing the evidence is not a part of the record; and that no question is presented for our consideration under appellant's fourth assignment of error. §657 Burns 1914, Acts 1897 p. 244; *Hoffman* v. *Isler* (1911), 49 Ind. App. 284, 286, 97 N. E. 188, and cases cited; *Nichols* v. *Central Trust Co.* (1908), 43 Ind. App. 64, 66, 86 N. E. 878; *Ladoga Can. Co.* v. *Corydon Can. Co.* (1912), 52 Ind. App. 23, 98 N. E. 849, 851; *Fireman's Fund Ins. Co.* v. *Finkelstein* (1904), 164 Ind. 376, 73 N. E. 814; *Taylor* v. *Schradsky* (1912), 178 Ind. 217, 97 N. E. 790.

Appellees insist that appellant's first assignment of error, viz., that the court erred in sustaining the demurrers to the second and fourth paragraphs of answer, is waived by appellant's failure to consider said error in its brief, and that the second and third assignments of error are not available because there is not in the record any exception to the court's action in sustaining the separate demurrers to said paragraphs of answer. As will be observed, demurrers

2. to the second and fourth paragraphs of answer were separate and several. The record on the ruling of the court, and the exception by appellant, reads as follows: "The court being fully advised in the premises now sustains the demurrer of the plaintiff to the second and fourth paragraphs of answer, heretofore filed, to which ruling of the court the defendant at the time objects and excepts. And the court being fully advised in the premises now overrules the demurrer of the plaintiff to the third paragraph of answer, to which ruling of the court the plaintiff at the time objects and excepts." This ruling of the court was on each of the separate and several demurrers to said paragraphs. The demurrers being separate and several, and the ruling of the court being on each of them, such ruling must be held, in our opinion, to be separate and several. If this is true, then appellant's exception must be held to be separate and several. *Whitesell·v. Strickler* (1906), 167 Ind. 602, 78 N. E. 845, 119 Am. St. 524. The authorities cited by appellees are not in point. They hold that an assignment of error, which calls in question several rulings of the court, is joint and not several. Appellant has not only assigned as error the rulings jointly, but separately, and we hold that the sufficiency of each of said paragraphs is thereby presented. Appellees, as heretofore noted, insist that the evidence is not in

3. the record, but they also insist that since evidence was introduced in support of the paragraphs of answer, to which demurrers were sustained, that the sustaining of said demurrers, if error, was harmless. We were required,

under the statute and authorities, to hold that the evidence was not in the record, and consequently, the evidence is not available for the purposes insisted upon by appellees. It is next insisted by appellees that even if the second and fourth parapraphs of answer, to which demurrers were sustained, stated facts sufficient to constitute a defense to appellees' complaint, that evidence to support such facts was admissible under the general denial. Section 361 Burns 1914, §356 R. S. 1881, provides: "All defenses, except the mere denial of the facts alleged by the plaintiff, shall be pleaded specially." It has been held repeatedly that the meaning of said section is that every fact which the plaintiff, in the first instance, is under the necessity of proving to sustain his action, or every matter of fact which must or may be alleged in a good complaint, is the proper subject of denial; but that all other matters, that is to say, matters which do not go merely to controvert a fact, or the facts in the complaint, must be set up affirmatively in the answer. 1 Woolen, Trial Procedure §2245, and cases cited. Again it has been held that the scope of the general denial under the code is merely to put in issue such of the averments of the complaint as the plaintiff is bound to prove in order to maintain his action. *Adams Express Co.* v. *Darnell* (1869), 31 Ind. 20, 99 Am. Dec. 582; *Baker* v. *Kistler* (1859), 13 Ind. 63. The above mentioned rule has been somewhat changed by statute in personal injury cases. §362 Burns 1914, Acts 1899 p. 58.

Appellant's second paragraph of answer, among other things, alleges that appellees, in their application, on which the policy sued upon was issued, and of which said application was made a part, made a false answer to a question, knowing that such answer was not a fact, and that the appellees warranted the answer to be true, and that appellant relied upon the answer as being true and relied upon said warranty, and was induced thereby to issue said policy; that

4.

appellant would not have issued said policy had it known that said answer was false; that when it learned that said answer was not true, within a reasonable time, rejected appellees' claim and tendered to appellees the premium which they had paid for said policy. Which tender was rejected and that appellant brought the same into court for appellees' benefit. The question and answer are as follows: "Have you in the last two years lost any live stock by death, accident or disease or theft? Answer: No."

The application upon which the policy in suit was issued was not made a part of appellees' complaint, nor was it necessary to do so; nor was it necessary for the appellees to allege or prove, in the first instance, that the answers in such application were true to entitle them to recover upon the policy. So, under the well-established rules, the matter alleged in said second paragraph of answer was not admissible under the general denial, but was matter of defense requiring a special answer. In *Phenix Ins. Co.* v. *Pickel* (1889), 119 Ind. 155, 21 N. E. 546, 12 Am. St. 393, it is decided: "In an action upon a policy of insurance, the plaintiff need not aver the truth of statements contained in the application, nor the performance or non-performance of conditions subsequent, nor negative prohibited acts; but it is sufficient for him to show fulfilment of the conditions of recovery, and the burden is then upon the defendant to show a breach of warranties." See, also, *Penn Mutual, etc., Co.* v. *Wiler* (1885), .00 Ind. 92, 50 Am. Rep. 769; *Louisville Underwriters* v. *Durland* (1890), 123 Ind. 544, 24 N. E. 221, 7 L. R. A. 399; *Continental Life Ins. Co.* v. *Kessler* (1882), 84 Ind. 310.

The mere falsity of the answer in the application, even if the same could have been shown under the general
5. denial, would have been insufficient to avoid the policy. But appellant was required to take steps to avoid the policy, by reason thereof, by tendering to appellees the premium which they had paid.

Appellees contend that defenses admissible under the gen-

eral denial are those which deny that there ever was a
6. cause of action. This contention is consistent with the
rules above laid down. The complaint in the case at
bar shows that a cause of action once existed, and would so
show even if the falsity of said answer had been admitted,
for such admission would not have rendered the policy absolutely void, *ab initio,* but only voidable, at the election of the
appellant. And in order to avoid the policy it was necessary
for appellant to tender back the premium. In the case of *Modern Woodmen, etc.* v. *Vincent* (1907), 40 Ind. App.
711, 715, 80 N. E. 427, 82 N. E. 475, 14 Ann. Cas.
89, it is said: "It follows that an answer which
seeks to defeat an insurance policy because of a breach
of warranty, must not only set up the warranty and the
breach, but also an election by the insurer to avoid such
policy because of such breach, and this ought certainly to
be true where the warranty was in regard to a fact immaterial to the risk, the breach of which in no way added to
the liability or burden of the insurer, and because of which
it is improbable that any election to avoid would ever be
made." See, also, *American Central Life Ins. Co.* v. *Rosen-
stein* (1910), 46 Ind. App. 537, 92 N. E. 380; *Metropolitan
Life Ins. Co.* v. *Johnson* (1911), 49 Ind. App. 233, 241, 94
N. E. 785, and cases cited. It remains only to be seen whether
said paragraphs of answer state facts sufficient to constitute
a defense to the complaint.

The fourth paragraph of answer is similar to the second,
including the allegation of a tender of the premium and alleges that appellees answered a certain question contained in
the application and thereby made certain promissory warranties which induced appellant to issue said insurance. The
question and answer, referring to said stallion, are as follows: "Is he to be handled by yourself or a keeper? Answer: Myself." Said paragraph further alleges that said
answer was not a fact but that said stallion was handled by
a keeper. It is true, as contended by appellees, that both of

said paragraphs of answer plead conclusions, but un-
7.   der §343a Burns 1914, Acts 1913 p. 850, this is permissible.  If appellees desired the facts pleaded required to sustain the conclusions, they would have been
entitled to such relief upon proper motion, as provided in
said section.

Some of the conditions of said policy are: ''This company shall not be liable if any fact or circumstances relating
to this risk has not been fully and correctly stated to this
company by the assured,  * * *  or if any of the warranties contained in the application, upon which this policy
is based, shall be found to be not a fact.'' The application
set out in appellant's said paragraphs of answer, and alleged
to have been a part of the policy, has these provisions: ''It
is understood that the applicant has answered all of the foregoing questions of his own knowledge, and warrants his answers to be facts, and that the policy to be issued hereon shall
be based entirely upon the answers contained in this application,  * * *.  I warrant the above answers to each of
the foregoing questions as they are written.''

A mere representation, as distinguished from a warranty,
in an application for insurance on the life of an animal, although false, will not necessarily avoid the policy in
8.   the absence of bad faith, unless it is substantial and
material to the risk, but if statements are warranted
to be true and the policy is issued upon the agreement that
such statements are warranted, the warranty must be strictly
satisfied.  25 Cyc 1519, and cases cited.  ''While a
9.   warranty relating to an existing fact must be literally true, or the policy does not attach, that which is
promissory in its nature is not so strictly construed.  In the
later cases it has been held sufficient if substantially true or
performed.  *Phoenix Ins. Co.* v. *Benton* (1882), 87 Ind. 132,
136.  ''Insurance contracts belong to a class which are
10.   to be strictly construed against the company whenever a strict construction is necessary to prevent the

forfeiture of the policy. * * * A warranty is created
only by the most unequivocal language, and where
11.  the words used will admit of two interpretations, that
which is most favorable to the assured will be
adopted." *Iowa Life Ins. Co.* v. *Haughton,* 46 Ind. App.
467, 477, 87 N. E. 702. These legal propositions are well
settled in this state. In many states legislation has made a
different rule with reference to warranties in insurance policies, requiring breaches thereof to be material to the risk,
in order to relieve the insurer. We do not hesitate to say that
such a rule ought to be the law in this state, but this court
cannot legislate. The application which is a part of
12.  the policy sued upon was evidently drawn with a
view of making the answers to the questions warranties, and of guarding against the numerous decisions in this
state to the effect that "where words are used that will admit of two interpretations, that which is most favorable to
the insured will be adopted."

Appellees contend that because it is shown that "Owens
& Patterson" signed the application and that the answer to
one of the questions is "myself," and that appellant's answers refer to the appellees as "plaintiff," that there is such
a failure to identify the appellees as to render the said paragraphs of answer bad. We cannot see that the use of these
words affect the question of warranty, but they do affect the
question of what construction should be put on the words in
determining whether the warranties are true. While a partnership between Owens and Patterson is not averred, there
can be but one inference drawn from the complaint and that
is that they were partners in the ownership, care and management of the stallion. A strict construction against the company of the first question and answer above set out would
require the appellant, in order to maintain its second paragraph of answer, to show that the partnership of Owens and
Patterson had lost live stock by death, accident, disease or
theft within two years prior to the time of the signing of

the application; while a strict construction of the last question and answer above set out would require the appellant, in order to maintain its fourth paragraph of answer, to show that neither Owens nor Patterson substantially performed the promise.

We are unable to find anything in the application, which contains the warranties, authorizing us in holding, under the well-established rules of construction, that the answer to either question set out in the second and fourth paragraphs of answer is a representation merely, requiring facts to be alleged showing that the falsity of such representations was material to the risk; and we are required to hold that the court erred in sustaining the demurrer to each of said paragraphs.

The cause is reversed, with instructions to overrule said demurrers, and to permit the parties to file such motions and pleadings as they may desire.

NOTE.—Reported in 113 N. E. 1024. Live stock insurance, validity and construction of policy, Ann. Cas. 1915A 614; 25 Cyc 1519; 44 L. R. A. (N. S.) 569. Distinction between a warranty and a representation in insurance, 4 Ann. Cas. 255. See under (10) 19 Cyc 656; 25 Cyc 821.

---

## KURTZ v. PHILLIPS.

[No. 9,622. Filed October 27, 1916.]

1. APPEAL.—*Right of Appeal.*—*Statute.*—Independent of statute, the right of appeal does not exist. p. 81.

2. APPEAL.—*Decisions Appealable.*—*Ruling on Motion to Set Aside Default.*—Where judgment was taken against defendant by default, and, after the expiration of the term, she filed a motion, under §405 Burns 1914, §396 R. S. 1881, to set aside the default and judgment on the ground of inadvertence, mistake and excusable neglect, and such motion was overruled, but no final judgment was rendered against defendant, the ruling of the court on the motion did not constitute a final judgment from which an appeal would lie under §671 Burns 1914, §632 R. S. 1881, relating to appeals from final judgments. p. 81.

3. JUDGMENT.—*Motion to Set Aside Default.*—*Pleadings.*—*Complaint.*—*Demurrer.*—While an action seeking to set aside a judg-

ment by default on the ground of inadvertence, mistake and excusable neglect should be determined in a summary manner and
no pleadings are contemplated other than the complaint or motion, yet such complaint or motion may be tested by demurrer.
p. 83.

4. APPEAL.—*Decisions Appealable.—Sustaining Demurrer.*—A ruling sustaining a demurrer to a complaint seeking to set aside
a judgment under §405 Burns 1914, §396 R. S. 1881, is not
appealable, in the absence of a judgment against the party
against whom the ruling is made, since it is not a final judgment within the meaning of §671 Burns 1914, §632 R. S. 1881,
relating to appeals from final judgments. p. 83.

5. APPEAL.—*Review.—Record.—Failure to Include Evidence.*—In
an action to set aside a judgment under §405 Burns 1914, §396
R. S. 1881, where it appeared from the record that the motion
was not denied until after the court had heard the evidence,
which was not made part of the record on appeal by a bill of
exceptions or otherwise, no question on the order of the court
is presented for review on appeal, even though appellant, who
made the motion, asserted that the facts set up in her motion
were not denied, and that the case was submitted on such verified motion alone. p. 85.

From Lake Superior Court; *Walter T. Hardy,* Judge.

Action by John B. Phillips against Flora Kurtz. Judgment for plaintiff by default and from an order overruling
a motion to set aside the judgment, the defendant appeals.
*Appeal dismissed.*

*Ora L. Wildermuth,* for appellant.

*E. G. Sproat* and *Crumpacker & Crumpacker,* for appellee.

HOTTEL, P. J.—The appellee brought suit in the trial court
on a note secured by chattel mortgage. Appellant was defaulted and a judgment rendered against her for $115,
for $30 attorney's fees, and for costs. A foreclosure of the
mortgage, and the sale of the mortgaged chattels were also
ordered and decreed. At the following term, appellant filed
her motion under §405 Burns 1914, §396 R. S. 1881, to set
aside the default and judgment, on the ground of "inadvertence, surprise and excusable neglect" of appellant and her
attorneys as therein set forth. This motion was overruled,
and from the ruling thereon this appeal is prosecuted.

Appellee has filed a motion to dismiss the appeal on the grounds: (1) That the marginal notes required by the rules of the court do not appear on the transcript; (2) because the attempted appeal is from a ruling of the trial court, and not from a final judgment.

Since the filing of said motion, appellant has filed her written petition, asking to be permitted to place upon the transcript the necessary marginal notes. It will be useless to grant this request, if, because of the other ground of appellee's motion or for any other reason, the appeal must be dismissed.

We will therefore first consider and determine whether the appeal is one which the law authorizes. Independent of statute, the right of appeal does not exist. It is not 1. claimed by appellant that the ruling appealed from is an interlocutory order from which an appeal is authorized by clauses 15 to 18 inclusive of §1392 Burns 1914, Acts 1907 p. 238, but it is, in effect, conceded, and properly so, that unless the appeal is authorized by the general section, §671 Burns 1914, §632 R. S. 1881, the right thereto does not exist. That part of this section upon which appellant must base her right to appeal provides as follows: "Appeals may be taken from circuit courts and superior courts to the supreme court by either party *from all final judgments.*" (Our italics.)

The transcript of the record in this case, after setting out appellant's petition or motion to set aside the default and judgment, shows that afterwards, to wit, on April 21, 2. 1916, the following further proceedings were had and entered of record, to wit: "Come now the parties hereto and this cause is now submitted to the court on the motion to set aside the default and judgment taken herein on December 13, 1915. *And the court having heard all the evidence* and argument of counsel now takes the same under advisement until next Monday morning April 24, 1916." (Our italics.) Then follows the record entry of April 24, overruling said motion, which entry omitting caption is as follows: "Come again the parties hereto, and the court now being fully advised in the premises, overrules defendant's motion to set aside the default and judgment herein, to which ruling of the court the defendant now duly excepts and prays an appeal to the Appellate Court of Indiana, which appeal is by the court granted upon the filing by the defendant of a bond in the sum of Three Hundred ($300.00) Dollars within thirty days from this date." This entry shows no final judgment, but nothing more than the ruling on the motion to set aside the default, and the exception to such ruling, a prayer for appeal therefrom, the granting of the appeal, and the fixing of the bond. No judgment of any kind is rendered against appellant.

It seems to be appellant's contention that an appeal will lie from an order overruling a motion to set aside a default and vacate a judgment when such judgment itself was final. In support of this contention appellant cites the following Indiana cases: *Beatty* v. *O'Connor* (1886), 106 Ind. 81, 5 N. E. 880; *Frost* v. *Dodge* (1860), 15 Ind. 139; *Hays* v. *Bank* (1863), 21 Ind. 154; *Western Union Tel. Co.* v. *Griffin* (1890), 1 Ind. App. 46, 27 N. E. 113; *Goldsberry* v. *Carter* (1867), 28 Ind. 59; *Sloan* v. *Faurqt* (1894), 11 Ind. App. 689, 39 N. E. 539.

The question here involved was not presented or decided in any of these cases. In the first case, *supra*, the language of the opinion indicates that there was a final judgment, and in the other cases the motion to set aside the default and vacate the judgment was made at the same term of court that such judgment was rendered, and hence, while the original action was *in fieri*. The court, in such a case, would still have jurisdiction of the original action, and independent of §405 Burns 1914, *supra*, it would be within the sound discretion of the court to set aside the default and vacate the judgment on a proper application and showing. *Masten* v. *Indiana Car, etc., Co.* (1900), 25 Ind. App. 175, 57 N. E.

148; *Domestic Block Coal Co.* v. *Holden* (1914), 56 Ind. App. 634, 640, 103 N. E. 73, and cases there cited.

And on appeal *from the judgment taken by default,* we think the ruling on such motion might be properly treated as a step in, and a part of, the proceedings of such original action, and hence be considered and passed upon by the appellate tribunal where presented by a proper assignment of error. Such is the effect of some of the cases, *supra.* They recognize the right of appeal from a judgment by default and also recognize that in such an appeal the ruling on the motion to set aside the default and vacate such judgment when made at the same term may be reviewed when properly assigned as error and presented to the appellate tribunal.

In the instant case, as we have already indicated, appellant's motion was made after the term at which the judgment by default was taken, and was based on §405 Burns 1914, *supra,* which requires that the court *shall* relieve a party from a judgment taken against him through his mistake, inadvertence, surprise or excusable neglect * * * *on complaint or motion filed within two years.''* This section gives an independent right or remedy, and when one seeks its benefit, after the court rendering the judgment sought to be vacated has lost jurisdiction of the original action, there must then be a final judgment in such new proceeding before an appeal will lie. While the action should be determined in a summary manner and no pleadings are contem-

3. plated other than the complaint or motion, yet both the Supreme Court and this court have held that such complaint or motion may be tested by demurrer. *Masten* v. *Indiana Car, etc., Co. supra,* p. 127; *Taylor* v. *Watkins* (1878), 62 Ind. 511; *Thompson* v. *Harlow* (1897), 150 Ind. 450, 50 N. E. 474; *Durre* v. *Brown* (1893), 7 Ind. App. 127, 34 N. E. 577. If there had been a demurrer filed to this complaint and the demurrer thereto sustained, ap-

4. pellant could not have appealed from the ruling on such demurrer, as it has been frequently held that

such a ruling, in the absence of a judgment against the party against whom the ruling is made, is not a final judgment within the meaning of §671 Burns 1914, *supra*. *Hollingsworth* v. *Hollingsworth* (1902), 29 Ind. App. 556, 64 N. E. 900; *James* v. *Lake Erie, etc., R. Co.* (1896), 144 Ind. 630, 43 N. E. 876; *State, ex rel.* v. *Lung* (1907), 168 Ind. 553, 80 N. E. 541. As indicating what are final judgments within the meaning of the said section of the statute, see, also, *Mak-Saw-Ba Club* v. *Coffin* (1907), 169 Ind. 204, 82 N. E. 461; *Gray* v. *Singer* (1894), 137 Ind. 257, 36 N. E. 209, 1109; *Jeffersonville* v. *Tomlin* (1893), 7 Ind. App. 681, 35 N. E. 29; *Nisius* v. *Chapman* (1912), 178 Ind. 494, 99 N. E. 785; Elliott, App. Proc. §§82-96, 334, and cases cited thereunder; Ewbank's Manual §82 and authorities cited.

In the case of *Mak-Saw-Ba Club* v. *Coffin, supra*, the court said: "It was decided in *Tatem & Canby* v. *Gilpin* (1816), 1 Del. Ch. 13, that an order made upon a point whereby a right was established was not appealable where it was only preparatory to a final order. We may here observe that Judge Freeman, in attempting to classify the orders which may be mistaken for final judgments or decrees, mentions, as belonging to one of such classes, orders, 'which, while they determine the rights of the parties either in respect to the whole controversy or some branch of it, merely ascertain and settle something without which the court could not proceed to a final adjudication, and the settlement of which is obviously but preliminary to a final judgment or decree.' 1 Freeman, Judgments (4th ed.), §29." Assuming that this case was submitted on the showing made by the complaint alone, it seems to us that the ruling would not be essentially or substantially different from that on a demurrer to the complaint, or a demurrer to the evidence, and in either case the ruling on such a demurrer is not a final judgment from which an appeal will lie. In addition to the cases cited above, see,

*Thomas, Admr.*, v. *Chicago, etc., R. Co.* (1894), 139 Ind. 462, 39 N. E. 44.

It has also been expressly held that a ruling *sustaining* a motion like that here involved is not a final judgment from which an appeal will lie. *Branham* v. *Fort Wayne, etc., R. Co.* (1856), 7 Ind. 524, 525; *Masten* v. *Indiana Car, etc., Co.* (1897), 19 Ind. App. 633, 49 N. E. 981. The reverse of this proposition would seem to follow necessarily.

However, there is another reason why this appeal should be dismissed. It will appear from the record indicated, *supra*, that this motion was not ruled on until after

5. the court had heard the evidence. Appellant states in his brief, in effect, that the facts set up in the application were not denied, and that the case was submitted on such sworn application alone. This may be true, but the record does not so show. The evidence is not in the record by bill of exceptions or otherwise. There is nothing in the record by bill of exceptions or otherwise, to show upon what evidence the court based the ruling complained of. So far as the record discloses, the court may have treated the facts stated in the application or motion as sufficient to entitle the appellant to the relief asked but, on hearing the evidence, found that the facts were not correctly stated therein. As the record comes to us, no question is presented by the appeal.

For each of the reasons indicated the appeal should be and is dismissed.

Note.—Reported in 113 N. E. 1016. See under (1) 2 Cyc 517; 3 C. J. 316; (5) 3 Cyc 174; 4 C. J. 550.

## BOSSON v. BRASH.

[No. 9,141. Filed November 9, 1916.]

1. PLEADING.—*Theory.—Determination.—Theory on Appeal.*—The theory of a pleading must be determined by a consideration of its general scope and tenor, and the theory adopted by the trial court will be adhered to on appeal where such pleading, from its plain terms, is susceptible of such construction and theory, particularly where it appears from the record that the parties themselves proceeded on such theory. p. 88.

2. ATTORNEY AND CLIENT.—*Compensation.—Action.—Jury Question.*—In an action by a client against an attorney for money collected, where the defendant contended that the money sought to be recovered was retained by him, with plaintiff's consent, as a reasonable attorney fee, it was for the jury to determine the amount, if any, due plaintiff. p. 89.

3. APPEAL.—*Review.—Evidence.—Verdict.*—Where there is some evidence to sustain the verdict, that is sufficient on appeal. p. 89.

4. ACCOUNT STATED.—*Agreement of the Parties.—Prior Dealings.*—Before there can be an account stated there must have been prior dealings between the parties, and, after an examination of all the items by each of the parties, they must have mutually agreed upon the items of the account and that the balance struck is just and due from the party against whom it is stated. p. 89.

5. ACCOUNT STATED. — *Nature of Action.* — An account stated amounts to more than an admission of an amount due, as it is a new cause of action, and in a suit upon such an account the inquiry is directed not to the original transaction out of which the account arose but to the questions of whether the parties had in fact agreed upon the amount due and whether it has been paid. p. 89.

6. ACCOUNT STATED.—*Action.—Evidence.—Presumption.*—Where, in the absence of an express agreement, an implied assent to the amount due is relied on for a recovery, the receipt and retention of a statement of account is proper evidence to be considered in determining whether the parties have agreed upon the amount due, but it is not necessarily conclusive, and amounts to no more than *prima facie* proof of agreement on a balance. p. 90.

From Marion Circuit Court; *Charles Remster*, Judge.

Action by Tirza B. Brash against William Bosson. From a judgment for plaintiff, the defendant appeals. *Affirmed.*

*William Bosson*, for appellant.

*W. W. Lowry*, for appellee.

FELT, J.—This is a suit to recover money alleged to be due appellee from appellant. The complaint was in four paragraphs. The first was for money had and received. The second paragraph alleges in substance that on January 11, 1908, appellant received from William Lowe Rice, receiver, $3,-441.63 belonging to appellee, and then and there agreed to pay the same to her; that before bringing this suit, on July 27, 1910, appellee demanded payment of said sum from appellant and payment was by him refused. The third paragraph avers that appellant, a practicing attorney, was employed by appellee to collect for her certain promissory notes; that he collected thereon $3,441.63 on January 11, 1908, and on January 16, 1908, paid appellee the sum of $2,306.90. and retained $1,135.73 as attorney's fees; that on July 27, 1910, appellee demanded from appellant the sum of $791.75 and payment was refused; that ten per cent. of the amount collected was a reasonable fee for appellant's services; that the amount retained by him was exorbitant and unreasonable. The fourth paragraph is substantially like the third except it is alleged that the notes provided for five per cent. attorney's fees, and that appellant agreed to accept that amount in payment for his services.

The complaint was answered by a general denial and by a paragraph of special answer, which set up in detail appellant's employment and services as attorney for appellee; that at the time of his employment he informed appellee that his fee would amount to from twenty to forty per cent. of the amount collected; that he charged and retained for his fees thirty-three per cent. of the amount collected; and that appellee stated that such fee was satisfactory to her and it was agreed that the sum of $1,135.73 was due him as attorney's fees. To the special answer appellee filed a reply of general denial. A trial by jury resulted in a verdict for appellee for $300.

The error assigned and relied on for reversal is the over-

ruling of appellant's motion for a new trial. A new trial
was asked on the ground that there was error in the assessment of the amount of recovery, it being too large; that the
verdict is not sustained by sufficient evidence and is contrary to law. The propositions urged by appellant are: (1)
That the acceptance by appellee without objection of the
amount collected, less the thirty-three per cent. retained by
him as attorney fees, was binding on her as to the amount of
such fee; (2) that the retention by him of his fee and the
remittance to and acceptance by appellee of the balance of
the amount collected resulted in an account stated, binding
upon both parties to the transaction; that the retention by
appellee for so long a time of the amount received by her
from appellant is conclusive evidence of her assent to the
settlement.

Appellee contends that the idea of an account stated between the parties is an afterthought of appellant, and that
there is nothing in the pleadings or proceedings of the trial
up to the filing of the motion for a new trial to suggest such
theory; that, on the part of appellee, the contention was that
appellant owed her money received by him as her attorney
and not accounted for to her; that the amount retained by
him as attorney fees was unreasonable and exorbitant and
was never agreed to by her; that appellant defended the suit
on the ground that the amount retained by him was a fair
and reasonable fee, and that appellee had given her assent
thereto.

The pleadings and records of the trial sustain appellee's
contention as to the theory of the pleadings and the theory
on which the case was tried below. The theory of a pleading must be determined by a consideration of its general
scope and tenor, and the theory adopted by the trial
court will be adhered to on appeal, where such
1. pleading, from its plain terms, is susceptible of
such construction and theory. The application of
this rule is emphasized where it also appears from the

record that the parties themselves proceeded on such theory, as in the present instance. *McKinley* v. *Britton* (1913), 55 Ind. App. 21, 24, 103 N. E. 349; *Euler* v. *Euler* (1913), 55 Ind. App. 547, 553, 102 N. E. 856; *Knight, etc., Co.* v. *Miller* (1908), 172 Ind. 27, 31, 87 N. E. 823, 18 Ann. Cas. 1146; *Studabaker* v. *Faylor* (1908), 170 Ind. 498, 507, 83 N. E. 747, 127 Am. Stat. 397; *Muncie, etc., Traction Co.* v. *Citizens Gas, etc., Co.* (1912), 179 Ind. 322, 329, 100 N. E. 65. On this theory it was a question for the

2. jury to determine from the evidence the amount, if any, due appellee from appellant. There is some evidence to sustain the verdict, and on appeal that is sufficient. Furthermore, if it were conceded that the

3. pleadings present the question of an account stated as a defense to the suit, we think the same results would follow in this case. Before there can be an account stated there must have been prior dealings between the

4. parties, and after an examination of all the items by each of the parties, they must have mutually agreed upon the items of the account and that the balance struck is just and due from the party against whom it is stated.

An account stated amounts to more than an admission

5. of an amout due. It is a new cause of action and in a suit upon such an account, the inquiry is not directed to the original transaction out of which the account arose, but is directed to the questions of whether the parties had in fact agreed upon the amount due and whether the same was unpaid. The account stated arose originally out of transactions between merchants and persons engaged in commercial transactions, and the rule was evolved that the receipt by one of the parties of an account showing a balance against him and the retention thereof for a reasonable length of time, sufficient to examine the same and make objections thereto, and a failure so to do, amounted to an approval of the statement rendered and it thereby became an account stated. There is considerable difference in the

application of this rule in different jurisdictions. In many states the rule has been extended to transactions between persons generally which result in accounts between them, but it has not been applied in such instances with the same strictness that obtained in the earlier decisions dealing with transactions between merchants. What will amount to a sufficient acquiesence to render an account current an account stated depends upon the facts and circumstances of each particular case, the relation of the parties, and the nature and extent of the dealings between them. Where there is no express agreement and an implied assent

6. to the amount due is relied upon for a recovery, the receipt and retention of the statement of account showing the amount due is proper evidence for the court or jury to consider in determining whether the parties have in fact agreed upon the amount, but it is not necessarily conclusive and in no case amounts to more than *prima facie* proof of such fact. 1 C. J. 596, 657, 695, 696; 1 Cyc 364, 380, 381; *Vanbebber* v. *Plunkett* (1895), 26 Ore. 562, 38 Pac. 707, 27 L. R. A. 811, and notes; *Anding* v. *Levy* (1879), 57 Miss. 51, 34 Am. Rep. 435; *Daytona Bridge Co.* v. *Bond* (1904), 47 Fla. 136, 36 So. 445, 447; *Rich* v. *Eldredge* (1860), 42 N. H. 153, 158; *Spellman* v. *Muehlfeld* (1901), 166 N. Y. 245, 247, 59 N. E. 817; *Mackin* v. *O'Brien* (1889), 33 Ill. App. 474; *Willard* v. *Bennet* (Iowa), 139 N. W. 914; *Pudas* v. *Mattola* (1912), 173 Mich. 189, 138 N. W. 1052, 45 L. R. A. (N. S.) 534; *Ripley* v. *Sage Land, etc., Co.* (1909), 138 Wis. 304, 119 N. W. 108, 23 L. R. A. (N. S.) 787.

So in either view of the case we should not be warranted in reversing the judgment for there is evidence tending to sustain it. Neither can we say the amount is excessive. We find no reversible error. Judgment affirmed.

NOTE.—Reported in 114 N. E. 6. Account stated, receipt of statement, effect, Ann. Cas. 1915A 694; 134 Am. St. 1021; 136 Am. St. 39. See under (2) 6 C. J. 708; (4) 1 C. J. 678; (5) 1 Cyc 450; 1 C. J. 705; (6) 1 Cyc 376; 1 C. J. 691.

BUETER, TREASURER, ET AL. *v.* AULBACH.

[No. 9,091. Filed November 10, 1916.]

1. DRAINS.—*Cleaning Ditch.—Expenses.—Action to Enjoin Collection.—Complaint.—Sufficiency.—*In an action to enjoin a county treasurer from collecting, under §6152 *et seq.* Burns 1914, Acts 1907 pp. 527, 600, relating to the repair and cleaning of ditches, the expenses of cleaning out a landowner's allotment of a public ditch, where the complaint alleges that the landowner had been notified by the township trustee to clean and repair according to the original specifications certain sections of a ditch which had been regularly allotted to him, that within the time specified in the notice the work allotted was completed in conformity with the specifications, and that the trustee, after notice of the performance of the work, accepted it as completed in accordance with the specifications, such complaint is sufficient as against objections that it does not sufficiently allege the acceptance of the work by the trustee as completed by the landowner, or when the work was done by him, or that he completed the work according to the requirements of the notice given by the trustee, and that the contents of the notice were not disclosed. p. 92.

2. APPEAL.—*Review.—Findings of Facts.—Contradictions in Evidence.*—Where findings of facts are supported by substantial evidence, they cannot be disturbed on appeal because there are contradictions in the evidence given at the trial. p. 94.

From Allen Circuit Court; *William C. Ryan*, Special Judge.

Action by Louis J. Aulbach against J. Herman Bueter, treasurer of Allen County, and others. From a judgment for plaintiff, the defendants appeal. *Affirmed.*

*Harper & Fuelber*, for appellants
*John H. Aiken*, for appellee.

CALDWELL, C. J.—Two alleged errors are sufficiently presented: The overruling of the demurrer to the complaint, and the denial of a new trial. The substance of the complaint is as follows: Appellee is the owner of certain described lands in Adams township, Allen county, which lands were owned by Hartzell in 1911. The lands are traversed by the

Schmidt and the Bender public ditches.  In July, 1911,
Fenker, as township trustee, notified Hartzell to clean and
repair to the original specifications certain sections of said
ditches, ·which sections had been regularly allotted to him
as landowner to that end.  Hartzell completed the work
as required by the notice and specifications and subsequently conveyed the lands to appellee.  Fenker, as trustee, claiming to have had such work done by some person other than
Hartzell, had caused the expense thereof to be placed upon the tax duplicate to be collected as other taxes are collected, and that appellant Bueter, as treasurer of Allen
county, was threatening to sell the lands to that end.  The
prayer was for an injunction.  On application duly made,
the court issued an order restraining the sale of the lands
until the further order of the court, which order, on a trial,
was made permanent as an injunction.

Of the points directed to the insufficiency of the complaint, the following are based on memoranda filed with
the demurrer thereto, and are therefore entitled to
1. consideration: That the complaint does not sufficiently allege the acceptance of the work as completed by Hartzell, or when the work was done by him, or
that he completed the work according to the requirements of
the notice, and that the complaint does not disclose the
contents of the notice.  There is a specific allegation that
certain described sections of each of the ditches had been
regularly alloted to Hartzell as landowner biennially to
clean and repair.  It is alleged also that in July, 1911, appellant Fenker, as trustee, notified Hartzell to clean and
repair such allotments, and that he presented to Hartzell
the specifications descriptive of the limits of the work to
be done, and "that said Hartzell did within the time so
specified do and complete said work on his said allotments,
and in conformity to said specifications, and immediately
thereafter notified the said defendant trustee that said work
was completed, whereupon said defendant trustee inspected

said work and found it performed and completed in conformity to the specifications and accepted said work from said Hartzell, and discharged this plaintiff's said land from further liability on account of said work." There follow allegations to the effect that, notwithstanding that Hartzell did said work and that it had been accepted by the trustee, the latter claims to have had the work done by some other person and that he had caused the alleged expense thereof to be placed upon the tax duplicate, etc.

In our judgment the complaint is not open to the objections urged. The statute provides that subject to exceptions not applicable here, all public ditches shall be cleaned and repaired under the supervision of the proper township trustee. The county surveyor when directed so to do by the trustee is required to fix and determine the portion of each of such ditches as is involved here, that each interested landowner shall biennially clean and repair. It is made the duty of the trustee to procure from the county surveyor a description of the allotments of each ditch within his jurisdiction, and biennially prior to August 1st to fix a time within which each allotment shall be completed, and to notify each affected landowner accordingly. Each landowner is required to appear before the trustee on a day fixed by the notice and declare his intention to clean his allotment and to execute to the trustee an undertaking providing for the completion of the work within the specified time, and according to the original specifications. The notice to the landowner is sufficient if it names the ditch, the owner of the land, describes the allotment, and specifies the time within which the work shall be done, and the time when the landowner shall appear to declare his intention, etc. There are provisions requiring the trustee to inspect the work on its completion, and other provisions to the effect that when a landowner fails to appear and declare his intention and execute such undertaking, or fails to complete the work, the trustee shall proceed to cause it to be done by others, and other provisions providing several remedies, including that pursued here, by which the expense of the work may be collected from the landowner. §6152 *et seq.* Burns 1914, Acts 1907 p. 527, 600.

The complaint here discloses that the trustee delivered to Hartzell, with the notice, specifications to guide him in cleaning the allotments assigned to him. It should be presumed that such specifications were in harmony with the original specifications under which the ditch was constructed, since the landowner's statutory undertaking as executed to the trustee is required to be to that effect. Hartzell thereupon completed the work according to such specifications and within the time specified by the notice. By so doing he performed the work as specified by the statute. §6157 Burns 1914, Acts 1907 p. 530. It was, however, the province of the trustee rather than Hartzell to determine whether the allotments had been properly cleaned and repaired. *Zimmerman* v. *Savage* (1896), 145 Ind. 124, 44 N. E. 252. In recognition of such fact Hartzell notified the trustee that the work was done, whereupon the latter inspected it and found it to be completed according to the specifications and presumably as required by the statute, and he thereupon accepted the work as completed and indicated such acceptance by discharging the appellee's land from further liability on account of such work. The court did not err in overruling the demurrer to the complaint.

At appellants' request, the court made a special finding of the facts and stated conclusions of law thereon. Appellants' exceptions to the conclusions were subsequent-

2. ly withdrawn. The assignment based on the overruling of the motion for a new trial presents for our consideration the single question of whether the facts were correctly found as measured by the evidence. While certain other comparatively immaterial questions relating to the sufficiency of the evidence are discussed in the brief, those of controlling importance are whether there was evi-

dence that Hartzell did complete such repair work to the
limits of the original specifications as designated by the notice and required by law, and whether appellant trustee
accepted the work as so completed. The finding on these
questions was in favor of appellee. A careful inspection
of the recorded testimony on these important questions dis-.
closes that there is some confusion and uncertainty, and
that in a number of respects there are contradictions. From
such a condition it is the province of the trial court to evolve
the facts. The trial court has done so. The finding is supported in every material and controlling matter by substantial evidence. The fact that such evidence is in some respects contradicted by other evidence does not authorize this
court to interfere. The judgment is affirmed.

NOTE.—Reported in 114 N. E. 8.

## GREATHOUSE ET AL. *v.* HARRISON.

[No. 9,093. Filed November 21, 1916.]

1. MORTGAGES.—*Action to Foreclose.*—*Release by Mistake.*—*Evidence.*—*Bona Fide Purchaser.*—In an action to foreclose a mortgage which plaintiff claimed he had released of record by mistake, where the complaint averred that one of the defendants,
who had obtained title to the real estate involved subsequent
to such release, paid no consideration for the transfer of the
property, and that he held the title as a volunteer for the benefit
of the mortgagor and for the fraudulent purpose of preventing
plaintiff from enforcing his lien against the real estate, plaintiff, in order to defeat such title, was required to show either
that such defendant held as a mere volunteer, or fraudulently,
or that no consideration was paid by him. p. 99.

2. DEEDS.—*Validity.*—*Presumption.*—A deed fair and valid upon
its face is evidence of an honest transaction, and until it is
assailed by evidence, effective as proof, that it was obtained by
the fraud of the grantee, he is not required to adduce any evidence in its support. p. 100.

From Shelby Circuit Court; *Alonzo Blair,* Judge.

Action by Theodore F. Harrison against Archie Great-house and others. From a judgment for plaintiff, the defendants appeal. *Reversed.*

*Charles B. Clarke* and *Walter C. Clarke,* for appellants.
*Franklin McCray, John A. Tindall* and *Alfred R. Hovey,* for appellee.

IBACH, J.—Appellee brought this action against appellant Greathouse and a number of other defendants to recover on a note executed by one Henderson and to foreclose a mortgage given to secure the same on property then owned and held by said Henderson, but which is now claimed by appellant Greathouse.

The amended complaint on which the case was tried is in one paragraph and was not challenged below. Its averments material to the questions presented by this appeal are in substance as follows: On September 30, 1902, Henderson executed his note for $1,300, together with certain coupon interest notes, to appellee and, his wife joining, mortgaged the property in dispute to appellee as security. The mortgage was recorded within forty-five days from its execution in the office of the recorder of Marion county, Indiana, in mortgage record No. 418 at page 121. There is now due and unpaid on said notes a total sum of $1,651 with attorney's fees. After this mortgage was executed and delivered to plaintiff (appellee), Henderson transferred the property to the defendants Puryear and Porter for the purpose of securing them as sureties on an appeal bond in an appeal from a judgment rendered against Henderson in the Marion Superior Court, the judgment in which cause has since been reversed and vacated. On March 11, 1912, Evelyn M. McAdams executed a quitclaim deed purporting to convey said real estate to defendants Puryear and Porter, and that said deed was afterwards, on April 23, 1912, recorded. After the execution of such deed the defendants Puryear and Porter and their respective wives executed a quitclaim deed to appellant Greathouse, purporting to convey said real estate to him, which deed was afterwards, on April 23, 1912, recorded. Defendant Henderson paid all the consideration for said transfers of said real estate, or arranged with Greathouse to pay said consideration for him, and Greathouse holds title to said real estate as a volunteer for the use and benefit of said Henderson and for the fraudulent purpose of preventing appellee from enforcing and collecting his lien sued upon herein as against said real estate. The property is in possession of the Hendersons.

Appellant Greathouse answered the complaint by general denial and a paragraph of special answer in which he avers in substance that as to so much of the complaint as seeks to foreclose the mortgage set out therein he is the owner in fee simple of the real estate described; that he became the owner of said real estate by a deed executed to him on March 11, 1912, by Puryear and Porter and their respective wives, which deed was recorded within forty-five days in the deed records of Marion county; that in consideration of the execution of such deed, he paid the full cash value of said real estate and took the title thereto; that appellee's mortgage was executed on September 30, 1902, and afterwards recorded in mortgage record No. 418 on page 121 of the records of Marion county; that on April 19, 1905, and long before the purchase of the real estate by him, appellee executed and caused to be recorded a full and complete release of said mortgage on the margin of the record wherein such mortgage was recorded; that said release is now and has been ever since April 19, 1905' of record in said mortgage record; that at the time he purchased the real estate said mortgage appeared to be released; that he had no notice or knowledge whatever that appellee had, or held a mortgage or other lien on such real estate; that he, relying wholly on the correctness and truthfulness of said entry of satisfaction, and in good faith and for valuable consideration, is a bona fide purchaser and holder of said real estate. There was a reply in general denial.  A trial by the court upon the issues thus formed resulted in a judgment in favor of appellee for $1,487.44 and a decree of foreclosure of the mortgage sued on and an order of sale of the property. Appellant Greathouse's motion for a new trial was overruled and such ruling is here assigned as error.  The only questions presented by such motion are that the decision of the court is not sustained by sufficient evidence and is contrary to law.

The undisputed facts, arranged in their sequence, are in substance as follows:  On September 30, 1902, William E. Henderson executed his note to appellee for $1,300, together with certain coupon interest notes.  On the same day, his wife joining, they executed a mortgage on the property in dispute, which Henderson then owned, to secure such note.  This mortgage was recorded on October 1, 1902, in record No. 418 page 121 in the recorder's office of Marion county.  On April 19, 1905, appellee released said mortgage (by mistake as he claims) by an entry on the margin of said record.  On June 19, 1906, Henderson, his wife joining, again mortgaged said real estate to Benjamin Dake to secure Henderson's note for $800 and certain interest notes accompanying it.  On January 25, 1908, Thomas McGruder obtained a judgment in tort against Henderson for $600, from which an appeal was taken to this court where it was reversed March 27, 1912.  On March 6, 1909, Henderson and wife, by a warranty deed, conveyed said real estate to John A. Puryear and Jacob M. Porter. On the same day Henderson, Puryear and Porter entered into an agreement by which Puryear and Porter were to have the property free from all claims in case the McGruder judgment should be affirmed and they should be compelled to pay it, but in case the judgment was reversed they were to reconvey the property to Henderson's wife.  On March 30, 1911, the sheriff of Marion county deeded the property in

question to Evelyn McAdams, such deed reciting, among
other things: That on November 24, 1908, in "the Appellate Court of the State of Indiana, in Cause No....., wherein Absent Bivens and Thomas McGruder are plaintiffs and
William E. Henderson is defendant, the said plaintiff recovered judgment against the said defendant William E. Henderson for the sum of one hundred and fourteen 05/100
dollars and costs and also an order for the sale of the real
estate hereinafter described, all without relief from valua-
tion and appraisement laws;" a sale of said property by the
sheriff to Jennie McGruder on January 29, 1910, the issuance
of a certificate to her, the assignment of this certificate to
Evelyn McAdams, and that said real estate was sold as the
property of William E. Henderson. On March 3, 1912,
Greathouse gave Puryear and Porter a certified check on
the Fidelity Trust Company for $1,060.31 in satisfaction
of the Dake mortgage. On March 11, 1912, Evelyn
McAdams conveyed and quitclaimed the property to Puryear and Porter. Afterwards on the same day Puryear
and Porter, their respective wives joining, released and
quitclaimed their interest in said property to appellant
Greathouse. On March 12, 1912, the defeasance contract
was assigned to appellant Greathouse by Henderson and
wife.

As indicated by the facts above set out appellant was
the apparent holder of the legal title to the property in
dispute. He was a remote grantee of Evelyn McAdams
and held all the title acquired by her by virtue of the
sheriff's deed. He was also the grantee of Puryear and
Porter and derived all title and interest vested in them by
virtue of the deed from Henderson and wife, and was also
the assignee of the contract of defeasance executed by Henderson and Puryear and Porter. Under the aver-
1.  ments of the complaint, in order to defeat appellant's
title, appellee was required to show, either that Greathouse held such title as a mere volunteer, or that it was

held fraudulently, or that the consideration was paid by Henderson. There has not been pointed out to us a scintilla of evidence on either of the above essentials that would even tend to support such allegations. A deed fair and valid upon its face is evidence of an honest trans-

2. action; and until it is assailed by evidence, effective as proof, that it was obtained by the fraud of the grantee, he is not required to adduce any evidence in its support. *Ewing* v. *Gray* (1859), 12 Ind. 64, 67; *Western Union Tel. Co.* v. *Krueger* (1905), 36 Ind. App. 348, 74 N. E. 25; *Sheets* v. *Dufour* (1841), 5 Blackf. 548. But aside from the presumption arising from the deeds there is uncontradicted evidence to show that appellant purchased the property in good faith, without notice of appellee's mortgage, and paid a valuable consideration therefor. Appellee contends, however, that it was within the province of the court to disbelieve the testimony of Henderson and of Greathouse as to an agreement for rent and the payment of a consideration other than the payment of the Dake mortgage and the assumed liability on the appeal bond which ceased to exist on the reversal of the judgment. Conceding that appellee's contention as to the credit to be given this testimony is correct, we think it apparent that this falls short of affirmative proof necessary to defeat the legal title shown in appellant.

It follows that the evidence is insufficient and the cause must be reversed. Judgment reversed, with instructions to the lower court to grant the motion for a new trial and for further proceedings not inconsistent with this opinion.

NOTE.—Reported in 114 N. E. 92. Mortgages, satisfaction of by mistake, revival, 5 Am. St. 703. See under (1) 27 Cyc 1433; (2) 13 Cyc 737.

## MARCOVICH *v.* O'BRIEN, AUDITOR OF STATE, ET AL.

[No. 9,286. Filed November 22, 1916.]

1. CORPORATIONS.—*Stockholders.*—*Suing or Defending Actions in Behalf of Corporations.*—As a general rule, the stockholders of a corporation, for the purposes of all litigation growing out of the relations of the corporation and a third person, surrender their personal or individual entity to the corporation, and when it is properly in court, the stockholders are also in court so far as is necessary for the purpose of adjudicating all matters incident to the issues between such corporation and other parties litigant, and it is only in exceptional cases that stockholders will be permitted to sue or defend a· suit for and on behalf of themselves as stockholders of such corporation. p. 111.

2. CORPORATIONS.—*Stockholders.*—*Suing or Defending Actions in Behalf of Corporations.*—*Conditions Precedent.*—Stockholders in a corporation are permitted to sue or defend actions growing out of the relations of the corporation with third persons only in cases in which appear one or more of the following conditions: (a) some action, or threatened action, by the board of directors or trustees, beyond their power; (b) a fraudulent transaction, contemplated or completed by the acting managers, in connection with some other party or among themselves causing injury to the corporation or stockholders; (c) action by the board of directors or a majority of them in their own interest, and in a manner destructive of the corporation or the rights of other stockholders; (d) where a majority of the stockholders are illegally or oppressively pursuing a course in the name of the corporation which is in violation of the right of other stockholders, and can be restrained only by a court of equity. p. 111.

3. CORPORATIONS.—*Stockholders.*—*Suing or Defending Actions in Behalf of Corporations.*—*Conditions Precedent.*—When conditions exist which will permit a corporate ,stockholder to sue or defend on behalf of the corporation, such stockholder must have had no share in the acts giving him the right to sue, nor have ratified them, the suit must be brought seasonably, and he must have made a good-faith and reasonable effort to induce the corporation itself to bring the suit. p. 112.

4. CORPORATIONS.—*Stockholders.*—*Suing or Defending Actions in Behalf of Corporation.*—*Conditions Precedent.*—Before a stockholder can sue or defend in behalf of a corporation it is ordinarily necessary to show a demand upon the board of directors to bring suit, and their refusal to do so; but the law does not

require a demand when it is made to appear that it would have been unavailing.  p. 112.

5. CORPORATIONS.—*Stockholders.*—*Suing or Defending Actions in Behalf of Corporation.*—*Corporation in Receiver's Hands.*—The rules governing stockholders of a corporation in bringing actions originally, for and in behalf of themselves, apply where the corporation is insolvent and its affairs are being managed and settled through a receiver appointed by, and acting under, the direction and orders of the court.  p. 112.

6. RECEIVERS.—*Insolvent Corporations.*—*Property as Trust Fund.* —Where a court has taken possession of the property of an insolvent corporation for administration, and appointed a receiver, the property of the corporation is a trust fund for the payment of its debts.  p. 112.

7. RECEIVERS.—*Officer of Court.*—*Functions and Duties.*—The receiver of an insolvent corporation is not the agent of either party to the action, but is regarded as an officer of the court, exercising his functions for the common benefit of all parties in interest.  p. 113.

8. RECEIVERS.—*Represents Both Stockholders and Creditors.*— *Duties.*—While for the purposes of determining the nature and extent of his title, a receiver represents the insolvent corporation itself, yet he represents both stockholders and creditors and is to be regarded as their trustee, charged with the duty of collecting, assembling, protecting and preserving the assets of such corporation for the benefit of those entitled thereto, subject to the orders and directions of the court whose officer he is. p. 113.

9. RECEIVERS.—*Action by or Against Insolvent Corporation.*— *Rights of Receiver.*—The receiver of an insolvent corporation is the proper party to bring any action which the corporation might have brought, and, as trustee for the creditors, can maintain and defend actions which the corporation could not.  p. 113.

10. CORPORATIONS.—*Insolvency and Receivers.*—*Parties to Receivership Proceedings.*—*Statute.*—In the absence of a showing of a refusal of the receiver to discharge his duty in collecting and protecting, by all proper means, the assets of an insolvent corporation for the benefit of those entitled thereto, or some showing of collusion or fraud on his part by which the court was misled or induced to act against, or to fail to act in, the interests of those for whom the corporate assets were held in trust, a stockholder in an insolvent corporation is not entitled to be made a party to a receivership proceeding, under §273 Burns 1914, §272 R. S. 1881, providing that when a complete determination of the controversy cannot be had without the pres-

ence of other parties, the court must cause them to be joined as
proper parties. p. 115.

11. CORPORATIONS.—*Insolvency and Receivers.—Parties.*—The trial
court might, in certain cases, permit a stockholder to intervene
in a receivership proceeding, where its refusal to do so would
not constitute reversible error. p. 115.

12. RECEIVERS.—*Application for Appointment for Insolvent Bank.
—Notice to Stockholders.—Statute.*—Under §3346 Burns 1914,
Acts 1895 p. 202, relating to the examination of banks, a notice
by publication to the stockholders of a bank, alleged to be insolvent, is a necessary prerequisite to the appointment of a
receiver therefor. p. 115.

13. CORPORATIONS. — *Insolvency and Receivers. — Allowances to
Creditors. — Rights and Remedies of Stockholders.* — Where a
stockholder in an insolvent bank sought to intervene in a receivership proceeding for the purpose of having reviewed the
allowance of claims to certain creditors, and it appears from
the record that such stockholder was given ample opportunity to
interpose any defense or objection to such claims, he should
have, if he had any valid defense to such allowances, presented
it to the court and prosecuted his appeal from the ruling thereon,
there being no charge that the allowance of the claims was
induced by fraud or collusion. p. 116.

14. CORPORATIONS,—*Insolvency and Receivers.—Actions.*—A stockholder of an insolvent corporation is properly refused the permission to bring suits in behalf of the corporation, when the
prosecution of such actions falls within the powers and duties
of the receiver, in the absence of a showing that the receiver
had ever been asked to bring such suits, or that he had refused
to bring them, or refused to ask and obtain the necessary orders
and directions of the court in reference thereto. p. 116.

15. APPEAL.—*Receivers.—Discharge of Duties.—Presumption.*—It
will be assumed on appeal, in the absence of a showing to the
contrary, that a receiver has or will discharge his duties as such,
and that the court under whose directions such receiver is acting
will make all orders necessary upon the receiver to the full protection of the corporation and the interests of its shareholders.
p. 116.

From Lake Superior Court; *Virgil S. Reiter,* Judge.

Action by William H. O'Brien, Auditor of State, and
another for the appointment of a receiver for the Indiana
Trust and Savings Bank. Wolf Marcovich sought to intervene and from a judgment striking out his petition, he
appeals. *Affirmed.*

*W. J. Murray* and *J. A. Stinson,* for appellant.

*L. D. Cravens,* for appellees.

HOTTEL, P. J.—The facts disclosed by the record herein, necessary to an understanding of the questions presented by this appeal are, in substance, as follows: Prior to and on October 29, 1913, the "Indiana Trust and Savings Bank," hereinafter referred to as the "insolvent bank," was a corporation engaged in the business of a loan and trust company in the city of Indiana Harbor. On said day the auditor of state caused an examination of said bank and found it to be in an insolvent and failing condition. Thereupon an agreement was made between such auditor, the "Citizens Trust and Savings Bank," the "Indiana Harbor National Bank," the "First National Bank of East Chicago," and the "First Calumet Trust and Savings Bank," whereby said banks were to advance money as needed to pay the debts and depositors of the insolvent bank, and to that end the Citizens Trust and Savings Bank was to be appointed liquidating agent and by said agreement was authorized, as such agent, to borrow from either or any of the banks that entered into said agreement the money necessary for the payment of the creditors and depositors of such insolvent bank and to give to the bank so loaning money for such purposes a note or notes therefor, which notes were to be the obligation of the insolvent bank, and were to bear seven per cent. interest payable semi-annually, the assets of the insolvent bank to be held in trust by such liquidating agent for the payment of the notes. It seems that this arrangement had the sanction of a petition of the stockholders purporting to be signed by persons representing more than eighty per cent. of the stock of such insolvent corporation. Said agent undertook and proceeded for a time with the discharge of its duties as liquidating agent, when the legality of many of its acts was questioned by some of the stockholders and creditors and such liquidating bank and the other banks above named petitioned for the appointment of a receiver for such insolvent bank. A receiver was appointed, whereupon appellant and another stockholder filed their petition asking to be made parties defendant to the petition of said banks and were admitted as parties defendant thereto, and thereupon they filed a demurrer to said petition, which demurrer was sustained by the court. Thereupon appellee, William H. O'Brien, auditor of state, filed his petition in the Lake Superior Court, asking for the appointment of a receiver for said insolvent bank and, after due notice of such petition had been properly given, such court by the agreement of the parties appointed William Wright and fixed his bond at $150,000. Wright duly qualified and proceeded with the duties of such receivership, whereupon the banks that had furnished money to pay the creditors and depositors of the insolvent bank under the agreement above indicated filed their respective claims against such receiver, in which each of such claimants in its claim set out in detail the agreement above indicated and alleged that pursuant thereto it had furnished money to such liquidating agent, which had been used to pay creditors and depositors of said insolvent bank, and had taken notes therefor properly signed by such liquidating agent, which were filed with and made part of such claim, and asked to be subrogated to the rights of the depositors of said insolvent bank and to have its claims take the priority of such depositors.

After the filing of these claims, to wit, on July 2, 1914, the record shows the filing of other claims and proceeds as follows: "Comes also" (naming the various claimants, the banks above named, the former receiver and the present receiver), *"and comes also Wolf Marcovich, another of said stockholders* and comes also the Indiana Securities Company."

"The receiver herein now files his verified petition for leave to compromise and adjust certain claims and for the disposition of other matters shown in said petition, which

petition is in these words, to-wit:—" This petition alleges, among other things, that the cause of the claimant
banks had been under inquiry for seven days, during
which time evidence had been heard "enlightening the
receiver and the court on all subjects hereinafter recom-
mended in this petition"; that both before and at the trial
the receiver and his attorney had "investigated as carefully
as possible the question of fact involved in the various matters hereinafter referred to, that this receiver has ascertained after a conference with the parties whose interests
would be concerned, that a compromise and adjustment can
be made of all subjects hereinafter referred to on the basis
of the recommendation contained herein, to-wit:" Then
follows recommendation of the allowance of the claims of
said banks in specified amounts aggregating $58,913.39;
that such claimants be subrogated to the rights of the depositors of such insolvent bank; that all costs and expenses of
the action heretofore by the claimant banks against the
Indiana Trust and Savings Bank, resulting in the appointment of H. C. Rutledge, receiver, be borne by said claimant
banks; that the report of the Citizens Trust and Savings
Bank as liquidating agent should be approved, with the
exception of certain enumerated items, which should be
disallowed; that no fees for the liquidating agent's services,
or the services of its attorneys should be allowed; that the
report of said Rutledge, receiver, in said other case be
approved, except that no charge for his services or that
of his attorney should be allowed. There are other provisions which we need not set out.

Over the separate and several objections of the receiver
and each of the said claimant banks, *appellant, Marcovich,
was permitted by the court to file objections to the allowance and compromise of the claims of such banks.* The
record shows that such objections were overruled by the
court, and exceptions saved by Marcovich, and an appeal
from such ruling prayed and granted, bond fixed and secur-

ity named and approved, and that the court "having examined said petition of the receiver and having heard the
evidence upon the matters petitioned for therein and being
fully advised in the premises now grants said petition."
Then follows the judgment that the petition of the receiver
be granted, setting out the several provisions thereof before
indicated. Following this entry is an entry of January 6,
1915, reciting that appellant by counsel filed herein an intervening petition, which is set out. This petition alleges
the filing of the claims by said banks, and that upon a hearing thereof "*an agreement was reached by the parties appearing in said action which was approved by the court
and entered upon the record as the order of the court*";
that appellant is a stockholder of the insolvent bank, being
the owner of ten shares of the capital stock thereof, and as
such is liable under the law for a stock assessment equal to
the amount of the stock held by him; that when the assets
of the insolvent bank are exhausted he will be sued by the
receiver on his stock liability. The petition then charges
that such insolvent bank through its officers committed acts
contrary to law, in that it made illegal loans, procured the
appointment of the liquidating agent and the first receiver
as above set out, after which this action was begun by
appellee and the present receiver, William H. Wright, was
appointed; that the claims of the above named banks are
found on notes given by John R. Farovid, as liquidating
agent for the Indiana Trust and Savings Bank, upon the
theory that said banks were entitled to be subrogated to
the rights of depositors of such insolvent bank; that upon
investigation appellant finds that the appointment of said
liquidating agent was not made according to law, and that
neither said insolvent bank or its stockholders ought to be
bound by the acts of such liquidating agent; that the law
requires eighty per cent. of the stockholders to join in a
petition for such appointment and that less than fifty per
cent. joined in the petition under which said liquidating

agent was appointed; that the Indiana Security Company and the Transylvania Company each voted fifty shares of stock for liquidation when neither of said companies was authorized to sign said petition; that notwithstanding the fact that there are $3,000 due the depositors, said claimants have asked and have been given a fifteen per cent. dividend on their claims above referred to; that the valuation of the assets of said insolvent bank was made by directors of banks which were competitors and claimants against said insolvent bank; that for several weeks prior to the closing of the doors of said insolvent bank, the officers of the three banks referred to, *supra*, which filed claims against the insolvent bank, were holding secret meetings at the First Calumet Trust and Savings Bank, with the bank examiners and banking clerk of the state department, devising ways and means of closing up and winding up the affairs of the insolvent bank, which meetings were held without the knowledge or consent of the officers of the insolvent bank, contrary to law and against public policy; that the stockholders of the insolvent bank had no knowledge of its affairs or conditions and were given no opportunity to straighten out its affairs; that the last examination made by the bank examiners of said insolvent bank showed it to be in a better condition than it had been for some time past; that no complaints were received from any source by the state department in reference to said insolvent bank, and yet directors of competing banks were called to Plymouth, Indiana, for the purpose of fixing the valuation of the assets of the said bank, and secret negotiations between the bank examiners and the chief bank clerk of the state department and the competitors of said insolvent bank began at that time; that whatever money has been paid by said claimant banks was a voluntary contribution for which they were fully repaid by the elimination of the insolvent bank as one of their competitors; that the stockholders of said insolvent bank have a cause of action against the three claimant banks for damages resulting from the actions of said banks in conspiring to close the doors of the insolvent bank; that appellant has a good meritorious defense against the claims of said banks, and if permitted to intervene, he will make such defense; that after said insolvent bank had been declared insolvent, Charles E. Fowler, president of Indiana Trust and Savings Bank, purchased from the directors thereof the real estate, loan and rental business, and the fixtures of said bank for a small sum, a small part of which he has paid, and the balance of which is held by the receiver in unsecured notes; that such transaction was illegal and appellant, if made a party hereto, will petition the receiver to commence an action to recover back the above named property; that one Cain, a stockholder of said insolvent bank, purchased fifty shares of capital stock of said bank on August 30, 1910, and on April 4, 1913, said stock was taken up by said bank, or some officer thereof, and eventually paid for out of the funds of said bank without any authority whatever; that appellant believes that such transaction was brought about by duress, and on account thereof said Cain is indebted to said bank in the sum of $5,000, and appellant, if allowed to intervene, will petition the receiver.to commence an action to recover the same; that the Indiana Security Company borrowed from said insolvent bank $13,000, secured by mortgage on a number of lots in Indiana Harbor, which your petitioner believes are worth considerably less than fifty per cent. of the amount for which they were mortgaged, and said Security Company is not keeping up the taxes and assessments upon said premises, and your petitioner believes that a receiver should be appointed for said Security Company for the protection of the interests of said insolvent bank, and if made a party defendant will petition this receiver to commence such action; that this insolvent bank, by its officers, loaned large sums of money to irresponsible persons on unsecured notes and.notes secured by worthless securities; that large mortgages were made on property owned or controlled by officers of the bank upon which the estate will suffer a loss of from fifty to sixty per cent.; that the directors of said bank are liable to the receiver for damages sustained by the bank in consequence of the negligence of said directors; that the petitioner, if permitted to intervene, will petition the receiver to bring actions in said cases.

A demurrer to this petition was filed and withdrawn, and a motion to strike out the petition was then filed by the receiver, which motion was sustained. To this ruling appellant excepted and prayed an appeal. This ruling is assigned as error in this court and relied on for reversal.

The ground upon which appellant predicates his right to be made a party to this suit is the showing made in his petition that he is a stockholder of the insolvent corporation, the property and business of which is being managed, directed and disposed of by said receiver under the orders of the court; that, as such stockholder, he, in common with other stockholders, is directly affected by each and all the proceedings had or taken in said receivership proceedings, and hence entitled to be made a party thereto under §273 Burns 1914, §272 R. S. 1881. This statute provides as follows: "The court may determine any controversy between the parties before it, when it can be done without prejudice to the rights of others or by saving their rights; but when a complete determination of the controversy can not be had, without the presence of other parties, the court must cause them to be joined as proper parties. And when, in an action for the recovery of real or personal property, a person not a party to the action, but having an interest in the subject thereof, makes application to the court to be made a party, it may order him to be made a party by the proper amendment."

There is no claim or showing made in said petition that appellant has any interest other than that of a stockholder, or that as a stockholder his interest is different from, or

may be affected differently from, that of any other stockholder. It follows that appellant when he filed his
1. petition was in a sense already in court; that is to
say, the corporation in which he is a stockholder was
in court, and generally speaking the stockholders of a corporation, for the purposes of all litigation growing out of
the relations between such corporation and a third person,
surrender their personal or individual entity to the corporation in which they are stockholders, and when such
corporation is properly in court, the stockholders are, under
the law, also in court, so far as is necessary for the purpose of adjudicating all matters incident to the issues tendered between such corporation and such other party or
parties litigant. It is only in exceptional cases that stockholders will be permitted to sue or defend a suit for and
on behalf of themselves as stockholders of such corporation.

These exceptional cases are those in which appears
2. one or more of the following conditions: "(1) Some
action, or threatened action, by the board of directors
or trustees, beyond their power; (2) a fraudulent transaction, completed or contemplated by the acting managers, in
connection with some other party or among themselves,
causing injury to the corporation or stockholders; (3) action by the board of directors, or a majority of them, in
their own interest, and in a manner destructive of the corporation, or the rights of the other stockholders; (4) where
a majority of the stockholders are illegally or oppressively
pursuing a course in the name of the corporation, which is
in violation of the right of the other stockholders, and can
only be restrained by a court of equity." *Tevis* v. *Hammersmith* (1903), 31 Ind. App. 281, 282, 66 N. E. 79, 66
N. E. 912, and cases there cited; *McFarland* v. *Pierce*
(1898), 151 Ind. 546, 549, 45 N. E. 706, 47 N. E. 1.

It is further said in *Tevis* v. *Hammersmith, supra,* that
in such cases the complaining stockholder "must have had
no share in the acts, nor have ratified them. He must

bring his suit seasonably. He must show to the court
3. that he has exhausted all the means within his reach
to obtain redress within the corporation. He must
make a good-faith and reasonable effort to induce the corporation to bring the suit itself. *Hawes* v. *Oakland, supra*
(104 U. S. 450, 26 L. Ed. 827); *Taylor* v. *Holmes,* 127
U. S. 489, 8 Sup. Ct. 1192, 32 L. Ed. 179; Cook, Corp.
(5th Ed.) §740; Clark & Marshall, Priv. Corp. §543.''

"It is ordinarily necessary to show a demand upon the
board of directors to bring suit, and a refusal upon their
part; but the law does not require idle ceremonies,
4. and when it is made to appear that a demand would
have been unavailing,—as when the corporation is
under the control of the wrongdoers, 'in the hands of its
enemies,'—such facts are sufficient. *Wayne Pike Co.* v.
*Hammons, supra* (129 Ind. 368); *Rogers* v. *Lafayette, etc.,
Works,* 52 Ind. 296; *Board, etc.* v. *Lafayette, etc., R. Co.,
supra* (50 Ind. 85, 100); *Carter* v. *Ford Plate Glass Co.,
supra* (85 Ind. 180); Thompson, Corporations, §4500;
Cook, Corporations, §741; *Knoop* v. *Bohmrich,* 49 N. J.
Eq. 82, 23 Atl. 118. The demand upon the board and its
refusal to act are stated by an. approved author 'material
and issuable, if controverted they must be proved. If proof
of them fails the whole foundation of the plaintiff's action
is gone'. Pomeroy, Eq. Jurisp., §1095.''

Such being the rules governing stockholders of a corporation in bringing actions originally, for and on behalf
of themselves, there would seem to be even more
5. reason for their application where the corporation
is insolvent and its affairs are being managed and
settled through a receiver appointed by and acting under
the direction and orders of the court. "When a court has
taken possession of the property of an insolvent cor-
6. poration for administration, and appointed a receiver, the property of the corporation is a trust
fund for the payment of its debts." (*Franklin, etc.,*

*Bank* v. *Whitehead* [1897], 149 Ind. 560, 583, 49 N. E.
592, 63 Am. St. 302, and cases there cited); and the receiver in such case "is not the agent or representa-
7. tive of either party to the action, but is uniformly
regarded as an officer of the court, exercising his
functions * * * for the common benefit of all parties
in interest." High, Receivers (4th Ed.) §1.

While for the purposes of determining the nature and
extent of his title, such receiver represents the corporation
itself, yet he represents both stockholders and credit-
8. ors and is to be regarded as their trustee, charged
with the duties of collecting, assembling, protecting
and preserving the assets of such corporation for the benefit of those entitled thereto, subject, of course, to the orders
and directions of the court whose officer he is. *Voorhees*
v. *Indianapolis, etc., Co.* (1895), 140 Ind. 220, 39 N. E.
738; *Big Creek, etc., Co.* v. *Seward* (1896), 144 Ind. 205,
42 N. E. 464, 43 N. E. 5; *National State Bank, etc.* v.
*Vigo, etc., Bank* (1895), 141 Ind. 352, 356, 40 N. E. 799,
50 Am. St. 330; *Northwestern, etc., Ins. Co.* v. *Kidder*
(1903), 162 Ind. 383, 390-392, 70 N. E. 489, 66 L. R. A.
89, 1 Ann. Cas. 509; *Coddington* v. *Canaday* (1901), 157
Ind. 243, 255-257, 61 N. E. 567. The receiver in such a
case is the proper party to bring any action which
9. the corporation might have brought, and, "as trustee for the creditors, can maintain and defend actions which the corporation could not." *Franklin, etc.,
Bank* v. *Whitehead, supra*, pp. 583, 584, and cases there
cited; *Voorhees* v. *Indianapolis, etc., Co., supra*, p. 239.

While our Supreme Court recognizes that a general
creditor, by reason of his lien upon the property so held
in trust by such receiver, "has the right to intervene and
contest the validity as well as the priority of other claims
or asserted liens," (*Franklin, etc., Bank* v. *Whitehead,*

*supra,* and cases cited), yet such court has also frequently held that such receiver "represents the creditors, and has the exclusive right to recover and protect the assets of the corporation, and that such actions can not be maintained by the creditors in their own names." *Northwestern, etc., Ins. Co.* v. *Kidder, supra,* 391, and cases there cited. It is likewise held that, in such cases, the right of action being one in favor of the corporation and not in favor of the individual shareholders, the latter cannot bring the action, but it may be brought by the receiver. *Coddington* v. *Canaday, supra,* p. 256.

In the case of *Voorhees* v. *Indianapolis, etc., Co., supra,* where a creditor of the insolvent corporation attempted to intervene, the court used the following language, which we think is pertinent and applicable to the petition under consideration: "The petition and proposed complaint, * * * were nothing more nor less than a proposal on the part of the rolling mill (petitioner) to usurp the functions of the receiver, or practically to appoint another receiver. The petitioner had no right to do this. Beach Rec., section 167. If one creditor could do so, each one could, and the purposes and objects of a receivership would be broken down and destroyed. All that is said in said petition against the receiver's conduct might be material to petition to remove him and appoint a successor, but those facts do not justify supplanting him by a person not a receiver. 20 Am. and Eng. Encyc. Law, 198, 199, 200, 201, 202, 3-4-5, and authorities there cited."

These cases, *supra,* seem to be conclusive as to the power and duty of the receiver to collect, protect and preserve all the assets of the insolvent corporation for the benefit of those entitled thereto, including stockholders as well as creditors, and to that end to maintain and defend all actions for or against such corporation, and where the interest of creditors requires, he may maintain and defend certain actions which the corporation itself could not. It

follows, we think, that in the absence of a showing
10.. of a refusal of the receiver to discharge his duty in
the respects indicated, or some showing of collusion
or fraud on his part, by which the court had been or was
being misled and induced to act against, or to fail to act
in, the interests of those for whom such corporate assets
were held in trust, appellant was not a necessary party to
said action, and hence not such a party as the first proviso
of the statute quoted above requires should be made a
party. There is no claim that the second proviso of the
statute has any application to the facts set up in said
petition.

The conclusion we have reached, we think, makes it proper
to observe that in our judgment the trial court, in the exercise of its discretionary power, might in certain cases
11. permit a stockholder to intervene, where its refusal
to do so would not constitute reversible error under
the statute, *supra*, and in this connection we may also
12. add that notice by publication to the stockholders of
a bank, alleged to be insolvent, is a necessary prerequisite to the appointment of a receiver for such bank
(§3346 Burns 1914, Acts 1895 p. 202), and we have no
doubt that after such bank has been thus brought into court
and a general receiver appointed, with complete authority
to take charge of the assets of such corporation and to manage and administer the same for the stockholders and
creditors, that either a stockholder, or a creditor that has
established his claim, has such a standing in court that he
may, on proper showing, ask and obtain from the court,
orders and directions on the receiver in furtherance of the
interests of stockholders and creditors and, if the receiver
disobeys such orders, such stockholder or creditor may ask
his removal by the court appointing him, and the refusal
of such court to take such action as would protect all concerned would be ground for complaint in the appellate
tribunal. *Voorhees* v. *Indianapolis, etc., Co., supra.*

It appears from the record and appellant's petition that the claims of the three banks, the allowance of which appellant in his petition seeks to have reviewed, were

13. allowed by the court upon the agreement of the parties, after it had heard the evidence and considered the petition and recommendation of compromise filed by the receiver; that appellant and another stockholder were present in court and appellant was allowed to file objections to said petition and excepted to the ruling on said objections, and asked an appeal therefrom. It appears, therefore, that as to such claims appellant was given ample opportunity to interpose any objection or defense, and, if he had any valid defense to such allowances he should have then presented it to the court and properly prosecuted his appeal from the ruling thereon. There is no charge in appellant's petition that the allowance of said claims, so made by the court, was induced by any fraud or collusion practiced upon the court by either the receiver or the claimants.

As to the other suits contemplated by appellant, his petition shows that they were suits, the bringing of which, under the authorities cited, *supra*, properly fall within the

14. powers and duties of the receiver, subject only to the orders and directions of the court in relation thereto, and there is no showing that the receiver had ever been asked to bring such suits, or that he had refused to bring them, or refused to ask and obtain the necessary orders and directions of the court in reference thereto. This

court will assume, in the absence of a showing to the

15. contrary, that the receiver has or will discharge his duties as such, and that the court under whose directions such receiver is acting will make all orders necessary upon the receiver to the full protection of the corporation and the interests of its shareholders and creditors. If, as appellant's brief seems to imply, there was collusion and fraud practiced upon the court in obtaining the allowance

of the claims of the said banks, appellant should have so alleged in his petition, and if such be the fact, appellant, and the other stockholders, are not without a remedy.

We find no error in the record, and the judgment of the trial court is therefore affirmed.

Note.—Reported in 114 N. E. 100. See under (1) 10 Cyc 963; (2, 3) 10 Cyc 967; (4) 10 Cyc 976; (6) 34 Cyc 230. Corporations, appointment of receiver, when proper, 72 Am. St. 48.

---

## Antioch Baptist Church *v.* Morton et al.

[No. 9,061. Filed June 30, 1916. Rehearing denied November 23, 1916.]

1. APPEAL.—*Vacation.—Parties.—Assignment of Errors.*—In a vacation appeal all parties to, and those affected by, the judgment must be named in the assignment of error, and there should be named therein as appellees all parties in whose favor the judgment appealed from was rendered, and those who are interested in having it maintained. p. 118.

2. APPEAL. — *Vacation.* — *Parties.* — *Dismissal.* — Where it affirmatively appears from the record of a vacation appeal that the judgment appealed from was rendered in favor of persons who are not named as appellees in the assignment of error, and that such persons are interested in maintaining the judgment, the appeal will be dismissed. p. 118.

From Marion Circuit Court (22,364); *Charles Remster,* Judge.

Action by the Antioch Baptist Church, by its trustees, Thomas Roberts and others, against Emma G. Morton and others. From a judgment for defendants, the plaintiff appeals. *Appeal dismissed.*

*W. E. Henderson,* for appellant.

*C. S. Denny, G. L. Denny* and *Robert W. McBride,* for appellees.

HOTTEL, P. J.—The Antioch Baptist Church, by its trustees, Thomas Roberts, Walter Carlock, John Parker, Frank Buckner, and John Gates, brought this action against the appellee, Emma G. Morton, and seven others, naming them, for the review of a certain judgment. The defendants demurred to the complaint for want of sufficient facts. The demurrer was sustained and, the plaintiff refusing to plead further, judgment was rendered thereon that plaintiff take nothing and that the defendants recover their costs. From this judgment appellant appeals.

In the assignment of errors the "Antioch Baptist Church, By its Trustees," is named as appellant and "Emma G. Morton, et al." are named as appellees. No other names appear either in the caption or in the body of the assignment. This is a vacation appeal. It is well settled that in a vacation appeal all parties to, and those affected by, the judgment must be named in the assignment of errors.

1. All persons in whose favor the judgment appealed from was rendered, and those who are interested in having it maintained must be named as appellees in the assignment of errors. *Lauster* v. *Meyers* (1908), 170 Ind. 548, 549, 84 N. E. 1087, and cases cited; *Deinhart* v. *Mugg* (1911), 176 Ind. 531, 96 N. E. 467; *West* v. *Goodwin* (1907), 41 Ind. App. 333, 81 N. E. 734; *Haag* v. *Deter* (1906), 167 Ind. 126, 78 N. E. 331; *Pope* v. *Voigt* (1911), 49 Ind. App. 176, 96 N. E. 984.

It affirmatively appears from the record in this case that the judgment appealed from was rendered in favor of persons who are not named as appellees in appellant's

2. assignment of error, and that such persons are interested in maintaining such judgment.

It follows, under the authorities cited, that we are without authority to determine the questions sought to be presented. Appeal dismissed.

NOTE.—Reported in 113 N. E. 309.

## YORK ET AL. *v.* COOPER.

[No. 9,088. Filed November 24, 1916.]

1. APPEAL.—*Review.—Questions Presented.—Motions.*—An assignment of error predicated on the trial court's refusal of a motion to modify its finding of facts by striking out certain special findings presents no question for review on appeal, since motions to modify, strike out or add to the special findings are not recognized by the code of procedure, the proper remedy being by a motion for a new trial. p. 120.

2. APPEAL.—*Briefs.—Sufficiency.*—Where appellant's brief fails to show that a motion for a new trial was filed or ruled on, and it is impossible to determine, without a search of the record, what questions were sought to be presented by the motion, the brief fails to comply with the fifth clause of Rule 22 of the Appellate Court, relating to the preparation of appellant's briefs, and no question is presented for review by an assignment of error based on the overruling of the motion for a new trial. p. 120.

From Starke Circuit Court; *Francis J. Vurpillat*, Judge.

Action by John Cooper against Miles M. York and others. From a judgment for plaintiff, the defendants appeal. *Affirmed.*

*Guy R. York, Charles Hamilton Peters* and·*John F. Lawrence*, for appellants.

*Burson & Burson*, for appellees.

IBACH, J.—Appellee brought this action against appellants to quiet title and to foreclose a lien on certain real estate. The complaint is in two paragraphs. The first paragraph is in the ordinary form of a complaint to quiet title, and the second seeks to reform a certain contract and to foreclose a lien created thereby. There was a trial by the court and on request a special finding of facts and conclusions of law stated thereon were filed, the court concluding as a matter of law that appellee was entitled to a reformation of the contract and a foreclosure of the same as a purchase-money lien. Judgment followed the conclusions of law.

The errors assigned and relied on for reversal are: (1) The overruling of appellants' motion to modify the court's finding of facts by striking out special finding No. 3. (2) The overruling of appellants' motion to modify the court's special finding of facts, by striking out special finding No. 4. (3) The overruling of appellants' motion for a new trial.

No question is presented by either the first or second assigned errors. Motions to modify, strike out, or add to the special findings are not recognized by our code 1. of procedure. The sole remedy is provided by a motion for a new trial. *Chicago, etc., R. Co.* v. *State, ex rel.* (1902), 159 Ind. 237, 241, 64 N. E. 860, and cases cited; *Citizens Trust Co.* v. *National, etc., Supply Co.* (1912), 178 Ind. 167, 177, 98 N. E. 865, 41 L. R. A. (N. S.) 695. As to the third assigned error there has 2. been no effort on the part of appellants to comply with clause 5, Rule 22, and without searching the record this court would be unable to determine what questions were sought to be presented by the motion for new trial, or whether in fact such a motion was filed or ruled on. No question is therefore presented by this assignment. *Reeves & Co.* v. *Gillette* (1910), 47 Ind. App. 221, 223, 94 N. E. 242. Judgment affirmed.

NOTE.—Reported in 114 N. E. 90.

---

INDIANAPOLIS ELECTRIC SUPPLY COMPANY *v.*
TRAPSCHUH ET AL.

[No. 9,209. Filed November 24, 1916.]

1. APPEAL.—*Motion for a New Trial.—Grounds.—Form of Assignment.*—Under §585 Burns 1914, §559 R. S. 1881, authorizing the granting of a new trial for the reason "that the * * * decision is not sustained by sufficient evidence, or is contrary to law," no question is presented for review on appeal, where trial was had without a jury, by an assignment of error predicated on the overruling of a motion for a new trial based on the

grounds that the judgment and order rendered by the court were contrary to the law and the evidence and that they were not sustained by sufficient evidence, since the word "decision," as used in the statute, has reference to the finding where the trial is by the court, and neither assigned cause for a new trial challenges the decision or finding of the court.

From Marion Superior Court (96,933); *Theophilus J. Moll*, Judge.

Action by the Indianapolis Electric Supply Company against Charles J. Trapschuh and others. Nicholas J. Lux, being made a party defendant, filed an intervening petition, and from a judgment in his favor, the plaintiff appeals. *Affirmed.*

*Hempstead C. Shaw*, for appellant.
*Frank S. Roby, Elias D. Salsbury, Edward W. Little* and *Earl W. Little*, for appellees.

CALDWELL, C. J.—Appellant commenced this action against appellee Trapschuh, doing business as The Trapschuh Lighting Fixture Company, to recover on certain promissory notes and accounts. On appellant's application, appellee J. Fred Masters was appointed receiver of the personal property and assets of Trapschuh. Subsequently, by order of court, appellee Nicholas J. Lux was made a party defendant, and he thereupon filed a pleading, designated as an intervening petition, by which he alleged facts to the effect that he was the owner of a stock of goods and certain personal property, of which Masters, as receiver, had taken possession as the property of Trapschuh.

The issues formed on the intervening petition were tried by the court. The finding was for Lux, and that he was the owner of the property described in his petition, and that he was entitled to possession thereof. The judgment follows the finding and includes an order that the receiver deliver the possession of the property to Lux. From such judgment appellant appeals, assigning the overruling of the motion for a new trial as the sole error. The motion for a

122    APPELLATE COURT OF INDIANA,

Indianapolis Electric Supply Co. v. Trapschuh—63 Ind. App. 120.

new trial is to the effect that thereby appellant moved the
court "to grant a new trial as from the finding and judgment rendered  *  *  *  which judgment and order directed" the receiver to deliver the property, etc., the grounds
of the motion being as follows:  (1) That said judgment
and order rendered by the court aforesaid are contrary to
law; (2) that the said judgment and order rendered by the
court were not sustained by sufficient evidence; (3) that
the judgment rendered and order made by the court on
December 11, 1914, were contrary to the law and the
evidence.

The statutory cause for a new trial to which appellant
evidently intends to appeal is the sixth subdivision of §585
Burns 1914, §559 R. S. 1881.  So much of that subsection
as is applicable where the trial is by the court without a
jury, is as follows:  "That the  *  *  *  decision is not
sustained by sufficient evidence, or is contrary to law."  The
word "decision" as used in such section has reference to
the finding where the trial is by the court.  *Gates* v. *Baltimore, etc., R. Co.* (1899), 154 Ind. 338, 56 N. E. 722; *Hillel*
v. *Buettner, etc., Co.* (1916), 62 Ind. App. 481, 113 N. E. 12.

It will be observed that by neither assigned cause for a
new trial does appellant challenge the decision or the finding of the court.  The causes in each case are directed
against the judgment, and the order, which in this case is
a part of the judgment.  "It may be that, upon verdicts
or findings in strict accord with the law and evidence,
judgments contrary to the law and evidence are rendered.
But the remedy against such errors is a motion to modify the judgment, and not a motion for a new trial."
*Lynch* v. *Milwaukee, etc., Co.* (1902), 159 Ind. 675, 65 N.
E. 1025.  A long line of decisions requires us to hold that
no question is presented for our consideration.  In addition to the decisions above cited, see the following, some of
which illustrate the spirit of liberality exercised by the
courts in an effort to hold sufficient causes irregularly as-

signed: *Rodefer* v. *Fletcher* (1883), 89 Ind. 563; *Hall* v. *McDonald* (1908), 171 Ind. 9, 85 N. E. 707; *Indiana, etc., Co.* v. *Caldwell* (1915), 59 Ind. App. 513, 107 N. E. 705; *Johnson* v. *Allispaugh* (1914), 58 Ind. App. 83, 107 N. E. 686; *Hillel* v. *Buettner, etc., Co., supra.* Judgment affirmed.

NOTE.—Reported in 114 N. E. 99.

---

ROYER ET AL. *v.* STATE OF INDIANA, EX REL. BROWN.

[No. 9,255. Filed April 5, 1916. Rehearing denied June 27, 1916. Transfer denied November 24, 1916.]

1. APPEAL.— *Briefs.—Omissions.— Supplied by Adverse Party.— Rules of Court.*—Although the points and authorities in appellant's brief are not applied to any specific ruling of the trial court relied on for reversal, yet where appellee has, by the statements in his brief, supplied the omissions of appellant, the questions sought to be presented may be considered without disregarding the rules for the preparation of briefs. p. 126.

2. DRAINS.—*Construction.—Objection to Contract.—Collusion and Fraud.—Legislative Power.*—It was the province of the legislature to designate who may institute and maintain the actions contemplated by the act of 1907 (Acts 1907 p. 490, §§3866-3877 Burns 1914), prohibiting fraud and collusion in the bidding for public work, and a taxpayer and property owner whose property is assessable for a drainage improvement is within the purview of the statute. p. 130.

3. DRAINS.—*Establishment.—Bidding for Contract.—Collusion or Fraud.—Remedies.—Statute.*—The purpose of the act of 1907 (Acts 1907 p. 490, §§3866-3877 Burns 1914), relating to combinations to restrain trade, is to prevent fraud and collusion in the bidding for contracts for public work, and to that end the legislature authorized not only that suits may be maintained by the proper persons to restrain violations of the act, but money paid under any contract procured in violation of the statute, before notice of fraud or collusion, may be recovered and that any person who has been injured by the doing of anything prohibited by the act may recover a penalty. p. 131.

4. DRAINS.—*Establishment.—Bidding for Contract.—Collusion or Fraud.—Statute.*—Under the act of 1907 (Acts 1907 p. 490, §§3866-3877 Burns 1914), directed to the prevention of fraud and collusion in the bidding for contracts for public work, if the successful bidder is a party directly or indirectly to collusion or fraud, no liability arises against the parties who would other-

wise be liable for the work contracted for, as a contract procured in violation of the act is void and unenforcible by the party who participated in the fraud or collusion by which the contract was procured, and anything remaining unperformed under the contract, or the awarding thereof, may be restrained if suit be instituted for that purpose by any of the persons designated by the statute, it being clear that the legislature intended to prevent a person who obtains a contract by fraud and collusion to derive any benefit therefrom directly or indirectly. p. 131.

5. INJUNCTION.—*Right to Relief.—Remedy at Law.*—Even in the absence of the statute giving the right to restrain the performance of a contract procured by collusion or fraud, the existence of a remedy at law would not necessarily deprive a party of injunctive relief, for, if the legal remedy is not as prompt, practical, efficient and adequate as that afforded by equity, an injunction will issue if the case is otherwise established. p. 132.

6. INJUNCTION.—*Grounds.—Multiplicity of Suits.*—Where there is a legal remedy, equity will frequently grant injunctive relief to prevent a multiplicity of suits. p. 132.

7. EQUITY.—*Jurisdiction.—Prevention of Fraud.*—Independent of statute, equity may be invoked to prevent fraud or to deprive a wrongdoer of the benefit of a fraudulent deal or transaction. p. 132.

8. DRAINS.—*Injunction.—Laches.—Public Interest.*—Where fraud and collusion have been employed to procure a contract for the construction of a public drain, the rule as to the effect of laches in dealings between individuals does not apply where public rights are involved. p. 132.

9. DRAINS.—*Establishment.—Injunction.—Laches.—Public Interest. Statute.*—In an action by the State, on the relation of a taxpayer, to annul the contract for the construction of a public drain, to enjoin the collection of assessments for the improvement and the payment of money by the drainage commissioner to the contractor, the remedy invoked under the statutes, §§3866-3877 Burns 1914, Acts 1907 p. 490, directed to the prevention of collusion and fraud in bidding for public contracts, was not intended to be limited to the private rights or interests of the taxpayer, but to reach all concerned in, or affected by, any particular contract or transaction tainted with fraud or collusion, and to secure or protect the interests of the public, so that those violating the statute cannot avoid the provisions thereof by showing that a party authorized to invoke the remedies afforded by such statute has not acted promptly. p. 133.

10. APPEAL.—*Petition for Rehearing.—Scope of Review.—Briefs.*—On a petition for a rehearing appellants may not present questions not presented by their original briefs. p. 134.

11. DRAINS.—*Construction.*—*Contract.*—*Action to Annul.*—*Necessary Parties.*—In an action under the act of 1907, Acts 1907
p. 490, §§3866-3877 Burns 1914, by the State, on the relation of
a taxpayer, to have a contract for the construction of a public
drain declared void and to enjoin the parties to the contract from
the performance thereof, the persons assessed for the improvement were not necessary party defendants, under §269 Burns
1914, §262 R. S. 1881, providing that any person may be made
a defendant who has, or claims, any interest in the controversy
adverse to the plaintiff, or who is a necessary party to the
complete determination or settlement of the questions involved,
since the persons so assessed were not parties to the contract,
and could not have prevented the relator obtaining the relief
sought, if he had brought himself within the provisions of the
statute, and as they neither had nor claimed any interest adverse to the right asserted by the relator they were not necessary parties to the determination of the questions involved in
the suit. p. 135.

From Starke Circuit Court; *Harley A. Logan,* Special
Judge.

Action by the State of Indiana, on the relation of
Nathaniel Brown, against Miles Y. Royer and another.
From a judgment for plaintiff, the defendant appeals.
*Affirmed.*

*John G. Reidelbach, Louis A. Reidelbach, John M. Span-
gler, William J. Reed* and *Henry A. Steis,* for appellants.
*Fansler & Foskett* and *Peters & Peters,* for appellee.

FELT, P. J.—This suit was brought by appellee against
appellants to annul the contract for the construction of a
public drain, to enjoin the collection of assessments for the
improvement and the payment of money by the drainage
commissioner to the contractor, appellant Royer. The complaint is in one paragraph and is based on the act of 1907.
Acts 1907 p. 490, §§3866-3877 Burns 1914. It was answered by general denial and a plea of estoppel to which a
reply in general denial was filed. On due request the court
made a special finding of facts on which it stated its conclusions of law. The errors assigned and presented by the
briefs call for a decision of the questions relating to the

right of the appellee to bring the suit and the correctness of the conclusions of law stated by the court on the finding of facts.

Appellees contend that no questions are presented by the briefs for the reason that the points and authorities are not

1. applied to any specific ruling of the trial court relied on for reversal. There is much merit in the criticism, but appellee has to some extent supplied the omissions of appellants by the statements in his brief, so that we may consider the questions above indicated without disregarding the rules for the preparation of briefs. *Geisendorff* v. *Cobbs* (1910), 47 Ind. App. 573, 577, 94 N. E. 236; *Chicago, etc., R. Co.* v. *Dinius* (1913), 180 Ind. 596, 626, 103 N. E. 652; *Schrader* v. *Meyer* (1911), 48 Ind. App. 36, 95 N. E. 335; *Inland Steel Co.* v. *Smith* (1906), 168 Ind. 245, 252, 80 N. E. 538.

The substance of the finding of facts so far as material to the questions presented is as follows: The relator, Nathaniel Brown, is a taxpayer of Van Buren township, Pulaski county, Indiana, and owns real estate abutting a public drain known as the "John F. Taylor ditch," which land is assessed for the construction of said ditch. Jerome B. Newman was, on October 6, 1910, duly appointed drainage commissioner or superintendent of construction of said ditch, which drain was duly established on October 6, 1910.

Said Newman duly qualified as such drainage commissioner and gave notice that he would receive bids for the construction of said ditch on November 5, 1910, and thereafter entered into a contract therefor with Miles Y. Royer for $6,490. Norman S. Denny, Edgar X. Boyles and said Royer each bid on said ditch. After making some bids Denny and Boyles retired and held a consultation, and Denny thereafter caused Royer to join them and thereupon Denny and Royer executed their note for $25 payable to Boyles and delivered it to him. That Denny had agreed with Boyles to give him the note in consideration of Boyles

refraining from bidding further on the ditch; that Royer
had knowledge of the consideration for the note and of the
aforesaid arrangement between Denny and Boyles; "that
the defendant Miles Y. Royer,. Norman S. Denny and Edward X. Boyles conducted themselves in the presence of
the drainage commissioner as competitive bidders and that
the agreements and understandings between them were col-
lusive and fraudulent and made for the purpose and intention of limiting and restricting the bidding on the John F.
Taylor ditch, a public work. That Edward X. Boyles and
Norman S. Denny stopped bidding by reason of the above
agreement and Miles Y. Royer was awarded the contract."
That after the contract was let Denny claimed to be a partner with Royer and performed some labor on the ditch;
that Denny's assessment on the ditch was $181 and Royer
made a full settlement with him for that amount in which
Denny agreed to and did pay Boyles $25 for said note;
that the relator, Nathaniel Brown, was present when the
contract was let to Royer on November 5, 1910, and on
April 2, 1911, obtained knowledge of the facts relating to
the letting of the contract in the manner aforesaid; that he
consulted attorneys about the same in June, 1911, and began
this suit on September 11, 1911; that he resided about a
quarter of a mile from the ditch and when he. commenced
the suit he knew that 2,160 feet of twenty-four-inch tile
and 3,800 feet of twenty-inch tile had been placed in the
ditch, and also knew that within thirty to sixty days after
the contract was let the commissioner purchased tile for
the ditch at a cost of $3,500; that on April 2, 1911, the
main line of the ditch was completed and about one-half of
the cost of the whole ditch had then been expended; that
Brown made no objection or complaint to Royer or said
Newman until September, 1911; that the ditch was completed according to contract and specifications on April 2,
1912, and was accepted by the commissioner in charge of
its construction; that Newman, the drainage commissioner,

unless restrained, will make payments on the contract for the construction of said ditch out of assessments made therefor against the real estate shown in the report on said ditch.

The conclusions of law on the finding of facts are as follows: "(1) The contract let by Jerome B. Newman, commissioner, to Miles Y. Royer is void as against the principal for which said commissioner was acting. (2) That the enforcement of said contract should be enjoined. (3) That the principal for which said commissioner was and is acting is not liable on said contract, and that Jerome B. Newman, commissioner, should be enjoined from making payments on said contract." The appellants each separately excepted to each conclusion of law.

The suit was brought under the statute. Acts 1907 p. 490, §§3866-3877 Burns 1914. The portions of the statute involved here provide as follows:

Section 3: "Any and all schemes, designs, understandings, plans, arrangments, contracts, agreements or combinations to limit, restrain, retard, impede or restrict bidding for the letting of any contract for * * * public work, directly or indirectly, or to in any manner combine or conspire to stifle or restrict free competition for the letting of any contract for * * * public work, are hereby declared illegal, and any person who shall directly or indirectly engage in any scheme, design, understanding, plan, arrangement, contract, agreement or combination to limit, restrain, retard, impede or restrict bidding for the letting of any contract for * * * public work, shall be deemed guilty of a misdemeanor, and upon conviction shall be fined * * *."

Section 4: "If there shall be collusion or fraud of any kind or character among the bidders at the letting of any contract or work as provided in section three of this act, then the principal who lets the contract or work, or for whom the contract was let, shall not be liable for such letting or on account of such letting or on account of said contract, or work, or any part thereof, to the successful bidder to whom the contract or work was let, * * * if such successful bidder be a party, directly or indirectly, to such collusion or fraud, on such contract, or letting, or for any work, materials furnished or thing done in discharge thereof, or with reference thereto, and if before notice of such collusion or fraud, payment or partial payment thereon or therefor shall have been made, such principal may at any time within five years from the date of the last payment made thereon or therefor, in an appropriate action in any court of competent jurisdiction in this state recover the full amount of such payment or payments with interest to date of judgment thereon, and attorneys fees, against such successful bidder, and such recovery shall not be a bar to any action, either civil or criminal, brought against such bidder on account of any violation of this act, on behalf of the state by the attorney-general, a prosecuting attorney or otherwise.

Section 5: "It shall be the duty of the attorney-general and of the prosecuting attorney of each judicial circuit to institute appropriate proceedings to prevent and restrain violations of the provisions of this act or any act of the common law relating to the subject-matter of this act. All such proceedings shall be in name of the state of Indiana upon relation of the proper party. The attorney-general may file such proceedings either in term time or in vacation, upon his own relation, or that of any private person, in any circuit or superior court of the state, without applying to such court for leave, when he shall deem it his duty so to do. Such proceedings shall be by information filed by any prosecuting attorney in a circuit or superior court of the proper county upon his own relation whenever he shall deem it his duty so to do, or shall be directed by the court or governor or attorney-general and an information may be filed by any taxpayer on his own relation."

Section 7: "Any person who shall be injured in his business or property by any person or corporation by reason of the doing by any person or persons, of anything forbidden or declared to be unlawful by this act, may sue therefor in the circuit or superior court of any county in which the defendant or defendants, or any of them, reside or are found without respect to the amount in controversy, and shall recover a penalty of threefold the damages which may be sustained, together with the costs of suit, including a reasonable attorney's fee."

Section 5 authorizes the suits contemplated by the act in question to be instituted by the Attorney-General on his own relation or that of a private person; by a prosecuting attorney on his own relation; or by any taxpayer on his own relation. In either case the act provides: "All such proceedings shall be in the name of the state of Indiana upon relation of the proper party" and the proper party must be held to be the Attorney-General, the prosecuting attorney, a private person or a taxpayer as designated in the statute. It was the province of the legislature to

2. designate who may institute and maintain the actions contemplated by the act, and relator Nathaniel Brown as a taxpayer is within the purview of the statute. 32 Cyc 625, note 62; *Matter of Fenton* (1908), 58 Misc. Rep. (N. Y.) 303, 109 N. Y. Supp. 321; *State, ex rel. v. Board, etc.* (1908), 170 Ind. 595, 608, 609, 85 N. E. 513; *Baldwin v. Moroney* (1909), 173 Ind. 574, 577, 91 N. E. 3, 30 L. R. A. (N. S.) 761.

The exceptions to the conclusions of law stated on the finding of facts present more serious questions. Appellant contends that it is not shown that the relator will suffer great injury or that he does not have an adequate legal remedy; that the statute (§3872, *supra*) provides a complete and adequate remedy at law which the injured party is bound to pursue; that the relator is shown to have been guilty of such laches as will deprive him of injunctive re-

lief; that the facts do not warrant an injunction affecting
the whole contract and the payment of all money due on
the contract; that the conclusions of law which authorize
a judgment affecting private persons not parties to the suit
are erroneous and the judgment *coram non judice* and void.

Appellee contends that the facts bring the case within
the provisions of the statute and warrant the relief granted;
that the public has an interest in such proceedings; that
the collusion shown by the facts is against public policy
and an injury to the public on account thereof will be conclusively presumed.

Under the statute a party who has paid money under any
contract procured in violation of the act "before notice of
such collusion or fraud," may, within five years from
3.  the date of the last payment, recover the full amount
    so paid with interest. The statute likewise author-
izes any person who has been injured by anything done in
violation of the act to recover as a penalty threefold the
damages sustained by him. But the statute also authorizes
suits to restrain and prevent violations of the act or the
common law relating to the subject-matter of the act. The
purpose of the act was to prevent fraud and collusion in
the letting of contracts and to protect trade and commerce
against unlawful restraints and monopolies. To accomplish
these ends the legislature has seen fit to incorporate into
the statute different remedies and drastic measures for the
punishment of those who violate its provisions, and for the
relief of those who suffer on account thereof. If the successful bidder is a party directly or indirectly to
4.  such collusion or fraud, no liability arises against
    the parties who otherwise would be liable for the
cost of the work covered by such contract. A contract procured in violation of this act is void and unenforcible by
the party who participated in the fraud or collusion by
which it was procured, and anything remaining undone
which is about to be done or performed in pursuance or

furtherance of such letting or contract may be restrained and enjoined if suit for that purpose is duly brought by any of the persons designated in the statute. The legislature clearly intended to prevent a person who obtains a contract by fraud and collusion from deriving any benefit therefrom either directly or indirectly.

Even in the absence of the statute, the existence of a remedy at law does not necessarily deprive a person of injunctive relief. If the legal remedy is not as prompt,

5.  practical, efficient and adequate as that afforded by equity, an injunction will issue if the case is otherwise established. *Shedd* v. *American Maize, etc., Co.* (1915), 60 Ind. App. 146, 108 N. E. 610, 622; *Cincinnati, etc., Railroad* v. *Wall* (1911), 48 Ind. App. 605, 609, 96 N. E. 389; *Indianapolis, etc., Traction Co.* v. *Essington* (1913), 54 Ind. App. 286, 289, 99 N. E. 757, 100 N. E. 765.

Where there is a legal remedy, equity will frequently grant injunctive relief to prevent multiplicity of suits. *Knickerbocker Ice Co.* v. *Surprise* (1912), 53 Ind.

6.  App. 286, 291, 97 N. E. 357, 99 N. E. 58. The statute recognizes and is in harmony with these well-established rules of equity jurisprudence, and the provisions for legal remedies in certain contingencies do not ·mitigate against the provisions for injunctive relief when a case is otherwise made out entitling the complaining party to such relief.

We have held that the suit may be maintained by the State on the relation of a taxpayer. It is claimed that the delay in bringing the suit under the circumstances shown evidences such laches as to deprive the relator of equitable relief. As already shown, the statute is intended to prevent fraud and collusion. Independent of statute,

7.  equity may be invoked to prevent fraud or to deprive a wrongdoer of the benefit of a fraudulent deal or transaction. The public has an interest in promot-

8.  ing honest dealing and in preventing fraud. This is

peculiarly true of transactions where fraud and collusion have been employed to procure a contract for public work and the contract in this instance comes within that class. Whatever may be the effect of laches in dealings between individuals where the public is not concerned, the rule does not apply where public rights are involved. This general proposition is fortified in the case at bar by the provisions of the statute. 16 Cyc 81 *et seq.;* 22 Cyc 794; *Sweeny* v. *Williams* (1883), 36 N. J. Eq. 627, 629; *Teft* v. *Stewart* (1875), 31 Mich. 367, 371; *Allen* v. *Henn* (1902), 197 Ill. 487, 493, 64 N. E. 250; *Kissel* v. *Lewis* (1900), 156 Ind. 233, 241, 59 N. E. 478; *O'Brien* v. *Central Iron, etc., Co.* (1901), 158 Ind. 218, 221, 63 N. E. 302, 57 L. R. A. 508, 92 Am. St. 305; *Bissel Chilled Plow Works* v. *South Bend Mfg. Co.* —— Ind. App. ——, 111 N. E. 932; *Reyburn* v. *Sawyer* (1904), 135 N. C. 328, 47 S. E. 761, 65 L. R. A. 930, 935, 102 Am. St. 555.

The suit at bar is brought by the State of Indiana on the relation of a taxpayer in pursuance of the provisions of the statute, and the remedy invoked was not intended to 9. be limited to the private rights or interests of such taxpayer, but to reach all concerned in, or affected by, any particular contract or transaction tainted with fraud or collusion, and to secure or protect the interests of the public. The remedy provided by the statute in a suit brought as in this case is identical with that available where the Attorney-General or prosecuting attorney proceeds in accordance with the provisions of the act.

The finding shows no wrong committed by the drainage commissioner, but the purpose of the statute is to prevent the party who procures a contract in violation of the statute from deriving any benefit therefrom either directly or indirectly. The provisions are broad enough to authorize an injunction to prevent the doing of anything which recognizes the validity of such contract. If the commissioner may step in and carry out the illegal contract, the purpose of the law will be defeated. He may be enjoined, not because of any wrong of his own, but because his action may have the effect of defeating the clearly expressed intention of the legislature in enacting the statute.

Viewed from the standpoint of the relator's private interests alone, the law may seem to work a hardship on appellant Royer; but, viewed from the standpoint of honest dealing and the public good, the beneficial character of the statute is apparent. The question of the hardship that may result in this or any other case is not a question for the courts, for the legislature had the right to provide the remedies it deemed most expedient and best calculated to accomplish the end in view. The penalties and remedies provided do not affect those who have done no wrong. Those who violate the statute take their chances and cannot escape the consequences by showing that some one authorized to invoke its remedies has not acted promptly, and that the work has proceeded to a point where the remedy seems severe and drastic. Evidently it was the intention of the legislature to make the law so severe that men would be deterred from violating it.

We conclude therefore that the court did not err in its conclusions of law. The views already announced make it unnecessary to consider other questions presented in the briefs. No reversible error is shown. Judgment affirmed.

## ON PETITION FOR REHEARING.

FELT, J.—Appellants earnestly urge their petition for a rehearing, and by it seek to present some new questions not presented by their original briefs. It is well settled 10. that this cannot be done. *Chicago, etc., R. Co.* v. *Roth* (1915), 59 Ind. App. 161, 108 N. E. 971. Most of the questions discussed are decided by the original opinion, and after a careful review of such questions we find no reason to change or modify the conclusions already announced. In our view, appellants' contentions are fully

answered·by the statute under which the suit was brought
and by virtue of which the ·judgment rendered is fully
authorized.

Appellants also insist that the court failed to decide the
question of defect of parties defendant presented by appellants' demurrer to the complaint. The point was not
decided because the court concluded that it was not duly
presented by the briefs. We have re-examined the briefs
and find that they do not strictly comply with the rules,
·but may be treated as showing a substantial compliance
sufficient to justify us in considering the question. The demurrer alleges such defect by showing that other
11. parties assessed for the construction of the ditch are
not made defendants, and sets out their names. The
suit was brought by the State of Indiana, on relation of
Nathaniel Brown, a taxpayer, against Royer, who .obtained
the contract for construction of the ditch, and Newman,
the drainage commissioner, who received the bids and
entered into the·contract with Royer for the construction
of the public ditch. The suit was brought to declare the
contract void and to enjoin the parties thereto from carrying
it out. The parties to the contract were made defendants
to the suit and the court granted the relief prayed as shown
in the original opinion.

The statute authorized appellee as a taxpayer to maintain the suit. The persons assessed for the construction of
the ditch were not parties to the contract and were not
necessary parties to the suit to declare the contract void
under the statute and to enjoin the parties thereto from
carrying out its provisions. §269 Burns 1914, §268 R. S.
1881; *Town of Windfall City* v. *First Nat. Bank* (1909),
172 Ind. 679, 687, 87 N. E. 984, 89 N. E. 311; *Cummings*
v. *Stark* (1894), 138 Ind. 94, 103, 34 N. E. 444; *Haggerty*
v. *Wagner* (1897), 148 Ind. 625, 636-639, 48 N. E. 366, 39
L. R. A. 384.

The persons assessed were not parties to the contract and

could not have prevented appellee from obtaining the relief prayed for, if he brought himself within the provisions of the statute. They neither had nor claimed any interest adverse to the right asserted by appellee and were not necessary parties to a complete determination of the questions involved in the suit. The court, therefore, did not err in its ruling on the demurrer to the complaint.

The petition for a rehearing is overruled.

NOTE.—Reported in 112 N. E. 122, 113 N. E. 312. See under (5) 22 Cyc 771; (6) 122 Cyc 766. Injunction, right of taxpayer to relief by: (a) for misapplication of funds (3 Ann. Cas. 1014), in absence of statute, 36 L. R. A. (N. S.) 1; (b) in letting of contracts for public work, 17 Ann. Cas. 653 (where favoritism is shown, 36 L. R. A. [N. S.] 10); (c) to prevent enforcement of ordinance claimed to be void, 118 Am. St. 372. Laches in taxpayer's actions, effect, Ann. Cas. 1913C 898.

---

## LAFAYETTE TELEPHONE COMPANY v. CUNNINGHAM.

[No. 9,057. Filed November 28, 1916.]

1. TELEGRAPHS AND TELEPHONES.—*Guy Wires.*—*Care Required by Telephone Company.*—The primary and general use of a highway is for travel, and, although a telephone company may have the right to occupy a highway with its poles, yet, if it secures them with guy wires, its duty is to use reasonable care to so erect and maintain such wires as not to endanger the public travel, or the safety of individuals in the reasonable and ordinary use of the highway. p. 142.

2. TELEGRAPHS AND TELEPHONES.—*Injuries from Guy Wire.*—*Complaint.*—*Averments.*—*Duty to Use Care.*—*Negligent Violation of Duty.*—In an action by a police officer against a telephone company for injuries incurred when plaintiff tripped over a guy wire, averments in the complaint that plaintiff, at the time of the injury, was walking along a city street in the performance of his duties and that defendant had erected its poles and wires in such street show that defendant was charged with the duty to use reasonable care to so maintain its guy wire that it would not endanger the use of the street by the public, including plaintiff, so that, such duty being shown, allegations that the guy wire was "carelessly, negligently and unlawfully constructed and

built in said highway * * * and has been carelessly, negligently and unlawfully maintained" by defendant, sufficiently charge a negligent violation of its duty to plaintiff, there being nothing shown by the complaint which would destroy the effect of such general allegations of negligence. p. 142.

3. TELEGRAPHS AND TELEPHONES.—*Maintenance of Guy Wire.— Care Required.—Crossing Street Between Street Intersections.*— In an action against a telephone company for personal injuries, the fact that the plaintiff, when injured by falling over a guy wire, was attempting to cross a public street at a place where there was no intersection of a street or alley, and at a place not provided for crossing, while pertinent to the question of whether plaintiff was guilty of contributory negligence, did not discharge the defendant from its duty to use reasonable care in maintaining its guy wire so as not to endanger the public in the use of the street. p. 143.

4. NEGLIGENCE.— *Contributory Negligence.— Crossing Street Between Street Crossings.*—Where a police officer in response to a call from another officer, attempted to cross a street at a place where there was no intersection of a street or alley, and at a place not provided for crossing and in so doing tripped over a telephone guy wire and was injured, it cannot be said, as a matter of law, that the officer was guilty of contributory negligence in crossing the street where no street crossing was provided. p. 143.

5. TELEGRAPHS AND TELEPHONES.— *Use of Highway.— Care Required.—License to Locate Poles and Wires in Highway.*—A telegraph or telephone company using a highway is under a duty to exercise care to prevent injury to persons using the highway, and a license from a municipal corporation to use the way does not relieve the company from that duty; but, on the contrary, the acceptance of the license implies a duty on the part of the electric company to exercise care and diligence to prevent injury to persons using the highway. p. 144.

6. MUNICIPAL CORPORATIONS.— *Streets.— Use by Public.— Control by Municipality.*—While the public is entitled to the free use of any portion of a public street, yet the municipal corporation may devote portions of the sidewalk to other purposes useful and convenient to the public. p. 144.

7. TELEGRAPHS AND TELEPHONES.— *License to Place Poles and Wires in Street.—Care Required by Licensee.*—The proper municipal officers may devote a portion of a city's sidewalks to the use of telephone poles, lines and guy wires, but such portions of the sidewalk are, in the absence of an ordinance showing the contrary, a part of the street which the pedestrian may use for

travel, and any authority or license to use such part of the street
for telephone poles and wires must be exercised with reference
to the possible uses thereof by pedestrians, which must be anticipated by the licensee, and his license will not absolve him
from the duty of using ordinary care not to expose pedestrians to
unnecessary danger in using such portion of the street. p. 145.

8. TELEGRAPHS AND TELEPHONES.—*Injuries to Pedestrian from Guy
Wire.—Crossing Street in Absence of Street Crossing.*—In an
action against a telephone company for injuries incurred by
plaintiff falling over a telephone guy wire, the fact, as established by the jury's answers to interrogatories, that plaintiff
went upon a grassplot for the purpose of crossing the street at
a point where there was no cross-walk, did not relieve the defendant of its responsibility to him, since a pedestrian is not
restricted to cross-walks or street intersections in crossing a
street, but he may cross at any place, and he is not necessarily
guilty of contributory negligence in so doing. p. 146.

9. TRIAL.—*Interrogatories to Jury Calling for Conclusions.—General Verdict.—Effect.*—While special interrogatories to the jury
which call for conclusions should be disregarded, yet a general
verdict for the plaintiff is a finding in his favor of every fact
within the issues tending to support such conclusions. p. 147.

10. TRIAL.—*Contradictory Interrogatories.*—The fact that interrogatories propounded to the jury are contradictory or inconsistent with each other tends to their own destruction and not
to that of the general verdict. p. 147.

11. TRIAL.—*Interrogatories.—Answers.—Reconciliation with General Verdict.*—When the answers to all proper interrogatories,
read as an entirety, can be reconciled with the general verdict
by any supposable evidence possible under the issues, they will
not be permitted to overthrow such verdict. p. 147.

12. TELEGRAPHS AND TELEPHONES.—*Injuries to Pedestrian from
Guy Wire.—Negligence.—Evidence.—Sufficiency.*—In an action
against a telephone company for injuries incurred by plaintiff,
a night police officer, tripping over a guy wire when attempting
to cross a street in the performance of his duties, where there
was evidence that the guy wire, which was located in a grassplot between the sidewalk and curb and could not be seen easily
at night, was strung from the top of a telephone pole to an
anchor which protruded about five inches above the ground, that
the wire was not properly constructed for use in a street, and
that it would have been practicable either to have fastened such
a guy wire to a stub-pole several feet above the ground or to
have so trussed the telephone pole so that no guy wire would
have been needed, such evidence was sufficient to warrant the
jury finding that the defendant was negligent in using the par-

ticular construction of guying its pole, rather than some construction which would have dispensed with the guy wire or which would have made it more conspicuous or elevated it so as to place it where it could not trip travelers on the street. p. 147.

13. TELEGRAPHS AND TELEPHONES.—*Injuries to Pedestrian from Guy Wire.—Contributory Negligence.—Evidence.—Knowledge of Obstruction.*—In an action against a telephone company by a police officer, who was injured by falling over a guy wire when attempting to cross a street, the fact that the plaintiff had previous knowledge of the obstruction does not, *per se*, establish his contributory negligence. p. 149.

14. TELEGRAPHS AND TELEPHONES.—*Injuries to Pedestrian from Guy Wire.— Knowledge of Obstruction.— Contributory Negligence.—Question for Jury.*—In an action by a police officer for injuries received in falling over a guy wire, evidence that plaintiff had previous knowledge of the presence of the wire and that he momentarily forgot it when summoned across the street by his superior officer were facts for the consideration of the jury in determining whether the injured party was exercising reasonable care. p. 149.

15. APPEAL.— *Harmless Error.—Admission of Incompetent Evidence.—Cure by Instruction.*—In an action for injuries sustained by plaintiff falling over a guy wire, error, if any, in permitting witnesses to testify that they had, since plaintiff's accident, tripped over the wire in question was cured by an instruction informing the jury that they should not consider such testimony in making up their verdict. p. 149.

16. TRIAL.—*Instruction.—Invading Province of Jury.—Preponderance of Evidence.*—An instruction that by the expression "preponderance of the evidence" as used in the instructions given, was not meant the greater number of witnesses and that the preponderance of evidence does not depend upon the number of witnesses nor does it mean the greater number of witnesses, but does depend upon the weight of the evidence and means the greater weight of the evidence, was not erroneous as invading the province of the jury, although the wording of the instruction was subject to criticism. p. 150.

From Tippecanoe Superior Court; *Henry H. Vinton,* Judge.

Action by John F. Cunningham against the Lafayette Telephone Company. From a judgment for plaintiff, the defendant appeals. *Affirmed.*

*George P. Haywood* and *Charles A. Burnett*, for appellant.

*Edgar D. Randolph*, for appellee.

HOTTEL, J.—This is an appeal from a judgment in appellee's favor in an action brought by him in the Tippecanoe Superior Court to recover damages for injuries resulting from his tripping and falling over a guy wire alleged to have been negligently erected and maintained by appellant in Romig street in the city of Lafayette. The complaint was in two paragraphs, each of which was demurred to on the ground that the facts stated therein were not sufficient to constitute a cause of action. Each demurrer was overruled, and appellant then filed an answer in general denial. The issues thus joined were tried by a jury, which returned a verdict in favor of appellee in the sum of $2,500, together with answers to interrogatories. A motion for judgment on said answers and a motion for new trial were each overruled. The several rulings above indicated are each assigned as error in this court and relied on for reversal.

The allegations common to each paragraph of complaint and pertinent to the questions presented by appellant's demurrer thereto are substantially as follows: The appellant, prior to January 23, 1911, negligently and unlawfully constructed a guy wire attached to a pole at an alley leading north off of Romig street, between Fourth and Fifth streets, and strung the guy wire east and fastened the same to an iron stake near the curbing on the north side of Romig street, and at the root of a large sycamore tree situated and standing between the sidewalk and the gutter on the north side of Romig street, and, about seventy-five or eighty feet east of said pole; that there are two other large trees between said alley and the sycamore tree at the root of which said guy wire is fastened; that the guy wire slopes from where it is fastened to said pole to where it is fastened to said iron stake in the ground, and is about a quarter of an inch in diameter, and was *carelessly, negligently* and *unlawfully* constructed and built in said highway by appellant long prior to January 23, 1911, and has been *carelessly, negligently* and *unlawfully maintained* by it in said highway as above described ever since; that the construction of said guy wire as aforesaid is an obstruction of Romig street and a public nuisance. Such wire obstructs the free and proper use of said street and highway by the public and the citizens of the city of Lafayette in this, to wit: that said wire is invisible at night, and is calculated to and does deceive and trip people and persons using said highway and street in crossing from one side of the street to the other. Appellee, on the occasion in question, was a member of the police force of the city of Lafayette, and while walking westward on the sidewalk on the north side of Romig street, between Fourth and Fifth streets, in the performance of his duty as such police officer, he was called by another officer on the south side of Romig street, and in response to said call started across said street, and not seeing and not being able to see said guy wire, was caught and tripped by it and injured, etc., all without fault on his part. The second paragraph of complaint contains the additional averments that at a regular meeting of the board of works of the city of Lafayette, Indiana, held on January 27, 1909, a motion was passed declaring said wire an obstruction to said highway and street "and that the company will be held liable for all damages caused by the same."

Appellant contends that neither of said paragraphs show that said guy wire was unlawfully placed or maintained by appellant, or that appellant had no right to maintain said pole and wire at the place described, but that it appears from the averments indicated that the wire was anchored outside the traveled part of the highway; that each paragraph shows that appellee was.injured in attempting to cross Romig street at a place where there was no intersection of a street or alley, and at a place not provided for crossing, and that, therefore, no liability of appellant to appellee is shown.

The primary and general use of a highway is for travel; and, although a telephone company may have the right to occupy a highway with its poles, yet, if it secures

1. them in the highway with guy wires, its duty is to use reasonable care to so erect and maintain such wires as not to endanger the public travel, or the safety of individuals in the reasonable and ordinary use of the highway. *Wilson* v. *Great Southern Telephone, etc., Co.* (1889), 41 La. Ann. 1041, 6 So. 781; *Poumeroule* v. *Cable Co.* (1912), 167 Mo. App. 533, 152 S. W. 114; 2 Shear. & Redf. Negligence (6th ed.) §359; 1 Thompson, Negligence §1239; Curtis, Electricity §504, p. 755.

Each paragraph of complaint avers that appellant had erected its poles and wires in said Romig street; that ap-

2. pellee was a police officer in the city of Lafayette, and, on the night in question, was walking on said Romig street in the performance of his duties as such officer. These averments show the duty of appellant to use reasonable care to so maintain its guy wire that it would not endanger the use of said street by the public (appellee included) and hence shows a duty from appellant to appellee. This duty being shown, the averments in the complaint that said wire was "carelessly, negligently and unlawfully constructed and built in said highway * * * and has been carelessly, negligently and unlawfully maintained" by appellant, sufficiently charge a negligent violation of said duty, there being nothing shown by the complaint which would destroy the effect of such general allegations of negligence. *Tippecanoe Loan, etc., Co.* v. *Cleveland, etc., R. Co.* (1914), 57 Ind. App. 644, 656, 657, 104 N. E. 866, 106 N. E. 739, and cases cited; *Cleveland, etc., R. Co.* v. *Clark* (1912), 51 Ind. App. 392, 404-405; 97 N. E. 822; *New York, etc., R. Co.* v. *Lind* (1913), 180 Ind. 38, 44, 45, 102 N. E. 449.

Appellant, however, contends that the complaint shows that appellee was injured while attempting to cross said street at a place where there was no intersection of

3.  a street or alley, and at a place not provided for crossing. The fact that appellee, when injured, was outside the usually traveled part of the highway, while pertinent to the question whether appellee was guilty of negligence contributing to his injury, does not discharge appellant from its duty to use the reasonable care before indicated. *Wilson* v. *Great Southern Telephone, etc., Co., supra; Dickey* v. *Maine Telegraph Co.* (1859), 46 Me. 483; Crosswell, Electricity §79; *McIlhenney* v. *Philadelphia* (1906), 214 Pa. 44, 45, 63 Atl. 368; *Raymond* v. *City of Lowell* (1850), 6 Cush. (Mass.) 524, 526, 53 Am. Dec. 57; *Stringer* v. *Frost* (1889), 116 Ind. 477, 479, 19 N. E. 331, 2 L. R. A. 614, 9 Am. St. 875; *Simons* v. *Gaynor* (1883), 89 Ind. 165.

Nor can this court, under the facts averred in either

4.  paragraph of the complaint, say, as a matter of law, that appellee was guilty of contributory negligence in crossing the street where he did. *Southern Bell Telephone, etc., Co.* v. *Howell* (1905), 124 Ga. 1050, 53 S. E. 577, 4 Ann. Cas. 707; *Moebus* v. *Hermann* (1888), 108 N. Y. 349, 15 N. E. 415, 2 Am. St. 440; *Simons* v. *Gaynor, supra;* Elliott, Roads and Streets 622; *Collins* v. *Dodge* (1887), 37 Minn. 503, 35 N. W. 368; *Raymond* v. *City of Lowell, supra.*

Appellant's contention that the court erred in overruling its motion for judgment on the jury's answers to interrogatories rests upon the assumption that such answers show: (1) that appellant was not guilty of any negligence causing appellee's injury; and (2) that appellee was guilty of negligence contributing to his injuries.

The answers pertinent to the first contention are to the following effect: The defendant, at the time of the accident, had a franchise in the city of Lafayette, under which it was authorized to construct and maintain along the lines of the streets and alleys of the city of Lafayette, its poles, wires, etc., necessary for supplying telephone service to the citizens of said city; one of appellant's poles was located on the north side of Romig street; said pole was braced by a guy wire; Romig street was improved and divided into a gutter, roadway and sidewalks; there was a cement sidewalk on the north side of said street; there was a space or grassplot, three feet, ten inches wide, between said sidewalk and the curb on the north side of Romig street; said guy wire was anchored just inside said curb in said grassplot, and three feet, ten inches from the edge of said sidewalk; said wire did not cross any part of said sidewalk, or the roadway of said Romig street, or any intersection of said street with any other street, or any roadway, cement walk or cross-walk on said street; said wire did not interfere with the passage of any animal, vehicle or person on any cement walk, roadway or cross-walk; there was no cross-walk at the place where appellee started to cross the street, when he met with the accident. The law applicable to the facts thus found by the jury, as expressed by the text books and recognized by the decided cases, is

5. as follows: "A telephone or telegraph company using a highway is under a duty to exercise care to prevent injury to persons using the highway. A license from the municipal corporation to use the way does not relieve the company from that duty, but, on the contrary, the acceptance of the license implies a duty on the part of the electric company to exercise care and diligence to prevent injury to persons using the highway."

It is, however, insisted by appellant, and correctly so, we think, that "the general proposition that the public is entitled to the free use of any portion of a public street

6. must be accepted with the qualifications that a municipal corporation may devote portions of the sidewalk to other purposes useful and convenient to the public." *Teague* v. *City of Bloomington* (1906), 40 Ind. App. 68, 73, 74, 81 N. E. 103; *Barnesville* v. *Ward* (1911), 85 Ohio St. 1,

96 N. E. 937, Ann. Cas. 1912 D 1234, 40 L. R. A. (N. S.) 94; *Dougherty* v. *Village, etc.* (1899), 159 N. Y. 154, 53 N. E. 799; *Dotey* v. *District of Columbia* (1905), 25 App. D. C. 232.

It is further contended by appellant, in effect, that under the authorities just cited, a municipal corporation has a right to designate and use a part of its street for a grassplot and shade trees, and that the facts found by the jury, indicated, *supra,* show that the municipal officers of the city of Lafayette had so designated that part of the street where appellee was injured; that they had licensed appellant to locate its poles and lines in and along such grassplots; that such location was a proper one; and, hence, that appellant is not shown to have been guilty of any actionable negligence.

While, as above indicated, the authorities recognize that the proper municipal officers may devote a part of the sidewalks of the city to the uses and purposes indicated,

7. such portions of the sidewalk are, in the absence of an ordinance showing the contrary, held to be a part of the street, which the pedestrian may use for travel, and any authority or license to use such part of the street for the other purposes indicated must be exercised with reference to the possible uses thereof by such pedestrians; and, such licensee must anticipate such possible use by the pedestrian, and his license will not absolve him from the duty of using ordinary care not to expose such pedestrian to unnecessary danger in his use of such portion of the street. *Barnesville* v. *Ward, supra; Johnson* v. *City of Bay City* (1910), 164 Mich. 251, 129 N. W. 29, Ann. Cas. 1912 B 866; *Townley* v. *City of Huntington* (1911), 68 W. Va. 574, 70 S. E. 368, 34 L. R. A. (N. S.) 118; *Poumeroule* v. *Cable Co., supra;* Curtis, Electricity §487, p. 717.

The right of the public to go upon such a grassplot was upheld in the case of *Johnson* v. *City of Bay City, supra,* where the defendant, a municipal corporation, maintained a row of poles on a city street between the sidewalk and the roadway, on that part of the street designed to be used as a grassplot for ornamental purposes. The poles were part of the defendant's electric lighting system, by means of which it furnished electricity for both public and private lighting. Plaintiff, a child of about five years of age, while on the grassplot, was injured by coming in contact with a wire which had fallen from one of the poles. It was alleged that the wire fell because of the negligent manner in which it was erected and maintained. It was held that the plaintiff was not a trespasser upon said grassplot, and that the defendant was liable for the negligence charged.

The fact, established by some of the answers, that appellee went upon said grassplot for the purpose of crossing the street at that point, where there was no cross-

8. walk, does not relieve appellant of its responsibility.

A pedestrian is not restricted to cross-walks or street intersections in crossing a street, but he may cross at any place, and he is not necessarily guilty of contributory negligence because he does so. *McIlhenney* v. *Philadelphia, supra; Raymond* v. *City of Lowell, supra; Moebus* v. *Hermann, supra; Simons* v. *Gaynor, supra; Stringer* v. *Frost, supra; Collins* v. *Dodge, supra.*

As affecting its second contention, *supra*, appellant insists, in effect, that the answers to interrogatories show that there were two street lights, each of 2,000 candle power, one at the intersection of Romig and Fourth streets, and one at the intersection of Romig and Fifth streets; that the accident was in the winter season, when there were no leaves on the trees, and nothing to interfere with the rays of these lights falling on the place where appellee received his injury; that appellee had served as policeman some eight or nine years; that his duties required him to pass the place of his injury frequently and that he knew of the existence and location of the wire over which he fell

and was injured.   It is insisted that these answers show that
appellee knowingly attempted to cross the street, passing
over the grassplot in question, where he knew the wire
was located, and thereby was guilty of negligence contributing to his injury.

In answer to this contention, it should be stated that the
jury expressly found that the place where appellee was injured was not lighted at the time of the injury by said
street lights; that appellee before coming in contact with
said wire used reasonable care; that such guy wire was an
unreasonable obstruction to said street; that the maintenance thereof on said street was unnecessary and was calculated to deceive and trip people in the lawful use of said
street.

It is insisted, and properly so we think, that some of the
interrogatories, the answers to which we have just indicated,
called for conclusions and should be disregarded.

9.  The fact remains, however, that without such answers
the general verdict is a finding in appellee's favor
of every fact within the issues tending to support such
conclusions.  The fact that interrogatories are con-

10.  tradictory or inconsistent with each other tends to
their own destruction and not to that of the general
verdict, and when the answers to all proper interrogatories,
read as an entirety, can be reconciled with the gen-

11.  eral verdict by any supposable evidence possible under the issues, they will not be permitted to overthrow such verdict.  *Pittsburgh, etc., R. Co.* v. *Lightheiser*
(1906), 168 Ind. 438, 78 N. E. 1033; *Dickason Coal Co.* v.
*Peach* (1903), 32 Ind. App. 33, 69 N. E. 189.  For the
reasons indicated, the trial court did not err in overruling
appellant's motion for judgment on said answers.

Appellant contends that the verdict of the jury is not
sustained by sufficient evidence and is contrary to law.

There is evidence that appellee, a police officer, was

12.  walking westward on Romig street, between Fourth

and Fifth streets, in the city of Lafayette, at about eight o'clock in the evening of January 23, 1911, being then in the performance of his duty as such police officer; that his superior officer called to him from the opposite side of said street; that appellee heard the call and recognized it as that of his superior officer, and in response thereto, started across said street, and in doing so fell over a guy wire maintained by appellant; that said guy wire extends from the top of a pole on said street to an anchor buried in the ground about seventy-five feet from said pole and just inside the curb and near the root of a tree; that said guy wire was about one-half or five-eighths inches in diameter; that said anchor was an iron rod about an inch in diameter, the upper end of which protruded from the ground about four or five inches and was bent back upon itself so as to form a loop to which said wire was fastened; that the vertical distance of this loop from the ground was about four or five inches; that the place where the anchor was buried was dark at the time of the accident, that said place is dark at night; that said wire could not easily be seen at night; that the construction of said wire was not a proper construction in a street; that pipes are sometimes put over such anchors; that it would have been practicable to have fastened such a guy wire to a stub pole at a point several feet above the ground; that the pole could have been trussed so that no guy wire would have been needed.

The jury was warranted in finding from such evidence that appellant was negligent in using the particular construction here used, rather than some construction which would have dispensed with said wire or which would have made it more conspicuous, or elevated it so as to place it where it could not trip travelers on the street. *City of Fort Worth* v. *Williams* (1909), 55 Tex. Civ. App. 289, 119 S. W. 137; *Louisville Home Telephone Co.* v. *Gasper* (1906), 123 Ky. 128, 93 S. W. 1057, 9 L. R. A. (N. S.) 548; *Poumeroule* v. *Cable Co., supra.*

It is insisted, however, by appellant that the evidence shows that appellee knew of the existence and location of said wire, and hence was guilty of contributory negligence in attempting to cross the street at a place where he knew he would come in contact with it. It is true appellee testified that he knew of the existence of the wire and that when he started to cross Romig street he did not think about it. He says, in this connection, that Captain Kluth, his superior officer, had called to him from the opposite side of said street, and that he thought only about getting to him; that he thought "that there was something up." The fact that appellee had previous knowledge of the obstruction does not, *per se*, establish his contributory negligence. Such knowledge and his momentarily forgetting it are facts for the consideration of the jury in determining whether the injured party was exercising reasonable care. *Henry County Turnpike Co.* v. *Jackson* (1882), 86 Ind. 111, 44 Am. Rep. 274; *Wilson* v. *Trafalgar, etc., Road Co.* (1884), 93 Ind. 287; *City of Evansville* v. *Thacker* (1891), 2 Ind. App. 370, 28 N. E. 559. This is true especially where the attention of such party has been diverted. *City of East Chicago* v. *Gilbert* (1915), 59 Ind. App. 613, 108 N. E. 29, 109 N. E. 404. In the course of his duties, a policeman often meets with emergencies requiring quick action on his part, engrossing his entire attention, and we are not, therefore, prepared to say that appellee, having been summoned by his superior officer, and thinking that his presence across the street was required immediately, was as a matter of law chargeable with remembering the wire, or that he was, *per se*, guilty of negligence in attempting to cross the street where he did.

13.

14.

Appellant complains of the action of the trial court in permitting certain witnesses, over appellant's objection, to testify that they, at different times since the accident to appellee, had tripped over the wire in question. The court, after such testimony had been admit-

15.

ted, instructed the jury "not to consider it at all in making up" their "verdict in this case." Any error committed in admitting this testimony was cured by this instruction.

The court gave the following instruction: "By the expression, 'preponderance of the evidence,' as used
16.  in these instructions, is not meant the greater number of witnesses. The preponderance of evidence
does not depend upon the number of witnesses and does not mean the greater number of witnesses. It does depend up-
on the weight of the evidence and it means the greater weight of the evidence." Appellant urges that the giving of this instruction was error, because it invaded the province of the jury.

In the case of *Hammond, etc., R. Co.* v. *Antonia* (1907), 41 Ind. App. 335, 83 N. E. 766, it was held that an in-
struction that " 'the preponderance of the evidence does not necessarily lie with the party who may have introduced the greater number of the witnesses, but it depends upon the greater weight of the evidence, in view of all the testimony and the facts and circumstances in evidence before you' " was not erroneous, as being an invasion of the province of the jury. See, also, *Indianapolis Street R. Co.* v. *Johnson* (1904), 163 Ind. 518, 525, 72 N. E. 571, 573, 574. While the wording of the instruction under consideration is open to criticism, we are of the opinion that under the authorities, *supra*, the giving of it did not constitute reversible error.

Finding no reversible error in the record, the judgment below is affirmed.

NOTE.—Reported in 114 N. E. 227. Telegraph and telephones, rights and duties of company in use of streets, liability for injuries to persons or property, 37 Cyc 1639-1647; Ann. Cas. 1917A 1006. See under (10, 11) 38 Cyc 1926, 1929; (15) 4 C. J. 991.

CRITTENBERGER, AUDITOR OF STATE *v.* STATE SAV-
INGS AND TRUST COMPANY ET AL.

[No. 9,718.  Filed November 28, 1916.]

1. APPEAL.—*Right of Appeal.—Power of Legislature.*—There is
no vested right of appeal, and such right is the subject of legislative discretion, to be given or withheld as the general assembly
sees fit.  p. 153.

2. TAXATION.—*Inheritance Tax.—Appeal from Determination of
Tax.—Statute.*—As the provisions of the inheritance tax law of
1913 (Acts 1913 p. 79 *et seq.,* §10143a *et seq.* Burns 1914), indicate
that the legislature intended to make the ascertainment and collection of inheritance taxes a part of our probate law, and since
the act contains no express denial of the right of appeal from
judgments rendered thereunder, an appeal from a judgment of
a probate court on the rehearing and redetermination of an inheritance tax may be taken under §2977 Burns 1914, §2454 R. S.
1881, providing that any person considering himself aggrieved
by any decision of a circuit court growing out of any matter
connected with a decedent's estate, may prosecute an appeal to
the Supreme Court; and §15, clause 3, of the inheritance tax
law, providing for a rehearing of the determination of an inheritance tax, refers only to the procedure in the trial court,
and does not bar an appeal.  p. 153.

3. APPEAL.—*Appeal without Bond.—Inheritance Tax Determination.—Statute.*—Where the auditor of state instituted an action
for the rehearing and redetermination of an inheritance tax
assessment, although the suit was not brought by the State, or
in its name on the relation of the Attorney-General, yet the trial
court and the parties treated it as an action so brought, and
it was, in fact, prosecuted by the Attorney-General, an appeal
by the auditor may be taken from the judgment rendered without bond under §9270 Burns 1914, Acts 1899 p. 219, providing
that in civil actions brought in the name of the state, or in its
name on the relation of the Attorney-General or on the relation
of any state board, any relief to which the state is entitled
therein may be obtained without filing any bond either for costs
or damages.  p. 155.

4. APPEAL.—*Perfecting Appeal when no Bond is Required.—Time.*
—When no bond is required to be given by a party appealing
under §2977 Burns 1914, §2454 R. S. 1881, relating to appeals
from decisions growing out of any matter connected with a

decedent's estate, the appellant has 120 days from the date of the decision complained of within which to perfect his appeal. p. 156.

From Marion Probate Court; *Mahlon E. Bash,* Judge.

Action by Dale J. Crittenberger, Auditor of State of the State of Indiana, against the State Savings and Trust Company of Marion county, Indiana, and others. From the judgment rendered plaintiff appeals, and defendants move to dismiss the appeal. *Motion to dismiss appeal overruled.*

*Evan B. Stotsenburg,* Attorney-General, *Charles J. Orbison* and *Thomas H. Branaman,* for appellant.

*Pickens, Cox & Conder,* for appellees.

IBACH, J.—Appellant appeals from a judgment rendered in the matter of the rehearing and redetermination of the inheritance tax in the estate of William L. Higgins, deceased.

After the filing of the transcript in this court and before the filing of appellant's brief, appellees, other than Charles Latham, whose death is suggested, have filed a motion to dismiss the appeal for each of the following reasons: "1. No right of appeal is by law provided from the judgment of the Probate Court of Marion County, Indiana, set forth in the transcript of the record in the above entitled cause, and no appeal from any such judgment of the Probate Court of Marion County, Indiana, is permitted by law. 2. No bond was filed with the clerk of Marion County, Indiana, or with the clerk of the Probate Court of Marion County, Indiana, as provided by law, as a condition upon which an appeal may be had from a judgment such as is disclosed in the said transcript of record, *it being a judgment growing out of a matter connected with a decedent's estate.* 3. No appeal bond was filed with any officer or person in connection with the said attempted appeal within thirty days after the decision complained of was made. 4. No transcript was filed in the office of the clerk of this court within ninety days after the filing of an appeal bond with any officer or person whatsoever in connection with an attempted appeal from the decision and judgment of the Probate Court of Marion County disclosed in the transcript of record, in the above entitled cause, as is by law provided as a condition upon which appeals are allowed in decisions of the Probate Court of Marion County, growing out of any matter connected with a decedent's estate, and in fact no appeal bond has been at any time filed in connection with this attempted appeal or any attempted appeal from the decision and judgment of the Probate Court of Marion County, disclosed in the transcript in the above entitled cause." (Our italics.)

The act in question (Acts 1913 p. 79 *et seq.*, §10143a *et seq.* Burns 1914) contains no express provisions authorizing an appeal. Proceedings had under the provisions of such act are in the nature of special proceedings. It is thoroughly settled that there is no vested right of
1. appeal and that such right is the subject of legislative discretion, to be given or withheld as the general assembly sees fit. It has also been held that the general right of appeal allowed from final judgments does not apply to special proceedings, and that statutory provisions for the improvement of streets and other highways, and for the assessment of the costs thereof against the property benefited are special in character and unless expressly granted, no appeal lies from any action or decision of the board or tribunal conducting such proceedings. *Stockton* v. *Yeoman* (1912), 179 Ind. 61, 65, 66, 100 N. E. 2; *Indianapolis Union R. Co.* v. *Waddington* (1907), 169 Ind. 448, 82 N. E. 1030; *City of Indianapolis* v. *L. C. Thompson Mfg. Co.* (1907), 40 Ind. App. 535, 81 N. E. 1156, 82 N. E. 540; *State v. Rockwood* (1902), 159 Ind. 94, 95, 64 N. E. 592, and cases cited.

An analysis of the act in question and a study of its provisions as a whole indicate that the legislature in-
2. tended to make the ascertainment and collection of inheritance taxes a part of our probate law, and to

vest our county courts with probate jurisdiction over such matters. The act provides, among other things, that the value of the estate and the amount of tax to which it is liable shall be determined by the court after notice and hearing; that such tax shall be a lien on the property transferred until paid and the administrator shall be personally liable therefor; that no administrator shall be entitled to a final accounting until he produces a receipt for its payment; that he shall have power to sell the property of his decedent to pay such tax; that he shall not deliver or be compelled to deliver any specific legacy or property subject to such tax to any person until he shall have collected the tax thereon; that in the collection of unpaid taxes the procedure shall conform, as near as may be, to the provisions of the law governing probate practice of this state; that the powers conferred on the circuit court shall be conferred on certain other courts having jurisdiction in probate matters. With this construction it follows that the right of appeal, if not expressly denied by the act itself, is provided by §2977 Burns 1914, §2454 R. S. 1881, which reads in part as follows: "Any person considering himself aggrieved by any decision of a circuit court, or judge thereof in vacation, growing out of any matter connected with a decedent's estate may prosecute an appeal to the supreme court," etc. As tending to sustain our conclusion, see *Bennett* v. *Bennett* (1885), 102 Ind. 86, 89, 1 N. E. 199; *Baker* v. *Edwards* (1900), 156 Ind. 53, 59 N. E. 174; *Rogers* v. *State* (1900), 26 Ind. App. 144, 59 N. E. 334; *Holderman* v. *Wood* (1904), 34 Ind. App. 519, 73 N. E. 199; *Vail* v. *Page* (1910), 175 Ind. 126, 130, 93 N. E. 705, and cases cited.

Appellees, while contending that no right of appeal is created by §2977, *supra*, also contend that the act contains language which practically forbids an appeal. The language referred to is found in §15, clause 3, of such act (§10143o Burns 1914), and is as follows: "The auditor of state, county treasurer, or any person dissatisfied with the appraisement or assessment and determination of such tax may apply for a rehearing thereof before the circuit court within sixty days from the fixing, assessing and determination of the tax by the circuit court as herein provided on filing a written notice which shall state the grounds of the application for a hearing. The rehearing shall be upon the records, proceedings and proofs had and taken on the hearings as herein provided and a new trial shall not be had or granted unless specially ordered by the court.'' The language indicated has reference to the procedure in the trial court, and not to the right of appeal. The act contains no express denial of the right of appeal.

The remaining reasons on which a dismissal is urged may be treated together. They in effect deny that any appeal has been perfected. It is urged that appellant has 3. not complied with §2977, *supra,* by failing to file an appeal bond. While it may be conceded that this action was not brought in the form of the ''State of Indiana'' or the ''State of Indiana on the relation of the Attorney-General,'' yet the trial court and both the parties treated it as an action so brought, and it was a matter of fact prosecuted by the Attorney-General, so we are of the opinion that the action falls within the provisions of §9270 Burns 1914, Acts 1899 p. 219, and an appeal bond was not required. Furthermore, by statute the state auditor is given authority to represent the state in these proceedings before the trial court, and we have held that the right of appeal existed in such cases. It would therefore be entirely foreign to the spirit of our law to hold that the state auditor, representing the state in an effort to obtain taxes, should be required to furnish a bond before the state's appeal could be perfected. 3 C. J. 1122, §1161; Ewbank's Manual (2d ed.) §9; *Humphreys* v. *State* (1904), 70 Ohio St. 67, 70 N. E. 957, 65 L. R. A. 776; 101 Am. St. 888, 1 Ann. Cas. 233; *People* v. *Sholem* (1909), 238 Ill. 203, 87 N. E. 390.

When no bond is required to be given by a party appealing under §2977, *supra,* the appellant has 120 days from the date of the decision within which to perfect his

4.  appeal.  The judgment in this case was rendered on May 29, 1916, and the transcript of the record filed

in this court on August 16, 1916, within the 120 days.

The motion to dismiss the appeal is overruled.

NOTE.—Reported in 114 N. E. 225. Statutes abridging right of appeal, constitutionality, 5 Ann. Cas. 860; Ann. Cas. 1912B 274. Inheritance tax statutes, construction, Ann. Cas. 1915C 322. See under (1) 2 Cyc 517; 3 C. J. 616; (2) 37 Cyc 1583.

---

MEYER ET AL. *v.* THE PITTSBURGH, CINCINNATI, CHICAGO AND ST. LOUIS RAILWAY COMPANY.

[No. 9,171. Filed June 8, 1916. Rehearing denied October 27, 1916. Transfer denied November 28, 1916.]

1.  EASEMENTS.—*Fee Simple in Easement.*—A fee may exist in an easement. p. 162.

2.  RAILROADS.—*Right of Way.—Title by Prescription.—Extent of Title.*—It is the general rule that where a railroad right of way is acquired by prescription, the company takes only an easement. p. 165.

3.  RAILROADS.—*Right of Way.—Title by Prescription.—Interest Acquired.—Grant Presumed.*—The charter of a railway company authorizing it to acquire lands in fee for right of way purposes and providing that when the right of way should be procured the company "shall be seized in fee simple of the right to such lands" did not prohibit the railroad and its successors in interest from acquiring a less interest or smaller estate in the lands desired, and where the company, claiming title by prescription, has been in possession and occupation of lands used in the operation of its railroad for tracks and embankments for more than twenty years, such user of the lands being continuous and adverse to the claim or interest of any owner thereof, the grant presumed, and the prescriptive title acquired, from such use and occupancy is not that of an estate in fee simple, but is only a fee in an easement sufficiently comprehensive to protect the railroad's use of the land as exercised during such occupancy. p. 165.

From Marion Circuit Court (23,015); *Charles Remster,* Judge.

Action by the Pittsburgh, Cincinnati, Chicago, and St. Louis Railway Company against August B. Meyer and others. From a judgment for plaintiff, the defendants appeal. *Reversed.*

*Charles W. Smith, Henry H. Hornbrook* and *Albert P Smith,* for appellants.
*Samuel O. Pickens* and *Owen Pickens,* for appellee.

CALDWELL, C. J.—Appellee brought this action against appellants to quiet its title, alleged to be in fee simple, to a certain parcel of real estate situated in the block bounded by Chestnut, Morris, Wenzel (now Delaware) and Hanway (now Downey) streets in the city of Indianapolis. The tract as described in the complaint is an irregular quadrilateral, situated in the southwest corner of the block, being within the northeast angle formed by the intersection of Chestnut and Downey streets, the latter forming its southern and the former its western boundary.

The errors relied upon are based on appellant's exceptions reserved to the conclusions of law. The first conclusion is in effect that appellee is the owner in fee simple of the tract of land described in such conclusion, the boundaries of which are not identical with the boundaries of the tract described in the complaint. The former excludes a triangular parcel of ground included in the latter, situated in the extreme southwest corner of the block, while the eastern line of the former does not exactly coincide with the eastern line of the latter. The remaining conclusion is in substance that appellee is entitled to recover costs. The decree follows the conclusions.

Appellants in their brief clearly outline the scope of the controversy submitted for our consideration as follows: "There is but one question presented by this appeal: That question is whether under the facts specially found by the court, the appellee acquired a fee-simple title to the lands covered by its tracks with proper clearance, or acquired but an easement.''

We proceed to consider such question. The finding to the extent necessary to a determination of such question is substantially as follows: By an act of the general assembly of the State of Indiana, approved February 2, 1832, the Madison, Indianapolis & Lafayette Railroad Company was created. In 1866, its successor, the Indianapolis & Madison Railroad Company, consolidated with the Jeffersonville Railroad Company, under the name of the Jeffersonville, Madison & Indianapolis Railroad Company. The latter, June 10, 1890, consolidated with certain other companies, thus forming appellee. Prior to October 9, 1890, the Jeffersonville, Madison & Indianapolis Railroad Company, or some one of its predecessors in title entered upon and extended in a northwesterly direction across the parcel of land described in the complaint a railroad consisting of a main track with a sidetrack paralleling it on either side, which tracks have been continuously maintained on such parcel of land and used for railroad purposes by such entering company and its successors in title, including appellee, to the present time. Rights acquired in such parcel of ground by virtue of the extension, maintenance and use of such railroad tracks thereon passed to such succeeding and consolidated companies in succession, including appellee. On said October 9, 1890, McCarty and others were the owners of the south part of the block bounded by the streets aforesaid, including the tract of land as described in the complaint, and as described in the conclusions and decree, subject, however, to the rights of the Jeffersonville, Madison & Indianapolis Railroad Company, and its assigns therein. On said day such owners conveyed the entire tract so owned by them to Elder. In 1892, Elder conveyed to Fahnley & McCrea, who on November 11, 1901, conveyed to appellants. Each of the deeds by which the successive conveyances from McCarty to appellants were accomplished, was duly recorded, and contained a clause excepting from its operation the rights of the railroad company and its assigns as aforesaid. Facts are specifically found respecting the boundaries of the parcel of land in said block, which such railroad companies in succession have continuously occupied and used in the operation and maintenance of such railroad, and for proper railroad purposes in connection therewith, the parcel of ground so outlined being the same as that described in the conclusions and decree. While Fahnley & McCrea were the owners of the tract, formerly owned by McCarty, the board of public works of Indianapolis placed against it by proper proceeding an assessment amounting to $520.50, for constructing a public sewer along Downey street. Fahnley & McCrea as owners signed the waiver authorized by the statute, and thereafter prior to conveying the tract to appellants paid the assessment in full. Appellants, after the conveyance of the tract to them in 1901 paid the taxes and municipal assessments against it as they arose, except that in September, 1910, appellee paid an assessment levied in its name in the sum of $525.19 for the construction of a sidewalk along the east side of Chestnut street, of which assessment and its payment by appellee appellants had no notice prior to the bringing of this action. In 1913, preparatory to the execution of a purpose to elevate its tracks, appellee entered into negotiations with appellants for the purchase and to procure the conveyance to it by appellants of the lands described in the complaint. Thereupon at appellee's invitation, appellants submitted in writing a proposition to sell and convey to appellee. Appellee received and retained such proposition without response, and such negotiations terminated and failed. Several days after such proposition was submitted, at a meeting before the board of public works of Indianapolis, appellee by attorney asserted a claim to the ownership of the lands described in the complaint. This was appellant's first knowledge that appellee claimed

to own the lands, except such knowledge as is implied from
the use of the lands as aforesaid.

There is included in the finding the following, respecting
the parcel of ground described in the conclusion and decree:
That it "has been in the possession of and used and occupied by the plaintiff in the operation of said railroad and
by its embankment and tracks laid thereon for more than
20 years prior to the bringing of this action, and such use
and possession by the plaintiff thereof has been continuous,
open, notorious and adverse to the claim or interest therein
of any owner thereof for more than 20 years prior to the
commencement of this action."      .

The parties apparently agree that the finding discloses
an adverse occupancy of the parcel of land described in the
decree for more than the statutory period for the uses and
purposes stated in the finding. They differ, however, respecting the nature of the right or title that exists in appellee by reason of such occupancy. Appellee contends that
through such use and occupancy, it is seized in fee of such
lands. It is appellants' position, however, that such
occupancy has been limited to certain specific uses and purposes, and that by reason thereof appellee has acquired in
such lands an interest in the nature of an easement or a
prescriptive right merely to hold and use such lands for
the purpose of maintaining and operating its railroad
thereon and proper railroad purposes incident thereto, subject to which the title in fee is in appellants. We are not
specifically advised by the finding as to the company with
which originated the possession and occupancy of such parcel of ground continued through a number of intermediate
and constituent companies to appellee. The finding on this
subject is that some time prior to October 9, 1890, the Jeffersonville, Madison & Indianapolis Railroad Company or some
one of its predecessors in title entered upon such lands
and constructed a railroad. The general assembly, by an
act approved February 1, 1834, changed the name of the

Madison, Indianapolis & Lafayette company to the Madison & Indianapolis Railroad Company. Acts 1834 p. 244. The parties agree that under the latter name, the company, in 1847, extended its line to and into the city of Indianapolis; that in so doing it entered upon the lands involved here and located and constructed its track over the same; and that the rights acquired by it and its successors including appellee in continuing the occupancy of said lands must be measured by the rights that the entering company would have acquired under the same circumstances, had the latter, rather than its successors, continued such occupancy and use as set out in the finding. As measuring the hypothetical rights of the entering company under the supposition aforesaid, and consequently the rights of appellee, and to sustain their respective contentions, the parties appeal to the said act of 1832 (Acts 1832 p. 181), by the provisions of which the Madison, Indianapolis & Lafayette Railroad Company, predecessor of the Madison & Indianapolis company, was created. To the end indicated, appellee points particularly to §19 of such act, which is as follows: "That when said corporation shall have procured the right of way as herein provided, they shall be seized in fee simple of the right to such land, and shall have the sole use and occupancy of the same; and no person  *  *  *  shall in any way interfere with, molest, disturb or injure any of the rights and privileges hereby granted or that could be calculated to detract from or affect the profits of such corporation." By reason of the reference in §19 to other provisions of the act an examination of certain other sections is necessary to a proper understanding of §19. Thus, §14 authorized the corporation to enter on any lands to make surveys and estimates for the purpose of locating its tracks. Section 15 declared it to be lawful for the corporation to obtain, by relinquishment in writing duly executed, the lands necessary for the construction and location of its road, and to receive by donations, gifts, grants and bequests, made in writing as aforesaid, land, money, materials, etc., for the benefit of the corporation. Section 16 provided that in case any land needed for right of way purposes could not be obtained by relinquishment, or where a contract could not be made between the parties, such lands might be acquired for the purposes aforesaid by condemnation under the right of eminent domain, a proceeding to that end being outlined.

It will thus be observed that the act of 1832 makes provision for but two ways in which the railroad company might acquire a right of way, namely, by relinquishment and by condemnation. Section 19 does not literally provide that where a right of way was procured by either of such methods, the lands covered by such right of way should be held and owned by the corporation in fee simple. The language is that the corporation "shall be seized in fee simple of the right to such lands." Literally construed, the language used seems to refer to a right in the land as distinguished from the land itself. "A fee may exist

1. in all estates in land; therefore, a fee may exist in an easement." *Branson* v. *Studabaker* (1892), 133 Ind. 147, 33 N. E. 98. The provisions that immediately follow are in harmony with such a construction, in that there are stipulations respecting exclusive use and occupancy and noninterference by others with the rights and privileges granted. It would seem that if the title acquired were a fee simple in the land, such added safeguards would follow as incidents of the fee, although not provided by express stipulation. However, the question of the title acquired by relinquishment or condemnation under the act is not an open one. Thus §§15, 16 and 19 of the act of 1846 (Local Laws 1846 p. 210 *et seq.*), by which the Peru & Indianapolis Railroad Company was created, are practically the same in effect as §§15, 16 and 19 of the act of 1832. Sections 15 and 16 of the former authorized the created corporation to acquire lands for right of way purposes by re-

lease, and by condemnation where a voluntary release could not be obtained. Section 19 of the act of 1846, in so far as concerns the questions involved here, is identical with §19 of the act of 1832. In *Newcastle, etc., R. Co.* v. *Peru, etc., R. Co.* (1852), 3 Ind. 464, it was held that where the created company proceeded by release or condemnation under the act of 1846, it acquired the lands by title in fee simple, the court saying respecting §19: "We think it simply intended as declaratory of the effect which the releases and condemnations of land spoken of in the 15th and 16th sections should have; that is, whether they should be taken to convey an easement, a right of way merely, or a fee-simple title, and declaring that it should be the latter."

*Newcastle, etc., R. Co.* v. *Peru, etc., R. Co., supra,* is recognized in *Cleveland, etc., R. Co.* v. *Coburn* (1883), 91 Ind. 557, as decisive of the construction of §19 involved in the former. In the Coburn case, the court was required to construe and determine the scope of §21 of the act of 1848 (Local Laws 1848 p. 182) creating the Indianapolis & Bellefontaine Railroad Company, which section is identical with §19 of the act of 1832, the latter, as we have said, being identical in legal effect with §19 of the act of 1846, construed in the Newcastle case. In the Coburn case the court speaks of the language of §21 as being somewhat obscure, and that had it not been judicially construed by the Newcastle case, it might be supposed to mean that the railroad company should be the owner of the right relinquished, "which might be a fee, or a less estate, or a mere easement, according to the terms of the written relinquishment." Respecting the construction placed on the corresponding section by the Newcastle case, the court said: "Under this construction, an unconditional relinquishment of the land undoubtedly would have vested in the railroad company the absolute fee simple of the land, but the statute under consideration can not be held to impair the right to make contracts." The court, in recognition of the right of the rail-

road company to accept by contract a conditional relinquishment or a conveyance of a right in lands less in quantity
than a fee, says, in substance, that if the company could
not procure an unconditional relinquishment, it was not
required to accept a relinquishment coupled with conditions, but they might proceed by condemnation to acquire
a fee; but that if it did accept a conditional relinquishment,
such conditions, if precedent, must be performed in order
that title might be complete, or that a failure to perform
them, if subsequent, might defeat the estate relinquished.
In that case lands were relinquished for right of way purposes, by written instrument held to create not an estate
in fee simple but an estate upon condition subsequent.

The Coburn case may have an important bearing here,
in that it holds that where the charter or the creating and
enabling act of a railroad company authorizes it to acquire
lands by specified methods for right of way purposes, and
provides that lands acquired by such methods shall be held
and owned in fee simple, such provisions of the charter or
creating act not being exclusive in character, do not destroy or prohibit the exercise of the common-law power to
contract. *Cincinnati, etc., R. Co.* v. *Geisel* (1889), 119 Ind.
77, 21 N. E. 470, also is instructive. That case involved the
question whether a deed of release and quitclaim containing special provisions, executed to appellant's predecessors,
conveyed the described lands in fee, or merely created therein an easement for right of way purposes. The court, in
holding that only an easement was created, said: "We do
not think the question before us is affected by the provisions
of the charter of the appellant's grantor, for here the right
is founded entirely upon contract, and not upon proceedings under the right of eminent domain. The question is
not what estate might have been acquired, but what estate
did the one party bargain for and the other convey? It
does not follow that because a railroad company may take
an estate in fee, or a right of way of defined width, it does

take such an estate, or such a right of way, for parties may by their contract create a less estate than a fee, or a right less in extent than that which the law authorizes the grantee to acquire.'' It would therefore seem to follow that while prescription creates the presumption of a grant, a grant of the corpus of the land in fee simple is not necessarily presumed where the holder by grant may legally acquire an estate less in quantity or different in quality. As we have said, a fee may exist in an easement. *Branson* v. *Studabaker, supra.* ''The doctrine generally accepted is, that the right acquired by the power of eminent domain extends only to an easement in the land taken, unless the statute plainly provides for the acquisition of a larger interest.'' *Quick* v. *Taylor* (1888), 113 Ind. 540, 16 N. E. 588. See, also, *Chicago, etc., R. Co.* v. *Huncheon* (1892), 130 Ind. 529, 30 N. E. 636; *Hoffman* v. *Zollman* (1911), 49 Ind. App. 664, 97 N. E. 1015.

It is also the general rule that where a railroad right of way is acquired by prescription, the company takes only an easement. 23 Am. & Eng. Ency. Law 704; 33 Cyc 150; Elliott, Railroads §402. As we have indicated, however, it is recognized that under the act of 1832 creating the Madison, Indianapolis & Lafayette Railroad Company, and the act of 1846 creating the Peru & Indianapolis Railroad Company, and the act of 1848, creating the Indianapolis & Bellefontaine Railroad Company, the courts hold that by condemnation or by release, in the absence of a contract to the contrary, the lands involved are acquired in fee. Likewise, under the Public Improvement Acts of 1835 and 1836 (Acts 1835 p. 25; Acts 1836 p. 6), construed in *pari materia,* it is held that the State by appropriation proceedings, under the power of eminent domain, acquired the appropriated lands in fee rather than an easement therein. *Water Works Co., etc.* v. *Burkhart* (1872), 41 Ind. 364. In recognition of the fact that title to the lands in fee is an interest or es-

2.

3.

tate therein in excess of the requirements of the public purpose involved, the Supreme Court, in *Indianapolis Water Company* v. *Kingan & Co.* (1900), 155 Ind. 476, 58 N. E. 715, cites a list of decisions to the effect that while the courts have abided by the decision in the Burkhart case as a rule of property, yet it has been reluctantly followed, and that the Supreme Court "has declared its unwillingness to extend the doctrine by construction beyond cases in which the State's grantee claims under the board's exercise of the power of eminent domain." Thus, in *Brookville, etc., Co.* v. *Butler* (1883), 91 Ind. 134, 46 Am. Rep. 580, the State, under the Public Improvement Act of 1836, had appropriated lands for canal purposes. The canal had been constructed in such a manner that at one point it overflowed a tract of low land forming a pond. In a suit involving the fee to the overflowed lands, commenced after such flowage had continued more than twenty years, it was held that while by the appropriation proceedings the state had acquired, and that it had transmitted to its grantees, title in fee to the land occupied by the canal and its appurtenances, yet (quoting from the Kingan case, *supra,* which reviews the Butler case), "that the flowage of water beyond the excavated channel did not evidence an appropriation, under the power of eminent domain, of the fee in the flooded land; that the right of flowage is merely an easement; that evidence of the fact of flowage for twenty years establishes of itself nothing more than a prescriptive right to such an easement."

The significance of the Butler case consists in the following: That under the act of 1836, the State, by appropriation proceedings, acquired title in fee to the lands appropriated. If the overflowed lands were necessary to the canal enterprise, the state by proceedings under that act would have acquired the lands in fee; the lands were in fact held by the state and its grantees for flowage purposes in connection with the canal enterprise for more than twenty years. From such use there originated a prescriptive right in the lands overflowed; the fact, however, that the state might have acquired the lands in fee, considered in connection with the exercise of such right for the prescriptive period, was not sufficient to raise the presumption that it had acquired the lands in fee, but established merely a right sufficiently broad to protect the use as it had been exercised; that is, that the prescriptive right was an easement of flowage rather than title to the lands in fee.

Whatever interest or estate appellee owns in the lands involved here is based on the fact of the use of such lands for the full prescriptive period, or in other words, such interest or estate is in the nature of a prescriptive right. It is the use of the lands as indicated which the court finds to have been continuously and adversely exercised. Appellee, in support of its contention that under the facts found it owns the lands in fee rather than an easement therein, constructs an argument in effect as follows: That prescription creates the presumption of a grant; that by the act of 1832, appellee's predecessor was authorized to acquire lands in fee by relinquishment equivalent to a grant; a prescriptive right being established, a grant coextensive in quantity and identical in quality with the grant which appellee's predecessor was authorized to take by the terms of the creating act must be presumed, and hence that appellee must be declared to be the owner of the land in fee. But, as we have established from a consideration of the decided cases, the fact that appellee's predecessor was authorized by its creating statute to acquire lands in fee for right of way purposes was not prohibitive of a right to acquire by contract, and hence by grant, a less interest or a smaller estate in the lands desired. The question therefore arises whether from the established prescriptive right a grant of the lands in fee must be presumed or merely a grant of an estate or interest sufficiently comprehensive to protect the use as it has been exercised. *Indianapolis Water Co.* v.

*Kingan, supra,* is in point here. That case involved the question of the overflow of lands incident to the construction and operation of a canal built under the Public Improvement Acts of 1835 and 1836. There, as here, appellant's predecessors were authorized by such acts in a proper proceeding to acquire lands in fee for canal purposes. The flowage having continued for more than twenty years, the canal proprietors claimed title to the overflowed lands in fee. In holding against such contention, the Supreme Court said: "After possession for twenty years, the conclusive presumption arises of a grant or right ample enough to protect the possession. 'A prescriptive right can never be broader than the claim evidenced by user.' * * * The user by flowage evidenced no broader claim than a right of flowage; and such a claim is a mere easement." See, also, *Consumers Gas Trust Co.* v. *American Plate Glass Co.* (1903), 162 Ind. 393, 68 N. E. 1020; *Peoria, etc., R. Co.* v. *Attica, etc., R. Co.* (1899), 154 Ind. 218, 56 N. E. 210. *Brookville, etc., Co.* v. *Butler, supra; Hoffman* v. *Zollman, supra.*

We conclude that appellee's estate in the lands described in the decree, under the facts found, is an easement to use and occupy such lands for the purpose of maintaining and operating its railroad on and over the same, rather than an estate in fee simple in the land. It results that the cause must be reversed. Judgment reversed, with instructions to restate the conclusions of law in harmony with this opinion and to decree accordingly.

NOTE.—Reported in 113 N. E. 443. Railroads, right of way, estate or interest acquired, 6 Ann. Cas. 242; 13 Ann. Cas. 432; Ann. Cas. 1916E 763. Interest acquired by condemnation for railroad as easement or fee, 20 Ann. Cas. 572. As to right to acquire by adverse possession, Ann. Cas. 1915C 772.

## COBE v. DARROW ET AL.

[No. 9,015. Filed April 19, 1916. Rehearing denied June 30, 1916. Transfer denied November 28, 1916.]

1. APPEAL.—*Assignment of Error.*—*Grounds.*—Alleged error of the trial court in directing a verdict is not ground for an independent assignment of error. p. 170.
2. PUBLIC LANDS.—*Swamp Lands.*—*Patents.*—A state patent conveying title to a certain described section of land, together with all rights, privileges, immunities and appurtenances of whatever nature thereto belonging, such patent having been made according to the act of 1852 regulating the sale by the state of swamp lands donated by the United States to the State of Indiana, is held, on the authority of the *State* v. *Tuesburg Land Company* (1915), 61 Ind. App. 555, not to convey title to the thread of a stream forming a boundary line of the section, even though the stream is a nonnavigable river. p. 172.

From Porter Superior Court; *Harry B. Tuthill,* Judge.

Action by Ira M. Cobe against Samuel Darrow and others. From a judgment for defendants, the plaintiff appeals. *Affirmed.*

*Stanley W. Swabey* and *Charles Hamilton Peters,* for appellant.

*E. D. Crumpacker, Grant Crumpacker* and *O. S. Crumpacker,* for appellees.

HOTTEL, J.—In a complaint to quiet title to certain real estate in Starke county, Indiana, and to cancel a mortgage thereon, appellant claims to be the owner in fee simple of the following described real estate situate in said county:

"Commencing at a point at the northwest corner of the northeast quarter of the northwest quarter of said section 13 (Tp. 33 north, range 3 west) and extending directly west to the thread of the stream of the Kankakee river; thence down the thread of said stream to a point directly west of the southwest corner of the southeast quarter of the northwest quarter of said section 13; thence due east to the southwest corner of the southeast quarter of the northwest quarter of said section 13; thence due north to the place of beginning."

Appellees admit by answer that appellant is the owner in fee of the west half of the northwest quarter of said section 13, consisting of eighty acres, bounded on the west by the west line of section 13, and that they are not claiming, and never have claimed, any interest therein, and are not in possession thereof; but they deny that appellant owns or has any interest in any of the land described in the complaint west of the boundary line of said section 13, as marked and established by the United States government survey west of what purports to be the meander line of the Kankakee river.

The cause was submitted to trial by jury, and at the close of plaintiff's (appellant's) evidence, appellees orally moved the court to instruct the jury to return a verdict in their favor. This motion was sustained, and under instruction of the court, to the giving of which the plaintiff excepted, the jury returned a verdict for the defendants (appellees). Appellant's motion for a new trial was overruled and judgment was rendered on the verdict.

The errors relied on for reversal are: "Error of the court in instructing the jury to return a verdict for defendants"; and error of the court in overruling plaintiff's motion for a new trial.

The first error assigned is not ground for independent assignment and presents no question. Appellant's motion for a new trial is based on three specifications or grounds, viz.: that the verdict is not sustained by sufficient evidence; that it is contrary to law; and that the court "erred in sustaining defendant's motion to instruct the jury to return a verdict for the defendant."

1.

The question which appellant attempts to present by his appeal, stated in his own words, is as follows: "The appellant claims title under two patents from the State of Indiana to E. M. Burch, dated February 6, 1858, conveying the west half of the northwest quarter of section thirteen (13), township thirty-three (33), range three (3) west, 'together with all rights, privileges, immunities and appurtenances of whatever nature thereto belonging,' which patents recite that they are made according to the provisions of an Act of the General Assembly of the State of Indiana, approved May 29, 1852, entitled, 'An Act regulating the sale of Swamp Lands donated by the United States to the State of Indiana, and to provide for the drainage and reclamation thereof, in accordance with the condition of said grant'; and also of the several acts supplemental thereto, and that as the owner of the uplands specifically described in said grants, and deraigning title from the United States, he is the owner of the bed of the Kankakee River to the thread of the channel thereof, and that his northern boundary extends from the northwest corner of the west half of the northwest quarter of section thirteen (13) due west to the center or thread of the river; that his western boundary is the center or thread of the Kankakee river, and that his south line is a line starting at the southwest corner of the said west half and running due west to the center of the same stream; the lines so claimed would include the north half of what would have been section fourteen (14), had not the space been occupied by the Kankakee River, and the northeast quarter of fractional section 15, had the latter been extended to a full section— the area depending upon the exact location of the middle or thread of the channel of the Kankakee river at the time of the government's survey of 1835." The appellant claims title to the land in controversy under the riparian theory, and by virtue of the common-law doctrine of riparian ownership.

On the other hand appellees contend "that the Kankakee river is not the west boundary of section 13, but that the line shown on the plat one mile in length, and which coincides with the government meander line, is the boundary line of that section and that appellant acquired no title to any lands west of that line; that while a meander line is not necessarily or usually a boundary line, a section line is always a boundary line, because it is made so by express declaration of law, which enters into and forms a part of every conveyance of land within a particular section, and the fact that the section line is also a meander line does not render it any the less a boundary line of the section and of all lands embraced therein." Appellees further contend "that appellant failed to make out a case which entitled him to go to the jury, for the reason that appellant's evidence failed absolutely to prove one material allegation of his complaint, and that is, that appellees were asserting or claiming title to the real estate in controversy."

Giving to appellant the full benefit of his contention herein, the question, *supra,* indicated as the one claimed by him to be presented by this appeal, is controlled by

2.  the principles of law announced in the case of *State v. Tuesburg Land Co.* (1916), 61 Ind. App. 555, 109 N. E. 530, 111 N. E. 342. That case now has the approval of the Supreme Court, the petition to transfer such case having been denied by the Supreme Court, April 6, 1916. The law announced in that case authorized the peremptory instruction given by the trial court in the instant case, and requires an affirmance of the judgment below. If appellees' contention and claim in the instant case be correct, the trial court had additional reasons for giving such instruction; but for the purposes of the question presented we need not inquire or enter into a consideration of appellees' contention. The judgment is therefore affirmed.

NOTE.—Reported in 112 N. E. 257. Government grant, nontidal. navigable river as boundary, extent of title, 24 L. R. A. (N. S.) 1240. See under (2) 5 Cyc 894-896; 61 Ind. App. 555, 608.

## HANCOCK v. HANCOCK, ADMINISTRATOR, ET AL.

[No. 9,220. Filed February 3, 1916. Rehearing denied April 25, 1916. Transfer denied November 28, 1916.]

1. EXECUTORS AND ADMINISTRATORS.—*Contract with Widow.—Constructive Fraud.—Fiduciary Relations.*—Where an administrator, an heir to the estate, voluntarily assumed the management of the business affairs of decedent's widow, who was aged, in feeble health, uneducated and wholly without business experience, he sustained toward her a fiduciary relation which charged him with acting in the utmost good faith respecting the management of the trust property in his care; and a contract between himself as administrator, and the widow, which she signed, under his persuasion and veiled threats, without proper advice as to the effect of its terms, and by its stipulations surrendered to the administrator, to her injury, her interest in the personalty to be administered in the estate, in which was included certain certificates of deposit which were her personal property, is void as being constructively fraudulent, on the failure of the administrator to show the good faith required of him in his fiduciary capacity. pp. 178, 180, 182.

2. EXECUTORS AND ADMINISTRATORS. — *Contracts. — Construction.— Fiduciary Relations.*—Where an administrator, an heir to the estate, voluntarily assumed the management of the business affairs of, and established his residence with, decedent's widow, who was uneducated, aged and without business experience, he sustained toward her a fiduciary relation which cast upon him the burden of showing good faith and fair dealing in the management of the trust property in his care, particularly where the result of his action enures to his own benefit and to the injury of the party whose interest he should protect, and, unless good faith is shown, any contract entered into by such administrator with decedent's widow concerning her trust property would be unenforcible as constructively fraudulent. p. 179.

3. EXECUTORS AND ADMINISTRATORS.—*Settlement of Family Controversy.—Transfer of Personalty to Estate.—Want of Consideration.*—Where a widow, through the efforts of the administrator, an heir to the estate, surrendered to him certificates of deposit which were her personal property by reason of a gift from her deceased husband during his life, and the administrator applied them to the estate to be administered with decedent's personalty, there was no reasonable ground of disputing the widow's title to such certificates, and, therefore, no real family controversy

concerning them requiring settlement, so that the transfer to the estate was without consideration. p. 181, 182.

4. HUSBAND AND WIFE.—*Gifts of Personalty.*—*Delivery by Husband to Wife.*—Where a husband delivered to his wife certificates of deposit and stated at the time that she should care for them as they were her property, he made a complete unconditional gift by delivery which passed title to her. p. 182.

5. EXECUTORS AND ADMINISTRATORS.—*Accounting.*—*Technicalities.*— In determining questions arising out of the administration of decedent's estates, courts will not permit an injustice to be sustained upon mere technical questions of practice. p. 182.

From Howard Circuit Court; *William C. Purdum*, Judge.

Charles E. Hancock, administrator of the estate of William Hancock, deceased, filed a current report and Ollie Hancock filed exceptions thereto. From an approval of the report as filed, the exceptor appeals. *Reversed.*

*Overton & Joyce*, for appellant.

*Bell, Kirkpatrick & Voorhis* and *McClure & Roll*, for appellees.

SHEA, J.—Appellee, as administrator of the estate of William Hancock, deceased, filed an amended current report, to certain items of which appellant filed exceptions as follows: By item No. 1 of amounts chargeable, appellee charges himself with $23,404. Appellant, as the widow of decedent, William Hancock, by her exception to this item, claims that the above amount included two certificates of deposit in her name, amounting to $8,000, which belonged to her. By credits Nos. 1 and 7 of said report, appellee claims to have paid $82 and $66, respectively, for administrator's bonds. Appellant's exceptions question these credits on the ground that, since item No. 1 of amounts chargeable included $8,000 belonging to her, the bonds were too large, and that these credits are therefore excessive. By credit No. 11 appellee claims he has paid appellant, as decedent's widow, all that is her due by reason of a certain contract with him. Appellant by her exception to this item claims that the agreement was without consideration, and is null and void. Upon the determination of this question depends the disposition to be made of the certificates of deposit aggregating $8,000 as hereinafter set out.

The court approved the report of the administrator as filed, and overruled each of appellant's exceptions thereto, also her motion for a new trial. These rulings are here assigned as error.

In "Exhibit A," attached to the current report, it is averred under oath, by appellee administrator in explanation of item No. 11 and voucher No. 11 for $1,000, that appellant is the second childless wife of decedent William Hancock, and under the law would be entitled to one-third of the personal estate; that all the heirs of William Hancock have attained their majority; that heretofore, following the death of decedent, appellant entered into a contract with the administrator, who was acting for all the heirs, by which she agreed to and did, in pursuance of that contract, make to said heirs deeds to certain property held by virtue of a joint deed between herself and decedent, reserving to herself a life estate therein, and did thereby release her interest in and to the personal estate of decedent; that in consideration thereof the administrator, acting for the heirs of decedent, made a deed to her for life, of certain other real property described in the contract, in which she had no interest, which deed was signed by all the heirs of decedent and acquiesced in by them, and as further consideration of said contract she retained the $500, widow's allowance which had been previously paid to her, receiving in addition thereto the $1,000 represented by item No. 11 and voucher No. 11 of the report, all in full consideration of her one-third interest in and to the personal estate of decedent; that this is the final and only distribution in which appellant will, under the terms of said contract, participate in, and closes her interest in said estate.

In her exceptions to the amended report appellant avers, in substance, among other things, that soon after decedent's death appellee administrator voluntarily assumed charge of her affairs, paid her taxes and managed her business for her; that soon after he had so assumed charge of her affairs, he asked her to give him the two certificates of deposit representing the $8,000 included in amounts chargeable, as administrator, which she did, without any knowledge that he intended to use them in any manner other than for her use and benefit; that she had great confidence in his honesty and business ability, and that she was without any business experience whatever, and for these reasons permitted him to take charge of and manage all her property and business affairs, and trusted him to manage and protect all her property and interests of every kind and character; that when she delivered the certificates to him, she believed that he intended to put them in a place of safety for her; that after obtaining possession of them, he inventoried them as a part of the estate, and that said amount rightfully belongs to her.

In connection with "Exhibit A" of appellee's amended report she avers that on or about July 31, 1913, appellee asked and persuaded her to sign a certain instrument of writing, which she has since learned contains an agreement that in consideration of certain services which he voluntarily performed for her in the care and management of her affairs, and for the further consideration of $1,000, she agreed to and by said contract did release, transfer and assign to him, as administrator of the estate, all her right, interest and title to all of the personal property described and set out in the inventory of the estate; that for the purpose of inducing her to sign said pretended contract he fraudulently concealed from her that it contained said agreement, or any agreement unfavorable to her interest; that at said time she could not see to read; that she was without business experience and did not know or understand the contents of the pretended agreement, and did not know or understand what it contained; that appellee did not, nor did he have anyone else, read said pretended agreement to her; that he represented to her that said pretended agreement was for her benefit, and advised and requested her to sign it; that she trusted and believed him, and said agreement was without any consideration.

The material parts of the agreement in question, are as follows:

"This agreement entered into this 31st day of July, by and between Ollie Hancock, Widow of William Hancock, party of the first part, and Charles E. Hancock administrator of the estate of William Hancock, deceased, party of the second part, Witnesseth: That,

Whereas, the first party has no child, or father or mother surviving and—

Whereas, all of the real estate which she owns was acquired through her marriage with said William Hancock, deceased, or by conveyance from the heirs of said William Hancock, deceased, and—

Whereas, said Charles E. Hancock, as such Administrator and in his individual capacity, cares for the property of the first party, collects the rents and causes the necessary repairs to be made, taxes paid, etc., on such properties; and—

Whereas, said Charles E. Hancock proposes, without charge on his part to superintend the construction of a dwelling house for first party on real estate in the City of Kokomo, Indiana; and—

Whereas, first party has received from second party her Five Hundred ($500) Dollars allowance as widow under the Statute of Indiana; and—

.Whereas, upon the reasons and considerations herein set out first party desires that said administrator, for and on behalf of said estate, shall receive her one-third (1/3) interest in all the personalty of said estate described in the inventory heretofore made and filed by second party,

Now, therefore, in consideration of the services heretofore rendered and hereafter to be rendered for first party by second party in his administrative and individual capacity, and in further consideration of One Thousand Dollars, $1000.00, the payment of which is hereby acknowledged, the first party hereby releases, relinquishes, transfers, assigns and sets over to the second party all her right, interest and title to all of the personal property described and set out in such inventory.  Said second party to use the same in the administration of said estate and for distribution among the heirs of said William Hancock, deceased, it being understood and agreed between the parties hereto that first party, as such widow, releases and relinquishes all her right to the personal property of said estate as far as the same is set forth in such inventory.

A further consideration for the execution of this release, being that first party has heretofore received from second party, in addition to said Five Hundred ($500) Dollars, without compensation, the household goods, one (1) cow, chickens and all personal property of said estate not set out in the inventory.

Witness the hands and seals of the parties hereto.

   Ollie Hancock

   Chas. E. Hancock, Administrator of estate of William Hancock, deceased.

Witness Lex J. Kirkpatrick.''

The evidence discloses that appellant was the childless second wife of William Hancock and that they had lived together for a period of thirty years; that by a former marriage decedent had six children, who were living; that prior to his death William Hancock had been in the habit of depositing money in the banks of the city of Kokomo, taking time certificates in the name of his wife, which he from time to time cashed or drew out, signing his own name together with that of his wife; that immediately prior to his death he had, in addition to other amounts, two certificates, for $7,000 and $1,000, respectively, which were in the name of his wife. These he delivered to his wife unconditionally, saying that she should take care of them, as they belonged to her. These certificates were put away by appellant. After her husband's death, Charles E. Hancock, her step-son and the oldest son of decedent, appellee in this case, was appointed administrator upon the statement, in his verified petition to be appointed such administrator, that appellant who was entitled to administer the estate if she so desired, was "an old and enfeebled woman." The evidence also shows without contradiction

that immediately he took up his residence with appellant
and assumed the management of her business affairs, paying taxes, etc.; that she was uneducated and wholly without business experience; that the business of the settlement
of the estate was discussed frequently between appellant
and administrator. The evidence discloses that efforts of
the administrator were frequent and persistent that she
should turn over the property, including the two certificates, to him, to be administered as part of the assets of
the estate; that as a result of the negotiations the written
contract, which she signed in the presence of Judge Kirkpatrick, the substance of which is herein set out, resulted.

It is argued on behalf of appellant that the contract is
void; that Charles E. Hancock sustained toward appellant
a relation of trust and confidence. He likewise sus-
2. tained toward her a fiduciary relation, which casts
upon appellee the burden of showing good faith and
fair dealing. Under such circumstances the contract will receive the closest examination. *Whitesell* v. *Strickler* (1906),
167 Ind. 602, 611, 78 N. E. 845, 119 Am. St. 524; *McCord*
v. *Bright* (1909), 44 Ind. App. 275, 87 N. E. 654; *Goodwin* v. *Goodwin* (1874), 48 Ind. 584; *Lindley* v. *Kemp*
(1906), 38 Ind. App. 355, 76 N. E. 798; *Mors* v. *Peterson*
(1914), 261 Ill. 532, 104 N. E. 216; *Beach* v. *Wilton* (1910),
224 Ill. 413, 91 N. E. 492; *Huffman* v. *Huffman* (1905),
35 Ind. App. 643, 73 N. E. 1096; *Copeland* v. *Bruning*
(1909), 44 Ind. App. 405, 87 N. E. 1000, 88 N. E. 877.
This trust relation charged upon appellee administrator the
utmost good faith respecting all conduct in the management
of the trust property in his care. Especially is this true
when the result of his action enures to his own benefit and
to the injury of the party whose interest he should protect.
This is fundamental in law and morals, and therefore the
authorities upon this proposition are uniform. He could
not enter into an enforcible contract with appellant concerning her trust property, unless good faith is shown, as

it amounts to constructive fraud, and gives appellant, who was injured by such breach of duty, a right to the relief sought. *Teegarden* v. *Ristine* (1914), 57 Ind. App. 158, 163, 106 N. E. 641; *McCord* v. *Bright, supra; Huffman* v. *Huffman, supra; Ikerd* v. *Beavers* (1886), 106 Ind. 483, 7 N. E. 326; *Yount* v. *Yount* (1896), 144 Ind. 133, 43 N. E. 136; *Whitesell* v. *Strickler, supra; Goodwin* v. *Goodwin, supra.*

It is argued that the contract was fully explained to her by Judge Kirkpatrick, who accompanied administrator to the home of appellant on the morning of the execu-

1. tion thereof. The evidence discloses clearly that appellant was not satisfied with the contract when it was read to her, and that she refused to sign it; that Judge Kirkpatrick very frankly stated to her that he was the attorney for the estate, and for the heirs, and could not advise her as to what she should do. He did state to her what she was entitled to under the law, and that she would receive less under the terms of the contract, and advised her to secure the advice of her own attorney, after which statement he left the house, stating that he came over for the purpose of having the contract signed, which he had already prepared upon information given him by the administrator, believing it was entirely satisfactory; that he sat in appellee Charles E. Hancock's automobile near the house for some time, during which time, the evidence discloses, that appellee administrator, by persuasion and veiled threats, stating that if she did not sign it at that time she could not sign it at all, and by changing the consideration from one dollar to $1,000, induced appellant to sign the contract. He then informed Judge Kirkpatrick that appellant was ready to sign the contract. This was about twelve o'clock in the morning. Judge Kirkpatrick then returned to the house, and the contract was signed, resulting in a loss to appellant of several thousand dollars. It must be borne in mind in this connection that appellant had, during

the early part of the day, asked to have an interview with her attorney, Mr. Joyce; that appellee administrator heard a neighbor inform appellant that Mr. Joyce could not come to see her until two o'clock in the afternoon. In response to this information appellee administrator said to her, "What has old John Joyce to do with this?"—thus showing annoyance and displeasure because appellant had sought the advice of an attorney. The whole attitude of the administrator, as shown by this evidence, discloses great anxiety to have this contract executed without giving appellant an opportunity to consult her own lawyer, although she was advised to do so by Judge Kirkpatrick. There was undue haste, under the undisputed facts shown, if not actual coercion by the administrator at a time when he stood in very intimate business and social relationship with appellant.

It must be remembered that this is not an action to rescind a contract, where the question of return of consideration is involved; neither is it an action of damages for the breach of a contract; but it is an action based upon exceptions to a report, where it is alleged that the assets of the estate are enhanced by $8,000 represented by the cash value of the two certificates of·deposit which belonged to appellant, and the charges for surety company bonds paid by the administrator, which are incidental to the main question. The controlling question presented is, Shall this court give its sanction to the conduct of the administrator in obtaining possession of these certificates from appellant in the manner shown? All other questions presented are incidental thereto.

It is further insisted by appellees that this is a settlement of a family controversy, and should therefore receive favor at the hands of this court. It must be borne 3. in mind, in the first instance, that there was no reasonable ground for dispute as to the rights of the parties with respect to the certificates of deposit amounting to $8,000. Putting aside all claims appellant may have had to title because they were made out in her name,

4. there was a complete unconditional gift by delivery, as shown by the evidence of Dora Wheatly, a daughter of decedent, which is undisputed; so that the title was in appellant for that reason, if for no other. *Teague* v. *Abbot* (1912), 51 Ind. App. 604, 100 N. E. 27; *Grant Trust, etc., Co.* v. *Tucker* (1911), 49 Ind. App. 345, 96 N. E. 487; *Snyder* v. *Frank* (1912), 53 Ind. App. 301, 101 N. E. 684; *Miller* v. *Neff* (1889), 33 W. Va. 197, 10 S. E. 378, 6 L. R. A. 515; *Doty* v. *Willson* (1872), 47 N. Y. 580. There-

fore, there being no real controversy, there was no

3. consideration for the transfer to the estate. *Emery* v. *Royal* (1889), 117 Ind. 299, 20 N. E. 150; *Moon* v. *Martin* (1890), 122 Ind. 211, 23 N. E. 668; *Armijo* v. *Henry* (1907), 14 N. M. 181, 89 Pac. 305, 25 L. R. A. (N. S.) 275. In cases that we have examined where settlements have been upheld because they involved family affairs, and were entered into with a view to promote harmony, there was some real contention as to the rights of the parties, and were sustained for that reason, as the settlement of the dispute was the consideration which passed. No such case is presented by the evidence here.

In determining questions arising out of the administration of decedents' estates, neither the trial court nor this court would be justified in permitting an injustice

5. to be sustained upon mere technical questions of practice. It is the judgment of this court that the

1. conduct of the administrator in this case comes clearly within the rule of constructive fraud, as shown by the authorities cited, and if sustained in this court, would result in injustice to appellant. The facts and circumstances in all essential particulars are undisputed. We need not go into questions presented upon the admission and refusal to admit evidence. The decision of the court is contrary to law.

A new trial is ordered, with instructions to the trial court to sustain the exceptions to the final report of the administrator with respect to the matters herein stated, and for further proceedings consistent with this opinion. Judgment reversed.

Note.—Reported in 111 N. E. 336. See under (1, 2) 21 Cyc 287, 296; (4) 21 Cyc 1296.

---

## NATIONAL FIRE PROOFING COMPANY *v*. IMPERISHABLE SILO COMPANY.

[No. 8,904. Filed April 27, 1916. Rehearing denied June 28, 1916. Transfer denied November 28, 1916.]

1. CONTRACTS.—*Construction.— Parol Evidence.— Ambiguity.*— Unless the court can say from a consideration of the entire contract that a clause contained therein is ambiguous, resort can not be had to extrinsic facts to determine its meaning. p. 189.

2. PATENTS.—*License Contract.—Construction.*—A contract licensing the defendant to manufacture and sell patented silos and silo blocks in accordance with the stipulations therein set forth and providing for the payment to plaintiff of a royalty of five per cent. on the gross sales of silos by the licensee, is held to mean, when the contract is construed as an entirety, that there could be a recovery of five per cent. of the proceeds of the sales of patented silos only, even though a clause of the contract provided that defendant was obligated to pay the stipulated royalty on the sales of "all vitrified block silos," since the general subject-matter of the contract, and of the recitals therein, was the patented silo blocks alone. pp. 189, 190.

3. CONTRACTS.—*Construction.*—When a contract is to be interpreted or when the effect of some separate provision thereof is involved, separate clauses and provisions will not be considered apart from the general context or apart from connected clauses, but the meaning of the entire contract and of each of its clauses will be determined from all the language used, and the parties will be held to have intended that meaning to each clause which makes the whole contract consistent, and which is reasonable in view of all the terms employed. p. 189.

From the Wells Circuit Court; *William H. Eichhorn,* Judge.

Action by the Imperishable Silo Company against the National Fire Proofing Company. From a judgment for plaintiff, the defendant appeals. *Reversed.*

*Leonard, Rose & Zollars* and *Simmons & Dailey*, for appellant.

*C. K. Lucas, Lesh & Lesh, C. W. Watkins* and *E. C. Vaughn*, for appellee.

IBACH, C. J.—This is an action to recover royalties. The contract under which the controversy arose, omitting the usual preliminary language found in such instruments, recites that certain letters patent had been issued by the United States government to Oliver Brumbaugh covering silo blocks and a method of constructing vitrified tile silos, and such letters patent being still in force, said Brumbaugh sold them to Eugene H. Baker in the year 1910, prior to the time of the organization of appellee company, except that said Brumbaugh reserved to himself all rights under the patents in certain localities. The said contract continues:

"Whereas, the said party of the first part (appellee) has an organization which has been selling vitrified silos and silo blocks made under the above described letters patent and has done a large amount of advertising which should result in large sales of silos in the future; and

"Whereas, The party of the second part (appellant) desires to *make and sell, or cause to be made and sold the silos and silo blocks described in said letters patent* (our italics) and now quite generally known as Imperishable Silos' and Imperishable Silo Blocks and Clamps; and

"Whereas, The party of the second part desires to avail itself of the sales organization of said party of the first part and of the advertising done by said party of the first part,

"Now, therefore, these presents witnesseth,

"First. That said party of the first part, for and in consideration of the covenants and agreements hereinafter set forth and mentioned to be performed by the party of the second part, hereby gives and grants unto

said party of the second part, the exclusive right now
owned under said letters patent by the party of the
first part, except as hereinafter provided, to manufacture and sell the said patented silos and silo blocks
and clamps incident thereto and a part thereof.

"Second. The said party of the first part further
undertakes and agrees that any improvements in silo
blocks or silo construction, whether patented or not, the
said party of the first part shall invent or devise, or
become possessed of, shall be for the exclusive use of the
said party of the second part, so long as this agreement shall continue in full force and effect.

"Third. The said party of the first part hereby
agrees to sell, assign, transfer and set over unto the said
party of the second part, all its office equipment, including the names of prospective purchasers of silos,
acquired by correspondence, at the fairs, or otherwise,
testimonials, cuts, engravings, miniature blocks, and
other matter used for advertising purposes, the dies
owned by said party of the first part used in manufacturing regular or miniature blocks, stock of doors,
roof frames and iron now owned by the said party of
the first part, and the silos erected on fair grounds for
advertising purposes.

"The said party of the second part in consideration
of the above exclusive license and the sale and transfer
of the property hereinbefore referred to, hereby agrees
as follows:—

"(a) The party of the second part agrees to utilize
at once and to maintain during the life of the above
mentioned patents, at its own expense, an efficient selling organization for the purpose of diligently pushing
the sales of the so-called Imperishable Silos and Blocks,
and that during that period it will make every reasonable effort to manufacture the number of silos that can
or may be sold by the said selling organization, it being
understood that the said party of the second part, during the life of this contract, will manufacture and keep
in stock at its plants where proper silo blocks can be
made, ready for delivery in seasonable time, that is, between January 1st and August 15th of each year, a
sufficient number of blocks that can or may be sold by
the selling organization, in order that the supply shall
equal the demand.

"(b) The said party of the second part hereby agrees
to retain or employ Eugene Baker, now or recently of
Huntington, in the State of Indiana, to be the general

186  APPELLATE COURT OF INDIANA,

Nat. Fire Proofing Co. v. Imperishable Silo Co.—63 Ind. App. 183.

manager of what shall be known as the 'Agricultural Department' of the National Fire Proofing Company, the party of the second part hereto, for a period of at least three years.

"(c) The said party of the second part hereby further agrees that during the life of this contract it will not assign or license to any other person or corporation whatsoever any of the rights herein conveyed, without making provision, to be approved in writing by the said party of the first part, whereby the latter may have accurate knowledge of all the sales made during each quarter year by any sub-licensee under said letters patent, and that the party of the second part further agrees that it will guarantee unto the party of the first part the payment in lawful money of the United States, of five per centum of the gross sales of silos by any and all sub-licensees under the above mentioned letters patent.

"(d) Said party of the second part hereby further covenants and agrees that it will keep, or cause to be kept books of account in which complete entries of all sales of *vitrified block silos or silo blocks manufactured or sold* by the said party of the second part, or its agents, and that the said books shall at all reasonable times be open to the inspection of an authorized representative of the party of the first part, or its duly appointed attorney; that the said party of the first part by its authorized attorneys, shall have the right to examine any and all of the books of account of the said party of the second part, containing any items, charges, memoranda or information relating to the manufacture or sale of said silos or blocks, and the party of the second part agrees that it will make and transmit to the party of the first part, full and true returns of the *gross sales of vitrified silos and blocks* made in the territory covered by the aforesaid patents, within fifteen days after the end of each quarter year.

"(e) The said party of the second part hereby further agrees that within fifteen days after the first day of January, April, July and October of each and every year during the life of this contract, it will pay or cause to be paid to the said party of the first part at its principal office in Huntington in the State of Indiana, five per centum of the gross sales of all *vitrified block silos* sold and shipped by it during the previous three months, in the territory covered by the license, or upon any silos manufactured by it in the state of Ohio and that part of the commonwealth of Pennsylvania lying west of the second degree of longitude west of Washington City, and which shall be sold in any part of the United States outside of the State of Ohio, and that part of Pennsylvania aforesaid, the term 'gross sales' to be interpreted to mean the price received for the price of the silos as shown by the orders or contracts given by the purchasers of silos, less the cost of freight incurred in the delivery thereof to the purchaser at the railway station; and it is further understood and agreed that where the term 'gross sales' appears in any part of this agreement, the interpretation as set forth in this clause of this contract shall prevail.

"(f) The said party of the second part hereby further agrees to pay or cause to be paid unto the said party of the first part, the amount of the cost of the equipment, cuts, miniature blocks, dies, doors, lumber and iron mentioned in this contract, which payment shall be made within thirty days after the date of this contract, by a representative of the said party of the second part.

"It is further understood and agreed by and between the parties hereto and the said party of the first part hereby covenants with the said party of the second part, that it has full rights to make the said license and sale in the manner and form as above written, and that the letters patent herein mentioned are free from all prior assessments, grants, mortgages or other incumbrances whatsoever, except as herein stated, and it is understood and agreed by the parties hereto that in the event that any person, company or corporation shall be guilty of an infringement of said letters patent herein referred to, or any improvements in connection therewith, the said party of the second part shall forthwith, upon receiving a notice of any such infringement, notify the said infringers of such infringement and proceed forthwith to protect the invention or inventions covered by said letters patent in any court or courts it may deem proper or see fit, at its own expense.

"It is further understood and agreed by and between the parties hereto that the said party of the second part will not at any time dispute the validity of the above mentioned patents, nor allege their invalidity as a cause for refusing to make any payments under this contract, and that it will during the existence of this license co-operate with the party of the first part in establishing as far as possible the integrity of such letters patent:

Provided, however, that if at any time during the life of this contract the said letters patent be infringed to the extent that more than one hundred silos shall be manufactured in any one year by persons or companies not licensees by either of the parties to this agreement, and proceedings at law shall have shown that it is impossible to protect the party of the second part in the exclusive rights herein granted, then any and all payments of the *license or royalty* fee as herein stipulated shall cease and determine.

"It is further understood and agreed by and between the parties hereto that in the event other silos shall be manufactured and placed upon the market by any person, company or corporation other than the said party of the second part, not actually infringing on the invention or inventions covered by the letters patent hereinbefore mentioned, or any improvement thereof, but rendering the sale of silos, or the manufacture of silo blocks and clamps under said letters patent financially impossible by reason of the royalty or license fee herein agreed to be paid by the party of the second part unto the party of the first part, then the so-called royalty of five per centum as hereinbefore stipulated shall be decreased and any reduction therein shall be referred to a board of arbitration to consist of three persons, one to be selected by the party of the first part, another to be selected by the party of the second part, and the two so chosen to select the third member of said board, and a majority of the board of arbitration so selected shall decide in the premises.

"It is further understood and agreed by and between the parties hereto that any and all matters of dispute arising under this contract shall be decided by a board of arbitration to consist of three persons, one of which shall be selected by the party of the first part, one by the party of the second part, and the third member thereof to be chosen by the two so selected.

"In Witness Whereof, The said parties have hereunto affixed their respective common corporate seals, duly attested by their respective officers, the day and year first above written.

(Seal) Imperishable Silo Company
By Eugene H. Baker, Pres.

Attest:—F. B. Bash, Sec.

(Seal) National Fire Proofing Company.
W. L. Henry, President.

Attest:—C. S. Jones, Sec."

The outstanding question in this case is whether the provisions of clause "e" of article third of the contract, by which appellant has obligated itself to pay five per cent. royalty on "all vitrified block silos" sold by it, expresses a definite meaning when read in connection with all the other provisions of the contract together with its recitals. Does it mean that the royalty provided for covers sales made of silos manufactured under the Brumbaugh patents alone, or, when so considered, is it an ambiguous contract and one of such doubtful meaning as to require the aid of extrinsic facts to ascertain the intention of the parties? If there is ambiguity, it is a patent one, and it is for the court to say as a matter of law, whether it exists. Unless the court can say from a consideration of the entire contract that the above mentioned clause is ambiguous,

1. other extrinsic facts are not a proper subject of inquiry, because, if unambiguous, the language of the contract itself is the only medium through which the court may ascertain its true meaning. *Vandalia Coal Co.* v. *Underwood* (1913), 55 Ind. App. 91, 101 N. E. 1047, 1049; *Sargeant* v. *Leach* (1910), 47 Ind. App. 318, 321, 94 N. E. 579; Elliott, Contracts §§1506-1510. When all the provisions of this contract, together with its recitals are

2. considered together, it was the duty as well as the sole province of the court to interpret it, for it is apparent that the provision refers to silos manufactured under the Brumbaugh patent and none other. It

3. is a familiar principle that when a contract is to be considered or when some separate provision thereof is involved, separate clauses and provisions will not be considered apart from the general context or apart from connected clauses, but the meaning of the entire contract and of each of its clauses will be determined from all the language used, and the parties will be held to have intended that meaning to each clause which makes the whole contract consistent, and which is reasonable in view of all the

190    APPELLATE COURT OF INDIANA,

Nat. Fire Proofing Co. *v.* Imperishable Silo Co.—63 Ind. App. 183.

terms employed. *Nave v. Powell* (1912), 52 Ind. App. 496,
96 N. E. 395, and cases there cited.  Applying these principles to the present case, we are satisfied that the
2. subject under consideration and which the parties
expressed in their final written agreement was the
Brumbaugh patent silo block, silos constructed therewith
and the purchase of the tangible property described in
such contract.  Consequently clause "e" must be held to
refer to silos manufactured under such patent.  Reference
to the several general recitals which precede the contractual
provisions necessarily leads to this conclusion.  It is recited
that Brumbaugh obtained the patents; that appellee acquired them from him, and by it appellant was granted
the exclusive right to manufacture the silos and blocks, in
*pursuance of the patents;* that appellee had a sales organization engaged in selling Brumbaugh silos; that they had
been generally advertised, and that appellant desired to
make and sell silos and silo blocks described in said letters
patent; and, to avail itself of such selling organization and
the advertising done by it, that appellant was to maintain
*during the life of the patent* an effective sales organization
for the purpose of selling the *Brumbaugh patent silo.*

The recitals in clause "c," which have to do with the
payment of royalties in case appellant licensed any other
person to manufacture silos and silo blocks *in conformity
with the patent above referred to,* clause "d" which provided for the keeping of accurate accounts of all silos and
silo blocks made and sold, and, immediately following thereafter, clause "e," which provided for the payment of five
per cent. royalty on the gross sales of silos and silo blocks,
clause "f," covenanting that appellee had authority to
license appellant to make such silos *under said patent,* and
if said patent is infringed to the extent mentioned, then
"all payments of the license or royalty fee as herein stipulated shall cease and determine," also indicate that the
parties were negotiating with reference to the Brumbaugh

patent. When consideration is given to each provision of
the contract in the light of all its other provisions, at the
same time bearing in mind that it is in clause "e" where
reference is made to the payment of "license fees or royalties," and that these terms are there frequently used in
connection with silos manufactured under the Brumbaugh
patents and none other, it seems to us that we would be
doing violence to the contract to hold that its provisions
required the payment of license fees or royalties upon sales
of other silos than those manufactured under the Brumbaugh patent. The effect of such a holding would be the
making for the parties a different contract from that which
they had made for themselves.

It is sufficient to state also that there is no averment in
either paragraph of the complaint to show that the purchase price of the tangible property mentioned in the contract remained unpaid, or that sales of silos manufactured
under the Brumbaugh patent had been made and that
royalties were due appellee. Neither is there an allegation
in either paragraph of the complaint based on the theory
of fraud in procuring the alleged contract, thereby elim-
inating appellee from the field of silo manufacturing to
appellant's advantage, so that it might be inferred that
with this purpose in mind the contract provided for the
payment of fees and royalties upon all silos sold by appellant, whether manufactured under the Brumbaugh patent
or otherwise. And there is no averment in either paragraph
of the complaint which could make it sufficient upon the
theory that the parties, by their own conduct, had placed
a different construction on the contract; and no other facts
are averred which would authorize a holding different from
the one here announced.

Other errors assigned by appellant need not be considered
in view of the conclusion we have reached on the main question. As to them, it is sufficient to say that the fundamental
error we have discussed is to be seen throughout the whole

case. The separate demurrers to each paragraph of the complaint should have been sustained. Judgment reversed.

Note.—Reported in 112 N. E. 408. Contracts, oral evidence to explain ambiguity, when proper, 122 Am. St. 546. See under (1) 17 Cyc 666; (2) 30 Cyc 956; (3) 9 Cyc 579.

---

# DENNEY v. REBER.

## [No. 9,159. Filed December 12, 1916.]

1. JUSTICE OF THE PEACE.—*Judgment.—Matters Adjudicated.—Title to Real Property.*—A judgment of a justice of the peace, rendered by agreement of the parties, awarding possession of certain lots did not adjudicate the title thereto; and an answer, in a subsequent action between the same parties to cancel and set aside a deed for such real estate as having been executed under duress, reciting the rendition of the judgment, is insufficient as a plea of former adjudication of title, since such question could not have been adjudicated by the justice of the peace. p. 196.

2. ESTOPPEL.—*Equitable Estoppel.—Action to Cancel Deed.—Payment of Rent.*—The fact that one claiming to have conveyed property under duress paid her grantee rent to occupy the premises for a time after an agreed judgment, which was not appealed from, for possession of the real estate in controversy had been rendered against her by a justice of the peace, did not estop her from subsequently prosecuting an action against her grantee to have the deed set aside for duress, where both parties had equal knowledge of all the facts in the transaction, and the grantee had not been induced to change his position to his damage by any act of the plaintiff. p. 197.

3. CANCELLATION OF INSTRUMENTS.—*Deeds.—Action.—Complaint.—Sufficiency.—Duress.—Consideration.*—In an action to cancel and set aside a deed alleged to have been executed by plaintiff under duress, a complaint averring that plaintiff conveyed certain lots to defendant to prevent his carrying out threats to prosecute her husband for a criminal offense, "and for no other purpose or consideration whatever," and that by the threats and promises of defendant she was coerced, put in fear and induced to convey her property, and not otherwise, sufficiently shows, under the rules of pleading, that no consideration was paid for the property, although there was no specific allegation to that effect, and that through fear plaintiff was deprived of her free agency in making the conveyance. p. 198.

Denney v. Reber—63 Ind. App. 192.

4. CONTRACTS.—*Validity.*—*Execution.*—*Duress.*—Duress is a species of fraud in which compulsion in some form takes the place of deception in accomplishing the injury, and where a deed, mortgage, or note is obtained from the wife upon a threat to prosecute, arrest or imprison her husband, the instrument so procured is voidable by the wife. p. 198.

5. CONTRACTS.—*Validity.*—*Duress.*—*Evidence.*—In determining the question of duress courts consider the age, sex, capacity, situation and relation of the parties and all the attending circumstances which throw any light upon the particular transaction under investigation. p. 199.

6. PLEADING.—*Amendment.*—*Withdrawal of Submission.*—*Discretion of Court.*—*Failure to Show Harm.*—Where the trial court, after the hearing of the evidence, permitted plaintiff to withdraw the submission of the cause and file an additional paragraph of complaint, the accrued costs having been assessed against plaintiff, the withdrawal was not a dismissal of the action, and the procedure was fully within the discretion of the court, under §403 Burns 1914, §394 R. S. 1881, relating to amendments to pleadings, especially when the complaining party fails to show that he was harmed by the action of the court, and where the judgment rendered was favorable to him. p. 200.

7. APPEAL.—*Prejudicial Error.*—*Overruling Demurrer to Bad Answer.*—*Presumption.*—Error in overruling a demurrer to a bad answer is presumed to be harmful and will constitute reversible error, unless it is affirmatively shown by the record that the ruling was not prejudicial, and the duty of making such showing rests upon the party who contends that the error was harmless. p. 200.

From Jay Circuit Court; *Clark J. Lutz,* Special Judge.

Action by Zelpha Denney against Milton D. Reber. From a judgment for defendant, the plaintiff appeals. *Reversed.*

*James R. Fleming,* for appellant.
*John F. LaFollette* and *Emerson McGriff,* for appellee.

FELT, C. J.—This is a suit by appellant, Zelpha Denney, against appellee, Milton D. Reber, to cancel and set aside a deed executed by appellant and her husband to appellee for certain real estate. The case was tried on the second and third paragraphs of complaint. An answer of three paragraphs was addressed to the second paragraph of complaint and one of two paragraphs to the third paragraph of complaint. A demurrer was sustained to the third paragraph of answer to the second paragraph of complaint. Appellant's demurrer to the second paragraph of answer to the third paragraph of complaint was overruled, to which appellant reserved an exception. Replies in general denial were filed to the affirmative paragraphs of answer. The case was tried by the court without a jury and a judgment rendered that appellant take nothing by her complaint, and that appellee recover costs. From such judgment this appeal was taken and the only error assigned is the overruling of appellant's demurrer to appellee's second paragraph of answer to the third paragraph of the complaint.

The second paragraph of complaint was drawn on the theory that the deed which appellant sought to have set aside was in fact a mortgage, executed by appellant, a married woman, to secure the debt of her husband.

The third paragraph of complaint proceeds on the theory that the deed in question was procured by the duress of appellee, and, in substance, charges that on December 30, 1912, appellant was the owner in fee simple of lot No. 7 in Meeker's addition to the city of Portland, Indiana; that prior thereto her husband, Riley H. Denney, had been employed by appellee as a salesman of cigars, and appellee then and there accused him of embezzling certain money belonging to him and unlawfully and fraudulently represented to appellant that he would cause her husband to be arrested and sent to the penitentiary unless the amount he claimed to have been embezzled was paid to him, or the real estate aforesaid conveyed to him in satisfaction thereof; that to induce her to make such conveyance appellee unlawfully promised and agreed not to prosecute her husband for said crime if she would make such conveyance; that her husband had been arrested on said charge, and was then under bond, and appellee promised her to procure the dismissal of the charge against him and to procure his release if she would make such conveyance to him; that for more than a week prior to the execution of said deed, she was in great fear, sick and confined to her bed on account of the threats against her husband, and on the date aforesaid, to prevent the carrying out of the threats of prosecution made against him, and for no other purpose or consideration whatever, she executed and delivered to appellee a deed, conveying to him the title to said real estate; that the threats and promises aforesaid, so made by appellee, were made for the purpose of cheating, defrauding and coercing appellee, and she was thereby coerced, put in fear and induced to so convey said real estate as aforesaid, and not otherwise.

The first paragraph of answer to the third paragraph of complaint was a general denial. The second paragraph of answer admits the ownership and conveyance of the real estate by appellant and alleged that the property was conveyed subject to a mortgage for $300 and subject to a mechanic's lien and to accrued taxes; that as a further consideration for the conveyance the parties agreed that appellant should occupy the premises and dwelling house thereon for six months without the payment of rent, at the expiration of which time she and her husband were to surrender possession to appellee; that appellant did so occupy and use said property for six months and then refused to vacate the same in accordance with the aforesaid agreement; that thereupon appellee brought suit before a justice of the peace for possession of said property, the details of which are alleged.

It is also averred that on July 10, 1913, by agreement of the parties, a judgment was duly rendered by said justice of the peace to the effect that appellee should have possession of the real estate in controversy, but provided also that if appellant should, within five days, pay to appellee $15 she should have the right to occupy the property until September 1, 1913; that the money was paid in accordance with said agreement; that appellant did not remove from the property on September 1, 1913, and on September 2, 1913, a writ of restitution was issued for the possession thereof and in October, 1913, appellee removed from the real estate and since that time has not occupied or used the same; that the parties to this suit are identical with the parties to the suit before the justice of the peace, and the judgment aforesaid is in full force and unappealed from. The demurrer to the aforesaid second paragraph of answer was for insufficiency of the facts alleged to constitute a defense to appellant's cause of action alleged in her third paragraph of complaint.

The memorandum accompanying the demurrer is, in substance, as follows: (1) The facts alleged do not show a former adjudication of appellant's cause of action. (2) Such facts do not constitute an estoppel against appellant. (3) The facts alleged do not show a ratification of the conveyance sought to be set aside.

Appellee does not contend that the answer is good as showing a ratification of the transaction and conveyance by
1. which he obtained title to the property, but asserts its sufficiency both as a plea of former adjudication and as an estoppel. Neither do the averments of the answer, viewed from their general scope and tenor, indicate any other possible theory than those asserted by appellee. We shall therefore consider the answer from the viewpoint of appellee's contention as to theory.

The answer in question is not good as a former adjudication of title. The question of title was not in issue under the averments, nor does it come within the rule that questions will be deemed adjudicated which might have been litigated and settled within the issues. The justice of the peace could not have adjudicated the question of title, and had the title been put in issue before him, it would have been his imperative duty to have certified the case to the circuit court. §1722 Burns 1914, §1434 R. S. 1881; *Deane v. Robinson* (1904), 34 Ind. App. 468, 472, 73 N. E. 169;

*Mitten* v. *Caswell-Runyan Co.* (1912), 52 Ind. App. 521, 525, 99 N. E. 47.

Neither do we regard the answer sufficient as a plea of estoppel. In the first place both parties to the transaction had equal knowledge of all the facts and circumstances involved in the transactions alleged. Appellee was not induced to change his position to his damage by anything said or done by appellant. He asserted his title both before and subsequent to the proceedings before the justice of the peace and the arrangement about possession of the property. Appellee's technical legal title was not, and is not, disputed by appellant; for her complaint proceeds on the theory that he has the legal title, but that it was procured by fraud and duress and should not be allowed to stand. Under such conditions the payment of the $15 and the occupancy of the property as alleged do not estop appellant from asserting her right to have appellee's evidence of legal title—the deed—set aside. *Penn, etc., Plate Glass Co.* v. *Schwinn* (1912), 177 Ind. 645, 656, 98 N. E. 715; *State* v. *Mutual Life Ins. Co.* (1910), 175 Ind. 59, 83, 93 N. E. 213, 42 L. R. A. (N. S.) 256; *Indianapolis Traction, etc., Co.* v. *Henby* (1912), 178 Ind. 239, 251, 97 N. E. 313; *Johnson* v. *Spencer* (1911), 49 Ind. App. 166, 171, 96 N. E. 1041; *Steele* v. *Michigan Buggy Co.* (1912), 50 Ind. App. 635, 642, 95 N. E. 435.

But appellee contends that the third paragraph of complaint is insufficient to state a cause of action, and that the demurrer to the answer should be carried back to the complaint and be sustained. A demurrer to the third paragraph of complaint was duly presented and overruled. Appellee could have assigned cross-errors, but has not done so. Whether, in such case, under our present demurrer law, the demurrer to the answer could be carried back to the complaint, and sustained, if the paragraph of complaint were insufficient, we do not decide, for the reason that we deem the paragraph sufficient to state a cause of action for procuring the deed by duress.

Appellee now asserts that the paragraph is bad for failure to aver the value of the real estate, and to show that appellee did not pay full value therefor; also that the averments do not show that appellant was deprived of her free agency and did not act voluntarily in executing the deed to appellee. The allegations show that appellant was the owner of the real estate, and that to prevent the carrying out of the threats against her husband, "and for no other purpose or consideration whatever," she executed the deed to appellee; that by the threats and promises of appellee she was coerced, put in fear, and induced to so convey her property and not otherwise. Under the rules of pleading now established in this state, these averments show that there was no consideration whatever moving to appellant for the conveyance of her property; that she was put in fear and made sick by the threats against her husband and by such threats and the promise of appellee to prevent the prosecution of her husband for embezzlement and to procure his release, she was coerced into executing the deed, and was moved to do so wholly on account of such threats and promises. Whether the value of the property was great or small is immaterial when the allegations show that no consideration moved to appellant and that, by threats and promises, as averred, she was deprived of her free will and induced to convey her property, in payment of an alleged debt which was in no sense an obligation she was bound to discharge, to accomplish a result appellee had no power, or legal right, to control, but which he unlawfully assured appellant he could and would control.

Cooley on Torts (vol. 2, 3d ed., 966, 967) says: 4. "Duress is a species of fraud in which compulsion in some form takes the place of deception in accomplishing the injury. * * * Where a deed, mortgage, or notes are obtained from the wife upon a threat to prosecute, arrest or imprison her husband, the instruments are void." The above statement is in harmony with the decisions of our own courts and the prevailing weight of authority generally, with the possible modification or explanation that contracts or other instruments so procured are not, strictly speaking, void, because they may be ratified, but are voidable by the party so induced to execute them. To give validity to any contract, the law requires the free assent of the parties to be bound thereby, and the trend of modern authority is to relieve a party from his obligation or deed when, through fear, terror, or violence, he has been deprived of free and voluntary action by the other contracting party, or by one acting for and in behalf of such party.

In determining the question of duress, the courts take into account the age, sex, capacity, situation and relation of the parties and all the attending circumstances

5. which throw any light upon the particular transaction under investigation. 2 Cooley, Torts 969; *Rose v. Owen* (1908), 42 Ind. App. 137, 141, 85 N. E. 129; *Bush v. Brown* (1875), 49 Ind. 573, 577, 578, 19 Am. Rep. 695; *Schee v. McQuilken* (1877), 59 Ind. 269, 278; *Line v. Blizzard* (1880), 70 Ind. 23, 25; *Adams v. Stringer* (1881), 78 Ind. 175, 180; *Baldwin v. Hutchison* (1893), 8 Ind. App. 454, 458, 35 N. E. 711; *Cribbs v. Sowle* (1891), 87 Mich. 340, 49 N. W. 587, 24 Am. St. 166, 171; *First Nat. Bank, etc. v. Sargeant* (1902), 65 Neb. 594, 91 N. W. 595, 59 L. R. A. 296, 299; *Bryant v. Peck, etc., Co.* (1891), 154 Mass. 460, 28 N. E. 678; *Turner v. State* (1911), 10 Ga. App. 18, 72 S. E. 604; *Benedict v. Roome* (1895), 106 Mich. 378, 64 N. W. 193; *Bank v. Hutchinson* (1900), 62 Kan. 9, 61 Pac. 443; *Woodham v. Allen* (1900), 130 Cal. 194, 62 Pac. 398; *Lomerson v. Johnston* (1888), 44 N. J. Eq. 93, 13 Atl. 8; *Galusha v. Sherman* (1900), 105 Wis. 263, 81 N. W. 495, 47 L. R. A. 417; *Brown v. Pierce* (1868), 7 Wall. 205, 19 L. Ed. 134, 137; 9 Cyc 443; 14 Cyc 1123.

Appellee asserts that in any event the judgment should

not be reversed for two reasons, viz.: (1) Because the
record shows that after the submission of the cause and the
hearing of evidence, the court permitted appellant to withdraw the submission and file the third paragraph of complaint, which was in effect a dismissal of the action; (2) because appellant must show that the ruling complained of
was harmful and has failed to do so. On the record before
us neither of these contentions can be sustained.

6. While the court permitted appellant to withdraw the
submission of the cause and file the third paragraph
of complaint, it adjudged the costs up to that time against
appellant before permitting her to file such third paragraph.
Appellee moved to strike out certain parts of the third
paragraph, and thereafter demurred thereto and obtained
the rulings of the court thereon. The case was duly put at
issue on the third paragraph of complaint as above shown,
the cause was resubmitted for trial without a jury, the evidence heard, the case taken under advisement and later the
finding of the court was announced and the judgment rendered as above stated. The procedure was fully within the
discretionary power of the court, and furthermore, appellee has not properly challenged the court's action and has
wholly failed to indicate that he was in any way misled or
harmed by the action of the court, but on the contrary he
obtained judgment in his favor. The case was not dismissed
by the withdrawal of the submission, and was not finally
disposed of by the trial court until the judgment was rendered from which this appeal was prayed. §403 Burns
1914, §394 R. S. 1881; *Burnett* v. *Milnes* (1897), 148 Ind.
230, 235, 46 N. E. 464. Where the court overrules a demurrer to a bad answer, the ruling is presumed to be harmful and will constitute reversible error, unless it is affirmatively shown by the record that the ruling was not

7. harmful. In making such ruling the court commits
an error of law which is presumed to be carried into
the final judgment unless the contrary is shown by the

record and the duty of making such showing rests upon the party who contends that the error was harmless. This rule is sometimes confused with the one which obtains where the court erroneously sustains a demurrer to a good answer and it appears that the same proof was admissible under another paragraph held good, or that the party in some way obtained the full benefit of such answer, in which event the error in sustaining such demurrer is held to be harmless. *Gregory* v. *Arms* (1911), 48 Ind. App. 562, 578, 96 N. E. 196; *Norris* v. *Tice* (1895), 13 Ind. App. 17, 21, 39 N. E. 1046; *Bowlus* v. *Phenix Ins. Co.* (1892), 133 Ind. 106, 118, 32 N. E. 319, 20 L. R. A. 400; *Cleveland, etc., R. Co.* v. *Case* (1910), 174 Ind. 369, 376, 91 N. E. 238.

For the error in overruling the demurrer to appellee's second paragraph of answer to appellant's third paragraph of complaint the judgment is reversed, with instructions to sustain appellant's motion for a new trial, to sustain the demurrer to said second paragraph of answer, and to permit the parties to amend their pleadings, if desired, and for further proceedings not inconsistent with this opinion.

Caldwell, Ibach, McNutt and Hottel, JJ., concur.

Moran, P. J., not participating.

NOTE.—Reported in 114 N. E. 424. Contracts: procurement of by threats of prosecution of relative, effect, 26 L. R. A. 48, 20 L. R. A. (N. S.) 484, 37 L. R. A. (N. S.) 539, L. R. A. 1915D 1118, 11 Ann. Cas. 385; voidable for duress, ratification, Ann. Cas. 1913E 438. See under (1) 24 Cyc 450; (2) 16 Cyc 746; (4) 9 Cyc 453; 14 Cyc 1123; (5) 9 Cyc 771; (6) 31 Cyc 402.

---

# HARRIS ET AL. *v.* RIGGS ET AL.

[No. 9,539. Filed May 31, 1916. Rehearing denied October 27, 1916. Transfer denied December 12, 1916.]

1. TRIAL.—*Findings of Fact.—Ultimate and Evidentiary Facts.—* Ultimate and not evidentiary facts should be stated in a finding of fact, and facts contained in conclusions of law must be disregarded. p. 208.

2. TRIAL.—*Findings of Fact.—How Considered.—Presumptions.*—A finding of fact should be considered as a whole, and all intendments and presumptions are in its favor rather than against it, and if, by considering one part in connection with other parts, relative to the same matter, the finding can be said to be sufficient, it will be upheld. p. 208.

3. TRIAL.—*Findings of Fact.—Evidentiary Facts.*—While evidentiary facts should not be included in a finding of facts, yet their presence therein does not necessarily render the finding insufficient to support conclusions of law. p. 208.

4. TRIAL.—*Findings of Fact.—Sufficiency.*—Where the primary facts contained in a finding of facts are of such a character that they necessitate the inference of an ultimate fact, such ultimate fact will be treated as found and as sufficient on appeal, even though there may be a technical defect of statement in the finding. p. 208.

5. TRIAL.—*Findings of Fact.—Ultimate Facts.—Sufficiency.*—If a finding of facts contains sufficient ultimate facts to support the judgment, it will be sufficient, though it may not find all the issuable facts and may contain primary or evidentiary facts. p. 208.

6. TRIAL.—*Conclusions of Law.—Sufficiency.*—In an action to enforce an oil and gas lease, a conclusion of law that on and prior to a certain date the lease had been forfeited and was null and void is not subject to criticism as containing a finding of facts. p. 209.

7. TRIAL.—*Conclusions of Law.—Sufficiency.*—In an action to quiet title based on an oil and gas lease, conclusions of law that plaintiffs had no right, title, or interest in the leased premises in controversy, are entitled to no relief in the action and should pay the costs of the suit are supported by the finding of the ultimate fact that the lease was abandoned. p. 209.

8. TRIAL.—*Findings of Fact.—Ultimate Facts.—Evidentiary Facts.* —Where, in an action on an oil and gas lease, the trial court in its findings of facts found as an ultimate fact that the lease had been abandoned by the lessees prior to a certain date, such finding is not invalidated by the court's statement of evidentiary facts which authorized the inference of the ultimate facts that the lease had been abandoned and forfeited under a construction thereof mutually agreed and acted upon by the parties. p. 209.

9. MINES AND MINERALS.—*Oil and Gas Leases.—Abandonment.*—A lease, giving the lessee the right to drill the leased premises for oil and gas for a fixed period of time and providing that, if a well shall not have been completed prior to a certain date, the lessee is obligated to pay the lessors a stipulated rental until the completion of a well, may be abandoned by the lessee, and, if

it is abandoned, he can not thereafter enforce any right thereunder without first securing the consent of the lessor or a renewal
of the lease. p. 209.

10. MINES AND MINERALS.—*Oil and Gas Leases.—Abandonment.*—
Because of the nature of the subject-matter, abandonment of oil
and gas leases may be more readily found than in most cases
and, as the rights granted thereunder are for exploration and
development, the lessee will not be permitted to fail in development and hold the lease for speculative or other purposes, except in strict compliance with his contract for a valuable and
sufficient consideration other than such development. p. 210.

11. MINES AND MINERALS.—*Oil and Gas Leases.—Actions.—Burden
of Proof.*—In an action on an oil and gas lease, the burden of
proof is on the plaintiffs to show their right to the relief sought,
and they cannot base a recovery on the weakness of defendant's
position. p. 210.

12. MINES AND MINERALS.—*Oil and Gas Leases.—Actions.—Failure
to Find Essential Facts.*—In an action to quiet title based on an
oil and gas lease, the failure of the trial court in its findings of
fact to find any material fact essential to plaintiff's recovery is
a finding against them as to such fact. p. 210.

13. MINES AND MINERALS.—*Oil and Gas Lease.—Abandonment.—
New Lease.—Effect.*—Where, after the abandonment of an oil and
gas lease, the lessor, who had never been out of possession of the
leased premises, so that he could not re-enter upon himself, again
leased the premises, such new lease sufficiently showed the lessor's intention to treat the first lease as annulled. p. 211.

From Knox Circuit Court; *Benjamin M. Willoughby,*
Judge.

Action by James F. Harris and others against Edgar R.
Riggs and others. From a judgment for defendants, the
plaintiffs appeal. *Affirmed.*

*Simmons & Dailey, McCarty & Arnold, James M. House*
and *Hunt & Gambill,* for appellants.

*Jay A. Hindman, Hays & Hays, John W. Lindley, James
Wade Emison, Lee F. Bays* and *Fred F. Bays,* for appellees.

FELT, P. J.—This suit was brought by appellants to quiet
their title and exclusive right to go upon certain real estate
and explore and operate for oil and gas.

The complaint was in seven paragraphs and appellants
based their claims on a lease executed on February 1, 1912.

Each paragraph of complaint was answered by general denial, and by special paragraphs of answer directed to each paragraph of the complaint, in which facts were alleged to show that appellants had ceased to have any right or claim under the aforesaid lease. A reply of general denial was filed to each paragraph of special answer. On due request the court made a special finding of facts, on which conclusions of law were stated that appellants should take nothing by their complaint and that they pay the costs of suit. Judgment was rendered on the conclusions of law from which this appeal was prayed and granted.

Appellants have assigned as errors: The overruling of their motion for a new trial; that the court erred in its conclusions of law and in each separate conclusion; that the court erred in overruling their motion for a *venire de novo*.

The finding of facts is in substance as follows: On February 1, 1912, Felix P. and Malissa J. Beard, husband and wife, were the owners as tenants in common of the 135 acres of real estate in controversy (describing it); that on said day they executed to Emery A. Snyder and Jasper Miller an oil and gas lease on said real estate which in substance provides: That for a valuable consideration said Beard and Beard let and leased to the second party, their successors and assigns—

"for the sole and only purpose of mining and operating for oil and gas and of laying pipe lines, constructing tanks and other structures thereon to take care of said products. * * * It is agreed that this lease shall remain in force for the term of three years from this date and as long thereafter as oil or gas or either of them is produced therefrom by the party of the second part, successors or assigns. * * * The party of the second part agrees to complete a well on said premises within nine months from the date hereof or pay at the rate of thirty dollars in advance for each additional three months, such completion is delayed from the time above mentioned for the completion of such well until a well is completed. The above rental shall be paid to the first party in person or to the credit of the first party at the Shelburn National Bank. For and in consideration of one dollar, the receipt of which is hereby acknowledged the first party hereto expressly waive their right to demand or declare a cancellation or a forfeiture of this lease except for the non-payment of rentals when due; and further agree that the party of the second part, their successors or assigns, shall have the right at any time on the payment of one dollar, to the party of the first part, their heirs or assigns to surrender this lease for cancellation, after which all payments and liabilities thereafter to accrue under and by virtue of its terms shall cease and determine.''

That at the time of the execution of the lease it was expressly agreed and understood by and between the parties thereto and the lease was by them expressly construed to mean that in case the lessees failed to complete a well for the production of oil or gas within nine months from the date of the lease it would be void if the lessees should thereafter fail to pay to the lessors the sum of $30 in advance for each three months' delay in completing such well; that other explorations were made in the vicinity of the leased land within nine months from February 1, 1912, and no oil or gas was found or known to exist in that vicinity; that appellants did not take possession of said premises under the lease and on October 25, 1912, the lessors requested the lessees aforesaid to either pay for an extension of the lease as therein provided or return the lease; that thereupon the lessees refused to make any payment and informed the lessors that they did not desire an extension of time in which to complete a well and did not intend to pay anything under the lease, but intended to let it lapse by their failure to complete a well or pay any rentals as therein stipulated; that on October 25, 1912, the lessees aforesaid notified the lessors that they intended to abandon the lease and allow it to become void; that on October 31,

1912, no well had been commenced or completed on said premises and there was then due on the lease $30 for a further extension thereof; that the conditions were the same and a like amount became due under the lease each succeeding three months and no amount was paid; that "said lease became void and forfeited on November 1, 1912, and was on said day abandoned"; that on February 7, 1913, the said Felix P. Beard died leaving Malissa J. Beard, his widow, surviving him; that prior to May 26, 1913, the lessees under the lease of February 1, 1912, had neither taken nor demanded possession of the leased premises, and had not commenced or completed a well, nor paid or tendered any money for an extension of the lease; that on May 26, 1913, said Malissa J. Beard executed to Edgar R. Riggs and Fred F. Bays another lease of said lands for oil and gas purposes conditioned that it should remain in force for the term of six months from date and as long thereafter as oil or gas should be produced therefrom by the lessees, their successors or assigns. One well was to be produced within sixty days from date of lease, and on failure to do so $100 was to be paid in advance for each month's delay; that at the time the second lease was executed the lessees therein had no actual knowledge of a prior lease on the land; that in pursuance of said second lease Riggs and Bays took possession of the leased premises and constructed eight wells, in which oil and gas were found in paying quantities; that said 'lessees have expended in testing and developing said property $19,125; that on May 27, 1913, the lessees in the lease of February 1, 1912, visited Malissa J. Beard and sought to get from her a new lease of said premises and expressed regret that they had abandoned their former lease, and then and there learned of the second lease aforesaid; that on May 28, 1913, Emery A. Snyder, lessee in the first lease, congratulated Riggs and Bays on the lease they had secured, and expressed regret that they had allowed their lease to become forfeited; that on May 22, 1913, oil was found in paying quantities on land adjoining said leased premises, and on May 31, 1913, the lessees in said first lease left at the bank mentioned therein $131.25, and requested the bank officials to place the same to the credit of Malissa J. Beard; that before the money was left at the bank, as aforesaid, Malissa J. Beard duly notified the bank not to receive any money from said parties for her on said former lease and said lessees knew thereof when they left the money at the bank; that she also notified the bank and said lessees in writing on June 1, 1913, that said lease had been forfeited and she would not accept any money thereunder; that she did not at any time accept any money from any one on said lease; that on April 14, 1914, Malissa J. Beard died leaving defendant William Ray Osborn, Gertrude Thompson and Grace Dark, her grandchildren, as her only heirs at law.

The court stated its conclusions of law on the facts found as follows: (1) That on and prior to May 26, 1913, the lease of date February 1, 1912, executed to Emery A. Snyder and Jasper Miller had been forfeited and was null and void. (2) That at the time this suit was commenced the plaintiffs had no right, title or interest in or to the real estate described in the amended complaint. (3) That the plaintiffs are entitled to no relief prayed for in this action and the defendants are entitled to judgment against them for costs. Judgment was rendered in accordance with the conclusions of law.

Appellants contend that the finding of facts is made up of evidentiary instead of ultimate facts; that ultimate facts are stated in the conclusions of law and must be disregarded; that the facts found do not support the conclusions of law.

It is true that ultimate and not evidentiary facts should be stated in a finding and that facts stated in the conclusions of law must be disregarded. While this is

1. true, a finding of facts must be considered as a whole, and is not to be dissected into fragmentary parts and assailed in such parts disconnected from other por-

2. tions of the findings relating to the same proposition.

All intendments and presumptions are in its favor rather than against it, and if, by considering one part in connection with other parts relative to the same matter, the finding can be said to be sufficient it will be upheld. While

evidentiary facts should not appear in a finding of

3. facts, yet their presence in a finding does not necessarily render the finding insufficient to support conclusions of law. In the case at bar, the court has in many instances stated both the evidentiary and the ultimate facts.

Where the primary facts found lead to only one con-

4. clusion, or where the primary facts found are of such a character that they necessitate the inference of an ultimate fact, such ultimate fact will be treated as found by the trial court and sufficient on appeal. In such instances the facts are sufficiently found, though there may be a technical defect of statement in the finding. *Mount v. Board, etc.* (1907), 168 Ind. 661, 665, 80 N. E. 629, 14 L. R. A. (N. S.) 483; *Judah v. Cheyne Electric Co.* (1913), 53 Ind. App. 476, 484, 101 N. E. 1039; *National Surety Co. v. State* (1913), 181 Ind. 54, 60, 103 N. E. 105; *Horn v. Lupton* (1914), 182 Ind. 355, 361, 105 N. E. 237, 106 N. E. 708; *Knight v. Kerfoot* (1915), 184 Ind. 31, 110 N. E. 206, 209; *Whitcomb v. Smith* (1890), 123 Ind. 329, 332, 24 N. E. 109; *DePauw Plate Glass Co. v. City* (1898), 152 Ind. 443, 453, 52 N. E. 608. If a finding of facts

5. contains sufficient ultimate facts to support the judgment it will be sufficient, though it may not find all the issuable facts and may contain primary or evidentiary facts. *Carnahan v. Shull* (1913), 55 Ind. App. 349, 351, 102 N. E. 144; *Whitcomb v. Smith, supra; DePauw Plate Glass Co. v. City, supra.*

In the opinion of this court the first conclusion of law is not justly subject to criticism. But if, as contended by appellants, the first part of it is the statement of an
6. ultimate fact rather than a conclusion of law, it might be treated as surplusage and the remaining portion, that the first lease was null and void before the second was executed, would still be a good conclusion of law and have the same legal effect. The other con-
7. clusions of law—that the plaintiffs have no right, title, or interest in the leased premises, are entitled to no relief in this suit, and should pay the costs of suit— necessarily follow the first conclusion. But, independent of the first conclusion, the second and third conclusions of law are correct and are supported by the finding of the ultimate fact that the lease was abandoned.

The findings show that the parties themselves placed a construction on the lease to the effect that the lease should be void if the lessees failed to complete a well within
8. nine months from its date, and likewise failed to pay a stipulated rental in advance as provided in the lease. The court also finds as an ultimate fact that the lease was abandoned by the lessees on November 1, 1912. True, the finding contains evidentiary facts which strongly support the facts of abandonment, and of forfeiture of the lease before the second lease was executed and before this suit was begun. The court having found and stated the essential ultimate facts did not annul or change them by stating evidentiary facts which clearly authorized the inference of the ultimate facts that the lease was abandoned and had been forfeited under the construction mutually agreed and acted upon by the parties. Such a lease may be abandoned, and when once abandoned by the les-
9. see, he cannot thereafter claim or enforce any right thereunder without first securing the consent of the lessor or a renewal of the lease. *Gadbury* v. *Ohio, etc., Gas. Co.* (1903), 162 Ind. 9, 16, 67 N. E. 259, 62 L. R. A.

895; *Island Coal Co.* v. *Combs* (1898), 152 Ind. 379, 387, 53 N. E. 452; *Ohio Oil Co.* v. *Detamore* (1905), 165 Ind. 243, 252, 73 N. E. 906; *Bartley* v. *Phillips* (1895), 165 Pa. St. 325, 30 Atl. 842; *Calhoon* v. *Neely* (1902), 201 Pa. St. 97, 50 Atl. 967; *Urpman* v. *Lowther Oil Co.* (1903), 53 W. Va. 501, 44 S. E. 433, 435, 97 Am. St. 1027; *Van Meter* v. *Chicago, etc., Mining Co.* (1893), 88 Iowa 92, 55 N. W. 108; 1 C. J. 5 *et seq.;* 1 Cyc 4 *et seq.;* Thornton, Law Oil & Gas §137.

It has been held and supported by sound reason that abandonment may be more readily found in cases of oil and
10. gas leases than in most other instances. The rights granted under such leases are for exploration and development. The title or interest granted is inchoate until oil or gas is found in quantities warranting operation, and courts will not permit the lessee to fail in development and hold the lease for speculative or other purposes, except in strict compliance with his contract for a valuable and sufficient consideration other than such development. *Gadbury* v. *Ohio, etc., Gas Co., supra,* p. 14; *Urpman* v. *Lowther Oil Co., supra; Huggins* v. *Daley* (1900), 99 Fed. 606, 40 C. C. A. 12, 48 L. R. A. 320, 325; *Dittman* v. *Keller* (1913), 55 Ind. App. 448, 451, 104 N. E. 40; *Risch* v. *Burch* (1911), 175 Ind. 621, 627, 95 N. E. 123; *Dill* v. *Fraze* (1907), 169 Ind. 53, 57, 79 N. E. 971; *Ramage* v. *Wilson* (1909), 45 Ind. App. 599, 604, 88 N. E. 862.

The burden was on appellants to show their right to the relief prayed. They cannot claim anything which depends
11. wholly upon the weakness of their adversaries' position. The failure to find any material fact essential to their recovery is a finding against them as to such fact. It is clear that the finding of facts would not
12. support a judgment in appellants' favor. While there is a dispute in the evidence as to some of the ultimate facts found, there is no failure of evidence to sustain the finding of the material facts.

In leases of the kind here involved where the lessor has continued to hold possession he cannot re-enter upon himself.  The execution of a new lease under the facts
13.  of this case sufficiently shows the lessor's election to treat the first lease as annulled and in no sense binding upon any of the parties thereto.  *Huggins* v. *Daley, supra; Twin-Lick Oil Co.* v. *Marbury* (1875), 91 U. S. 587, 23 L. Ed. 328, 331; *Guffy* v. *Hukill* (1890), 34 W. Va. 49, 11 S. E. 754, 8 L. R. A. 759 and notes, 26 Am. St. 901.

The conclusions already announced make it unnecessary to consider many questions discussed in the briefs.  The court did not err in its conclusions of law or in overruling appellants' motion for a *venire de novo,* or for a new trial.  The case seems to have been fairly tried and a correct result reached on the merits of the controversy.  No error has been pointed out which deprived appellants of any substantial rights.  Judgment affirmed.

Caldwell, C. J., Moran, Ibach, McNutt and Hottel, JJ., concur.

NOTE.—Reported in 112 N. E. 36.  Mining leases, breach of covenant, relief from, 20 Ann. Cas. 1172.  See under (1, 3) 38 Cyc 1980, 1982; (11) 27 Cyc 655.

---

# NATIONAL LIVE STOCK INSURANCE COMPANY *v.* CRAMER.

### [No. 9,116.  Filed December 13, 1916.]

1. INSURANCE.—*Parol Contracts.—Validity.*—Parol contracts of insurance may be valid and of binding force. p. 215.
2. INSURANCE.—*Contract to Renew Policy.—Validity.*—An insurance company can, by a preliminary oral contract, bind itself to issue or renew a policy of insurance in the future. p. 216.
3. INSURANCE.—*Renewal of Policy.—Authority of Agent.—Oral Contract.*—Where an agent for an insurance company has apparent power to solicit insurance, collect premiums, deliver policies, and do all things necessary to transact the company's business intrusted to his care, and no restriction is brought to the knowledge of an applicant, the company is bound by the agent's oral contract to renew an existing policy of insurance. p. 216.

4. INSURANCE.—*Authority of Agent.—Renewal.—Notice of Expiration of Policy.*—A letter from an insurance company to a policy holder, informing him of the date of the expiration of his policy and requesting him to see the company's agent concerning a renewal and let him take care of his interests, justified the assured in assuming that the agent had full and general authority to act for his principal. p. 216.

5   INSURANCE.—*Contracts of Insurance.—Power of Agents.—Restrictions in Policy.*—Provisions in policies of insurance limiting the powers of agents have reference to that policy only, and have no application to preliminary agreements to insure or to renew existing insurance. p. 217.

6.  APPEAL.—*Action on Insurance Policy.—Judgment.—Error in Favor of Appellant.*—A defendant appealing from an adverse judgment cannot object that the judgment is for a smaller amount than should have been allowed under the findings of fact. p. 217.

From Henry Circuit Court; *John F. LaFollette,* Special Judge.

Action by Joe Cramer against the National Live Stock Insurance Company. From a judgment for plaintiff, the defendant appeals. *Affirmed.*

*M. S. Meyberg,* for appellant.
*Forkner & Forkner,* for appellee.

IBACH, J.—Appellant issued a live-stock insurance policy to appellee for a term of one year and for the sum of $500, covering two certain horses, particularly describing them.

The first paragraph of the complaint, to recover for the death of one of the horses, proceeds upon the theory that, the same agent who obtained the first policy orally agreed to reinsure the horses described in the first policy in the same amount for another year on the same terms and conditions contained in the original policy, and that such old policy would be renewed; that no new policy was ever issued, and on May 19, 1913, one of the horses died. The second paragraph proceeds upon the theory that appellant's agent made an original parol contract of insurance with appellee.

Appellant answered in two paragraphs, a general denial

and a denial that any policy of insurance was issued, or that any insurance was effected through the negotiations between appellee and appellant's agent and, if any insurance had been thereby consummated, there was no liability because the horse for which loss is claimed was sick from eight o'clock a. m. one day until three o'clock a. m. of the next day, and no notice of such sickness was given appellant, as the terms of the policy required.

Replies were filed closing the issues. The cause was submitted to the court and by request a special finding of facts was returned, together with conclusions of law thereon. Appellant excepted to each of the conclusions of law and then filed a motion for a *venire de novo,* which was overruled. A motion for a new trial was then filed, which was also overruled and exceptions reserved to each of such rulings. Judgment was rendered for appellee in the sum of $381.72, from which this appeal is taken.

The facts are fully found by the court and are sustained by the evidence. We, therefore, are not required to give further thought to the errors assigned relating to the overruling of appellant's separate motions for a *venire de novo* and for a new trial. We proceed to the further assignment that the court erred in its conclusion of law on the facts found. These findings show the existence of appellant company; that it was organized to insure live stock and that it appointed as its agent in Newcastle and vicinity Nathan Cummins. The appointment was in writing and by its terms the authority of such agent was limited to soliciting and forwarding applications of insurance to appellant for approval or rejection. In compensation for his services he was to be paid in commissions provided for in his appointment.

On April 16, 1912, defendant issued to plaintiff a policy of insurance by the terms of which defendant, in consideration of the sum of $50 as premium, agreed to insure plaintiff against the loss of two horses by death for a period of

one year to the amount of $100 on one horse, and $400 on
another, named Turban. Before the expiration of the
policy defendant mailed a letter to plaintiff wherein he was
informed of the time his policy would expire and a request
was made that he renew his policy and he was directed to
reach the local agent and *"have him take care of his interests."* On the same day defendant also wrote its local agent,
Cummins, directing him *to use his best endeavors to secure
a renewal of the policy if he still considered the risk desir-
able.* Upon receipt of his letter plaintiff called upon the
agent Cummins and informed him of his desire to again
insure with his company for the same amount, "but that
he desired the entire sum placed on the one horse Turban."
The agent instructed plaintiff to bring him the card giving
the description and number of the horse and that they
would arrange to reinsure him. Afterwards, and before
the expiration of the old policy, plaintiff provided defendant with the requested information, and thereafter, and in
the absence of plaintiff, the agent Cummins prepared an
application for him which was mailed to defendant at its
office in the city of Indianapolis. Plaintiff then offered to
pay the premium to the agent but he was told by him not
to pay it until he received the policy and *that he could consider himself insured.* Immediately after the expiration of
the policy plaintiff again called on the local agent for his
new policy, but was informed that it had not been received
from the home office, but *agreed and promised that he
should consider himself insured in the sum named in his
application on the horse Turban.* While all these matters
were happening defendant was holding out to the public and
to appellee that Cummins was its agent; that plaintiff *had
no knowledge of any limitation on his authority.* Plaintiff
relied on the agreement believing that Cummins was defendant's agent, and was induced to rely on said insurance
and not to take insurance in any other company. About eight
o'clock a. m. of May 18, 1913, the horse Turban became

sick. He was then on plaintiff's farm about one mile from Millville, Henry county, and about seven miles from Hagerstown. Plaintiff immediately called a veterinary surgeon at Hagerstown, by telephone, and he came at once to attend the horse. Plaintiff was required to telephone through the exchange at Millville and, May 18, being Sunday, the exchange was closed after nine o'clock of that day. The veterinary remained with the horse the greater part of that day and until two o'clock next morning, when the horse died. Plaintiff immediately notified defendant of the death of the horse and asked what disposition should be made of him, and was told by Cummins to bury him. He had the horse moved, however, to Hagerstown, where an autopsy disclosed that he had died from acute indigestion. The horse had never been sick before, was a pedigreed stallion, and was worth $1,000. After the death of the horse and within a reasonable time, on May 22, plaintiff wrote a letter to defendant in which he narrated all the business transactions had with their agent; that he relied upon the statement made by the agent that the horse was insured; that he had died shortly after the new insurance had been placed; that he had notified the agent of his death, and demanded the new policy and the amount of insurance which had been placed on the horse. All of which was refused by the defendant on the ground of nonliability.

Upon the foregoing facts the court stated conclusions of law as follows: First, the law is with the plaintiff on the finding of facts hereinbefore found. Second, that the plaintiff should recover the sum of $381.72 together with costs.

Parol contracts of insurance have been many times held valid and of binding force by both the Supreme and Appellate Courts of this State. *Angell* v. *Hartford Fire*
1. *Ins. Co.* (1874), 59 N. Y. 171, 17 Am. Rep. 322; *Western Assurance Co.* v. *McAlpin* (1899), 23 Ind. App. 220, 55 N. E. 119, 77 Am. St. 423; *Ohio Farmers Ins. Co.* v. *Bell* (1912), 51 Ind. App. 377, 99 N. E. 812.

The proposition is well settled that an insurance company can, by a preliminary contract, bind itself to issue
or renew a policy of insurance in the future. The
2. controlling question then in this case is, Do the facts
constitute such a contract? Insurance companies
3. ·contract through their agents, and whether he be
called a general or special agent, if he had apparent
power to solicit insurance, collect premiums, deliver policies,
and do all things necessary to transact the business of his
company given to his care, and no restriction is brought to
the knowledge of the person dealing with him, such
agent, under such circumstances, will bind the company by
a verbal contract with the assured made at or prior to the
expiration of an insurance policy covering live stock, which
the assured desired to again insure either in whole or in
part. *Kerlin* v. *National Accident Assn.* (1894), 8 Ind. App.
628, 35 N. E. 39, 36 N. E. 156; *Kitchen* v. *Hartford Fire
Ins. Co.* (1885), 57 Mich. 135, 23 N. W. 616, 58 Am. Rep.
344; *Commercial Union Assurance Co.* v. *State* (1888), 113
Ind. 331, 15 N. E. 518. The letter from appellant to
appellee, in which he was requested to see its agent and let
him take care of his interests, justified him in assuming
that such agent had full and general authority to act
4. for it. He had a right from this and other facts
proven and found by the court to infer that appellant had authorized all that its agent did and said to appellee concerning insurance. *Ruggles* v. *American Central
Ins. Co.* (1889), 114 N. Y. 415, 21 N. E. 1000, 11 Am. St.
674.

We are satisfied that the finding of facts, considered
together, are sufficient on the question of the authority of
Cummins to make an oral contract of insurance and of
appellee's right to rely, and that he did rely on such authority when the oral contract of insurance contended for was
made. But it is appellant's contention that since the original policy of insurance which appellee had received from

it in 1912 contained limitations of the agent Cummins' authority, such limitations in that policy would be notice generally of his limited authority.

It has been held, however, and rightly so, that provisions in policies limiting powers of agents, have reference only to the policy itself, and have no application 5. to the preliminary agreements to insure or to renew existing insurance. *Zell* v. *Herman, etc., Ins. Co.* (1890), 75 Wis. 521, 44 N. W. 828; *Renier* v. *Dwelling House Ins. Co.* (1889), 74 Wis. 89, 42 N. W. 208, 210; 1 Wood, Insurance (2d ed.) §11. Appellant, although denying that there was a contract of insurance at the time the stallion Turban died, yet contends that if such oral contract of insurance had been consummated, it must be presumed that the parties contemplated such form of policy as to conditions as was used by the parties originally, and since such policy provided that the company would not be liable if the insured failed to render at once, by telegraph, notice of any sickness with which the horse might become afflicted, there was no liability because of failure to give such notice. In view of the disposition we have made of the last contention we are not required to discuss this proposition.

There was evidence, although contradicted, supporting the court's finding. These findings cover all the issues tried and they are favorable to appellee, and sustain the conclusions of law and the decision.

It appears from the finding of facts in this case that appellee should have been given a judgment for $500, 6. but appellee does not contend for this and no point is made in the briefs. Appellant is in no position to object. Judgment affirmed.

NOTE.—Reported in 114 N. E. 427. Insurance, oral contracts, validity and effect, 6 Ann. Cas. 624. General agencies, apparent authority of agent, 88 Am. St. 782; 22 Cyc 1429, 1430.

## HAEHNEL ET AL. v. SEIDENTOPF.

### [No. 9,424.    Filed December 13, 1916.]

1. Costs.—*Bond.—Permission to Sue as a Poor Person.—Nonresidence of Plaintiff.*—A party granted the right to prosecute an action as a poor person under §261 Burns 1914, §260 R. S. 1881, relating to the appointment of attorneys for persons without means to prosecute or defend actions, cannot be required to give a bond for costs because he thereafter becomes a nonresident of the state.  p. 220.

2. Appeal.—*Presentation of Error.—Motion for New Trial.—Assignment of Error.*—A specification in a motion for a new trial, alleging that the trial court erred in not requiring a bond for costs to be filed by plaintiff, who became a nonresident of the state subsequent to the commencement of his action, does not present any question for review as to the court's ruling permitting plaintiff, after the motion for a cost bond, to prosecute his action as a poor person, since such ruling must be challenged by an independent assignment of error.  p. 221.

3. Costs.—*Bond.—Permission to Sue as a Poor Person.—Nonresidence of Plaintiff.—Ruling of Trial Court.—Presumption.*—In the absence of an assignment of error challenging the action of the trial court in permitting plaintiff, after a motion had been filed to require him to furnish a cost bond because he was a resident of another state, to prosecute his suit as a poor person, it will be assumed on appeal that the ruling of the trial court was proper, and it was not, therefore, error to overrule the motion for a bond for costs.  p. 221.

4. Exceptions, Bill of.—*Time of Presenting for Signing.—Recitals in Bill.*—The recital in a bill of exceptions of the day it was presented to the judge for signing, which was after the time given to file the bill, will be taken as correct, regardless of a recital that it was presented within the time allowed for filing.  p. 221.

5 Appeal.—*Presenting Questions for Review.—Bill of Exceptions.—Time for Signing and Settlement.*—The bill of exceptions containing the evidence must be presented to the trial judge for his signature within the time fixed for filing the bill in order to present for determination on appeal any questions requiring a consideration of the evidence.  p. 222.

6. Appeal.—*Questions Reviewable.—Sufficiency of Complaint.—Waiver of Defects.—Statute.*—Since the enactment of §3481 Burns 1914, Acts 1911 p. 415, an assignment of error challenging the complaint for not stating facts sufficient to constitute a cause of action is no longer available.  p. 222.

7. PLEADING.—*Complaint.—Motion to Make More Specific.—Knowledge.*—Where, in an action to foreclose a mechanic's lien, the complaint alleged that the property on which the lien was taken was owned by the defendants, husband and wife, as tenants by entireties, that the buildings erected on the premises were constructed under a contract with the husband with the full knowledge, consent and acquiescence of the wife, and that in all things relating to the contract the husband acted as her agent, a motion to make the complaint more specific as to what knowledge, if any, the plaintiff had given to the wife concerning the contract for the erection of the buildings was properly overruled, since the averments of the complaint, in effect, charge the wife with having all knowledge possessed by the husband. p. 222,

8. MECHANICS' LIENS.—*Husband and Wife.—Tenancy by Entireties.—Liability of Wife for Improvements.—Statute.*—Section 7860 Burns 1914, §5123 R. S. 1881, which requires the written consent of the wife in order to charge her personally and alone with repairs or improvements made on her separate real estate by order of the husband, has no application to real estate which the wife and husband own as tenants by the entireties. p. 223.

From Lake Superior Court; *Walter T. Hardy*, Judge.

Action by Frank Seidentopf against Herman Haehnel and another. From a judgment for plaintiff, the defendants appeal. *Affirmed.*

*John M. Stinson*, for appellants.
*Milo M. Bruce*, for appellee.

HOTTEL, J.—Appellee, in a complaint in one paragraph, sought to recover of appellant a balance alleged to be due him on account of work and labor performed and material furnished in the erection of certain buildings on appellants' real estate described in the complaint, and to foreclose a mechanic's lien on said premises. A motion to make the complaint more specific, and a demurrer to the complaint were each overruled. The appellants filed an answer in denial and a counterclaim. There was a trial by the court and a general finding that there was due appellee on his complaint the sum of $440, and a finding for appellants on their cross-complaint in the sum of $190, that appellee should have judgment for $250, plus an attorney fee of

$40, which sum was declared to be a lien upon said real estate. Judgment was rendered for appellee in accord with the finding. Appellants filed a motion for new trial which was overruled. During the progress of the trial, it developed that appellee, after filing his suit, had changed his residence from that part of the city of Hammond which is located in the State of Indiana, where he resided when his action was begun, to a part of said city located in the state of Illinois. Thereupon appellants moved the court to require appellee to give a cost bond. The appellee then filed a petition to prosecute his action as a poor person, and supported the same by an affidavit, whereupon the court permitted him to so prosecute his action, to which ruling of the court the appellants excepted.

The several rulings of the trial court above indicated, except the last, are each separately assigned as error in this court and relied on for reversal. The ruling last above indicated is attempted to be presented by the first ground of appellants' motion for a new trial, in the following words, viz.: "That the Court erred in not requiring plaintiff to file bond for costs, the plaintiff being a non-resident at the time of the beginning of the trial."

This is not the ruling shown by the record to have been made by the court. The only ruling disclosed by the record affecting this question is the ruling permitting appellee to prosecute his action as a poor person. Assuming, however, that the ruling made had the effect of a refusal by the court to require appellee to file a cost bond, and assuming also, without so deciding, that such ruling is properly presented by the ground of the motion for new trial, *supra*, rather than by an independent assignment of error, the record discloses that appellee, to relieve himself of the necessity of giving such bond, made an application, supported by affidavit, to prosecute his action as a poor
1.  person. If, before becoming a nonresident of the State, he had made a proper application to prosecute

his action as a poor person, and such application had been granted by the court, his removal from the State afterwards would not have necessitated the giving of a cost bond. *Wright, Admr.*, v. *McLarinan* (1883), 92 Ind. 103, 105; *Fuller, etc., Co.* v. *Mehl* (1893), 134 Ind. 60, 62, 63, 33 N. E. 773; *Pittsburgh, etc., R. Co.* v. *Jacobs* (1894), 8 Ind. App. 556 *et seq.*, 36 N. E. 301; §261 Burns 1914, §260 R. S. 1881. We do not see any substantial difference between the question here attempted to be presented and that determined in the cases cited, *supra*. In any event,

2. the action of the court in permitting appellee to prosecute his action as a poor person is not challenged by said ground of appellants' motion for a new trial, and could not be properly challenged thereby, as such ruling constitutes a cause for independent assignment of error. *Pittsburgh, etc., R. Co.* v. *Jacobs, supra*, p. 557.

Assuming, therefore, as we must, in the absence of such a challenge, that the action of the trial court, permitting appellee to prosecute his action as a poor person,

3. was proper, it follows as a matter of course that no error resulted from refusing to require appellee to give a cost bond.

The other grounds of appellants' motion for new trial challenge the admission ·and exclusion of evidence, and attempt to present such questions as can be presented only by the general bill of exceptions containing the evidence.

The record discloses that the judgment was rendered March 30, 1915, and the motion for a new trial overruled June 30, 1915, from which time the appellants

4. were given sixty days to file their bill of exceptions. There is nothing in the record to show that this time was ever extended under §661 Burns 1914, Acts 1911 p. 193. The bill of exceptions shows that it was presented to the judge for his signature August 31, 1916, more than sixty days after the overruling of the motion for new trial, and

hence not within the time granted by the trial court. The bill recites that "on this the 31st day of August 1915 and *within the time allowed by the Court for the filing of their bill of exceptions* * * * the said defendants presented to the Judge * * * their bill of exceptions," etc. (Our italics.)

The recital in the bill of the day it was presented will be taken as correct regardless of the italicized language, *supra,* which follows: *Malott* v. *Central Trust Co.* (1906), 168 Ind. 428, 431, 79 N. E. 369, 11 Ann. Cas. 879.

In order to present any question, the proper determination of which in any way depends on the evidence, the bill

5. of exceptions containing such evidence must be presented to the trial judge within the time fixed for filing the same. *Joseph* v. *Mather* (1887), 110 Ind. 114, 115, 116, 10 N. E. 78; *Cornell* v. *Hallett* (1895), 140 Ind. 634, 646, 40 N. E. 132; *Stoner* v. *Louisville, etc., R. Co.* (1893), 6 Ind. App. 226, 228, 33 N. E. 242; *Indiana, etc., Oil Co.* v. *O'Brien* (1902), 160 Ind. 266, 278, 65 N. E. 918, 66 N. E. 742.

Appellants' first assignment of error, which challenges the complaint on the ground that it does not state

6. facts sufficient is no longer available. §348 Burns 1914, Acts 1911 p. 415.

The second assigned error challenges the overruling of the motion to make more specific. The only matter suggested in appellants' brief under this heading is that

7: the complaint should have been made to state "what if any knowledge he (appellee) had given to defendant Catherine Haehnel of the contract for the erection of said building." As affecting this question, the complaint alleges that on November 11, 1914, Herman Haehnel and Catherine Haehnel were the owners in fee simple, as tenants by entireties of the lots in question (describing them); that on said day, appellee and said Herman entered into the written contract filed with and made part of the complaint. Averments follow showing the performance of the work and the furnishing of the material under said contract, and also an agreement with said Herman Haehnel for the performance of work and furnishing of material for another building and for certain changes in the first, a bill of particulars for which is filed with and made a part of the complaint. It is then averred that *"said buildings were constructed with the knowledge consent and acquiescence of the defendant Catherine Haehnel, and that in all things herein mentioned said Herman Haehnel acted for himself and also for his said wife as her agent."*

These averments, in effect, charge the wife with all the knowledge possessed by the husband affecting said contract, and hence meet appellants' said objection to the complaint. *Taggart* v. *Kem* (1898), 22 Ind. App. 271, 277, 279, 53 N. E. 651; *Wilson* v. *Logue* (1892), 131 Ind. 191, 30 N. E. 1079, 31 Am. St. 426; *Dalton* v. *Tindolph* (1882), 87 Ind. 490.

Appellants' third assigned error challenges the ruling on the demurrer to the complaint, and in their brief, under points and authorities, applied to such alleged error, their objection to the complaint is stated as follows: "The complaint on its face showed that the plaintiff had contracted with one of the owners by entirety without the consent or knowledge of the other owner." The averments of the complaint, quoted *supra,* show the contrary. In this connection, we might add that §7860 Burns 1914, §5123 R. S. 1881, which requires the written consent of the wife in

8.    order *to charge her personally and alone with repairs or improvements made on her separate real estate* by order of the husband, has no application to real estate which the wife and husband own as tenants by the entireties. *Taggart* v. *Kem, supra,* 275. Finding no reversible error in the record, the judgment below is affirmed.

NOTE.—Reported in 114 N. E. 422.

## PHILLIPS *v.* BALL ET AL.

[No. 9,703. Filed December 13, 1916.]

1. APPEAL.— *Vacation.— Statute.— Coparties.*— The word "coparties," as used in §674 Burns 1914, Acts 1899 p. 5, relating to vacation appeals, which provides that a part of several coparties may appeal but must serve notice on all the other parties, means coparties to the judgment appealed from. p. 227.

2. APPEAL.—*Vacation.—Parties.—Coappellants.*—On a vacation appeal all parties against whom judgment was rendered must be made coappellants or the appeal will be dismissed. p. 227.

3. APPEAL.— *Dismissal.—Determination.— Defect of Parties.* — In passing on a motion to dismiss an appeal for defect of parties the court can only consider the question whether all the parties were properly before the court on the day of submission, even though it appears from the record that the party whom it is claimed should have been made a coappellant could not have appealed because more than 180 days had elapsed between the time of overruling the motion for a new trial and the filing of the motion to dismiss the appeal. p. 228.

4. APPEAL.—*Parties.—Defect.—Waiver.*—Where, in a vacation appeal, a defendant to whom the judgment appealed from was adverse was not made a coappellant in the assignment of errors, the defect in parties was not waived by the principal defendant, who moved to dismiss the appeal, joining in an agreement for immediate submission of the cause, since the defect in parties was jurisdictional, and could be waived only by the party affected by the judgment. p. 229.

5. APPEAL.—*Vacation.—Parties.—Defect.—Jurisdiction.—Dismissal.* —Where, in an action against several defendants to foreclose a real-estate mortgage, the judgment, from which a vacation appeal was taken, decreed that one of the defendants had no interest in the land in controversy, such defendant had a right to appeal, and should have been made a coappellant in the assignment of errors, and notified, as provided in §674 Burns 1914, Acts 1899 p. 5, relating to vacation appeals, and where the appeal was taken without making him a coappellant, it must be dismissed for want of jurisdiction. (*Rooker* v. *Fidelity Trust Company* [1915], 185 Ind. 172, distinguished.) p. 229.

From Elkhart Superior Court; *James L. Harman,* Judge.

Action by Effie I. Phillips against Fernando W. Ball and

others. From the judgment rendered, the plaintiff appeals.
*Appeal dismissed.*

*C. C. Raymer* and *Carlton T. Olds,* for appellant.
*Proctor & Calley,* for appellees.

McNUTT, J.—This was an action in the court below by
appellant against appellees Fernando W. Ball and Mary A.
Ball, his wife, and Sidney A. Uncapher and R. C. Beck,
whose christian name is alleged to be unknown.

The complaint alleges, in substance: That on May 16,
1912, Uncapher purchased certain real estate described,
and thereupon Fernando W. Ball loaned him $1,700 and,
as security, received a conveyance of said real estate; that
at the same time said Ball and Uncapher entered into a contract which provided, in substance, that the former should
reconvey said real estate upon payment of said loan, with
interest, together with the taxes on the real estate; that
if said Uncapher failed to perform said contract, then it
should be considered a lease of the premises; that on October 29, 1913, said Ball assigned said contract to appellant
and conveyed to her said real estate to secure a loan of
$1,700, which sum said Ball agreed to pay in case of
Uncapher's failure; that defendant Beck claimed some right,
title and interest in said real estate and claimed to hold
an assignment of said contract, and he was made a party
defendant to answer to his interest, if any. The prayer
asks for a personal judgment against Ball and Uncapher;
that the contract be declared forfeited and annulled as to
any rights and interests of defendants Uncapher and Beck,
and that appellant's deed be declared a mortgage and be
foreclosed.

Said Fernando W. Ball filed an answer in denial and
also a cross-complaint against defendant Uncapher. The
cross-complaint was afterwards withdrawn and said Ball
filed a disclaimer as to the real estate. Defendant Mary
Ball filed a disclaimer. Defendant Beck was served by

publication notice and was defaulted. Defendant Uncapher filed an answer in denial. The cause was submitted to the court and, after hearing the evidence, the court rendered the following judgment, which follows the finding: "It is therefore considered, ordered and adjudged by the court that said plaintiff take nothing as to the defendants, Ball and Ball.

"It is further ordered, adjudged and decreed by the court that the defendant, R. C. Beck, has no interest in or to the real estate described in the plaintiff's complaint or in the contract set forth therein.

"It is further considered, adjudged and decreed by the court that the contract described and set forth in plaintiff's complaint be, and the same is hereby declared forfeited and determined as to the defendant, Uncapher, and that said defendant, Uncapher, has no further right, title or interest in and to said contract and the real estate.

"And it is further ordered, adjudged and decreed by the court that said plaintiff do have and recover of and from said defendant, Sidney A. Uncapher, her costs and charges herein laid out and expended, taxed at———dollars."

Afterwards plaintiff filed her motion for a new trial and in the title of said motion she named all of the original defendants. The reasons assigned are: (1) The decision of the court is contrary to law; (2) the decision of the court is not sustained by sufficient evidence, and the other reasons assigned relate to the admission and rejection of evidence.

This is a vacation appeal, as authorized by §674 Burns 1914, Acts 1899 p. 5, which is as follows: "A part of several co-parties may appeal to the supreme or appellate court, but in such case they must serve written notice of the appeal upon all the other co-parties or their attorneys of record, and file proof thereof with the clerk of such court, and whenever it shall be made to appear to such court by satisfactory proof that such other co-parties, or any of them, are not residents of the state and have no attorneys of record in the court below, or that such attorneys can not be served with such notice in the state, the court may order that notice of the pendency of the appeal be given to such non-resident co-parties in some newspaper printed and published in the state, for three weeks successively; after which, if proper notice has been given the appellees, the court shall proceed in all respects as if said non-resident co-parties had been personally served with notice of said appeal. After notice to said co-parties in either of the ways provided in this section, unless they appear and decline to join in said appeal, they shall be regarded as properly joined, and shall be liable for their due proportion of the costs. 'If they decline to join, their names may be stricken out, on motion; and they shall not take an appeal afterwards, nor shall they derive any benefit from the appeal, unless from the necessity of the case, except persons under disabilities; *Provided, however,* That nothing in this act shall be construed to repeal or modify an act entitled, An act in relation to appeals to the supreme and appellate courts, approved March 8, 1895 (Acts of 1895, page 179), or any part thereof, but the provisions of said act shall continue in force the same as if it had been enacted after the taking effect of this act.''

It has been frequently held that "coparties," as used in said section providing for vacation appeals, means coparties to the judgment. *Hadley* v. *Hill* (1881),

1. 73 Ind. 442; *Hildebrand* v. *Sattley Mfg. Co.* (1900), 25 Ind. App. 218, 57 N. E. 594. "It is well settled that in vacation appeals all parties against whom judgment was rendered must be made coappellants in this court,

2. or the appeal will be dismissed, for the reason that in such case we have no jurisdiction to determine the case on its merits." *Brown* v. *Brown* (1907), 168 Ind. 654, 656, 80 N. E. 535. See, also, *Polk* v. *Johnson* (1906), 167 Ind. 548, 78 N. E. 652, 79 N. E. 491; *Chicago, etc., R.*

*Co.* v. *Walton* (1905), 165 Ind. 642, 74 N. E. 988; *Moore* v. *Ferguson* (1904), 163 Ind. 395, 72 N. E. 126; *Rich Grove Tp.* v. *Emmett* (1904), 163 Ind. 560, 72 N. E. 543; *Haymaker* v. *Schneck* (1902), 160 Ind. 443, 67 N. E. 181; *North* v. *Davisson* (1901), 157 Ind. 610, 62 N. E. 447; *Brown* v. *Sullivan* (1901), 158 Ind. 224, 63 N. E. 302; *Mellott* v. *Messmore,* (1901), 158 Ind. 297, 63 N. E. 451; *Smith* v. *Fairfield* (1901), 157 Ind. 491, 61 N. E. 560; *Owen* v. *Dresback* (1899), 154 Ind. 392, 56 N. E. 22, 848; *McKee* v. *Root* (1899), 153 Ind. 314, 54 N. E. 802; *Crist* v. *Wayne,. etc., Assn.* (1898), 151 Ind. 245, 51 N. E. 368; *Midland R. Co.* v. *St. Clair* (1896), 144 Ind. 363, 42 N. E. 214; *Shuman* v. *Collis* (1896), 144 Ind. 333, 43 N. E. 257; *Gregory* v. *Smith* (1894), 139 Ind. 48, 38 N. E. 395; *Holloran* v. *Midland R. Co.* (1891), 129 Ind. 274, 28 N. E. 549; *Mascari* v. *Hert* (1912), 52 Ind. App. 345, 100 N. E. 781; *Helberg* v. *Dovenmuehle* (1905), 37 Ind. App. 377, 76 N. E. 1020; *Harrison* v. *Western Construction Co.* (1907), 41 Ind. App. 6, 83 N. E. 256; *Continental Ins. Co.* v. *Gue* (1912), .51 Ind. App. 232, 98 N. E. 147; *Belk* v. *Fossler* (1908), 42 Ind. App. 480, 85 N. E. 990.

In the last cited case the court said: "The true and equitable test would seem to be the rule as laid down in some of the decisions, 'that all parties who are entitled to appeal from the judgment must be joined as coappellants in one and the same appeal.' "

It is contended by appellant that it affirmatively appears that more than 180 days have elapsed between the time of overruling the motion for a new trial and the filing

3. of the motion to dismiss and, therefore, said Beck could not possibly appeal. In passing on the motion to dismiss we can only consider the question whether all the parties were properly before the court on the day of submission.

It is further contended by appellant that because appellee Uncapher, who moves to dismiss the appeal, has joined in

an agreement for immediate submission of the cause,
4. he has waived the defect of parties, but the defect
of parties which has been pointed out involves the
jurisdiction of the court to hear and determine the cause
on its merits and such question cannot be waived, except
by the party who is affected by the judgment. This
proposition is so well settled that citation of authority is
unnecessary.

Appellant relies upon the case of *Rooker* v. *Fidelity
Trust Co.* (1915), 185 Ind. 172, 109 N. E. 766, to support his contention that it was unnecessary to in-
5. clude said Beck as a party to this appeal. An
examination of the Rooker case, and especially the
record in the case, discloses that two of the defendants
in Rookers' complaint filed disclaimers. This action on
their part took them out of the case. Neher, the other
defendant, was defaulted and the court found that he had
no interest in the real estate, but the court renders no judgment against him, except that Rookers recover their costs.
The judgment appealed from in the Rooker case was the
judgment of the Fidelity Trust Company against the
Rookers on said company's cross-complaint which was
against the Rookers alone. Under the facts, therefore, in
the Rooker case it was not necessary to make Neher a party
to the appeal, and the Supreme Court so held. The case
does not support appellant's contention. In the instant
case the judgment was against Beck, and from this judgment
he had a right to appeal. He should have been made a
coappellant in the assignment of errors and notified as
provided in said section. Because of his absence as such
a party we have no jurisdiction to determine the cause on
its merits. The appeal is, therefore, dismissed.

Note.—Reported in 114 N. E. 647.

PAUL, GUARDIAN, v. DICKINSON TRUST COMPANY, GUARDIAN, ET AL.

[No. 9,019.  Filed April 19, 1916.  Rehearing denied December 13, 1916.]

1. WILLS.—*Construction.*—*Words of Postponement.*—*Vesting of Estates.*—The law looks with disfavor on postponing the vesting of estates, and the intent to do so must be clear and not depend upon inference or construction, the presumption being that words in a will postponing the estate relate to the beginning of the enjoyment of the remainder and not to the vesting of the estate, unless the contrary clearly appears. p. 233.

2. WILLS.—*Construction.*—*Vesting of Estates.*—The law favors the vesting of remainders absolutely, rather than contingently or conditionally. p. 233.

3. WILLS.—*Construction.*—*Words of Survivorship.*—Words of survivorship in a will generally refer to the death of the testator where the first taker is given a life estate and the remainder over is devised to another. p. 233.

4. WILLS.—*Construction.*—*Remainders.*—*Estates Created.*—Where a testator devised to his daughter for life certain lands which, at her death, were to go to her children, should any survive, and, if not, to her grandchildren in fee simple, the child of the devisee, born subsequent to the execution of the will but prior to the death of the testator, is vested at the death of the testator with the fee, subject only to the life estate and to the one-third interest therein taken by the testator's widow under the laws of descent. p. 233.

From Wayne Circuit Court; *Daniel W. Comstock,* Special Judge.

Action for partition by Sarah Myers against Essie Paul, guardian of Neva Paul, and others.  Essie Paul, guardian, filed a cross-complaint to quiet title, and from a judgment sustaining demurrers to her cross-complaint, she appeals. *Reversed.*

*Shively & Shively,* for appellant.

*Byram C. Robbins* and *Philip H. Robbins,* for appellees.

FELT, P. J.—In a suit for partition of real estate brought by the widow of Moses Myers, deceased, appellant filed

a cross-complaint to quiet her title to two-thirds of the
real estate in controversy, subject to the life estate of Essie
Paul, mother of Neva A. Paul. Separate demurrers were
filed to the cross-complaint by each of the appellees on the
ground of the insufficiency of the facts alleged to state a
cause of action. The court sustained each of the demurrers,
to which appellant duly excepted and has assigned those
rulings as the errors upon which she relies for reversal of
the judgment against her.

Moses Myers was the grandfather of both appellant and
appellees, and all parties concede that the correctness
of the court's ruling on the demurrer to appellant's cross-
complaint depends upon the construction of the will of
Moses Myers, deceased, and particularly upon item No. 4
thereof.

By item No. 2 of his will the testator devised to his son
Moses E. Myers a certain tract of real estate for life, and
then to his children in fee simple, share and share alike.
By item No. 3 he devised to his daughter Rose A. Howard
a specific tract of real estate for the period of her natural
life, and after her death the same to go to her children,
share and share alike in fee simple. In other parts of the
will he made provision for an annuity for his widow, but
she elected to take under the law. By item No. 4 he
devised to his daughter Essie Myers (who afterwards
became Essie Paul by marriage) a tract of real estate
containing 107 acres, "to have and to hold the same for
her own use and benefit during the period of her natural
life, and at her decease the same to go to her children
should she leave any living, and if not, then the same to
go to her grandchildren in fee simple, share and share
alike," subject to the annuity mentioned above. In item
No. 5 he devised to his son Jeremiah Myers seventy-eight
acres of real estate for his own use and benefit during the
period of his natural life and then "the same to go to his

children in fee simple, share and share alike," subject to the annuity aforesaid.

The averments of the cross-complaint show that at the time of the execution of the will, the testator had four children, viz., two sons, Moses and Jeremiah, and two daughters, Rose and Essie. At that time, his son Moses had two children of full age, to wit, Nora M. Myers and John E. Myers, appellees herein; and his son Jeremiah had two children, Herbert and Charles, who were minors. His daughter Rose then had two children, Mabelle M. Howard and Ruth M. Howard, both under age. His daughter Essie was then unmarried but prior to the death of the testator she intermarried with Arvel Paul, and the appellant Neva Paul is their child, born prior to the death of the testator. All of said children and grandchildren were living at the death of the testator.

Appellant contends that by the terms of her grandfather's will she became the owner of a remainder in the real estate devised by item No. 4 of his will, in fee simple absolute, and that his other grandchildren have no interest whatever therein. On the other hand, appellees contend that by item No. 4 of his will the testator desired and intended to devise a life interest in said real estate to his daughter Essie Myers, now Essie Paul, and the fee thereof to her children living at the time of her death, if any should survive her, and if she left no children, then the fee should go to all the testator's grandchildren, share and share alike; that the intention is plain, lawful, and so expressed as not to violate any rule of property, and does not make a case where it is necessary to invoke rules of construction to give effect to the intention of the testator.

The question turns upon the proposition of the vesting of the title to the remainder devised by item No. 4. If it vested at the death of the testator, appellant's contention must be sustained. If the vesting is contingent and dependent upon the daughter of the testator, Essie Paul, leaving children surviving her at the time of her death, then appellant does not have an absolute, vested title to the remainder, and the ruling of the trial court should be sustained.

In view of the numerous decisions relating to the question involved, and especially the more recent decisions of our Supreme Court, we are compelled to hold that the language of item No. 4 is such as to make it necessary to resort to rules of construction to properly interpret it and give effect to the intention of the testator. The rules have been so frequently and fully stated that we shall be content with a statement of those most pertinent to the question presented. The law looks with disfavor on postponing the vesting of estates, and the intent to do so must be

1. clear and not depend upon inference or construction. It presumes that words postponing the estate relate to the beginning of the enjoyment of the remainder and not to the vesting of the estate, unless the contrary clearly appears. It favors the vesting of remainders abso-

2. lutely, rather than contingently or conditionally. Words of survivorship generally refer to the death

3. of the testator where the first taker is given a life estate and the remainder over is devised to another. *Aldred* v. *Sylvester* (1915), 184 Ind. 542, 111 N. E. 914, and cases cited; *Taylor* v. *Stephens* (1905), 165 Ind. 200, 203, 74 N. E. 980; *Myers* v. *Carney* (1908), 171 Ind. 379, 383, 86 N. E. 400; *Aspy* v. *Lewis* (1898), 152 Ind. 493, 498, 52 N. E. 756; *Hoover* v. *Hoover* (1888), 116 Ind. 498, 501, 19 N. E. 468; *Campbell* v. *Bradford* (1905), 166 Ind. 451, 453, 77 N. E. 849; *Alsman* v. *Walters* (1915), 184 Ind. 565, 106 N. E. 879, 111 N. E. 921.

Under the foregoing rules, in the light of decisions applying them to similar testamentary provisions, there is little, if any, room to doubt that the fee-simple title

4. to two-thirds of the 107 acres of real estate devised by item No. 4 of the will of Moses Myers, deceased,

vested in appellant at the time of the death of the testator, subject only to the life estate therein of Essie Paul.

The judgment is therefore reversed, with instructions to the lower court to overrule the demurrers to appellant's cross-complaint and for further proceedings not inconsistent with this opinion.

NOTE.—Reported in 112 N. E. 256. Remainders: (a) whether vested or contingent, Ann. Cas. 1917A 859; (b) character of, as affected by direction in will that children, etc., of a deceased remainderman shall take parent's share, 37 L. R. A. (N. S.) 728. See under (1, 2) 40 Cyc 1668, 1678, 1679.

---

## CHRISTIE v. WALTON.

[No. 9,087. Filed October 3, 1916. Rehearing denied December 13, 1916.]

1. PHYSICIANS AND SURGEONS. — *Malpractice.* — *Complaint.* — *Sufficiency.*—In an action against a physician for malpractice in treating a burn on plaintiff's foot, a complaint containing allegations showing the nature and extent of the injury, that the only cure was a certain treatment which the defendant unskilfully and negligently failed to employ, that he negligently used, and continued to use, an insufficient remedy and failed to observe that it was not healing the wound, and that as a result of defendant's negligence and unskilfulness plaintiff suffered great pain, etc., and the foot was amputated, sufficiently states a cause of action for improper diagnosis, from want of skill or care, for use of an improper remedy and the continuance thereof after it should have been observed to be ineffectual. p. 235.

2. APPEAL.—*Review.*—*Evidence.*—*Sufficiency.*—Where there is some competent evidence to support a verdict for plaintiff, it must be sustained on appeal, even though the weight of the evidence was favorable to the defendant. p. 237.

From Jennings Circuit Court; *Robert A. Creigmile,* Judge.

Action by Eva Walton against James M. Christie. From a judgment for plaintiff, the defendant appeals. *Affirmed.*

*Alexander G. Cavins* and *William Fitzgerald,* for appellant.

*H. C. Meloy, F. M. Thompson* and *George H. Batchelor,* for appellee.

IBACH, J.—Appellee recovered damages from appellant, a physician and surgeon, for malpractice in treating a burn on her foot. In substance, it is averred in the complaint, among other things, that the burn which she had received was so severe that eight or ten square inches of the skin on her foot was deadened and destroyed; that the bones of the ankle and instep were scorched, charred, burned and deadened; that the only cure or safe course in the treatment of such injury was the amputation of the foot, or the grafting of skin over the parts which had been burned after the removal of the deadened and charred parts of the bones; that she first went to a hospital and secured the services of Dr. George Denny, a competent physician; that then she went to the home of a relative to wait until the foot was ready for operation; that there she placed herself under the care of appellant, who undertook to treat her foot, but he failed to graft skin where the skin had been destroyed; that, as a result of such improper treatment and unskilful and negligent conduct of appellant, the foot did not heal and was not cured, and that it became useless, deformed and drawn, and subject to suppurating sores; that although she told him the advice and suggestions she had received from Dr. Denny, he told her they were unsound and that he could cure her foot without skin grafting, and without the removal of the charred bones, by the use of Scarlet Red salve, and by tricks and artifices kept Dr. Denny from visiting her; that appellant negligently and unskilfully continued to use his Scarlet Red salve, which was not adapted for use on a burn of such degree, but was a remedy for superficial burns where the bones were not deadened or large parts of skin destroyed; that he negligently failed to observe that his Scarlet Red remedy was insufficient for the purpose for

1.

which it was being used, and negligently failed to observe that the burns were not healing with new skin, and negligently and unskilfully continued to use the same, assuring appellee that her foot was healing; that he advised her to remain away from home for many months, confined to her bed, and negligently and unskilfully permitted her injured limb to remain in a drawn position for such a length of time that it was drawn upward and backward, shortening such limb, and greatly deforming her; that at all times during such treatment she suffered excruciating pain, the period of which was unnecessarily extended and prolonged by reason of the negligent and unskilful conduct of defendant, and by reason of such conduct she suffered and still suffers great pain and mental anguish, her health has become impaired, her nervous system shattered and shocked, and her foot a corrupt mass of suppurating sores and hopelessly useless for any purpose.

By a supplemental complaint it was alleged that since the filing of the complaint the foot and ankle became further diseased on account of appellant's negligent and unskilful conduct; that in order to prevent blood poison and the further impairment of her health and to save her life, it was necessary to amputate her leg above the ankle, and that such amputation would have been prevented, if defendant had properly treated the limb by removing the deadened portions of bone and grafting skin.

The complaint sufficiently states a cause of action on the theory that appellant improperly diagnosed the case, from a want of skill or care, and used an improper remedy, and continued to use it after he should have observed that it was ineffectual, and that such treatment made her condition worse. It is also averred in the complaint that the grafting of skin after the removal of the charred bones would have been a proper remedy in the case. *Longfellow* v. *Vernon* (1914), 57 Ind. App. 611, 105 N. E. 178; 30 Cyc 1570.

The next question is as to the sufficiency of the evidence to sustain the verdict. It may as well be admitted that the weight of the evidence, most of which was given by

2. physicians, was favorable to appellant, and did not tend to show that he was negligent in diagnosis or treatment, or that skin grafting would have been successful if used. However, this court is bound to sustain the verdict if there is any competent evidence on which it can rest, without considering evidence which conflicts with that which tends to sustain it. There was evidence, some of which was expert, that Scarlet Red salve was not a standard remedy for such a burn as that on appellee's foot; that if proper in such a case, the injured and charred bones should have been first removed. There was also some evidence of the same character tending to show that appellant was negligent in failing to remove the charred bones and in continuing to use the Scarlet Red salve after it was apparent that it was not a proper remedy. There being some evidence to support the verdict, the judgment of the lower court must be affirmed. Judgment affirmed.

NOTE.—Reported in 113 N. E. 750. Physicians and surgeons: (a) care and skill required, 1 Ann. Cas. 21, 306, 14 Ann. Cas. 605, 30 Cyc 1570; (b) sufficiency of complaint to charge negligence, 59 L. R. A. 209, 30 Cyc 1583.

---

# CHICAGO, SOUTH BEND AND NORTHERN INDIANA RAILWAY COMPANY ET AL. *v.* DUNNAHOO.

[No. 9,016. Filed May 12, 1916. Rehearing denied June 28, 1916. Transfer denied December 13, 1916.]

1. PLEADING.—*Complaint.—Exhibits.*—Where, in an action to recover a deposit made to indemnify defendant, the complaint alleged that plaintiff had, in another suit, obtained judgment against defendant company as garnishee, that the judgment had been paid by check and the money immediately placed in the keeping of the company by plaintiff to indemnify it against loss by reason of having satisfied such judgment, and that the purpose of the indemnity had been accomplished and payment thereof

had been refused plaintiff on his demand, such complaint was not based on the judgment, since it was shown by the averments therein to have been satisfied, nor was it necessary to set forth a copy of the check, as a recovery was not sought thereon. p. 242.

2. PLEADING.—*Cross-Complaint.—Insufficient Allegations.—Motion to Strike Out.*—Insufficiency of a cross-complaint to state a cause of action is not a ground for striking it out, since such question can only be raised and presented by a demurrer for want of facts alleged. p. 246.

3. PLEADING.—*Motion to Strike Out.*—A motion to strike out a pleading ordinarily reaches formal defects only, and where the pleading tends to state a cause of action or defense, though insufficient when tested by demurrer, it should not be stricken out, thereby barring the right to amend. p. 246.

4. PLEADING.—*Cross-Complaint Not Germane to Action.—Motion to Strike Out.*—If the facts averred in a pleading are so palpably irrelevant to the matter in controversy that the pleading could not, by amendment, be made germane thereto, it would not be error to strike it out. p. 246.

5. PLEADING.—*Sham.—Motion to Strike Out.*—It is proper to strike out a sham pleading. p. 246.

6. PARTIES.—*Joining Additional Parties.—Mode of.—Cross-Complaint.—Motion to Strike Out.*—Where, in an action to recover a deposit made to indemnify defendant company against loss or damage by reason of its having paid a judgment obtained against it as garnishee in a prior suit, defendant filed a cross-complaint against plaintiff and additional parties containing averments showing the existence of various conflicting claims to the money held as a deposit, that defendant could not safely go to trial unless the additional parties were joined, so that the proper claimant to the money involved might be determined, and that it might be compelled to litigate the several claims in separate suits unless all claimants were joined in the present action, the cross-complaint, since the facts alleged therein tended to state a cause of action against some of the defendants thereto and were germane to the subject-matter of the transaction in controversy, should have been allowed to prevent multiplicity of suits, and it was error for the trial court to strike out the pleading. pp. 246, 249.

7. JUDGMENT.—*Satisfaction.—Vacating.*—An entry of satisfaction of a judgment does not necessarily bar its collection, since the entry might be vacated for sufficient cause or otherwise be shown to be ineffectual against parties claiming to own the judgment. p. 248.

From St. Joseph Circuit Court; *Thomas W. Slick*, Special Judge.

Action by Frank H. Dunnahoo against the Chicago, South Bend and Northern Indiana Railway Company and another. From a judgment for plaintiff, the defendants appeal. *Reversed.*

*Perry L. Turner, Ira H. Church* and *Deahl & Deahl*, for appellants.

*Hubbell, McInerny & Yeagley* and *Graham & Crane*, for appellee.

,FELT, P. J.—Appellee brought this action against appellants, the Chicago, South Bend and Northern Indiana Railway Company and the Northern Indiana Railway Company, to recover money alleged to be due him. The complaint is in five paragraphs. The first is in the form of a common count for money had and received. The remaining paragraphs are substantially alike and in substance are as follows: The Northern Indiana Railway Company was a corporation duly organized under the laws of Indiana, and owned and operated street and interurban railways in Indiana. The Chicago, South Bend and Northern Indiana Railway Company is also a similar corporation engaged in like business. On February 6, 1906, in the St. Joseph Circuit Court, appellee recovered a judgment against one Dillworth, a nonresident of the State, for $3,873.41, and also against the Northern Indiana Railway Company as garnishee defendant. It was found and adjudged that the railway company owed Dillworth a certain nonnegotiable note due February 15, 1906, in a sum in excess of appellee's judgment against Dillworth, and that other garnishee defendants were sureties of the railway company on said note. The railway company was ordered to pay appellee's judgment in the sum of $3,873.41 when the aforesaid note became due and to pay the balance due on the note to the City National Bank of South Bend for the use and benefit of the owner of said note.

Between the date of the judgment and February 15,

1906, when the note became due, certain rumors and suggestions came to the Northern Indiana Railway Company that the aforesaid note might possibly have been assigned and that the Lincoln National Bank of Pittsburg, Pennsylvania, claimed some right, title or interest in the note and might make demand upon the company for payment of the same and bring suit for the collection thereof.  On February 15, 1906, said railway company, through its vice president and general manager and treasurer, informed appellee of such rumors and suggestions and that it was desirous of complying with the order of the court, but would demand indemnity and protection from any liability to the Lincoln National Bank, and likewise demanded indemnity and protection from any costs and expenses of litigation that might arise from a suit by that bank.  Whereupon appellee and said company entered into the following parol agreement, to wit:

"That in consideration of the payment of said judgment at this time, this plaintiff would indemnify and save harmless the said defendant railway company from any further or additional payment growing out of any claim of ownership or right, title or interest in said note of said Lincoln National Bank; that said plaintiff further agreed to defend all actions or suits at law which might arise upon said claim of the Lincoln National Bank; that this plaintiff further agreed to pay all expenses of any litigation which might arise from said claim of said Lincoln National Bank, and to defend any suit or suits so brought at his own expense; that for the purpose of indemnifying said Northern Indiana Railway Company against said alleged claim of said Lincoln National Bank, it was agreed that the funds and moneys paid upon said judgment should be delivered back to said defendant, Northern Indiana Railway Company and be retained by it as a protection against any claim or suit brought against said defendant by the said Lincoln National Bank, and growing out of said note, which said money, so long as it remained in the hands of said defendant railway company, was to bear interest in favor of this plaintiff at the rate of six per cent per annum, and which said money and funds were to be delivered over to this plaintiff, together with interest thereon, upon the termination or settlement of any suit to be brought by the said Lincoln National Bank.''

In compliance with said agreement, on February 15, 1906, the railway company issued its check (No. 5624) in the amount of $3,873.41, drawn on the Citizens National Bank of South Bend, Indiana, in favor of the clerk of the St. Joseph Circuit Court, which check was delivered and accepted by the clerk in payment of said judgment and afterwards endorsed by him to appellee, who immediately endorsed and delivered it back to the Northern Indiana Railway Company to be held as indemnity as above stated. Appellee then released the judgment against said company upon the record. Thereafter the Lincoln National Bank brought suit in the St. Joseph Circuit Court against the Northern Indiana Railway Company for the collection of said note. The claim was litigated, an appeal taken, and thereafter again litigated in said circuit court. On April 2, 1913, the Lincoln National Bank abandoned its alleged claim to said note and dismissed its suit against said company, and the suit finally ended without loss, expense or damage to said company. Pursuant to his agreement, appellee, with the knowledge and consent of said company, employed attorneys to defend the suit, and paid all expenses of such litigation; he and the attorneys so employed consulted frequently with the officers and agents of the Chicago, South Bend and Northern Indiana Railway Company, which company succeeded to the rights, properties, debts and liabilities of the Northern Indiana Railway Company. On January 26, 1907, appellant, Chicago, South Bend and Northern Indiana Railway Company, was incorporated under the laws of this state for street railway purposes and particularly for the purpose of taking over all the stock, assets and property, and succeeding to all the rights, duties and liabilities of the Northern Indiana Railway Company.

At the time of taking over such properties the suit of the Lincoln National Bank against the Northern Indiana Railway Company was pending in the St. Joseph Circuit Court. It is alleged that appellee fully performed his said agreement with the railway company and made demand for payment of the money due him before instituting this suit, and payment was refused. Separate demurrers by each of the appellants to each paragraph of the complaint were overruled. Each of the appellants answered by general denial. The Chicago, South Bend and Northern Indiana Railway Company also filed four paragraphs of special answers, the substance of which is that appellee was not the real party in interest; that prior to the beginning of the suit he had sold, assigned and transferred his alleged claim and demand sued upon to Calvert H. DeFrees, Edward A. Morse and Gabriel R. Summers. The Chicago, South Bend and Northern Indiana Railway Company also filed a cross-complaint and sought to bring in new parties. Appellee moved to strike out the cross-complaint and his motion was sustained. The appellants have assigned separate errors and each has filed a separate brief.

The only error assigned and not waived by the Northern Indiana Railway Company is the overruling of its demurrer to each paragraph of the complaint. The only error assigned and not waived by the Chicago, South Bend and Northern Indiana Railway Company is the striking out of its cross-complaint. The Northern Indiana Railway Company presents and urges two points to sustain its contention that the court erred in overruling its demurrer to each paragraph of the complaint: (1) Each paragraph, except the first, shows that the judgment referred to was not paid. The action, if any, should have been upon the judgment. (2) Neither paragraph of plaintiff's complaint sets forth a copy of the check referred to in the complaint. The first paragraph is clearly for money had and received. The other paragraphs allege the facts and circumstances under which the money was received by the Northern Indiana Railway Company and by which the Chicago, South Bend and Northern Indiana Railway Company became liable to appellee therefor. Neither paragraph is based upon the judgment, but each shows that the judgment had been paid and satisfied and the money immediately placed in the keeping of the Railway Company as an indemnity; that the purpose of such indemnity had been accomplished and appellee was entitled to the money, had demanded the same, and payment had been refused. Each of the paragraphs of complaint is good as against both the appellants for the recovery of the money placed in the keeping of the Northern Indiana Railway Company under the conditions alleged. Neither paragraph seeks to recover on the check and there was no occasion for setting forth a copy of it with the complaint. The court did not err in overruling the demurrer to the complaint

The cross-complaint is very long, goes into the history of the original suit in garnishment, the sale and transfer of the property of the Northern Indiana Railway Company, and the arrangement and conditions under which the transfer was accomplished. It is against appellee and Northern Indiana Railway Company and the following additional parties, viz.: William L. Taylor, Arthur Kennedy, The Federal Union Surety Company, The Western Indemnity Company, the Citizens National Bank of South Bend, Calvert H. DeFrees, Charles Dietrich, Gabriel R. Summers, Edward A. Morse, Samuel T. Murdock, Charles M. Murdock and Mary Murdock Cory. The pleading shows that Arthur Kennedy, party of the first part, and Charles F. Dietrich and James Murdock entered into the original contract by which the Northern Indiana Railway Company sold and transferred its property, and the parties to the contract other than James Murdock, who has since deceased, are made parties to the cross-complaint because of their relation to that transaction. The descendants of James Mur-

dock are likewise made parties for the same reason. A
bond was given to guarantee the purchasers against liens
and claims not assumed by the purchasers and the surety
companies are made parties to determine their liability, if
any, should appellee's claim be adjudged valid. Certain
of the defendants are alleged to have indemnified the
surety company. Others are alleged to have been stockholders in the selling company and to have wrongfully distributed to themselves large sums of the purchase money
that should have been held for the payment of unsatisfied
claims. It is also averred that at the time of the purchase
by said railway company the records were examined and
appellee's judgment against the Northern Indiana Railway
Company was found to be duly satisfied upon the record
and the transfer of the property was thereafter made in
reliance thereon and in the belief that the same was a full
satisfaction of any claim due appellee and the purchasers had
no knowledge or notice to the contrary. The cross-complaint
also repeats the averment relating to the claim and suit of
the Lincoln National Bank and the arrangement of appellee to indemnify the Northern Indiana Railway Company
against loss on account thereof. It is also averred that
after appellee filed this suit Calvert H. DeFrees, Edward
A. Morse and Gabriel R. Summers, each served upon cross-
complainant written notices to the effect that appellee, in
1913, had duly assigned to each of said parties the judgment previously rendered in his favor for $3,873.41; that
the judgment was unpaid and they intended to enforce
collection thereof against cross-complainant; that the Citizens National Bank of South Bend also notified cross-
complainant that it was the owner of the note upon which
said judgment in garnishment was rendered against the
Northern Indiana Railway Company and intended to enforce
its collection. It is also averred that said Chicago, South
Bend and Northern Indiana Railway Company cannot
safely go to trial upon the complaint of appellee, which

proceeds upon the theory that said former judgment had been paid and satisfied, without the hazard of being liable to said Morse, Summers and DeFrees, each of whom claims to be the equitable owner of said judgment and that the same has not been paid or discharged; that the trial between appellee and cross-complainant of the issues joined on the complaint cannot determine the question whether as between appellee and said alleged assignees of the judgment, it was in fact discharged and likewise as to the claim of the Citizens National Bank; that cross-complainant, unless permitted to adjudicate all said claims and demands in this suit, will be compelled to do so in separate suits if the claimants persist in their threats and demands. Cross-complainant also avers facts on which it denies the validity of some of said claims and asks that they be tried and adjudicated; also that as to some of the claims it is not advised as to whether appellee or the claimants are right in their contentions; that ''to avoid circuity of actions and to prevent multiplicity of suits and to settle for once and all the complex questions involved * * * a court of equity should assume jurisdiction and require all of said cross-defendants to be made parties hereto * * * and be required to appear and to plead in this cause'' their several claims and demands. The pleading concludes with a detailed statement of the relief prayed against the several parties asked to be made defendants thereto.

Appellant insists that the court erred in sustaining the motion to strike out the cross-complaint. Appellee contends that the matter set up in such pleading is not germane to the questions at issue on his complaint; that the facts averred, which are in any way related to the subject-matter of the transactions in issue were also in issue on the complaint and answers, and the ruling of the court in striking out the pleading, if wrong, ·was a harmless error for which the judgment should not be reversed.

The correctness of the ruling of the trial court in sus-

taining the motion to strike out the cross-complaint does
not depend upon the sufficiency of the pleading to state
    a cause of action against the defendants named
2.  therein, since that question can only be raised and
    duly presented by a demurrer for insufficiency of the
facts alleged. *Moorhouse* v. *Kunkalman* (1911), 177 Ind.
471, 481, 96 N. E. 600; *Toledo, etc., Traction Co.* v. *Toledo,
etc., R. Co.* (1908), 171 Ind. 213, 223, 86 N. E. 54; *Guthrie*
v. *Howland* (1904), 164 Ind. 214, 221, 73 N. E. 259. A
    motion to strike out a pleading ordinarily reaches
3.  formal defects only. If the averments tend to state
    a cause of action or a defense, though the pleading
may be insufficient in substance when duly tested by
demurrer, it should not be stricken out; for the party has
the right to amend after a demurrer is sustained, and this
right is cut off when the pleading is struck out.

If, however, the facts averred in a pleading are so palpably irrelevant to the matter in controversy that the plead-
    ing could not, by amendment, be made germane to
4.  the controversy it would not be error to strike it
    out; likewise where it clearly appears that the
5.  pleading against which the motion is directed is a
    sham pleading. *Guthrie* v. *Howland, supra*, p. 225;
*Hart* v. *Scott* (1907), 168 Ind. 530, 532, 81 N. E. 481;
*Chicago, etc., R. Co.* v. *Summers* (1887), 113 Ind. 10, 16,
14 N. E. 733, 3 Am. St. 616; *Clark* v. *Jeffersonville, etc.,
R. Co.* (1873), 44 Ind. 248, 263; *McCoy* v. *Stockman* (1896),
146 Ind. 668, 46 N. E. 21.

While not passing on the sufficiency of the cross-complaint, we think the facts averred tend to state a cause of
action against some of the defendants thereto and are ger-
    mane to the subject-matter of the transaction in con-
6.  troversy. The affirmative answers to the complaint
    aver that appellee is not the real party in interest,
and that he had assigned and transferred his claim against
the railway company before beginning this suit. The find-

ings and the judgment settle the question adversely to appellants and in favor of appellee, but the question is not determined as to persons not parties to the suit.

The assignment of the judgment by appellee to other parties, long after he had placed upon the record a satisfaction thereof, is open to the inference that, notwithstanding such satisfaction, he still claimed to own or have some assignable interest in the judgment. The judgment rendered in this suit does not bar such assignees from an effort to enforce the collection of the judgment. The cross-complaint tendered this issue against such assignees and also tendered other alleged issues. Some of them may not be germane to the subject of the legal controversy growing out of appellee's demand, but the fact remains that appellee's demand in this suit is based upon the fact that he satisfied and released a valid judgment upon receipt of the amount due thereon and thereupon placed the money in the keeping of the judgment defendant until he met certain conditions which in this suit he claims to have satisfied, and is therefore entitled to his money, not on the original judgment, but from the fact that the party who received it from him, now wrongfully refuses to pay it to him. The money due represents the same original claim. If in fact he had sold and transferred the judgment, and in that way obtained payment of his original claim, he is not in equity entitled to receive it again. If that judgment may be enforced against appellants or if there is reasonable ground to assert that they may be called upon to resist its collection as alleged in the cross-complaint, then the controversy should have been ended in this suit, in all its phases, as to all possible parties to the transaction or controversy, to avoid a multiplicity of suits and to reach and satisfy the ends of justice as to all who assert, or are likely to claim, some interest in the subject-matter of the transactions involved in the suit.

It is the policy of the law to avoid multiplicity of suits.

The relief demanded by the cross-complaint goes beyond
a defense to appellee's claim and seeks affirmative relief
against persons not parties to the original suit. The facts
averred at least tend to state a cause of action growing
out of the transactions involved which should have been
adjudicated in this suit. The motion should have been
overruled, the parties should have been brought in to answer
the cross-complaint or take steps to test its sufficiency as
seemed advisable to them. This practice in such instances
is fully sustained by the decisions of our Supreme Court.
Many subsidiary questions are suggested in the briefs which,
in view of the conclusion reached, need not be considered.
The following decisions in addition to those already cited
seem decisive of such questions and also support the conclusion that the trial court erred in sustaining the motion
to strike out the cross-complaint of appellant, Chicago,
South Bend and Northern Indiana Railway Company.
Pomeroy, Code Remedies (4th ed.) 845-847; *Ellison* v.
*Branstrator* (1909), 45 Ind. App. 307, 311, 88 N. E. 963,
89 N. E. 513; *Burk* v. *Taylor* (1885), 103 Ind. 399, 3 N.
E. 129; *Fletcher* v. *Crist* (1894), 139 Ind. 121, 124, 38 N.
E. 472; *Excelsior Clay Works* v. *DeCamp* (1906), 40 Ind.
App. 26, 37, 80 N. E. 981 and cases cited; *Standley* v. *North-
western, etc., Ins. Co.* (1884), 95 Ind. 254, 260; *Todd* v. *Ogle-
bay* (1901), 158 Ind. 595, 601, 64 N. E. 32; *Cambria Iron
Co.* v. *Union Trust Co.* (1899), 154 Ind. 291, 296, 55 N. E.
745, 56 N. E. 665, 48 L. R. A. 41; *Hunter* v. *First Nat.
Bank* (1908), 172 Ind. 62, 67, 87 N. E. 734; *Larue* v. *Ameri-
can, etc., Engine Co.* (1911), 176 Ind. 609, 613, 96 N. E. 772;
*Chapman* v. *Lambert* (1911), 176 Ind. 461, 467, 468, 96 N. E.
459; 20 Ency. Pl. & Pr. 988; 14 Ency. Pl. & Pr. 92.

The entry of satisfaction of the judgment upon the
record by appellee would not necessarily bar its collection.

7. The entry might be vacated for sufficient cause or
   otherwise be shown to be ineffectual against the
   parties who claimed to own the judgment. At least

there could be an issue formed to determine the validity of
the satisfaction and the ownership of the judgment.  23
Cyc 1500; *Dunning* v. *Galloway* (1874), 47 Ind. 182;
*Wheeler* v. *Emmeluth* (1890), 121 N. Y. 241, 24 N. E.
285; *Read's Appeal* (1889), 126 Pa. St. 415, 17 Atl. 621.

In the case at bar the ruling cannot be held to be harmless on the ground that this court can say, on the record
presented, that a correct result was reached.   While
6.  we might so declare as to the parties who were before
the court, we cannot say as a matter of law that the
original judgment satisfied upon the record by appellee,
was in fact paid, as against the claims to the contrary of
the alleged assignees, as to whom there has been no adjudication of that question.  On this point appellees rely
especially upon the decisions in *Harris* v. *Randolph County
Bank* (1901), 157 Ind. 120, 129, 60 N. E. 1025, and *Horace
F. Wood Transfer Co.* v. *Shelton* (1913), 180 Ind. 273, 277,
101 N. E. 718.  The cases do not deal with persons not
parties to the suit, who are asserting claims and have served
notice thereof as in the case at bar.  The questions there
decided are not identical with the one presented by striking out the cross-complaint in this case.  Giving full credit
to the cases cited, they do not sustain appellee's contention.
To avoid multiplicity of suits and adjudicate all claims
growing out of the transactions involved in this suit, the
alleged assignees of the judgment were necessary parties
to a full determination of all phases of the controversy.
It may be unfortunate to so hold, but appellee has himself
made possible the situation presented, first, by his attempted
assignment of the judgment he had previously satisfied and,
secondly, by moving to strike out the cross-complaint instead
of meeting any issue properly presented by it and seeing
that all conflicting claims germane to the transactions
involved in the suit were tried and adjudicated.

The judgment is therefore reversed, with instructions

to overrule the motion to strike out the cross-complaint and for further proceedings not inconsistent with this opinion.

Ibach, C. J., Caldwell, Moran, Hottel and McNutt, JJ., concur.

Note.—Reported in 112 N. E. 552. See under (2-4) 31 Cyc 619-625; (5) 113 Am. St. 639; 31 Cyc 625. (6) New parties, right to bring in by cross-bill, 20 Ann. Cas. 1151; 16 Cyc 200; (7) 23 Cyc 1500.

---

# DOAK-RIDDLE-HAMILTON COMPANY v. RAABE.

### [No. 9,146. Filed December 14, 1916.]

1. INSURANCE.—*Agent.—Contract.—Unpaid Premiums.—Liability of Agent.*—Under a contract between an insurance company and its agent whereby he was required to collect first premiums on applications taken by him and was prohibited from extending the time for the payment thereof, the agent is not chargeable with premiums unpaid by applicants on insurance written by him, in the absence of any provision in the contract evidencing an intention to make him liable therefor. pp. 254, 255.

2. APPEAL. — *Presumptions. — Master Commissioner's Findings.— Adoption by Court.*—In an action by an insurance company against its agent to recover money alleged to be due under an agency contract, the court on appeal cannot presume, even though certain provisions of the contract made it defendant's duty to collect premiums on insurance written by him, that the agent collected the premiums in controversy, where the master commissioner's report adopted by the court found that the agent did not collect such premiums. p. 254.

3. INSURANCE.—*Contract with Agent.—Commissions.—Accounting for Premiums.—Master's Report.—Construction.*—Where in an action by an insurance company against an agent to recover money alleged to be due under an agency contract, a master commissioner found certain "commissions due or allowed defendant from plaintiff," such commissions being on uncollected premiums, the word "or" was used, not in its alternative sense, but as a connective, and the word "allowed" as meaning "to concede, consent to, or to grant," so that the report of the master could be construed as meaning that the company consented to allow such commissions to defendant, though unpaid, notwithstanding a provision in the contract that commissions should be payable only on premiums collected in cash on policies issued on applications procured by the agent and accounted for by him. p. 255.

4. APPEAL.—*Review.—Master Commissioner's Report.—Evidence*

*Not in Record.—Presumption.*—Where the evidence is not in the record, the master commissioner's report of the facts, having been adopted by trial court, must be presumed to be correct. p. 256.

5. APPEAL.—*Master Commissioner's Report.—Conclusions.*— Mere conclusions in the report of a master commissioner, in a case referred to him for a finding of facts, must be excluded. p. 256.

6. APPEAL.—*Presumptions.—Action of Trial Court.*—Presumptions should be indulged in favor of the action of the trial court until it is made to appear that the court erred therein. p. 257.

From Vigo Superior Court; *John E. Cox*, Judge.

Action by the Doak-Riddle-Hamilton Company against Herman Raabe. From a judgment in part for plaintiff, the plaintiff appeals. *Affirmed.*

*Beasley, Douthitt, Crawford & Beasley,* for appellant.

CALDWELL, J.—Appellant, an Indiana insurance company, brought this action against appellee, who was formerly its agent, to recover on account of certain expense money advanced to appellee and certain insurance premiums alleged to have been collected by him and not accounted for. The cause having been placed at issue was referred to a master commissioner, appointed under the provisions of §1677 Burns 1914, §1397 R. S. 1881 "to hear the evidence, ascertain the facts and report his findings." The court adopted the report as made, except specification No. 8 thereof, and on the report as adopted found for appellant in the sum of $69.03, with interest in the sum of $12.42 and rendered judgment for $81.45, the aggregate. Appellant presents, among other questions, that the amount of the recovery is too small.

Specification No. 8 of the report, rejected by the court as aforesaid, was to the effect that a named sum was due appellant in cash, if the court should place a certain construction on the contract of employment executed by the parties February 8, 1910. A proper construction of the contract determines the entire controversy. It is made a part of the master's report as adopted by the court.

The following abstract of the contract includes the substance of its provisions material to the controversy: It specifies that the agent's services should commence February 8, 1910, and that either party might terminate the contract by giving seven days' notice to the other in writing, and that if so terminated, the power of the agent to collect and receive premiums should cease; that if the contract should be terminated by either party for any cause, the compensation which should then have been paid to the agent, together with the amount then due him under the contract, should be in full settlement of all demands against the company in favor of the agent, except as otherwise provided by the contract. The company agreed to advance to appellee $18 per week for living expenses, commissions as earned to be applied in payment thereof. In the event of the cancellation of the contract by either party, the agent agreed to pay to the company any balance of such advancements remaining unpaid. The agent bound himself diligently to canvass the territory assigned to him for applications for life, accident and health insurance, to collect and account for premiums, and to forward applications and report collections to the company. The contract prohibited the agent from extending the time for the payment of premiums and from accepting payment of them other than in current funds, and from receiving any money on the company's account, except on policies and receipts sent to him for collection. There is a provision that in the life department "during the continuance of this contract, the company will pay on business transacted by and through the agent, as full compensation for all services," certain specified graduated per cents. estimated on the amounts of the premiums in the first year of insurance, and in the accident department certain other graduated per cent's estimated on premiums "in the first year of insurance reported and paid to the agent during the continuance of the contract," the stipulated per cent. of commissions in each case depending on the character of the policy. It is stipulated that "commissions shall be payable only on premiums collected in cash on policies issued on applications procured by the agent and accounted for by him," and also a provision that "no collection fee shall be charged by the company for the collection of premiums subject to commission under this contract"; also a provision that in case the company should return to the insured a premium upon which the agent had been paid a commission, he should return to the company the amount of such commission.

The material part of the report of the master as adopted by the court is to the following effect: Appellee's services as agent commenced February 8, 1910, and terminated in April, 1911, the cause and circumstances of the termination not being reported. Appellant advanced to appellee sums totalling $423. Facts are reported rendering appellee liable for $8.61 on account of policies cancelled and premiums returned. Appellee collected and paid to appellant on applications written by him premiums amounting to $1,241. His commission on such premiums amounted to $291.78, which commissions he did not reserve but paid to appellant. He wrote other applications on which premiums subject to commission amounted to $215.07. His commission thereon amounted to $70.80. The premiums last named, however, including the commissions thereon, have not been paid to either appellant or appellee, but are due from applicants and unpaid. Respecting the commissions last named, the report of the master is that they are commissions "due or allowed to defendant from plaintiff."

Specification No. 9 of the report is in substance that if the contract should be construed that, by the terms thereof, appellee is not chargeable with uncollected premiums but that such premiums are the property of appellant, then the balance due appellant is $69.03. Specification No. 8 rejected by the court as aforesaid is, in substance, that if appellee is chargeable with such premiums, the balance due is $284.10.

It will be observed that if appellee be charged with the $423 advanced to him, and with the $8.61 due from him on account of premiums returned, and if he be credited with commissions in the sum of $291.78 and also $70.80, the balance due from him is the amount of the judgment exclusive of interest. It is, therefore, apparent that the court construed the contract as suggested by specification No. 9 of the report.

Appellant contends that appellee should be charged also with such uncollected premiums as suggested by specification No. 8, and that as a consequence there is due from him $284.10, exclusive of interest; and that, if he should not be charged with such premiums, he should not be credited with commission thereon, and that on such hypothesis there is due from him $139.83, exclusive of interest.

Two questions then are presented: first, Should appellee be charged with such uncollected premium? and, secondly, if not, Should he be credited with $70.80 commission thereon?

By the terms of the contract, it was appellee's duty, at least primarily, to collect first premiums on applications taken by him, and other premiums also when policies or receipts were forwarded to him for that purpose. We find nothing in the contract, however, evidencing an intention to charge him with the amounts of the premiums which he in fact had not collected. It is urged that in view of certain provisions of the contract making it appellee's duty to collect premiums we should presume that he did collect the premiums involved in this transaction amounting to $215.07. We cannot indulge such presumption in the face of the master's report adopted by the court, to the effect that appellee did not collect the premiums composing such item, but that they were due from applicants and unpaid. The record

does not convince us that the court erred in refusing
1. to charge appellee with such item. It is well to
observe that in its relation to premiums the action is
predicated on the theory that appellee collected and failed
to account for certain premiums, rather than on alleged
omission of duty, whereby appellant was damaged.

We proceed to determine whether the court erred in
crediting appellee with the commission item of $70.80.
Commissions on the item of $215.07 of uncollected
3. premiums constitute this item. We are not advised
by what arrangement or omission such premiums
remained uncollected. It sufficiently appears that they were
premiums on policies issued by the company and based on
applications written by appellee. The contract between
appellant and appellee, while not expressly so stipulating,
apparently contemplated that applicants for insurance
should pay first premiums in cash. As we have indicated,
the contract prohibited the agent from extending the time
of the payment of premiums, and from receiving payment
thereof otherwise than in current funds. No such inhibition, however, was placed on the company. It, in any case,
might have extended credit to any applicant, or it might
have taken a promissory note to represent any unpaid
premium. As we have said, there was a stipulation in the
contract that the company should not charge a fee for collecting premiums which were subject to commission under
the contract. Such provision contemplated that under some
circumstances, the company might collect premiums on
which the agent was entitled to commission. Such provision is therefore in harmony with a supposition that under
some circumstances the company might extend the time for
the payment of such premiums, and thereafter collect them.
It is true that there was another provision in the contract
that commissions should be payable only on premiums collected in cash on policies issued on applications procured
by the agent and accounted for by him. Such provision,

however, does not necessarily mean that the agent should
be paid commission only on premiums collected by him in
cash, since such other provision recognized his right to commission in some cases on premiums collected by the company. The provision that commission should be payable
only on premiums collected in cash, like any other provision of an ordinary written contract, was subject to a
subsequent parol modification on sufficient consideration.
There are indications of such a modification in the master's
report as adopted by the court, in that thereby the master
reported as a fact that the item of $70.80 was constituted
of "commissions due or allowed defendant from plaintiff."
While the word "or" is frequently used in an alternative
sense, in our judgment it is used here to connect two words
expressing the same idea. It is frequently used in such a
sense also. 29 Cyc 1502. Webster's International Dictionary. The word "allow" includes the following meanings:
"To concede," "consent to," "to grant," etc. 2 C. J.
1154. The report of the master then may very properly be
construed to mean that the appellant conceded or granted
such commissions to appellee, or consented to them as a
credit in appellee's favor, or that they were commissions
which appellant had allowed to appellee.

The evidence is not before us. The master by the terms
of the order appointing him was not required to, and did
not, report it to the trial court. The order was that
4. the master should "hear the evidence, ascertain the
facts, and report his findings." In the absence of
the evidence, the master's report of the facts having been
adopted by the court must be presumed to be correct.
*Stanton* v. *State, ex rel.* (1882), 82 Ind. 463; *Bremmerman*
v. *Jennings* (1885), 101 Ind. 253; *McKinney* v. *Pierce*
(1854), 5 Ind. 422; *Midland R. Co.* v. *Trissal* (1902), 30
Ind. App. 77, 65 N. E. 543. The master's report,
5. excluding therefrom mere conclusions, as we are required to do (*Smith* v. *Harris* [1893], 135 Ind. 621,

35 N. E. 984) includes the facts respecting the amount of the advancements made by appellant to appellee, and the amount with which the latter should be charged on account of commissions received on premiums subsequently returned to insured persons, and respecting the amount of premiums collected by appellee and paid to appellant, and the former's commission thereon, and also the facts respecting uncollected premiums, and that appellant had allowed appellee commissions thereon in the sum of $70.80. It is true that the report is not in all respects as full and specific as might be desired, but it is not attacked on such grounds. The court adopted it as sufficient and entered judgment accordingly. Presumptions should be indulged in favor of the action of the trial court until it is made to appear that the court erred therein. Appellant does not convince us that error was committed. Judgment affirmed.

Note.—Reported in 114 N. E. 415. Insurance, liability of agent to company for failure to collect premiums, Ann. Cas. 1916D 651. See under (3) 2 Cyc 134; 2 C. J. 1154; 29 Cyc 1502; (4) 3 Cyc 309.

---

CROUCH ET AL. v. FAHL ET AL.

[No. 9,038. Filed October 25, 1916. Rehearing denied December 14, 1916.]

1. SALES.—*Contracts.*—*Breach of Warranty.*—*Remedies.*—*Return of Property.*—A written contract of warranty of a stallion, providing that in case of a breach thereof the vendor will take the stallion back and that the buyer will accept another stallion of equal value and return the former to the seller in as sound condition as at the time of delivery, provides an exclusive remedy for a breach of the warranty, which is available to the purchaser, under the contract, only in case he returns or offers to return the stallion. pp. 263, 265.

2. SALES.—*Contracts.*—*Breach of Warranty.*—*Remedies.*—*Exclusive Remedy.*—*Return of Property.*—Where a warranty confers on the purchaser of personal property the mere right or privilege of returning the property in case it does not comply with the

warranty and making settlement on specified terms, but does not require him to do so to avail himself of a breach, it is the general rule that such stipulation confers merely an optional or cumulative remedy, so that the purchaser may retain the property and maintain an action for damages based on the breach of the warranty; but where the stipulation for the return of the property, if not as warranted, is mandatory, the remedy afforded thereby is exclusive. p. 264.

3.  SALES.— *Contracts.— Warranty.— Remedy for Breach.— Extension.*—Where a contract of warranty provided that the purchaser should return the property before a specified date if found not to be as warranted, a subsequent agreement between the parties that the purchaser should try the property another year extended the warranty for that length of time and required a return of the property at the expiration thereof to make available an action for a breach of the warranty; and, in the absence of proof that the buyer returned or offered to return the property within the time stipulated, the evidence is insufficient to sustain a verdict in favor of the purchaser for damages for breach of the warranty. p. 266.

4.  CHATTEL MORTGAGES.—*Remedies of Mortgagee.—Replevin.—Sale of Property.—Application of Proceeds.*—Where a buyer of personal property gives notes for the purchase price secured by a chattel mortgage authorizing the mortgagee to take possession on default, the mortgagee may, upon failure to pay the notes, maintain an action in replevin to regain possession of the mortgaged chattel and, having thus acquired possession, could cause the property to be sold, purchase the same at the sale, and apply the proceeds to the discharge of the notes. p. 267.

5.  BANKRUPTCY.—*Sale of Mortgaged Property.—Purchase by Mortgagor.—Lien of Mortgages.*—Where a buyer of personal property secured the purchase price by a chattel mortgage authorizing the mortgagee to take possession in case of default, and, upon the mortgagor becoming bankrupt, the mortgaged property was scheduled as a part of his assets, the purchase by the mortgagor of the mortgaged chattel at the sale in bankruptcy did not defeat the mortgagee's right to recover the property, since the sale could only be made subject to the lien of the mortgage. p. 267.

6.  BANKRUPTCY.—*Action Against Bankrupt.—Parties.—Substitution of Trustee.*—Where, in an action in replevin, the defendant, a bankrupt, counterclaimed for a breach of warranty originating prior to his bankruptcy, it was proper for the trial court to substitute defendant's trustee in bankruptcy as a party to prosecute such claim, since it passed to the trustee by reason of the bankruptcy proceedings and he was, therefore, the real party in interest. p. 268.

From Huntington Circuit Court; *Samuel E. Cook*, Judge.

Action by Jeptha Crouch and others against George S. Fahl and others. From a judgment for defendants, the plaintiffs appeal. *Reversed.*

*Wilson & Quinn* and *Branyan & Branyan*, for appellants. *Fred H. Bowers, Milo N. Feightner, H. B. Spencer* and *J. W. Moffett*, for appellees.

CALDWELL, C. J.—The following undisputed facts are disclosed by the record: On January 14, 1911, appellants sold and delivered to appellee George S. Fahl a certain stallion at an agreed price of $2,500, for which amount Fahl executed his two promissory notes, each in the sum of $1,250, payable with six per cent. interest January 14, 1912, and January 14, 1913, respectively. To secure the payment of the notes Fahl executed a chattel mortgage on the horse. The mortgage was duly recorded. As a part of the transaction of sale, appellants executed to Fahl a certain written guaranty or warranty hereinafter set out, respecting the condition and qualities of the stallion. In payment of a part of the purchase price, Fahl, at the time of the purchase, sold and delivered to appellants a certain other stallion owned by him at an agreed price of $1,100, which amount was credited on the notes above mentioned, $550 on each of them. Appellee Fahl made the following additional payments on the note first maturing: April 9, 1912, $500; August 26, 1912, $50; October 9, 1912, $50. No additional payments were made on the other note.

On April 14, 1914, appellants commenced this action against Fahl to recover possession of the stallion sold to him. The complaint is in the ordinary form of replevin. A writ was issued on affidavit duly made, under which the sheriff took possession of the horse. Fahl having failed to execute an undertaking in time and manner as specified by the statute (§1334 Burns 1914, §1270 R. S. 1881), and appellants having executed such an undertaking, the stallion was delivered into their possession. Proceeding under certain provisions of the chattel mortgage above mentioned, appellants subsequently caused the stallion to be sold at public auction on notice given, they becoming the purchasers, on a bid of $800, which sum was credited on the notes above mentioned. Appellee Fahl, in due course, answered the action by four paragraphs: first, general denial; second, payment of the notes before suit brought; third, failure of consideration as to the notes and mortgage, in that the stallion was sold and recommended as a breeder, and that on a trial it proved worthless as such; fourth, that appellants' claim to the stallion is based only on the chattel mortgage; that in November, 1913, Fahl filed his petition in bankruptcy, and was subsequently adjudged a bankrupt; that in the proceeding he scheduled the stallion as part of his property, and listed appellants as creditors by reason of said notes; that appellee Charles F. Keefer was duly chosen as trustee in bankruptcy, and as such took possession of the stallion, and by virtue of an order of the bankruptcy court, and pursuant to notice given, sold him at public auction, Fahl becoming the purchaser at $125, which amount he paid by a credit on his exemption of $600 as a resident householder; that appellants, with notice and knowledge of the facts, permitted Fahl to buy the horse, without asserting any right to him, and that they relied on their claim for the balance due on the notes, alleged to have been filed with the referee in bankruptcy.

Fahl filed also two paragraphs of counterclaim: First, that he purchased the stallion on a written guaranty that he was a satisfactory, sure breeder, if properly cared for and kept in healthy condition. The guaranty which is made a part of each paragraph of counterclaim is as follows:

"We have this day sold the imported percheron stallion Hermann No. (73776) 70235, to George S. Fahl of Huntington, Indiana, and we guarantee the said stallion to be a satisfactory, sure breeder, provided the said stallion keeps in as sound and healthy condition as he now is and is properly exercised. If the said stallion should fail to be a satisfactory, sure breeder with the above treatment, we agree to take the said stallion back, and the said George S. Fahl agrees to accept another percheron stallion of equal value in its place, the said stallion Hermann No. (73776) 70235 to be returned to us at Lafayette, Indiana, in as sound and healthy condition as he now is, by April 1, 1912. If the above named stallion should become disabled before he is delivered, the said George S. Fahl agrees to accept another imported percheron stallion of equal value in his place.''

(Signed) J. Crouch & Son.''

"Accepted: George S. Fahl.

Facts are pleaded to the effect that the stallion, although in sound and healthy condition and properly cared for, proved to be practically worthless as a breeder during the season of 1911; that Fahl thereupon informed appellant of the facts, whereupon, at appellants' request, he kept the stallion another season; that during such season, although surrounded by proper conditions, no improvement was shown; that had the stallion been as represented, he would have been worth the purchase price, but that under the circumstances he was valueless as a breeder, and that Fahl had so informed the appellants.

There are general averments that said appellee performed all the terms and conditions of the contract by him to be performed, and that he is willing to return the horse to appellants upon a return by them of the consideration paid and compliance by them with the contract of purchase. There are averments that Fahl has paid the purchase price in full and other averments of special damages based on labor and expense in caring for the horse. '

The second paragraph of counterclaim is substantially the same as the first, containing an additional specific averment, however, to the effect that after Fahl had ascertained that the horse had proved to be worthless as a breeder during the season of 1912, he informed appellants of the fact, and asked them to take the horse back, and give him another one of equal value, the stallion being at the time in a sound and healthy condition, but that appellants failed and refused to do so. Each paragraph of counterclaim prays judgment for $5,000.

Subsequently, the court on a verified showing made by Fahl that Keefer had been his trustee in bankruptcy since January, 1914, sustained the former's motion that the latter be substituted to prosecute the cause of action presented by the counterclaims, and entered an order substituting Keefer, trustee, in place of Fahl, to prosecute the action set up by way of counterclaim. Appellants reserved an exception to the order of substitution, and subsequently filed an answer of general denial to the counterclaim. The sufficiency of the pleadings was not challenged in the trial court.

The verdict was in favor of Fahl and Keefer on the issues formed on the complaint. On the issues joined on the counterclaim, the jury returned a verdict for $1,000 in favor of Fahl for the use of Keefer as trustee. Judgment was rendered on the verdict.

The sufficiency of the evidence is challenged. In addition to the facts set out in the early part of this opinion, evidence was introduced in support of the various defenses and counterclaims pleaded, in substance as follows: The horse, although properly handled, failed materially as a breeder during the season of 1911. On March 25, 1912, Fahl called on appellants at Lafayette, informed them specifically respecting the failure of the horse, and expressed his dissatisfaction. Appellants reminded Fahl that the horse had been imported recently before his purchase by Fahl, and stated that they frequently had trouble with horses the first season after they were imported, and suggested that Fahl try the horse another year, and give him plenty of exercise. Fahl agreed to do so, and said nothing about appellants taking the horse back.   The horse's record in 1912 was not so good as in 1911.   In August or September, 1913, Fahl again called on appellants and expressed his dissatisfaction with the horse, whereupon appellants offered to sell the horse on Fahl's account, and pay him the surplus, if any, over what was unpaid on the notes. There was no evidence that Fahl at any time tendered or offered to return the horse to appellants, or that they offered another in exchange.   There was evidence that the horse would have been worth the selling price of $2,500 had it been as warranted, but that he was in fact valueless as a breeder.

The only evidence respecting the proceeding in bankruptcy consisted of certain testimony by Fahl as a witness, in substance, that he filed his petition in bankruptcy in December, 1913, and that he was subsequently adjudged a bankrupt, Keefer being trustee; that Fahl scheduled the horse as a part of his property, and that on March 25, 1914, he bought the horse at bankruptcy sale for $125, and made payment by credit on his exemption as a resident householder.   To determine the sufficiency of the evidence necessitates a construction of the written guaranty hereinbefore set out.   In ascertaining the rights of the parties

1.   under such instrument as applied to the facts of this case, it must be assumed that the horse remained at all times in as sound and healthy condition as when sold to Fahl, and that he received proper care and that he was properly exercised.   Such assumption must be indulged because the uncontradicted evidence was to that effect.   It will be observed that the written guaranty as above set out consists of three paragraphs of three full sentences. The scope of the guaranty is primarily defined by the first sentence.   The second sentence specifies a remedy for a breach.   As to whether such remedy is exclusive or merely cumulative or optional in its relation to Fahl, we shall hereafter consider.   The remedy is in substance that, in case

of a breach of the warranty, appellants agreed that they would receive the stallion back, and Fahl agreed that under such circumstances he would accept another in the place of the one purchased, the remedy to be available only in case Fahl returned the horse to appellants at Lafayette by April 1, 1912. The third sentence is important under the facts of this case only to the extent that it illuminates the second sentence. The third sentence consists of an agreement by Fahl relating to a possibility of the purchased horse becoming disabled before delivery. It is couched in the same language as Fahl's agreement expressed in the second sentence, and is in effect that he would accept another horse under the circumstances named in place of the one purchased. We think it apparent that had the horse become disabled as provided in the third sentence, Fahl would have been obliged to accept another horse, and that failing to do so, he would have been without remedy. Returning to a consideration of the second sentence, where a stipulation annexed to a contract of warranty by its terms confers on the purchaser of personal property the mere

2. right or privilege of returning the property in case it does not prove to be as warranted, and making settlement on specified terms, but does not require him to do so in case he desires to avail himself of the breach, it is at least the general rule that such stipulation extends to the purchaser merely an optional or cumulative remedy, and that if he elects to do so, he may retain the property and maintain an action for damages based on the breach of the warranty. But where the stipulation for the return of the property in case it does not prove to be as warranted is mandatory, the remedy afforded by the stipulation is exclusive. *J. I. Case Threshing Mach. Co.* v. *Badger* (1914), 56 Ind. App. 399, 105 N. E. 576; 35 Cyc 437; *Wasatch, etc., Co.* v. *Morgan, etc., Co.* (1907), 32 Utah 229, 89 Pac. 1009, 12 L. R. A. (N. S.) 540, and note. Contracts of warranty containing provisions for the return of the prop-

erty in case it is found to be otherwise than as war-
1.   ranted by the vendor present themselves in such vary-
ing shades of meaning and expression that courts find
it at times a difficult task to classify a particular contract
in the one group rather than the other.  However, in each
of the following the contract involved was either very
similar to, or identical with, the instrument under consideration, and in each case it was held that in the absence of
fraud the return of the property and a settlement as specified excluded all other remedies for a breach of the warranty.  *Nave* v. *Powell* (1912), 52 Ind. App. 496, 96 N. E.
395; *Hickman* v. *Richardson* (1914), 92 Kan. 716, 142 Pac.
964; *Walters* v. *Akers* (1907), (Ky.) 101 S. W. 1179;
*Oltmanns Bros.* v. *Poland* (1912), (Tex. Civ. App.) 142 S.
W. 653; *Highsmith* v. *Hammonds* (1911), 99 Ark. 400, 138
S. W. 635; *Merchants Nat. Bank* v. *Grigsby* (1915), 170
Iowa 675, 149 N. W. 626.

The question involved is fully considered in the cases
above cited, and we, therefore, omit further discussion here.
The cited decisions appeal to us as sound.  We are con-
strained to follow them.  We hold that the contract here
provides its own exclusive remedy for a breach of warranty
as made.  The horse having proven to be otherwise than
as warranted, and assuming for the present that there was
no countervailing fact or circumstance, it became Fahl's
duty, if he desired to avail himself of the breach, to take
the initiative and return the horse to appellants at Lafayette
by April 1, 1912.  Had he done so, it would then have
become appellants' duty to deliver to Fahl another imported
percheron stallion equal in value to the one sold had it
been as warranted.  Had appellants failed or refused to
do so, Fahl would have had ample grounds for relief, but
failing to return the horse, he was deprived of all remedy,
in the absence of some additional controlling fact.  If
there was such additional controlling fact, it consisted in
the transaction of March 25, 1912.  We therefore proceed

to determine the force and effect of the arrangement made
by the parties at that time, which was in substance
3. as follows: Fahl had ascertained that the horse
was not a satisfactory, sure breeder, and thereupon
called upon appellants at Lafayette. The horse was left
at Huntington, and Fahl did not return or offer to return
him to appellants. Fahl merely stated the facts and
expressed his dissatisfaction. Appellants, drawing on
their experience, theorized somewhat respecting the causes
of the horse's failure, and suggested that Fahl try him
another year. To this Fahl consented. By this new additional arrangement, it cannot be plausibly contended that
Fahl continued under the obligation to return the horse by
April 1, 1912, in order that he might avail himself of a
breach of the warranty. Appellants by such arrangement
waived the return of the horse at that time. Nor can it
be successfully contended that after April 1, 1912, appellants were relieved of liability under the warranty. The
only reasonable holding is that by such arrangement the
parties contemplated an extension of the warranty for
another year or until April 1, 1913. The warranty being
so extended, the remedial portion thereof was extended with
it. *Merchants Nat. Bank* v. *Grigsby, supra.* It follows
that if Fahl desired to avail himself of the breach of warranty, he was under the same obligation to return the horse
by April 1, 1913, as indicated respecting the return by April
1, 1912, in the absence of such arrangement. Some averments of the counterclaim disclose that such was his view of
the situation. From March 25, 1912, to April 1, 1913, Fahl
was silent. Although he made payments on the notes as we
have indicated, he took no action. In fact he at no time
returned or offered to return the horse to appellants at
Lafayette. He did make some complaint to appellants in
August or September of 1913, but even at that late day did
not tender or offer to return the horse. In view of the
foregoing, it is apparent that the evidence was insufficient

to sustain the verdict as returned on the counterclaim. We proceed to consider the sufficiency of the evidence in its relation to the issues formed by the complaint and answer.

It is conceded that Fahl failed to pay the interest on 4. the notes representing the purchase price of the stallion and also $800 of the principal. The notes were long past maturity. Under such circumstances, the chattel mortgage given to secure payment of the notes, expressly authorized appellants to take possession of the stallion and to sell him on notice at either public or private sale. There having been default, and demand for possession having been made, appellants *prima facie* were authorized to maintain replevin to regain possession of the horse. Possession having been thus acquired, proceeding as specified by the mortgage, the regularity of which is not challenged, appellants were within their rights in causing the stallion to be sold and in becoming the purchasers at the sale, and in applying the proceeds to the discharge of the notes. *Whitehead* v. *Coyle* (1890), 1 Ind. App. 450, 27 N. E. 716; *Lee* v. *Fox* (1888), 113 Ind. 98, 14 N. E. 889; *Broadhead* v. *McKay* (1874), 46 Ind. 595; *Nichols, etc., Co.* v. *Burch* (1891), 128 Ind. 324, 27 N. E. 737; *Syfers* v. *Bradley* (1888), 115 Ind. 345, 16 N. E. 805, 17 N. E. 619.

As against such *prima facie* rights of appellants, appellee Fahl interposes three special defenses. The first presented by the second paragraph of answer is unproven and disproven. Our discussion discloses that the second, presented by the third paragraph of answer, is in part unproven, and also that considered as a whole and measured by all the facts, it is not a defense. Assuming for purposes of discussion the sufficiency of the fourth para-5. graph of answer, presenting the third special defense, its theory as we interpret it, is new title in Fahl, based on the purchase at the bankruptcy sale, an estoppel as against appellants, and a waiver of their rights under the mortgage. There was no evidence to support the cstoppel or waiver features of the answer. As to the other elements of the new title pleaded, it may be said that the mere fact that the horse was scheduled in the bankruptcy proceeding as a part of Fahl's property did not affect appellants' lien. The trustee took the property subject to the lien, and Fahl, as a purchaser at the bankruptcy sale, acquired title of no higher degree than the trustee acquired from him. 7 C. J. 185 and cases cited. The evidence is not sufficient to sustain the verdict as returned on the issues joined on the complaint.

The court's action in substituting the trustee in bankruptcy to prosecute the cause of action presented by the counterclaim is challenged. It is not controverted that the claim declared on by the counterclaim, if it existed, passed to the trustee by virtue of the bankruptcy proceeding. Such being the case, the trustee is the real party in interest as to such claim. The substitution, therefore, appears to have been proper. Appellants' briefs are criticized, but they are sufficient to present the questions decided. Other questions are not considered or decided.

The judgment is reversed, with instructions to sustain the motion for a new trial.

NOTE.—Reported in 113 N. E. 1009. Sale of animals for breeding purposes, warranty, effect, Ann. Cas. 1916A 573. See under (1-3) 35 Cyc 437-439; (4) 7 Cyc 20; (6) 5 Cyc 378. Sales, privilege of returning goods as to claim for breach of warranty, Ann. Cas. 1915D 1159. Replevin, action of, rules as to title and parties, 1 Ann. Cas. 984.

---

## SMITH v. WESTON.

[No. 9,075. Filed October 5, 1916. Rehearing denied December 14, 1916.]

1. APPEAL.—*Waiver of Error.*—*Briefs.*—An assignment of error predicated on the overruling of the demurrer to the complaint is waived by failure to present it in appellant's briefs. p. 269.

2. APPEAL.—*Review.*—*Evidence.*—*Sufficiency.*—*Conflicting Evidence.*

—If there is some evidence to sustain the verdict, it is neither the right nor duty of the court on appeal to weigh conflicting evidence. p. 271.

3. TRIAL.—*Instructions.—Statement of Law.—Scope.—Considered Together.*—In an action to recover for damages to a motorcycle caused by a collision with an automobile on a public highway, an instruction that a violation of the law regulating travel on public highways would constitute negligence, which, if the proximate cause' of the damage complained of, would warrant a recovery if plaintiff was free from contributory negligence, states a correct proposition of law, and is not objectionable for failure to make allowance for sudden emergencies and the effect thereof on the question of liability, where the subject was covered by other instructions, as all the law need not be given in a single instruction, but all should be considered together. p. 271.

From Huntington Circuit Court; *Charles K. Lucas,* Special Judge.

Action by Boston Weston against William F. Smith. From a judgment for plaintiff, the defendant appeals. *Affirmed.*

*C. W. Watkins* and *George M. Eberhart,* for appellant.
*Fred H. Bowers* and *Milo Feightner,* for appellee.

FELT, J.—This is a suit for damages to personal property brought by appellee against appellant. The jury returned a verdict for $180, and over appellant's motion for a new trial judgment was rendered on the verdict.

Appellant has assigned as error the overruling of his demurrer to the complaint and the overruling of the motion for a new trial. The first alleged error is waived by failing to present the same in the briefs. Under the motion for a new trial appellant questions the sufficiency of the evidence and the giving of certain instructions and the refusal to give others tendered by appellant.

The gist of the complaint is that appellee, while riding a motorcycle west on a public street in the city of Huntington, Indiana, met appellant driving an automobile in the opposite direction; that appellant negligently drove his automobile to the left of the center of said highway and negligently ran the same into and against appellee's motorcycle, and thereby broke and damaged the same; that when so struck appellee was on the right-hand side of the center of the street and the collision was not caused, or contributed to, by any fault or negligence on his part and was wholly due to the aforesaid negligence of appellant.

Appellant contends that the evidence conclusively shows that the collision was caused or contributed to by the negligence of appellee; that he came suddenly from an alley at a rapid rate of speed and drove in such a zigzag course as to cause appellant to believe it was necessary for him to turn to the left to avoid a collision; that he did so and then turned to the right in a good-faith effort to avoid a collision, when appellee suddenly turned his motorcycle to the left and collided with his machine near the center of the street.

We have examined the evidence and find that there is a sharp conflict upon many material propositions. While there is some evidence tending to support appellant's contention, it is by no means uncontradicted. There is evidence tending to show that appellee came from an alley opening into the south side of the street where the collision occurred, when appellant was driving east along the highway, but west of the mouth of the alley; that appellee crossed the street to the north side and then turned west and drove a distance, variously estimated at from forty to seventy feet, before he met appellant; that in going that distance the motorcycle kept within three or four feet of the curb on the north side of the street; that as appellant approached appellee he turned his automobile to the left side of the street and so near the curb that appellee did not have room to pass; that the collision occurred north of the center of the street and near the curb; that the motorcycle was dragged about eighteen feet in a diagonal direction across the street before the car stopped, and when stopped it was near the center of the street. Some of the witnesses say appellee turned slightly to the left around a defect in the street just before the collision occurred, but most of such witnesses say the collision occurred only four or five feet from the north curb, and north of the center of the traveled or paved portion of the street; that appellant did not turn back toward the center of the street until about the time of the collision. There is no evidence that

2.  the view of either was obstructed after appellee came into the street. There is evidence to sustain the verdict, and in such case it is neither our right nor duty to weigh conflicting evidence.

Appellant complains of the giving of instruction No. 2, which in substance told the jury that a violation of the

3.  law regulating travel on public highways by appellant, as alleged, would constitute negligence, which if shown to be the proximate cause of appellee's injury would warrant a recovery if appellee was himself free from negligence contributing to the injury complained of. The objection urged against the instruction is that it makes no allowance for sudden emergencies which may arise and affect the application of the general rule.

The instruction states a correct proposition of law. The court is not required to give all the law in a single instruction. In other instructions the court very fully covered the proposition of sudden emergencies and conditions that may arise and affect the question of liability. Instructions are to be considered together and when read in the light of the other instructions, the one complained of is not objectionable, but entirely proper under the issues and facts of the case.

Complaint is also made of the refusal of the court to give the jury instructions Nos. 6, 8, 9, 10, 11 and 13, tendered by appellant. We have examined all the instructions tendered and refused and those given by the court. Instructions Nos. 6, 9, 10, and 13 tendered by appellant, so far as correct and applicable to the case, were fully covered by others given. Instructions Nos. 8 and 11, so tendered, are not accurate statements of the law and were properly refused for that reason and also for the reason'last above stated. Instruction No. 11 also invades the province of the jury. Several of the instructions refused were in substance duplications of others tendered by appellant and given by the court. Instructions Nos. 12 and 14, tendered by appellant and given by the court, fully cover the propositions mainly relied on by appellant, of sudden peril, unusual conditions and good-faith effort on the part of appellant to avoid a collision. The case seems to have been fairly tried. Appellant was deprived of no substantial right which in any way affected the result. No reversible error is shown. Judgment affirmed.

NOTE.—Reported in 113 N. E. 757. See under (3) 38 Cyc 1778, 1781.

---

## TROOK v. TROOK ET AL.

[No. 9,287. Filed January 4, 1916. Rehearing denied October 5, 1916. Transfer denied December 14, 1916.]

1. NEW TRIAL.—*New Trial as of Right.—When Granted.*—In an action seeking to have a trust in land declared and an accounting by defendant for rents and profits, wherein defendant by cross-complaint asked to have his title quieted to the land involved, but the decree rendered did not grant such relief, defendant was not entitled to a new trial as of right. p. 276. •

2. NEW TRIAL.—*New Trial as of Right.—Joinder of Causes in Same Case.*—Where two causes of action are joined and proceed to judgment in the same case, in one of which a new trial as of right is allowable, and in the other it is not, the statute is not applicable, and a new trial as of right will not be granted. p. 277.

3. NEW TRIAL.—*New Trial as of Right.—Vacating Order for.*—Where a motion for a new trial as a matter of right is improperly sustained, the same court may thereafter vacate the order. p. 278.

4. COURTS.—*Superior Courts.—Jurisdiction.—Setting Aside Order for New Trial Made by Circuit Court.*—Where an order for a new trial as a matter of right was made by the Grant Circuit Court

and the cause was thereafter transferred to the Grant Superior Court on change of venue, the latter had authority to inquire into the correctness of the order for a new trial and to vacate the same if improperly granted. pp. 278, 279.

5. NEW TRIAL.—*New Trial as of Right.—Joinder of Several Causes of Action.*—A complaint seeking to have a trust declared in land and asking also for an accounting by the defendant for rents and profits states two substantive causes of action and if the first mentioned cause so involves the questions of title and possession that, if standing alone, defendant would be entitled to a new trial as of right, such right is properly denied where, as in this case, both causes have proceeded to judgment; since a new trial as of right is not permissible in a suit for an accounting. p. 280.

6. APPEAL.—*Rehearing.—New Question.*—Where appellant on rehearing seeks for the first time to challenge the complaint as being insufficient under the statute relating to the creation of trusts in real estate, such question cannot be considered. p. 281.

From Grant Superior Court; *Robert M. VanAtta*, Judge.

Action by Orrin H. Trook against William H. Trook and others. From an order of the superior court of Grant County setting aside an order for a new trial as of right made by the circuit court before a change of venue, the defendant named appeals. *Affirmed.*

*Woodson S. Marshall, George A. Henry, Wilson D. Lett, John A. Kersey* and *Meyers & Gates,* for appellant.

*Marshall Williams, G. D. Dean* and *Blacklidge, Wolf & Barnes,* for appellees.

MORAN, J.—On July 8, 1910, appellee Orrin H. Trook commenced an action in the Grant Circuit Court against his coappellee, Richard M. Crouch, and appellant, William H. Trook. From the complaint it appears that appellee Crouch was the owner of several tracts of land in Miami and Grant counties, Indiana, which were heavily incumbered. One Milton Shirk held a mortgage on all of said real estate, and appellee Orrin H. Trook held a mortgage on a part of the same, which was a prior lien to the Shirk mortgage as to the real estate covered. Prior to February 8, 1898, appellee Crouch entered into an agreement with Shirk, by which Shirk was to foreclose his mortgage, purchase the real estate, and hold the title under certain conditions for Crouch. While the foreclosure proceedings were pending, and on the date last mentioned, appellee Crouch and wife entered into an agreement with appellee Orrin H. Trook whereby his mortgage was to be foreclosed in connection with the foreclosure of the Shirk mortgage as junior, although it was senior, as to the real estate included therein. In consideration thereof, appellees, Crouch and Orrin H. Trook, were to own the rest of the real estate or proceeds derived therefrom in common after the payment of an indebtedness of some $14,000, which included the mortgages and other indebtedness owing by Crouch. Part of the real estate was platted into lots as an addition to the town of Converse, Indiana, and by the agreement Crouch was to sell the part platted into lots, or so much as was necessary to discharge the indebtedness, the money derived from the sale of the lots to be placed in bank at Converse in the name of Crouch as trustee for Orrin H. Trook and Shirk. Pursuant to the agreements the mortgages were foreclosed and the real estate sold at sheriff's sale; the certificate of purchase of the various tracts of real estate were taken in Shirk's name. Thereafter Crouch sold several of the lots and applied the proceeds to discharge the liens. The transfer of the title to the lots sold was by assignment of the certificates of purchase held by Shirk at the request of Crouch and Orrin H. Trook. After part of the liens specified were discharged, the balance of the real estate by assignment of the sheriff's certificate passed to one Wilson with the consent of Orrin H. Trook and Crouch, under an agreement that Wilson was to convey said real estate thereafter to Crouch and Trook or to whomsoever they directed, after Wilson's indebtedness to the amount of $1,200 was paid, .and Wilson was to hold the real estate in trust for

Orrin H. Trook and Crouch. Orrin H. Trook and Crouch turned over to appellant, William H. Trook, as their attorney, the sum of $1,500, which was used by him as far as necessary to discharge the Wilson indebtedness, and thereupon he took the conveyance of the real estate in his own name from Wilson, as trustee for his clients, which real estate consisted of several lots in Central Park addition to Converse, Indiana, together with two tracts of farming land. While he was holding the real estate as trustee for said parties he acquired certificates of purchase at tax sales for many of the lots. The money to purchase the same was furnished by Crouch and Orrin H. Trook. After taking the title as trustee, William H. Trook collected rent and failed to account for the same, disposed of lots without the consent of the owners and denied holding the real estate as trustee, and offered the real estate for sale. A trust was asked to be declared in favor of appellees, Orrin H. Trook and Crouch, that he be ordered to convey the same to appellees, Orrin H. Trook and Crouch, and to account for the moneys collected for rent and the sale of lots; and that a receiver be appointed during the pendency of the litigation. The pleading embodying these facts was verified. Appellee Crouch refused to join with Orrin H. Trook as a party plaintiff, but filed a cross-complaint, which set up practically the same facts and asked the same relief.

Appellant, William H. Trook, filed a cross-complaint setting up that he was the owner of the real estate described in the complaint and asked that the title to the real estate be quieted in him. The issues being closed as to the complaint and cross-complaints by answers of general denial by the respective parties, a trial resulted in judgment for appellees, Orrin H. Trook and Crouch, that they were the owners of the real estate described in their pleadings and were entitled to the immediate conveyance from William H. Trook, as their trustee; that he had no right or title to the real estate, except as held for the benefit of Orrin H.

Trook and Richard M. Crouch, and that they were entitled to recover the rents and profits that accumulated, less any credits due William H. Trook as trustee; that they were entitled to recover the sum of $312 of the Flint Elevator Company, which was made a party to the action, the value of grain sold from the real estate. That Orrin H. Trook was indebted to Richard M. Crouch under their agreement, and that certain real estate was set off to Crouch and certain other real estate to Orrin H. Trook and Crouch as tenants in common, the division being made as agreed by them, and that appellant, William H. Trook, convey to Crouch certain real estate, and convey jointly to Orrin H. Trook and Richard M. Crouch certain real estate within ten days from July 1, 1911, and William H. Carroll was appointed commissioner to make the conveyance if not made within that time. Judgment was rendered against appellant on his cross-complaint.

A new trial as of right was granted appellant and thereupon the cause was transferred from the circuit court to the Grant Superior Court. At the October term of the Grant Superior Court, on motion of Orrin H. Trook and Richard M. Crouch, the order granting the new trial as of right was set aside, and the decree and judgment of the circuit court was in all things restored, on the ground that the cause was one in which a new trial as of right was not demandable. The several errors assigned by appellant all go to the right and authority of the court to set aside the order granting a new trial as of right.

The complaint of appellee Orrin H. Trook, and the cross-complaint of appellee Richard M. Crouch, clearly disclose that appellant held the title to the real estate

1. described in the pleadings as trustee for the use and benefit of appellees, Trook and Crouch, and paid no consideration therefor, and, while he held the title as trustee, he sold a portion of the same, and collected rent for

a part occupied by tenants.　For the money received from real estate sold and rent collected from tenants an accounting was asked, and that a trust be declared in favor of appellees.　No relief was asked in the way of quieting title, either in the complaint or the cross-complaint of Crouch, nor did the decree rendered grant such relief.　It is clear that under the issues joined on the complaint and cross-complaint of Crouch, appellant was not entitled to a new trial as of right.　The issues on the part of appellees, Orrin H. Trook and Richard M. Crouch, embraced a suit for an accounting and to establish a trust and, on the part of appellant, an action to quiet title.　The decree and judgment covered all of the issues joined.　"Notwithstanding the cross-complaint in which one of the appellants asked to have his title quieted, there were other substantive causes of action embraced in the judgment, upon which a new trial as of right was not allowable."　*Wilson* v. *Brookshire* (1891), 126 Ind. 497, 25 N. E. 131, 9 L. R. A. 792; *Bradford* v. *School Town, etc.* (1886), 107 Ind. 280, 7 N. E. 256; *Schlichter* v. *Taylor* (1902), 31 Ind. App. 164, 67 N. E. 556; *Hofferbert* v. *Williams* (1903), 32 Ind. App. 593, 70 N. E. 405.　Where two causes of action are joined and proceed to judgment in the same case, in one of

2.　which a new trial as of right is allowable and in the other it is not, the statute is not applicable, and a new trial as of right will not be granted.　*Larrance* v. *Lewis* (1912), 51 Ind. App. 1, 98 N. E. 892; *Nutter* v. *Hendricks* (1898), 150 Ind. 605, 50 N. E. 748; *Garrick* v. *Garrick* (1908), 43· Ind. App. 585, 87 N. E. 696, 88 N. E. 104; *Bennett* v. *Closson* (1894), 138 Ind. 542, 38 N. E. 46; *Schlichter* v. *Taylor, supra; Wilson* v. *Brookshire, supra; Richwine* v. *Presbyterian Church, etc.* (1893), 135 Ind. 80, 34 N. E. 737.

The power of the court to set aside its order granting a new trial as of right is questioned, but it seems to be

settled that,. where a motion for a new trial as a
3. matter of right is improperly sustained, the order
allowing it may thereafter be vacated. *Butler University* v. *Conard* (1884), 94 Ind. 353; *Jenkins* v. *Corwin* (1876), 55 Ind. 21; *Hofferbert* v. *Williams, supra.*

This leaves for consideration the question as to whether the Grant Superior Court had authority to set aside
4. the order of the Grant Circuit Court granting a new trial as of right. Counsel have not called our attention to, nor has our research disclosed, an authority upon this precise question.

By §9 of an act defining the jurisdiction of the Grant and Delaware superior courts (Acts 1909 p. 79, §1566 Burns 1914), it is provided, among other things, that, "all orders, judgments and decrees of said superior court shall have the same virtue, force and effect as the orders, judgments and decrees of the circuit courts of this state."

In *Foster, Admr.,* v. *Potter* (1865), 24 Ind. 363, it was said, in speaking of the power of the court to which the cause had been venued, that: "If the venue had not been changed, it can hardly be doubted that that court might have corrected its own mistake, and it is equally clear that the court to which the venue was changed was possessed of the same power." This was where the Fountain Circuit Court vacated a judgment, and after the case reached the Tippecanoe Circuit Court on change of venue, the Tippecanoe Circuit Court set aside the order vacating the original judgment as made by the Fountain Circuit Court.

In *Niagara Oil Co.* v. *Jackson* (1911), 48 Ind. App. 238, 91 N. E. 825, it was held that, after the venue of the cause had been changed from the Randolph to the Delaware Circuit Court, where a new party plaintiff was made by the filing of an amended complaint, over the objection of the defendant, that the Delaware Circuit Court had the same jurisdiction and power to make any order or ruling that it would have had had the cause been properly brought in said court in the first instance.

"A court to which a cause is properly removed by change of venue acquires jurisdiction of the cause and subject-matter, co-extensive with that of the court from which the venue was removed, and may inquire into anything connected with the subject-matter of the action, and render any judgment which might have been rendered by the court in which the case originated." *Hazen* v. *Webb* (1902), 65 Kan. 38, 68 Pac. 1096, 93 Am. St. 276; *United Zinc, etc., Co.* v. *Morrison* (1907), 76 Kan. 799, 92 Pac. Rep. 1114. The fact that the cause reached the Grant Superior Court on change of venue did not deprive that court of authority to inquire into the correctness of an order made before the cause reached such court as to the granting of the new trial as of right. *Hazen* v. *Webb, supra.*

We find no reversible error in the record. Judgment is therefore affirmed.

## On Petition for a Rehearing.

Moran, J.—Appellant, by his petition for a rehearing and briefs supporting the same, insists that the court erred in its original opinion in holding: (1) that appellant was not entitled to a new trial as of right; and (2) that the Grant Superior Court had authority to set aside an order of the Grant Circuit Court granting a new trial as of right after the cause was transferred to the superior court by agreement of the parties.

As to the latter contention, the argument now advanced in this behalf is in the main the same as advanced 4. by appellant originally, and what we have said in our former opinion fully covers such questions.

As to the first proposition, appellant contends that, notwithstanding much is said in the complaint to the effect that appellant took title to the real estate in question in trust

for appellee and a trust is asked to be declared in
5. their favor, the real controversy involves the title
and possession of the real estate. We are of the
opinion that the complaint states a substantive cause of
action on the theory that appellant held the real estate in
trust for appellees and that the court should have so
declared upon the facts pleaded if they were established,
and which the court did so find and so declare. Yet, if
it be conceded for the sake of argument that the complaint
does not state a substantive cause of action in this respect,
and that it does state a cause of action involving the question of title and possession of real estate as to entitle
appellant to a new trial as of right, if this cause of action
stood alone, appellant would not be entitled to a new trial
as of right in this cause.

The decree in the case at bar is quite comprehensive in its
scope. It adjusted the entire transaction mentioned in the
original opinion as between the parties, not alone between
appellant and appellees, but as between the appellees, as
appellant was directed to convey a part of the real estate
to the appellees jointly and a part to them in severalty, and
in the same decree the court found that appellant was
indebted to appellees in the sum of $175 for money that
came into his hands while acting as trustee for the appellees, for which a personal judgment was rendered against
him. Likewise it was found that appellees were entitled
to receive the sum of $312 from the Flint Elevator Company
for grain sold from the real estate in controversy by appellant in the course of his trust.

The personal judgment rendered for $175 against appel-
lant and the finding that the appellees were entitled to the
sum of $312 due from the Flint Elevator Company were
within the issues, as the complaint in this respect stated
a substantive cause of action for an accounting. Hence,
the complaint stated two substantive causes of action even
on appellant's theory, one of which would, and the other

would not, entitle appellant to a new trial as of right. The new trial as of right was properly denied. *Henry* v. *Frazier* (1913), 53 Ind. App. 605, 100 N. E. 770.

Appellant for the first time now seeks to raise the question that, by virtue of the statute of the state in reference to the creation of trusts in real estate, the complaint 6. could not under the facts pleaded be held sufficient on the theory of establishing a trust in appellant to the real estate in favor of appellees. This question, not having been heretofore raised, cannot be considered upon a petition for a rehearing.

The petition for a rehearing is overruled.

NOTE.—Reported in 113 N. E. 730. See under (1-3) 29 Cyc 1037-1043; (4) 40 Cyc 176.

---

PARKER ET AL. *v*. HUMFLEET ET AL.

[No. 9,396. Filed April 19, 1916. Rehearing denied June 27, 1916. Transfer denied December 4, 1916.]

SCHOOLS AND SCHOOL DISTRICTS.—*Joint Elementary and High School.—Relocation.—Township Trustee.—Powers.—Statute.* — It is within the discretionary power of a township trustee to change the site of a joint elementary and high-school building by constructing another elsewhere, and injunction will not issue to restrain him from so doing where it does not appear that the trustee has exceeded the scope of his discretionary authority and there is no charge of bad faith or fraud, §6417 Burns 1914 *et seq.*, Acts 1893 p. 17, which provides that a petition for the relocation of a school building shall be signed by a majority of the patrons of the school, applying only to the relocation of district schools, and it is not necessary for a majority of the patrons of a high school to join with a trustee in a petition for its relocation.

From Shelby Circuit Court; *Alonzo Blair*, Judge.

Action by George W. Parker and others against William Humfleet, as trustee of Buck Creek township, Hancock county, and others. From a judgment for defendants, the plaintiffs appeal. *Affirmed.*

*R. L. Mason, Cook & Walker, Tindall & Tindall* and *Hord & Adams,* for appellants.

*L. Ert Slack, Isaac Carter* and *Samuel J. Offutt,* for appellees.

MORAN, J.—Appellants as taxpayers of Buck Creek-township, Hancock county, Indiana, sought to enjoin appellees, the trustee and advisory board of said township, and Howard C. Elliot, the contractor, from carrying out a contract for the construction of a school building in the township and the sale of bonds to defray the cost of the same. A demurrer was sustained to the complaint, and upon appellant's failure to plead further, judgment was rendered against them, from which an appeal has been prosecuted, presenting for consideration the sufficiency of the complaint to withstand a demurrer.

The complaint discloses: that appellants, three in number, were taxpayers of Buck Creek school township, and that the trustee and advisory board entered into a contract in violation of law with Howard C. Elliot to construct a school building; that, in 1899, a joint elementary and high school building was erected in district No. 5 and paid for by the taxpayers of the township, and since that time a noncommissioned high school has been maintained; that $5,000 was expended over and above what it would have cost to construct the building solely for the purpose of holding an elementary district school; that on March 2, 1914, eighteen persons, representing themselves as residents and patrons of the district, and the trustee, filed a petition with the superintendent of schools of Hancock county for an order authorizing the trustee to relocate the district school building on another tract of real estate, and pursuant thereto the superintendent made the following order:

"And it is now therefore considered and ordered by the county superintendent of schools and the said trustee of Buck Creek township is hereby ordered and authorized by the said county superintendent to change the site and location of said schoolhouse in said District No. 5 and remove said schoolhouse to the new site. Dated this 2nd day of April, 1914, George J. Richmond, Co. Supt.''

That the trustee and advisory board prepared plans for the construction of the school building for the new site and the advisory board appropriated $35,000 for erecting and fitting the building to be used as a district and township high school, $20,000 of which was necessary to make the building suitable for high-school purposes; that bids were advertised for the construction, and on the day fixed for receiving the same Howard C. Elliot was awarded the contract for $34,470.90, and the board authorized the trustee to issue and sell bonds to raise funds with which to construct the same, and the trustee issued bonds and was threatening to sell the same when suit was filed. It is further disclosed that at the time of the filing of the petition with the county superintendent, there were 150 patrons of the high school who had children enumerated for school purposes that were entitled to attend high school, and the trustee was attempting to abandon the high school and relocate the same; that the petition was not signed by a majority of the heads of families having children enumerated for school purpose in the township, and the petition filed did not request, nor did the order of the county superintendent authorize, an abandonment or a relocation of the high school; that no authority existed to construct and maintain the building upon the new site. Upon the facts pleaded, of which the foregoing is the substance, injunctive relief is demanded.

The objections urged to the complaint by appellees may be classified under two subdivisions: First, the petition addressed to the county superintendent, as disclosed by the complaint, was not signed by a majority of the patrons, guardians and heads of families having charge of all persons of school age in the township who would be affected by the relocation; that its being signed by a majority of the patrons of district No. 5 was not sufficient; secondly, that the removal of the district school building only was asked by the petition, and not the removal of the site of the township high school.

To these objections appellants answer that the change of site of a high school is for the township trustee alone, subject to an appeal to the county superintendent of schools, and that the statute authorizing a petition to the county superintendent in reference to a relocation of a school applies to the change of site of a district school, which requires only a majority of the patrons of the district.

Thus the controversy is narrowed down to the legality of the action taken by the school officers in attempting to relocate and build a high-school building as a part of, and in connection with, the graded-school building. Numerous sections of the statute are referred to by the parties in support of their respective contentions, and which are discussed in so far as they throw light on the question involved.

Under §6410 Burns 1914, Acts 1899 p. 424, it is made the duty of the township trustee to take charge of the educational affairs of the township; and, among other duties enumerated by this section, the trustee may establish and maintain, as near the center of the township as seems wise, at least one separate graded high school, to which shall be admitted all pupils who are sufficiently advanced. But as a prerequisite to the exercising of authority in this respect by the trustee, there must be within the township at least twenty-five common-school graduates of school age. Instead, however, of building a separate school building, the statute provides a method of transferring the pupils to another school corporation where they may receive a high-school education; and the statute likewise provides that two or more trustees may establish a joint graded high school in lieu of a separate graded high school.

By §1 of an act of 1913, Acts 1913 p. 331, §6584a *et seq.*
Burns 1914, it is provided that a township having taxable
property of $600,000, with no high school, and having eight
or more graduates of the township elementary school for
two years last preceding, the township trustee may establish
a high school, or a joint high school and elementary school;
and, when a majority of the persons having charge of
children enumerated for school purposes petition the trustee
to establish and maintain such school, the trustee shall
establish the same. Section 2 provides that where there
is no high school within three miles of any boundary line
of such township, and there have been eight or more
graduates of the elementary schools, as aforesaid, the trustee
shall establish a high school. Section 3 provides that the
location shall be determined by the trustee, except in the
event that ten persons, having charge of children who are
graduates of the elementary schools and enumerated for
school purposes, may petition for a location other than the
one determined by the trustee, whereupon an appeal shall
be taken to the county superintendent of schools, whose
decision shall be final.

This enactment, as well as the prior act (Acts 1899 p.
424, *supra*), deals with the construction of high-school
buildings and the maintaining of high schools. Neither of
the acts deal with the relocation of a high school already
established. Both enactments, in a general way, disclose
the duties, scope and discretionary powers of the trustee in
relation to the educational affairs of his township and the
maintaining of high-school facilities, and in this respect only
are the enactments instructive as to the question involved.

Section 6417 *et seq.* Burns 1914, Acts 1893 p. 17, provides that whenever it becomes necessary to re-establish the
site of any school building, the trustee shall present to the
county superintendent a petition setting forth the place
to where it is desired to change the school building, together
with reasons for such change, and shall procure an order

from the county superintendent to relocate the school building. The petition shall be signed by the trustee and the majority of the patrons of the school where said building is located; proofs of notice by posting for twenty days prior to the day set for the hearing being required.

It is argued by appellants that §6417, *supra*, which provides for the relocation of the site of a school building, has reference to any and all schools and calls for a majority of all affected, the same as where a relocation is sought in the district; that otherwise those interested would have no voice in the relocation. To further elucidate, appellant's position is that a majority of the patrons of the township affected by a relocation of a high school must join in a petition asking for such relocation. As we have seen, §6417, *supra*, contains the language "any school" and "a majority of the patrons" of the school, and upon the language thus used appellants lay much stress and insist that when taken in connection with the various statutes and the entire subject-matter covered, it can be fairly implied to mean any school within the general supervision of the township trustee, which would include the township high school.

On the part of appellees, this language, it is contended, means any district school, inasmuch as the statute using the same was enacted several years prior to the enactment of the statute creating the township high school.

By §6410, *supra*, there is no initial step required of the taxpayers or patrons of the township to be taken by petition to invoke the authority of the trustee to erect a building for high school purposes. The condition prerequisite thereto is that there be twenty-five common-school graduates of school age in the township; and by the acts of 1913, *supra*, the trustee may, in townships having taxable property to the amount of $600,000, establish a high school, if there are eight or more graduates of the township elementary schools residing within the township, etc. Here we have instances under the statute where, in the construction of high schools, the authority of the trustee to so construct does not depend upon any affirmative action being taken by the taxpayers of the township, which, in a measure, argues against appellants' contention that the whole scope and tenor of the statutes under consideration fairly implies that the voice of the patrons or taxpayers must first be heard before the trustee proceeds in the matter.

In *Kessler, Trustee,* v. *State, ex rel.* (1896), 146 Ind. 221, 45 N. E. 102, cited by appellants as supporting their contention, the court makes use of the following language, in construing §6417, *supra:* "The language of the act shows that the intention was to give the majority of the patrons of the school a controlling voice in the removal of their school from the place where it had once been located. The judgment of the trustee and that of the county superintendent must also be united to that of the majority of the school patrons before such removal shall be allowed. * * * The legislature saw fit to take this matter from the arbitrary control of the school officers and to restore it to those to whom it originally belonged, the people of the school district itself." The facts in this case, as well as the conclusions reached by the court, clearly disclose that the decision has reference only to the relocation of a district school.

In *Carnahan, Trustee,* v. *State, ex rel.* (1900), 155 Ind. 156, 57 N. E. 717, also relied upon by appellant, it was held that, prior to the enactment of the statute under consideration, the trustee had the arbitrary power to relocate a school and the only authority reserved in the patrons of the district was advisory, but that by the Acts of 1893 p. 17, *supra,* the action of a majority of the patrons, township trustee and the county superintendent was necessary for the relocation of a school. This decision likewise deals with a district school. There is nothing in either the Kessler or Carnahan cases, *supra,* that supports appellants'

contention that §6417, *supra*, is subject to the construction
that the trustee cannot act in the matter of the relocation of
a township high school until a majority of those having children eligible to attend petition for such change of location.

In *State, ex rel.* v. *Wilson, Trustee* (1897), 149 Ind.
253, 48 N. E. 1030, in reference to §6417, *supra*, it was
said: "It is clear from an examination of the provisions
of the act cited, that it only applies when it is proposed to
change the site of a schoolhouse from one point to another
in the same school district."

In *Willan* v. *Richardson* (1912), 51 Ind. App. 102, 98
N. E. 1094, involving the relocation of a school by the
township trustee, it was held by this court that where
patrons were referred to in §6417, *supra*, reference was to
patrons of the district schools; that there was no statute
which referred to patrons of a high school; and this was in
accord with the holding of the Attorney-General of the
State, as the opinion discloses.

A township trustee, while not possessing exclusive control in many respects, has the general control and supervision of the educational affairs and the management of the
schools of his township. This is true as to the construction,
location, removal, abandonment, consolidation and kindred
subjects falling within this general duty.

The graded school and the high school under consideration
were conducted for several years in the same building. The
relocation of the building contemplated will continue this
system, one building serving both purposes. There is no
contention that it will not be to the best interests of the
patrons of the district and the public to relocate the graded
school, for as to this we have seen there is no objection, only in so far as the relief sought, if granted, would
necessarily operate to defeat both the building of the graded
school and the high school. It does not appear that the
trustee has exceeded the scope of his discretionary authority,
and no bad faith or fraud is charged against appellees, and

the allegations of the complaint, when applied to the law, disclose that no statute was violated. nor was there an infringement of any legal rights of appellants.

Appellants, apparently with much feeling, argue that if school officers at will may expend large sums of money, as here attempted, the way is clear to a dissipation of public funds without the sanction or approval of the taxpayers. This would be weighty argument to address to the law-making body of the state if there is a lack of restraint upon public officers that have the handling and expenditure of public funds, as officers possessed with authority to expend public funds should do so economically, keeping in view the necessity for so doing; but relief in this respect cannot come through the courts.

Finding no error that calls for a reversal of the judgment, the judgment is affirmed.

NOTE.—Reported in 112 N. E. 253. See 36 L. R. A. (N. S.) 16; 35 Cyc 936.

---

# THE CLEVELAND, CINCINNATI, CHICAGO AND ST. LOUIS RAILWAY COMPANY v. GANNON.

[Filed April 27, 1916. Rehearing granted January 30, 1916. Transfer denied December 14, 1916.]

1. APPEAL. — *Briefs.—Rules of Court.—Substantial Compliance.—* Although the rules for the preparation of appellant's brief have not been strictly followed, the errors presented will be considered where there has been a substantial compliance therewith. p. 293.

2. APPEAL.—*Review.—Instructions.—Consideration.—Misleading Instruction.*—In an action for unlawful appropriation of a tract of real estate and for damages, an instruction that the burden was on defendant to prove by a fair preponderance of the evidence that the material allegations of its several paragraphs of answer, which pleaded the different statutes of limitations, while misleading, if standing alone, was not prejudicial to defendant when read in connection with other instructions, given by the court on its own motion, which covered specifically each paragraph of answer, except that pleading the ten-year statute of limitations. p. 293.

3. APPEAL.—*Review.—Instructions.—Burden of Proof.—Preponder-*

*ance of the Evidence.—Harmless Error.*—In an action for unlawful appropriation of real estate and for damages, an instruction which informed the jury that the "burden of proof" and the "fair preponderance of the evidence" did not mean that either party must prove any particular fact by a greater number of witnesses than the opposing party, but meant the facts testified to by the witnesses that carried the greater weight, was not prejudicial to defendant as confusing the burden of proof with the preponderance of the evidence, or as excluding documentary evidence from the consideration of the jury, when read in connection with other instructions that "if you find from a fair preponderance of the evidence," and that, in determining whether defendant had been in possession of the real estate in controversy, the jury should consider all the evidence and be governed by a fair preponderance thereof, and to consider, among facts shown by all the evidence, defendant's use of the realty. p. 294.

4. APPEAL. — *Review.—Instructions.—Harmless Error.—Appropriation of Lands.—Measure of Damages.*—In an action for possession of lands unlawfully appropriated and for damages, an instruction that, if it should be found that defendant unlawfully appropriated the real estate in controversy, the measure of damages would be the value of the land appropriated, while not a correct statement of law, was more favorable to defendant than one could have been embodying the general rule that the measure of damages was the difference in the value of the whole tract of real estate before the alleged appropriation and thereafter, as the defendant was not required by the instruction complained of to answer for any damages that might have resulted to the residue of the land by reason of the taking of a part thereof. p. 295.

5. APPEAL.—*Review.—Excessive Damages.—Presenting Questions for Review.*—In order to present for review on appeal an objection that an instruction states an erroneous measure of damages, there must have been an assignment, as a ground for a new trial, that the damages recovered were excessive. p. 295.

6. APPEAL.—*Review.—Instructions.—Refusal.*—In an action for the unlawful appropriation of a tract of real estate and damages, the refusal of defendant's requested instructions on the question of the burden of proof as to the title of the land in controversy and the different elements to be considered in arriving at the measure of damages was proper, where the court informed the jury, in an instruction on the subject of ownership, that plaintiff, to recover, must show by a fair preponderance of the evidence that he was the legal owner of the real estate in controversy at the time of its appropriation, and where the instructions given as to the measure of damages were more favorable to defendant than it was entitled to. p. 296.

7. APPEAL.—*Review.*—*Jury Question.*—In an action for the unlawful appropriation of realty, the weight to be given the evidence relied on by plaintiff to establish ownership was, if such evidence were competent, for the jury, and, as the general verdict necessarily found for plaintiff upon such issue, the court on appeal is precluded from further inquiry.  p. 296.

8. EMINENT DOMAIN.—*Appropriation of Land.*—*Action by Owner.* —*Burden of Proof.*—*Title.*—In an action for possession of land alleged to have been unlawfully appropriated and for damages, where plaintiff was not in possession of the realty in controversy at the time the action was commenced and had not been for a long time prior thereto, the burden was on him to establish title as alleged.  p. 297.

9. APPEAL.—*Review.*—*Evidence.*—*Public Records.*—*Deeds.*—*Certification.*—*Admissibility.*—*Statute.*—In an action for the unlawful appropriation of land, where plaintiff relied on certified copies of certain deeds to establish his title, it was not error for the trial court to admit in evidence certified copies of deeds upon which appeared, above the recorder's certificates attached thereto, the words "Decatur County Recorder's Seal. Indiana," since this was a substantial compliance with §478 Burns 1914, §462 R. S. 1881, which requires that copies of deeds and other instruments required by law to be recorded in public offices, to be admissible in evidence, must be duly certified by the officer having the custody thereof, and authenticated by the officer's seal, which should be attached to the certificate of the officer to the instrument exemplified.  p. 297.

From Shelby Superior Court; *Pliny W. Bartholomew,* Judge.

Action by Michael Gannon against the Cleveland, Cincinnati, Chicago and St. Louis Railway Company. From a judgment for plaintiff, the defendant appeals. *Affirmed.*

*Carter & Morrison,* for appellant.

*John E. Osborne, Frank Hamilton* and *M. O. Sullivan,* for appellee.

MORAN, J.—The subject of controversy in this cause is a small tract of real estate, located on the outskirts, but within the corporate limits, of Greensburg, Indiana. On March 20, 1911, appellee filed a complaint against appellant in two paragraphs, one for damages for the unlawful appropriation of this tract of real estate, and the other for possession of the same and for damages for unlawfully with-holding the possession thereof. Upon issue being joined, a trial was had before a jury in the Shelby Superior Court, where the cause had been venued. Verdict was returned for. appellee, awarding damages in the sum of $500, and denying him the right to possession of the real estate. Judgment was rendered on the verdict. The overruling of appellant's motion for a new trial is the error relied upon for reversal.

Briefly, the facts disclose that the Michigan division of appellant's railroad crosses the Chicago division at a point within the corporate limits of the city of Greensburg. At the point of intersection, the Chicago division runs east and west, and the Michigan division runs northeast and south-west. For convenience in the operation of cars, a switch was constructed from the east side of the Michigan division to the north side of the Chicago division, leaving a tri-angular space between the tracks of the two divisions. Appellant filled up the triangular space and erected a modern station thereon. Appellee claimed to be the owner of a lot, the greater portion of which extended north of the Michigan division, and a very small portion extending south of the track of this division. The portion of land in controversy is bounded on the northwest by the right of way of the Michigan division of appellant's railroad, and on the east and south by land owned by appellant.

The giving of instructions Nos. 3, 4, 5 and 6 by the court of its own motion, and the refusal to give instructions Nos. 5, 7, 8, 12, 13, 14, 14½, 16 and 18, tendered by appellant, together with the admission and rejection of certain evidence, are the questions presented for review under the motion for new trial.

Appellee seeks to obviate the errors relied upon by appellant on the ground that neither the bill of exceptions containing the instructions nor the bill of exceptions containing a transcript of the evidence are properly authenticated.

and that appellant's brief does not comply with the rules
prescribed for the briefing of causes in this and the Supreme
Court. An examination of the record discloses that the
bills of exceptions containing the instructions and transcript of the evidence are duly authenticated, and if the
rules have not been strictly followed by appellant
1. in the preparation of its brief, there has at least been
a substantial compliance with the same. The errors
presented must be considered upon their merits.

Instruction No. 3, given by the court of its own motion,
informed the jury that appellee had the burden of proving
by a fair preponderance of the evidence the material
2. allegations of at least one of his paragraphs of complaint, and that the burden was upon appellant to
prove by a fair preponderance of the evidence the material allegations of its second, third, fourth, sixth, seventh
and ninth paragraphs of answer. It can readily be seen
how the latter part of this instruction, if standing alone,
could have been misleading; for it, in effect, told the jury
that, in order for either paragraph of answer to be available
as such, the material allegations of the same, together with
the material allegation of each of the other paragraphs,
must have been established by a fair preponderance of the
evidence.

In stating the issues, the jury's attention was called to
each of the affirmative paragraphs of answer, which pleaded
in various forms the different statutes of limitations that
might be available to appellant.

By instruction No. 8, given by the court of its own motion, the jury was informed that if the damage accrued
within six years before the commencement of the action,
the finding should be for the defendant. By instruction
No. 9, given by the court of its own motion, the fifth, sixth
and seventh paragraphs of appellant's answer were covered,
the jury being informed that, if appellant had the possession of the real estate for twenty years undisturbed, and

the possession had been open, visible and continuous, there
could be no recovery by the appellee. Each of the paragraphs of answer, save the eighth paragraph, which pleads
the ten-year statute of limitations, was specifically covered
by the court's instructions. The objectionable part of
instruction No. 3, when read in connection with all of the
other instructions that dealt with the subject-matter covered
by the various paragraphs of answer, could not have misled the jury to the prejudice of appellant. By instruction No. 4, given by the court of its own motion, the jury
was told that by the "burden of proof" and the "fair
3.  preponderance of the evidence" is not meant that
the plaintiff or the defendant must prove any particular fact by a greater number of witnesses than the opposing party must prove the same fact, but by the "burden of
proof" and "fair preponderance of the evidence" is meant
the facts testified to by the witnesses that carry the greater
weight. In addition to confounding the burden of proof
with the preponderance of the evidence, it is insisted that
the effect of this instruction was to exclude from the consideration of the jury the value of documentary evidence.
At various places in the instructions given to the jury by
the court is found the expression, "if you find from a fair
preponderance of the evidence," which, by inference at
least, informed the jury that all the evidence, whether oral
or documentary, should be considered. Instruction No. 9,
given by the court of its own motion, contains the following expression: "In determining whether or not the defendant has or has not been in possession of the real estate in
controversy herein, you must consider all of the evidence
in this cause upon said subject, and be governed by a fair
preponderance of the same, and you may, among other facts
shown by all the evidence, consider as to what use the
defendant has or has not made of the real estate in controversy herein." Here again all of the evidence was
referred to, which included the documentary as well as oral

evidence. Appellant was not harmed by the giving of this instruction.

Instructions Nos. 5 and 6, given by the court of its own motion, informed the jury that, if they found that the real estate was unlawfully appropriated by appellant, the

4. measure of appellee's damages would be the value of the real estate appropriated. Appellant insists that the correct rule as to the measure of damages was the difference in value of the whole tract of real estate before the alleged appropriation and the value after the appropriation. This is the general rule as disclosed by the authorities ·in this State.

"Where a part of a tract of land is taken, the owner is entitled to the value of the land actually appropriated and any injury to the residue of the land naturally resulting from the appropriation and the construction and operation of the road thereon." *White* v. *Cincinnati, etc., Railroad* (1904), 34 Ind. App. 287, 71 N. E. 276; *Louisville, etc., R. Co.* v. *Sparks* (1895), 12 Ind. App. 410, 40 N. E. 546; *Evansville, etc., R. Co.* v. *Swift* (1891), 128 Ind. 34, 27 N. E. 420.

The instructions given upon the measure of damages impress us as being more .favorable to appellant than one embodying the general rule could have been, as appellant was not required by the instruction given to answer for any damages that might have resulted to the residue of the real estate by reason of the part appropriated. And,

further, appellant's brief does not disclose that any

5. complaint was made by the appellant in its motion for a new trial that the damages were excessive, which should have been made in order to present the question for review in this court. *Pittsburgh, etc., R. Co.* v. *Macy* (1915), 59 Ind. App. 125, 107 N. E. 486, and authorities cited.

The instructions requested by appellant went to the question of the burden of proof as to the title to the real

estate in question, and the different elements to be
6. considered in arriving at the measure of damages
in the event they should find that the appellee was
damaged. The court informed the jury that appellee, in
order to recover, must show by a fair preponderance of
the evidence that he was the legal owner of the real estate
in dispute at the time of the appropriation. This covered
in a general way the subject-matter covered by the instructions tendered by appellant upon the ownership of the real
estate. What we have heretofore said on the measure of
damages disposes of the other questions presented by the
instructions tendered by appellant.

Many of the instructions given to the jury, when standing alone, lack clearness of expression. Taking the instructions as a whole, however, the jury was informed as to the
law applicable to the issues joined and the facts involved.
There was no error in refusing to give either of the instructions tendered by appellant.

The principal objection to the admission of the evidence
complained of is directed to the admission in evidence of
        four certified copies of deeds of conveyances by which
7. appellee sought to establish title to the real estate
        described in his complaint. The ownership of the
real estate was a controverted question. Appellee's remote
grantors, in conveying the real estate of which the small
tract in question was a part, exempted from their deeds
in favor of the railroads, which were located adjacent
thereto, certain portions of the real estate for right of way
purposes; and there is much uncertainty as to the ownership of the small tract in question, which lies between the
two divisions of appellant's railroad. However, if the evidence relied upon to establish the ownership was competent,
the weight to be given to the same was for the jury. The
general verdict necessarily found for appellee upon this
issue, and we are precluded from further inquiry under
the facts and circumstances disclosed by the record.

We direct our attention to the competency of the evidence by which the ownership of the real estate was sought to . be established. Appellee was not in possession of the real estate at the time the action was commenced, nor had he been for a long time prior thereto. The burden was upon him to establish title as alleged. 15 Cyc 1006; *Dean* v. *Metropolitan, etc., R. Co.* (1890), 119 N. Y. 540, 23 N. E. 1054; *City of LaFayette* v. *Wortman* (1886), 107 Ind. 404, 8 N. E. 277.

The real estate in question is located in Decatur county, and the trial was had in Shelby county. It is earnestly urged by appellant that certain certified copies of deeds, by which appellee sought to establish title to the real estate in question, were erroneously admitted in evidence over the objection of appellant, on the ground that they were not properly authenticated by the recorder of Decatur county; the specific objection being pressed that the recorder's seal of office was not attached to the certificates. By §9507 Burns 1914, §5943 R. S. 1881, the recorder of a county is required to provide himself with a seal to be used in attesting certificates and other instruments necessary and proper to be sealed, to which full faith and credit shall be given. "Copies of instruments and proceedings required by law to be recorded therein (in public offices), to be admissible as evidence, must be duly certified by the officer having the custody thereof." *Knotts* v. *Zeigler* (1914), 58 Ind. App. 503, 106 N. E. 393; §478 Burns 1914, §462 R. S. 1881. "Where the law requires that a record or paper to make it admissible as evidence, shall be certified by the official custodian and attached by the seal of his office, the omission of the seal is fatal, and the document is not admissible." *Elliott,* Evidence §1380. *Painter* v. *Hall* (1881), 75 Ind. 208; *Sykes* v. *Beck* (1903), 12 N. D. 242, 96 N. W. 844.

In the light of the construction given the statute, which provides for the admission in evidence of exemplification or copies of records, and the authorities generally, if appellant's contention is true that there was an omission of the recorder's seal, the certified copies of the deeds were not properly authenticated and were erroneously admitted in evidence, and the error would be reversible, as this was the only method resorted to by appellee to establish the title to the real estate in question. A close examination of the record discloses that, while the seal of the recorder was not attached to the certificates of the recorder to the copies of the deeds, but just above the certificates and upon the copy of the deeds appear the words, "Decatur County Recorder's Seal, Indiana." The better practice would have been to have placed the seal upon an appropriate place on the certificate. However, from the examination we have made of the record we cannot say, under the circumstances, that there was not a substantial compliance with the statute; therefore there was no error in admitting the certified copies of said deeds in evidence.

We have carefully examined each of the questions presented by appellant and find no error that calls for a reversal of the judgment. Judgment affirmed.

NOTE.—Reported in 112 N. E. 411. See under (9) 17 Cyc 339.

---

## JOSE ET AL. *v.* HUNTER ET AL.

[No. 7,881. Motion to retax costs overruled December 15, 1916.]

1. STATUTES.—*Repeal by Implication.—Recovery of Costs.—Premiums on Bonds Executed by Corporate Sureties.*—The repeal of a statute by implication is not favored, and, in the absence of a repealing clause, the act of 1901, Acts 1901 p. 63, §5737 *et seq.* Burns 1914, concerning the incorporation and regulation of bonding and surety companies, did not repeal the act of 1897, Acts 1897 p. 192, §5728 *et seq.* Burns 1914, relating in part to the charging by litigants, as costs, the expense of procuring sureties on bonds or undertakings required in any action; and, although §7 of the latter act, concerning the recovery, as costs, of money paid as premiums on bonds executed by surety companies, was

declared invalid, when embodied in the act of 1901, as not being embraced within the scope of the title of such act, it is still in full force and effect as part of the act of 1897. (*Indianapolis, etc., Traction Co. v. Brennan* [1909], 174 Ind. 1, distinguished.) pp. 300, 302.

2.  STATUTES.—*Validity.—Title.*—The title of the act of 1897 (§5728 *et seq.* Burns 1914, Acts 1897 p. 192, 196), is sufficiently comprehensive to embrace the subject-matter of §7 thereof, which relates to the taxing, as costs of premiums paid by litigants to corporate surety companies for the execution of bonds or other undertakings. p. 302.

3.  COSTS. — *Bonds. — Premiums.— Taxation as Costs.—Statutes.*— Section 7 of the act of 1897 (§5728 *et seq.* Burns 1914, Acts 1897 p. 192, 196), which, after authorizing a receiver, etc., to include as part of the expense of executing his trust, money paid to a corporate surety company for becoming surety on his bond, provides that in all actions or proceedings the party entitled to recover costs may include such reasonable sum as may have been paid a surety company by such party for executing any bond therein, allows all litigants who are entitled to recover costs to have taxed as a part thereof premiums paid to surety companies for the execution of bonds or undertakings required in the action. p. 303.

From Marion Superior Court (79,933); *Pliny W. Bartholomew,* Judge.

Action by Erskine E. Hunter and another against Oscar A. Jose and another. From an adverse judgment defendants appealed, and there was a reversal, with costs ordered taxed against appellees. The latter move that the costs as taxed be retaxed. *Motion to retax costs overruled.*

*Charles A. Dryer,* for appellants.

*Williams & Schlosser,* for appellees.

HOTTEL, J.—The appellees recovered a judgment against appellants in the court below, which judgment was reversed by this court on November 26, 1913, and costs in the trial court and this court were taxed to appellees, under §706 Burns 1914, §664 R. S. 1881. A petition for rehearing was denied by this court January 16, 1914, and a petition to transfer to the Supreme Court was by such court denied January 27, 1916. Appellees now move to retax certain costs taxed against them by the clerk of this court. As shown by this motion, the total costs taxed against appellees by such clerk aggregates $221.60, two items of which represent premiums paid by appellants for the appeal bond filed by them, viz., $20 for the original premium, and $40 for the accumulated premiums. Appellees, by their motion, seek to be relieved from the items of cost represented by such premiums. In support of their motion, appellees insist that no authority can be found in this State which authorizes the taxing of such items as costs against them, and also cite authority in other jurisdictions holding that such items are improper, in the absence of statutory provisions authorizing them to be taxed. *Bick* v. *Reese* (1889), 5 N. Y. Supp. 121; *Somerville* v. *Wabash R. Co.* (1896), 111 Mich. 51, 69 N. W. 90; *Lee Injector, etc., Co.* v. *Pemberthy, etc., Co.* (1901), 109 Fed. 964; *Osborn* v. *Newberg, etc., Assn.* (1900), 36 Ore. 444, 59 Pac. 711, 60 Pac. 994.

Appellants insist that appellees' motion is not sufficient and that they have been guilty of such negligence and laches in its presentation that they should not now be permitted to obtain any benefit from it, and that, in any event, the taxing of said items as part of the costs of this ligitation is authorized by §5734 Burns 1914, Acts 1897 p. 192, 196.

As affecting the first question, we think the motion is sufficient to indicate to the court the particular items of costs which appellees seek to challenge. The case was not finally disposed of by the Supreme Court until January 26, 1916, and the delay since such final disposition does not show such laches as would warrant the court in refusing to relieve appellees from the payment of said items of costs if there is, in fact, no authority for taxing them therewith. As affecting this question the legislature, by

1. §7 of an act approved March 6, 1897, *supra*, provided as follows: "Any receiver, assignee, guardian, committee, trustee, executor, administrator, or other fidu-

ciary, required by law or the order of any court or judge
to give a bond or obligation as such, may include, as a part
of the lawful expense of executing his trust, such reasonable
sum paid a company authorized under this act so to do,
for becoming his surety on such bond or obligation, as may
be allowed by the court in which he is required to account,
or a judge thereof, not exceeding, however, one per centum
per annum on the amount of such bond or obligation; *and
in all actions or proceedings the party entitled to recover
costs may include therein and recover such reasonable sum
as may have been paid such company by such party for
executing or guaranteeing any bond, undertaking or obligation therein.*" The act, of which this section is a part, is
entitled as follows: "An act relative to bonds and other
obligations, with surety or sureties, and the acceptance as
sureties .thereon of companies qualified to act as such, and
the release of such surety, and the safe depositing of assets
for which such surety may be liable, and to the *charging by*
fiduciaries and *litigants of the expense of procuring sureties*,
and repealing all laws in conflict therewith, and declaring
an emergency."

In 1901, the legislature, by an act approved March 2,
1901, and entitled: "An act for the incorporation of bonding and surety companies, defining their powers, prescribing the duties of certain officers in connection therewith,
authorizing the acceptance of bonds made by an incorporated company, providing penalties for the violation of this
act, and declaring an emergency," incorporated, as §25
thereof, §7, above quoted, of the act of 1897, changing the
wording thereof so as to make it apply to corporations organized under the latter act, but in other respects, adopting substantially if not the same language of §7 of the
former act. Acts 1901 p. 63, §5761 Burns 1914.

In the case of *Indianapolis, etc., Traction Co.* v. *Brennan*,
(1909), 174 Ind. 1, 87 N. E. 215, 90 N. E. 65; Id. 68, 91
N. E. 503, the Supreme Court had before it the question

now under consideration, and there held that the premium for the appeal bond, taxed in that case, was improperly taxed. In that case, however, it is stated that the appellant based its right to recover of the appellees such costs, upon the act of 1901, *supra,* and the court based its conclusions on the fact that the portion of §7 italicized, *supra,* as incorporated in §25 of the act of 1901 was not within the scope of the title of such later act, and for this reason was invalid and void as violating Art. 4, §19, of the Constitution of the State. No reference was made in the opinion to §7 of the previous act of 1897, and we have examined the briefs on file in that case, and find that the court's attention was in no way called or directed to such previous act, until after the filing of a petition for a rehearing on the motion to retax costs, when the appellant, in briefs then filed, called the attention of the court to the fact that the former act had escaped the attention of the appellant and the court, and asked the court to reconsider said motion. We must therefore conclude that said act of 1897 was not considered by the court in that case, and hence that said decision does not control the question as now presented, though the items of cost be of the same character. The title of the act of 1897 is more comprehensive than that of the later act, and

2. seems to be sufficiently comprehensive to embrace the subject-matter of said section. In fact, the title of the former act seems to include the very matter (viz., litigants) which the opinion, *supra,* held to be essential to and omitted from the title of the act of 1901, and on account of which omission the court held said part of the section of the latter act invalid and void.

There is no repealing clause in the act of 1901, and hence the former act could not be repealed by the latter except by implication. Repeals by implication are

1. not favored *(Baltimore, etc., R. Co.* v. *Hagan* [1915], 183 Ind. 522, 109 N. E. 194, 196; *Mor-*

*rison* v. *State, ex rel.* [1913], 181 Ind. 544, 552, 105 N. E. 113; *Blain* v. *Bailey* [1865], 25 Ind. 165, 166) and, in any event, there is nothing in the later act that indicates any intention to repeal the former. On the contrary, §7 of the former act seems to have been incorporated in the latter as §25 thereof to make sure that corporations organized under the latter act should have the benefits extended by §7 of the former act to the companies mentioned in that act. Said sections of the two acts are in perfect harmony and, if both were valid, could be and should be construed together. *Cahill* v. *State* (1905), 36 Ind. App. 507, 512, 76 N. E. 182; *State, ex rel.* v. *Graham* (1914), 183 Ind. 53, 108 N. E. 111; *Quality Clothes Shop* v. *Keeney* (1914), 57 Ind. App. 500, 503, 106 N. E. 541; *Ensley* v. *State, ex rel.* (1909), 172 Ind. 198, 203, 88 N. E. 62.

The rules governing the construction of statutes as announced in these cases compel the conclusion that §7 of the act of 1897 (Acts 1897 pp. 192, 196, §5734 Burns 1914) is in full force and effect.

It is, however, insisted by appellees that even though such section be in force, the last provision thereof has application to only such litigants as fall within the class 3. before enumerated, viz., receivers, assignees, guardians, etc. It seems to us that no such intention on the part of the legislature is indicated, either by the language of the enacting clause, or the language of the act. The language of each indicates that all litigants required to give bond were intended to be included within the provisions in question.

The reasonableness of the amount taxed for said premiums is not questioned and, for the reasons indicated, we are of the opinion that such premiums were properly taxed as a part of the costs incurred by appellants in their appeal. The motion to retax costs is therefore overruled.

NOTE.—For opinion on merits, see 60 Ind. App. 569.

## HYPES v. NELSON ET AL.

[No. 9,280.   Filed December 19, 1916.]

1. APPEAL.—*Joint Exceptions.*—Where the exceptions to conclusions of law are joint, the judgment must be affirmed if any one of such conclusions is correct. p. 305.

2. TRIAL.—*Findings of Fact.—Failure to Find.—Effect.*—The absence of a finding on any material issuable fact is by presumption a finding against the party having the burden on that issue. p. 307.

3. TAXATION.—*Tax Deeds.—Validity.—Burden of Proof.*—Under §10380 Burns 1914, Acts 1891 p. 199, 275, making tax deeds *prima facie* evidence of the regularity of the sale of the land and all prior proceedings, and *prima facie* evidence of a valid title in fee in the grantee, a party assailing the validity of a tax deed has the burden of proof. p. 307.

4. TAXATION.—*Tax Sales.—Validity.*—To convey title, a tax sale must be conducted in accordance with the statute, and if any material act required has been omitted, or has been improperly done, the sale is ineffectual and insufficient to convey title to the purchaser. p. 307.

5. TAXATION.—*Tax Sales.—Search for Personal Property.—Demand.—Statute.*—Where a county treasurer, prior to making a sale of realty for delinquent taxes, not knowing that one in possession of the property involved was the real owner or claimed any interest therein, searched the tax duplicates for personal property belonging to the owner of record, but found none listed in her name for taxation, and made no further search or demand for property to pay the delinquent taxes, this was sufficient under §10324 Burns 1914, Acts 1903 p. 49, 60, making it the duty of the county treasurer to make demand and a search for personal property out of which to pay delinquent taxes of each resident delinquent, since the statute refers to delinquents whose names appear on the tax duplicate. p. 308.

6. TAXATION.—*Tax Sales.—Place of Holding.—Validity.—Statute.*—Under §10355 Burns 1914, Acts 1891 p. 199, 269, providing that tax sales shall be at public auction at the door of the county courthouse, a sale is valid, although conducted inside the courthouse near the door, which was closed at the time on account of cold weather. p. 308.

7. TAXATION.—*Tax Sales.—Conduct of Sale.—Validity.—Statute.*—Under §10356 Burns 1914, Acts 1891 p. 199, 269, providing that on the day fixed in the notice the county treasurer shall commence the sale for delinquent taxes and continue the same until so much of each parcel assessed shall be sold as will pay the taxes, a sale was valid where made by an auctioneer in the

presence and under the direction of the county treasurer, even though such auctioneer had no written appointment and did not take any oath as deputy treasurer. p. 308.

From Hendricks Circuit Court; *George W. Brill*, Judge.

Action by Allen G. Hypes against Horace Nelson and others. From a judgment for defendants, the plaintiff appeals. *Affirmed.*

*James W. Nichols* and *Orville W. Nichols*, for appellant.

*George C. Harvey, Drenan R. Harvey, George R. Harvey* and *Samuel Ashby*, for appellees.

IBACH, J.—This is an action to quiet title to certain lots and to set aside a tax deed held by appellee Horace Nelson. There was a cross-complaint to quiet title under such tax. deed. Upon request the court filed a special finding of facts with conclusions of law stated thereon.

1. The only question presented for the decision of this court is the correctness of the conclusions of law. The exceptions are joint and if any one of such conclusions is correct the judgment must be affirmed.

The facts found by the court are, in brief, as follows: On April 30, 1908, appellant was the owner of the real estate in controversy and on that date conveyed the property to John W. Trotter. On August 31, 1908, Trotter and wife conveyed it to Effie M. O'Donnell. Each of these deeds was recorded in the recorder's office of Hendricks county within forty-five days after their execution. On December 15, 1908, Mrs. O'Donnell, her husband joining, deeded the property to James R. Gum. On December 18, 1909, Gum and wife deeded the property to appellant. The two last-mentioned deeds were recorded on July 10, 1914. While the property was in the name of Effie M. O'Donnell and while it so appeared on the tax duplicate, the taxes became delinquent for the years 1909 and 1910, and the property was sold for taxes by the treasurer on February

14, 1911, to appellee Horace Nelson for $6.79, the amount of taxes due thereon and penalties. Nelson at that time took a tax certificate as evidence of the sale. "The sale as conducted by the treasurer was made by one William L. Wilson, an auctioneer, in the presence and under the direction of said treasurer, the said Wilson holding no written appointment, nor having taken any oath as deputy county treasurer, on the inside of the east courthouse door in the hallway of the courthouse, and near to the door; the day upon which the sale was made was cold and the door at the time was closed." Before the sale the treasurer searched the tax duplicate for personal property in the name of Effie M. O'Donnell and found no personal property listed by her for taxation, and he made no further search or demand for personal property. The treasurer, at the time and prior to the sale, had no knowledge that appellant was the owner or claimed to be the owner of the property and made no search for personal property in his name. If he had done so, he could have found personal property sufficient to pay the taxes delinquent on said real estate. The property was sold for delinquent taxes. Appellant is now and has been in possession of the property since December 18, 1909, claiming to be the owner thereof. Since the sale of the property for taxes appellee Nelson has paid all taxes due thereon, in all $14.47. Appellant has not paid or offered to pay any taxes on such property since the same became delinquent, except on May 30, 1914, he tendered to appellee Nelson the sum of $16, which lacked $1.63 of being the amount of the principal, interest and subsequent taxes paid at that date by Nelson. The sum of $16 was brought into court for the use of appellee. On April 5, 1913, the then auditor of said county executed and delivered to appellee Nelson a tax deed to the real estate in controversy which was recorded the same day on the deed records of said county. At the time of the sale the property was of the fair value of $400. Appellant had no actual knowledge of the sale. Appellee Nelson is claiming to be the owner under the tax deed.

The court concludes as a matter of law: "(1) That the defendant and cross-complainant Horace Nelson is the owner in fee simple of the real estate in question and entitled to have his title quieted thereto; (2) that the law is against the plaintiff and that he take nothing by this action; and (3) that the defendant recover his costs from the plaintiff."

The absence of a finding on any material issuable fact is by presumption a finding against the party having the burden on that issue. Section 10380 Burns 1914,

2. Acts 1891 p. 199, 275, provides that a tax deed shall be *prima facie* evidence of the regularity of the sale

3. of the land and of all prior proceedings, and *prima facie* evidence of a valid title in fee in the grantee named in the tax deed. A person assailing the validity of such deed has the burden of proof. *Knotts* v. *Zeigler* (1914), 58 Ind. App. 503, 106 N. E. 393; *Henderson* v. *Bivens* (1911), 50 Ind. App. 384, 98 N. E. 421; *Richard* v. *Carrie* (1895), 145 Ind. 49, 43 N. E. 949.

"The manner of conducting a delinquent tax sale to make the same effective to convey title must be in accordance with the statute, and each step required from

4. the first publication notice to the delivery of the deed must be taken. If any material and essential act required to be done has been omitted, or has been improperly done, the entire sale must be held ineffectual and insufficient to convey title to the purchaser." *Dixon* v. *Thompson* (1912), 52 Ind. App. 560, 563, 98 N. E. 738, 739.

Appellant's contentions are based on two propositions: (1) That there was no demand or search for personal property (belonging to appellant) prior to the sale; and

(2) that the manner of sale was not in conformity with the statute in that the statute contemplates a sale by the treasurer, whereas the facts in this case show a sale by an auctioneer in the presence and under the direction of the treasurer, such auctioneer having no written appointment and not having taken any oath as deputy treasurer; and further that the sale was held in the courthouse instead of on the outside.

In answer to the first, it may be said that the facts show that the record title at the time of the sale was in the name of Effie M. O'Donnell; that the treasurer

5. searched the tax duplicate for personal property in that name and found none listed by her for taxation; that the treasurer at the time and prior to the sale had no knowledge that appellant was the owner, or claimed to be the owner, of the property. The findings do not show, and it is not claimed, that Effie M. O'Donnell had any personal property out of which the delinquent taxes might have been collected. Section 10324 Burns 1914, Acts 1903 p. 49, 60, which makes it the duty of the county treasurer to make search and demand for personal property out of which to pay delinquent taxes of each resident delinquent, refers to delinquents whose names appear on the tax duplicate.

The provisions of the statutes affecting the questions presented by the second proposition, *supra,* read as follows:

"The auditor shall cause a copy of such (delinquent)

6. list to be posted * * *. To such list shall be attached * * * a notice that * * * said

7. lands * * * will be sold at public auction at the courthouse door of such county," etc. §10355 Burns 1914, Acts 1891 p. 199, 269. "On the day mentioned in the notice, the county treasurer shall commence the sale of such lands, and shall continue the same from day to day," etc. §10356 Burns 1914, *supra.*

The contention of appellant cannot be upheld. The

findings of fact show a substantial, if not a strict, compliance with the requirements of the statute. Judgment affirmed.

Note.—Reported in 114 N. E. 459. Tax sales, where made, 33 L. R. A. 96; 37 Cyc 1334. See under (2) 38 Cyc 1985; (4) 37 Cyc 1479.

---

## WAINRIGHT TRUST COMPANY, RECEIVER, *v.* UNITED STATES FIDELITY AND GUARANTY COMPANY.

### [No. 9,579. Filed December 19, 1916.]

1. **FRAUDS, STATUTE OF.**—*Contractor's Bond.*—Under the statute of frauds (§7462 Burns 1914, §4904 R. S. 1881), a contractor's bond indemnifying the obligee against loss resulting from a breach of the contract must be in writing, since its purpose is to charge one person upon a special promise to answer for the default of another. p. 314.

2. **FRAUDS, STATUTE OF.**—*Contractor's Bond.—Waiver of Condition by Parol.*—An oral waiver by a surety of a provision in a contractor's bond relative to the time within which suit must be brought is not binding, since the bond itself is required to be in writing by the statute of frauds (§7462 Burns 1914, §4904 R. S. 1881), and cannot be varied by parol. p. 315.

3. **PRINCIPAL AND SURETY.**—*Bonds.—Construction.*—Where a bond is ambiguous or open to two constructions, the interpretation most favorable to the obligee should be adopted, but this rule does not apply to bonds, the terms of which are certain, definite and unambiguous. p. 315.

4. **PRINCIPAL AND SURETY.**—*Contractor's Bond.—Notice of Breach. —Failure to Give.*—Where a contractor's bond provided that no liability should attach to the surety unless, in the event of the principal's default, notice thereof should be given the surety not later than thirty days after knowledge of such default such condition was valid. p. 315.

5. **PRINCIPAL AND SURETY.**—*Contractor's Bond.—Conditions.—Notice of Default.*—Where, in an action against a surety company on a road contractor's bond, the complaint contained allegations showing that on May 13, the board of county commissioners notified the obligee that work under the contract should begin within ten days in order to complete it by August 1, to which date the board had extended the time limit fixed in the contract, and that immediately upon receipt of such notice the obligee had written notice of the contractor's alleged default to the surety company and informed it of the board's order, such allegations do not show a

310    APPELLATE COURT OF INDIANA,

Wainright Trust Co. v. U. S. Fidelity, etc., Co.—63 Ind. App. 309.

compliance with a condition in the bond requiring, in order that liability should attach to the surety, that notice of the principal's default be given to the guarantor by the obligee not later than thirty days after knowledge of default, as the alleged notice of default was given more than two and one-half months before the expiration of the time limit fixed for the completion of the work. p. 316.

6. PRINCIPAL AND SURETY.—*Contractor's Bond.—Notice of Default.* *—Acceptance of Premium.—Effect.*—The acceptance and retention by a surety company of a renewal premium on a contractor's bond was not a waiver of the company's right to a notice of the contractor's default, as provided in the bond, where the alleged default did not occur until several months after the payment of the premium. p. 316.

From Hamilton Circuit Court; *Meade Vestal*, Special Judge.

Action by Wainright Trust Company, receiver for the firm of Holleran, Haverstick, Wheeler and Patterson, against the United States Fidelity and Guaranty Company. From a judgment for defendant, the plaintiff appeals. *Affirmed.*

*Gentry & Campbell,* for appellant.

*Pickens, Moores, Davidson & Pickens* and *Fred C. Hines,* for appellee.

McNUTT, J.—This was an action by appellant, as receiver for the firm of Holleran, Haverstick, Wheeler & Patterson, in the court below, against appellee, as surety upon a contractor's bond, the contractor being one Black. The appellee demurred to appellant's complaint, the same being the fourth amended, for want of sufficient facts, which demurrer was sustained. This action of the court is the only error assigned.

The contract, which is made a part of the complaint by exhibit, required said Black to place the gravel on two public highways of Hamilton county, known as the Eiler road and the Hunter road, which appellant's firm had contracted with the board of commissioners of said county to construct according to certain plans and specifications.

Said Black agreed to place the gravel on said roads on or before January 1, 1913, and the contract was entered into on July 17, 1912.

The bond, which is also made a part of the complaint by exhibit, reads as follows:

"Know all Men by these Presents, That W. P. Black of Fishers, Indiana, (hereinafter called the Principal), and the United States Fidelity and Guaranty Company, a corporation created and existing under the laws of the State of Maryland, and whose principal office is located in Baltimore City, Maryland, (hereinafter called the Surety), are held and firmly bound unto Holleran & Haverstick, Noblesville, Indiana, (hereinafter called the Obligee,) in the full and just sum of Five thousand ($5000.00) Dollars, lawful money of the United States, to the payment of which sum, well and truly to be made, the Principal binds himself, his heirs, executors and administrators, and the said Surety binds itself, its successors and assigns, jointly and severally, firmly by these presents.  Signed, sealed and delivered this 30th day of September, A. D. 1912.

"WHEREAS, said Principal has entered into a certain written contract with the Obligee dated July 17th 1912, to furnish labor and material for completion of a gravel road, known as the Eiler Road, in accordance with contract which is made a part of this bond.

"Now therefore, The condition of the foregoing obligation is such that if the said Principal shall well and truly indemnify and save harmless the said Obligee from any pecuniary loss resulting from the breach of any of the terms, covenants and conditions of the said contract on the part of the said Principal to be performed, then this obligation shall be void; otherwise to remain in full force and effect in law.

"PROVIDED, however, that this bond is issued subject to the following conditions and provisions:

"First,—That no liability shall attach to the Surety hereunder unless, in the event of any default on the part of the Principal in the performance of any of the terms, covenants or conditions of the said contract, the obligee shall promptly, and in any event not later than thirty days after knowledge of such default, deliver to the Surety at its office in the City of Baltimore, written notice thereof, with a statement of the

312 APPELLATE COURT OF INDIANA,

Wainright Trust Co. v. U. S. Fidelity, etc., Co.—63 Ind. App. 309.

principal facts showing such default and the date thereof; nor unless the said Obligee shall deliver written notice to the surety at its office aforesaid, and the consent of the Surety thereto obtained, before making to the Principal the final payment provided for under the contract herein referred to.

"Second, That in case of such default on the part of the Principal the Surety shall have the right, if it so desire, to assume and complete or procure the completion of said contract; and in case of such default, the Surety shall be subrogated and entitled to all rights and properties of the Principal arising out of the said contract and otherwise, including all securities and indemnities theretofore received by the Obligee and all deferred payment, retained percentages and credits, due to the principal at the time of such default or to become due thereafter by the terms and dates of the contract.

"Third,—That in no event shall the Surety be liable for a greater sum than the penalty of this bond, or subject to any suit, action or other proceeding thereon that is instituted later than the 30th day of July, A. D. 1913.

"Fourth,—That in no event shall the Surety be liable for any damage resulting from, or for the construction or repair of any work damaged or destroyed by act of God, or the public enemies, or mobs, or riots, or civil commotion, or by employes leaving the work being done under said contract, on account of so-called "strikes" or labor difficulties.

"In testimony whereof, the said Principal has hereunto set his hand and seal and the said Surety has caused these presents to be executed by its Attorney-in-fact, sealed with its corporate seal, the day and year first written."

The complaint alleges, in substance, that on March 10, 1915, the appellant was appointed receiver for said firm; that on July 17, 1912, said firm entered into said contract; that in consideration of said contract and as a part thereof said appellee, as surety for the contractor, Black, executed to said firm said bond for the faithful performance of said contract; that said contractor complied with the terms of said contract relating to said Hunter road and received the consideration therefor, but failed to perform any part

of the work on said Eiler road; that on or before said
January 1, 1913, said Black and said firm mutually agreed
to and did extend the time for the completion of said work,
and in consideration of such extension said firm agreed to
waive any claim for damages for the work not being completed on or before said January 1, 1913, and that said
Black upon his part agreed to pay, and did pay, to appellee
the sum of $25 for the extension and security of said bond,
of all of which facts said appellee then had knowledge;
that after the extension of the time for the completion of
said work appellant, said Black and appellee appeared
before the board of commissioners of Hamilton county and
obtained from it an order extending the time for the completion of said Eiler road; that appellee, knowing that said
bond contained a provision "that in no event shall the
surety be subject to any suit or action or other proceeding thereon that is instituted later than July 30th, 1913,"
did, on or about November 20, 1913, accept from said Black
an additional premium of $25 for the continuation and
extension of the terms of said bond, and that appellee has
ever since retained said sum; that on November 21, 1913,
said firm, believing said bond was still in force and relying
upon its security, together with said Black and one Hines,
who was then and there the duly authorized local agent
of appellee, appeared before said board, and that said Hines,
as spokesman for said parties, asked for and was granted
an order by said board extending the time for the completion of said Eiler road to August 1, 1914, that on May
13, 1914, said board notified said firm that work should
begin on said road within ten days thereafter, in order to
complete it by the time allotted; that immediately upon
receipt of notice of said demand, and within thirty days
after knowledge of default by said Black, or on or about
May 13, 1914, written notice of such default and the order
of said board was given to appellee, at its office in Baltimore, Maryland; that said Black neglected and wholly

314 APPELLATE COURT OF INDIANA,

Wainright Trust Co. *v.* U. S. Fidelity, etc., Co.—63 Ind. App. 309.

failed to perform any part of his work on said Eiler road; that appellee failed and refused to perform any of said work; that by reason thereof said firm, by its legal representative, was compelled to, and did, perform said work at a cost of $1.05 per cubic yard, which was sixty-eight cents per cubic yard in excess of said Black's contract, to plaintiff's damage in the sum of $3,757.68; that appellant, on September 14, 1914, demanded of appellee said sum, but that appellee refused to pay any part thereof; that said sum, with interest, is long past due and unpaid, and judgment therefor is demanded.

Appellant, in its brief, under "Points and Authorities," states only two points, which are as follows: "1. A condition in a bond executed by a surety company, limiting the time within which an action may be brought on such bond, being for the benefit of the company, may be waived. 2. Contracts of surety companies are contracts of indemnity, and as such fall under the rules of construction applicable to contracts of insurance."

Appellee does not dispute the correctness of either of said points as abstract legal propositions, but insists that, while a condition in a surety bond, limiting the time within which an action thereon may be brought, may be waived, no waiver of such condition is shown in the complaint for the reason that the requirement that suit be brought within a certain time is shown to be in writing, while the alleged waiver is shown to be in parol, and, therefore, within the statute of frauds. The bond in suit was not only in writing, but was for the purpose of charging appellee upon a special promise to answer for the default of another, 1. and, therefore, under the statute of frauds had to be in writing. §7462 Burns 1914, §4904 R. S. 1881; *Knight & Jillson Co.* v. *Castle* (1908), 172 Ind. 97, 87 N. E. 976, 27 L. R. A. (N. S.) 573.

In the case of *Wellinger* v. *Crawford* (1911), 48 Ind. App. 173, 89 N. E. 892, 93 N. E. 1051, it is held that

NOVEMBER TERM, 1916. 315

Wainright Trust Co. v. U. S. Fidelity, etc., Co.—63 Ind. App. 309.

because contracts for a commission for a sale of real estate
must be in writing (§7463 Burns 1914, Acts 1913 p. 638),
such contracts cannot be varied or waived by parol. In *Burgett* v. *Loeb* (1908), 43 Ind. App. 657, 660, 88 N. E. 346, it is
held that since a lease for more than three years is required
to be in writing (§7462 Burns 1914, *supra*), it could only
be changed or modified by a written instrument. See, also,
*Bradley* v. *Harter* (1900), 156 Ind. 499, 60 N. E. 139;
*Napier Iron Works* v. *Caldwell, etc., Iron Works* (1915),
60 Ind. App. 317, 110 N. E. 714.

It is only by inference from conduct that the complaint
attempts to show an oral waiver of the provision in the
bond relative to the time within which suit must be
2. brought; but even if a positive, direct waiver of this
provision were alleged, we are of opinion, under the
authorities, that such a waiver is not binding upon appellee
since it is not shown to be in writing.

Appellant has pointed out no ambiguity or uncertainty in
the bond, nor does it contend that the bond admits of more
than one interpretation. It is the law that where a
3. bond is ambiguous or uncertain or is open to two
constructions, one favorable to the surety and one
to the obligee, that a construction favorable to the obligee
should be adopted. These principles of construction are
based on reason and authority, and in cases where they have
any application are important, but they have no application to contracts, the terms of which are certain, definite
and unambiguous. *Beech Grove Imp. Co.* v. *Title Guaranty, etc., Co.* (1911), 50 Ind. App. 377, 98 N. E. 373.

Points presented by appellee show the complaint to be
insufficient on account of other conditions in the bond not
shown to have been complied with. It is not con-
4. tended that the first condition in the bond is not
valid, and under the authorities it is a valid condition. *Knight & Jillson Co.* v. *Castle, supra; Beech Grove
Imp. Co.* v. *Title Guaranty, etc., Co., supra. Caywood* v.

*Supreme Lodge, etc.* (1908), 171 Ind. 410, 86 N. E. 482, 23 L. R. A. (N. S.) 304, 131 Am. St. 253, 17 Ann. Cas. 503.

It is alleged in the complaint that appellant's firm and the contractor, before the time for completing the work expired, as provided by the original contract, agreed

5.   that the time should be extended in which the work was to be finished to August 1, 1914, and that said parties and appellee, through its agent, requested and secured from the board of commissioners an order for such extension. It is further alleged: "That on May 13, 1914, said Board of Commissioners notified said firm that work should begin on said road within ten days thereafter in order to complete it by the time allotted; that immediately upon receipt of notice of said Board, and within thirty days after knowledge of default by said Black, or on or about May 13, 1914, written notice of such default and the order of said Board was given to appellee, at its office in Baltimore." Since it is shown that the time for completion of the work under the contract was extended to August 1, 1914, could there be any default before that date? The alleged notice or default was given appellee more than two and one-half months before the time within which the contractor had to do the work. It is our opinion that this was not a compliance with the first condition of the bond. Nor do we think the acceptance and retention by appellee of a renewal premium paid by the principal in November,

6.   1913, was a waiver of appellee's right to a notice of the contractor's default for the reason that it is not contended that there was any default on the contractor's part until several months after the payment of such premium, in view of the allegations that the time for furnishing the work had been extended to August 1, 1914.

In *Bennecke* v. *Insurance Co.* (1881), 105 U. S. 355, 360, 26 L. Ed. 990, the court said: "A waiver of a stipulation in an agreement must, to be effectual, not only be made intentionally, but with knowledge of the circumstances.

This is the rule when there is a direct and precise agreement to waive the stipulation. A *fortiori* is this the rule when there is no agreement either verbal or in writing to waive the stipulation, but where it is sought to deduce a waiver from the conduct of the party. Thus, where a written agreement exists and one of the parties sets up an arrangement of a different nature, alleging conduct on the other side amounting to a substitution of this arrangement for a written agreement, he must clearly show not merely his own understanding, but that the other party had the same understanding." See, also, *Georgia Home Ins. Co.* v. *Rosenfield* (1899), 95 Fed. 358, 37 C. C. A. 96; *Insurance Co.* v. *Wolff* (1877), 95 U. S. 326, 333, 24 L. E. 387; *Marion, etc., Bed Co.* v. *Empire State Co.* (1912), 52 Ind. App. 480, 100 N. E. 882. "A waiver involves the idea of assent; and assent is primarily an act of the understanding. We cannot assent to a proposition without some intelligent apprehension of it. It presupposes that the person to be affected has knowledge of his rights but does not wish to enforce them." *Jewell* v. *Jewell* (1892), 84 Me. 304, 307, 24 Atl. 858, 859, 18 L. R. A. 473. See, also, *Gibson Electric Co.* v. *Liverpool, etc., Ins. Co.* (1899) 159 N. Y. 418, 54 N. E. 23; *Strange* v. *Fooks* (1863), 4 Gif. 408, 413; *Berman* v. *Fraternities, etc., Assn.* (1910), 107 Me. 368, 78 Atl. 462; *U. S. Fidelity, etc., Co.* v. *Ridgely* (1903), 70 Neb. 622, 97 N. W. 836.

It is not necessary to notice other questions presented by appellee. The court below did not err in sustaining the demurrer to the complaint. Judgment affirmed.

NOTE.—Reported in 114 N. E. 470. See under (3) 32 Cyc 176; (4) 115 Am. St. 94.

## ESSIG ET AL. *v*. PORTER.

[No. 9,559. Filed May 31, 1916. Rehearing denied October 26, 1916. Transfer denied December 19, 1916.]

1. VENDOR AND PURCHASER.—*Remedies of Vendor.—Vendor's Lien. —Purchase Price of Realty.*—Where plaintiff, in an action to enforce a vendor's lien, after having purchased and paid for a tract of land and entered into possession, caused a deed of conveyance to be made directly from his vendor to his purchaser, he was entitled to a vendor's lien for the purchase price, for when the actual vendor of realty holds only a title in equity and the conveyance is made directly from the party holding the legal title in trust, a vendor's lien arises in favor of the actual vendor. p. 319.

2. BILLS AND NOTES.—*Promissory Note.—Construction.—Negotiability.*—An instrument promising to pay, for value received, a specified sum of money and containing the expression "negotiable and payable" at a bank named, is a negotiable note, even though it does not contain the words "or order," "or bearer," or other like words of negotiability, since the wording of the note clearly shows that it was intended to be negotiable. p. 320.

3. VENDOR AND PURCHASER.—*Remedies of Vendor.—Lien.—Waiver.* —Where one holding a vendor's lien accepted the vendee's note for the unpaid portion of the purchase price of land, he did not thereby waive his lien. p. 321.

4. VENDOR AND PURCHASER.—*Vendor's Lien.—Notice to Purchaser.* —Where a grantee of land, the defendant in an action to enforce a vendor's lien, was present when her grantor gave her note, and knew of its execution and that it was for unpaid purchase money for the land involved, and that the note was unpaid at the time such land was conveyed to her, such grantee took the land with notice that it was subject to a vendor's lien in favor of the payee of the note. p. 321.

5. VENDOR AND PURCHASER.—*Vendor's Lien.—Purchaser Without Notice.—Rights of Parties.*—A remote grantor may enforce his vendor's lien against a subsequent purchaser without notice, who is afterwards notified of the lien, to the extent of the purchase price unpaid by him at the time he receives notice. p. 322.

6. APPEAL. — *Vendor's Lien. — Action to Enforce.—Conclusions of Law.—Failure to Except.—Effect on Appeal.*—Where, in an action to enforce a vendor's lien, the trial court found that land in the hands of a grantee was subject to a vendor's lien in favor of a remote grantor to the extent of the unpaid money due from such grantee, who neither excepted to the conclusions of law nor

made any motion to modify the judgment rendered thereon, it is
unnecessary for the court on appeal to consider whether the
grantee, who gave his note to his grantor for the unpaid portion
of the purchase price, was an innocent purchaser as to the entire
purchase price, as any error in the conclusions of law in this
respect would not be prejudicial to his immediate grantor, who
is a coappellant. p. 322.

7. VENDOR AND PURCHASER.—*Vendor's Lien.—Enforcement.—Remedies of Vendor.—Judgment.*—Where, in an action to enforce a
vendor's lien, it was found by the trial court that the grantor of
the land involved knew at the time of the conveyance that it
was subject to a vendor's lien, a judgment decreeing that the
grantor pay into court a sufficient amount to satisfy the lien out
of money in her possession derived from the sale of the land,
and providing that she should be subject to citation and punishment for disobedience of the decree, was proper, since, in such
a case equity will transfer the lien to the funds received from the
sale of the land. p. 322.

From Hamilton Circuit Court; *Meade Vestal*, Judge.

Action by Samuel J. Porter against Samantha P. Essig
and others. From a judgment for plaintiff, the defendants
appeal. *Affirmed.*

*O. H. Mendenhall* and *Christian & Christian*, for appellants.

*J. F. Neal* and *N. C. Neal*, for appellee.

IBACH, J.—This was an action by appellee against appellants to enforce a vendor's lien against certain real estate.
The errors assigned in overruling appellant's demurrers to
the complaint will not be discussed, since the arguments as
to such errors are met by what will be said concerning the
facts of the case as found by the court and its conclusions
of law thereon.

In 1877 appellee owned forty acres of real estate in
Hamilton county, in which Barbara Hertzler had a life
estate. She and appellee agreed that if appellee would purchase a certain ten-acre tract of land in the vicinity,
1. and construct on it a dwelling house, and convey it
to her, she would release to him her life estate in
the forty-acre tract, surrender possession of it to him, and

pay him the difference in value between the ten acres and dwelling house, and the life estate. Appellee purchased the ten acres, entered into possession, and built the house in accordance with his agreement, and then had the deed of conveyance made directly from the former owners to Mrs. Hertzler, and she surrendered her life estate in the forty acres to him, and was indebted to him on account of the excess of the value of the ten-acre tract and cost of the dwelling house which had been paid by him.

This was sufficient to cause to exist in appellant's favor a lien against the ten-acre tract of land for the purchase price. When the actual vendor holds only a title in equity, and the conveyance is made directly from the party holding the legal title in trust, a vendor's lien arises in favor of the actual vendor. "Where a purchaser has paid the whole purchase-money, he is, in equity, regarded as the real owner of the land for every purpose. He is so in very substance, and a conveyance to him is but a compliance with a form of law. It would be a surprising doctrine, that a court of equity would so stick upon form, in utter disregard of right, as to deny to him the implied lien for purchase-money, which it would give if he had held also the legal title." *Johns* v. *Sewell* (1870), 33 Ind. 1, 4. See, also, *Dwenger* v. *Branigan* (1884), 95 Ind. 221; *Otis* v. *Gregory* (1887), 111 Ind. 504, 515, 13 N. E. 39.

In 1896 the amount owing by Barbara Hertzler to appellee as purchase money had not been paid, nor secured in any manner, and it was agreed between her and appellee that she owed him $318, and she executed to him her note therefor, in part in the following language:

2.

"One day after death * * * for value received * * * promise to pay S. J. Porter the sum of $318 and attorneys' fees, negotiable and payable at the Union Bank at Tipton, Indiana, with interest at the rate of six per cent per annum from date until paid."

This instrument must be held to be a negotiable note. If a note does not contain the words "or order," "or bearer," or other like words of negotiability, it is non-negotiable. Tiedeman, Commercial Paper §21; *Maule* v. *Crawford* (1878), 14 Hun (N. Y.) 193; *Hackney* v. *Jones* (1842), 3 Humph. (Tenn.) 611. But if it contains words which clearly show that it was intended to be negotiable, it is not necessary that the words "order" or "bearer" be used. It is clearly stated that this note shall be "negotiable and payable at the Union Bank at Tipton, Indiana," and therefore it must be held to be a negotiable instrument. Tiedeman, Commercial Paper §21; *Raymond* v. *Middleton & Co.* (1858), 29 Pa. St. 529. However, the taking of this note did not operate as a waiver of the vendor's lien previously held by appellee. "The presumption of payment,

3. which ordinarily arises from the giving of a note governed by the law merchant, will be controlled when its effect would be to deprive the party who takes the note of a collateral security, or any other substantial benefit. In such cases the presumption of payment is rebutted by the circumstances of the transaction itself." *Jouchert* v. *Johnson* (1886), 108 Ind. 436, 9 N. E. 413. See, also, *Bradway* v. *Groenendyke* (1899), 153 Ind. 508, 55 N. E. 434; *Scott* v. *Edgar* (1902), 159 Ind. 38, 63 N. E. 452; *Aldridge* v. *Dunn* (1844), 7 Blackf. 249, 41 Am. Dec. 224; 39 Cyc 1842.

On October 3, 1911, Barbara Hertzler executed a deed conveying the above mentioned ten-acre tract of land to appellant Samantha P. Essig, her daughter. This

4. tract of land was Mrs. Hertzler's only property. The consideration for the deed was services rendered to Mrs. Hertzler and a home furnished to her, of ample value for the land. Appellant Essig was present when her mother gave the note in question to appellee, and knew of its execution, that it was for unpaid purchase money, and that it

was unpaid when the land was deeded to her. Hence she took the land with notice that it was subject to a vendor's lien in favor of appellant. On February 2, 1912, Barbara Hertzler died insolvent, and on March 1, 1912, appellant Essig conveyed the aforesaid ten-acre tract to appellant Cocain for the consideration of $2,000 of which he

5. paid her $1,500 in cash, of which amount she now has $1,300 in cash, and the remaining portion was evidenced by his promissory note for $500 secured by mortgage on the real estate sold. On March 5, 1912, he was notified of appellee's claim against the real estate. It is undoubtedly true that appellant Cocain would not be an innocent purchaser as to the amount of the purchase price unpaid by him at the time he received notice of appellee's lien against the land, but such rule can have no application in this case unless the promissory note was not payment. *Certain* v. *Smith* (1912), 53 Ind. App. 163, 101 N. E. 319; *Higgins* v. *Kendall* (1881), 73 Ind. 522. The court found

6. that appellee has, and is entitled to, a vendor's lien on the land to the extent of the unpaid purchase money owing by appellant Cocain, and also upon the purchase money in the hands of appellant Essig, and stated conclusions of law accordingly. It is unnecessary for us to consider whether appellant Cocain, having given his promissory note for the unpaid portion of the purchase price, can by that fact be said to be an innocent purchaser as to the entire purchase price. This appellant has not excepted to the conclusions of law, or made any motion to modify the judgment rendered thereon, and any error in this respect as to him would not be prejudicial to appellant Essig. The court as a part of its judgment decreed that appellant Essig should within thirty days pay into court the sum of $689.98,

7. which it found to be due on the note, with interest, in discharge of appellee's lien and in case of her failure to do so, she should be subject upon appellant's motion to citation and punishment for disobedience

of the decree. Appellant Essig moved the court to strike out this portion of the judgment rendered. The overruling of this motion was not error. Appellants were neither personally liable for the debt represented by the vendor's lien held by appellee; but, as appellant Essig, with knowledge of such lien, sold the land upon which it was attached, equity will transfer the lien to the funds received from the sale of the lands, and require her to pay the lien therefrom.

The death of appellee while this appeal has been pending having been suggested, the judgment is therefore affirmed as of the date of submission. Judgment affirmed.

Note.—Reported in 112 N. E. 1005. See under (1) 39 Cyc 1801. Negotiable note, what constitutes, Ann. Cas. 1912D 4. See under (2) 7 Cyc 606; (3) 39 Cyc 1834; (4) 39 Cyc 1823.

---

## Vandalia Coal Company *v.* Ringo, Administrator.

[No. 9,178. Filed December 20, 1916.]

1. Appeal.—*Briefs.—Omissions by Appellant.—Supply by Appellee. Sufficiency.*—Where appellant's brief, in seeking to question the sufficiency of the complaint, fails, in its statement of the record, to set out enough of the complaint to properly present the objections thereto, it is subject to criticism as not complying with the rules of the Appellate Court, but when the omissions from the record are supplied by appellee, such brief is sufficient to present the objections urged against the complaint. p. 324.

2. Death.—*Action for Wrongful Death.—Damages.—Loss of Prospective Benefits.*—Damages, in case of wrongful death, may be the loss by the beneficiary of any pecuniary benefit which he might reasonably have expected to receive by gift during the lifetime of the deceased, so that it is competent, in an action for the death by negligence for the benefit of the parents and brothers and sisters, to show decedent's earnings and that he gave a large part thereof to his parents and their children for their maintenance and support. p. 326.

3. Appeal.—*Briefs.—Sufficiency.*—Where the only proposition or point mentioned in appellant's brief applying to questions arising under the motion for a new trial is a general statement that instructions must be confined to the issues made by the pleadings,

and must be based on the evidence, and neither the pleadings nor the evidence is set out, no question is presented for review as to the instructions or motion for a new trial based on error therein. p. 326.

4. APPEAL.—*Review.*—*Searching the Record.*—The court on appeal will search the record to affirm a cause, but not to reverse it. p. 326.

From Knox Circuit Court; *Benjamin M. Willoughby,* Judge.

Action by Nathan W. Ringo, administrator of the estate of James Cross, deceased, against the Vandalia Coal Company. From a judgment for plaintiff, the defendant appeals. *Affirmed.*

*James M. House* and *Henry W. Moore,* for appellant.

*Oscar E. Bland, L. M. Wade* and *A. J. Padgett,* for appellee.

IBACH, J.—This is an action for the wrongful death of appellee's decedent while working in appellant's coal mine. The negligence charged is the failure on the part of appellant to supply and circulate sufficient air in its mine as required by statute.

The complaint is in two paragraphs. A demurrer to each for want of facts was overruled, and such rulings are separately assigned as error. A trial resulted in a verdict and judgment for appellee for $600. Appellant's motion for a new trial was overruled and such ruling is also assigned as error. The sufficiency of appellant's brief to present any question is attacked by appellee.

It is insisted that the rulings on the demurrers are not presented for the reason that appellant has failed to set out the complaint or its substance in its brief as required by the rules of this court. In its statement of the record to present such questions appellant says: "We desire especially to challenge the sufficiency of the complaint in so far as it pretends to set up the damages sustained by the next of kin. The only allegation of either

paragraph of the complaint which refers in any way to the
next of kin or their dependence is as follows: 'That at the
time plaintiff's said decedent was injured he was twenty-
two years of age and was a strong, healthy, able-bodied
man, and a skilled workman in his profession of coal mining, and that he left at his death surviving him and wholly
dependent upon him for support, his father, Alexander
Cross, his mother, Jenette Cross and six brothers and sisters
whose names and ages are as follows: Mary 13 years,
Jennette 11 years, Alex 9 years, Jermimma 7 years, John 4
years and Agnes 1½ years.' '' ' •

That part of the memorandum accompanying the demurrers set out in appellant's brief is as follows: "8· There
is no sufficient allegation of fact or facts showing that the
deceased left any one depending upon him for support, or
that any one sustained a pecuniary loss by the death of
the deceased. 9. The general allegation that the father and
mother and six brothers and sisters were dependent upon
the deceased for support is overcome by the fact disclosed
in the complaint that the six brothers and sisters are all
under age and have a father and mother living, and that the
deceased was more than twenty-one years of age."

Appellee also insists that each paragraph states a cause
of action, and supports such insistence by the further
statement from each paragraph of complaint: "That plaintiff's decedent, during his lifetime and up to the time of
his death, earned on an average of $40 every two weeks,
and gave the same or most of it to his father and mother,
and children for their support and maintenance."

While appellant's briefs are subject to criticism, the statement of the record contained therein, when supplied by that
of appellee, is sufficient to present the specific objections
urged against the complaint. *Adams* v. *Betz* (1906), 167
Ind. 161, 164, 78 N. E. 649.

The loss which a man suffers by the death of a relative
may be the loss of something which he was legally entitled

to receive, or may be the loss of something which it
2. was reasonably probable he would receive. The
second description of loss includes the loss by the
beneficiary of any pecuniary benefit which he might reasonably have expected to receive during the lifetime of the
deceased by gift. It was competent, therefore, under the
averments of each paragraph of the complaint in question,
to show the earnings of decedent and that a large part of
them were given to his father, mother, brothers and sisters
for their support and maintenance. There are no specific
allegations which overcome the general allegations. See
*Standard Forgings Co.* v. *Holmstrom* (1914), 58 Ind. App.
306, 316, 317, 104 N. E. 872; *Louisville, etc., R. Co.* v.
*Goodykoontz* (1889), 119 Ind. 111, 21 N. E. 472, 12 Am.
St. 371; *Diebold* v. *Sharp* (1897), 19 Ind. App. 474, 49 N.
E. 837.

It is next insisted that the brief is insufficient to present any question arising under appellant's motion for a
new trial for the reason that all the instructions are not set
out in the brief, and that it does not contain a condensed
recital of the evidence in narrative form.

Appellant has not complied with the rules in its statement
of the evidence. The only proposition or point mentioned in
appellant's brief, under "Points and Authorities,"
3. that could be held to apply to questions arising
under its motion for a new trial is as follows:
"Instructions must be confined to the issues made by the
pleadings, and must be based upon the evidence." In the
absence of the pleadings and the evidence, such objection,
if sufficiently specific to present any question, would
4. require a search of the record. This court will search
the record to affirm but not to reverse. *March* v.
*March* (1911), 50 Ind. App. 293, 295, 98 N. E. 324.

Other errors are assigned, but in view of the disposition
made of other questions, their discussion here becomes un-

necessary. No reversible error having been shown, the judgment below is affirmed.

NOTE.—Reported in 114 N. E. 466. See under (1) 3 C. J. 1447; (2) 13 Cyc 355.

---

## BROWN v. TERRE HAUTE, INDIANAPOLIS AND EASTERN TRACTION COMPANY.

[No. 8,581. Filed December 16, 1915. Rehearing denied June 8, 1916. Transfer denied December 20, 1916.]

1. CARRIERS.—*Carriage of Passengers.—Action for Wrongful Ejectment.—Fares.—Evidence.*—Where a carrier's published schedules of fares, as filed with the Railroad Commission, fixed the fare from A to B at ten cents, from A to C at twenty cents, and from B to C at five cents, the schedules not mentioning two stops between B and C, known as stops Nos. 8 and 9, and when passengers boarded trains at other than established fare points, authorized the collection of five cents to the first fare point plus the fare from the first fare point to the destination, while a supplementary schedule fixed the fare at fifteen cents between A and stop No. 8, but fixed no fare between such stop and any other station, such schedules did not definitely or certainly establish the fare between stop No. 9 and B, so that, in an action against the carrier for wrongful ejectment, evidence was admissible to show the fare actually charged by defendant between such points on the day in question for the purpose of ascertaining the interpretation and construction placed on the schedules by the carrier. pp. 335, 336.

2. EVIDENCE.—*Best and Secondary Evidence.—Railroad Fares.—Schedules Filed With Railroad Commission.*—A carrier's published schedules of fares as filed with, and approved by, the Railroad Commission, such body being invested with control thereof, are the best and, therefore, the proper evidence by which to prove the established fares between stopping places on the carrier's line. p. 336.

3. CARRIERS.—*Carriage of Passengers.—Action for Wrongful Ejectment. — Evidence. — Admissibility. — Res Gestæ.* — In an action against an interurban railroad for wrongful ejectment, the statement made to plaintiff by the conductor on the occasion of the occurrence involved, concerning fares charged by defendant, was admissible as part of the res gestæ. p. 337.

4. CARRIERS.—*Carriage of Passengers.—Action for Wrongful Ejectment.—Passenger Fares.—Splitting up Journey.—Instructions.—Statutes.*—Section 1 of the act of 1911 (Acts 1911 p. 545), §§3,

cl. g, 7, 13 and 14, cls. a, b, of the act of 1907 (Acts 1907 p. 454) only make it unlawful for a carrier to charge or collect any rate or tariff different from that fixed in the tariff schedule or by the use of any special rate, rebate, etc., to demand or receive from any person a greater or less fare than it charges any other person for like transportation, and forbids the acceptance by any person or firm of a rebate, but such statutes do not prohibit a passenger from making his journey by stages, regardless of his motive for so doing, and when a carrier offers the traveling public both a local and a through tariff in the duly published schedules, and the sum of the local fares between any two points on the carrier's line is less than the through rate, a passenger, although he cannot elect at the commencement of his journey to pay the sum of the local fares for a through passage, may make his journey by stages in order to get the benefit of the local tariffs, and it is the duty of the carrier to accept a fare to any regular stopping point that a passenger may indicate; hence, in an action against an interurban railroad for wrongful ejectment instructions stating that one becoming a passenger is obligated to pay the through fare to the final destination intended when boarding a car is erroneous as making the passenger's original intention controlling, and depriving him of the right to change his destination. pp. 337, 346.

5. CARRIERS. — *Carriage of Passengers.* — *Passenger Fares.*—*Local and Through Fares.—Duty of Carrier.*—Where a passenger on an interurban railroad when first approached by the conductor indicated a desire to contract for a through passage to a certain station on the carrier's line, but upon learning the amount of the through fare expressed his intention to contract for transportation to an intermediate stop and tendered the fare to such point, the conductor should have received the same and carried him to such intermediate stop, even though the passenger's purpose was to obtain the benefit of the scheduled local fares, which aggregated less than the through fare to the destination originally named by him. p. 345.

6. CARRIERS.—*Carriage of Passengers.—Action for Wrongful Ejectment.—Splitting of Journey.—Evidence.*—Where a passenger on an interurban railroad has the right to make his journey by stages and to pay the local fares between the various stops, evidence, in an action for wrongful ejectment, that the passenger alighted at the point to which the first local fare covered his transportation is of no controlling importance, except as part of plaintiff's conduct tending to show that he stood on his right to take advantage of the local fares, which aggregated less than the through fare to his destination. p. 345.

7. CARRIERS.—*Carriage of Passengers.—Action for Wrongful Ejectment.—Trial.—Instructions.—Retention of Fare.*—A conductor on

NOVEMBER TERM, 1916.        329

Brown *v.* Terre Haute, etc., Traction Co.—63 Ind. App. 327.

an interurban car is not authorized to eject a passenger for failure to pay the proper fare while retaining the fare tendered by
the passenger, so that, in an action for wrongful ejectment, instructions purporting to state facts which would justify defendant in ejecting plaintiff from its car, but ignoring evidence tending to prove that the conductor had received and retained the
fare tendered by plaintiff, are erroneous. p. 346.

8. CARRIERS.—*Carriage of Passengers.—Local and Through Fares.
—Selection by Passenger.—Discrimination.*—Where a railroad's
published schedule of fares offers to the traveling public two
different fares, one a local and the other a through fare, each
having the same legal sanction and authority, a passenger may
elect which fare he will take, and, where the carrier permits one
passenger to contract for a through passage at the through rate,
and another for local passage at the local rate, it is not guilty of
discrimination, although the aggregate of the local fares between
two points on the carrier's line may be less than the through fare
for the same journey. p. 348.

From Marion Superior Court (87,704); *Charles J.
Orbison,* Judge.

Action by James A. Brown against the Terre Haute,
Indianapolis and Eastern Traction Company. From a
judgment for defendant, the plaintiff appeals. *Reversed.*

*M. M. Bachelder* and *E. E. McFerren,* for appellant.

*W. H. Latta,* for appellee.

HOTTEL, J.—This is an appeal from a judgment in appellee's favor in an action brought by appellant to recover
damages for an alleged illegal ejectment from appellee's
car. The issues of fact were tendered by a complaint in
one paragraph and an answer in two paragraphs, the first
of which was a general denial.

The only error assigned and relied on for reversal is
the overruling of appellant's motion for new trial. The
grounds of this motion insisted upon as presenting reversible error are those challenging the sufficiency of the evidence and the action of the trial court in excluding certain
evidence, and in giving certain instructions.

We indicate the averments of the complaint and special
answer necessary to an understanding of the questions thus

presented by the appeal. The averments of the complaint pertinent to said questions are, in substance, as follows: On September 5, 1911, at Ben Davis, Indiana, where one of appellee's. cars stopped to take on passengers, appellant boarded said car with the desire to be carried from said point to the terminal station at Indianapolis, and to that end tendered to appellee's conductor on such car the sum of.... cents, the usual and regular fare between said points; that such conductor refused to accept said fare, and wrongfully and maliciously refused to permit appellant to travel on said car, and seized him in a rude, insolent and violent manner and attempted to eject him.

The averments of the special answer pertinent to said questions are in substance as follows: On September 5, 1911, appellee had in force established tariffs and schedules which it had filed with the Railroad Commission of this State, and was then charging and collecting the fare provided in such schedules, to wit, the fare provided in "Local and Interdivision Passenger Tariff No. 12," effective August 24, 1911, with "Supplement No. 1" thereto, effective August 31, 1911; that the first station on appellee's line of road, west of Ben Davis, is stop No. 8, and the next stop west is stop No. 9; that by the terms of said tariff and rate sheet the rate of fare between stop No. 8 and Indianapolis, in either direction, was fifteen cents; and under the provisions of said tariff and schedule conductors on appellee's cars were authorized and required to collect from points not shown in tariff schedules to fare points shown thereon, five cents; that stop No. 9 was not a fare point mentioned in said passenger tariff No. 12 or in supplement No. 1, or in any tariff regulation or schedule then in force on said line of road; that under said tariff schedule appellee's conductor was required to collect of all through passengers from stop No. 9 to Indianapolis, twenty cents, to wit, five cents from stop No. 9 to the first fare point which was stop No. 8, plus fifteen cents, the schedule fare from stop No. 8 to

Indianapolis. That the distance from Indianapolis to stop No. 8 is 8.16 miles and to stop No. 9, 8.52 miles. That appellant boarded appellee's car at stop No. 9 and announced to the conductor that he desired to go to Indianapolis, and appellee *"alleges the fact to be that (appellant) then and there became a through passenger upon said car from said Stop No. 9 to the City of Indianapolis, and became obligated under said tariff to pay to this defendant for his said carriage the said sum of twenty cents."* That appellant upon boarding said car at stop No. 9 tendered to appellee's conductor the sum of fifteen cents as and for his fare to Indianapolis, and was informed by such conductor that the fare was twenty cents; that the conductor refused to accept fifteen cents and appellee refused to pay twenty cents. That for the purpose of avoiding his obligation to pay the latter sum and without any good faith or intention to be a passenger to Ben Davis, but solely for the fraudulent purpose just indicated, appellant alighted at Ben Davis and immediately reboarded the same car and thereafter tendered to said conductor the sum of fifteen cents to be carried to Indianapolis; that the conductor again refused said sum and demanded twenty cents, and informed appellant that he must either pay such sum or get off the car; that appellant refused to do either, and thereupon the conductor and motorman attempted to eject appellant when another passenger on said car paid to such conductor five cents and appellant paid his fifteen cents, after which no further attempt was made to eject appellant; that such attempted ejectment was made without malice, violence or undue force and was made in the manner and for the purpose herein alleged.

The facts disclosed by the evidence pertinent to said questions presented by the appeal are, in substance, as follows: It was agreed that exhibits 1 and 2 (these were the tariff schedule and supplement sheet referred to in appellee's answer, *supra*) "taken together constitute the duly author-

ized rates of fare and passenger tariff" duly filed with the
Railroad Commission of the State of Indiana, in force and
effect from the time shown therein up to and including
September 5, 1911. Tariff schedule No. 12, effective August 24, 1911, shows the following mileage and fares between
points here involved, viz.: From Indianapolis to Ben Davis,
six miles, fare ten cents; from Indianapolis to Bridgeport,
the first station shown west of Ben Davis, nine miles, fare
twenty cents; from Ben Davis to Bridgeport, three miles,
fare five cents. This schedule makes no mention of either
stop No. 8 or stop No. 9, both of which are between the last
named stations, but, under heading "Plan for Collecting
Fares and Tickets," authorizes conductors to "collect five
* * * cents to first fare point plus fare shown in tariff
from the fare point to destination. Ben Davis and Bridgeport are the only stops west of Indianapolis, here involved,
which are referred to or mentioned as fare points in said
schedule No. 12, and under such schedule the fare to Indianapolis from any point east of Bridgeport and west of Ben
Davis could be but fifteen cents; that is, the conductors
could collect five cents from such non-fare point to Ben
Davis, and ten cents, the published fare, from Ben Davis
to Indianapolis.

Supplement No. 1 to said tariff schedule No. 12, referred
to in the answer as having gone into effect August 31, 1911,
provided that, "The rate between Indianapolis and stop
8, either direction, will be fifteen * * * cents." Under
this supplement stop No. 8 became a fare point for the purpose of determining the fare to and from such point and Indianapolis, but no fare or tariff was fixed between such point
and any other station on appellee's line, nor was there any
other change or modification of the tariff fares fixed by tariff
schedule No. 12. The fare from Ben Davis to Bridgeport
still remained five cents. Under tariff No. 12 and supplement the fare for through passage from stop No. 9 to Indianapolis became twenty cents. This is so because stop

No. 9 is not a fare point, and hence, under schedule No. 12, a fare of five cents should be collected to the first fare point, which under the supplement is stop No. 8, and the fare between stop No. 8 and Indianapolis is by said supplement.fixed at fifteen cents.

It should be stated, also, in this connection, that the exact distance between Indianapolis and the stops herein involved is admitted by appellee in its special answer and brief to be as follows: From Indianapolis to points respectively, as follows, viz.: to Ben Davis 6.47 miles; to stop No. 8, 8.16 miles; and to stop No. 9, 8.52 miles. For the purposes of fixing tariffs in accord with the two-cent mile law (§5196 Burns 1914, Acts 1913 p. 156) said distances and tariffs were, therefore, as before indicated herein, and such tariffs, as fixed by said schedule, are within the provisions of said law. It will also appear from the above figures that the distance between Ben Davis and stop No. 9 is only 2.05 miles, and hence the rate between such stops, to be within the two-cent mile law, could not exceed five cents.

The oral evidence affecting the questions involved is as follows: Appellant, on direct examination, testified, in effect, that on September 5, 1911, he got on one of appellee's cars at Ben Davis to go to Indianapolis; that when the conductor came to collect his fare he (appellant) tendered him fifteen cents—a dime and nickel—and the conductor demanded another nickel, which he (appellant) refused to pay; that the conductor then pulled the bell rope, stopped the car and proceeded to eject him; that after some struggle between them the conductor called to his aid the motorman; that during the time the conductor was trying to put appellant off the car he (the conductor) retained the fifteen cents given him by appellant; that a fellow passenger tendered the extra nickel demanded by the conductor after which appellant was released and permitted to go on to Indianapolis.

Appellant's answers on cross-examination are, in part,

334     APPELLATE COURT OF INDIANA,

Brown *v.* Terre Haute, etc., Traction Co.—63 Ind. App. 327.

to the following effect: "Stop No. 9 is called Riggins' Crossing. It is just a private crossing for the farm that it runs through. There is a waiting station, but no agent there. Stop No. 8 is between stop No. 9 and Ben Davis. I got on the car at stop No. 9 and the conductor came for my fare. I offered him fifteen cents to go to Indianapolis and the conductor said it was not enough. I told him to take out to Ben Davis, and in place of taking out any, he put it all back in my hand and said, 'I will collect later,' and was gone before I had time to say anything. That is all the conversation I had with him prior to the car reaching Ben Davis. Just before the car stopped at Ben Davis he came forward and slapped me on the shoulder and says, 'Ben Davis, feller; get off,' in rather a rude manner, one that would attract the attention of all the passengers in the car. I was sitting in the front part of the rear coach. I got up and got off, just as he demanded and got down on the platform. When the Ben Davis passengers got on I got on, and we hadn't gone far from Ben Davis, perhaps a mile or so, when the conductor came to me for my fare; I was then in the smoker. I gave him a dime and a nickel. I knew that the fare from Ben Davis to Indianapolis was ten cents, and yet I tendered him a dime and a nickel. I offered him the extra nickel because my nerves were unstrung; after he asked me to get off the car, I knew I was a passenger from that station. I might have thought the nickel was the fare from stop 9 to Ben Davis."

Appellant's statement, in its essential features, is corroborated by most of the witnesses and contradicted by none except the conductor, who testified, in part, to the following effect: "After Mr. Brown got on the car at stop 9 I went to get his fare and he handed me fifteen cents. I says 'Where to?' He says, 'Indianapolis.' I says, 'It is twenty cents to Indianapolis,' and he made some remark—'It is not right,' or something—and somebody else says to him, 'Pay to Ben Davis.' Some passengers got on at stop

8 and I handed his dime and nickel back, and I said, 'I will get your fare after while.' That is all that took place between stop 9 and Ben Davis. When we approached Ben Davis, I did not address anyone personally. I said, 'Ben Davis!' and called it twice. I positively did not punch appellant. When the car stopped at Ben Davis appellant started to get off the car, and went down to the first or second step and turned around and went back in, and walked up to the smoker. I asked him for the fare and he held out fifteen cents to me. I says, 'It is twenty cents from where you got on to Indianapolis,' and he says, 'I will not pay it.' I says, 'You will have to pay it or get off.' He said 'I will not get off and you cannot put me off.' I took hold of him and started to take him to the front end of the car because I could not get him through the back end of the car. The motorman came and opened the door. At this time some one else paid me a nickel and appellant gave me fifteen cents. I cut a receipt out and gave it to him, and did not say anything else to him. When I got to Ben Davis I hollered out twice right up close to the smoker, 'Ben Davis!'—had the smoker door open. I was almost at the side of Mr. Brown. If I touched him, I did so accidentally and did not know it. I positively did not say: 'Ben Davis, fellow; get off.' When the other man gave me the nickel, he had the fifteen cents ready, and I took the fifteen cents.''

It will be seen, from the issues, tendered and the evidence pertinent thereto above set out, that one of the disputed questions in the trial court was whether appellant,

1. when appellee's conductor attempted to eject him, had paid or tendered a fare which entitled him to be carried on appellee's car to Indianapolis. In determining such question, under one phase of the case, it was important for the jury to know the amount of the fare for the distance between stop No. 9 and Ben Davis on the day in question. As pertinent to this question, appellant

offered to prove by one or more witnesses the fare charged between said stops on the day in question by conductors on appellee's cars, and offered to prove by appellant that the conductor on the car on which appellant took passage stated to appellant on the occasion in question that the fare from stop No. 9 to Ben Davis was five cents. An objection to this evidence was sustained, and it is insisted by appellee that such action of the court was proper because the question of passenger fares or tariffs is now under the control of the Railroad Commission and that proof of such fares can only be made in the regular way, viz., by the published schedules of fares as filed with, and approved by, such commission; that tariffs so fixed cannot be attacked collaterally, but can be adjudged illegal and improper only by direct action brought for such purpose. In support of this contention appellee cites: *Southern Ind. R. Co.* v. *Railroad Commission* (1908), 172 Ind. 113, 87 N. E. 966; *State, ex rel.* v. *Florida, etc., R. Co.* (1909), 58 Fla. 524, 50 South. 425.

The legal principles for which appellee contends are, we think, sound and supported by authority. The general rule that the published tariff schedules approved by
2. such commission are the best, and hence the proper, evidence by which to prove such tariffs, has application to those cases where the schedules or tariffs so filed and published fix the fare between the points involved in the litigation. We have already indicated that, in the instant case, the fare between stop 9 and Ben Davis is not
1. certainly or definitely fixed by appellee's schedule of fares effective on the day in question. True, it might be inferred from such schedule that the fare between such points was five cents, because of the presumption that such tariff would be made to conform to the two-cent fare law, and, because also, that the tariff between Bridgeport (which is west of Ben Davis) and Ben Davis is fixed by such schedule at five cents, and hence that the fare from an

intermediate point would not be a greater amount. However, in view of the fact that the schedule, here involved, does not fix the fare between stop No. 9 and Ben Davis, or at least does not expressly fix such fare, but leaves it in doubt and uncertainty, we think that the jury trying the case was entitled to know the fare actually charged and collected by appellee between said points, not for the purpose of contradicting or disputing said tariff schedule, but for the purpose of ascertaining the interpretation and construction placed thereon by appellee. For this reason the offered evidence was proper and should have been

3.  admitted. The offered statement of appellant as to what the conductor stated to him on the occasion in question was, in any event, competent as a part of the *res gestœ.*

It is, however, contended by appellee, in effect, that inasmuch as the through fare between stop No. 9 and Indianapolis was fixed by the tariff schedule as twenty cents, the question of appellee being justified in its attempt to eject appellant from its car, in its last analysis, turns solely on the question whether appellant was a passenger from stop No. 9 or from Ben Davis when the attempt to eject him was made, and hence that the exclusion of said evidence was harmless in any event. For reasons that will appear later in this opinion we do not agree with this contention. We next consider the error predicated on the instructions given. Of those challenged No. 5, originally given, and No. 4 of the reinstructions, given by the court after the jury had

4.  been once instructed and sent to their room, are, we think, the most vulnerable. The first paragraph of instruction No. 5, which is particularly objected to, and said reinstruction No. 4 in its entirety, are as follows:

"No. 4. The court instructs the jury that if the plaintiff got on the car at stop No. 9 on the Brazil Division, and desired to ride to Indianapolis, and that it was his intention when he boarded the car to go to Indianapolis, on that car, he then and thereby became obligated to pay to the defendant the fare which it was entitled to charge under the schedule and tariff then in force, and which, under the evidence in this case, was twenty cents. And if the jury find that the said Brown tendered to the conductor of said car fifteen cents as and for his fare to the City of Indianapolis, and said conductor demanded twenty cents, then said Brown could not evade the payment of the through fare from stop No. 9 to the City of Indianapolis by getting off of said car at Ben Davis and getting back on the car, but he was under a continuing duty and obligation throughout the entire distance from stop No. 9 to Indianapolis to pay the through fare between said points, and even if you find that the conductor of the car called Ben Davis and told the plaintiff to get off and the plaintiff did get off, yet if you find from the evidence that the plaintiff continually intended to be a through passenger to Indianapolis, on that car, and never in fact relinquished his intention to do so, but his getting off at Ben Davis was merely to attempt to gain an advantage in fares and he did not have a good faith intention of being a passenger to Ben Davis, then the court instructs you that unless the plaintiff at some time paid or offered to pay to the conductor twenty cents, the conductor had a right to eject him, using no more force than was necessary to do so.''

''No. 5. The court instructs the jury that if the plaintiff got on the car at stop 9, on the Brazil Division, and desired to ride to Indianapolis, and that it was his intention when he boarded the car to go to Indianapolis on that car, he then and thereby became obligated to pay the defendant the fare which it was entitled to charge under the schedule and tariff then in force, and which under the evidence in this case, was twenty cents. * * *''

It is insisted by appellant that these instructions make the question of his original intention as to destination controlling, and that by them the jury was told that if, when he entered appellee's car at stop No. 9, he intended to go to Indianapolis, he then became obligated to pay the through tariff between said points though, after entering the car, he changed his intention and sought and offered to pay his fare to an intermediate stop.

Appellee insists that said instructions, when read in their entirety, do no more than tell the jury that, if appellant in fact intended to be a *through passenger* from stop No. 9 to Indianapolis, he was required to pay a *through fare*. The importance of this contention is particularly dwelt upon, and the legal questions involved therein exhaustively and ably presented by appellee in its brief.

The first paragraph of instruction No. 4 and that part of No. 5 above quoted, standing alone, are open to appellant's criticism. Assuming, however, that the instructions, when read in their entirety, could not have misled the jury or have been misunderstood by it as to the question of appellant's right to, in good faith, change his destination after becoming a passenger, they, in any event, do more than appellee concedes. They, in effect make the question *of intended final destination* controlling, and as such question is important and must necessarily arise on another trial of the case it should be now determined and decided.

As affecting said question, appellee contends that the undisputed evidence shows that appellant entered appellee's car at stop No. 9 then intending, and continuously thereafter intending, Indianapolis as his final destination, and that he thereby became a through passenger from stop No. 9 to Indianapolis, and became obligated to pay the through fare between said points as fixed by appellee's tariff schedule; that appellant's tender of fare to Ben Davis and his alighting at such stop was a subterfuge and trick resorted to for the purpose of avoiding the payment of such through fare, and hence did not operate to separate his journey into stages, whereby he could obtain any advantage of the local fare between such stops, and did not relieve him from paying the regular fare from the place of original entry on the car to his final destination. In support of this contention, it is argued that, inasmuch as interurban roads operate local cars, stopping at frequent intervals at country-road crossings, separated by fractions of miles, it is impossible for such roads to comply with the two-cent fare law, and at the same time make the sum of the local fares equal in all cases the through fare; that, in view of this fact, the law contemplates, and public policy requires, that a through passenger shall pay the through fare and that the obligation to pay such through fare continues, unless, after getting on the train, such passenger, in good faith, makes up his mind to stop at an intermediate point; that a stop at some intermediate point and a payment, or tender, of fare to such point, made for the sole purpose of obtaining the advantage of a lower local tariff, and then boarding the same car to be carried to the destination originally and always intended, is a trick and device of the passenger by which he attempts to do by indirection that which he may not directly do, and hence that such practice should not be given the sanction of the courts; that an acceptance by the carrier of the local fare from the passenger who thus attempts to evade the payment of the through fare would be a violation by it of the letter and spirit of the Railway Commission Law (§1, cl. b) of an act approved March 6, 1911 (Acts 1911 p. 545, 547, *post*) which would subject it to the penalty therein provided.

As supporting this contention, appellee specially relies on the following section of the statute: §1 of an act approved March 6, 1911, Acts 1911 p. 545, §5540 Burns 1914; §3, cl. (g), of an act approved March 9, 1907, Acts 1907 p. 454, §5533 Burns 1914; §7, Id. p. 470, §5537 Burns 1908; §13, Id. p. 478, §5543 Burns 1908; §§14, cls. (a) and (b), Id. p. 481, §5544 Burns 1908. These sections are too lengthy to set out in this opinion. It is sufficient to say that we

NOVEMBER TERM, 1916.        341

Brown *v.* Terre Haute, etc., Traction Co.—63 Ind. App. 327.

have examined them, and, in so far as they affect the questions under consideration, they do no more than make it *unlawful for the carrier* to charge, demand or collect, either directly or indirectly, any rate or tariff *different from that fixed in the tariff schedule* and, also provide against unjust discrimination, making it unlawful for such carrier or any of its agents, officers or employes ·by special rate, rebate, . drawback, device, or other methods enumerated, to charge, demand, collect or receive from any person, firm or corporation *"a greater or less fare than it charges, demands, receives or collects from any other person, firm or corporation for like transportation under substantially similar circumstances and conditions."* A provision, similar to that last quoted, is made to apply to any person, his agent or employe, any member of a firm, or any corporation or any officer, agent or employe of such firm or corporation who intentionally accepts or receives such rebate, etc. Penalties are also provided for the violation of each of said several sections.

We find nothing in any of such sections indicating any intention of the legislature to prohibit the passenger, when two tariffs (one "local" and one "through") are published, from making his journey by stages, regardless of his motive for so doing.

The cases cited and relied on by appellee are, we think, easily distinguishable from the instant case. The case of *St. Louis, etc., R. Co.* v. *Waldrop* (1909), 93 Ark. 42, 123 S. W. 778, was a suit to recover from the carrier the penalty under a statute prohibiting the carrier from collecting from the passenger a greater fare than that permitted by the statute. It was held, and properly so we think, that it was the duty of the agent to know the correct tariff and that the mistake of the agent in such respect did not relieve the carrier from the payment of the penalty. The case of *Reynolds* v. *United States* (1878), 98 U. S. 145, 25 L. Ed. 244, simply announces the general principle that, where every act necessary to constitute a crime is knowingly done, the crime itself is, in law, knowingly committed, that ignorance of fact may sometimes be taken as evidence of want of criminal intent, but not ignorance of the law.

The case of *Armour Packing Co.* v. *United States* (1908), 209 U. S. 56, 28 Sup. Ct. 428, 52 L. Ed. 681, involved a prosecution under the Elkins Act (Act Feb. 19, 1903, 32 Stat. at L. 847, ch. 708, U. S. Comp. St., Supp. 1907, p. 880). The packing company had been convicted in the district court of a violation of said act on a charge of obtaining from the Chicago, Burlington & Quincy Railway Company an unlawful concession of twelve cents per 100 pounds from the published and filed rate of that .portion of the route between the Mississippi river and New York for transportation of the packing company's product from Kansas City to New York for export. The United States Supreme Court discusses the Elkin's Act in connection with the previous acts leading up to it, and holds in effect that the purpose and intent of the later' act was to put all shippers on an equal footing and prevent discrimination in favor of or against any shipper and to "prohibit any and all means that might be resorted to to obtain or receive concessions and rebates *from the fixed rates duly posted and published,*" and that any "device" or "method of dealing" by the carrier by which the forbidden result could be brought about, though not fraudulent was within the inhibition of the statute. (Our italics.) To the same effect is the case of *New York, etc., R. Co.* v. *Whitney Co.* (1913), 215 Mass. 36, 102 N. E. 366, 368, which holds that both shipper and carrier "are bound inexorably to follow *the rate published.*" (Our italics.)

In *Layne* v. *Chesapeake, etc., R. Co.* (1909), 66 W. Va. 607, 67 S. E. 1103, it was held that: "A passenger does not, however, lose his status as such by merely alighting at a regular station for exercise, for lunch or for any business not inconsistent with the pursuit of *the journey con-*

*tracted for.''* (Our italics.) To the same effect is the case of *Austin* v. *St. Louis, etc., R. Co.* (1910), 149 Mo. App. 397, 130 S. W. 385.

In our judgment none of these cases fit the facts of the case under consideration, and hence furnish little or no reason or support for appellee's contention. Indeed, some of these cases, by implication at least, are against appellee's contention in that they hold in effect that, in determining whether the statute in such cases has been violated by the carrier, the real question is whether a tariff *different from the published tariff* was charged or received, etc., or whether there had been discrimination in the collection of tariffs by giving a particular shipper a special *rate, rebate or drawback,* not given to other shippers under the same circumstances and conditions, in either of which events the statute would be violated, regardless of the method used by the carrier to obtain the forbidden result, and regardless of the question whether there was a fraudulent purpose and intent on the part of the carrier to obtain such result.

In the instant case there were two published tariffs, one a *local* and one a *through* tariff, offered by the carrier to the traveling public with the sanction and approval of the Railroad Commission. Such tariffs stood upon the same footing. They, each alike, had the approval of the commission, and were each the *legally published tariffs of such carrier,* open to acceptance by the traveling public. We do not mean by the last statement that the through passenger may choose to pay for through passage the sum of the local fares; but, if the sum of the local fares is less than the through fare, and the passenger desires to make his journey by stages in order to get the benefit of such local fare, we find nothing in the law that will prevent him from so doing. In such a case the agent of the carrier, whether at the ticket office window selling tickets, or the conductor on the car collecting fares, is under obligation, in the one case, to sell to the traveler the ticket which entitles him to trans-

344    APPELLATE COURT OF INDIANA,

Brown *v.* Terre Haute, etc., Traction Co.—63 Ind. App. 327.

portation to the destination for which he seeks to purchase a ticket, and, in the second case, to charge and accept a fare to such destination as the passenger may indicate, provided, of course, that· the destination be one at which such car stops. Nor do we believe that public policy requires, or demands, the construction placed on such law insisted on by appellee, but, on the contrary, favors a construction in such case that will look to the actual transaction, the contract, or attempted contract, for passage rather than to the unexpressed, but intended final destination of the passenger. If the legislature had intended to prevent a through passenger from breaking his journey into stages in order to get the advantage of a local fare, it, by appropriate and apt language, could have so provided in the act in question, or, if the Railroad Commission in adopting the tariff in question had thus intended, it could have made the tariff so show, and to say that the acceptance by the carrier of its published tariff, under such circumstances, would be a trick or device by the carrier, resorted to for the purpose of discriminating in favor of the particular passenger which would render it subject to the penalty provided in either section of the act in question would, in our judgment, be a strained construction of the act wholly unwarranted by its language, and never intended or thought of by the legislature. If there could be said to be any device or trick on the part of the carrier, in connection with charging, demanding or receiving such a tariff, it would seem to have had its origin and inception in the promulgation of the two fares, and such fares having the sanction of the Railroad Commission, there is no reason for the carrier apprehending prosecutions for collecting and receiving the local tariff under the circumstances here indicated.

We have no doubt but that, under the tariff rates above indicated, as adopted and published by appellee, where a passenger has boarded one of its cars at stop No. 9, and

NOVEMBER TERM, 1916. 345

Brown *v.* Terre Haute, etc., Traction Co.—63 Ind. App. 327.

the conductor attempts to collect the fare of such passenger, if the passenger indicates a desire to go to Indianapolis, with no expressed desire or demand to take advantage of the local rate, and no offer to pay fare to the intermediate stop, such conductor is required to collect the through fare between stop No. 9 and Indianapolis, which is twenty cents; but this is not the question here presented.

It is true that appellee, after boarding the car at stop No. 9, when first approached by the conductor, indicated a desire to contract for through passage to Indianapolis; but,

5. upon learning the tariff for such through passage was twenty cents, he then indicated a desire to contract for passage and to pay fare to the intermediate stop—Ben Davis—and tendered the fare necessary to carry him to such stop. For the reasons herein stated, we think appellant was entitled, if he so desired, to change his place of destination regardless of his motive for so doing, and that the conductor should have received his fare when tendered and carried him to Ben Davis without further question. He did in fact carry him to Ben Davis, and under appellant's statement required him to get off there. The conductor denied this statement, but the motive prompting appellant to change his destination—whether he left the car at Ben Davis voluntarily or at the demand of the conductor—is not in our judgment of controlling importance. The fact that he got off at Ben Davis

6. was of no controlling importance, except as a part of appellant's conduct tending to show that he stood on his right to take advantage of the local rate and contract for passage to Ben Davis. In support of our conclusion see the following cases: *Kurtz* v. *Pennsylvania Co.* (1909), 16 Inters. Com. Com. Rep. 410; *Railroad* v. *Klyman* (1902), 108 Tenn. 304, 67 S. W. 472, 56 L. R. A. 769, 91 Am. St. 755; *Phettiplace* v. *Northern Pacific R. Co.* (1893), 84 Wis. 412, 54 N. W. 1092, 20 L. R. A. 483; *Chicago, etc., R. Co.* v. *Parks* (1857), 18 Ill. 460, 68 Am. Dec. 562; *Gulf,*

*etc., R. Co.* v. *Texas* (1907), 204 U. S. 403, 27 Sup. Ct. 360, 51 L. Ed. 540, and cases cited.

4.
For the reasons indicated, the instructions above set out, as well as some of those not indicated, incorrectly stated the law, and hence necessitate a reversal of the judgment below.

It should be further stated with reference to the instructions that some of them are open to the criticism that they attempt to state to the jury the facts which, if found

7.
by it, would justify it in finding that appellee had a right to eject appellant from its car, and ignore the element of appellee's receiving and retaining the fare tendered by appellant. The appellant testified that, after he got on the car at Ben Davis, appellee's conductor came to him for his fare and that he gave him fifteen cents; that the conductor had and retained this fare while attempting to eject him. The conductor denied this, but such question was one of fact to be determined by the jury, and should not have been ignored in an instruction which attempted to enumerate the facts which would authorize the conductor to eject appellant. The law would not authorize an ejectment by the conductor for failure to pay proper fare while the fare tendered was retained by such conductor. *Bland* v. *Southern Pac. R. Co.* (1880), 55 Cal. 570, 36 Am. Rep. 50; *Wardwell* v. *Chicago, etc., R. Co.* (1891), 46 Minn. 514, 49 N. W. 206, 13 L. R. A. 596, 24 Am. St. 246, 248-249; 6 Cyc 559, 560.

Our conclusion as to the instructions renders unnecessary a consideration of the other grounds of the motion for new trial. On account of the error predicated on the giving of the instructions indicated, the motion for new trial should have been sustained. The judgment below is therefore reversed, with instructions to the trial court to grant a new trial, and for such other proceedings as may be consistent with this opinion.

## ON PETITION FOR REHEARING.

HOTTEL, J.—Appellee in an able brief earnestly and vigorously insists that this court has erred in its original opinion, and that rehearing should be granted. It is urged that every railroad operating within the jurisdiction of this court has been seriously and adversely affected by the decision; that their difficulties with their passengers have been multiplied and innumerable controversies actual and· potential have been brought into existence. It should be stated in. this connection that this insistence is not urged by appellant as an argument or reason for its contention that the decision is wrong, but rather as a means of impressing on the court the importance of the question involved. In this connection we deem it proper to say that the court has fully recognized and appreciated the importance of such question, and has seen that hardship might result from its decision, but it seriously doubts whether the condition would be bettered by adopting appellant's contention, and making the question of the passenger's right to contract for a local or through passage depend on his secret intent and motive rather than upon the character of passage demanded.

Appellee now says in his brief for rehearing that: "It does not matter whether a man gets on the car at stop No. 9, on our Brazil Division, to ride to Indianapolis, or whether he gets on the car at Indianapolis, to ride to Chicago, if in truth and in fact he pursues his journey by one continuous, unbroken series of acts, which result in his being carried from one point to the other; by every test of definition, reason or authority he is and ought to be regarded as a through passenger." It may be that the law ought to be as stated, and that such a law or regulation would obviate many of appellant's difficulties, but such a law would ignore the question of the passenger's intent which· was made prominent and controlling in the instructions which were held to be erroneous in the original opinion. We do not question the wisdom of a law or regulation which would provide that, in cases where a railroad company, having the proper legal sanction and authority so to do, publishes and offers to the traveling public a local and a through tariff or rate, a passenger on one of such company's trains who continues his passage on the same train to his place of destination should be required to pay the through fare, regardless of what may have been his intention either before or after he entered the car, and even though he had purchased a ticket to an intermediate stop and got off the train at such stop, provided, of course, he again entered the same train and continued his passage thereon. Such a law or regulation might, and doubtless would, avoid some of the hardships which appellant suggests, and it would not be open to the criticism that it makes the passenger's right to the advantage of fares depend on his intent rather than on the contract demanded or the passage itself. Such a law or regulation, however, is a matter proper for legislative consideration, or for the consideration of the Public Utilities Commission, if the legislature has clothed it with the necessary power to make such regulations. Courts construe the law as they find it, and we find no legisla-

8. tive enactment and know of no law or precedent that requires, or would justify the court in holding that, where two different fares or rates are published by a railroad company, each of which have the same legal sanction and authority, the passenger may not select and contract for the character of passage which will secure to him the most advantageous rate. Every passenger has the same right, if he desires to exercise it, and where, in such a case, a railroad company permits one passenger, who so demands, to contract for through passage at a through rate, and permits another passenger, who so demands, (though his final destination may be the same as the first) to contract for local passage at the local rate, it has been guilty of no discrimination between such passengers in the absence of

legal enactment or regulation defining and limiting the character of passengers entitled to the respective rates of fare so authorized and published. In each case the passenger is given what he demands, and is charged a fare that has the sanction of the law.

We therefore overrule the petition for rehearing.

NOTE.—Reported in 110 N. E. 703, 113 N. E. 313. Carriers, discrimination of passengers between localities, as to rates of fare, 18 Ann. Cas. 149; 11 Am. St. 647. See under (3) 16 Cyc 1148.

---

## BARNUM *v.* RALLIHAN ET AL.

[No. 9,437. Filed May 18, 1916. Rehearing denied October 6, 1916. Transfer denied December 20, 1916.]

1. APPEAL.—*Review.*—*Rulings on Demurrers.*—*Memorandum of Defects.*—*Scope of Review.*—Although the court on appeal, in reviewing the overruling of a demurrer to a complaint, can consider only the defects pointed out in the memorandum required by §344, cl. 6, Burns 1914, its review is not so limited where a demurrer to a complaint is sustained for insufficiency of facts alleged, and it will uphold such a ruling if the complaint is insufficient for any reason. p. 356.

2. TAXATION.—*Tax Sales.*—*Failure to Exhaust Personalty.*—*Sale of Realty.*—*Injunction.*—Where one liable for taxes has personal property in the county out of which his taxes may be collected, he may enjoin the sale of his real estate for the payment of such taxes. p. 358.

3. TAXATION. — *Collection of Taxes.* — *Injunction.*—*Pleading and Proof.*—One seeking to enjoin the collection of taxes must show by averment and proof either that the property upon which the taxes are assessed is not subject to taxation, or that such taxes have been paid. p. 358.

4. TAXATION.—*Collection of Taxes.*—*Resort to Personalty.*—Under §10324 Burns 1914, Acts 1903 p. 49, relating to the sale of property for nonpayment of taxes, personalty is the primary source of funds out of which to pay all taxes, and, if the person liable for taxes has personal property in the county, it is the duty of the officials charged with the collection of taxes to exhaust it before selling the assessed realty. p. 358.

5. TAXATION.—*Taxes on Realty.*—*Death of Owner.*—*Liability of Estate.*—Taxes accruing on realty before the owner's death but

not those accruing thereafter, become a charge against him, as well as a lien upon all his property, and should be paid by his executor out of the decedent's personal estate.  p. 358, 359, 363.

6.  TAXATION.—*Lien for Taxes.—Date of Attachment.*—The lien for taxes attaches to the property assessed upon the date that the taxes accrue.  p. 359.

7.  TAXATION.—*Tax Sales.—Validity.*—Where an owner of land dies leaving ample funds in his estate with which to pay delinquent taxes assessed against his realty in his lifetime, but his executrix fails to pay the same and the county treasurer sells the land to satisfy such taxes but fails in various ways to comply with the law relating to the collection of delinquent taxes and the sale of land therefor, the purchaser could not acquire title to the real estate by virtue of such sale, since there was a failure to follow the law governing the collection of delinquent taxes. p. 359.

8.  TAXATION.—*Payment of Taxes.—Conditions.—Effect.—Recovery.*—Where the owner of lands sold to satisfy delinquent taxes tendered to the county treasurer the full amount of money necessary to redeem the land from the tax sale and it was received by him, an attempted imposition of certain conditions in the tender as to a refund of part of the money was of no effect, and on failure to comply with the conditions there could be no recovery of the money so paid.  p. 360.

9.  TAXATION.—*Tax Sales.—Invalid Sales.—Rights of Purchaser.*—Where a sale of land for taxes is invalid and ineffectual to convey title because the law for the collection of delinquent taxes was not followed, although the tax was valid and constituted a lien on the realty sold, the lien of the State is transferred to the purchaser at the sale.  p. 360.

10.  TAXATION.—*Tax Sales.—Invalid Sales.—Payment of Redemption Money to County Treasurer.—Effect.*—The payment to the county treasurer of the amount necessary to redeem land sold for taxes at an irregular sale inures to the benefit of the purchaser at such sale, and satisfies the lien acquired by him.  p. 361.

11.  PLEADING. — *Complaint.— Relief Granted.—Prayer.*—The relief to which a party is entitled is determined by the facts averred and not by the prayer of the pleading.  p. 361.

12.  PLEADING.—*Theory.—Determination.*—In determining the theory of a pleading, the relief demanded may be considered in connection with the averments.  p. 361.

13.  EVIDENCE.—*Public Officers.—Performance of Official Duties.—Presumption.*—In considering the sufficiency of a pleading, it is presumed that public officials have done and will do their duty unless the contrary appears from the allegations.  p. 362.

14. EXECUTORS AND ADMINISTRATORS.—*Accounting and Settlement.
—Collateral Attack.*—The settlement of a decedent's estate, although irregular or invalid, cannot be attacked collaterally. p. 363.

15. TAXATION.—*Tax Sales.—Action to Redeem.—Complaint.—Sufficiency.*—A complaint, in an action to set aside a sale of land for taxes, is insufficient so far as seeking redemption from the tax sale, where it appears from the averments that the redemption is in legal contemplation already consummated, since there is no need of invoking the power of the court. p. 363.

16. SUBROGATION.—*Payment of Taxes.—Liability.—Rights of Payor.*—Where an executrix was obligated to pay the taxes on her decedent's realty, but permitted them to become delinquent, and the purchaser of the real estate paid such taxes after final settlement of the estate to prevent the loss of part of his lands, he is entitled to recover the money so paid, on the principle of subrogation, from those who should have paid it. p. 363.

17. EXECUTORS AND ADMINISTRATORS.—*Filing Claims Against Estate.
—Taxes.—Collection.*—While ordinary claims against an estate can only be collected through administration as provided by statute, claims for taxes need not be filed by the county treasurer and may be collected from the administrator out of funds in his hands, or the treasurer may seize and sell property assessed to liquidate the amount due. p. 364.

18. EXECUTORS AND ADMINISTRATORS. — *Claim Against Estate.—Failure to File.—Liability of Devisees.*—Where the taxes on a testator's real estate should have been paid by his executrix out of the funds of the estate, but she permitted the same to become delinquent, and one purchasing such realty from testator's devisees paid the tax to protect his property, such purchaser, on failure to enforce his claim against the estate for the money so paid, cannot recover such money from the devisees after the settlement of the estate, at least in the absence of a showing that they still have the property received by them in their possession at the time the action was instituted. p. 364.

From Noble Circuit Court; *Emmet A. Bratton*, Special Judge.

Action by Orlo P. Barnum against Timothy Rallihan and others. From a judgment for defendants, the plaintiff appeals. *Affirmed.*

*H. G. Zimmerman* and *Robert W. McBride,* for appellant. *Otto E. Grant* and *George L. Foote,* for appellees.

FELT, P. J.—This is a suit brought by appellant against appellees to set aside a sale of real estate for taxes made by appellee Hines, as county treasurer, to quiet title, and for other relief. The complaint was in one paragraph. The several demurrers of appellees thereto for insufficiency of the facts alleged to state a cause of action against them were sustained, to which appellant duly excepted and appealed from the judgment rendered against him on such ruling.

The errors assigned and relied on for reversal of the judgment are: (1) Sustaining the demurrer of appellee Rallihan; (2) sustaining the demurrer of appellees Mary and Abel Barnum; (3) sustaining the demurrer of appellees Wilbert T. Hines, county treasurer, and Joseph C. Kimmel, county auditor. The other. assignments are unauthorized and present no question.

The complaint is very long and its material averments are, in substance, as follows: On September 10, 1894, one Abel Barnum was the owner in fee simple of the northwest quarter of section 18, in township 34, north of range 10 east, in Noble county, Indiana, and on that date conveyed to appellant by warranty deed the undivided one-half of said real estate, reserving to himself a life estate therein. On March 1, 1910, said grantor was a resident taxpayer of said county and then owned an undivided one-half interest in said quarter section, and other real estate in said county, of the value of $1,000, together with a large amount of personal property of the aggregate value of $30,000. On March 5, 1910, he died testate the owner of said real estate and personal property, and also of other real estate in said county of the value of $5,000. On March 12, 1910, his will was duly probated, by which he devised all his personal property and his real estate in fee simple, to his widow, Mary Barnum, and his son, Abel. Appellee Mary Barnum was appointed executrix of his will, was duly qualified, and she entered upon her duties as such, March 16, 1910. On

April 22, 1910, appellant purchased from the said devisees their undivided one-half interest in said northwest quarter, and their deed therefor was duly recorded on April 23, 1910, and appellant is now the owner in fee simple thereof. On March 1, 1911, the said executrix filed her final report showing the payment of costs and expenses of administration, without filing any inventory or showing the amount of money received or paid out by her or the amount or value of the estate, which report was approved by the court on March 22, 1911, and the estate was declared settled and the executrix discharged from her trust. The amount of the personal property in the hands of the testatrix at the date of her discharge as aforesaid was $30,000. The taxes for the year 1910 assessed against the undivided one-half of said northwest quarter section so owned by the testator as aforesaid on March 1, 1910, amounted to $46.41. The executrix failed, neglected and refused to pay said taxes, which became due and payable on the first Monday in May, 1911, although at all times she had sufficient money and assets in her hands belonging to said estate out of which she could have paid the same. The total amount of taxes assessed upon and charged against said northwest quarter for the year 1910 was $92.83. On April 29, 1911, appellant paid to the county treasurer one-half of the first installment, which was the amount due on his individual one-half interest owned by him on and prior to March 1, 1910, and thereafter paid the second installment. The county treasurer at each of said dates issued to appellant a receipt stating therein the fact that such payments were made on appellant's former individual interest in such real estate. The unpaid tax of $46.41 was carried over by appellee Kimmel, as county auditor, and entered upon the duplicate tax list for 1911, together with the penalty and charges, amounting in all to $53.83. At the following tax-paying time appellant paid all taxes assessed against said

tract of land for the year 1911, but refused to pay the
aforesaid delinquent tax, which was not paid and was again
carried over and entered upon the tax duplicate for the
current year 1912, together with costs and penalties, amounting to $54.03.   Thereupon appellee Kimmel, as county audi-
tor, added such delinquent tax to appellant's current tax
for the year 1912, aggregating $154.62, charged against
said real estate and entered upon the delinquent list of
lands for sale in the name of appellant.   Thereafter appellee Kimmel, as such auditor, advertised the same for sale
for the nonpayment of said delinquent tax amounting to
$53.83.   On February 10, 1913, appellee Hines, as county
treasurer, sold ten acres in the northwest corner of said
tract to appellee Rallihan for the sum of $154.62, and
said Kimmel executed to such purchaser a certificate of sale
therefor.

It is also averred in the complaint that said tax sale
was illegal and void, for numerous reasons, in substance as
follows:  That no demand was ever made by appellee Hines,
as county treasurer, upon said devisees, or either of them,
for personal property to satisfy and pay delinquent tax,
and no effort was made by said treasurer to levy upon and
sell any of said personal property.   No delinquent list was
ever made by said treasurer after the first Monday in May,
1912, of the delinquents for unpaid taxes in said county and
certified to appellee Kimmel, as county auditor.   The
county treasurer did not call upon either of said devisees
and demand payment of said taxes or make any return
showing diligent search for personal property.   No notice
of the sale of appellant's lands on February 10, 1913, was
given by the county auditor as required by law.   The
treasurer's sale of said land was made in the interior of
the courthouse, and not at the door, as required by law.
The quantity of land sold was excessive, being of the value
of $1,000.   At the time of said sale, and during the entire
preceding year of 1912, appellant was the owner and in

possession of personal property in said county of the value of $1,500, and he has fully paid all taxes on his original undivided one-half interest in said northwest quarter section and such one-half interest therein is not subject to sale for said delinquent taxes. On May 5, 1913, appellant tendered to appellee Hines, as such county treasurer, the sum of $172.83, the same being the amount named in the certificate of sale, $154.62, together with ten per centum additional and lawful interest from date of sale. One hundred and nineteen dollars thereof were tendered absolutely and unconditionally, and the residue of $53.83, subject to the condition that, if the same could not be collected from said Mary and Abel Barnum, Jr., on demand or made by distraint or by levy and sale of personal or other property, namely, the real estate derived by them as devisees under the will of said testator, Abel Barnum, or by the necessary and required statutory proceedings against said Mary Barnum, as such former executrix, to set aside her final settlement account, then to be retained for said purchaser, Rallihan; otherwise to be returned to appellant. The aforesaid treasurer has not since the date of said tender made any effort to collect said delinquent tax from said devisees or either of them. Appellee Hines, as such county treasurer, received from appellant on May 5, 1913, the sum so tendered as aforesaid, and has ever since retained, and still retains, the same, by reason of which fact appellant is unable to pay the same into court.

Appellant asks that the court declare said tax sale illegal and void; that it be vacated and set aside and his title quieted against each and all of said defendants; "that the said $53.83 be ordered returned to plaintiff, and said certificate of sale issued to defendant Timothy Rallihan be cancelled; that the defendant Mary Barnum be ordered and required to answer concerning the kind, quantity and value of personal property which came into her hands as executrix of the last will of the testator, Abel Barnum, also the kind, quantity and value of the personal estate distributed by her on final settlement of said estate and that said defendants Mary and Abel Barnum be ordered and required to answer what disposition has been made by them of said personal estate, the nature, quantity and value of the chattel property remaining in their hands and in said county or in the hands of others, and where situated, and to show cause why the same should not be applied to the payment of said delinquent tax, and the judgment for costs, and for all proper relief.''

The court sustained the several demurrers, and the presumptions in favor of the rulings of the trial court require us to sustain the ruling if we find the complaint

1. insufficient for any reason, whether contained in the memorandum or not, notwithstanding the rule that limits this court to points made in the memorandum in cases where the demurring party complains of the overruling of his demurrer. §344, cl. 6, Burns 1914, Acts 1911 p. 415. *Bruns* v. *Cope* (1914), 182 Ind. 289, 105 N. E. 471, 474; *Boes* v. *Grand Rapids, etc., R. Co.* (1915), 59 Ind. App. 271, 108 N. E. 174, 176. Section 10343 Burns 1914, Acts 1909 p. 158, provides that the lien of the state for taxes ''shall attach on all real estate on the first day of March annually''. Sections 10344, 10345, 10346 Burns 1914 (Acts 1903 p. 49; Acts 1891 p. 199) are as follows: ''10344. All the property, both real and personal, situated in any county, shall be liable for the payment of all taxes, penalties, interest and costs charged to the owner thereof in such county, and no partial payment of any such taxes, penalties, interest or costs shall discharge or release any part or portion of such property until the whole is paid; which lien shall in nowise be affected nor destroyed by any sale or transfer of any such personal property, and shall attach on the first day of March, annually, for the taxes of the year.

"10345. If any such partial payment be made, and the payer desires it to be applied on any particular property, real or personal, the property so designated shall not be sold for the residue of the taxes due, if property of the same description can be found sufficient to make the balance due.

"10346. The treasurer shall receive the tax on a part of any real estate charged with taxes, provided the person paying such tax shall furnish a particular specification of such part and shall pay a like proportion of all the several taxes charged thereon for state, county, road or other purposes; and if the tax on the remainder of such real estate shall remain unpaid, the treasurer shall enter such specification on his return to the county auditor, to the end that the part on which the tax remains unpaid may be clearly known; but such payment shall not discharge any lien of the state, as provided for in this act."

Section 10324 Burns 1914, Acts 1903 p. 49, makes it the duty of the county treasurer to make search and demand for personal property out of which to pay delinquent taxes of each resident delinquent and to make due return setting forth the fact of his search in case he is unable to find personal property out of which to make such taxes.

Section 10354 et seq. Burns 1914, Acts 1891 p. 199, provide for the making of a list of lands liable for delinquent taxes, posting, notice and sale.

Section 2901 Burns 1914, §2378 R. S. 1881, provides the order of paying debts and liabilities of solvent estates, the fourth clause of which is as follows: "Taxes accrued upon the real and personal estate of the deceased at his death, and taxes assessed upon the personal estate during the course of the administration."

Section 10340 Burns 1914, Acts 1897 p. 226, provides that "It shall be the duty of every administrator, executor * * * to pay the taxes due upon the property of such decedent * * * and, in case of his neglecting to pay any installment of taxes when due, when there is money enough on hand to pay the same, the county treasurer shall present to the circuit court or other proper court of the county * * * a brief statement in writing, signed by him as such county treasurer, setting forth the fact and amount of such delinquency * * *."

When a party liable for taxes has personal property in the county out of which his taxes may be made, he may
2. enjoin the sale of his real estate for the payment of such taxes. *Weaver* v. *Kaufman* (1914), 57 Ind. App. 59, 106 N. E. 398. But where one seeks to
3. enjoin the collection of taxes altogether, he must show by averment and proof either that the property upon which the taxes are assessed is not subject to taxation, or that such taxes have been paid. *Weaver* v. *Kaufman, supra*; *McCrory* v. *O'Keefe*, (1903), 162 Ind. 534, 536, 70 N. E. 812; *Fell* v. *West* (1904), 35 Ind. App. 20, 29, 73 N. E. 719; *Nyce* v. *Schmoll* (1907), 40 Ind. App. 555, 558, 82 N. E. 539; *Beard* v. *Allen* (1895), 141 Ind. 243, 248, 39 N. E. 665, 40 N. E. 654.

Personal property is the primary source of funds out of which to pay all taxes, and, if the person liable for taxes has personal property in the county, it is the duty
4. of the officials charged with the collection of taxes to exhaust it before selling real estate upon which such taxes are a lien. §10324 Burns 1914, *supra*; *Weaver* v. *Kaufman, supra*, p. 60; *Abbott* v. *Edgerton* (1876), 53 Ind. 196, 200; *Cones* v. *Wilson* (1860), 14 Ind. 465; *McWhinney* v. *Brinker* (1878), 64 Ind. 360, 363; *Gable* v. *Seiben* (1894), 137 Ind. 155, 158, 36 N. E. 844.

Where taxes have accrued upon the real estate of a person before his death, they become a charge against him, as well as a lien upon all his property, and such taxes
5. should be paid by his executor or administrator out of the personal estate if sufficient for that purpose. Taxes which accrue on real estate after the death of the owner are not a charge against him in his lifetime, his

estate is not liable therefor, and his administrator or executor is not required to pay them.

By the statute the taxes for each year attach and become a lien upon both real and personal property on the first day of March annually, though the same are not due 6. and payable until the following year, and will not become delinquent until after the first Monday in May. While not expressly so stated, our decisions seem to treat all taxes as accruing on the first day of March when the lien thereof attaches to the property assessed. *Cullop* v. *City of Vincennes* (1904), 34 Ind. App. 667, 670, 72 N. E. 166; *Henderson* v. *Whitinger* (1877), 56 Ind. 131; *Graham* v. *Russell* (1898), 152 Ind. 186, 193, 52 N. E. 806; *Elliott* v. *Cale* (1888), 113 Ind. 383, 404, 14 N. E. 708, 16 N. E. 390; *Cones* v. *Wilson, supra*; *Schrodt* v. *Deputy* (1882), 88 Ind. 90, 92; *Smith* v. *Kyler* (1881), 74 Ind. 575, 586.

The taxes which accrued and became a lien upon the testator's undivided one-half of the aforesaid northwest quarter section of real estate on March 1, 1910, prior 5. to his death, were a claim against him, and should have been paid by the executrix out of his personal estate.

The complaint avers facts which show that there were ample funds out of which such payment could have been made; that the county treasurer made no search or 7. demand for personal property of decedent out of which to pay the aforesaid taxes; that the sale was not made at the door of the courthouse, and .also avers other facts tending to show that the sale was irregular and that the law for the collection of such delinquent taxes was not followed. We therefore hold that on the facts of this case the purchaser cannot acquire title to the real estate by virtue of such sale. *McWhinney* v. *Brinker, supra*; *Weaver* v. *Kaufman, supra*; *St. Clair* v. *McClure* (1887),

111 Ind. 467, 469, 12 N. E. 134; *Dixon* v. *Thompson* (1912), 52 Ind. App. 560, 564, 98 N. E. 738.

The complaint also shows that appellant tendered to the county treasurer the full amount of money paid by the purchaser with interest and penalty added. It also

8. shows that he attempted to impose certain conditions as to the part of the taxes he claims should have been paid by the executrix. However, the money was turned over to the county treasurer and he received it as such official. The original tax belonged to the State and it was not affected or bound by the conditions attempted to be imposed upon the treasurer. The State received the money when paid to the official authorized to receive it, and could not be required to refund it to appellant because of the treasurer's failure to comply with the conditions attempted to be imposed upon such official by appellant. The effect of such conditions, if any, was to show that the payment so made was not voluntary, but was made under protest. *Graham* v. *Russell, supra,* 195; *Beard* v. *Allen, supra.*

We thus have a situation where the sale is invalid and ineffectual to convey title, but in such instances the lien of the state is transferred to the purchaser. In this

9. case the owner has paid the full amount of the tax with interest and penalty, and we know of no way by which he may recover any part thereof from the county or state, for though the sale was irregular, the tax was valid and constituted a lien upon the real estate sold, as well as upon the personal property of the testator owned by him at the time of his death on March 5, 1910. §10388 Burns 1914, Acts 1901 p. 366; *Dixon* v. *Thompson, supra; Gable* v. *Seiben, supra; Green* v. *McGrew* (1904), 35 Ind. App. 104, 115, 72 N. E. 1049, 73 N. E. 832, 111 Am. St. 149; *St. Clair* v. *McClure, supra; City of Logansport* v. *Case* (1890), 124 Ind. 254, 24 N. E. 88.

The facts averred show that the sale cannot ripen into a title to the purchaser. The lien on the land which the

purchaser acquired has been satisfied by the payment
10. by appellant to the county treasurer of the amount
necessary to redeem from the sale. Such payment
inures to the benefit of the purchaser since the state and
county have already received the full amount of the taxes
from the purchaser at the tax sale.

The relief to which a party is entitled is determined by
the facts averred and not by the prayer of the pleading.
But, where the court is seeking to determine the
11. theory of a pleading, the relief demanded may be
looked to, in connection with the averments, to aid
12. in determining that question. *Sharpe* v. *Dillman*
(1881), 77 Ind. 280, 284; *Houck* v. *Graham* (1886),
106 Ind. 195, 202, 6 N. E. 594, 55 Am. St. 727; *Baker* v.
*Armstrong* (1877), 57 Ind. 189, 191; *Monnett* v. *Turpie*
(1892), 132 Ind. 482, 485, 32 N. E. 328; *Martin* v. *Martin*
(1889), 118 Ind. 227, 236, 20 N. E. 763; *Muncie, etc., Traction Co.* v. *Citizens Gas, etc., Co.* (1912), 179 Ind. 322,
329, 100 N. E. 65; *Indianapolis, etc., Traction Co.* v. *Henderson* (1906), 39 Ind. App. 324, 328, 79 N. E. 539; *Sebienske*
v. *Downey* (1910), 47 Ind. App. 214, 216, 93 N. E. 1050;
*Halstead* v. *Stahl* (1910), 47 Ind. App. 600, 602, 94 N. E.
1056; *Gates* v. *Sweet* (1914), 58 Ind. App. 689, 108 N. E.
881, 883.

While the complaint prays that title be quieted, it is
devoid of some of the usual and necessary allegations of
such suit, unless such facts be inferred. The prayer is
somewhat vague and contradictory and is of little, if any,
assistance in construing the pleading. The facts averred,
when considered in their general scope and tenor, seem to
invoke the equitable powers of the court. Equity looks
through form to substance, and the substance here is primarily the restoration of the title to appellant and sec-
ondarily the recovery of the part of the taxes appellant
claims should have been paid by the testatrix as aforesaid.

*Houck* v. *Graham, supra; Monnett* v. *Turpie, supra; Sharpe*
v. *Dillman, supra; Martin* v. *Martin, supra.*

Appellees in their briefs say: ''There is no contention that
the land in question was not liable to be taxed and no contention that the taxes which had become a lien had been
fully paid, unless the payment to the county treasurer be
considered an absolute payment to the treasurer for the
purchaser, Rallihan. This is probably the legal effect of
said payment for the reason that the county treasurer has
no authority to accept conditional payments * * *
while the legal effect of the facts averred would be to
establish an absolute payment and a redemption, the purpose of the pleader as gathered from the prayer of the complaint * * * is otherwise.''

We therefore conclude that the complaint as against the
purchaser at the tax sale and the county auditor and
treasurer is a proceeding in equity to redeem from the tax
sale.

It is not shown that either the auditor or treasurer has
refused to discharge any official duty necessary to complete the redemption. The averments do show an attempt
on the part of appellant to have the final application of a
part of the redemption money held in abeyance subject to
certain conditions which we have held he could not legally
impose. If the complaint showed a failure or refusal
13. of the officials to perform any part of their duties
connected with the redemption, it might entitle
appellant to some relief. The law presumes that public
officials have done and will do their duty until the contrary appears. If they have not made the necessary record
to evidence the redemption accomplished by appellant's
payment of the money to the county treasurer, we must
presume that they will do so, as soon as they are advised
of their duty in that respect. The conclusion is not changed
by the fact that appellant prays that the treasurer proceed to collect the disputed tax from other parties.

The averments show that the estate of the testator was settled in 1911, and, though such settlement may be irregular or invalid, if directly attacked, it cannot successfully be assailed collaterally or by indirection as appellant is here attempting to do. We therefore hold the complaint insufficient as against the purchaser at the tax sale and the auditor and treasurer of the county, for the reason that the redemption is in legal contemplation already fully consummated and there is no need of invoking the power of the court to do that which is already accomplished.

14.

15.

We have yet to consider the sufficiency of the complaint against Mary and Abel Barnum. As above indicated, the complaint shows that the disputed tax for 1910 should have been paid by the executrix and has, in fact, ultimately been paid by appellant. Appellant did not pay voluntarily but under the necessity of saving himself from the loss of a part of his real estate. He is therefore, by subrogation, entitled to recover the disputed tax so paid by him from the parties who under the law should have paid the same. *Chamness* v. *Chamness* (1912), 53 Ind. App. 225, 229, 101 N. E. 323; *Owen Creek, etc., Church* v. *Taggart* (1909), 44 Ind. App. 393, 396, 89 N. E. 406, *Fast* v. *State, ex rel.* (1914), 182 Ind. 606, 608, 107 N. E. 465; *Cullop* v. *City of Vincennes, supra.* Appellant had the right to pay the disputed tax and enforce his claim for the amount so paid against the estate, if the county treasurer failed to collect the taxes from the testator's estate. What his remedies are under present conditions cannot be determined in this case except as indicated by the averments of the complaint. We have already held that the disputed tax should have been paid by the executrix because it accrued before the death of the testator.

16.

5.

Ordinary claims against an estate can only be collected through administration as provided by statute. Taxes

need not be filed as a claim by the treasurer, and
17. may be collected from the administrator or administratrix out of funds in his or her hands, or the
treasurer may seize upon and sell property assessed to provide funds to liquidate the amount due. Appellant cannot
in this case enforce his claim against the estate for he is
not proceeding on that theory and the estate has been
settled. §2828 Burns 1914, Acts 1883 p. 153; §2925 Burns
1914, §2403 R. S. 1881; §2965 Burns 1914, §2442 R. S. 1881;
*Rinard* v. *West* (1884), 92 Ind. 359, 365; *Leonard* v. *Blair*
(1877), 59 Ind. 510, 514; *Clevenger* v. *Matthews* (1905),
165 Ind. 689; 76 N. E. 542; *Fisher* v. *Tuller* (1890), 122
Ind. 31, 23 N. E. 523; *Cullop* v. *City of Vincennes, supra;*
*Graham* v. *Russell, supra.*

The complaint shows that appellees Mary and Abel
Barnum were the devisees under the will of the personal
estate of the decedent, which at the time of the
18. settlement of the estate amounted to $30,000. It is
not averred that they received the personal property
but the fact is a necessary inference from all the facts
averred. In view of these averments the question arises,
Does the complaint state a cause of action against them?
As already shown, claims against an estate cannot be
enforced except in the way provided by statute, and the .
persons failing to so enforce their claims have no personal
liability against the heirs or devisees who take the property
upon final distribution. The kind and character of the personal estate is not shown, nor is it shown to have been in
existence and in the hands of appellees when this suit was
begun. If these facts were shown we should feel called
upon to determine whether appellant's right of subrogation would preserve to him the lien upon such personal
property notwithstanding the payment of the taxes as shown
and the satisfaction of the lien upon the land sold, and
whether such lien could still be enforced against the specific
property in the hands of such devisees. But, in the

absence of such averments, we must conclude that the complaint does not state a cause of action against said appellees, either of personal liability or for the enforcement of a lien against property received by them as such devisees. *McCoy* v. *Payne* (1879), 68 Ind. 327, 333; *Cincinnati, etc., R. Co.* v. *Heaston* (1873), 43 Ind. 172; *Clevenger* v. *Matthews, supra.* Judgment affirmed.

NOTE.—Reported in 112 N. E. 561. Taxation: (a) assessment of, on property of decedent's estate, 56 L. R. A. 634; (b) right of person paying tax to be subrogated to tax lien, 17 Ann. Cas. 1134; (c) recovery of taxes paid, 94 Am. St. 425. Right of one that advances money for payment of debt or incumbrance against decedent's estate to be subrogated to creditor's rights, 11 Ann. Cas. 676; Ann. Cas. 1915C 130. See under (2, 4) 37 Cyc 1285; (3) 37 Cyc 1276; (5) 18 Cyc 420; (6) 37 Cyc 1142; (7) 37 Cyc 1479; (8) 37 Cyc 1415; (9) 37 Cyc 1531; (13) 16 Cyc 1076; (14) 18 Cyc 1192; (15) 37 Cyc 1420; (16) 37 Cyc 443; (17) 18 Cyc 467.

---

# THE CHESAPEAKE AND OHIO RAILWAY COMPANY OF INDIANA v. JORDAN.

[No. 9,163.  Filed December 21, 1916.]

1. **CARRIERS.**—*Carriage of Goods.—Interstate Shipment.—Action for Damages.—Common-law Liability.*—There may be a cause of action under the common law against a common carrier for its negligence or wrongful acts resulting in damages to an interstate shipper, although there is a federal statute governing interstate shipments. p. 370.

2. **CARRIERS.**—*Carriage of Goods.—Action for Damages.—Defenses.*—Under §8592, cl. 11, U. S. Comp. St. 1913, 34 Stat. at Large p. 595, providing that every common carrier receiving property for transportation from one state to another shall issue a receipt or bill of lading therefor and shall be liable to the lawful holder thereof for any loss or damage to such shipment, the duty is imposed on the carrier of issuing a receipt or bill of lading for an interstate shipment of freight, and, in an action for damages thereto, it can not predicate a defense on its failure to issue the receipt required by the statute. p. 371.

3. **APPEAL.**—*Waiver of Error.—Briefs.*—An assignment of error predicated on the overruling of the motion for judgment on the

interrogatories is waived by failure of appellant to present any point or proposition relating thereto in its brief. p. 371.

4. CARRIERS.—*Carriage of Goods.—Limiting Liability.—Special Contracts.*—Notwithstanding the federal statute governing interstate shipments common carriers may make contracts whereby they limit and define the extent of their liability for interstate shipments under specified conditions, but such carriers cannot, by contract, relieve themselves from liability for damages caused by their negligence or that of their employes. p. 375.

5. COMMERCE.—*Interstate Shipments.—Federal Legislation.*—Where shipments of freight are interstate, the state law is superseded by the federal statutes relating to interstate commerce as to all questions of liability or defense covered by such statutes. p. 375.

6. COURTS.—*Jurisdiction of State Courts.—Interstate Commerce.— Carriage of Goods.—Action for Damages.*—Although there are federal statutes governing the liability of common carriers for interstate shipments of freight, the state courts are not thereby deprived of jurisdiction in actions for damages to such shipments, for the federal law is a part of the law of the state and, in such actions, may be applied by the state courts and the relief warranted given. p. 375.

7. CARRIERS.—*Carriage of Live Stock.—Damages.—Liability.—Limiting by Special Contract.*—Where, in an action against a common carrier for damages to an interstate shipment of live stock, the defendant answered that its liability was limited by a special contract issued and accepted by the shipper several months after the shipment and payment of the freight charges, no receipt or bill of lading having been issued at the time of the shipment, the acceptance of the special contract under such circumstances was without consideration unless it was in accordance with a custom, as claimed by defendant, established by prior similar transactions between the parties. p. 376.

8. TRIAL.—*Verdict.—Scope and Effect.*—A general verdict for plaintiff is a finding in his favor of every issuable fact and is conclusive on all questions where there is any evidence tending to support the verdict. p. 377.

9. CARRIERS.—*Carriage of Live Stock.—Action for Damages.—Evidence.*—In an action against a common carrier for damages to a shipment of live stock, evidence that on a few occasions prior to the transaction in controversy plaintiff had shipped live stock under a special contract limiting the carrier's liability, but that the contracts were procured at the time of the shipment and that in some instances bills of lading had been obtained after shipments were made, was insufficient to show the establishment of a custom, as claimed by defendant, permitting the carrier, where a shipment of live stock was made under an oral agreement, to

issue to the shipper several months thereafter a special contract restricting its liability as to such shipment. p. 377.

10. CARRIERS.—*Carriage of Goods.*—*Shipping Under Oral Agreement.*—If a bill of lading is not furnished a shipper until after the goods are fully accepted by the carrier under an oral agreement, the bill of lading constitutes no part of the contract and the oral agreement controls. p. 379.

11. APPEAL.—*Review.*—*Harmless Error.*—*Admission of Evidence.*— In an action for damages to a shipment of live stock, where the verdict and the jury's answers to the interrogatories showed that the jury found adversely to defendant's contention that the shipment was made under a special contract restricting carrier's liability and that the shipper was bound thereby, the defendant could not have been harmed by the ruling of the trial court, even though erroneous, on certain instructions, the admission of evidence, etc., relating to the provisions of such special contracts. p. 379.

12. APPEAL.—*Review.*—*Harmless Error.*—*Admission of Evidence.*— *Submission of Issues.*—*Verdict.*—*Scope and Effect.*—In an action by a shipper for damages to a shipment of live stock, where the carrier claimed that the shipment was made under a special contract restricting its liability, but the shipper contended that he was allowed to exercise no option as to rates or other conditions of transportation, but was compelled to ship under the special contract or not at all, the general verdict for plaintiff was a finding in his favor on such issue, so that any error by the trial court in the instructions or admissions of evidence relating to such special contract was harmless. p. 380.

From Delaware Superior Court; *Myron H. Gray*, Special Judge.

Action by Seward W. Jordan against the Chesapeake and Ohio Railway Company of Indiana. From a judgment for plaintiff, the defendant appeals. *Affirmed.*

*Warner & Warner, McClellan, Hensel & Guthrie* and *Robbins, Starr & Goodrich,* for appellant.

*Ward Marshall, George H. Koons* and *George H. Koons, Jr.,* for appellee.

FELT, C. J.—This is a suit to recover damages for failure to furnish transportation, and to safely transport certain live stock from Medford, Indiana, to Chicago, Illinois. The complaint was in three paragraphs, which was answered by a general denial and by a second paragraph of special answer. Appellee filed a reply to the second paragraph of answer in four paragraphs, the first of which was a general denial. The case was tried by a jury, and a verdict was returned for $500, also answers to interrogatories. Appellant's motion for a new trial and for judgment on the answers of the jury to interrogatories were overruled; judgment was rendered for appellee on the general verdict and this appeal was prayed and granted.

Appellant has assigned as error the overruling of its separate demurrer to each paragraph of the complaint; the overruling of its separate demurrer to each of the second, third and fourth paragraphs of reply to the second paragraph of its answer; the overruling of its motions for a new trial and for judgment on the answers of the jury to the interrogatories, and the overruling of its several motions to require the jury to return to its room and to more definitely and correctly answer certain interrogatories designated in the motion.

Omitting the formal allegations about which there is no controversy, the first paragraph of complaint, in substance, charges that: on January 11, 1912, appellee tendered to appellant, at its station at Medford, 325 sheep for shipment to Chicago, Illinois, and offered to pay the reasonable and established charges for such shipment; that appellant failed and refused to so transport the sheep within a reasonable time, although it could have done so, and did not ship the same until January 16, 1912; that appellant then agreed to safely transport the sheep to Chicago within a reasonable time but did not issue appellant any bill of lading or receipt therefor, and wholly failed to transport the sheep within a reasonable time, by reason of which the sheep became emaciated, sick and crippled and some of them died and the market declined during the delay, the details of which are alleged, by reason of all of which appellee was damaged in the sum of $700 for which he demands judgment.

The second paragraph is substantially like the first and differs only in details which are not important in deciding the questions presented for decision.

The third paragraph contains substantially the same general allegations as the other paragraphs and charges that: on January 16, 1912, appellee delivered to appellant at Medford, Delaware County, Indiana, 325 fat sheep to be transported to Chicago, Illinois, and appellant then and there received them for such shipment and agreed to safely transport them to Chicago but did not issue to appellee any receipt or bill of lading therefor; that the sheep were loaded at Medford at nine o'clock a. m. on January 16, 1912, and were not delivered at the stockyards in Chicago until six o'clock p. m. January 18, 1912, and were negligently kept in said cars all the time, or fifty-seven consecutive hours, without food, water, or rest, in violation of the federal statute duly enacted and in force from and after June 29, 1906, which provides, in substance, that any railway company or common carrier shall not confine any cattle, sheep, or other animals in cars for more than twenty-eight consecutive hours without unloading them in a humane manner into properly equipped pens for rest, water and feeding, for at least five consecutive hours, unless prevented by storm, etc., provided, on the written request of the owner or custodian, the time may be extended from twenty-eight to thirty-six hours; that neither appellee nor any custodian of said sheep signed any such request; that said sheep were given no rest, food, or water during the time aforesaid which was exclusive of the time consumed in loading and unloading, and by reason thereof they were almost starved, had lost flesh and were greatly reduced in weight and became unsightly in appearance, and some of them were crippled and others dead and missing; that owing to the negligence of appellant in so confining said sheep for the time aforesaid they deteriorated in value $380; that the value of sheep not delivered was $56; that the sheep that died on account of the neglect aforesaid were of the value of $45 and the loss in the sheep that were crippled amounted to $25, for all of which appellee demanded damages in the sum of $700.

The memorandum accompanying the demurrer to the complaint states, in substance: (1) That neither paragraph sets out a copy of the bill of lading or contract covering the shipment, and the averments show it was an interstate shipment and governed by the federal law and not by the laws of the State of Indiana, and therefore insufficient without a copy of such bill of lading or contract; (2) that the allegations fail to show that appellee made due application for cars as required by the statute; that it is not shown that appellant failed or refused to issue a receipt or bill of lading for the sheep or that appellee made demand for such receipt or bill of lading.

Appellant urges the proposition that each paragraph shows that the shipment was interstate and governed by the Carmack Amendment to the Hepburn Act, which requires the issuance of a receipt or bill of lading by the carrier, the issuance of which cannot be waived; that the liability, if any, is based upon a breach of the contract evidenced by such receipt or bill of lading, without which the complaint is sufficient, unless it appears that demand was made for such receipt or bill of lading by the shipper and refused by the company. The complaint does not purport to state a cause of action under the statute, though it does appear in each paragraph that the shipment was interstate. It has been held that there may be a

1.  cause of action for damages, under the common law, against a common carrier for its negligence or wrongful acts resulting in damages or loss to the shipper of an interstate shipment, notwithstanding the federal statute governing such shipment. According to the aver-

ments appellant accepted the live stock for ship-

2. ment and failed to issue any receipt or bill of lading therefor to the shipper.

The United States Statutes at Large (vol. 34 p. 595, §8592, cl. 11, U. S. Comp. St. 1913) provides: "That any common carrier, railroad, or transportation company receiving property for transportation from a point in one state to a point in another state shall issue a receipt or bill of lading therefor and shall be liable to the lawful holder thereof for any loss, damage, or injury to such property caused by it or by any common carrier, railroad, or transportation company to which such property may be delivered or over whose line or lines such property may pass, and no contract, receipt, rule or regulation shall exempt such common carrier, railroad, or transportation company from the liability hereby imposed; Provided, that nothing in this section shall deprive any holder of such receipt or bill of lading of any remedy or right of action which he has under existing law."

The statute clearly imposed on the carrier the duty of issuing the receipt or bill of lading and it cannot shield itself from liability by a failure to discharge a statutory duty. Each paragraph states a cause of action under the common law. *Toledo, etc., R. Co.* v. *Milner* (1915), 62 Ind. App. 208, 110 N. E. 756, and cases cited.

The assignment that the court erred in overruling

3. appellant's motion for judgment on the answers of
the jury to the interrogatories is waived by failure to present any point or proposition relating thereto in appellant's briefs.

The second paragraph of answer to each paragraph of complaint admits the shipment by appellant of the sheep from Medford, Indiana, as alleged, but avers that it then had two rates for the shipment of such live stock, one of which applied when shipments were made under its uniform live-stock contract, and the other, a higher rate, used when shipments were made without such contract, whereby the shipper became subject to the liability imposed by the common law and the federal and state statutes applicable thereto; that at the time of the shipment aforesaid these rates were evidenced by appellant's rate sheets, or tariffs, filed with the Interstate Commerce Commission and published according to law; that appellee was entitled to ship at either of said rates and then and there did ship at the lower rate, in compliance with the conditions of appellant's uniform live-stock contract, or at thirteen cents per hundredweight for 42,000 pounds, amounting to $54.60; that appellant, on January 16, 1912, the day of the shipment, was ready and willing to issue such uniform live-stock contracts but appellee failed to call for them at the freight office in the city of Muncie, Indiana, at which office he made his request for cars, and did not call therefor until March 15, 1912, when appellant's agent issued to him three of such contracts, one for each carload of stock shipped, which he then signed under the name and style of Web Jordan, copies of which contracts are made parts of the answer, and dated January 16, 1912; that prior thereto there had been a long course of dealings between the two parties as carrier and shipper of live stock and all of appellee's shipments were made at the lower freight rate and subject to the terms and conditions of the aforesaid contracts which were well known to appellee; that it had been the custom and practice of appellee to call at the freight office at Muncie, Indiana, after the shipment of live stock and procure said contracts; that he lived about six miles from Muncie and appellant for a long time prior to January 16, 1912, had permitted him to ship without such contracts or any receipt or bill of lading and to procure the contract afterwards as an accommodation to him; that appellee accepted the aforesaid contracts, which provide that, in case of unusual delays "caused by the negligence of the said carrier or its employes or its connecting carrier, or their employes or otherwise, the shipper agrees to accept as full compensation for all loss or damage sustained thereby the amount actually expended by said shipper in the purchase of food and water for the said stock while so detained,'' and also provide that no claim for damages shall be allowed or paid unless a verified claim therefor shall be made in writing and delivered to the general claim agent of the carrier at his office in Richmond, Virginia, within five days from the time the stock is removed from the cars; that the shipper shall see that all doors and openings in the cars are kept closed so as to .prevent the escape of any of the live stock and the carrier shall not be liable for the escape of any of the stock so shipped or for loss from overloading, crowding, kicking, goring, suffocating, fright, or from fire, heat, cold, or changes of weather; that appellee failed to so make and present his claim within five days for any of the damages he now seeks to recover in this action, by reason whereof appellant is not liable for any of the sheep that were missing or for any of the damages alleged.

To this answer a reply of general denial was filed, and a special reply in which it was alleged that the contracts relied upon were executed without any consideration. There was also filed a paragraph which alleges in detail all the facts of the shipment and the subsequent transactions and, among other things, alleges that appellee was ready and willing to pay and did pay the full and reasonable freight charges demanded by appellant for such shipment, and no option was given him of shipping at a higher rate and he had nothing to do with fixing the rate of freight charged by appellant and did not at any time agree to ship at a lower rate and limit appellant's liability in any respect whatever; that appellant did not, on January 16, 1912, when said sheep were shipped, issue to appellee any receipt or bill of lading therefor; that on March 15, 1912, appellee demanded of appellant a receipt or bill of lading for the

live stock so shipped and appellant failed and refused to
issue the same and did not do so, but instead thereof issued
the aforesaid contracts and refused to issue any other
receipt or bill of lading for said shipments and then procured appellee's signature thereto, all without any consideration therefor; that appellee did not accompany the
sheep to Chicago, nor did any one in his behalf, and appellant at the time knew that such was the case and then and
there undertook to take care of the sheep during transportation and it was the duty of appellant to care for,
feed and water the sheep; that the provisions of said contracts relied on are in extremely fine print, were not read
by, or known to appellee at the time, and his attention
was not called thereto by appellant or its agents; that said
provisions were and are illegal, unreasonable, against public policy, fraudulent and void; that appellee did not undertake to feed, water, or care for the sheep, or look after
the cars during the time of the shipment, nor did he at any
time agree to relieve appellant from liability for its negligence, or the negligence of its employes or connecting
lines, nor from liability for any of the causes or reasons
alleged and based on said contracts so issued after the shipments were made as aforesaid.

While the sufficiency of the affirmative paragraphs of
reply to the second paragraph of answer is not presented
by appellant's briefs, and questions relating thereto are
thereby waived, nevertheless we have deemed it necessary
to state the substance of those pleadings as a means of
comprehending and deciding the questions presented under
the assignment that the court erred in overruling appellant's motion for a new trial.

The first proposition urged under this assignment is that
the verdict of the jury is not sustained by sufficient evidence, for the reason that the complaint proceeds on the
theory of a common-law liability for violation of a parol
contract of shipment and the uncontradicted evidence

shows the shipment was made under the written contract
set out in appellant's special answer. Many of the general
propositions advanced in support of this contention are
beyond dispute and need not be discussed because they
are supported by authority. *Walker* v. *Larkin* (1890), 127
Ind. 100, 26 N. E. 684; *Snow* v. *Indiana, etc., R. Co.*
(1887), 109 Ind. 422, 426, 9 N. E. 702; *Stewart* v. *Cleveland, etc., R. Co.* (1898), 21 Ind. App. 218, 226, 52 N. E.
89; *Cleveland, etc., R. Co.* v. *Hollowell* (1909), 172 Ind.
466, 469, 88 N. E. 680.

Notwithstanding the federal statute, common carriers
may make contracts whereby they limit and define the extent
 of liability against them under specified conditions,
4. but they cannot, by contract, relieve themselves from
 liability for damages caused by their negligence or
the negligence of their employes. *Wabash R. Co.* v. *Priddy*
(1912), 179 Ind. 483, 494, 101 N. E. 724; *Adams Express
Co.* v. *Croninger* (1913), 226 U. S. 491, 33 Sup. Ct. 148, 57
L. Ed. 314, 44 L. R. A. (N. S.) 257.

Reference is made to the act of 1905 (§3918 *et seq.* Burns
1914, Acts 1905 p. 58) relating to the practice in suits
against common carriers of freight for damages resulting
from failure to safely transport property delivered to such
carriers for shipment. This act has been held to be valid
and constitutional. *Cleveland, etc., R. Co.* v. *Blind* (1914),
182 Ind. 398, 419, 105 N. E. 483. But the case at bar does
 not depend upon its provisions. Where the shipments
5. are interstate, the state law is superseded by the federal statute on the subject as to all questions of liability or defenses covered by the statute and applicable
6. to any given case, but this does not interfere with
 the jurisdiction of the state courts, for the federal
law is a part of the law of the state, and in suits of the
character here involved the state courts may apply such law
and give the relief warranted by the law and the facts. As
already shown the complaint counts on a common-law liability.

The special answer sets up facts to show that the shipment was not only interstate, but that the nature and extent of appellant's liability was fixed by a special contract duly entered into and binding on both the carrier and shipper. The answer shows that the contract was not actually executed until about two months had expired after the shipment was made. To connect the contract with the shipment the answer avers an established custom between the parties by which shipments were made without any receipt, bill of lading or contract in writing being delivered to the shipper and whereby subsequent to such shipments appellee executed and accepted contracts identical with those under which it is alleged these shipments were made.

One paragraph of reply to the answer alleged no consideration and another sets out the details of the transaction and charges that on March 15, 1912, appellee demanded the issuance of a bill of lading or receipt for the sheep so shipped by him on January 16, 1912, and appellant refused to issue the same and would not and did not do so, but instead thereof issued the special contracts set up in the answer, which were then so issued without any consideration and without any knowledge on the part of appellee as to the provisions relied on by appellant to defeat his recovery of damages sustained by the alleged negligence and want of care in making such shipment.

Under these pleadings several issuable questions of fact were presented to the jury for decision, among which were the following: (1) Was the shipment made in pursuance of the special contract? (2) Does the evidence conclusively show the custom alleged in the answer? (3) Did appellee demand the ordinary receipt or bill of lading used in such shipments, and did appellant refuse to issue the same and give appellee no choice but to accept the special contract limiting liability as alleged in the answer? The answer to the first question is necessarily dependent upon the second question, for, in the absence of such custom, the shipment in January, without any bill of lading, receipt or contract in writing issued to appellee by appellant, would be wholly disconnected from the issuance and acceptance of the contract in March subsequent to such shipment, and would therefore be without consideration since it is not claimed to rest upon any other consideration than that of the shipment of the stock and payment of the freight in January. Without the establishment of such custom the evidence fails to show the meeting of the minds of the contracting parties upon the alleged contract and appellant would fail in the defense alleged in its special paragraph of answer. The

8. general verdict is a finding in appellee's favor of every issuable fact, and is conclusive on all questions where there is any evidence tending to support the finding.

There is testimony tending to show that appellee ordered the cars from appellant's freight agent by telephone and

9. that the agent agreed to furnish them; that when the sheep were loaded on January 16, appellee reported to the agent, over the telephone, the cars and number of sheep in each car and their destination; that rates were not mentioned and nothing was said or done at the time about a receipt, bill of lading or special contract in writing; the freight was paid at Chicago but appellee was not present and had nothing to do therewith; that the sheep were shipped under a verbal arrangement; that on March 15, 1912, at the request of his attorney, appellee called upon appellant for a bill of lading for the sheep shipped in January and the agent of appellant refused to give it to him but offered him the special contracts set out in the answer and said he would not give him such contracts unless he signed them; that he then signed them without reading them or knowing their contents; that on a few occasions when he shipped fat hogs to eastern markets he had accepted special contracts but

procured them at the time the shipments were made; that
he "always got the contracts at the time he shipped the
stock, except the one shipment of sheep" now in controversy; that he shipped live stock from Medford, about
six miles from Muncie, and in some instances, obtained
bills of lading at Muncie after the shipments were made
and sometimes when they were made; that he had never
read one of the special contracts, did not know their provisions and appellant's agents did not at any time call
his attention thereto; that neither appellee, nor any one
in his behalf accompanied the shipment to Chicago and
appellant knew such was the case at the time of the shipment.

There is little if any evidence tending to prove the
alleged custom and the proof fully sustains the finding
that there was no established custom as alleged in the
answer.

Furthermore, in answer to interrogatories, the jury in
substance found the following: That there was no established
custom between the parties by which appellee executed
special contracts as alleged after shipments of live stock
had been made to Chicago; that at the time of the shipment in controversy nothing was said about rates; and
appellee was not offered his choice of two rates; that
appellee demanded of appellant a bill of lading on March
15, after the shipment in January and appellant refused
to issue it; that appellee received no consideration from
appellant for signing and accepting the three uniform
live-stock contracts on March 15, 1912; that there was no
written or printed instrument in existence which contained the exact terms of the agreement under which the
sheep of appellee were shipped to Chicago; that no part
of the damages allowed appellee were for delay in furnishing cars at Medford, Indiana. On this state of the
record the finding of the jury may be sustained on the
theory that the special answer was not established because

of the failure to prove the alleged custom, and likewise
that the special contracts relied upon by appellant were
executed without consideration and therefore not binding
on appellee. The answers to the interrogatories show
that such was the theory upon which the jury found its
verdict, and that nothing was allowed for delay in furnishing cars before the shipment was actually made as
alleged in the first and second paragraphs of complaint;
and therefore that the judgment rests upon the third
paragraph of the complaint for damages due to appellant's negligence in failing to care for and make timely
delivery of the sheep at Chicago. Futhermore, it is the
rule of the law in this state that if a bill of lading
10. is not furnished the shipper until after the goods
are fully accepted by the carrier under an oral
agreement, the bill of lading constitutes no part of the contract, and the oral agreement controls. *C. F. Adams Co.*
v. *Helman* (1914), 58 Ind. App. 394, 106 N. E. 733, and
cases cited.

The findings and conclusions already announced make
it unnecessary for us to consider in detail several questions suggested by appellant relating to the instruc-
11. tions, the alleged failure of the jury to fully and
fairly answer certain interrogatories, the admission
of certain evidence and certain questions relating to shipping rates, for the reason that appellee could not have
been harmed by any ruling of the court so complained of,
unless it appeared that the jury might have arrived at
its verdict on the theory that the shipments were made
in pursuance of the provisions of the special contracts,
since all of the questions referred to relate to such contracts,
and could only be available to assist appellant on the theory
that appellee was bound by the contracts. Having expressly found to the contrary, and it clearly and conclusively
appearing from the record that the verdict was based on
a finding that the alleged custom did not exist and that

the shipments were not made under the alleged contracts
set up in the answer, the rulings of the court aforesaid,
even if erroneous, could not have influenced the verdict or
in any way have deprived appellant of any substantial
right.   Furthermore, if the record did not con-
12.  clusively show that the verdict was reached on the
theory above stated, and we were required to view
the question from the standpoint of such contracts, the
general verdict is a finding that appellee was given no
choice and was compelled to ship under the provisions of
the contracts, or not at all, in which event appellant would
be liable for the damages under the common law.  *Toledo,
etc., R. Co. v. Milner, supra.*

On the whole record a correct result seems to have been
reached, and we find no intervening error that will warrant a reversal.  Judgment affirmed.

NOTE.—Reported in 114 N. E. 461.  Carriers: (a) "Carmack
amendment" as affecting state regulations limiting liability of common carriers, notes, 44 L. R. A. (N. S.) 257; 50 L. R. A. (N. S.)
819; (b) limitation of carrier's liability for injury to or loss of
goods as affected by Interstate Commerce Act, Ann. Cas. 1912B 672,
1915D 612, 7 Cyc 421; (c) jurisdiction of state courts of an action
for damages for violation of the Interstate Commerce Act, 4 Ann.
Cas. 773; (d) state regulation as to shipment of live stock or goods
as interference with interstate commerce, Ann. Cas. 1917A 973; (e)
contract of carriage, supplementing of, by proof of collateral oral
agreement, Ann. Cas. 1914A 458; (f) duties of, in carriage of live
stock, 63 Am. St. 548.  See under (4) 6 Cyc 394; (5) 7 Cyc 421.

HARTZELL ET AL. *v.* PRANGER.

[No. 9,067.  Filed May 12, 1916.  Rehearing denied November 22,
1916.  Transfer denied December 21, 1916.]

1.  APPEAL.— *Review.— Verdict.— Conclusiveness.— Conflicting Evidence.*—Where there is a conflict in the evidence, the decision of
the trial court is conclusive.  p. 383.
2.  MECHANIC'S LIEN.—*Time for Filing.—Last Work Done.*—Where
plaintiff, under a contract fixing no time for the completion of
the work, installed a heating plant in a residence, and several
months thereafter, under the direction and with the consent of

the owner, removed a section of the boiler for the purpose of remedying defects in the plant, a notice of an intention to hold a mechanic's lien, filed within the statutory time after the completion of such additional work, was within the proper time and plaintiff was entitled to a foreclosure of the lien. p. 384.

From Allen Circuit Court; *John W. Eggeman,* Judge.

Action by Frank Pranger against John R. Hartzell and another. From a judgment for plaintiff, the defendants appeal. *Affirmed.*

*John H. Aiken, Lee J. Hartzell* and *Ray McAdams,* for appellants.

*William C. Ryan,* for appellee.

McNUTT, J.—This was a suit by appellee Pranger, against appellants, to recover a balance alleged to be due him for installing a heating plant in appellants' residence, and to foreclose a mechanic's lien against the real estate upon which the residence is located.

Briefly, the complaint alleges that in 1912 appellee entered into a contract with appellants by which they agreed to pay him $638 to install a hot-water plant for heating their dwelling house, and to furnish all materials therefor; that he performed said contract, and completed the work on May 23, 1913; that said materials, work and labor were of the reasonable value of $638; that appellants paid $400 on said contract leaving $238 unpaid, which, on demand, they refused to pay; that on July 19, 1913, within sixty days after completing the work, he filed notice of a mechanic's lien, which was duly recorded, and is made a part of the complaint by exhibit, praying judgment for said balance, $100 attorneys' fees and for foreclosure of said lien.

To this complaint appellants filed an answer in two paragraphs, the first being a general denial, and the second a plea of payment to which appellee replied in general denial. Appellants also filed a counterclaim setting up in substance that appellee was employed by the P. & H. Sup-

ply Company, a corporation from whom appellants purchased a hot-water heating plant, to install said plant in
appellants' house for $632, and that said plant was
guaranteed by appellee to be of sufficient capacity to heat
appellants' twelve-room residence at a temperature of
seventy-two degrees in zero weather, and to burn less coal
than any hot-air furnace and to properly heat said residence; that it was agreed that one-half of the contract
price, or $316, should be paid when the work was com-
pleted, and the other half when the heating plant was
tested out to seventy-two degrees in zero weather; that it
was also agreed that appellee was to do said work in a
workmanlike manner; that said work was not done in a
workmanlike manner and said plant was not properly
installed and did not properly heat said house during the
winters of 1912 and 1913; that the plant was not inspected
in zero weather, and was not installed so that appellants
could so inspect it; that it will be necessary to have said
plant repaired or a new plant installed, and it will cost $500
to put said plant in working order; that after repeated
efforts to get said plant in working order, appellee finally
left said work in May, 1913, and that appellants have been
unable to test the same in zero weather; that by reason of
said improper installation, appellants have been damaged
in the sum of $500 for which amount they pray judgment.

Appellee filed a reply in general denial to the counterclaim. The cause was submitted to the court for trial,
resulting in a finding and judgment in appellee's favor for
$167, and for foreclosure of appellee's lien and sale of
the real estate described in the complaint.

The only error relied on for a reversal is the overruling of appellants' motion for a new trial, in support of
which it is urged that the decision and finding of the
court is contrary to law, and is not supported by sufficient evidence.

Appellants in their brief make no contention that the

contract for the installation of the heating plant in question was between appellants and the P. & H. Supply Company, a corporation, and the cause seems to have been tried on the theory that the contract was between appellee and appellants as alleged in the complaint.

The contract between appellee and appellants for the installation of the heating plant was a verbal one, and there is a direct conflict in the evidence by the parties as to what the contract was with reference to the time when the work should be paid for. Appellee contends that he was to be paid for the work when the same was completed, and that his contract to install a heating plant that would heat appellants' residence to seventy-two degrees in zero weather was not a condition precedent to his receiving payment for the work.

Appellants contend that one-half of the contract price was to be paid when the heating system was installed, and the other half when the plant was tested out and heated the house to seventy-two degrees in zero weather. Appellants admit that $300 of the contract price was paid before the heating system was installed and that an additional $100 was paid about the time the system was installed. The sum paid by appellants was almost two-thirds of the contract price, and their conduct in that respect is wholly inconsistent with their contention here.

Appellants cite and rely on the case of *Reed, etc., Furnace Co.* v. *State* (1904), 34 Ind. App. 265, 72 N. E. 615, but an examination of that case shows that the contract was in writing, and that the state was to have ninety days in which to test out the heating plant, and if it was accepted after such test, the contract price was to be paid. There was no dispute as to the time when the plant was to be tested. In the case now under consideration

1. there is a conflict, and where there is a conflict in the evidence, we must accept the conclusion of the trial court. This rule is so well settled that citation of authority is unnecessary.

It is earnestly insisted, however, by appellants, that the last work under the contract was done in October, 1912, and that the notice of lien was not filed until July 2.• 19, 1913, more than sixty days after the completion of the work. Appellants admit that appellee removed a section of the heating plant in May, 1913, but insist that this was done for the sole purpose of making the plant conform, if possible, to the guarantee, and was not such work and labor entering into the contruction of the plant as would give appellee the right to a lien filed within sixty days thereafter, relying upon the case of *Conlee* v. *Clark* (1896), 14 Ind. App. 205, 42 N. E. 762, 56 Am. St. 298, to support their contention. The court in the Conlee case decided that the work done by a contractor to remedy a defect in the performance of his work, caused by his own negligence, for which he makes no charge, but which is necessary to complete the performance, may be considered the last work done for the period of fixing the time for filing the lien under the statute giving sixty days after performing the labor or furnishing the material. It will be seen that the decision in the Conlee case does not support appellants' contention, but on the contrary supports the contention of appellee.

It is not contended by either party to this appeal that any time was fixed by the contract in which the work was to be performed. It is admitted by appellee that the heating plant was installed in the fall of 1912. The evidence shows that during the following winter appellants were making complaint that the plant did not work satisfactorily, and appellee on different occasions secured the services of experts to examine the plant, and along in March was advised by one of such experts that a change should be made in the boiler by removing a section. This advice was communicated to appellant Hartzell and appellee was thereupon directed to "go ahead and take that section of the boiler out of there." It is not disputed that this was done on May 25, 1913. It would appear, therefore, from the evidence that this work was done by appellee in good faith, for the purpose of bettering the plant, and was done not only with the consent, but by the direction of appellant John Hartzell.

In the case of *Stephenson* v. *Ballard* (1882), 82 Ind. 87, the court said: "In the case at bar, the claim is for work and also for materials in repairing a dwelling-house, and the suit is by the original contractors, who did the work and furnished the materials under one entire contract, and the notice was filed within sixty days after the last work done, but not within sixty days after the materials were furnished; they were furnished two months before the last work was done. In such a case, upon such an entire contract, the statute is satisfied if the notice is filed, as it was in this case, within sixty days after the last work done."

In the case of *Jeffersonville Water Supply Co.* v. *Riter* (1894), 138 Ind. 170, 37 N. E. 652, a standpipe was so far completed as to be ready for testing and inspection in September, but it was not actually tested by filling with water until November, when leaks were found which were closed and the work finally received. The court held that the work was only then finished, the additional labor being in fact necessary and performed by the mechanic. See, also, *Whitcomb* v. *Roll* (1907), 40 Ind. App. 119, 81 N. E. 106.

We are of the opinion that the court below was clearly right in concluding that appellee filed his notice of lien in time, and was entitled to foreclosure of the lien. As stated before, the other questions involved in appellants' motion for a new trial were decided in appellee's favor upon conflicting evidence, and in such case this court is powerless to disturb such finding. Judgment affirmed.

NOTE.—Reported in 112 N. E. 530. Mechanic's lien: (a) whether work done or material furnished in perfecting original work are lienable items to establish period for filing claim, note, 12 L. R. A. (N. S.) 864; (b) time for filing, as extended by substituting new materials for those already furnished, Ann. Cas. 1912C 217, 27 Cyc 148; (c) last work done as fixing time for filing, note, 62 App. 382.

## COLUMBIA SCHOOL SUPPLY COMPANY *v.* LEWIS.

### [No. 9,791.   Filed December 21, 1916.]

1. **MASTER AND SERVANT.**—*Workmen's Compensation Act.—Scope.— Employe.*—Under §76 of the Workmen's Compensation Act (Acts 1915 p. 392), which defines an employe as every person in the service of another under any contract of hire or apprenticeship written or implied, except casual laborers, etc., one who is an independent contractor is not included within the protection of the act. p. 388.

2. **MASTER AND SERVANT.**—*Independent Contractor.—Determination. —Questions of Law and of Fact.*—The question of what constitutes an independent contractor is ordinarily one of mixed law and fact. Where the evidence with respect to the relation is oral, and is sufficient to establish the existence of some relation, and if it be uncontradicted and reasonably susceptible of but a single inference, the question of what relation is thereby shown to exist is a law question, but if the evidence is conflicting, or is such that different deductions may reasonably be drawn therefrom leading to different conclusions as to what relation is established, it is a question of fact, in the sense that the triers of the facts must determine the facts and draw the inferences and make the deductions, but even in such a case certain legal standards and principles must be applied to the facts after they are ascertained and a question of law is thereby involved, so that the ultimate question of whether a person is an employe or an independent contractor under certain facts involves a law question. p. 389.

3. **MASTER AND SERVANT.**—*Workmen's Compensation Act.—Injury in Course of Employment.—Question of Law.*—Where the facts, including all reasonable inferences to be drawn therefrom, are ascertained, the ultimate question from such facts of whether an injury under consideration was an injury by accident arising out of and in the course of the employment within the meaning of the Workmen's Compensation Act involves a law question. p. 390.

4. **MASTER AND SERVANT.**—*Workmen's Compensation Act.—Award for Injury.—Appeal.*—If, in an action for an award under the Workmen's Compensation Act (Acts 1915 p. 392) the uncontradicted evidence, when measured by legal standards that must be

applied, established the relation of contractee and independent contractor rather than that of employer and employee, as those terms are used in the act, or if such uncontradicted evidence established that the injury complained of was not an injury arising out of and in the course of employment, an award involves errors of law, and the cause is appealable under §61 of such act, providing that appeals may be taken from awards of the industrial board to the Appellate Court for errors of law. p. 390.

From the Industrial Board of Indiana.

Action by Charles Lewis under the Workmen's Compensation Act against the Columbia School Supply Company. Defendant appeals from a judgment for plaintiff, and the latter moves to dismiss the appeal. *Motion to dismiss appeal overruled.*

*McKay, Turner & Robertson,* for appellant.
*Willard Robertson,* for appellee.

CALDWELL, J.—Appellee, while hauling goods for appellant, suffered certain physical injuries. His cause having been regularly brought before the Industrial Board, under the provisions of the act of 1915 (Acts 1915 p. 392), a hearing before a member of the board resulted in a finding and award in appellee's favor. The cause having been reviewed by the full board on application to that end, there was a like finding and award, from which award this appeal is prosecuted. Appellee has filed a motion to dismiss the appeal, on the ground that appellant presents for our consideration no error of law.

Section 61 of the act provides, in substance, that an award, if not reviewed in due time, or an award of the board upon such review shall be conclusive and binding as to all questions of fact, "but either party to the dispute may within thirty days from the date of the award, appeal to the appellate court for errors of. law under the same terms and conditions as govern appeals in ordinary civil actions."

The finding is in part that appellee "was in the employment" of appellant, and that he "received a personal injury by an accident arising out of and in the course of his employment." On the finding appellee was awarded a certain weekly compensation for 100 weeks.

Appellant's assignment of error in this court is in part to the effect that there was no evidence tending to show that the relation of employer and employe existed between appellant and appellee, but that the evidence affirmatively established that such relation was that of contractee and independent contractor; and that there was no evidence from which it might be determined that appellee received his injuries by accident arising out of and in the course of his employment.

An inspection of the act discloses that it deals with employers and employes. By §76 an employer is defined as including "any individual, firm, * * * using

1. the services of another for pay"; and an employe is defined as including "every person * * * in the service of another under any contract of hire or apprenticeship written or implied," except casual laborers, etc. The same section of the act limits the injuries for which there may be an award under the act to injuries "by accident arising out of and in the course of the employment."                    •

It seems to be conceded by appellee's counsel that, if appellee were in fact an independent contractor, rather than an employe, he is not included within the protection of the act. Such seems to be the effect of the definition of an employe as contained in the act, and as above set out. The courts so hold under similar acts. See cases collected in note to *Rayner* v. *Sligh Furn. Co.* (1914), L. R. A. 1916A 118, 247; *Matter of Powley* v. *Vivian & Co.* (1915), 169 App. Div. 170, 154 N. Y. Supp. 426; *Matter of Rheinwald* v. *Builders, etc., Co.* (1915), 168 App. Div. 425, 153 N. Y. Supp. 598.

Appellee contends, however, that as to whether he was an independent contractor rather than an employe within the meaning of the act was a question of fact for the Industrial Board, and that the board determined that he was an employe by finding that he was "in the employment" of appellant. Appellant, however, contends that the question of what constitutes an independent contractor is a question of law, and not a question of fact.

It may be said, however, that such question is ordinarily one of mixed law and fact. Where the evidence with respect to the relation under investigation is oral as 2. here, and is sufficient to establish the existence of some relation, and if it be uncontradicted and reasonably susceptible of but a single inference, the question of what relation is thereby shown to exist is a law question; but if the evidence is conflicting, or is such that different deductions may reasonably be drawn therefrom leading to different conclusions as to what relation is established, it is a question of fact, in the sense that the triers of the facts must determine the facts and draw the inferences and make the deductions.

But even in such case, in order that the ultimate question of what relation is shown to exist may be determined, there must be applied to the facts, after they are so ascertained, including inferences and deductions reasonably drawn, a certain legal standard and certain legal principles, and hence a question of law is involved. It follows that the ultimate question of whether a person is an employe or an independent contractor under certain facts involves a law question. *Board, etc.* v. *Bonebrake* (1896), 146 Ind. 311, 318, 45 N. E. 470; *Dodge Mfg. Co.* v. *Kronewitter* (1914), 57 Ind. App. 190, 199, 104 N. E. 99; *Lagler* v. *Roch* (1914), 57 Ind. App. 79, 86, 104 N. E. 111; *Richmond* v. *Sitterding* (1903), 101 Va. 354, 43 S. E. 562, 65 L. R. A. 445, note 508, 99 Am. St. 879; *Knicely* v. *West Virginia, etc., R. Co.,* 17 L. R. A. (N. S.), note

382. A like course of reasoning establishes that,
3. where the facts, including all reasonable inferences
to be drawn therefrom, are ascertained, the ultimate
question from such facts of whether a certain injury under
investigation was an "injury by accident arising out of and
in the course of the employment" also involves a law question. It is so regarded and treated by the courts. See
the following: *Rayner* v. *Sligh Furn. Co., supra,* note 227,
232; *Vennen* v. *New Dells Lumber Co.* (1915), 161 Wis.
370, 154 N. W. 640, L. R. A. 1916A 273; *Hurle's case*
(1914), 217 Mass. 223, 104 N. E. 336, L. R. A. 1916A
279, Ann. Cas. 1915C 919; *Adams* v. *Acme, etc., Works*
(1914), 182 Mich. 157, 148 N. W. 485, L. R. A. 1916A
283, Ann. Cas. 1916D 689; *Zappala* v. *Industrial Ins.
Comm.* (1914), 82 Wash. 314, 144 Pac. 54, L. R. A. 1916A
295; *Industrial Comm.* v. *Brown* (1915), 92 Ohio St. 309,
110 N. E. 744, L. R. A. 1916B 1277.

If, as charged by appellant in its assignment of errors,
the uncontradicted evidence, when measured by legal standards that must be applied, established the relation of
4. contractee and independent contractor rather than
that of employer and employe, as those terms are
used in the act, or if such uncontradicted evidence established that the injury complained of was not "an injury
by accident arising out of and in the course of the employment," the award here involves errors of law, and the cause
is appealable. It results that the motion to dismiss must be
overruled.

We would not be understood as determining anything
at this time respecting the scope of the terms "employer"
and "employe," as used in the act, or as indicating anything respecting the line dividing the relation thereby
expressed from the relation of contractee or independent
contractor, in proceedings brought under the act. The
courts, however, in proceedings brought under similar acts

have manifested a disposition in favor of the former relation in doubtful cases.

The motion to dismiss the appeal is overruled.

NOTE.—Reported in 115 N. E. 103. Master and servant, persons
deemed independent contractors, see notes, 65 L. R. A. 445; 17 L. R.
A. (N. S.) 371; 26 Cyc 1546.

---

NEW ALBANY NATIONAL BANK ET AL. *v.* BROWN
ET AL.

[No. 8,773. Filed December 21, 1916.]

1. PLEDGES.—*Elements.—Possession.*—Possession of a chattel is the
essence of a pledge, and without it no privilege can exist against
third persons. p. 400.

2. PLEDGES.—*Surrender of Possession for Special Purpose.—Possession Wrongfully Obtained.—Effect.*—Possession and control of
pledged property acquired without the assent of the pledgee, or
by deception and false pretenses, will not create a forfeiture of
his lien, nor will the delivery of the pledged chattel to the
pledgor for merely a temporary or special purpose divest the
pledgee's lien as against the pledgor or attaching creditors, although it would have that effect as against bona fide purchasers
from the pledgor while in such temporary possession. p. 400.

3. INTERPLEADER.—*Cross-Complaint.—Nature of Proceedings.* — In
interpleader, the cross-complaint of a claimant asserting a first
lien on the fund is a proceeding *in rem,* and where such pleading
alleges that another claims an adverse interest in the fund it is
sufficient to require the other claimant to answer. p. 401.

4. INTERPLEADER. — *Cross-Complaint. — Demurrer.—Laches.*—In interpleader, where one party claims a first lien on the fund in
controversy by a cross-complaint alleging that another is wrongfully asserting an adverse interest therein, the other claimant cannot raise the question of laches by demurrer, but only by answer
showing an interest in the fund. p. 401.

5. PLEADING.—*General Denial. — Scope. — Laches.* — Under §361
Burns 1914, §356 R. S. 1881, providing that all defenses, except
the mere denial of the facts alleged by plaintiff, shall be pleaded
specially, the defense of laches is not provable under the general
denial, but must be specially pleaded. p. 402.

6. INTERPLEADER.—*Pleading. — Answer. — Sufficiency. — Interest in
Action.*—Where, in interpleader, the cross-complaint of a claimant
to the proceeds of a life insurance policy merely alleged that an-

other wrongfully asserted an adverse interest therein, the other claimant's answer, pleading the statute of limitations, but failing to show that he had interest in the fund, was insufficient. p. 402.

7. PLEDGES.—*Renewal of Notes.—Effect.*—Where notes secured by a pledge are renewed, the pledge remains as security for the new notes, in the absence of anything showing that the parties intended that the original debt should be regarded as paid. p. 402.

8. LIMITATION OF ACTIONS.—*Pledge.—Right to Foreclose Lien.*— The right to foreclose the lien of a pledge given to secure notes is not barred until the expiration of the ten-year period fixed by the statute of limitations (§295 Burns 1914, §293 R. S. 1881) in which action may be brought to recover on the notes. p. 403.

9. LIMITATION OF ACTIONS.—*Action to Foreclose Lien on Pledge.— Fraud.—Possession of Pledge.*—Where, in interpleader, a claimant to the proceeds of a policy of life insurance assigned to her as security for notes alleged that possession of the policy was obtained by the assignor through fraudulent representations, fraud was not the basis of the action, so that claimant's right to recover is not barred within six years by §294, cls. 3, 4, Burns 1914, §292 R. S. 1881. p. 403.

10. APPEAL.—*Briefs.—Sufficiency.—Questions Presented for Review.*—An assignment of error based on the overruling of a demurrer to an answer presents no question for review where appellant's brief sets out neither the complaint nor the answer, nor the substance of either, and fails to show that such answer was filed. p. 404.

11. APPEAL.—*Witnesses.—Objection to Competency.—Sufficiency.— Presumptions.*—An objection to the competency of a party as a witness presents no question for review on appeal where the party objecting failed to point out any reason for the alleged incompetency, since the presumption is that all parties to an action are competent to testify in their own behalf. p. 404.

12. APPEAL.—*Review.—Evidence.—Sufficiency.—Scope of Review.*— In determining the sufficiency of the evidence on appeal the court will not weigh the evidence, but will determine whether there is any evidence to support the finding in appellee's favor, and will consider only the evidence which tends to support such finding. p. 405.

13. INSURANCE.—*Assignment of Policy.—Right to Proceeds.—Bona Fide Purchaser.—Prior Equities.*—The assignment of a life insurance policy as collateral to secure a pre-existing debt does not make the assignee a holder for value as against prior equities. p. 407.

14. INSURANCE.—*Policy.—Surrender of Possession.—Right to Proceeds.*—Where the assignee of a life insurance policy surrendered

possession thereof to the assignor upon his representation that he desired to have a proper assignment executed and that he would then return the policy to her, the assignee did not thereby lose her lien, and a subsequent assignment by the assignor to secure a pre-existing debt was ineffectual as against such original assignee. p. 410.

15. INSURANCE.—*Policy.—Assignment.—Right to Proceeds.—Assignees.—Laches.*—An assignee who took an assignment of a life insurance policy to secure a pre-existing debt, but parted with no new consideration therefor, did not change his position in any way to his injury, and could not, in interpleader to determine the ownership of the proceeds of the policy, rely on the alleged laches of a prior assignee, who had been induced by the false representations of the assignor to return the policy to him. p. 410.

From Clark Circuit Court; *Harry C. Montgomery,* Judge.

Interpleader by the Northwestern Mutual Life Insurance Company against the New Albany National Bank, Lizzie Brown and others. From a judgment allowing Lizzie Brown and others priority in the fund involved, the New Albany National Bank and others appeal. *Affirmed.*

*Alexander Dowling,* for appellants.

*Stotsenburg & Weathers* and *George H. Voight,* for appellees.

McNUTT, J.—In 1908 the Northwestern Mutual Life Insurance Company filed its complaint in the Floyd Circuit Court against appellants and appellees, alleging that one Gebhart had previously died the owner of an insurance policy issued upon his life by said company in 1882, and that the same was payable to his estate or his assigns; that said defendants were each claiming the proceeds of said policy, and asked that it be allowed to pay said proceeds, amounting to $5,620, into court and that said defendants be required to interplead among each other to settle the ownership of said proceeds. The court made an order accordingly.

Thereafter the venue of the cause was changed to the

Clark Circuit Court, and thereupon the appellant bank
filed its complaint against said other parties, alleging, in
substance, that said company, on May 11, 1882, issued to
said Gebhart a policy of insurance for $15,000; that the
premium had not been paid thereon after 1898, and for
failure to pay premiums the said policy had, by its terms,
become a paid-up policy for $5,620; that said Gebhart died
on March 27, 1907, intestate, and that said $5,620 had been
paid by said company into court for the use of the parties
entitled thereto; that on December 19, 1893, said Gebhart
was indebted to it in the sum of $15,000, for borrowed
money, which debt was evidenced by his promissory note for
said sum, dated December 18, 1893, and on said date
pledged said policy to it, which said pledge was stated in
said note, which was made part of the complaint by exhibit;
that at said time said Gebhart was in possession of the
policy and delivered it to the bank as collateral security
for the note, and that it had received the policy believing that said Gebhart had a right to pledge the same to
it, and that it had ever since had the actual possession of
said policy and held same as security; that, during 1894
and 1895, $2,000 were paid on the principal of said debt,
and that from time to time renewal notes were given containing the same pledge agreement; that after the execution of said first note it was advised by said company that
in case of an assignment of a policy, or where a policy
was held as security, a duplicate assignment should be
given the company, and thereupon it procured from said
Gebhart a written assignment thereof, which is set out and
dated December 19, 1893, and that the same was attached
to said policy, which is made a part of the complaint by
exhibit; that on March 1, 1907, said debt amounted to
$22,354.93, and was renewed by said Gebhart, by his execut-
ing several notes aggregating said amount; that the other
defendants to the company's complaint each wrongfully
claim some interest in, title to, or lien upon said sum of

$5,620 so paid into court by said company; but that it denies that any of said other defendants have any interest in, title to, or claim or lien upon said fund, or any part thereof, and that the whole of the fund rightfully belongs to it by virtue of said pledge, and prays for a foreclosure thereof.

Appellees answered the bank's complaint in six paragraphs. The first was a general denial; the second, a plea of payment; the third, a plea of the three-year statute of limitations; the fourth, a plea of the ten-year statute of limitations; the fifth, a partial answer "to so much of the complaint as is founded upon the written assignment of said policy set out on page five of the complaint"; that said pretended assignment was not executed by said Gebhart on December 19, 1893, and was not delivered by said Gebhart to said bank on said December 19, 1893, but, on the contrary, said assignment was executed by said Gebhart, and was delivered by him to the bank, on February 18, 1902. This paragraph of answer was verified.

The sixth paragraph of answer was filed to so much of the complaint of the bank as is founded upon the alleged assignment to the bank of the policy of insurance, and which seeks to enforce a lien upon said policy and the proceeds thereof. This paragraph of answer alleges, in substance, that prior to January 1, 1893, said Gebhart was indebted to Elizabeth Brown in the sum of $3,500, evidenced by his promissory note; that, at the time of the execution of said note, Gebhart delivered to her the policy, mentioned in the bank's complaint, as security for its payment long before the assignment to the bank; that on March 1, 1895, Gebhart executed two notes to Elizabeth Brown for the purpose of renewing said debt; that on June 8, 1896, for the purpose of further securing these notes and perfecting his agreement, he executed a written assignment of said policy as follows:

APPELLATE COURT OF INDIANA,

"New Albany, Ind., June 8, 1896.
I hereby assign to Elizabeth Brown, her heirs or assigns, the life insurance policy attached as collateral for two notes covering $3,500, together, money given me in cash.                          J. F. Gebhart."

It is further alleged that the assignment, the two notes, and the policy were pinned together, and that Elizabeth Brown retained possession of the policy until July 1, 1899, when Gebhart obtained it from her by representing to her that it was not properly assigned; that he requested possession of it to have it properly assigned on the books of the company; that Elizabeth Brown delivered the policy to Gebhart for the purpose of having it properly assigned to her and for no other purpose; and that, though many times thereafter requested, he refused and neglected to redeliver said policy to her; that, on August 2, 1899, Gebhart did deliver to her another written assignment of said policy as follows:

"Assignment as Collateral Security.
In consideration of thirty-five hundred dollars, the receipt of which is hereby acknowledged, I hereby sell, assign, transfer and set over unto Elizabeth Brown of New Albany, in the State of Indiana, and her executors, administrators, and assigns, as their interest may appear, all right, title, and interest in and to policy No. 113972, issued by the Northwestern Mutual Life Insurance Company, subject to all the terms and conditions in the said policy contained. The interest of the assignee in the policy hereby assigned is limited to said assignee's valid pecuniary claim against the assignor, existing at the time of the settlement of the policy; the remainder of said policy, if any, being unaffected by this assignment.
Witness my hand and seal at New Albany, in the State of Indiana, this second day of August, 1899.
                                    J. F. Gebhart."

Said answer further alleges that, after obtaining possession of the policy, he delivered it to the New Albany National Bank to secure the indebtedness mentioned in its cross-complaint; that the debt to the bank was incurred prior

to the delivery of the assignment of the policy to it; that
this indebtedness was subsequent to the time of indebtedness to Elizabeth Brown; that, at the time of delivery of the
assignment of the policy to the bank, it parted with no
consideration for it, but that it was delivered solely for
the purpose of securing the old indebtedness of Gebhart
to the bank; that Elizabeth Brown died October 1, 1902,
leaving the said appellees as her sole heirs; that her estate
had been fully administered, including said notes, which
were turned over to said heirs; that about December 1,
1904, the said notes were renewed by said Gebhart and
four new ones were executed to appellees, aggregating the
amount due on the old ones, two notes of $1,000 each dated
September 1, 1904, and two notes of $750 each dated
December 1, 1904, all payable one day after date and all
bearing interest at seven per cent.; that a copy of said last
assignment was filed with said company; that the assignment of said policy to said bank purporting to be dated
December 19, 1893, was, in fact, executed on or about
February 18, 1902, and that the assignment of the policy
was made to Elizabeth Brown long before its assignment
to said bank.

The appellant bank replied to appellees' answers, except
the first. The replies to the second, fifth and sixth paragraphs were general denials, and the replies to the third
and fourth paragraphs of answer allege that the cause of
action did accrue within a period in which the action was
not barred.

Appellees also filed a cross-complaint against all the other
defendants in the complaint of the insurance company. It
alleges the execution of the policy of the company; the
payment of all premiums falling due before November 11,
1898; the failure to pay premiums thereafter and by reason
thereof becoming a paid-up policy for $5,620; that before
January 1, 1893, said Gebhart was indebted to Elizabeth
Brown, as evidenced by his note for $3,500; that, at said

date, he delivered to her the policy of insurance referred
to as security for said debt and note and that she took possession of and held the same; that on March 1, 1895, Gebhart renewed said note and debt by executing to Elizabeth
Brown his two notes; that it was agreed that said Elizabeth Brown should continue to hold the policy as security
for the payment of said notes; that on June 8, 1896, for
the purpose of further securing said notes, Gebhart executed
the first assignment heretofore set out in appellee's answer;
that in order to identify the said assignment it was pinned
to said policy; that Elizabeth Brown believed that Gebhart had a right to pledge said policy; that she retained it
until July 1, 1899, when Gebhart notified her that it was
not properly assigned and that he would have to have possession of it to have it assigned on the books of the company,
and so requested her to deliver it to him for that purpose;
that she thereupon delivered the policy to him and that
afterwards, though often requested, he failed, neglected and
refused to deliver said policy to her; that on August 2,
1899, he delivered to her a written assignment thereof
(same as heretofore set out in appellees' answer.) Said
cross-complaint further alleges that Elizabeth Brown died,
intestate, October 1, 1902, in Floyd county, Indiana, leaving appellees, her daughters, as her sole heirs at law; that
her estate had been fully administered and that said notes
were turned over to appellees, after which said Gebhart
executed four new notes (the same as alleged in appellees'
answer), and that said notes executed to Elizabeth Brown
were surrendered to said Gebhart at the time of the execution of the new notes to appellees; and that Elizabeth
Brown caused copies of the two assignments to be delivered
to said company. A copy of the insurance policy is
made a part of the said cross-complaint by exhibit. Said
cross-complaint further alleges that the notes executed to
appellees, with interest and attorney's fees, are due and
unpaid; that said Gebhart died, intestate, March 27, 1907;

that said appellees offered to make proof of death, but the same was waived by the company; that the proceeds of the policy were paid into court; that appellees claim the first lien on the policy and that the defendants to the cross-complaint wrongfully claim interest in it adverse to them, but that the cross-complainants are entitled to the entire proceeds of the policy.

Appellant bank demurred to appellees' cross-complaint for insufficient facts which demurrer was overruled. Said appellant then filed an answer in three paragraphs. The first was a general denial, the second the six-year statute of limitations, the third the ten-year statute of limitations. Appellees demurred to said second and third paragraphs for want of sufficient facts, which demurrer was overruled as to the third and sustained as to the second. The cause was tried by the court and a finding was made for appellees, on which judgment was rendered after appellant's motion for a new trial was overruled.

Appellant bank assigns errors as follows: Overruling of the demurrer of the bank to the cross-complaint of appellees; sustaining the demurrer of appellees to the second paragraph of the answer of the bank; overruling the demurrer of the bank to the sixth paragraph of the answer of the appellees to the second paragraph of the complaint of the bank; and overruling the motion of the bank for a new trial.

The first error challenges the sufficiency of the cross-complaint of appellees. It is contended by appellant that when said Gebhart procured possession of the policy in 1899, said Elizabeth Brown thereby lost title to it, and by not taking timely steps to repossess the same, she and appellees were guilty of laches, and that appellees' claim was barred by the statute of limitations of six years at the time of the filing of the cross-complaint.

As an abstract proposition of law, possession is the essence of pledge, and, without it, no privilege can exist as against

third persons. *Casey* v. *Cavaroc* (1877), 96 U. S.
1.  467, 490, 24 L. Ed. 779; Edwards, Bailments (2d
ed.) §246; 22 Am. & Eng. Ency. Law 855; *Ex Parte
Fitz*(1876), 2 Lowell (U. S.) 519; *Saint Joseph Hydraulic
Co.* v. *Wilson* (1893), 133 Ind. 465, 474, 33 N. E. 113;
*Geilfuss* v. *Corrigan* (1897), 95 Wis. 651, 70 N. W. 306,
37 L. R. A. 166, 60 Am. St. 143; *Moore* v. *Moore* (1887),
112 Ind. 149, 13 N. E. 673, 2 Am. St. 170. But it is well
settled that the delivery by the pledgee to the
2.  pledgor for a mere temporary purpose, or a special
purpose, does not, in legal contemplation, interrupt
the pledgee's possession; and the fact that the policy was
turned over to the pledgor for a temporary or special purpose does not take away the possession from the pledgee
any more than if the pledgee had turned the policy over to
a stranger for the same purpose. "Possession and control
of the pledge, without the assent of the pledgee will not
create a forfeiture of the lien, nor defeat his right to recover
damages for an injury to the pledge or for a conversion
of it. The pledgee cannot be deemed to have released his
lien when the pledge has been obtained by the pledgor
through deception and false pretenses." Jones, Collateral
Securities §41. "A pledgee does not lose his lien by permitting the pledgor to have possession of the property for
a special and limited purpose, and not merely for his own
use and benefit." Jones, Collateral Securities (3d ed.)
§44. "The delivery, however, of the property by the
pledgee to the pledgor for merely a temporary or special
purpose, as for example for some temporary use, for the
performance of some work on it, for sale, for lease for the
pledgee's account, for pledge to another creditor of the
pledgor, for collection, or to be exchanged for other property to be held in pledge, does not divest the pledgee's lien
as against the pledgor or attaching creditors, although it
would have that effect as against *bona fide* purchasers for
value from the pledgor while in such temporary posses-

sion, without notice of the pledgee's right." 31 Cyc 818. See, also, 22 Am. & Eng. Ency. Law 860.

"Where the pledgor surreptitiously or fraudulently obtains possession of the property from the pledgee, such wrongful dispossession does not affect the pledge, and the lien will continue to subsist." 22 Am. & Eng. Ency. Law 862. See, also, *Goodwin* v. *Massachusetts Loan, etc., Co.* (1890), 152 Mass. 189, 25 N. E. 100.

The delivery of the policy by Mrs. Brown to Gebhart, under the circumstances shown in the complaint, was not such a surrender of the policy as would show that she intended to give up her security.

The cross-complaint of appellees was a proceeding *in rem.* It was alleged that the bank claimed some interest in, or lien upon, the proceeds of the policy. It is our opinion that the pleading was sufficient to require the bank to answer. It is contended by appellees that without some showing by the bank that it was a subsequent holder of the policy for value, it was in no position to claim that the complaint showed laches. In this contention we feel bound to concur, and, therefore, that such question could only be raised by an answer. In *Corbey* v. *Rogers* (1898), 152 Ind. 169, 52 N. E. 748, it is decided that where a complaint to foreclose a mortgage recites that a certain defendant claims some interest in the mortgaged property, but if he has any interest it is subject to plaintiff's mortgage, such defendant cannot plead the statute of limitations unless he alleges facts showing that he has an interest in the property. In *Scherer* v. *Ingerman* (1887), 110 Ind. 428, 11 N. E. 8, 12 N. E. 304, held that it is only where the laches of a party are of such a character as to work an equitable estoppel, that his right of action will be limited to a less period than that fixed by the statute of limitations.

Section 361 Burns 1914, §356 R. S. 1881, provides: "All

defenses, except the mere denial of the facts alleged by the
plaintiff, shall be pleaded specially." In *Baker* v.

5. *Kistler* (1859), 13 Ind. 63, the Supreme Court said:
"The code says: 'All defenses, except the mere
denial of the facts alleged by the plaintiff, shall be pleaded
specially.' 2 R. S. p. 42, §66. This evidently means,
facts which the plaintiff, to sustain his action, is bound
to prove; and we have decided that 'every matter of fact
which goes to defeat the cause of action, and which the
plaintiff is not under the necessity of proving, in order to
make out his case, must be alleged in the answer.'" See,
also, *Adams Express Co.* v. *Darnell* (1869), 31 Ind. 20;
99 Am. Dec. 583; *National, etc., Ins. Co.* v. *Owens* (1916),
*ante* 70, 113 N. E. 1024; *Storer* v. *Markley* (1904),
164 Ind. 535, 73 N. E. 1081; *Peters* v. *Griffee* (1886), 108
Ind. 121, 8 N. E. 727. From these authorities, it seems
clear that the defense of laches is one which is not provable
under the general denial, and which must be specially
pleaded to be available as a matter of defense. It therefore follows that even if there had been laches, it would not
be available to the bank in this case.

The contention of the bank that the cross-complaint of
appellees shows that their claim was barred by the six-
year statute of limitations is also raised by the sec-

6. ond assignment of error, viz., that it was error to
sustain the demurrer of appellees to the second
paragraph of appellant bank's answer to appellees' cross-
complaint. Since the cross-complaint of appellees merely
alleged that appellant bank was claiming some interest in
the fund, it was necessary to show in such answer that it
was entitled to the benefit of the statute of limitations.
This the answer does not do.

It is alleged in appellees' cross-complaint that after the
death of Mrs. Brown, or in 1902, renewal notes were

7. executed to appellees by said Gebhart, aggregating
the amount due on the original note. If the original

note were secured by the policy, the renewal notes carried
the pledge with them.

"When a promissory note secured by a pledge becomes
due and a new note is given in renewal, the pledge remains
as security for the new note, in the absence of anything
showing that the parties intended that the original debt
should be regarded as paid or discharged.  When it appears
that it will be for the benefit of the creditor that the old
debt should be kept alive, the presumption of payment, by
the taking of the new note for the old note, does not arise,
and the original debt is not discharged."  Jones, Collateral Securities (3d ed.) §355a.  The limitation

8. of the action on the notes being ten years, the right
to foreclose the pledge would not sooner expire.
§295 Burns 1914, §293 R. S. 1881.

The appellant bank contends that appellees' cross-complaint was one based on fraud and was for the recovery
of possession of personal property, and, therefore,

9. under clauses three and four, §294 Burns 1914, §292
R. S. 1881, the second paragraph of answer was
sufficient.  However, fraud was not the basis of appellees'
claim; fraud is a mere incident in the cause.  In such case
the six-year statute of limitations does not apply.  *Wilson* v.
*Brookshire* (1891), 126 Ind. 497, 25 N. E. 131, 9 L. R. A.
792; *Eve* v. *Louis* (1883), 91 Ind. 457; *Caress* v. *Foster*
(1878), 62 Ind. 145.  We are of opinion that, as long as
the notes were not barred, appellees' right to their

8. lien, if they had one, was enforcible.  §295 Burns
1914, *supra; Bottles* v. *Miller* (1887), 112 Ind. 584,
14 N. E. 728; Jones, Collateral Securities (3d ed.) §581.

In the last cited case it is held that a payment upon a
note secured by a mortgage, if sufficient to take the note
out of the operation of the statute of limitations, will have
a like effect upon the mortgage; and, so long as any part
of the debt remains unpaid and not barred, the lien of
the mortgage continues unimpaired.  It is our opinion,

therefore, that the court did not err in overruling the demurrer to the cross-complaint of appellees or in sustaining their demurrer to appellant bank's second paragraph of answer.

Appellant bank's brief wholly fails to show that appellees filed a sixth paragraph, or any other answer, to its second paragraph of cross-complaint or interpleader. Such 10. second paragraph of cross-complaint or interpleader is not set out in said brief, nor is such answer, or the substance of it, set out, and no demurrer to any such answer is mentioned, except in the assignment of errors, and the point is made that it should have been sustained. No question is, therefore, presented on the third assignment of error.

The questions presented by the motion for a new trial are that the judgment of the court is not sustained by sufficient evidence; that it is contrary to law; and that the court erred in permitting appellee Lizzie H. Brown to testify as a witness on behalf of appellees.

After said witness had testified to some preliminaries the bill of exceptions discloses the following: "Q. Prior to your father's death, was Gebhart indebted to 11. your father in any amount? The plaintiff, through its attorney objects for the reason that the witness is not competent to testify to any indebtedness on the part of John F. Gebhart, which objection is by the court overruled, to which ruling of the court, the plaintiff, at the time, excepts." The presumption is that all parties to an action are competent to testify in their own behalf, and where it is sought to exclude a party it is incumbent upon the party objecting to point out to the trial court the reason or reasons why such party is incompetent to testify. No reason whatever was given by appellant bank, upon the occasion now complained of, why the witness was incompetent, and no question can be raised by the objection in this court. Elliott, Work of the Advocate 222, and cases

there cited.  We might say in this connection that no reason
is now given by appellant bank why said witness was not
competent to answer the question objected to.  The question in no way referred to the insurance policy, the proceeds of which were in controversy.  The court found that
appellees' claim should be paid in full, and the remainder
of the proceeds of the insurance policy be paid to the
appellant bank.

On appeal this court will not weigh the evidence, but
will determine whether there is any evidence to support the
finding in appellees' favor, and will consider only
12. the evidence which tends to support such finding.
*Pittsburgh, etc., R. Co.* v. *Nicholas* (1905), 165 Ind.
679, 76 N. E. 522; *Union Traction Co.* v. *Buckland*, (1904),
34 Ind. App. 420, 72 N. E. 158; *Diamond Block Coal Co.*
v. *Cuthbertson* (1905), 166 Ind. 290, 76 N. E. 1060;
*Knoefel* v. *Atkins* (1907), 40 Ind. App. 428, 81 N. E. 600.
This evidence shows that about 1883 said Gebhart borrowed
of appellees' father the sum of $3,500, for which he gave
him a note, and also his insurance policy in the Northwestern Mutual Life Insurance Company for $15,000 as
collateral security; that their father gave the note and
policy to their mother in 1892; that their father died in
1894, and soon afterwards said policy was placed in the
Louisville Trust Company and an assignment of the policy
was made on a slip of paper and pinned to the policy;
some time about 1897 or 1898 Gebhart came to appellees'
mother and informed her, in substance, that the assignment which he had theretofore made to her was not good
or proper in form and said if she would let him have the
policy he would have a proper assignment made and return
both to her; about one month later he brought her another
assignment of the policy which was sent to the company,
but never did return the policy; this assignment was on
the company's blank and identified the policy by number
and the debt by amount; it is admitted by the bank that

it did not procure a written assignment of the policy until
after the second written assignment was delivered to Mrs.
Brown, and it is also admitted that this written assignment
was dated back to December 19, 1893, and before making
an effort to get such written assignment it had information from the company that Mrs. Brown had a written
assignment of the policy as collateral; but on the other
hand it is shown that appellees did not have any knowledge that the bank had an assignment of the policy until
after the death of Gebhart in 1907. A letter from the
company was put in evidence showing that the policy was
assigned to Elizabeth Brown, mother of appellees, on August
2, 1899, by duplicate received and recorded by the company
August 23, 1899, and was assigned to the bank, dated
December 19, 1893, and not recorded by the company until
February 2, 1902. The evidence further shows, by the testimony of Lizzie H. Brown, that she had not seen the
policy from the time Gebhart obtained possession of it from
her at the Louisville Trust Company until she was on
the witness stand, when the policy was handed to her
and she found the place where the assignment given her
mother in 1896 had been pinned to it, and the pin holes
in the policy corresponded with the pin holes in the assignment. The evidence further shows that after Mrs. Brown
died her estate was fully settled and the Gebhart debt was
turned over to her daughters as the only heirs, and that
afterwards Gebhart executed four notes to appellees aggregating the amount of the debt. There was evidence to show
that appellees' father and mother had the policy as collateral long before the bank claims to have received it in
1893. And there is evidence from which the trial court
could find that the bank never had possession of the policy
until about the time the assignment to it was received by
the company in February, 1902, and that when it did get
possession of the policy it had knowledge that Mrs. Brown
had an assignment of it on the books of the company.

But without such knowledge on the part of the bank when it procured the policy as collateral, it is contended by appellees that inasmuch as no new debt was 13. created at the time the bank procured the policy, it was not a *bona fide* purchaser so as to cut off the prior equities of the Browns. The evidence shows that, prior to the time the bank claims to have procured the policy in 1893, Gebhart was indebted to it in the sum of $15,000, and that a note for this sum was executed to it by Gebhart dated December 18, 1893; that, during 1894 and 1895, $2,000 were paid on the principal of the note by Gebhart; that about this time or a little later, but before 1899, the bank let Gebhart have the money to pay two or three semi-annual payments of premiums, amounting to much less than $2,000, and that it quit loaning Gebhart any more money with which to pay premiums because it was figured that if Gebhart lived as long as some of his ancestors, more would be paid out in premiums and interest than the policy would be worth at Gebhart's death. It is also shown that interest accumulated on the bank paper executed by Gebhart and renewal notes were executed by Gebhart from time to time, the last renewal being only about one month before his death in 1907.

It will be seen, therefore, that whether the bank procured the policy in 1893 or in 1902 as collateral, it was to secure an existing debt. As between Gebhart and the bank there can be no question but that a precedent debt would constitute a valuable consideration for the assignment of the policy. An assignment, however, as security for a precedent debt does not make such an assignee a holder for value as against prior equities. In the late work of Jones on Pledges and Collateral Securities, §360a, the author says: "A pre-existing debt is not a sufficient consideration to constitute a pledgee a holder for value." In support of the text he cites *Goodwin* v. *Massachusetts Loan, etc., Co., supra; Loeb & Bro.* v. *Peters & Bro.* (1879), 63

Ala. 243, 35 Am. Rep. 17; *Sleeper* v. *Davis* (1886), 64
N. H. 59, 6 Atl. 201, 10 Am. St. 377; *Linnard's Appeal*
(1886), (Pa.) 3 Atl. 840; *Merchants' Ins. Co.* v. *Abbott*
(1881), 131 Mass. 397; *Lesassier & Wise* v. *Southwestern*
(1874), 2 Woods 35; *Currie* v. *Misa* (1875), L. R. 10
Ex. 153; *Leask* v. *Scott* (1877), L. R. 2 Q. B. D. 376;
*Rodger* v. *Comptoir d'Escumpte de Paris* (1869), L. R. 2
P. C. 393; *Chartered Bank, etc.* v. *Henderson* (1874), L.
R. 5 P. C. 501.

In Indiana, the rule has long since been established that
a precedent debt does not constitute one a holder or purchaser for value. "The fact, conceding it to be the fact,
that the notes were assigned to appellee in payment of a
precedent debt, does not show that there was no valid consideration for the assignment. A precedent debt is unques-
tionably a valuable consideration for a contract, but is not
such a consideration as will make a grantee or assignee a
*bona fide* purchaser against prior equities. *Hewitt* v.
*Powers*, 84 Ind. 295; *Louthain* v. *Miller*, 85 Ind. 161;
*Fitzpatrick* v. *Papa*, 89 Ind. 17. As against one who has
no prior equity, a precedent debt will support a contract
otherwise valid." *Boling* v. *Howell* (1884), 93 Ind. 329,
331.

"As to mortgages of land taken to secure a precedent
debt it is well settled in Indiana, that, although a precedent debt is a valuable consideration for a mortgage given
to secure it, yet it will not make the mortgagee a *bona fide*
purchaser, as against prior equities of which he had no
notice. That such a mortgage is founded upon a valuable
consideration was decided in *Work* v. *Brayton*, 5 Ind. 396;
*Wright* v. *Bundy*, 11 Ind. 398, and *Babcock* v. *Jordan*, 24
Ind. 14, and upon this point these cases have been repeatedly followed; but so far as these cases asserted that the
holder of such a security was entitled to protection against
secret equities they have been virtually overruled by
*Busenbarke* v. *Ramey*, 53 Ind. 499; *Gilchrist* v. *Gough*,

63 Ind. 576; *Davis* v. *Newcomb,* 72 Ind. 413; *Hewitt* v. *Powers,* 84 Ind. 295; *Louthain* v. *Miller,* 85 Ind. 161; *Boling* v. *Howell, ante,* page 329. The doctrine of these later cases is that an antecedent debt is a valuable consideration and will support a mortgage, but is not such a consideration as will make the mortgagee a *bona fide* purchaser, so as to cut off prior secret equities. This doctrine is supported by abundant authority elsewhere. See the cases cited in *Busenbarke* v. *Ramey, supra,* and *Gilchrist* v. *Gough, supra.''* *Wert* v. *Naylor* (1884), 93 Ind. 431, 433.

"In Hare & W. Lead. Cas., vol. 2, page 104, 3 Am. ed., it is said, that 'it is equally well settled, * * * that, although a sale, vitiated by fraud, cannot be set aside in the hands of a *bona fide* purchaser, from the fraudulent vendee; yet, that no one can claim the benefit of this doctrine, who has not parted with value, or who has taken the goods as security for an antecedent debt; *Buffington* v. *Gerrish,* 15 Mass. 156; *Hodgeden* v. *Hubbard,* 18 Vt. 504; *Poor* v. *Woodburn,* 25 Vt. 234; *Clark* v. *Flint,* 22 Pick. 231. In *Upshaw* v. *Hargrove, Adm'r,* 6 Sm. & M. 286, *Boone, Adm'r,* v. *Barnes,* 23 Miss. 136, and *Halstead* v. *The President, etc., of the Bank of Kentucky,* 4 J. J. Mar. 554, the same rule was applied to the conveyance of land by a debtor to a creditor, which was said not to render the latter a purchaser for value, unless something was given up or relinquished on the faith of the conveyance, or the transfer accepted in absolute payment or satisfaction for the debt!'' *Busenbarke, Executor,* v. *Ramey* (1876), 53 Ind. 499, 502.

"It is insisted, that, as the mortgage was executed to secure a pre-existing debt which Heffner owed the appellee, it is not supported by a sufficient consideration, and we are referred to *Busenbarke* v. *Ramey,* 53 Ind. 499; *Gilchrist* v. *Gough,* 63 Ind. 576; *Davis* v. *Newcomb,* 72 Indiana 413. We do not regard the cases as declaring the doctrine for which appellants contend. We understand

them to hold that a pre-existing debt is not such a consideration as will make a purchaser a *bona fide* one in such a
sense as to cut off prior equities; but we do not understand them to hold that an antecedent debt may not constitute a valuable consideration." *Louthain* v. *Miller* (1882),
*supra*, 161, 163.

It is very evident under the authorities cited that the bank
is not a holder for value. The question then arises, Did
the Browns lose their security by reason of the
14. delivery of the policy to Gebhart under the circumstances of such delivery? The evidence clearly shows
that Gebhart came to Mrs. Brown and told her the assignment of the policy, in the shape it was, would do her no
good; that it must be assigned on a blank of the company
and on their books; that he would take it and have it
properly assigned and return it to her. Upon this promise
and for this purpose she let him have possession of the property. If Gebhart had pledged the policy to the bank for
cash, without any notice of prior equities by the bank,
instead of a debt already in existence, it is probable that
it would be entitled to the proceeds as against appellees,
but, as shown by the authorities cited under a discussion
of the first assignment of error, a pledgee does not lose his
lien by permitting the pledgor to have possession of the
property for a special and limited purpose, and not merely
for his own use and benefit, unless it is subsequently
pledged for value, without notice.

The evidence does not show any laches on the part of
the Browns which in any way injured the bank. The evidence shows that the bank was not a holder for value.
15. It gave up nothing on the strength of the policy,
and the Browns knew nothing of the claim of the
bank until after Gebhart's death. Laches implies something more than mere lapse of time; it requires some actual
or presumable change of circumstances rendering it inequitable to grant relief. The Supreme Court of the United

States in *O'Brien* v. *Wheelock* (1901), 184 U. S. 450, 22
Sup. Ct. 354, 46 L. Ed. 636, thus states the rule: "The
doctrine of courts of equity to withhold relief from those
who have delayed the assertion of their claims for an
unreasonable length of time is thoroughly settled. Its
application depends on the circumstances of the particular
case. It is not a mere matter of lapse of time, but of
change of situation during neglectful repose, rendering it
inequitable to afford relief."

The rule governing the defense of laches is thus stated
in *Galliher* v. *Cadwell* (1891), 145 U. S. 368, 12 Sup. Ct.
873, 36 L. Ed. 738: "The cases are many in which this
defense has been invoked and considered. It is true, that
by reason of their differences of fact no one case becomes
an exact precedent for another, yet a uniform principle
pervades them all. They proceed on the assumption that
the party to whom laches is imputed has knowledge of his
rights, and an ample opportunity to establish them in the
proper forum; that by reason of his delay the adverse
party has good reason to believe that the alleged rights are
worthless, or have been abandoned; and that because of the
change in condition or relations during this period of delay,
it would be an injustice to the latter to permit him to now
assert them. * * * They all proceed upon the theory
that laches is not like limitation, a mere matter of time;
but principally a question of the inequity of permitting
the claim to be enforced—an inequity founded upon some
change in the condition or relations of the property or the
parties." In *Townsend* v. *Vanderwerker* (1895), 160 U.
S. 171, 16 Sup. Ct. 258, 40 L. Ed. 383, it is said: "The
question of laches does not depend, as does the statute of
limitations, upon the fact that a certain definite time has
elapsed since the cause of action accrued, but whether,
under all the circumstances of the particular case, plaintiff is chargeable with a want of due diligence in failing
to institute proceedings before he did."

The bank has never changed its position on account of the conduct of the Browns. It parted with nothing when it took the policy from Gebhart. It has parted with nothing since. Before a right of action can be barred by a less period than the statute of limitations, the laches must have been of such a character as to work an equitable estoppel. "There may be cases of statutory proceedings, or cases of purely equitable cognizance where the laches of a party may be of such a character, and under such circumstances, as will bar his right to prosecute his action, in less time than that fixed by the statute of limitations. But that is only in cases where the laches are of such a character and under such circumstances as to work an equitable estoppel. *State, ex rel.,* v. *Gordon,* 87 Ind. 171; *City of Logansport* v. *Uhl,* 99 Ind. 531, 50 Am. R. 109; *Earle* v. *Earle,* 91 Ind. 27." *Scherer* v. *Ingerman* (1887), 110 Ind. 428, 433, 11 N. E. 8, 12 N. E. 304.

We have heretofore shown that the claim of appellees was not barred by the statute of limitations. There was some evidence to support the finding of the court, and such finding is not contrary to law. The judgment is affirmed.

NOTE.—Reported in 114 N. E. 486. Pledges: (a) validity of, without delivery as against pledgor or person claiming through him, 11 Ann. Cas. 793; (b) recourse against pledge after bar of principal obligation, 2 Ann. Cas. 271, 14 Ann. Cas. 847. Collaterals, title acquired by holder, 32 Am. St. 711. See under (1, 2, 14) 31 Cyc 800, 818, 819; (8) 25 Cyc 1000; (13) 25 Cyc 777.

---

# DEISTER CONCENTRATOR COMPANY *v.* DEISTER MACHINE COMPANY ET AL.

[No. 8,979. Filed May 22, 1916. Rehearing denied December 22, 1916.]

1. TRADE-MARKS AND TRADE-NAMES.—*Unfair Competition.*—*Use of Surname in Business Enterprises.*—A person may make a fair and reasonable use of his own name in commercial pursuits, and in so doing he cannot be held liable for incidental damages to a

competitor in business using the same name, but he must be honest in such use and not injure the good will of a rival by palming off his goods as that of such rival; nor can he employ his name fraudulently so as to appropriate the good will of an established business of his competitor. p. 418.

2. TRADE-MARKS AND TRADE-NAMES.—*Name of Inventor.*—*Use by Rival Companies.*—Where one Deister, an inventor of certain mining machinery called a concentrator, after organizing a company known as the Deister Concentrator Company and assigning to it his patents and giving it the right to manufacture and sell machinery made thereunder, disposed of his interest in such concern but was not by contract or otherwise precluded thereafter from the use of his name in connection with another business, injunction will not issue at the instance of such company to restrain the mere use of the name "Deister" by a new corporation, known as the Deister Machine Company, subsequently organized by the inventor to fabricate and dispose of his improved patented concentrator. p. 419.

3. TRADE-MARKS AND TRADE-NAMES.—*Unfair Competition.*—Nothing less than conduct tending to pass off one man's merchandise or business as that of another will constitute unfair competition, the essence of the wrong being the sale of goods of one manufacturer for those of a competitor. p. 419.

4. TRADE-MARKS AND TRADE-NAMES.—*Unfair Competition.*—*Intent.*—In order to constitute unfair competition by conduct tending to pass off the goods of one person for that of another, it is not necessary that one should take some affirmative action in that respect, or that he should intend to sell his goods for those of his rival, as actual deception is not necessary; for, if the name under which he disposes of his products, together with the method of disposing of the same, is manifestly liable to deceive purchasers, the result would be accomplished. p. 420.

5. TRADE-MARKS AND TRADE-NAMES.—*Unfair Competition.*—*Deception.*—*Knowledge of Purchasers.*—The class of persons who buy the particular kind of articles manufactured, such as servants or children, upon the one hand, or persons skilled in the particular trade, upon the other, must be considered in determining the question of probable deception. p. 421.

6. TRADE-MARKS AND TRADE-NAMES.—*Unfair Competition.*—*Use of Name.*—*Injunctive Relief.*—*When Granted.*—Where one Deister, an inventor and patentee of certain mining machinery called a concentrator, organized a company known as the Deister Concentrator Company, to manufacture and sell such machinery, and assigned his patents to it, retaining the right to manufacture the concentrators for sale in foreign countries, and thereafter disposed of his interest in the company, with no restrictions as

414    APPELLATE COURT OF INDIANA,

Deister Concentrator Co. v. Deister Mach. Co.—63 Ind. App. 412.

to his right to again engage in the manufacture and sale of mining machinery under the name "Deister" or the use of that name in connection therewith, injunction for unfair competition will not issue at the instance of such company to restrain a corporation, known as the Deister Machine Company, subsequently organized by the inventor to manufacture his concentrators under new patents in this country and under the old patents for the foreign market, from using the name "Deister" in the title of the corporation or upon its manufactured product, where the machines made under the new patents were easily distinguished from the type made under the old patents, and the concentrators were sold to those familiar with mining machinery, thereby diminishing the likelihood of purchasers being deceived, and in view of the fact that the new company's advertisements contained the words, "Note carefully the new name," and its catalogues were of a different color from those circulated by the older company. p. 421.

7. TRADE-MARKS AND TRADE-NAMES.—*Unfair Competition.—Resemblance Between Devices.—Use of Name.—Questions of Fact.*—No inflexible rule can be formulated as to what conduct will constitute unfair competition, and, as the degree of resemblance between the names of articles made and sold, as well as the precaution taken to differentiate one article from another, or the name, is not capable of exact definition, it becomes, from the nature of the case, a question of fact to be determined by the circumstances as they are brought before the court in each particular case. p. 424.

From Dekalb Circuit Court; *Frank M. Powers,* Judge.

Action by the Deister Concentrator Company against the Deister Machine Company and others. From a judgment for defendants, the plaintiffs appeal. *Affirmed.*

*Elmer Leonard, James H. Rose, Fred E. Zollars, Robert S. Taylor* and *Elwin M. Hulse,* for appellant.

*Barrett, Morris & Hoffman,* for appellees.

MORAN, J.—This was a suit by appellant Deister Concentrator Company against Deister Machine Company, Emil Deister, William F. Deister and Charles G. Williams, appellees, seeking injunctive relief and damages for unfair competition in trade. No error is predicated as to the rulings upon the pleadings. Therefore it is sufficient to state that the complaint is in one paragraph, to which was addressed a general denial and an affirmative paragraph of answer, to which affirmative paragraph of answer a reply in general denial was filed.

The facts were found specially by the court, and conclusions of law stated thereon, which were adverse to the appellant, and from a judgment upon the conclusions of law that appellant take nothing by its suit and that appellees recover costs, an appeal has been taken by appellant, assigning as error the action of the court in stating the conclusions of law on the facts specially found, and in overruling appellant's motion for a new trial.

The facts specially found by the court material to an intelligent presentation of the questions arising thereon may be summarized as follows: Appellee Emil Deister for several years prior to the bringing of this suit had been engaged in designing a machine called a concentrator for the separation of gold, silver, copper, and other minerals from foreign substances, which, in general appearance, resembles a wooden table inclosed on three sides, with retaining boards, and when in operation has a vibrating movement by which the minerals, on account of their specific gravity being greater than that of foreign substances accompanying the same, drop into riffles or pools in the table and the foreign substance or refuse is discharged at the lower inclination of the table; that prior to May 21, 1906, he had obtained certain patents from the United States government, and on that date incorporated appellant company with a capital of $200,000 for the purpose of manufacturing and selling such machinery, the patents of which he assigned to the company in consideration of fifty-one per cent. of the stock, retaining the rights to manufacture the same in the United States for sale in foreign countries; one-fourth of the stock was assigned to William H. Bensman and Walter G. Burns, who had rendered him valuable assistance financially; the balance of the stock other than a small amount that had been issued to secure additional funds was

416    APPELLATE COURT OF INDIANA,

Deister Concentrator Co. *v.* Deister Mach. Co.—63 Ind. App. 412.

held as treasury stock and thereafter sold; appellee Emil
Deister through his inventive genius designed new and valuable mining machinery after the incorporation of the company, and assigned the patents therefor to the company without further consideration; by a process of advertising in
trade journals and catalogues, the business developed so that
on December 15, 1911, the company had transacted business
to the amount of $500,000; the numerous patents all bore
in some manner the name "Deister," so that the name
became a valuable property right; on account of a dissen-
sion that arose between appellee Emil Deister and other
stockholders, he and his brother, appellee William F.
Deister, sold all of their stock in the company to the other
stockholders about the first of the year of 1912, appellee
Emil Deister receiving for his stock the sum of $92,000,
but neither of the Deister brothers were in any way
restricted from using the name "Deister" thereafter, nor
from engaging in the manufacture and sale of mining
machinery under this name; about the time of the organization of the appellant company, appellee Emil Deister sold
the same patents assigned to appellant company to certain
parties for the republic of Mexico, and appellant company
sold to Emil Deister from time to time a large number of
catalogues to be used in advertising his trade beyond the
borders of the United States. The Deister Brothers, after
withdrawing from appellant company, continued in business at Fort Wayne, selling mining machinery in foreign
countries; and on June 15, 1912, they organized a corporation, with a capital stock of $200,000, under the name of
"Deister Machine Company," and, in the meantime, they
procured new patents for improved mining machinery,
which they assigned to the new corporation, which latter
company proceeded to manufacture for the trade throughout the world, and proceeded to manufacture machinery
under the old patents for the trade beyond the United States
and Mexico; the new machine used the name "Deister" in

connection with other characters and words, and were made
on the same general principle as those manufactured by
appellant company, differing, however, as to the construction and method of operation; the business was advertised
in trade journals and catalogues, designating wherein the
machinery manufactured and sold differed from all other
similar machinery for this purpose; the catalogues were of
different color than that used by appellant company, and
the advertising matter contained nothing to mislead or
deceive the public, and bore the further statement, "Note
carefully the new name"; that since the commencement of
this suit, appellees have advertised that the "Deister Machine Company" was a separate and distinct company from
appellant company; that appellee company was organized
in good faith, and with no intention of injuring appellant
company, and has not attempted to sell any of its machines
as the product of appellant company; the machinery made
and sold by both companies is not sold through retailers
generally, but as a usual thing is sold direct to the operators
of mines; slight confusion has resulted in the correspondence of the respective companies, and this was due principally by reason of appellee Emil Deister purchasing catalogues of appellant company, and circulating the same in
the Dominion of Canada to advertise his foreign business.

As to the assignment of error based upon the exceptions
to the conclusions of law, appellant takes the position that
Emil Deister, the patentee of the mining machinery made
and sold by it, after selling his stock to the stockholders
of appellant company and severing his relations therewith,
could not, without making himself amenable to the law, use
the name "Deister" as a part of the name of the competing company, as this was a part of the corporate name
of appellant company; and especially would the law forbid
him to do so without sufficient explanation that the two
companies were separate corporations, in order that the

public be not deceived, and further that it was not necessary that fraud was intended or that the public or any person was actually deceived; that if appellant's machinery was imitated by appellees by name, word or symbol, so as to produce confusion in the trade and injure appellant's business, such conduct would constitute unfair competition.

On the other hand, appellees take the position that a person's name is his property, and he has the right to use it in any legitimate way that he sees fit, and that when Emil Deister disposed of his stock, he did not agree that he would not again engage in the invention, manufacture and sale of mining machinery, nor that he would not use the name "Deister" in connection therewith; that the essence of the wrong in unfair competition consists in the sale of goods of one vendor for those of another, and appellees in placing their product upon the market designated the same in such a manner that a purchaser could readily trace the source of its manufacture; that the character of the mining machinery under consideration is such that it is purchased through experts skilled in the business and not at retail, which fact greatly diminishes, if not entirely removes, the likelihood of a purchaser being deceived.

It may be stated as a general proposition that a man's name is his own property and he has the right to its use and enjoyment the same as any other property right,

1.  and so long as such use be a fair and reasonable exercise of such right, he cannot be held liable for incidental damages to a rival in business using the same name, but he must make an honest use of his name, and not injure the good will and reputation of a rival by palming off his goods or business as that of such rival. Nor will he be permitted to use his name fraudulently so as to appropriate the good will of an established business of his competitor. *Pemberthy Injector Co.* v. *Lee* (1899), 120 Mich. 174, 78 N. W. 1074; *Rogers* v. *Rogers* (1885), 53 Conn. 121, 1 Atl. 807, 5 Atl. 675, 55 Am. Rep. 78; 38 Cyc 809;

*Brown Chemical Co.* v. *Meyer* (1890), 139 U. S. 540, 11 Sup. Ct. 625, 35 L. Ed. 247; *Howe Scale Co.* v. *Wyckoff, etc.* (1905), 198 U. S. 117, 25 Sup. Ct. 609, 49 L. E. 972; *International Silver Co.* v. *Rogers* (1907), 72 N. J. Eq. 933, 67 Atl. 105, 129 Am. St. 722; *Waterman Co.* v. *Modern Pen Co.* (1914), 235 U. S. 88, 35 Sup. Ct. 91, 59 L. Ed. 142.

In *Howe Scale Co.* v. *Wyckoff, etc., supra,* Chief Justice Fuller, speaking for the court said: "But it is well settled that a personal name cannot be exclusively appropriated by any one as against others having a right to use it; and as the name "Remington" is an ordinary family surname, it was manifestly incapable of exclusive appropriation, * * *"; and, in concluding the opinion, said: "We hold that, in the absence of a contract, fraud or estoppel, any man may use his own name, in all legitimate ways, and as a whole or a part of a corporate name."

Without extending our view further on this branch of the case, it must be regarded as settled by the authorities that Emil Deister, not parting with the use of his name by

2. contract or otherwise, when he disposed of his stock in appellant corporation was not precluded thereafter from the use thereof in connection with another business; that is, the mere use of the name "Deister" in the new corporation did not of itself confer any right upon appellant to injunctive relief.

This brings us to the investigation of the main question—whether appellee's conduct in the use of the name "Deister" was such as to constitute unfair competition. It

3. seems to be well settled that nothing less than conduct tending to pass off one man's merchandise or business as that of another will constitute unfair competition within the meaning of the term; the essence of the wrong is the sale of the goods of one manufacturer for those of a competitor. *Standard Paint Co.* v. *Trinidad Asphalt Mfg. Co.* (1911), 220 U. S. 446, 31 Sup. Ct. 456, 55 L. Ed.

536; *Rathbone, Sard & Co.* v. *Champion Steel Range Co.*
(1911), 189 Fed. 26, 110 C. C. A. 596, 37 L. R. A. (N. S.)
258; *Howe Scale Co.* v. *Wyckoff, etc., supra; Goodyear Co.*
v. *Goodyear Rubber Co.* (1888), 128 U. S. 598, 9 Sup. Ct.
166, 32 L. Ed. 535; 38 Cyc 784; *Computing Cheese Cutter
Co.* v. *Dunn* (1909), 45 Ind. App. 20, 88 N. E. 93; *Hartzler*
v. *Goshen, etc., Ladder Co.* (1913), 55 Ind. App. 455, 104 N.
E. 34; *International Silver Co.* v. *Rogers, supra.* In the case
of *Goodyear Co.* v. *Goodyear Rubber Co., supra,* the court
uses the following language: "The case at bar cannot be
sustained as one to restrain unfair trade. Relief in such
cases is granted only where the defendant, by his marks,
signs, labels, or in other ways, represents to the public that
the goods sold by him are those manufactured or produced
by the plaintiff, thus palming off his goods for those of
a different manufacture, to the injury of the plaintiff."
And in *Howe Scale Co.* v. *Wyckoff, etc., supra,* it was said:
"The essence of the wrong in unfair competition consists
in the sale of the goods of one manufacturer or vendor for
those of another, and if defendant so conducts its business
as not to palm off its goods as those of complainant, the
action fails."

Thus the inquiry naturally arises, Did appellees' conduct in disposing of the machinery manufactured by it
tend to or have the effect of passing the same to
4.    purchasers as the machinery manufactured by appellant? In order that this result be accomplished, it
was not necessary that appellees, or either of them, actually
take some affirmative action in this respect, or that they,
or either of them, so intended, as actual deception was
not necessary. If the name under which appellees disposed of their machinery, together with the method of disposing of the same, was manifestly liable to deceive purchasers, the result would be accomplished. *Northwestern
Knitting Co.* v. *Garon* (1910), 112 Minn. 321, 128 N. W.
290; *Fuller* v. *Huff* (1900), 104 Fed. 141, 43 C. C. A. 453,
51 L. R. A. 332.

The facts found by the court disclose that the machinery under consideration is of necessity purchased by those skilled in this particular line of business and not by
5. the average consumer of articles of property or commodities sold at retail generally. "The class of persons who buy the particular kind of articles manufactured, such as servants or children, upon the one hand, or persons skilled in the particular trade upon the other, must be considered in determining the question of probable deception." 38 Cyc 777; *W. F. & John Barnes Co.* v. *Vandyck-Churchill Co.* (1913), 207 Fed. 855; *International Silver Co.* v. *Rogers, supra.*

The appellant put its machinery upon the market as manufactured by the Deister Concentrator Company and appellees put their machinery upon the market as
6. manufactured by the Deister Machine Company.

Concluding as we have that Emil Deister was not compelled to abandon his own name (*Howe Scale Co.* v. *Wyckoff, etc., supra*), and had the right to use the same under proper restrictions, it becomes material to examine the steps taken, if any, by appellees to differentiate their machinery from that manufactured and sold by appellant, so that prospective purchasers would have sufficient information to distinguish the machinery sold by appellees from that manufactured and sold by the old concern, and thus avoid unfair competition and confusion.

In *Singer Mfg. Co.* v. *June Mfg. Co.* (1896), 163 U. S. 169, 16 Sup. Ct. 1002, 41 L. Ed. 118, after citing with approval authorities recognizing the right one has to use his own name in business, so long as he does not resort to artifice or deception, the court held: "Where the name is one that has previously thereto come to indicate the source of manufacture of particular devices, the use of such name by another, unaccompanied with any precaution or indication, in itself amounts to an artifice calculated to produce the deception alluded to in the foregoing adjudications."

422 APPELLATE COURT OF INDIANA,

Deister Concentrator Co. *v.* Deister Mach. Co.—63 Ind. App. 412.

It was held in *International Silver Co.* v. *Rogers, supra,* that in order to save complainant's rights and to avoid hardship on the defendant that the goods manufactured and sold by the defendant should be stamped "Not the original Rogers," or "Not connected with the original Rogers." In the Waterman Fountain Pen case (*Waterman Co.* v. *Modern Pen Co., supra*), it was held that the defendant should distinguish its goods from the complainant's goods by employing the name "Arthur A. Waterman & Co." and follow the name with "Not connected with L. E. Waterman & Co." Here the right to use the name "Waterman" was recognized by the court under the foregoing restrictions. In each of the cases quoted from and last referred to, the names under consideration had acquired a secondary signification in connection with the product or article manufactured, yet the use of the name itself was not prohibited, but those resorting to the use were required to differentiate the same from that of the original use to which the name was put.

In *Pemberthy Injector Co.* v. *Lee, supra,* where the facts were similar to the facts before us, it was held that Pemberthy, the patentee of the articles manufactured by the company from which he withdrew, had a right to use his name in his own business thereafter without interference, but that such right should be guarded by language sufficiently clear and explicit to notify all persons that his business was not that of his rival's. Upon this proposition the general trend of the adjudicated cases seems to be harmonious; and it will serve no useful purpose to carry the analysis or elucidation of the authorities further. The facts found by the court disclose that appellees took the necessary precaution in the disposition of the mining machinery made by appellee company to notify the trade that it was a separate concern from appellant company, especially in view of the fact that the court found that its articles of property were not disposed of to those likely

to be deceived, and in view of the further finding of the
court that when Emil Deister originally sold his patents
to appellant company, he reserved the right to the trade in
foreign countries, and when he withdrew from the company and sold his stock, there were no restrictions as to
his right to again engage in business or against the use
of the name "Deister"; and after severing his connection
with appellant company he continued to supply foreign
trade as he had theretofore, and after the incorporation
of appellee company the advertisements generally as to its
business contained the words, "Note carefully the new
name," and the catalogues were of different color, and the
machinery made under the new patents, which he claimed
the right to sell in the United States, were readily distinguishable from the machines made under the original
patents; that appellant has sustained no loss or injury on
account of the similarity of the corporate names or representations and statements made as to the machines; and
since the incorporation of the appellee company it has
advertised in catalogues, periodicals and trade journals
that the Deister Machine Company was a separate and
distinct company from that of the Deister Concentrator
Company and not connected therewith.

The conclusions of law are correct when the law is
applied to the facts specially found.

The propositions of law addressed by appellant to the
error presented on the conclusions of law, we are asked to
consider as being applicable to the error based upon the
overruling of the motion for a new trial, on the ground
that the decision of the court is not sustained by sufficient
evidence and is contrary to law.

We need not reiterate what has been said as to the right
under the law of appellees using the name Deister as a
part of its corporate name. This leaves for consideration
under the assignment of error based on the overruling of
the motion for a new trial appellees' conduct in placing

its machinery upon the market in competition with that of its rival concern, which comes to us through a very voluminous record of some 1,400 pages of evidence.

No inflexible rule can be laid down as to what conduct will or will not constitute unfair competition. As to what degree of resemblance between the names or devices 7. of articles made and sold, as well as the precaution taken to differentiate the one article from the other or the name, as the case may be, is not capable of exact definition; thus from the very nature of the case, it becomes a question of fact to be determined by the circumstances as they are brought before the court in each particular case. 38 Cyc 770; *Chas. S. Higgins Co.* v. *Higgins Soap Co.* (1895), 144 N. Y. 462, 39 N. E. 490, 27 L. R. A. 42, 43 Am. St. 769; *Atlas Assurance Co.* v. *Atlas Ins. Co.* (1908), 138 Iowa 228, 112 N. W. 232, 114 N. W. 609, 15 L. R. A. (N. S.) 625, 128 Am. St. 189.

It would unnecessarily incumber the opinion to attempt to review and analyze the evidence. Our examination of the same, however, has been carried to the extent that we are satisfied that the evidence sufficiently supports the judgment of the trial court and the judgment is not contrary to law, when the law heretofore announced is applied to the evidence. From the evidence in the record and the facts found by the court it is disclosed that at the time the court denied appellant the relief sought by it appellees were using the necessary precaution to distinguish the machinery manufactured and offered for sale by it from that of appellant. This disposes of each of the questions presented by appellant's learned counsel. Judgment affirmed.

## On Petition for Rehearing.

Moran, P. J.—Appellant in its brief on petition for rehearing insists that the court held in its original opinion, and erroneously so, that at the time the trial court denied the relief sought by it and rendered its decision appellees were then using the necessary precaution to distinguish the machinery made and sold by them from the machinery made and sold by appellant, and that this was not sufficient; that if the necessary precaution had not been taken before suit was filed, appellant was entitled to the relief sought, and, further, that if appellant was not entitled to injunctive relief at the time the lower court reached its decision by reason of additional precaution having been taken subsequent to the filing of the complaint, and prior to the decision of the lower court, that this would not preclude appellant from recovering damages for the wrong suffered theretofore.

The complaint alleges generally that appellant was damaged by reason of the conduct of appellees, but injunctive relief only is demanded thereby, and under "Points and Authorities" in appellant's brief upon the merits of the cause there is no insistence for damages or for an accounting against appellees. Neither of the five propositions relied upon in the brief are addressed to the question of damages in any manner. There is nothing in appellant's brief on the merits to show that there was any proof offered upon the theory that appellant suffered damages or that an accounting should be had as to profits, if any, that were realized by appellees by reason of using the name they did in disposing of the machinery which they manufactured and sold. It was not intended to hold by the original opinion, nor does it hold, that at the time suit was filed by appellant as against appellees that appellees were not then using the necessary precaution to distinguish the machinery made and sold by them from that made and sold by appellant. From the special finding of facts and conclusions of law announced by the court thereon, it is evident that the decision reached in the court below was on the theory that appellees were taking the necessary precaution at the time suit was filed to distinguish the machinery made and sold by them, and in putting the same on the market, from that made and sold by appellant, and not upon the steps taken by appellees subsequent to the filing of the suit; nor was the judgment affirmed upon the additional precautions that were taken subsequent to the filing of the suit and before the decision was reached by the trial court.

After suit was brought, however, additional precaution was taken by appellees, as disclosed by the special finding of facts, which, when taken into consideration with the precaution that had been taken before the filing of the suit, clearly informed the public that the machinery manufactured and sold by appellees was different from that manufactured and sold by appellant, and that such additional precaution was proper, and to the end that doubt was removed as to the duty that was owing from appellees to appellant and the public. The original opinion is not subject to the infirmity contended for by appellant in this respect.

Each question raised in the petition for rehearing has been carefully considered, and it is the judgment of the court that a correct conclusion was reached in the original opinion, to which we now adhere. The petition for rehearing is overruled.

NOTE.—Reported in 112 N. E. 906, 114 N. E. 485. Unfair competition: (a) fraudulent intent as a necessary element, 3 Ann. Cas. 32; (b) use of personal or corporate name, 2 Ann. Cas. 415, 16 Ann. Cas. 596. Trade-marks and trade-names, similarity of name as constituting infringement, Ann. Cas. 1915B 327. Right of one selling business and good will to use similar name in competing business, 19 L. R. A. (N. S.) 765. See under (1, 2) 38 Cyc 809, 810, 817, 818; (3) 38 Cyc 756; (4) 38 Cyc 784; (5) 38 Cyc 777: (7) 38 Cyc 779.

## DAMMEYER ET AL. *v.* VORHIS.

[No. 9,076. Filed October 13, 1916. Rehearing denied December 22, 1916.]

1. LANDLORD AND TENANT.—*Injury to Pedestrian.—Liability of Landlord.—Doors in Sidewalk.—Guarding Opening.*—In an action for injuries received by a pedestrian falling into a cellarway leading from the sidewalk to the basement of a leased building, the landlord is not liable for negligence in not guarding the opening over the cellarway where the tenant in possession left open the iron grating covering it, nor for failure to provide stops or blocks which would hold the grating in a perpendicular position when raised, thus affording a partial guard to the opening. p. 430.

2. LANDLORD AND TENANT.—*Repairs to Premises.*—It is not the duty of the landlord to keep the leased premises in repair, in the absence of an agreement with the tenant to that effect. p. 431.

3. LANDLORD AND TENANT.—*Injury to Pedestrian.—Nuisance.—Opening in Sidewalk.*—Where, in an action by a pedestrian for personal injuries received by falling into an unguarded cellarway leading from the sidewalk to the basement of a building, the right of recovery is predicated on the theory that the cellarway was a nuisance when the cover was raised, but it was not contended that, during the ownership of the landlord, the cellarway and doors were not properly constructed or not in good condition, and that the sidewalk was not safe when the doors were closed, the premises did not constitute a nuisance *per se*, but became so by the act of the tenant in leaving the doors open. p. 431.

4. LANDLORD AND TENANT.—*Opening in Sidewalk.—Duty of Tenant.*—Where doors which cover a cellarway leading from the sidewalk to the basement of a leased building are raised, it is the duty of the tenant in possession to guard the opening. p. 431.

5. LANDLORD AND TENANT.—*Injuries to Third Persons.—Liability of Landlord.—Nuisance.*—Where property, at the time it is leased, is not in such a condition as to constitute a nuisance in and of itself, but becomes so only by the act of the tenant in possession, and injury to a third person occurs during such possession, the owner is not liable; but where the owner leases premises which are a nuisance in and of themselves, or must, from their nature, become so by use, and the owner receives rent, he is liable, regardless of whether he is in possession, for injuries to third persons flowing from such negligence. p. 433.

6. APPEAL.—*Bill of Exceptions.—Certificate of Judge.—Sufficiency.*—The evidence is properly in the record even though the certificate of the trial judge to the bill of exceptions fails to show that

be examined the bill before allowing and signing it, since the presumption is that he did so, and the sufficiency of the certificate is not affected by the failure to recite the fact therein. p. 434.

From Marion Superior Court (85,729); *John J. Rochford,* Judge.

Action by Mollie Vorhis against Charles G. Dammeyer and others. From a judgment for plaintiff, the defendants appeal. *Reversed.*

*Hooton & Hack,* for appellants.
*White & Jones,* for appellee.

McNUTT, J.—This was a suit by appellee against appellants and also one Stark for personal injuries alleged to have been received by her in falling into a cellarway leading from a sidewalk to a basement of a building in the city of Indianapolis, on the night of September 28, 1911. The cause was tried upon a second amended first paragraph and a second paragraph of complaint.

A demurrer to the second paragraph of complaint, for want of facts, was overruled, and this action of the court and the overruling of appellants' motion for a new trial are assigned as errors in this court.

The second amended first paragraph of complaint charges, in substance, that appellants were the owners of said building and rented the first floor and basement of the same to said Stark; that under said building was a basement which was reached by a stairway leading from an opening in the sidewalk along the side of the building, which covered almost the entire width of said walk and was used by said Stark to enter said basement, all of which was known to said owners; that said owners had provided and maintained iron grating doors over said opening which had to be lifted and laid back to a point beyond the perpendicular to gain access to the basement; that said owners negligently failed to provide any guard or light around said opening and that a guard could have been erected to protect pedestrians against injury when said cellar doors were open; that said Stark opened said doors on said night and negligently failed to provide any guard or danger signals and while they were open appellee fell into the opening and down the stairway and received the injuries for which she sues.

The second paragraph of complaint is similar to the second amended first paragraph and, in addition, alleges that said owners knowingly and negligently permitted said iron grating doors to become out of repair, in this, that the stops or blocks which formerly had been on the side of the building against which said doors rested when open, were allowed to become insufficient for said purpose; that when such blocks were not upon the side of said building, the doors, when open, instead of standing perpendicular, and thus forming a guard about the opening, would lie almost flat upon the sidewalk, in which position they formed no guard or protection; that when said doors were raised the opening constituted a highly dangerous place, and was a nuisance, as said walk was much used by the public, all of which was known to said owners.

As will be seen, the second amended first paragraph of complaint seeks to hold appellants liable as owners of the building for their failure to provide a guard or light around said opening, when the doors were raised or open; and said second paragraph seeks to hold appellants liable, as owners of the building, for negligence, in knowingly permitting the blocks, formerly on the side of the building, which held the doors nearly upright when open, to become out of repair and ineffectual for the purpose, and that, when the doors were open, they, and the opening, constituted a nuisance.

It is not contended by appellee, in either paragraph of the complaint, that the doors over the cellarway were not properly constructed or were not in good condition or that the walk over them was not safe for use by the public, when the doors were closed. It is not disputed that Stark was a tenant in possession at the time of the injury, nor is it disputed that he left the cellar doors open and failed to guard the opening. For this negligence the tenant is liable, it being shown that appellee's injury was caused thereby.

The only negligence charged against appellants, in the second amended first paragraph of the complaint, is their

1. failure to guard the opening, when the doors were open. Appellants were not negligent in this regard, as will hereinafter appear by the authorities cited, and as appellee admits by her failure to cite any authority, or to contend otherwise, in her brief; and it follows, in our opinion, that appellants were not negligent, as charged in the second paragraph of complaint, in their failure to provide the block on the side of the building, which, at best, could furnish only a partial guard to the opening.

But the second paragraph of the complaint not only charges appellants with negligence in failing to provide the blocks on the side of the building, but charges "that when said guard or cover over said opening was raised, said opening and the cover thereof constituted a highly dangerous place, and the same was a nuisance." It is not charged in said second paragraph of complaint that appellants, in the construction and maintenance of said stairway and covering, violated any statute of this state or any ordinance of said city, so if they are to be held guilty of maintaining a nuisance they must be so held under the common law. We have examined all the authorities cited by appellee, which hold the landlord liable in such cases, and find them to be cases where the doors or covering to the entrance were either not properly constructed or had been allowed to become defective and were in such condition as to constitute a nuisance *per se,* at the time of the letting, except cases where the landlord had agreed to keep the premises in repair. In the later cases we find none holding that such an opening is a nuisance, when properly covered, and the covering is in good condition.

In the instant case there is no charge in the complaint that appellants agreed to keep the leased premises in repair, but appellee proceeds on the assumption that such 2. was their duty. Such assumption is unwarranted as that duty rested upon the tenant under the allegations of the complaint. *Purcell* v. *English* (1882), 86 Ind. 34, 44 Am. Rep. 255; *Monnett* v. *Potts* (1894), 10 Ind. App. 191, 37 N. E. 729; *Lake Erie, etc., R. Co.* v. *Maus* (1898), 22 Ind. App. 36, 51 N. E. 735; *Hanson* v. *Cruse* (1900), 155 Ind. 176, 57 N. E. 904.

Since it is not contended otherwise than that the cellarway and doors were properly constructed, were in good condition, and that the walk over the doors was safe 3. when the doors were closed, during all the time appellants owned the building, it cannot be held that the premises constituted a nuisance *per se,* but became so by the act of the tenant in leaving the doors open. Under the facts alleged in the complaint, the question of duty to repair and negligence in failing to repair does not 4. arise, but the only question is as to the duty to guard the opening when open. This duty, we must hold, devolved upon the tenant.

In the case of *Joyce* v. *Martin* (1887), 15 R. I. 558, 10 Atl. 620, it is held: "Where property is demised and at the time of the demise is not a nuisance, and becomes so only by the act of the tenant while in his possession, and injury happens during such possession, the owner is not liable". The above case is followed in the case of *Adams* v. *Fletcher* (1890), 17 R. I. 137, 20 Atl. 263, 33 Am. St. 859 and *Henson* v. *Beckwith* (1897), 20 R. I. 165, 37 Atl. 702, 38 L. R. A. 716, 78 Am. St. 847.

In *Schroeck* v. *Reiss* (1900), 61 N. Y. Supp. ,1054, 46 App. Div. 502, it is held that a landlord who lets a store and basement to a tenant, who had exclusive possession and control thereof, is not liable to third persons for management of the cellar door covering steps from sidewalk to basement.

In *Opper* v. *Hellinger* (1906), 101 N. Y. Supp. 616, 116 App. Div. 261, it is held that where a cellarway under a sidewalk was constructed by permission of the municipal authorities, and was provided with doors to completely cover it, it was not a nuisance, so far as the owner was concerned, and he was not liable for injuries sustained by a pedestrian who fell into it while it was uncovered, where the premises were under the exclusive control of the tenant.

In *Duffin* v. *Dawson* (1905), 211 Pa. St. 593, 61 Atl. 76, it is held that where a person is injured by the tilting of a cellar door, and it appeared that the accident was caused by reason of the door to the cellarway not being properly closed, and not because of any defect in the construction of the door, the remedy is against the tenant in possession and not against the owner.

In *Frischberg* v. *Hurter* (1899), 173 Mass. 22, 52 N. E. 1086, it is held that the owner of premises occupied by a tenant, and which the owner has not agreed generally to keep in repair, is not liable for injuries caused to a third person by falling into a coal-hole on the premises through the neglect of the tenant to fasten the cover, which of itself is in good condition.

In the case of *Taylor* v. *Loring* (1909), 201 Mass. 283, 87 N. E. 469, 470 the court said, on page 285: "The defendants had nothing to do with the care and management of the premises at the time of the accident. The only ground for a contention that they were liable for the accident is that the mode of construction of the vestibule made it a nuisance by reason of the use for which it was intended and to which it was put by the tenants in accordance with the plan and purpose of the defendants when they executed the lease. * * * If at any time there were conditions which made it dangerous, the defendants had a right to assume that the tenants would use it in such a way as would be safe, either by keeping it closed or by putting a barrier before it, or would otherwise protect those who might be in danger from it. The defendants had no reason to expect such a use of the premises by the tenants as would make the vestibule a nuisance or expose to danger persons lawfully using the premises.

In *Reynolds* v. *King* (1911), 74 Misc. Rep. 439, 132 N. Y. Supp. 273, it is held that where a cellarway under the sidewalk was covered with iron doors, which were in perfect condition, and safe so long as closed, and the doors were in control of the tenant, the owner was not liable for injuries received by a pedestrian because of the falling of the doors, which the tenant opened and left insecurely fastened.

In *Fisher* v. *Thirkell* (1870), 21 Mich. 1, 4 Am. Rep. 422, it is held that where there is no provision in a lease in regard to injuries, it is the duty of the person having control of the premises to keep a scuttle in a sidewalk in repair; and the owner of the premises will not be held liable for injuries caused by neglect to keep the scuttle in repair, if it was in good condition when possession was given under the lease.

The principal question involved in this case has not been decided by either of the Indiana courts, but from an examination of the many authorities from other jurisdictions, we feel warranted in stating the rule to be that: where property is leased, and at the time is not in such a condition as to constitute a nuisance in and of itself, but becomes so only by the act of the tenant while in possession, and injury occurs during such possession, the owner is not liable; but where the owner leases premises which are a nuisance in and of themselves or must, in the nature of things, become so by their use, and receives rent, then, whether in possession or out, he is liable. In

5.

addition to the above authorities, see *Owings* v. *Jones* (1856), 9 Md. 108; *Martin* v. *Pettit* (1889), 117 N. Y. 118, 22 N. E. 566, 5 L. R. A. 794; *Babbage* v. *Powers* (1891), 130 N. Y. 281, 29 N. E. 132, 14 L. R. A. 398; *West Chicago, etc., Assn.* v. *Cohn* (1901), 192 Ill. 210, 61 N. E. 439, 55 L. R. A. 235, 85 Am. St. 327.

Appellee contends in her brief that her complaint, if not good under the common law, is good under Acts 1911, page 597, known as the "Dangerous Occupations Act." Whether said act applies to coal-holes and cellarways in sidewalks we do not regard as necessary to decide. It is sufficient to say that, if it were intended to apply to such cases, the complaint and evidence shows that appellants fully complied therewith by maintaining a good covering for the cellarway.

Appellee further contends that the evidence in the cause is not properly in the record because the certificate of the trial judge to the bill of exceptions fails to show
6. that he examined the bill before allowing and signing it. With this contention we cannot agree. The presumption is that the judge examined the bill before signing it, and the failure of the certificate to recite the fact does not affect the sufficiency of the certificate. *Tombaugh* v. *Grogg* (1900), 156 Ind. 355, 59 N. E. 1060; *Dodge* v. *Morrow* (1895), 14 Ind. App. 534, 41 N. E. 967, 43 N. E. 153; *Howe* v. *White* (1903), 162 Ind. 74, 69 N. E. 684; *Standard Life, etc., Ins. Co.* v. *Martin* (1893), 133 Ind. 376, 33 N. E. 105.

It follows from what we have said that the second paragraph of complaint does not state facts sufficient to constitute a cause of action against the appellants, and that the verdict is contrary to law and is not sustained by sufficient evidence.

The judgment of the lower court is reversed, with instructions to grant a new trial, sustain appellants' demurrer to the second paragraph of complaint and for further proceedings not inconsistent with this opinion.

NOTE.—Reported in 113 N. E. 764. Liability of landlord to a third person for condition of premises in possession of tenant, 20 L. R. A. 197, 198; 92 Am. St. 502; 24 Cyc 1128.

---

OHIO FARMERS INSURANCE COMPANY v. WILLIAMS.

[No. 9,028. Filed May 10, 1916. Rehearing denied December 22, 1916.]

1. INSURANCE.—*Fire Insurance Policy.—Stipulation Against Other Insurance.—Validity.*—Stipulations in a fire insurance policy to the effect that the policy shall be void if the insured has or procures any other contract of insurance on the property covered are valid and reasonable, and when they are violated, the insurer may defend against loss on the ground of breach of the contract. p. 438.

2. INSURANCE.—*Fire Insurance Policy.—Stipulation Against Other Insurance.—Use of Word "Void."—Effect.*—Where a stipulation in a fire insurance policy provides that the policy shall be void if the insured shall procure additional insurance on the property covered, a breach of such stipulation does not render the policy void, but only voidable at the election of the insurer. p. 438.

3. INSURANCE.—*Policy.—Breach.—Avoidance of Contract.—Return of Premiums.*—Where an insurance company's defense to an action on a policy is based upon a breach thereof that renders the contract ineffectual from its inception, so that, the risk never having attached, there was no consideration for the premium received, the insurer, upon learning of the breach, must seasonably offer to return the premium, or it cannot insist upon a forfeiture of the policy. p. 439.

4. INSURANCE.—*Policy.—Breach.—Avoidance of Contract.—Return of Premium.*—Where an insurer's liability attaches upon the execution of the policy, the return of the premium by the insurer is not necessary to avoid the contract for a breach of its stipulations by the insured. p. 439.

5. INSURANCE.—*Fire Insurance Policy.—Breach of Insured.—Return of Premium.—Cancellation.*—An insurer's denial of liability on a policy because of a breach of its stipulations by the insured does not amount to a cancellation of the policy requiring the return of the *pro rata* share of the premium, under a provision of the contract stating that upon cancellation of the policy by

the company, it shall only retain a *pro rata* share of the premium for the time elapsed. p. 442.

6. INSURANCE.—*Fire Insurance Policy.—Construction.*—Fire insurance contracts are strictly construed as against the insurer, so as to prevent a forfeiture, and liberally construed in favor of the insured to the end that the contract may serve its purpose of furnishing indemnity in case of loss. p. 442.

7. INSURANCE.—*Fire Insurance.—Action on Policy.—Pleading.*— Where, in an action on a fire insurance policy, the defense of forfeiture because of a breach of the stipulations in the contract, interposed by answer, was waived by the insurer, a reply setting up such waiver properly presents the same. p. 443.

From Bartholomew Circuit Court; *Hugh Wickens,* Judge.

Action by Samuel Hamer Williams against the Ohio Farmers Insurance Company. From a judgment for plaintiff, the defendant appeals. *Reversed.*

*Charles S. Baker* and *Frank N. Richman,* for appellant. *C. J. Kollmeyer* and *Julian Sharpnack,* for appellee.

MORAN, J.—This is an appeal from a judgment in the sum of $1,135.53 against appellant upon an insurance policy issued by appellant to indemnify appellee against loss by fire or lightning to certain chattel property owned by appellee. A review is sought as to the action of the trial court in holding insufficient as against demurrer appellant's second and eighth paragraphs of answer addressed to appellee's second paragraph of amended complaint and appellee's amended complaint respectively. The action of the court complained of was brought about by demurrers addressed to affirmative paragraphs of reply being carried back and sustained to the paragraphs of answer to which the replies were respectively addressed. The record discloses a paragraph of complaint designated as an amended complaint, and a second paragraph of amended complaint. They differ not in theory and but slightly in phraseology. The sufficiency of neither paragraph being challenged, reference hereafter will be made, as a matter of convenience, to the complaint and not to the separate paragraphs.

It is disclosed by the complaint that in consideration of a premium of $39, appellant issued to appellee a policy of insurance insuring against loss by fire or lightning appellee's chattel property consisting (1) of furniture, clothing, provisions and household goods of all kinds and character specifically described; (2) hay, grain, fodder and seeds; (3) live stock; (4) farming implements. That on October 29, 1911, the property insured was totally destroyed by fire. A compliance with the conditions of the policy is pleaded and a copy of the policy and an itemized bill of particulars of the property destroyed is made a part of the complaint.

The following part of stipulation No. 8 of the policy is material to the questions presented for consideration: "This entire policy, unless otherwise provided by agreement, endorsed hereon added hereto, shall be void if the insured now has or shall hereafter make or procure any other contract of insurance, whether valid or not, on the property covered in whole or in part by this policy, etc."

The second paragraph of appellant's answer embodies that part of stipulation No. 8 of the policy heretofore set out, and in substance alleges, that the insured, on July 21, 1910, violated this stipulation by procuring additional insurance from the German Fire Insurance Company of Indiana, in the absence of an agreement authorizing the same, as provided by the policy. A disposition of the error predicated upon the sustaining of the demurrer to this paragraph of answer will dispose of the error predicated upon a similar ruling as to the eighth paragraph of answer, as the paragraphs are identical, except addressed to different paragraphs of complaint, which paragraphs of complaint seek the same relief, and differ, as we have said, but slightly in phraseology.

It is appellant's position that by appellee procuring additional insurance in the manner and under the circumstances as set forth in the answer, under consideration, he breached a condition in the policy which relieves it from liability. The reason underlying the insertion of a stipulation such as here under consideration in policies of insurance covering indemnity for loss by fire is to prevent over-insurance, and "upon the assumption that the insured will be less careful to protect his property from loss in proportion as to the amount his insurance is increased," and further that the moral hazard should not be increased without the knowledge of the insurer. 19 Cyc 764; 5 Elliott, Contracts §4240; *Havens* v. *Home Ins. Co.* (1887), 111 Ind. 90, 12 N. E. 137, 60 Am. Rep. 689; *American Ins. Co.* v. *Replogle* (1888), 114 Ind. 1, 15 N. E. 810; Elliott, Insurance §245.

Such stipulations are regarded as valid and reasonable, and when violated, the insurer may, when a loss occurs, defend on the ground of a breach of the contract

1. in this respect. Thus far there is no ground for controversy.

Appellee's main objection to the answer is that the procuring of additional insurance did not render the contract void, but only voidable at the election of the insurer, and hence that it became appellant's duty as a condition precedent to defend upon this ground to return, or offer to return, the unearned portion of the premium; and that the absence of such averment in the answer rendered it insufficient to state a defense to the complaint.

Appellee's contention that the stipulation against procuring additional insurance does not render' the policy void, but voidable at the election of the insurer is,

2. as well as kindred stipulations, abundantly supported by the authorities. *Saville* v. *Aetna Ins. Co.* (1889), 8 Mont. 419, 20 Pac. 646, 3 L. R. A. 542; *Carpenter* v. *Providence, etc., Ins. Co.* (1842), 16 Pet. 495, 10 L. Ed. (U. S.) 1044; *Glens Falls Ins. Co.* v. *Michael* (1906), 167 Ind. 659, 74 N. E. 964, 79 N. E. 905, 8 L. R. A. (N. S.) 708; *Turner* v. *Meridan Fire Ins. Co.* (1883), 16 Fed. 454; *Com-*

*mercial Life Ins. Co.* v. *Schroyer* (1911), 176 Ind. 654; 95 N. E. 1004, Ann. Cas. 1914A 968; *Germania Fire Ins. Co.* v. *Klewer* (1889), 129 Ill. 599, 22 N. E. 489.

This as well as the Supreme Court and the courts of other jurisdictions generally have frequently held that both as to fire and life insurance policies where a defense 3. is based upon a breach of the policy that renders the contract ineffectual from its inception, and where, in fact, no risk attached, that under such circumstances there is no consideration for the premium received, and that the insurer upon learning of the breach should seasonably offer to restore the premium received by it; and failing to do so, it could not insist upon a forfeiture of the policy. *Glens Falls Ins. Co.* v. *Michael, supra; Catholic Order of Foresters* v. *Collins* (1912), 51 Ind. App. 285, 99 N. E. 745.

That liability attached, under the policy in suit, upon its execution and delivery is not denied by either party, and this is true up to the date of the procuring of 4. the additional insurance; at this date appellant takes the position that liability ceased on its part, while on the part of appellee it is contended that there was no cessation of liability, in the absence of an election on the part of appellant to avoid the contract by a return or offer to return the unearned premium. In view of the fact that this subject has been before the courts of this state heretofore, nothing further need be said than that this jurisdiction is committed to the doctrine that finds support in various jurisdictions that there is a distinction resting upon a legal principle between where a liability attached upon the execution of the policy, and where it did not, in reference to a return of the premium. In one instance the return of the premium is essential, in the other it is not. "Premiums paid to secure insurance cannot be recovered if the risk has once attached. If a policy is valid at its inception, then the company cannot be required to refund the premiums received." *Standley* v. *Northwestern, etc., Ins. Co.* (1884), 95 Ind. 254; *Continental Life Ins. Co.* v. *Houser* (1883), 89 Ind. 258; *Northwestern, etc., Assn.* v. *Bodurtha* (1899), 23 Ind. App. 121, 53 N. E. 787, 77 Am. St. 414; *American Ins. Co.* v. *Replogle, supra.*

Cooley in his briefs on the Law of Insurance, page 1043, says: "It is a principle of almost elementary character that, if the risk has once attached, there can be no return of the premium". And further, at page 1048, he says: "On the principle that when the risk has once attached a premium must be considered as earned, a valid forfeiture of a life policy will not justify a recovery of the premium paid, in the absence of an agreement giving the insured such a right."

In *Georgia Home Ins. Co.* v. *Rosenfield,* (1899), 95 Fed. 358, 37 C. C. A. 96, Lurton J., speaking for the court, uses the following language: "So, if the risk attached and the policy became void subsequently through the conduct of the insured, no part of the premium can be recovered." This case involved the question of additional insurance in violation of the provisions of the policy.

In the recent case of *Marion, etc., Bed Co.* v. *Empire State Surety Co.* (1912), 52 Ind. App. 480, 100 N. E. 882, a review of the authorities was had as to when and under what circumstances it was necessary for the insurer to tender back the premiums in order to defend upon certain grounds, and it was there announced as the judgment of the court that, the policy having taken effect, the insured was not entitled to a return of the premium; that it was only when the policy was void *ab initio* that the premium must be tendered or returned to the insured.

In *Aetna Life Ins. Co.* v. *Paul* (1881), 10 Ill. App. 431, in an action in assumpsit to recover premiums paid, it was said, after discussing the conditions under which the insured was entitled to a return thereof: "But where a risk is entire, and has once commenced to run, though it be for ever so short a period, there can be no apportionment or return of the premium.''

The policy before us indemnified appellee against loss by fire and lightning to his property for a period of three years for the gross sum of $39.60, and appellant was not, under the authorities, required to return any part of the $39.60 under the circumstances, unless the provision of the policy in reference to the cancellation thereof can be construed to require such return. The provision of the policy as to cancellation, so far as it relates to appellant, is: ''If cancelled by the company, it shall only retain a pro rata share of the premium for the time elapsed.'' It might be further added that the policy provides for cancellation by both the insured and insurer at any time. In *Colby v. Cedar Rapids Ins. Co.* (1885), 66 Iowa, 577, 24 N. W. 54, the insured sought to cancel certain policies of insurance and apply the unearned premiums on a new policy in another company; his method of attempting to do so was by assigning the unearned premiums to the agent of the company issuing the latter policy, and in discussing the irregularity of the method resorted to to cancel or attempt to cancel the former policy, the court said: ''It is not denied by plaintiff, and could not be properly, that if the Phoenix insurance was obtained before the virtual cancellation of the policies in the defendant company, these policies would be avoided by Marray's act in violating the condition, and there would be nothing left to cancel, and no claim would accrue for unearned premiums.'' This was where there was a stipulation in the policy against additional insurance, and it was held that the violation of the contract against additional insurance avoided the policy and there was nothing left to cancel. The Supreme Court of Minnesota in discussing a provision in a policy that gave the insurer the right to terminate the contract at any time, at its option, by giving notice and refunding a ratable proportion of the premium for the unexpired term, where there was a loss by fire after additional insurance was effected in violation of a condition in the policy, said: "The provision in the policy authorizing the company to terminate the contract at any time, at its option, bore no special relation to that concerning other insurance. By the plain terms of the policy, other insurance without the consent of this company would *ipso facto* avoid the contract; and in the case of a contract thus avoided, it would not be obligatory upon the insurer to repay any of the unearned premium * * *. It required no affirmative act of election on the part of the company to make operative the clause avoiding the contract whenever the specified conditions should occur." *Johnson* v. *American Ins. Co.* (1889), 41 Minn. 396, 43 N. W. 59.

Both upon authority and reason it seems that appellant's action in denying liability, by reason of the conduct of appellee in effecting other insurance, cannot be

5. treated as a cancellation of the policy, calling for a return of the pro rata share of the premium for the time between the date appellee effected the insurance to the date when the policy would expire, as disclosed upon its face. This disposes of the main question presented for consideration, and in so concluding, we are mindful

6. that contracts of insurance, such as are here under consideration, are strictly construed as against the insurer, so as to prevent a forfeiture of the contract, and liberally construed in favor of the insured to the end that the contract serve the purpose for which it was intended— that of indemnity in case of loss. But the provision here under consideration against procuring additional insurance is clearly expressed and in unambiguous terms, and to disregard the same would be to disregard the contract entered into between the parties. Additional insurance having been procured, and the loss having occurred thereafter, which is disclosed by the answer under consideration, the same states a defense to the complaint. An answer similar

in all respects to the one under consideration was held good
in the cases of *Bowlus* v. *Phenix Ins. Co.* (1892), 133 Ind.
106, 115, 32 N. E. 319, 20 L. R. A. 400, and *Sisk* v. *Citizens'
Ins. Co.* (1896), 16 Ind. App. 565, 45 N. E. 804.

Holding the answer sufficient virtually holds that the
question is properly raised in this manner, and disposes of
appellant's further contention that the complaint was so
drafted that appellant should have raised the question of
additional insurance by demurrer, and by not doing so it
was waived.

The sufficiency of the replies to avoid the paragraphs of
answer on the ground of waiver is not before the court for
consideration; however, if the defense interposed by

7.  the answers was waived by the insurer, a reply set-
ing up such waiver would properly present the same.
*Continental Ins. Co.* v. *Vanlue* (1891), 126 Ind. 410, 26 N.
E. 119, 10 L. R. A. 843; *Fort Wayne Ins. Co.* v. *Irwin*
(1899), 23 Ind. App. 53, 54 N. E. 817; *Evans* v. *Queen
Ins. Co.* (1892), 5 Ind. App. 198, 31 N. E. 843.

It follows that the court erred in carrying the demurrer
addressed to the replies back and sustaining the same to
the paragraphs of answer to which the replies were addressed respectively. The judgment is reversed, with
instructions to the trial court to overrule the demurrers
to the second and eighth paragraphs of answer; and for
further proceedings consistent with this opinion.

NOTE.—Reported in 112 N. E. 556. Insurance: (a) acts sufficient
to effect the cancellation of a fire insurance policy by insurer, 17
Ann. Cas. 795, Ann. Cas. 1915A 1233; (b) necessity of the return
or tender of unearned premium to effect cancellation of a fire insurance policy by insurer, 12 Ann. Cas. 1007, Ann. Cas. 1913D 490;
(c) retention of policy as a waiver of mistake or fraud of insurer
or its agent, especially as to other insurance, 67 L. R. A. 726. See
under (1, 2) 19 Cyc 703, 764, 765; (3) 19 Cyc 798; (6) 19 Cyc 656,
716; (7) 19 Cyc 980.

## DAYWITT ET AL. *v.* DAYWITT.

[No. 9,182.  Filed January 2, 1917.]

1. HUSBAND AND WIFE.—*Alienation of Affections.—Measure of Damages.*—The services, conjugal affection and society of a husband is valuable property, and, in a suit by the wife for the alienation of her husband's affections, the measure of damages is the value of the husband of whom she has been deprived.  p. 446.

2. APPEAL.—*Review.—Invited Error.—Instructions.*—In an action by the wife for alienation of her husband's affections, defendants cannot complain of an instruction directing a finding for plaintiff if either of them maliciously alienated the husband's affections, where the error, if any, in such instruction was invited by an instruction of the same nature requested by defendants. p. 449.

3. APPEAL.—*Review.—Waiver of Objections.—Instructions.*—Where, in an action by the wife for alienation of her husband's affections, ample opportunity was afforded two defendants to submit a form of verdict to find against one only if found liable, in addition to the two forms submitted, one to find for plaintiff and the other for defendants, but they made no request therefor at the proper time, they cannot complain of an instruction directing a verdict against both, if either of them maliciously did the acts charged.  p. 449.

4. TRIAL.—*Instructions.—Malice.—Invading Province of Jury.*—In an action for alienation of the husband's affections, an instruction defining malice and informing the jury that, if it found that defendants did the acts charged in the complaint and thereby caused the alienation of the husband's affections, and if it found that such acts were done purposely without just or probable cause, it could infer that such acts were done maliciously, but that in case it should so find, whether such inference should be drawn from the acts of the defendants was for the jury to determine from all the evidence, was not objectionable as invading the province of the jury to determine whether it should infer that the acts charged were malicious.  p. 449.

5. APPEAL.—*Review.—Refusal of Instructions.*—It is not error to refuse requested instructions where the subject-matter thereof is fully covered by the instructions given.  p. 450.

6. HUSBAND AND WIFE.—*Alienation of Affections.—Action.—Evidence.—Admissibility.*—In an action by a wife against her husband's parents for alienation of affections, testimony of the wife as to certain acts of her husband and sister-in-law just prior to plaintiff's separation from her husband is inadmissible in the

absence of other evidence connecting defendants with such acts. p. 450.

7. **HUSBAND AND WIFE.**—*Alienation of Affections.*—*Parent and Child.*—*Advice.*—*Presumptions.*—A parent may always in good faith and for the best interest of his child advise and counsel with him, and, where advice is given, the presumption is that it was induced by feelings of the highest parental affections and only for the child's good. p. 452.

8. **EVIDENCE.**—*Res Gestae.*—*Alienation of Affections.*—*Malice.*—In an action by a wife against her husband's parents for alienation, defendants should have been permitted to show as part of the *res gestae* that they allowed the son at the time of his marriage to bring his wife to the parental home to reside, and furnished him money for medical expenses during her illness and that when informed by the doctor that an operation on plaintiff was necessary they instructed the doctor to perform such operation, for which the evidence showed they subsequently paid. p. 452.

9. **EVIDENCE.**—*Res Gestae.*—*Alienation of Affections.*—*Malice.*—Where, in an action by a wife against her husband's parents for alienation, plaintiff contended that defendants permitted their daughter to move into a house provided by them for the purpose of driving her out, defendants should have been permitted to show, as a part of the *res gestae*, the arrangement made concerning the occupancy of the house. p. 454.

10. **TRIAL.**—*Witnesses.*—*Credibility.*—*Jury Question.*—In action for alienation, declarations which are part of the *res gestae* are admissible in evidence, and it is for the jury to determine whether they were made in good faith by the party offering them or were merely manufactured evidence for use at the trial, it being no objection to such declarations that they were self-serving. p. 454.

11. **EVIDENCE.**—*Res Gestae.*—The term *res gestae* includes the surrounding facts of a transaction, and also the accompanying declarations, to explain the act done, or for showing motive for acting, although such declarations aside from this doctrine may be in the nature of hearsay evidence. p. 454.

12. **APPEAL.**—*Review.*—*Witnesses.*—*Credibility.*—*Jury Question.*—It is for the jury to determine the credibility of witnesses, and not for the court on appeal. p. 455.

From Clinton Circuit Court; *Joseph Combs*, Judge.

Action by Helen Daywitt, by her next friend, Jane Stewart, against Albert Daywitt and another. From a judgment for plaintiff, the defendants appeal. *Reversed.*

*James V. Kent* and *Thomas M. Ryan*, for appellants.

*Leonard J. Curtis, John W. Strawn* and *William Robison,*
for appellee.

IBACH, J.—This action was brought by appellee, an infant
and wife of Lawrence Daywitt, by her next friend, against
appellants, who were the parents of said Lawrence, to
recover damages because they had wilfully, maliciously
and wrongfully alienated the affection of her husband, and
had maliciously and wrongfully induced him to drive her
from their home, and had wrongfully persuaded him to
abandon her and their children without support. The
questions in the record, presented for our determination,
relate to the court's refusal to give to the jury certain
instructions requested by appellants, and in giving others
on the court's own motion, for admitting irrelevant testimony and for excluding competent testimony.

Appellants first contend that instruction No. 11 requested
by them should have been given, and is as follows: "You
are instructed that the damages in a case of this character
is to be measured by the value of the husband of whom
the wife has been deprived and if you should find for the
plaintiff in this case you would have the right to consider,
in determining the question of damages, the treatment of
the plaintiff by her husband during their marital life and
before the alienation of the husband's affections, if such
alienation has been shown by the evidence, and you may
also consider in that connection the happiness or lack of
happiness which prevailed in the home of the plaintiff and
her husband before such alienation and any other facts
shown by the evidence which show the domestic relations
of the plaintiff and her said husband prior to such alienation, if you find in fact that such alienation has occurred."

Without approving the form of this instruction, we concur in the legal proposition involved, that the services, conjugal affection and society of a husband are valuable
1.   property, and in a suit by the wife for the alienation
     of her husband's affections, the measure of damages

is the value of the husband of whom she has been deprived. A man who demeans himself toward his wife as a dutiful, kind and loving husband is much more valuable to her than one who has been cruel, indifferent and neglectful of her. And it is evident that the trial court considered an instruction embodying such legal proposition proper in view of the facts of the case, for on its own motion, the following instruction was given: "In case you find for the plaintiff you may take into consideration what if any damages she has sustained on account of the loss, if any, of the services of her husband, also you may consider, if the evidence shows, what, if any damages she has sustained on account of the loss, if the evidence shows, of the society, companionship, affection, and protection of her husband."

The record discloses that the appellants were permitted to show the character of the home life of plaintiff and her husband, and with this evidence before them, the jury was told in the instruction that, if they found for the plaintiff, they might, in calculating her damages, consider both loss of service and loss of companionship. Such terms and expressions embrace the elements which go to make up the value of the husband; consequently the instruction given contained substantially all that was included in the instruction refused although not so clearly stated.

It is also contended that there was error in the giving of instruction No. 3 of the court's own motion. This instruction is as follows: "In order for the plaintiff to recover in this cause, it must be shown by the evidence that the defendants, or one of them, alienated the affections of the plaintiff's husband from her, or by some acts of theirs caused the separation of the plaintiff and her husband. And it must also be shown by the evidence that the defendant's conduct in so doing, was malicious, or that the acts causing the said alienation of affections, or separation, were done through malice. And, if you find from the evidence that the defendants, or either of them, did cause the aliena-

tion of affections of plaintiff's husband, and did thereby
cause the plaintiff and her husband to separate, then it
is a question of fact for you to determine from all of the
evidence given in the cause whether or not the acts of the
defendant, or defendants, were done maliciously, or were
done in good faith for the best interests of their son. When
a father and mother are charged with the alienation of a
husband's affection, the 'quo animo' is the important consideration. That is, from what motive did the parents act—
was it malicious, or was it inspired by a proper regard for
the welfare and happiness of the child? The reciprocal
obligations of parent and child last through life, and the
·duty of discharging them does not cease by the marriage
of the child. When trouble and disagreements arise between the married pair, the most natural prompting of the
child direct it to find solace and advice under the parental
roof. All legitimate presumptions in such cases must be that
the parent will act only for the best interests of the child.
The law recognizes the right of the parent in such cases to
advise the son or daughter, and when such advice is given
in good faith, and results in a separation, the act does not
give the injured party a right of action. In such a case
the motives of the parents are presumed to be good until
the contrary is made to appear. This presumption of good
faith on the part of the parents is like any other presumption that may arise and it may always be overcome by evidence to the contrary. So it is for you to determine from
the evidence in this cause whether or not the defendants,
or either of them did cause the alienation or separation
charged in the complaint and if so whether or not their
motive in so doing was malicious. If you find from the
evidence that the defendants, *or either of them,* did the
acts charged and with the result as charged and that the
acts were done through malice, then your verdict should
be for the plaintiff. But unless you find that they, or
either of them did cause the alienation or separation charged

and that it was done through malice then you should find
for the defendants."

The next to the last sentence of this instruction is the
portion particularly criticized, and the objection is that the
jury is not instructed as to a finding against the
2. defendants separately and that only two forms of
verdict were submitted, one a finding for the plaintiff
and the other a finding for the defendants. In other words,
appellants contend that the instruction directed a verdict
against both defendants if the proof showed only one of
them guilty. The charge is subject to this criticism, but
the state of the entire record shows that the giving of it
was harmless and that appellants are in no position to ask
for a reversal because it was given.

The record shows that an instruction tendered by appellants and given to the jury was of the same nature, so that
even if there was error in the form of the instruction now
contended for, it was an invited error and appellants must
be charged with it and they cannot now complain. *Domestic Block Coal Co.* v. *DeArmey* (1913), 179 Ind. 592,
100 N. E. 675, 102 N. E. 99.

Again ample opportunity was afforded appellants to have
three forms of verdict submitted to the jury instead of two
and not having made such request at the proper
3. time, it seems to us in view of the entire record that
such contention is without merit at this time.

Appellants also condemn instruction No. 4 given on the
court's own motion. In this instruction the court said:
"Malice is defined as a disposition or intent to injure
4. another or others for the gratification of anger, jeal-
ousy, hatred, revenge or the like; active malevo-
lence. A deliberate intention to do evil either with or without personal ill-will. A willfully framed design to do
another an injury. If you find that the defendants or
either of them did the acts charged in the complaint and

thereby caused the alienation or separation as alleged, and
if you find that the said acts were done purposely and
without just or probable cause, then you may infer that
such acts were done maliciously. But in case you so find
whether or not such inference should be drawn from the
acts of the defendants is for you to determine from the
evidence in this cause.''

The objection raised is that the court invaded the province
of the jury and it is argued that it was for the jury to
determine not only whether or not it should draw the
inference of malice but whether or not any given state of
facts would warrant such inference.

In this instruction, in defining malice, the court followed
the instruction used by the court and approved by this
court in the case of *Kelso* v. *Kelso* (1908), 43 Ind. App.
115, 86 N. E. 1001. The jury was there informed, if they
found that the wrongful acts charged in the complaint were
committed as charged, and were done purposely and without probable cause, then they might infer malice, but in any
event it was for them to determine from all of the evidence
whether such inference should be drawn. There is no
direction for them to so find; no such words as ''must'' or
''ought'' are used. There could have been no objection
urged if the court had simply informed the jury that malice
need not be proven by direct evidence but it may be inferred
from all the evidence introduced, and we believe that that,
in effect, is what the jury were told and that they so understood it.

Other instructions tendered by appellants were
5. refused but there is no ground for complaint for
the reason that the court fully covered them by other
instructions given.

Objection is made to the action of the court in admitting
in evidence, over appellants' objection, certain acts
6. of appellee's husband on the day of, and the day
preceding, their separation, also the conduct of her

sister-in-law toward her on the same days, all of which acts were done in the absence of appellants, and also in admitting in evidence over objection the following statement made by appellee's husband to appellee's mother in her presence: "My father says if you don't take the woman and kids and get off the place he will kick you off."

We are not unmindful of our statute and the universal rule which requires the protection of marital communications, but we do not consider that the class of evidence objected to falls within the letter or spirit of the statute or within the rule that confidential communications between husband and wife are not admissible in evidence in favor of the wife in a suit by her against the parents of her husband for the alleged alienation of his affections. Neither does it fall within the rule that conversations between persons not parties to the action, had in the absence of the parties against whom the same are introduced, are not competent evidence.

To support one of the material averments of the complaint it was essential for appellee to show the loss of the affections of her husband and that she was driven from her home on account thereof. The evidence objected to was competent for that purpose and none other, and to make her case it was necessary for appellee to go further and show that the cause of their separation was occasioned by the misconduct of the husband's parents. But what the husband and sister-in-law did, in the absence of other evidence, in some manner connecting the appellants with it, would have no probative value against appellants and would be no proof to support that issue. The fact that appellee's husband reported that his father had made a threatening statement, which report may have had some influence on appellee's conduct, could not be taken as any evidence that the parents had actually made such a statement and would be no proof that appellants' conduct occasioned the withdrawal of her husband's affections.

It is further contended that the court erred in refusing to admit in evidence declarations of the appellants as part of the *res gestae* showing the absence of malice. Our courts have many times held that declarations made at the time of the transaction inquired about, and which are a part of the *res gestae*, are admissible. *Gifford* v. *Gifford* (1914), 58 Ind. App. 665, 107 N. E. 308; *Doe* v. *Reagan* (1839), 5 Blackf. 217, 33 Am. Dec. 466; *Lockwood* v. *Rose* (1890), 125 Ind. 588, 595, 25 N. E. 710; *Bingham* v. *Walk* (1891), 128 Ind. 164, 172, 27 N. E. 483. In all cases like the present malice must be shown; the *quo animo* is the chief subject

7.  of inquiry. A parent may always in good faith and for the best interests of his child advise and counsel with him, and, where advice is given, the presumption is that it was induced by feelings of the highest parental affection and only for the child's good. *Reed* v. *Reed* (1893), 6 Ind. App. 317, 33 N. E. 638, 51 Am. St. 310.

Appellee had been permitted to show acts of disapproval of her marriage with appellants' son when they were informed that such marriage was a necessity, but

8.  it was shown that shortly thereafter they both lived with appellants in their home for some considerable time and were living there when the baby was born. Appellants then offered to show that when their son, who was only eighteen years of age and was without money or work, requested permission to bring his wife to their home appellants told him he could and that they might live with them as their children and when he was twenty-one years of age the father would help him to get a start on the farm.

There was evidence that appellants had at different times shortly after his marriage given their son money. They offered to show that this was done on the request of their son and because he had reported to them that appellee was sick; that he was out of work and needed the money to take care of her. They also offered to show that immediately after appellee's baby was born a serious operation became necessary on account of lacerations due to childbirth and that the doctor came to appellants and informed them that an operation was necessary and that such doctor was then instructed by them to prepare for and operate upon appellee. This offer was refused, but the court did allow the fact to be shown that appellants had paid all the expenses occasioned by appellee's sickness.

Appellee introduced evidence that while she and her husband lived on the farm and while appellants were living on an adjoining farm, appellants permitted their daughter and son-in-law to move into the same house occupied by appellee and her husband. Appellants offered to prove, for the purpose of showing absence of malice, a contract made with their own daughter and her husband, at a time when it was believed that appellee had finally left her husband, and appellee's husband concerning the occupancy of the house and the operation of the farm.

Since the question of good faith controls in these cases we believe that the proof offered was a part of the *res gestae* and should have gone to the jury. In the case of *Hamilton* v. *State* (1871), 36 Ind. 280, 282, 10 Am. Rep. 22, this language is used: "It is well established * * * that in all cases, civil and criminal, where evidence of an act done by a party is admissible, his declarations, made at the time, having a tendency to elucidate, explain, or give character to the act, are also admissible. They are a part of the transaction, and for that reason are admissible; and it makes no difference, so far as the admissiblity of the declaration is concerned, whether it be in favor of, or against the party making it."

If the money was given to the husband, it was competent for the purpose of showing the absence of malice that it was furnished for the express benefit of appellee and to relieve her wants. If large sums of money were paid for her by appellants on account of her serious illness, it was

competent to show the absence of malice by proving by the
physician that he had informed appellants of the serious
condition of appellee and that her health could only be restored through an operation. That the fact that appellants
received information of appellee's critical condition and that
such information caused them to act, was as much a part
of the case as the fact that she was brought to appellant's
home, there operated upon, and all expenses paid by appellants, and this is especially true since appellee insisted that
she was forced to return to appellants' farm against her
will. Again appellee strongly contended that appel-

9. lants allowed their own daughter to move into a part
of the house occupied by herself and husband for the
purpose of driving her out. The arrangement made
between the parties concerning the occupancy of the house
and the conduct of the farm were also a part of the *res
gestae* and it should have been shown to disprove malice.
There are many kindred declarations which should not have
been excluded, the jury should have received them,

10. and it was for them to say whether the declarations
offered as a part of the *res gestae* were made in
good faith or were merely manufactured evidence to be
used in their own behalf. It has been held that " 'it
is no objection to such declarations that they are self-serving, if they are part of the *res gestae*.' " *McConnell* v.
*Hannah* (1884), 96 Ind. 102, 106. The term *"res gestae"*
includes the surrounding facts of a transaction, and

11. accompanying declarations as well, to explain the
act done, or for showing a motive for acting, although
such declarations aside from this doctrine may be said to
partake of hearsay. 24 Am. & Eng. Ency. Law (2d ed.)
662; 34 Cyc 1642; *Porter* v. *Waltz* (1886), 108 Ind. 40,
46, 8 N. E. 105, and cases cited; *Carr* v. *State* (1884), 43
Ark. 99, 103. In the case last cited the rule is announced
in the following language: "Circumstances and declarations which are contemporaneous with the main fact under

consideration or so nearly related to it as to illustrate its character and the state of mind, sentiments or dispositions of the actors are parts of the *res gestae.*"

Appellee's case rests very largely on her own evidence, and she was strongly contradicted on every fact testified to by her. The question of credibility, however, was 12. one for the jury and not for this court. We cannot say that the result reached by the jury would have been the same had the trial court limited the probative force of the evidence objected to and had admitted the proof offered by appellants, and for these reasons we believe the ends of justice require the granting of a new trial.

Judgment reversed, and new trial granted.

Note.—Reported in 114 N. E. 694. Husband and wife: (a) action by wife for alienation of affections, 6 Ann. Cas. 661; 14 Ann. Cas. 47; Ann. Cas. 1912C 1179; Ann. Cas. 1916C 748; 46 Am. St. 478. Liability of parent for alienation of affections, 8 Ann. Cas. 813; for causing separation of husband and wife, 9 L. R. A. (N. S.) 322, 46 L. R. A. (N. S.) 467. Competency of one spouse to testify as to misconduct of the other in an action for alienation of affections, 2 L. R. A. (N. S.) 708; 39 L. R. A. (N. S.) 317. See under (1) 21 Cyc 1622; (2) 3 Cyc 248, 4 C. J. 708, 709; (3) 2 Cyc 700, 3 C. J. 850; (6, 7) 21 Cyc 1625.

---

## ROBBINS ET AL. *v*. BRAZIL SYNDICATE R. AND B. COMPANY.

### [No. 9,174. Filed January 8, 1917.]

1. SALES.—*Delivery to Carrier.*—*Effect.*—Where goods are bought at one place to be consigned and transported to the purchaser at another place, it is the general rule, in the absence of a contrary arrangement, that delivery by the seller to a common carrier is a delivery to the purchaser, since the carrier thereby becomes the agent of the purchaser and title to the property passes to him at the time of such delivery. p. 460.

2. SALES.—*Delivery to Carrier.*—*Effect.*—*Right of Inspection.*—The right of inspection, in the absence of any established custom or agreement to the contrary, does not prevent the title from passing to the purchaser on delivery to the carrier of goods duly consigned to the purchaser, but if, on inspection the goods are

not found to be such as were purchased, that fact may authorize
a rescission of the contract for sale.  p. 461.

3.  SALES.—*Delivery to Carrier.—Effect.—Recovery of Purchase
Price.*—If goods are sold to be delivered by the seller at the residence or place of business of the purchaser, a delivery to the
carrier is not a delivery to the purchaser, since in such case the
carrier is the agent of the seller, and failure to deliver the goods
to the purchaser according to the terms of the sale will defeat
recovery of the purchase price of the goods.  p. 461.

4.  SALES.—*Contract.—Construction.—Action for Purchase Price.*—
Where, in an action to recover the purchase price of goods sold,
plaintiff relies on a contract made up of letters and telegrams,
effect must be given to all parts of the contract alleged, if it can
be done without doing violence to the evident intention of the
parties, as ascertained from a consideration of all portions of
the writings.  p. 463.

5.  CONTRACTS.—*Contracts in Writing.—Construction.—Intention.*—
Where a contract is in writing and the language employed is unambiguous, it must be so interpreted as to carry into effect the
intention of the parties as expressed by the writings.  p. 463.

6.  CONTRACTS.—*Contracts in Writing.—Ambiguities.—Intention.—
Parol Evidence.*—If the language, or any portion thereof, used in
a written contract is ambiguous or of uncertain meaning or application, parol evidence may be heard not to vary or contradict the
writings, but to ascertain the sense in which the language was
used and its application to the subject-matter of the contract.
to determine the true intention of the parties at the time the
contract was entered into, and, in ascertaining such intention,
the court will, if necessary, consider the relation and situation
of the parties, the character of the transaction and all the surroundings and conditions attending the execution of the contract.
p. 463.

7.  SALES. — *Contract. — Construction. — Certainty. — Action to Recover Purchase Price.—Answer.—Sufficiency.*—Where, in an action to recover the purchase price of goods sold, plaintiff alleged
a contract consisting of letters and telegrams, wherein defendant
wrote "Quote us 25-50's Santos 4's same as last," and plaintiff
wired "Santos fours sixteen and half subject to return confirmation," and defendant then replied by telegram, "Ship twenty-five
fifties Santos fours at quotation," such contract is so ambiguous,
especially the meaning of the phrase "same as last" that parol
evidence must be resorted to in order to ascertain the interpretation to be placed on the contract; hence an answer averring
that the words "same as last" had a special meaning established
by prior dealings between the parties and was understood as
signifying delivery at the city where defendants resided, with

the right to inspect the goods, and that delivery was not so made, is sufficient as against demurrer. p. 464.

From Decatur Circuit Court; *Hugh Wickens*, Judge.

Action by the Brazil R. and B. Company against Will H. Robbins and Charles H. Johnston, doing business under the firm name of W. H. Robbins & Company. From a judgment for plaintiff, the defendants appeal. *Reversed.*

*George L. Tremain* and *Rollin A. Turner*, for appellants. *Thomas E. Davidson*, for appellee.

FELT, C. J.—This action was brought by appellee against appellants, Will H. Robbins and Charles H. Johnston, doing business under the firm name of W. H. Robbins & Co., to recover the purchase price of 1,250 pounds of coffee alleged to have been sold to appellants by appellee. The demurrer to the amended second paragraph of complaint for insufficiency of facts was overruled. Appellants filed an amended second paragraph and an additional third paragraph of answer to the amended second paragraph of complaint. Appellee demurred to each of such paragraphs of answer for insufficiency of facts alleged to constitute a defense to its cause of action and each of such demurrers was sustained. Thereupon appellee withdrew its first paragraph of complaint and appellants withdrew their first paragraph of answer. Appellants failed and refused to plead further and elected to stand on their said answers and the rulings of the court on the demurrers thereto, and the court rendered judgment for appellee against appellants in the sum of $207.50.

From this judgment appellants appealed and have assigned as error the overruling of their demurrer to the amended second paragraph of complaint, the sustaining of appellee's separate demurrer to the second amended and the additional third paragraph of appellants' answer.

Omitting formal and unquestioned allegations, the complaint is, in substance, as follows: Appellee was a wholesale dealer in coffee in the city of New York and among the brands of coffee sold by it to dealers was that known as ":Santos 4'S," which was sold in bags of fifty pounds each, commonly designated to dealers as "50'S"; that appellants, Will H. Robbins and Charles H. Johnston, under the firm name of W. H. Robbins & Co., were engaged in the wholesale grocery business in Greensburg, Indiana; that in 1913 appellee entered into a written contract with appellants through the following letter and telegrams, for the sale and purchase of twenty-five bags of fifty pounds each of said "Santos 4'S," at the agreed price of sixteen and one-half cents per pound, which letter and telegrams are as follows:

Letter:

"Will H. Robbins                    Charles H. Johnston
        "W. H. Robbins & Company
        Wholesale Grocers and
        Commission Merchants,
        Clover and Timothy Seed.
                        Greensburg, Indiana, 3-8, 1913.
"Brazil Syndicate,. New York,
Gentlemen:
        Quote us 25-50's Santos 4's same as last.
                        Yours truly,
                              W. H. Robbins & Co.

Telegram:

                              New York, Mar. 10, 1913.
"W. H. Robbins & Co.,
        Greensburg, Indiana,
        Santos fours sixteen and half subject to return confirmation.
                        Brazil Syndicate R. & B. Co., Inc."

Telegram:

                "Greensburg, Indiana, Mar. 10, 1913.
"Brazil Syndicate R. & B. Co. New York.
        Telegram received. Ship twenty-five fifties Santos fours at quotation.        W. H. Robbins & Co."

On March 19, 1913, in response to said letter and telegrams, appellee shipped to appellants by the usual and ordinary routes of carriage, twenty-five bags of fifty pounds each of the coffee designated and so ordered by appellants; that the same was addressed and consigned to W. H. Robbins & Co., Greensburg, Indiana, and delivered to the Erie Railroad Company for transportation to appellants, and said railroad company accepted said coffee and undertook the delivery thereof; that appellee caused the same to be billed to appellants and mailed to them an invoice and bill of lading for the coffee so shipped as aforesaid, which invoice and bill of lading were received by appellants; that said railroad company was at said time a common carrier of goods and merchandise from the city of New York to Greensburg, Indiana, and other points; that it was understood by appellants that appellee was selling and appellants were buying twenty-five bags of fifty pounds each of coffee known as "Santos 4'S" at the agreed price of sixteen and a half cents per pound.

The memorandum accompanying the demurrer to the complaint is, in substance, as follows: The complaint does not aver that the goods sold were delivered to the purchasers; the averments do not show an unconditional purchase of the goods f. o. b. New York City; the averments do not show that the coffee shipped was the "same as last," nor do they explain the meaning of such phrase; the complaint shows that the goods were never delivered to the purchaser but were delivered to the Erie Railroad Company; the averments do not show an unconditional sale of the coffee without the right of inspection at Greensburg, Indiana, and confirmation or rejection and compliance with conditions of payment; the averments do not show that appellants received notice of the shipment or that the seller performed all the conditions of the sale to be performed by it. The theory of the complaint is that the letter and telegrams constitute a contract of sale; that appellants accepted the proposition and terms of appellee for the sale of twenty-five bags of the brand of coffee designated, at the price quoted, and that appellee thereupon duly consigned the shipment to appellants, sent them a bill of lading therefor, and delivered the coffee to the Erie Railroad Company, a common carrier of such goods from New York to Greensburg, Indiana, for transportation and delivery to appellants, and thereby they became the owners of the coffee at the time of its delivery to the railroad company as aforesaid.

Where goods are bought at one place to be consigned and transported to the purchaser at another place, in the absence of any arrangement or agreement to the contrary, the

1. general rule is that delivery by the seller to a common carrier of such goods, duly consigned to the purchaser, is a delivery to the purchaser, for the carrier thereby becomes the agent of the purchaser and title to the property passes to him at the time of such delivery. There are exceptions to this general rule, but, in the absence of facts showing a different agreement or arrangement, the presumption is that the general rule prevails. *Pennsylvania Co.* v. *Holderman* (1879), 69 Ind. 18, 26; *Pennsylvania Co.* v. *Poor* (1885), 103 Ind. 553, 554, 3 N. E. 253; *Sohn* v. *Jervis* (1885), 101 Ind. 578, 582, 1 N. E. 73; *Butler* v. *Pittsburgh, etc., R. Co.* (1897), 18 Ind. App. 656, 660, 46 N. E. 92; *Tebbs* v. *Cleveland, etc., R. Co.* (1897), 20 Ind. App. 192, 199, 50 N. E. 486; *Kilmer* v. *Moneyweight Scale Co.* (1905), 36 Ind. App. 568, 571, 76 N. E. 271; *Hill* v. *Fruita Mercantile Co.* (1908), 42 Col. 491, 497, 94 Pac. 354, 126 Am. St. 172; *Kelsea* v. *Ramsey & Gore Mfg. Co.* (1893), 55 N. J. Law 320, 26 Atl. 907, 22 L. R. A. 415, and notes; 4 Elliott, Railroads' (2d ed.) §1414; 5 Elliott, Contracts §5042.

The general rule above stated may be changed by agreement of the seller and purchaser, either express, or implied from facts and circumstances or an established course of dealing, but the rule is not changed by a mere right of inspection to ascertain whether the goods delivered are,

in fact, such as were purchased. The right of inspection,
in the absence of any established custom or agree-

2.  ment to the contrary, does not prevent the title from
passing to the purchaser on delivery to the carrier
of the goods duly consigned to the purchaser, but, if on
inspection the goods are not found to be such as were purchased, that fact may authorize a rescission of the contract
of sale. *Wind* v. *Iler & Co.* (1895), 93 Iowa 316, 61 N. W.
1001, 27 L. R. A. 219, 220; *Foley* v. *Felrath* (1892), 98
Ala. 176, 13 South. 485, 39 Am. St. 39; *Boothby* v. *Plaisted*
(1871), 51 N. H. 436, 437, 12 Am. Rep. 140; 4 Elliott, Railroads (2d ed.) §1414; 35 Cyc 195.

If goods are sold to be delivered by the seller at the
residence or place of business of the purchaser, a delivery
to the carrier is not a delivery to the purchaser, for

3.  in such case the carrier is the agent of the seller
and not of the purchaser. In such instance failure
to deliver the goods to the purchaser according to the terms
of the sale will defeat recovery of the purchase price of the
goods. 2 Benjamin, Sales (1889) §1040; 35 Cyc 195, and
cases cited; *Braddock Glass Co.* v. *Irwin* (1893), 152 Pa.
440, 25 Atl. 490; *McNeal* v. *Braun* (1891), 53 N. J. Law
617, 23 Atl. 687, 26 Am. St. 441; *Devine* v. *Edwards* (1881),
101 Ill. 138, 141; *Murray* v. *Nichols Mfg. Co.* (1890), 11 N.
Y. Supp. 734; *Bartlett* v. *Jewett* (1884), 98 Ind. 206; *Sohn*
v. *Jervis, supra.*

The amended second paragraph of answer admits the
execution of the letter and telegrams set out in the complaint, but it avers that the phrase "same as last" in
appellants' letter of March 8, 1914, had reference to
a former shipment of coffee by appellee to appellants
and that both parties then and there understood the same
and that it had a special meaning and referred to the condition and terms of delivery and payment for said former
shipment and both parties knew and understood that by the
quotation asked for in said letter the coffee was to be

delivered to the purchasers in Greensburg, Indiana, as former shipments had been delivered, and that "Santos 4'S" was a standard grade of coffee quoted and sold generally on the market and was so designated by all dealers in coffee; that in November, 1912, a shipment of such coffee was made to appellants upon the express agreement that said coffee should be delivered to appellants at Greensburg, Indiana, and there to be examined by them and, if satisfactory, to be accepted and paid for within ninety days from the date of such delivery to them in Greensburg, and such former shipment was delivered to and paid for by appellants on such conditions; that in January, 1913, appellants made another similar purchase and the same was shipped, examined, accepted and paid for within ninety days from the date of delivery in Greensburg, under the aforesaid terms and conditions; that when the purchase was made in November, 1912, as aforesaid, it was expressly agreed by and between appellants and appellee that any future purchase of coffee made by appellants should be upon the condition that the same would be delivered by appellee to appellants at Greensburg, Indiana, subject to inspection and payment as above stated; that appellee did not deliver the aforesaid purchase of coffee of March 10, 1913, or any part thereof, to appellants in Greensburg, Indiana, and the same has never been delivered to them. The third paragraph of answer is substantially the same as the amended second paragraph.

The gist of the memoranda accompanying the demurrers to the special answers is that the answers do not show that the contract of sale is indefinite, uncertain or ambiguous; that the meaning of the phrase "same as last" is not uncertain, indefinite, or ambiguous, when read in connection with the whole contract set out in the complaint.

Accepting the theory of the complaint as indicated by its general tenor, the contract of sale must be determined by a consideration of the letter and telegrams set out therein

in the light of the other averments, and in so doing
4. effect must be given to all parts thereof if it can be
done reasonably without doing violence to the evident intention of the parties as ascertained from a due
consideration of all portions of the writings. Where the
contract is in writing and the language employed
5. is unambiguous, it is a cardinal rule of construction
that it shall be so interpreted as to carry into effect
the intention of the parties as expressed by the writings.
If the language or any portion thereof is ambiguous
6. or of uncertain meaning or application, parol evidence may be heard, not to vary or contradict the
writings, but to ascertain the sense in which the language was used and its 'application to the subject-matter of the contract, to arrive at the true intention of the
parties at the time the contract was entered into. In
ascertaining such intention the court will, if necessary, consider the relation and situation of the parties, the character
of the transaction and all the surroundings and conditions
attending the execution of the contract. *Warrum* v. *White*
(1908), 171 Ind. 574, 577, 86 N. E. 959; *Hitz* v. *Warner*
(1910), 47 Ind. App. 612, 618, 93 N. E. 1005; *Chapman* v.
*Lambert* (1911), 176 Ind. 461, 467, 96 N. E. 459; *Olds
Wagon Works* v. *Coombs* (1890), 124 Ind. 62, 65, 24 N. E.
589; *Martindale* v. *Parsons* (1884), 98 Ind. 174, 179; *Leiter*
v. *Emmons* (1897), 20 Ind. App. 22, 25, 50 N. E. 40; *Thomas*
v. *Troxel* (1900), 26 Ind. App. 322, 327, 59 N. E. 683; *Kann*
v. *Brooks* (1913), 54 Ind. App. 625, 101 N. E. 513.

In *Olds Wagon Works* v. *Coombs, supra,* (p. 65) Judge
Mitchell used language appropriate to the case at bar, viz.:
"In interpreting a contract the language employed therein
is the exclusive medium through which to ascertain its meaning; but in case the terms employed are ambiguous, or
susceptible of more than one meaning, the situation of the
parties and the circumstances under which the contract was
made may become a proper subject of inquiry in order to

arrive at the sense in which the language was employed. *Cravens* v. *Eagle Cotton Mills Co.,* 120 Ind. 6, and cases cited. This in nowise militates against the rule that the meaning of the parties is to be ascertained from the language used in the writing, and that the interpretation of the instrument is a duty resting upon the court. The court may, however, in a proper case, direct the jury that the instrument may mean one thing or the other, depending upon extraneous circumstances to be found by them from the evidence.''

In *Leiter* v. *Emmons, supra,* (p. 25) this court, by Robinson, C. J., said: ''As it was a contract made with reference to a particular business, it is presumed that it was made with reference to the ordinary course of such business. In such case it would be proper to consider the general and known course of business of appellants. While it is true that usage cannot control an express contract, yet where a contract is ambiguous, the presumption is that it was made with reference to the known usage or general course of the particular business. In such case the question becomes one of fact to be determined as any other question of fact.''

In our view the contract under consideration is ambiguous and especially the phrase "same as last" in the letter of March 8, 1913. This phrase is susceptible of more than one meaning. It was used by appellants in connection with a particular business, and was addressed to appellee with whom the answer shows appellants had established a course of dealing in which the phrase so used may have been understood by all the parties to have the meaning alleged in the answer. In such instance the previous established course of dealing and agreements between the parties, their situation and the circumstances under which the contract was made, became proper subjects of inquiry to ascertain the application of the phrase and the sense in which the language was employed.

If, as alleged in the answer, appellee undertook to deliver

the goods to appellants at Greensburg, the shipment would not be controlled by the general rule above announced, and failure to so deliver them would be a complete defense to appellee's suit. We therefore hold that each of the special answers states a defense to the cause of action alleged in the complaint and it was error to sustain the demurrers thereto.

The judgment is reversed, with instructions to overrule each of the demurrers to the special answers, and for further proceedings not inconsistent with this opinion.

Note.—Reported in 114 N. E. 707. Sales, delivery of goods to carrier as delivery to purchasers, 20 Ann. Cas. 1027; Ann. Cas. 1916A 1046; 35 Cyc 193. See under (2) 35 Cyc 289; (3) 35 Cyc 195; (4) 35 Cyc 97; (5) 9 Cyc 577.

---

## HERALD PUBLISHING COMPANY *v.* STATE OF INDIANA, EX REL. BOARD OF COMMISSIONERS OF THE COUNTY OF MADISON.

[No. 9,200. Filed January 4, 1917.]

1. PAYMENT.—*Recovery of Payments.—Mutual Mistake.—Fraudulent Claim.—Demand.*—The rule that, where there has been a mutual mistake in the payment of money, the party receiving it must first be given an opportunity to return it before an action will lie for its recovery applies only in cases in which there has been neither a breach of a contract nor a duty, and not where money has been paid on items which the defendant knowingly and fraudulently included in bills rendered to plaintiff. p. 467.

2. COUNTIES.—*Illegal Payments.—Recovery.—Auditor's Certificate. —Statutes.*—Under §§5955, 5962 Burns 1914, Acts 1899 pp. 343, 357, 362, a claim against a county must be accompanied by a certificate from the auditor showing that the quality of the goods furnished and the price corresponded with the provisions of the contract under which they were purchased, and money paid by a county on claims not so certified to may be recovered by it. p. 467.

3. COUNTIES.—*Claims.—Partial Allowance.—Acceptance.—Effect.*— Where a bill against a county is allowed in part by the board of

county commissioners and the part so allowed is accepted and receipted for by the claimant, the acceptance is a settlement or determination of the claim. p. 468.

4. APPEAL. — *Harmless Error.* — *Ruling on Demurrer.* — *Want of Memorandum of Defects.*—While it is error for the trial court to sustain a demurrer not accompanied by the memorandum required by statute, yet such ruling is not prejudicial where the pleading attacked is defective in many respects, and in such case the court on appeal will look beyond the mere form of the demurrer to uphold the ruling of the trial court. p. 468.

5. APPEAL.—*Questions Presented.—Record.—Refusal of Instructions.*—Error cannot be predicated on the trial court's refusal to give requested instructions, unless it appears affirmatively from the record that they were offered at the proper time and in the appropriate mode. p. 469.

6. APPEAL. — *Instructions Refused.* — *Absence of Evidence.* — *Presumption.*—Where the evidence is not in the record, it will be presumed on appeal that requested instructions were not applicable to the evidence and were properly refused for that reason. p. 469.

From Madison Superior Court; *H. Clarence Austill,* Judge.

Action by the State of Indiana, on the relation of the Board of Commissioners of the County of Madison, against the Herald Publishing Company. From a judgment for relator, the defendant appeals. *Affirmed.*

*Paul P. Haynes* and *Oswald Ryan,* for appellant.
*Walter Vermillion,* for appellee.

IBACH, J.—This was an action by appellee against appellant to recover a sum of money alleged to have been allowed by appellee in violation of law. There was also a cross-complaint filed by appellant in which it sought to recover a sum of money alleged to be due for the printing of supplies for appellee for other years. This went out on demurrer. Upon a trial had there was judgment for appellee for $95 and $10 attorney fees. To reverse this judgment appellant prosecutes this appeal.

The complaint alleges substantially that appellant is a printing company, and that in the year 1910 appellee contracted with it for the printing of tax receipts to be used in the year 1911. The contract provided that the receipts were to be furnished at the rate of sixty-five cents per hundred. Appellant furnished a large number of such receipts and filed its bill with appellee for the same at the rate of eighty cents per hundred and was allowed therefor $151.72 more than it was under its contract entitled to receive. It is charged that "the defendant in violation of the terms of his contract presented said bill for such receipts at the rate of eighty cents per hundred and that the defendant knowingly, unlawfully and fraudulently included in said bill so filed the sum of $151.72 more than it was entitled to receive and that it failed to obtain the certificate required in such cases."

A demurrer to the complaint for insufficient facts, accompanied by a memorandum specifying that no demand was made, was overruled and excepted to. This action of the trial court is the first error assigned.

The well-known rule that where there has been a mutual mistake in the payment of money, the party receiving the same must first be given an opportunity to return
1. it before an action will lie for its recovery, applies only where there had been neither a breach of contract nor a duty. It has no application here, where it is averred that the money had been paid on items which the defendant "knowingly, unlawfully and fraudulently" included in said bills so filed. These averments do not indicate a mutual mistake of the parties, but rather a wrongful presentation of an unlawful claim to appellee by appellant and the wrongful acceptance of the money paid it. *Worley* v. *Moore* (1881), 77 Ind. 567; *Sharkey* v. *Mansfield* (1882), 90 N. Y. 227, 43 Am. Rep. 161.

It is also averred in the complaint that appellant did not procure to be filed with its claim the certificate
2. of the auditor certifying that the quality of the goods and the price corresponded to the provisions of the

contract. It is expressly provided by statute that under such state of facts payment of appellant's claim was illegal. And it is also expressly provided by statute that claims, if paid, may be recovered in an action at law against the person receiving the same. §§5955, 5962 Burns 1914, Acts 1899 pp. 343, 357, 362. It is apparent that the action under consideration is based on these statutes.

It is next insisted that the court erred in sustaining appellee's demurrer to appellant's cross-complaint. The cross-complaint seeks to recover for receipts printed and used under a different contract for the year 1910. The averments disclose the fact that the bill for such printing was filed and allowed in part, which appellant obtained and receipted for. Since it is made to appear from the cross-complaint itself that appellant's bill for print-

3.  ing for the year 1910 was allowed in part and refused in part, and the part allowed was accepted and receipted for, such acceptance constitutes a settlement or determination of the claim so filed. *Butler* v. *Board, etc.* (1911), 177 Ind. 440, 98 N. E. 185; *Western Construction Co.* v. *Board, etc.* (1912), 178 Ind. 684, 98 N. E. 347.

Appellant's chief contention, however, is that the court should not have considered the demurrer to this pleading

4.  for the reason that no memorandum was filed with the demurrer. This precise question has not been passed upon by either of the courts of appeal of this state. Both courts, however, have held that it may look beyond the grounds stated in the memorandum which accompanies the demurrer to uphold the ruling of the trial court in sustaining a demurrer, and if such ruling of the trial court is correct on any ground it will be upheld, although the memorandum did not point out the particular ground on which the demurrer was sustained. *Boes* v. *Grand Rapids, etc., R. Co.* (1915), 59 Ind. App. 271, 108

N. E. 174, 109 N. E. 411; *Bruns* v. *Cope* (1914), 182 Ind. 289, 105 N. E. 471. Under these holdings, following the same line of reasoning, it would seem that, while a demurrer for want of facts containing no memorandum should not have been considered, but was considered, and the pleading to which it was addressed was defective for want of some essential allegation, the action of the trial court in sustaining the demurrer would not be held reversible error.

In this case the cross-complaint was bad in many respects. No harm could possibly come to appellant on account of the ruling complained of. Under such circumstances this court will look beyond the mere form of the demurrer to uphold the trial court.

Finally appellant contends that there was error in overruling its motion for a new trial, particularly with reference to the refusal of the court to give certain tendered

5. instructions. The record fails to disclose any request prior to the commencement of the argument that the offered instructions be given. Appellant is therefore in no position to complain. Error cannot be based on the refusal to give tendered instructions unless it appears affirmatively from the record that they were offered in due season and in the appropriate mode. *German Fire Ins. Co.* v. *Columbia, etc., Tile Co.* (1896), 15 Ind. App. 623, 638, 43 N. E. 41, and cases cited. Again the evidence is not before us, so that, if the instructions had been tendered opportunely, it would be presumed that they were not

6. applicable to the evidence and were refused on that account. *Jenkins* v. *Wilson* (1895), 140 Ind. 544, 40 N. E. 39; *Hamline* v. *Engle* (1895), 14 Ind. App. 685, 42 N. E. 760, 43 N. E. 463.

An examination of the instructions referred to clearly show they are not applicable to the theory of the complaint, which, as we have said, is clearly an action under the statute to recover illegal payments made by the board of commissioners.

We find no reversible error in the record. Judgment affirmed.

NOTE.—Reported in 114 N. E. 703. See under (1) 30 Cyc 1323; (3) 11 Cyc 599. Effect of allowance or rejection by county of claim presented against it, 55 Am. St. 203.

---

## GREER v. LAKE ET AL.

[No. 9,140. Cause transferred to Supreme Court January 4, 1917.]

COURTS.—*Appellate Jurisdiction.—Statutes.—Construction.* — Under §1389 Burns 1914, Acts 1903 p. 280, providing that appeals shall not be taken to the Supreme or Appellate Courts in any civil case where the amount in controversy, exclusive of interests and costs, does not exceed $50, except as provided in §1391 Burns 1914, Acts 1901 p. 565, declaring that in every case where the question of the validity or proper construction of a statute is presented, and which case would be otherwise unappealable under §1389 Burns 1914, shall be appealable directly to the Supreme Court, and the Appellate Court has no jurisdiction in a case where the judgment appealed from is less than $50, and such case is appealable to the Supreme Court for the sole and express purpose of procuring the construction of a statute.

From Morgan Circuit Court; *Nathan A. Whittaker,* Judge.

Action by Martin Lake and another against James C. Greer. From a judgment for plaintiffs, the defendant appeals. *Transferred to Supreme Court.*

*S. C. Kivett* and *G. J. Kivett,* for appellant.

*H. L. McGinniss* and *Will H. Pigg,* for appellees.

CALDWELL, J.—The board of commissioners of Morgan county, in proceedings brought to that end, ordered a certain public highway to be graded, rebuilt and surfaced, under the provisions of §7711 *et seq.* Burns 1908, Acts 1905 p. 521, 550, commonly known as the three-mile road law. Appellant was the contractor. In performing the work he destroyed certain fences on appellees' lands and made certain extensive excavations thereon, by reason of which appellees brought this action against him in the Morgan

Circuit Court to recover damages alleged to have been suffered by them. A trial resulted in a verdict for $40, on which judgment was rendered.

The fact that the judgment does not exceed $50 invokes the application of §§1389, 1391 Burns 1914. The former is §6 of the act of 1901 (Acts 1901 p. 565), as amended in 1903 (Acts 1903 p. 280). Originally this section was to the effect that appeals in civil cases within the jurisdiction of a justice of the peace should not be taken to the Supreme or Appellate Court, except as provided in §8 of the act. As amended in 1903, it is as follows: "No appeal shall hereafter be taken to the Supreme or Appellate Court in any civil case where the amount in controversy, exclusive of interest and costs, does not exceed $50, except as provided in §8 of this Act. Section 8 of the act of 1901 (§1391, *supra*) remains unchanged, and is as follows: "Every case in which there is in question, and such question is duly presented, either the validity of a franchise, or the validity of an ordinance of a municipal corporation or the constitutionality of a statute, state or federal, or the proper construction of a statute, or rights guaranteed by the state or federal constitution, and which case would be otherwise unappealable by virtue of section six (6) or section seven (7), shall be appealable directly to the Supreme Court, for the purpose of presenting such question only."

Section 7 referred to in the foregoing section is §1390 Burns 1914. It deals only with criminal cases, and is, therefore, not applicable here. Section 9 of the act of 1901 was in part as follows: "No appealable case shall hereafter be taken directly to the Supreme Court, unless it be within one of the following classes: First. Cases in which there is in question, and such question is duly presented, either the validity of a franchise, or the validity of an ordinance of a municipal corporation, or the constitutionality of a statute, state or federal, or rights guaranteed by the state or federal constitution. * * * All other appealable cases shall be taken to the Appellate Court.'' The quoted portion of §9 was amended in 1907 (Acts 1907 p. 237), to read as follows: ''Hereafter all appeals in appealable cases in the following classes shall be taken directly to the Supreme Court, viz.: First. All cases in which there is in question, and such question is duly presented, either the validity of a franchise or the validity of an ordinance of a municipal corporation, or the constitutionality of a statute, state or federal, or the rights guaranteed by the state or federal constitution. * * * All appealable cases, other than those herein mentioned, shall be taken to the Appellate Court.'' The section as amended is §1392 Burns 1914.

Of the exceptions specified by §1391, *supra,* by virtue of the existence of which this cause might be appealable, there is no contention that any are involved except it be a question of the proper construction of a statute. If such question is involved and duly presented, the cause is appealable by virtue of such section. As we must first ascertain whether this court has jurisdiction to hear this appeal in the event that it is appealable, we do not at this time determine whether the proper construction of a statute is involved and presented.

This court has assumed jurisdiction of like appeals at least to the extent of determining that the question involved therein did not come within any of the exceptions specified by §1391, *supra. Schultz* v. *Alter* (1915), 60 Ind. App. 245, 110 N. E. 230; *Mantle Lamp Co.* v. *Bonich* (1915), 60 Ind. App. 275, 110 N. E. 558; *Yakey* v. *Leich* (1905), 37 Ind. App. 393, 76 N. E. 926. Like cases have been appealed directly to the Supreme Court also, and final disposition has been made of them by such court. *Pittsburgh, etc., R. Co.* v. *Sneath Glass Co.* (1914), 183 Ind. 138, 107 N. E. 72; *Chicago, etc., R. Co.* v. *Anderson* (1914), 182 Ind. 140, 105 N. E. 49; *Chicago, etc., R. Co.* v. *Ebersole* (1909), 173 Ind. 332, 90 N. E. 608; *Stults* v. *Board, etc.* (1907),

168 Ind. 539, 81 N. E. 471, 11 Ann. Cas. 1021; *Hood* v.
*Baker* (1905), 165 Ind. 562, 76 N. E. 243.

Section one of the act creating the Appellate Court (Acts
1891 p. 39), as amended in 1893 (Acts 1893 p. 29, §1382
Burns 1914), conferred jurisdiction on such court over all
appeals in actions for the recovery of a money judgment
only where the amount in controversy, exclusive of costs,
did not exceed $3,500.  Certain causes were excepted, how-
ever, as those involving the constitutionality of a statute,
etc.  The effect of §9 of the act of 1901, *supra*, however,
was to extend to the Appellate Court jurisdiction in such
cases regardless of the amount in controversy, subject to
exceptions as indicated by the quoted portions of such sections, *supra*.  Such section, as amended in 1907 (Acts 1907
p. 237, §1392 Burns 1914), provides in its fourteenth subdivision, however, that all cases wherein the amount of
money in controversy, exclusive of interest and costs on the
judgment of the trial court exceeds $6,000 shall be taken
directly to the Supreme Court.  There are exceptions here
also as indicated by the quoted portion of said section,
*supra*.  The effect of the amendment is to limit the jurisdiction of the Appellate Court in such cases to appeals
wherein the amount in controversy does not exceed $6,000.
It will be observed that under the various statutes and
amendments to which we have last referred in the absence of
the applicability of some exception, jurisdiction in this
appeal would be in the Appellate Court.  But by the terms
of §1389, *supra*, this cause is not appealable to either the
Supreme or Appellate Court, unless it comes with an exception specified by §1391, *supra*.  If §1392, *supra*, should be
considered alone, jurisdiction in this appeal would be in the
Appellate Court, by reason of the fact that the amount in
controversy does not exceed $6,000.  But by the terms of
§1389, *supra*, this cause is not appealable to the Appellate
Court, and as a consequence, the Appellate Court has no
jurisdiction over it, unless such a result is prevented by

recourse to some exception contained in §1391, *supra,* or by some other statute. There is no such other statute. Section 1391 does not refer to the Appellate Court, but provides that if this cause comes within any of the exceptions noted by such section, · it shall be appealable directly to the Supreme Court.

From the organization of the Appellate Court, there have been provisions under the various acts by which in effect causes might be appealable to the Supreme Court from trial courts through the Appellate Court. §1392 Burns 1914, *supra;* §10, Acts 1901 p. 565, §1394 Burns 1914; §25, Acts 1891, *supra;* §3, Acts 1893, *supra;* §1429 Burns 1914. In view of such fact, the language contained in §1391, *supra,* that causes coming within any exception outlined by that section "shall be appealable directly to the Supreme Court," is significant. Like language is used in §1392, prescribing the jurisdiction of the Supreme Court, as "hereafter all appeals in appealable cases in the following classes shall be taken directly to the Supreme Court." Such language apparently is used in recognition that there may be not only a direct appeal to the Supreme Court, but also what may be denominated an indirect appeal from the trial court through the Appellate Court to the Supreme Court. If so, §1392 apparently authorizes the former. In our judgment sections 1391 and 1392 should be construed together, with the result that the jurisdiction of the Supreme Court is confined to appeals in causes that are included in the classes specified by the latter, except that jurisdiction is in that court also over causes appealable for limited purposes by virtue of the exceptions indicated by the former. Otherwise the two sections are to an extent contradictory, unless by the term "appealable cases" as used in §1392, *supra,* the legislature did not intend to include causes appealable only for limited purposes by virtue of §1391, *supra.* A construction as indicated is in harmony with very substantial reasons why jurisdiction should be in that court over causes appealable for the sole and express purpose of procuring the construction of a statute. We therefore conclude that this court has no jurisdiction over this appeal.

Per Curiam: It is ordered on the foregoing opinion that this cause be transferred to the Supreme Court for want of jurisdiction in this court to hear and determine it.

NOTE.—Reported in 114 N. E. 699.

---

## TOWN OF CARLISLE *v.* PIRTLE.

[No. 9,301. Filed January 5, 1917.]

1. PLEADING.—*Demurrer to Answer.—Memorandum of Defects.— Failure to File.—Waiver.*—The right to question an answer for insufficiency of facts is waived by failure to file with a demurrer thereto the memorandum of defects required by statute, and no question is presented for review on appeal by an assignment of error challenging the action of the trial court in overruling such demurrer. p. 477.

2. NUISANCES.—*Public Nuisance.—Private Nuisance.—Distinction.* —The distinction between a public and a private nuisance does not necessarily consist in the nature of the thing done or of the character of the structure maintained, either of which may constitute a public nuisance if prejudicial to the general public, and also a private nuisance as to some particular person if he suffers an injury not common to the general public. p. 480.

3. MUNICIPAL CORPORATIONS. — *Public Nuisance. — Obstruction in Street.—Abatement.*—An unauthorized and unlawful obstruction of a public street in a town or city is a public nuisance, and as such may be abated. p. 480.

4. MUNICIPAL CORPORATIONS.—*Public Nuisance.—Power of Incorporated Towns to Declare and Abate.—Statute.*—Under §9005, cl. 4, Burns 1914, Acts 1909 pp. 359, 363, incorporated towns are authorized to declare, by general ordinance, what shall constitute a nuisance and to prevent, abate or remove it, and they may also at their election resort to the courts to abate a public nuisance. p. 481.

5. MUNICIPAL CORPORATIONS. — *Public Nuisance. — Obstruction in Street.—Abatement by Incorporated Town.—Burden of Proof.—* Where an incorporated town resorted to the courts to have declared a nuisance and abated as such a cement sidewalk which was built on a higher grade than the walks adjoining at either end, the town assumed the burden of establishing that the walk,

by reason of its comparative elevation, was a public nuisance, in that its use was perilous to pedestrians. p. 481.

6. APPEAL.—*Briefs.—Specification of Errors.—Rules of Court.*— Where appellant assigns as error the overruling of its motion for a new trial, and its brief under such assignment contains four points, each general in its nature, to the effect that it is error to admit evidence of a certain nature, and such points are not directed to any particular ruling complained of, there is a failure to comply with the rules of the Appellate Court and no question is presented for review on appeal. p. 481.

From Greene Circuit Court; *Cyrus E. Davis*, Special Judge.

Action by the Town of Carlisle against George W. Pirtle. From a judgment for defendant, the plaintiff appeals. *Affirmed.*

*J. R. Cauble, Webster V. Moffett* and *Fred C. Braun*, for appellant.

*John W. Lindley, Louis Meyer, Claude E. Gregg, William L. Slinkard* and *Will R. Vosloh*, for appellee.

CALDWELL, J.—In the summer of 1913, appellee constructed, in front of his premises in the town of Carlisle, Sullivan county, a concrete sidewalk, extending along the side of a public street. The sidewalk was somewhat more elevated than the sidewalks to which it joined at each end. In November, 1913, appellant brought this action in the Sullivan Circuit Court. The complaint charges, in substance, that appellee, by constructing his sidewalk elevated as aforesaid, formed at either end a sudden rise or step where it joined the walks in front of the adjoining properties; that the walk as constructed constituted a dangerous obstruction to the sidewalk on the north side of the street, and that persons walking along such sidewalk were in constant peril of stumbling against such sudden rise or step, and thereby suffering injuries, and that appellant would thereby be rendered liable to respond in damages to the persons so injured. The relief sought is that the structure be declared to be a public nuisance and that the court order it abated and the obstruction removed.

By regular proceedings the cause was venued to the Greene Circuit Court where it was tried before a special judge. By request of the parties, the court made a special finding of facts, and stated conclusions of law thereon. Judgment was rendered on the conclusions in favor of appellee. Five errors are assigned in this court: the first, third and fourth being, in substance, that the court erred in overruling appellant's demurrer to appellee's amended fourth paragraph of answer; the court erred in each conclusion of law and in overruling the motion for a new trial. The second and fifth errors are not properly assigned. The questions sought to be raised by such assignments, however, are properly presented by the third assignment.

The demurrer filed to the amended fourth paragraph of answer sought to challenge the sufficiency of the facts thereby pleaded to constitute a defense. A memorandum 1. stating wherein such facts were insufficient was not filed with the demurrer. The right to question the answer for insufficiency of facts was therefore waived. It follows that the first assignment presents no question for our consideration. *Pittsburgh, etc., R. Co.* v. *Home Ins. Co.* (1915), 183 Ind. 355, 108 N. E. 525; *Quality Clothes Shop* v. *Keeney* (1914), 57 Ind. App. 500, 106 N. E. 541.

The special finding of facts is, in substance, as follows: Appellant is a municipal corporation. Ledgerwood street, extending east and west, is one of the principal streets in the town of Carlisle. Eaton and Harrison streets, one block apart, and an alley midway between them, intersect Ledgerwood street at right angles. The latter street has a gradual fall eastward from Harrison street to the alley. Westward from the alley to Harrison street, the following persons own properties abutting on the north side of Ledgerwood street: Curtner, 19 feet; appellee, 40 feet; Trimble, 12 feet; Squires, 24 feet; National Bank, 32 feet; Ridgeway, 32 feet. On each lot there is a business building. Appellant has never established a grade for sidewalks in front of the Curtner, Pirtle and Trimble properties. In 1899, appellee, without consent of or objection from appellant, constructed a cement sidewalk in front of his property on the natural grade. In 1904, appellant, by ordinance, but without establishing any grade. for same, ordered a cement sidewalk constructed in front of the Curtner, Pirtle and Trimble properties. Pursuant to such ordinance, Curtner and Trimble constructed a cement sidewalk on the natural grade, under the direction and to the satisfaction of appellant's sidewalk committee, appellee's sidewalk not being changed. When such construction had been completed the sidewalk in front of the three properties sloped by regular fall on the natural grade of the street. In 1906, appellant, by ordinance, caused sidewalks to be constructed in front of the remaining properties in the half block, by the owners of such properties, on the grade of the sidewalks constructed in 1904, and under the direction of the committee on sidewalks, so that the sidewalks along the entire half block conformed to the natural grade of the street. Thereafter appellant graded and graveled Ledgerwood street, and thereby elevated it about four inches above the sidewalks on the north. Thereafter cement sidewalks were constructed along the south side of the street opposite the half block above mentioned, the grade of which conformed to the raised grade of the street. Thereafter, appellee, of his own volition and without obtaining the consent of appellant, constructed a cement crossing from the south side of the street north to the east end of the sidewalk in front of his property. The crossing conformed to the grade of the sidewalks on the south side of the street, but was four or five inches higher than the sidewalk on the north where the two structures joined. Appellant acquiesced in such work, and paid appellee his expenses thereof. After the grade of the street was raised, and before appellee raised his sidewalk as hereinafter set out, and because of the raising of the grade

of the street, water in time of heavy rains overflowed the
gutters in front of appellee's and Curtner's properties and
flowed in considerable quantities upon such properties.   To
prevent such overflow was one of appellee's purposes in raising the sidewalk, and the work was successful to that end.
From the north end of the crossing above mentioned to
appellee's sidewalk before he raised it, there was a step of
four or five inches, creating a condition to some extent
dangerous to pedestrians in the exercise of ordinary care.
Prior to August, 1913, appellee's buildings were destroyed
by fire, and his sidewalk damaged.   He thereupon, in August, 1913, removed the old sidewalk and constructed a new
concrete sidewalk conforming to the grade of said concrete
crossing.   The new walk, as constructed by appellee, is three
and one-half inches on its outer edge and four inches on its
inner edge higher than the Curtner walk to which it joins,
at a point seventeen inches west of the junction, and slopes
thence by regular grade to conform to the Curtner walk at
the junction.   The slope of the sidewalk at the junction is
open and obvious to persons traversing the same, unless left
in darkness.   The sidewalk is not dangerous to pedestrians
passing over it and exercising ordinary care for their own
safety, and it is not unsightly or otherwise offensive in
appearance.   The sidewalk is a permanent structure.   Appellant was not requested to and did not fix or establish
the grade of such sidewalk, and appellee did not have appellant's consent to construct the new sidewalk on higher grade
than the old one.   Appellant, before commencing this suit,
notified appellee in writing to make said sidewalk safe for
travel within ten days.   Appellee thereupon notified appellant that he stood ready to reconstruct the sidewalk to conform to any grade which appellant would establish by
ordinance.   He thereupon, by the use of some sharp instrument, nicked and permanently roughened the seventeen-inch
slope where said sidewalk joined the Curtner sidewalk.

The court stated as conclusions of law that the sidewalk

described in the complaint and finding is not a public nuisance, and that appellant is not entitled to have it abated as such; that the law is with appellee, and that appellant is not entitled to recover.

The exceptions to the conclusions of law present the single question whether the sidewalk under the finding is a public nuisance. It is provided by statute that whatever is injurious to health, or indecent, or offensive to the senses, or an obstruction to the free use of property so as essentially to interfere with the free enjoyment thereof is a nuisance and the subject of an action, and that such action may be brought by any person whose property is injuriously affected or whose personal enjoyment is lessened by the nuisance, and that where a proper case is made the nuisance may be enjoined or abated. §291 *et seq.* Burns 1914, §289 R. S. 1881.

While the statutory provision is broad enough to include both classes, the statutes referred to apparently afford a remedy for a private rather than a public nuisance.

2. The distinction between a public and a private nuisance, however, does not necessarily consist in the nature of the thing done or the character of the structure maintained. The thing done or structure maintained may be prejudicial to the general public, and thus it may constitute a public nuisance, and yet as to some particular person it may also be a private nuisance, in that by it he suffers an injury not common to the general public. 29 Cyc 1153; *Kissel* v. *Lewis* (1900), 156 Ind. 233, 59 N. E. 478; *Haggart* v. *Stehlin* (1893), 137 Ind. 43, 54, 35 N. E. 997, 22 L. R. A. 577; *City of New Albany* v. *Slider* (1898), 21 Ind. App. 392, 52 N. E. 626.

This action is prosecuted on the theory that the structure involved here is a public nuisance. An unauthorized and unlawful obstruction of a public street in a town

3. or city is a public nuisance, and as such may be abated. *State* v. *Louisville, etc., R. Co.* (1882), 86 Ind. 114; *Burk* v. *State* (1867), 27 Ind. 430; *O'Brien* v. *Cen-*

*tral Iron, etc., Co.* (1901), 158 Ind. 218, 63 N. E. 302, 57 L. R. A. 508, 92 Am. St. 305; *Zimmerman* v. *State* (1892), 4 Ind. App. 583, 31 N. E. 550; *Langsdale* v. *Bonton* (1859), 12 Ind. 467.

The cases above cited deal with the erecting and maintaining of buildings, fences, etc., in such a manner as to obstruct or infringe upon the limits of public streets. The structure involved here is an essential, or, at least, a very proper part of a public street, and if it constitutes a public nuisance, such fact consists in the manner of its construction. The complaint proceeds on such a theory.

Incorporated towns are authorized to declare, by general ordinance, what shall constitute a nuisance, and to prevent, abate, or remove the same. §9005, cl. 4, Burns 1914,

4. Acts 1909 p. 359, 363. They may also at their election resort to the courts to abate a public nuisance. *American Furniture Co.* v. *Town of Batesville* (1894), 139 Ind. 77, 38 N. E. 408; *Cheek* v. *City of Aurora* (1883), 92 Ind. 107; *City of Valparaiso* v. *Bozarth* (1899), 153 Ind. 536, 55 N. E. 439, 47 L. R. A. 487; *Billings Hotel Co.* v. *City, etc.* (1916), L. R. A. 1916D 1020, note.

Appellant here resorted to the courts, and in so doing assumed the burden of establishing that the sidewalk, by

5. reason of its comparative elevation, was a public nuisance, in that its use was perilous to pedestrians.

The finding of the court, as hereinbefore indicated, is against appellant on such question. It follows that the court did not err in the conclusions of law.

Appellant assigns error on the overruling of the motion for a new trial. Appellant's brief under such assignment

6. contains but four points, each general in its nature, and to the effect that it is error to admit evidence of a certain nature. The points are not directed to any particular ruling complained of, and, under a strict construction of the rules of this court, present no question.

*Standard Live Stock Ins. Co.* v. *Atkinson* (1916), 185 Ind.
34, 111 N. E. 913; *Rosenbaum Bros.* v. *Devine* (1916), 271
Ill. 354, 111 N. E. 97; *Cole Motor Car Co.* v. *Ludorff* (1915),
61 Ind. App. 119, 111 N. E. 447; *Warner* v. *Reed* (1916),
62 Ind. App. 544, 113 N. E. 386. We have, however, examined the motion for a new trial in an effort to apply such
general propositions, but find no material error. Judgment
affirmed.

NOTE.—Reported in 114 N. E. 705. Public nuisance, nature and
elements, 107 Am. St. 199. Private nuisance, nature and elements,
118 Am. St. 869; note 62 Ind. App. 676. See under (2) 29 Cyc
1152, 1153; (3) 28 Cyc 893.

---

## EVANSVILLE RAILWAYS COMPANY *v.* COOKSEY, ADMINISTRATRIX.

[No. 8,993. Filed May 11, 1916. Rehearing denied November 29,
1916. Transfer denied January 5, 1917.]

1. APPEAL.—*Briefs.—Questions Presented for Review.—Ruling on
Demurrer.—Scope of Review.*—Where appellant assigns as error
the overruling of its demurrer to the complaint but in its brief,
under "Points and Authorities," the complaint is challenged as
being insufficient in only one respect, the appellate tribunal is not
required to determine the sufficiency of the pleading on any other
point than the one attacked. p. 486.

2. MASTER AND SERVANT.—*Injuries to Servant.—Action.—Complaint.—Negligence.—Proximate Cause.*—Where, in an action for
wrongful death, the complaint avers that the injury to the decedent and his death was caused by the negligence of the defendant in operating its freight car on a defective track, which was
laid in violation of a city ordinance, and that all the wrongs and
grievances set out, particularly the death of decedent, were entirely due to the negligence of the defendant as set out in the
pleading, such complaint sufficiently charges that the negligence
alleged was the proximate cause of the injury suffered. p. 486.

3. MASTER AND SERVANT.—*Injuries to Servant. — Action. — Complaint.—Negligence.—General and Specific Allegations.*—Where, in
an action against a street railway company for wrongful death,
the complaint contains a general averment directly charging that
defendant's negligence in unlawfully constructing its tracks in too
close proximity to its poles was the proximate cause of the injury suffered, such general averment is not overcome by a spe-

cific allegation that decedent received his injury because the swaying of the car threw him through the door thereof and against a pole, and the complaint is sufficient as against demurrer, since the swaying of the car was but an incident in its operation which extended the negligence charged so as to result in the death. p. 487.

4. APPEAL.—*Review.*—*New Trial.*—*Effect.*—*Errors Prior Thereto.* —Where defendant procured the court below to grant it a new trial, it waived any error in that court's ruling, made prior to the order for the new trial, on its motion for judgment on the interrogatories. p. 488.

5. MASTER AND SERVANT.—*Injuries to Servant.*—*Contributory Negligence.*—*Answers to Interrogatories.*—Where, in an action against a street railway company for the wrongful death of a conductor who was injured when struck by a trolley pole, negligence is predicated on the alleged construction of the tracks too close to the trolley poles, the jury's answers to interrogatories showing that decedent knew that in passing the particular pole causing the injury it was dangerous to put one's head outside the car door, a motion for judgment on the interrogatories as showing decedent guilty of contributory negligence was properly denied, where the answers do not show that decedent voluntarily, unnecessarily or negligently extended any part of his person beyond the car, or that he was negligent in occupying a position near the door, as it must be assumed, in the absence of answers to the contrary, that decedent occupied such position in the discharge of his duties, and that while so engaged he was thrown through the door and against the pole by the swaying of the car, as alleged in the complaint. pp. 488, 490.

6. MASTER AND SERVANT.— *Injuries to Servant.* — *Assumption of Risk.*—*Violation of Ordinance.*—Where, in an action against a street railway company for the wrongful death of a conductor who was struck by a trolley pole, the negligence charged consisted in the violation of a city ordinance, the doctrine of assumption of risk is not applicable notwithstanding decedent's knowledge of the risk. p. 490.

7. MASTER AND SERVANT. — *Injuries to Servant.* — *Action.* — *Jury Questions.*—*Contributory Negligence.*—*Weighing Evidence.*—In an action against an electric line for the death of a conductor who was killed when struck by a trolley pole, where several witnesses testified that at the time of the accident decedent had his head out of the car door, and a single witness testified that while he was standing in the doorway, but wholly within the car, the swaying of the car threw him out of the door and against the pole, the weighing of the evidence and the credibility of the witness was for the jury to determine, and the court on appeal can

not disregard the evidence of the single witness and say as a matter of law that decedent was guilty of contributory negligence. p. 490.

8. MASTER AND SERVANT.—*Injuries to Servant.—Action.—Master's Negligence.—Violation of City Ordinance.—Proximate Cause.—Evidence.*—In an action against a street car company for the wrongful death of an employe, defendant's negligence, as established, in maintaining its tracks in violation of a city ordinance was actionable only if the proximate cause of decedent's injury, so that it was proper to permit an expert witness to testify that the manner in which the tracks were maintained at the place of the accident was improper construction, such evidence being pertinent to the question of proximate cause. p. 492.

9. MASTER AND SERVANT.—*Injuries to Servant.—Master's Negligence.—Violation of Municipal Ordinance.*—The violation by a street car company of a city ordinance requiring that double tracks be laid an equal distance from the center of the street, resulting in the death of an employe, constitutes negligence. p. 492.

10. MASTER AND SERVANT.—*Injuries to Servant.—Duty of Master.—Safe Place to Work.—Delegation of Duty.*—A street railway company using the tracks of another company is not relieved of liability for injury to its employes due to defective or negligent construction of the tracks because they are maintained by the other company, since the duty to provide a safe working place for employes is nondelegable. p. 493.

11. TRIAL.—*Refusal of Instructions.—Conformity to Pleading and Proof.*—It is proper to refuse requested instructions which are not applicable to the theory of the case and the evidence. p. 494.

From Warrick Circuit Court; *Ralph E. Roberts*, Judge.

Action by Minnie S. Cooksey, administratrix of the estate of Walter Cooksey, deceased, against the Evansville Railways Company. From a judgment for plaintiff, the defendant appeals. *Affirmed.*

*Albert W. Funkhouser, Arthur F. Funkhouser, Woodfin D. Robinson, W. E. Stilwell* and *U. W. Youngblood*, for appellant.

*G. V. Menzies* and *J. E. Williamson*, for appellee.

CALDWELL, J.—The following statement of facts disclosed by the complaint is sufficient for the determination of questions presented in support of the assignment that the court erred in overruling the demurrer thereto: On September 9,

1909, and for a number of years prior thereto, the Evansville Electric Railway Company was operating an electric street railway in the city of Evansville under an ordinance of the city. The Evansville and Mt. Vernon Electric Railway Company, appellant's predecessor, was organized to operate an interurban electric railway between the two cities indicated by its name. On September 11, 1905, it entered into a contract with the Evansville Electric Railway Company and the city of Evansville, by which it acquired the right to operate its cars, both freight and passenger, from the western limits of the city to a point therein over certain designated tracks of the latter company, which contract was in the form of an accepted ordinance of the city. On September 9, 1909, appellant, as the successor of the Evansville & Mt. Vernon Electric Railway Company, was operating the line connecting Evansville and Mt. Vernon, entering the former city under and by virtue of the terms of said contract. Franklin street extends eastward through said city, intersecting St. Joseph avenue at right angles. That part of Franklin street east of St. Joseph avenue is wider than the part which lies west of said avenue. Double tracks were laid and maintained on Franklin street. The tracks extending eastward along Franklin street described a compound curve at and near such intersection, such construction being necessary in order that the tracks might be kept near the center line of the street. On September 9, 1909, Walter Cooksey, appellee's decedent, was an employe of appellant as conductor of one of its freight cars. On said day, while the car of which decedent was conductor was traveling eastward into said city, and as it approached said intersection, decedent was standing at or near the north door of the car looking westward, whereupon the car, as it was traversing said curve, suddenly swayed, whereby decedent was thrown off his balance, and caused to pitch forward and outward, thereby bringing his head in violent contact with a trolley pole standing near the eastern terminus of the curve, whereby his skull was fractured and from which injury he died. The pole stood so near to the track that a car such as the one of which decedent was conductor cleared it by only five and one-half inches. The negligence charged consists in the violation of an ordinance of the city requiring that double tracks be laid so that the center line of the space between the two tracks should be the center line of the street, and whereby the tracks were brought in close proximity to such pole aforesaid, and also of the violation of another ordinance requiring that all tracks, trolley poles, etc., should be kept in safe condition, and that all cars should be adapted to operation upon said tracks without injury thereto, and that they should be suitable for the safe transportation of passengers. The car involved here was forty-five feet long and eight and one-half feet wide. The physical situation resulting from the negligence charged, as disclosed by the complaint, was to the effect that, as the south track was maintained nearer the center line of said street than the north track, the car, being of the dimensions aforesaid, cleared said pole only as alleged.

Appellant assigns error on the overruling of its demurrer to the complaint. In its brief, under "Points and Authorities," the complaint is attacked only on the ground

1. that it fails to disclose that the negligence charged was the proximate cause of the injury suffered. We are, therefore, not required to determine the sufficiency of the complaint from any other viewpoint. *Buffkin* v. *State* (1914), 182 Ind. 204, 106 N. E. 362; *Holler* v. *State* (1914), 182 Ind. 268, 106 N. E. 364; *Mutual Life Ins. Co.* v. *Finkelstein* (1914), 58 Ind. App. 27, 107 N. E. 557.

A sufficient charge of negligence being thus impliedly conceded, to ascertain whether a proximate relation of cause and effect between the negligence charged and the

2. injury alleged to have been suffered is disclosed by the complaint, is the limit of our duty if not of our power. As bearing on this subject, it is directly averred in the complaint that "the injury to the decedent and his

death were caused by the negligence of the defendant in operating said freight car on the said defective track, which track was laid in violation of said ordinance of the city of Evansville, as aforesaid.'' There is a further allegation that ''all the wrongs and grievances herein set out, particularly the death of her decedent, was entirely due to the negligence of the defendant as herein set out.'' The complaint is therefore sufficient as against the objection urged. *Baltimore, etc., R. Co.* v. *Peterson* (1900), 156 Ind. 364, 59 N. E. 1044; *Board, etc.* v. *Mutchler* (1894), 137 Ind. 140, 36 N. E. 534; *Chicago, etc., R. Co.* v. *Stephenson* (1903), 33 Ind. App. 95, 69 N. E. 270; 29 Cyc 573.

It is urged, however, that the complaint specifically discloses that the swaying of the car rather than the negligence charged was the proximate cause of the injury. The former is not alleged to have been caused by any negligent conduct or unusual act on appellant's part or by the intervention of any agency independent of the operation of the car in the usual way. The accident happened then in the ordinary operation of the car. It sufficiently appears from the complaint that in the absence of the wrongs averred, there would have been no injury and that the accident was of a nature that it, or some similar occurrence, might reasonably have been anticipated by appellant. As a practical proposition, it seems to us apparent that the predominating and efficient cause of the injury was the negligence charged by reason of which the car cleared the pole by the narrow margin alleged. The swaying of the car, like its onward movement, was but an incident in the operation of the car, and by which the negligence charged was extended effectively to its natural result. The specific averment therefore respecting the swaying of the car does not overcome the general averments on the subject of proximate cause. *Board, etc.* v. *Mutchler, supra; Bessler* v. *Laughlin* (1906), 168 Ind. 38, 79 N. E. 1033; *Cincinnati, etc., R. Co.* v. *Worthington* (1902), 30 Ind.

App. 663, 65 N. E. 557, 66 N. E. 478, 96 Am. St. 355;
*Terre Haute, etc., R. Co.* v. *Buck* (1884), 96 Ind. 346, 49
Am. Rep. 168; *Ohio, etc., R. Co.* v. *Trowbridge* (1890), 126
Ind. 391, 26 N. E. 64; *Louisville, etc., R. Co.* v. *Nitsche*
(1890), 126 Ind. 229, 26 N. E. 51, 9 L. R. A. 750, 22 Am.
St. 582.

This cause was first tried in the Gibson Circuit Court.
The former trial resulted in a verdict in favor of appellee.
Appellant thereupon in such court met with an
4. adverse ruling on its motion for judgment on the
answers to certain interrogatories returned with the
general verdict. Such ruling is assigned as error in this
court. Following such ruling, a new trial was granted on
appellant's motion. Appellant by procuring the Gibson Circuit Court to grant it a new trial waived the error, if any,
in the ruling on the motion for judgment. *King* v. *Inland
Steel Co.* (1911), 177 Ind. 201, 96 N. E. 337, 97 N. E. 529.

Appellant assigns error also on the overruling of its
motion for judgment on the answers to interrogatories
returned with the general verdict in the trial in the
5. Warrick Circuit Court. In support of such assignment, appellant states generally that the answers are
conclusive that decedent's own negligence was the proximate
cause of the injury. Appellant, to sustain such contention,
refers in argument to certain of the answers whereby the
jury found that decedent had cautioned other employes of
appellant to avoid injury to themselves by coming in contact with the poles on Franklin street, and that he had
warned them respecting the peril they would incur should
they extend their bodies outside the cars on the side next
to the poles, and that decedent knew that in passing this
particular pole the side of the freight car would come so
near it as to render it dangerous for a person to put his
head outside of the door of the car. These answers are
sufficient to establish that decedent knew that should he
extend any part of his person outside the car at the place

involved here on the side next to the pole and while the car
was moving toward it, he would be in danger of receiving serious injury by coming in contact therewith.  Moreover, should he voluntarily and when the proper discharge
of his duties did not require it, extend his body beyond the
line of the car, and as a consequence receive injury by coming in contact with the pole, such fact would go very far at
least toward convicting him of contributory negligence.  The
answers to interrogatories, however, do not establish that
decedent voluntarily, abstractedly or unnecessarily extended
any part of his person beyond the car, or that he was negligent in occupying his position near the door immediately
prior to the accident.  There being an averment in the complaint to that effect and the answers not disclosing the
contrary, it must be assumed in the present discussion that
appellee's decedent in occupying such position was acting
in harmony with the proper discharge of his duties as an
employe.  Under such circumstances, it cannot be said that
the fact that he occupied such position convicts him of contributory negligence.  This is true, although he had full
knowledge of the position of the pole and of its proximity
to the track, by reason of the negligence charged.  It is true
that, as so circumstanced, he subjected himself to the perils
growing out of the negligence charged, rendered potent by
certain incidents accompanying the operation of the car, as
its swaying, but to such a situation the principle of assumption of risk, rather than that of contributory negligence is
applicable; that is, although decedent knew that the track
was being maintained in violation of the ordinance, and that
the car would as a consequence pass very near the pole, yet,
if his occupying such position was consistent with his obligations as an employe, he could not be convicted of contributory negligence by reason of the mere fact that he occupied
such position.  If he exercised reasonable care for his own
safety while in such position, he was not guilty of contributory negligence.  If the action here were based on a common-

law liability, rather than on the violation of a city

6. ordinance, decedent's mere situation and knowledge
would have aroused the principle of assumption of
risk rather than that of contributory negligence, but as the
negligence charged consisted in the violation of city ordinances, the doctrine of assumption of risk is not applicable,
and the risk of the perils which decedent incurred by reason
of his position was not, as a legal proposition, assumed by
him notwithstanding his knowledge. *Chicago, etc., R. Co.* v.
*Lawrence* (1907), 169 Ind. 319, 327, 79 N. E. 363, 82 N.
E. 768; *Davis Coal Co.* v. *Polland* (1901), 158 Ind. 607, 62
N. E. 492, 92 Am. St. 319. In order that the principle of
contributory negligence might arise against decedent,

5. he must have been guilty of negligent conduct when
so situated, as, for example, that he voluntarily or
negligently extended his person beyond the car. The answers to the interrogatories do not establish that he was
guilty of any such action. On the contrary, it must be
assumed in the consideration of said motion that, while in
the discharge of his duties, his person was projected beyond
the car, and thus brought in contact with the pole, by reason
of the swaying of the car as alleged in the complaint. Under
such circumstances, the answers to interrogatories do not
establish contributory negligence, and the motion was properly overruled. For distinction between assumption of risk
and contributory negligence, see *Pittsburgh, etc., R. Co.* v.
*Hoffman* (1914), 57 Ind. App. 431, 439, 107 N. E. 315, and
cases cited.

Under the assignment in the motion for a new trial that
the evidence is insufficient to sustain the verdict, appellant
directs specific points only to the issue of contribu-

7. tory negligence. Our discussion will therefore be
confined to the same limits. The evidence bearing
on this issue is contradictory. Several witnesses testified
that as the car approached the pole decedent stood in the
north door, with his hand resting on the frame, his head

extended beyond the car, and that he was apparently gazing back at some object in the street, and that while in such position his head came in contact with the pole. If there were no other evidence bearing on this subject, appellant would probably be correct in its contention that decedent's contributory negligence is established. A witness, however, who was near, testified to a different state of facts. His testimony was to the effect that when the car was within a half-block of the street intersection, he observed decedent within the body of the car, opposite the doorway, engaged in stacking boxes of freight or some such work; that just before the car arrived opposite the pole, decedent stepped to the doorway and stood within the line of the car, his right hand resting on the west side of the frame, his back northward, and that he was apparently looking at some object in the west end of the car; that while in such position the car swayed, and that thereby decedent was thrown outward, his head coming in contact with the pole. Appellant apparently does not controvert the proposition that, if this testimony be considered as evidence, the record presents some evidence supporting the verdict on the issue of contributory negligence, and hence that this court could not say as matter of law that decedent was guilty of contributory negligence. Appellant's argument, as we interpret it, is to the effect that testimony is not necessarily evidence, and that, viewing the evidence as a whole bearing on such issue, this court should say as matter of law that the testimony of such witness is not credible, and hence that contributory negligence is established. The testimony of such witness was relevant. If true, it cannot be said as matter of law that decedent contributed to his injury by his own negligence. His credibility was for the jury. The weighing of his testimony with that of other witnesses who testified to a different state of facts was also for the jury. His testimony being relevant, it was for the jury rather than this court to say whether it arose to the dignity of evidence. The jury by their general verdict determined that question. We cannot say as matter of law that decedent was proven guilty of contributory negligence.

The evidence established that the trolley pole with which decedent came in contact was in the center of the street, but that by reason of the tracks at that point being 8. maintained in violation of the ordinance, the south track was substantially closer to the pole than the north track. Under such circumstances, the court permitted a qualified witness to testify over objection that the maintaining of the track in the close proximity to the pole indicated by the evidence was improper construction. We are inclined to agree with appellant in its contention that its negligence in this case cannot be determined by an application of the standard of proper or improper construction as fixed by the principles of railroad engineering. Its 9. negligence, as charged, is based on the alleged violation of certain ordinances. If it violated the ordinances, it was guilty of negligence. If it acted in 8. obedience to such ordinances, it was not in that respect guilty of negligence, regardless of the opinions of railroad engineers on the subject of proper track construction. However, appellant may have violated the ordinances and thereby have been guilty of negligence, and yet the negligence may not have been actionable because not the proximate cause of the injury. In this case the question of proximate cause was and is controverted. If a certain track construction is negligent because in violation of a statute or ordinance, then the fact as to whether, independent of the ordinance, and fundamentally considered, it was a proper or improper construction might have an important bearing in the process of determining whether such negligence was the proximate cause of the injury. The court, therefore, did not err in admitting the evidence under consideration.

Complaint is made also that certain offered testimony was

refused. Neither in appellant's statement of the record, in the motion for a new trial, nor in points made in support of errors assigned, are we referred to the respective places in the transcript where the alleged erroneous ruling may be found. We have, however, from certain references contained in the department of the brief devoted to the argument, endeavored to search out such rulings but find no material error.

The court refused instructions Nos. 4 and 11 requested by appellant. The substance of instruction No. 4 is that

10. proof that appellant maintained the track and pole at the place involved here was essential to a recovery.

This instruction is somewhat obscure. As we interpret it, however, it is to the effect that, regardless of the track's defective condition, by reason of its location, or of the extent to which its existence constituted a violation of the ordinance of the city of Evansville, or of appellant's knowledge along these lines, if some other company was in fact looking after the track and keeping it in repair, appellant, for such reason alone, is not liable in this action. It appears that appellant by virtue of a lease or running privilege was regularly using the track involved here in the operation of its cars. It therefore adopted such instrumentality as its own. It constituted a part of the place furnished by appellant to decedent in which to work, and where he was required to work. Appellant therefore owed decedent a duty to exercise reasonable care to place and keep such track in a reasonably safe condition. Such duty must be classed among those that are nondelegable. Appellant could not relieve itself from such duty by entrusting its performance to another corporation. The instruction was therefore properly refused. *Brady* v. *Chicago, etc., R. Co.* (1902), 114 Fed. 100, 52 C. C. A. 48, 57 L. R. A. 712; *Illinois Central R. Co.* v. *Sheegog* (1909), 215 U. S. 308, 30 Sup. Ct. 101, 54 L. Ed. 208; 33 Cyc 715; *Stetler* v. *Chicago, etc., R. Co.* (1879), 46 Wis. 497, 1 N. W. 112; *Wisconsin Central R. Co.* v. *Ross*

(1892), 142 Ill. 9, 31 N. E. 412, 34 Am. St. 49; *Story* v. *Concord, etc., R. Co.* (1900), 70 N. H. 364, 48 Atl. 288; *Hamilton* v. *Louisiana, etc., R. Co.* (1906), 6 L. R. A. (N. S.) 787, note.

Instruction No. 11 is to the effect that there could be no recovery in this action if decedent knew of the proximity of the pole to the track, and that one who extended 11. any part of his person beyond the car was likely to suffer injury by coming in contact therewith, and with such knowledge continued in appellant's employ without any promise that conditions would be changed. This instruction was properly refused. As we have indicated, there was evidence justifying the jury in finding that decedent's person was thrown from or extended beyond the car through no fault of his, and while in the discharge of his duties. That theory of the case is ignored by the requested instruction. We find no material error in the instructions given. There is no question presented from a consideration of which we should be justified in reversing this case. The judgment is therefore affirmed.

NOTE.—Reported in 112 N. E. 541. See under (2) 26 Cyc 1389; (5) 26 Cyc 1514; (6) 26 Cyc 1181; (7) 26 Cyc 1482; (10) 26 Cyc 1104. Violation of statute or ordinance not intended for plaintiff's benefit as actionable negligence, 9 Ann. Cas. 427; Ann. Cas. 1912D 1106; Ann. Cas. 1916B 301.

---

## EXCEL FURNITURE COMPANY *v.* BROCK.

[No. 9,162.   Filed January 5, 1917.]

1. APPEAL.—*Review.—Overruling Demurrer to Bad Answer.—Reversible Error.*—Overruling a demurrer to a bad answer is reversible error, even though the evidence admissible thereunder might have been presented under a general denial. p. 498.

2. SALES.—*Action for Price.—Answer.—Sufficiency.*—In an action on account to collect for goods sold, the averments of the answer are held sufficient to show that plaintiff's agent, who was indebted to defendant, assumed to have authority to sell the goods

and have the price charged to his account with defendant, and that the written order, which advised plaintiff of such assumption of authority, was the only order given for the goods and that they were delivered thereunder. p. 499.

3. SALES.—*Written Order.—Conditions.—Acceptance by Seller.— Effect.*—Where a seller receives a written order for goods showing that the price was to be charged to his agent and not to the buyer, the seller cannot accept the order and deliver the goods thereunder without being bound by such condition. p. 500.

4. PRINCIPAL AND AGENT.—*Authority of Agent.—Presumption.*— There is no presumption that a special agent selling the goods of his principal has authority to pay his personal debts with the goods he sells. p. 500.

5. PRINCIPAL AND AGENT.—*Authority of Agent.—Burden of Proof.*— Where, in an action for the price of goods sold, the buyer relies on the agent's authority to sell the principal's goods in payment of his personal obligations, the burden is on the buyer to show that the agent had the right to so sell the goods, or that such sale was acquiesced in, or ratified by, the principal. p. 500.

6. SALES.—*Action for Price.—Answer.—Sufficiency.*—In an action on account to collect the price of goods sold, defendant's answer that the goods were purchased from the seller's agent under an agreement that they were to be charged to him, and not to defendant, and that such stipulation was embodied in the written order for the goods received and accepted by the seller, is sufficient as against demurrer. p. 501.

From Madison Superior Court; *H. Clarence Austill,* Judge.

Action by Excel Furniture Company against Frank H. Brock. From a judgment for defendant, the plaintiff appeals. *Affirmed.*

*Isaac Carter* and *Francis A. Walker,* for appellant.

*Charles R. Bagot,* for appellee.

HOTTEL, J.—This is an appeal from a judgment for appellee in an action brought by appellant to recover an amount alleged to be due it on account of goods sold and delivered to appellee.

The complaint is in two paragraphs, each of which alleges, in substance, that on November 13, 1913, the appellant sold and delivered to appellee under the name and style of

the "Larrimer Furniture Company" at the special instance
and request of the latter, five No. 15 top cabinets at $14.25
each, making $71.25, and five No. 10 cabinets at $16.50 each,
making $82.50, a total of $153.75. A demand for this
amount and a refusal to pay is alleged. Judgment for said
sum and interest thereon from January 13, 1914, is asked.

The paragraphs differ in that the first proceeds upon the
theory that the prices set out and indicated, *supra,* are correct and that the value of the property sold was that indicated by such prices, while the second paragraph proceeds
upon the theory that the prices so indicated and stated were
the prices which appellee agreed to pay for said goods, and
that such payment therefor was to be made on January
13, 1914.

To each of these paragraphs, appellee filed an answer
in four paragraphs, the first being a general denial, and
the second a plea of payment.

The third paragraph alleges, in substance, that on October 25, 1913, one A. V. Randall (herinafter referred to
as R) was the agent and salesman of appellant, and as such
called on appellee and solicited from him an order for the
purchase from appellant of the goods enumerated in each
of the paragraphs of the complaint; that R was then
indebted to appellee in a sum in excess of the price of
said goods, and appellee was desirous of collecting said
indebtedness and then and there informed R that if the
price of said goods might be credited by appellee upon
his, R's, said indebtedness, that he, appellee, would order
said goods; *that R then told appellee that he would sell
him said goods for appellant under such arrangement,* and
that appellee, in payment therefor, should credit R on his
indebtedness with the purchase price thereof, and R, as
such agent and salesman for appellant, then and there
made out and executed in duplicate a written memorandum
of said transaction, one copy of which he delivered to appel-

·lee, and the other he retained, in the words and figures following, towit:

"Order No.                               Date 3-25 1913.
Ship to Larrimer & Co.
City ·       Anderson, Ind.
Terms 10% 30 Ship at once.

| Quantity | Number | Finish | Price | Amount. |
|----------|--------|--------|-------|---------|
| 5 | 15 | N. T. S. | $14.25 | 71.25 |
| 5 | 15 | | 16.50 | 82.50 |
|   |    |   |   | 153.75 |

Dull Finish
Charge net amount to
    A. V. R.          ·
Please send me your mail orders, they will be appreciated and promptly attended to whether I am at home or not.

                        A. V. Randall, Mfg. Agt.
Bell Phone 824-K.       Shelbyville, Indiana."

That the initials "A. V. R." in said order were intended and understood to mean the said A. V. Randall, and the articles ordered and described are the same articles sued for by appellant; that appellee gave no other order and made no other or different arrangement for the purchase of said goods, and would not have ordered or purchased said goods under any other or different terms or conditions; "*that after giving said order and making said deal and transaction with the plaintiff's said agent and salesman, the plaintiff shipped and delivered said goods and property to defendant* and defendant then and there credited said debt of said Randall to him with the purchase price thereof, to wit, one hundred fifty-three dollars and seventy-five cents ($153.75) all in accordance with and pursuant to said agreement and arrangement."

The fourth paragraph differs from the third in that it contains, instead of the italicized averments above indicated as appearing in the third paragraph, substantially the following averments: R then told appellee that if he would

order said goods he might order them and have them ·
charged by appellant to R and said goods were delivered by
appellant and received by appellee under and pursuant to
said arrangement by and between appellee and appellant's
said agent and said written order and not otherwise. In
all other respects, the averments of the two paragraphs are
substantially, if not identically, the same.

A demurrer to each of these paragraphs of answer was
overruled. There was a reply in general denial and an
affirmative reply, but as said rulings on the demurrer to
said answers are the only errors assigned in this court,
the averments of the reply need not be indicated.

In its discussion of the ruling on the demurrer to said
answers, it is suggested by appellee that evidence of the
facts pleaded in each paragraph of said answer was
1. admissible under the general denial. Assuming, without deciding, that this is true, it does not follow that
reversible error did not result from such rulings. *Thompson* v. *Lowe* (1887), 111 Ind. 272, 278, 12 N. E. 476; *Lockwood, Admr.,* v. *Woods* (1892), 3 Ind. App. 258, 29 N. E.
569; *Epperson* v. *Hostetter* (1884), 95 Ind. 583, 587; *Sims*
v. *City of Frankfort* (1881), 79 Ind. 446, 448, 449; *Over*
v. *Shannon* (1881), 75 Ind. 352, 353.

In its memorandum accompanying said demurrer, appellant, states as its reason why said demurrer should be sustained the following, in substance: (1) It is not alleged in
either of said paragraphs that R claimed to have authority
to sell the goods on the conditions set out in said answers.
(2) It is not alleged that appellant had knowledge that the
goods were to be charged to the account of R and that
appellant shipped the goods with the knowledge of the representations made by R to appellee. (3) That the averments of the answer show that appellee was dealing with
an agent of appellant, and that the agreement alleged in
such answers was not one ordinarily within the authority
of an agent to sell, and hence could not bind the principal

unless it had knowledge of such agreement when it shipped the goods. (4) Neither of said paragraphs alleges that the order set out therein was forwarded to the appellant and that the goods were shipped thereunder. The fifth reason is substantially the same as the first, *supra.*

It will be observed that the averments of the fourth paragraph of answer are a little more specific as to the agreement between appellee and R, that the goods were 2. to be charged by appellant to R and that such goods were delivered by appellant and received by appellee under said arrangement. However, the order for the goods is set out in each paragraph, and, under the more recent decisions of the Supreme Court and of this Court (*Domestic Block Coal Co.* v. *DeArmey* [1913], 179 Ind. 592, 601, 100 N. E. 675, 102 N. E. 99), which permit reasonable inferences in favor of a pleading, we think that, when said order is read in connection with the averments of said third paragraph, it sufficiently appears from said paragraph that the goods ordered were to be charged to R, that said order was the only order given for said goods, and the one under which said goods were shipped by appellant and received by appellee. It is evident that appellant regards the theory and effect of the paragraphs as being the same, as the reasons stated in its memorandum, indicated *supra,* are addressed to each paragraph alike, and in his argument appellant treats the paragraphs as proceeding on the same theory.

We therefore deem it unnecessary to take up separately each of the several objections and discuss their respective merits as applied to each paragraph of answer; but deem it sufficient to say, in answer to said objections collectively, as applied to each or either paragraph of said answer, that each of such paragraphs show that R assumed to have authority to sell the goods upon the conditions averred in the answer, and, as before stated, such answers aver, in effect, that the sole and only order for the goods given or authorized by appellee, and the sole and only authority

which appellant had for the shipment and delivery of the
goods to appellee was the written order, which on its face advised both appellee and appellant that R had assumed to
have authority to sell the goods and have them charged to
himself. Each paragraph of the answer avers, in substance,
that appellee gave no order other than that set out in the
answer and *that the goods were delivered by appellant and
received by appellee and credit given on R's indebtedness
"all in accordance with and pursuant to said agreement
and arrangement."*

If R in fact had no authority to sell appellant's goods
upon the conditions alleged in each of said answers and

3. embodied in the written order pursuant to which
the goods were sold and delivered, as shown by such
answers, appellant was under no obligation to fill the
order, but it could not accept the order and ship the goods
thereunder without being bound by the conditions therein.
In other words, it could not accept the benefit of the order
which gave it a customer for, and an opportunity to sell,
its goods and avoid the conditions upon which such customer
agreed to purchase the goods.

It is true, as appellant contends, that there is no presumption that a special agent who has authority to

4. sell the goods of his principal also has authority to
pay his own debts with the goods he thus sells, and,
hence, that where one seeks to obtain the benefit of a

5. credit given on the agent's account for the goods of
the principal purchased through such agent, the burden is on such purchaser either to show that the agent had
authority to so sell his principal's goods or that the act of
the agent in the matter of such sale was known by and
acquiesced in, or ratified by, his principal. *Runyon* v. *Snell*
(1888), 116 Ind. 164, 167, 18 N. E. 522, 9 Am. St. 839;
*Davis* v. *Talbot* (1894), 137 Ind. 235, 238, 36 N. E.
1098; *Robinson* v. *Anderson* (1886), 106 Ind. 152, 156, 6
N. E. 12.

These cases and the legal propositions therein announced would be of controlling influence if appellee's said paragraphs of answer proceeded upon the theory of a

6. purchase by appellee of the goods from appellant through its agent in the usual way which permitted the goods to be charged to appellee, but with a private agreement or understanding that the goods thus purchased were to be paid for by giving credit on the agent's indebtedness. Such, however, is not the theory of either paragraph of the answer. On the contrary, each paragraph of the answer shows that that part of the agreement between appellee and R which required the price of the goods to be charged to R was in effect embodied in the written order, and such answers contain the further averments, above indicated, which put upon appellee the burden of proving that the goods were purchased and received by appellee and were delivered by appellant under and pursuant to said order and agreement. It follows that each paragraph of said answer states a complete defense to the cause of action stated in the complaint to which it was addressed, and that no error resulted from the ruling on said demurrer. The judgment below is affirmed.

NOTE.—Reported in 14 L. R. A. 234. Principal and agent, power of agent to use property of principal for payment of his own debts, 14 L. R. A. 234; liability of principal for unauthorized contracts of his agent, 88 Am. St. 780. See under (3) 35 Cyc 55.

---

## LAYMAN v. DIXON.

[No. 9,214. Filed January 9, 1917.]

1. ELECTIONS.—*Petition for Recount.—Dismissal.—Right of Appeal.*—An order dismissing a petition based on §6991 Burns 1914, §4739 R. S. 1881, for a recount of ballots cast for township trustee is not appealable, since the proceedings for a recount is under a special statute (§§6990-6994 Burns 1914, §§4738-4742 R. S. 1881) containing no provision for an appeal. p. 503.

2. ELECTIONS.— *Recount.— Petition—Sufficiency.— Statute.*— Under §6990 Burns 1914, §4738 R. S. 1881, relating to proceedings to obtain a recount of ballots cast at an election, where the petition provided for fails to show that the candidate desires to contest the election it is insufficient to invoke the action of the court in the matter, since one seeking the benefit of a statute must bring himself within its terms. p. 504.

From Jennings Circuit Court; *Robert A. Creigmile,* Judge.

Proceedings on the petition of Frank Layman for a recount of ballots cast for the office of township trustee. From an order dismissing his petition, the petitioner appeals. *Appeal dismissed.*

*William Fitzgerald,* for appellant.

*H. C. Meloy,* for appellee.

IBACH, P. J.—This is an attempted appeal from an order of the judge of the Jennings Circuit Court made in chambers dismissing appellant's petition based on §6991 Burns 1914, §4739 R. S. 1881, for a recount of the ballots cast for township trustee.

The recount statute, §§6990-6994 Burns 1914, §§4738-4742 R. S. 1881, has recently come under the review of the Supreme Court in the case of *Williams* v. *Bell* (1915), 184 Ind. 156, 110 N. E. 753. In that case the question arose upon the admission in evidence of the commissioners' certificate on a recount in a proceeding to contest, the question for determination being whether or not such certificate was a judgment. In disposing of such question the court said: "An examination of the recount statute makes it obvious that, while the instruments used are different, the recount is not different in character or purpose from that of the original count. It is merely to ascertain, if that may be, from the ballots as cast, who received the highest number of votes for the office or offices involved. It is not a judicial proceeding, nor a final adjudication of the title to the office. It is no more final than the original count and the sum of the returns based thereon as certified by the canvassing board. Manifestly, no appeal is contemplated by the statute, for none is provided, and the proceeding is a special statutory one in the nature of a discovery of evidence to be used in a judicial trial of the title to an office by statutory contest or information wherein the result may be overturned by the ballots themselves. It is only in aid of one who desires to contest with another the title to an office and not an independent judicial proceeding. On application by one desiring to contest who had complied with the statute, the circuit court, if in session, or the judge thereof in vacation, has no discretion but to appoint commissioners for the purpose and to order the recount. The number and qualifications of these commissioners the statute fixes, and the court may appoint none other. ·So we see that the circuit court or judge in appointing commissioners to recount is acting in no essentially different character than those ministerial officers who appoint those election officials who have the duty placed on them by law to count and canvass the ballots and returns. Nor are the duties of the recount commissioners of a different character in the matter of counting from those of election boards and canvassers of the first instance. It would seem evident therefore that the recount statute involves the exercise of ministerial functions and not judicial ones.''

The first question to be determined in this case is whether we have any jurisdiction over this proceeding, or, in short, whether such an appeal will lie. As we view such

1. question, it is conclusively settled by the holding of the Supreme Court in the case above quoted. We have here a proceeding under a special statute, containing no provision for appeal, and manifestly none contemplated. It is in no sense a civil action. It is unnecessary for us to extend this discussion; but in support of our conclusion, we refer to the following additional authorities: *Lafayette, etc., R. Co.* v. *Butner* (1903), 162 Ind. 460, 70 N. E. 529;

and authorities cited; *Collins* v. *Laybold* (1914), 182 Ind.
126, 132, 133, 104 N. E. 971, and authorities cited; *Noblesville Hydraulic Co.* v. *Evans* (1904), 163 Ind. 700, 72 N. E.
126. We conclude that an appeal does not lie from the
order of the court in this case.

Appellant's petition does not comply with the provisions
of the statute (§6991 Burns 1914, *supra*). It is evident,
from a reading of the act in question, that it is only
2. when the candidate desires to contest an election that
he may invoke the aid of such statute. §6990 Burns
1914, *supra*.

Among other things, the legislature has said that the petition must show "that he (the candidate) desires to contest
such election." This element appellant's petition does not
contain in express terms and there is no language from
which it may be fairly inferred. One who seeks the benefit of a statute must bring himself fairly within its terms.
Until a petition in compliance with the statute was filed, no
duty rested upon the judge of the circuit court to act in
the matter. Appeal dismissed.

NOTE.—Reported in 114 N. E. 698.

---

# S. W. LITTLE COAL COMPANY *v.* O'BRIEN,
## ADMINISTRATRIX.

[No. 9,012. Filed January 29, 1916. Rehearing denied November
23, 1916. Transfer denied January 9, 1917.]

1. PLEADING.—*Complaint.*—*Facts.*—*Conclusions.*—In an action for
   wrongful death, an allegation in the complaint that decedent, at
   the time of his injury, was in the discharge of the duties of
   employment, but not averring that he was performing any of
   the services set forth in the complaint as such states a conclusion.
   p. 511.

2. PLEADING.—*Complaint.*—*Facts.*—*Conclusions.*—In an action for
   death by negligence, an allegation that decedent, who was crushed
   between a car and a scale house, was compelled to cross a railroad track in front of a moving car and to pass between it and
   a scale house, but no facts are pleaded showing the necessity
   which compelled decedent to so do, states a conclusion. p. 512.

3. PLEADING.—*Pleading Conclusions.—Motion to Make More Specific.*—Since the enactment of §343a Burns 1914, Acts 1913 p. 580, providing that any conclusion stated in any pleading must be considered and held to be equivalent to the allegation of all the facts required to sustain such conclusion if necessary to the sufficiency of the pleading, but that a motion may be made to require the party filing such pleading to state the facts necessary to sustain the conclusion alleged, motions to make more specific in such cases should be liberally granted.   p. 512.

4. PLEADING.—*Complaint.—Motion to Make More Specific.—Pleading Conclusions.*—Where, in an action for wrongful death, the complaint pleads conclusions to the effect that decedent, at the time he was killed, was on the farther side of a railroad track "in the discharge of the duties of his employment" and that he was "compelled" to cross such track in front of an approaching car and to pass between it and defendant's scale house, but no facts are alleged showing the necessity which compelled deceased to so do, it was error for the trial court to overrule a motion to make the complaint more specific.   p. 513.

5. MASTER AND SERVANT.—*Injuries to Servant.—Contributory Negligence.—Negligence of Master.—Liability.—Burden of Proof.*—The mere fact that hazards inherent or apparent in the employment contributed to the injury involved, or the mere fact of the existence of defects in the working place, etc., of which the employer had knowledge, actual or constructive, and because of which defects the employe was injured, does not render the employer liable under §§2 and 3 of the Employers' Liability Act of 1911 (Acts 1911 pp. 145, 146, §§8020b, 8020c Burns 1914), providing that dangers or hazards inherent or apparent in the employment shall not be a defense for the employer in an employe's action for injuries, and that the employer has the burden of proving that he did not know of the defect causing the injury, either actually or constructively, in time to have remedied the same.   p. 515.

6. MASTER AND SERVANT.—*Injuries to Servant.—Negligence of Master.—Liability.—Assumed Risk.—Statute.*—Under the Employers' Liability Act of 1911 (Acts 1911 p. 145, §8020a *et seq.* Burns 1914) the employer is not liable unless the hazards of the employment and the defects in the working place, tools, etc., are chargeable to his negligence, and in the absence of negligence of the employer, the question of assumed risk is immaterial.   p. 515.

7. MASTER AND SERVANT.—*Injuries to Servant.—Negligence of Master.—Elements.—Notice of Defects.*—Where a cause of action for injury or death is predicated upon the existence of defects in the working place, tools, etc., the employer's knowledge of such

defects, actual or constructive, is an essential element of negligence, both under the Employers' Liability Act of 1911 (Acts 1911 p. 145, §8020a *et seq.* Burns 1914) and at common law. p. 515.

8. MASTER AND SERVANT.—*Injuries to Servant.—Action.—Complaint.—Allegations of Knowledge of Defect.—Sufficiency.*—Where, in an action for wrongful death caused by decedent being crushed, owing to insufficient clearance between a scale house constructed by defendant and a car on a switch track, the complaint alleges that all the facts concerning the defect complained of, which was the proximity of the scale house to the switch track, were known to defendant, sufficiently charges the employer with notice to bring the case within §8020c Burns 1914, Acts 1911 pp. 145, 146, relating to actions for injuries to employes, although the complaint contains no express averment that defendant knew of the defect in time to have remedied it, since, the defect alleged being structural in nature and neither latent nor concealed, defendant was chargeable with knowledge thereof from its inception. p. 515.

9. MASTER AND SERVANT.—*Injuries to Servant.—Action.—Defenses. —Contributory Negligence.—Statute.*—The defense of contributory negligence is not abolished in all cases by the act of 1911 (Acts 1911 p. 145, §8020a *et seq.* Burns 1914), relating to employers' liability for injuries to servants, and it is available in an action for wrongful death where the facts show that decedent who was crushed and killed between a moving car on a switch track and defendant's scale house which he was attempting to enter to weigh the car in pursuance of his duty, voluntarily and under no requirement of his employment placed himself in the perilous position occupied when killed so that death resulted not from the alleged defect in the working place due to the proximity of the scale house to the track, but rather from the use decedent made of the place to work. p. 516.

10. MASTER AND SERVANT.—*Injuries to Servant.—Action.—Complaint.—Allegations.— Defenses.—Contributory Negligence.— Burden of Proof.—Statute.*—In an action for personal injury, under §362 Burns 1914, Acts 1899 p. 58, the plaintiff is not required either to allege or prove that he was in the exercise of reasonable care at the time of the injury, and that he did not exercise such care is matter of defense and may be made under the general denial. p. 517.

11. MASTER AND SERVANT.—*Injuries to Servant.—Action.—Complaint.— Disclosure of Contributory Negligence.— Sufficiency.*—Where the complaint in an action brought under the Employers' Liability Act of 1911 (Acts 1911 p. 145, §8020 *et seq.* Burns 1914) affirmatively shows that the person injured or killed was guilty of contributory negligence which proximately caused or con-

tributed to such injury or death, it discloses a defense and is insufficient on demurrer. p. 517.

12. PLEADING.—*Demurrer.—Complaint.—Sufficiency.—Inferences.—* Where, in an action for wrongful death, the complaint is demurred to as affirmatively disclosing that decedent was guilty of contributory negligence, all inferences reasonably permissible under the allegations of the complaint must be indulged in favor of the sufficiency of the pleading. p. 517.

13. MASTER AND SERVANT.—*Injuries to Servant.—Action.—Complaint.—Sufficiency.—Contributory Negligence.—*Where, in an action for death by negligence, the complaint alleges facts showing that deceased, who was employed to weigh cars of coal as they were moved over a scale, attempted, for the purpose of weighing an approaching car, to enter defendant's scale house by passing between it and the moving car and in so doing was caught and crushed between the building and the car because of insufficient clearance, and that decedent voluntarily, and under no requirement of his employment, placed himself in the perilous position occupied when killed, there being no averments that his fellow servants were guilty of negligence or misconduct, or that there was anything unusual in the approach of the car, or its speed or control, such complaint discloses affirmatively decedent's contributory negligence and is not sufficient as against demurrer. pp. 517, 518.

14. MASTER AND SERVANT.—*Injuries to Servant.—Place to Work.—* The term "place to work," as used in employe's actions against the master for personal injuries, usually means the premises where the services are performed. p. 518.

15. MASTER AND SERVANT.—*Injuries to Servant.—Verdict.—Answers to Interrogatories.—*In an action for the wrongful death of an employe, a general verdict for plaintiff is not overcome by the jury's answers to interrogatories, where such answers do not disclose the existence of an obvious hazard in such a degree as necessarily convicted decedent of contributory negligence in making an attempt to pass between a moving car and a structure in such proximity to the track that he was caught and crushed because of insufficient clearance. p. 519.

16. TRIAL. — *Instructions. — Special Interrogatories. — When Answered.—*Where interrogatories are submitted to the jury under the provisions of §572 Burns 1914, Acts 1897 p. 128, it is proper, when requested, to instruct the jury that "the law does not prescribe when you shall consider and answer the interrogatories which will be submitted to you, and you are at liberty to take into consideration and answer them either before or after you have agreed upon a general verdict, according to your own desire and convenience." p. 520.

17. TRIAL. — *Instructions.* — *Special Interrogatories.* — *When Answered.—Statute.*—Section 572 Burns 1914, Acts 1897 p. 128, requiring that a general verdict be rendered in all cases tried by a jury, except cases in equity, and that where requested by either party, the court shall instruct the jury "when they render a general verdict to find specially upon particular questions of fact to be stated to them in the form of interrogatories," requires only that the interrogatories be answered and is not directory as to when, during the jury's deliberation, this shall be done, since the clause, "when they render a general verdict," is not to be interpreted as meaning after the jury has agreed on a general verdict, as the word "render" as used in the statute means not only the arrival at an agreement, but also reporting the verdict in due form, and the word "when" is to be construed as being used in the sense of "provided" or "if". pp. 522, 523.

18. TRIAL.—*Verdict.—Answers to Interrogatories.—Failure of Jury to Agree.—Discharge.*—Under §572 Burns 1914, Acts 1897 p. 128, requiring the rendition of a general verdict and providing for the submission of interrogatories in cases tried by jury, where interrogatories are submitted, and the jury fails to agree on either the general verdict or the answers to interrogatories, there is no verdict and the jury should be discharged for failure to agree. p. 523.

19. APPEAL.—*Harmless Error.—Refusal of Requested Instruction.*—Although a requested instruction that the jury could consider and answer the special interrogatories submitted either before or after agreeing upon the general verdict might properly have been given, its refusal was harmless error, where the interrogatories were answered. p. 524.

20. MASTER AND SERVANT.—*Injuries to Servant.—Liability.—Contributory Negligence.—Statute.*—Under §1 of the act of 1911 (Acts 1911 p. 145, §8020a Burns 1914), providing that liability against the employer may be established for the death or injury of a servant "when such injury or death resulted in whole or in part from the negligence of such employer, or his, its or their agents, servants, employes or officers," etc., does not under all circumstances eliminate the defense of contributory negligence, for where such defense is not expressly abolished it remains available, and it is recognized by §2 of the act (§8020b Burns 1914) providing that the burden of proof under that issue rests on the defendant. p. 525.

21. MASTER AND SERVANT.— *Injuries to Servant.— Action.— Defenses.—Contributory Negligence.—Servant's Obedience to Order.*—Under §2 of the act of 1911 (Acts 1911 p. 145, §8020b Burns 1914), where the injury complained of resulted from obedience to any order or direction of the employer, the employee shall not

be held guilty of contributory negligence by reason of the mere fact that he conformed or was obedient to the order, but in case an employee is injured because his manner of carrying out an order is not characterized by due care, rather than because he did obey the order, such section does not eliminate the defense of contributory negligence. p. 525.

22. MASTER AND SERVANT.—*Injuries to Servant.—Actions.—Questions for Jury.—Statute.*—Section 7 of the act of 1911 (Acts 1911 p. 145, §8020g Burns 1914)', providing that all questions of contributory negligence in employes' actions for personal injuries shall be questions of fact for the jury, or for the court where the cause is being tried without a jury, is simply a restatement of the law in relation to trials by jury, as it existed prior to the enactment of such section. p. 526.

From Gibson Circuit Court; *Simon L. Vandeveer,* Judge.

Action by Alta O'Brien, administratrix of the estate of William A. O'Brien, deceased, against the S. W. Little Coal Company. From a judgment for plaintiff, the defendant appeals. *Reversed.*

*Lucius C. Embree* and *Morton C. Embree,* for appellant.
*Samuel E. Dillin, Ely & Corn* and *T. Morton McDonald,* for appellee.

CALDWELL, C. J.—Appellee's complaint, in so far as is necessary to a determination of the questions raised respecting it, is in substance as follows: November 23, 1911, appellant was operating a coal mine in Blackburn, Pike county, employing therein fifty men. The mine was located on the line of the Evansville & Indianapolis Railroad Company, which extended north and south, and consisted of a main track and several side or switch tracks, the one involved here being east of the main track. The switch track was used both by appellant and by the railroad company in conducting their respective enterprises. Appellant's tip house was located on the sidetrack, at a point 300 feet south of which appellant maintained its track scale and scale house "theretofore constructed by it at said place, for the purpose of weighing railroad cars loaded with coal as they were moved

southward over said scale, over and upon said switch track.''
Appellant in operating its mine brought empty cars down,
by force of gravity, from the north to the tip house, and
there loaded them, and thence over such switch track to the
scale house to be weighed. William O'Brien, appellee's
decedent, was an employe of appellant, and as such it was
his duty to weigh the coal as it was loaded on the railroad
cars to be shipped; to move loaded and empty railroad cars
back and forth whenever necessary on the railroad tracks
at the mine; to send props and other material into the mine
as needed, and ''to do and perform all the things and duties
necessary to be done in the operation and conduct of said
tipple, railroad switch track, cars and track scales at said
mine.'' The wrongful conduct charged against appellant is
to the effect that it negligently constructed, maintained and
operated the scale house so close to the switch track that the
west side of the former was not more than two feet from the
east rail of the latter, and that as a consequence railroad
coal cars scraped against the side of the former in moving
along the switch track, and that such situation was extremely
dangerous to employes required to work in and about the
scale house, for the reason that they were likely to be caught
and crushed between the scale house and passing cars while
performing their ordinary duties. It is charged that ''all
the foregoing facts were to said defendent well known at all
the times herein mentioned.''

On November 3, 1911, appellant loaded a railroad car with
coal at the tipple and thereafter dropped it southward along
the switch track towards the main line. ''As said car
passed over said track scale, it became and was the duty of
plaintiff's decedent to weigh said car of coal; that in order
to do so, it was necessary for him to go inside said scale
house for that purpose; *that at said time said decedent was
in the discharge of the duties of his employment*, and was on
the west side of said switch and south of said scale house;
that the door opening into said scale house was on the north

side of said scale house at the northwest corner thereof, and next to said switch; *that said decedent was compelled to and did cross said switch track in front of said approaching car and to go between said car and said scale house, in order to get within said scale house and weigh said car as it passed over said scale;* that said defendant required said decedent to weigh said car while moving, and there was no other practicable or available means of getting into said scale house in time to weigh said car.'' It is further alleged that while decedent was attempting to enter the scale house, as aforesaid, he was caught between it and the moving car and crushed and killed. Decedent was twenty-three years old, and left surviving him appellee, his wife, and also an infant daughter. A trial of the cause resulted in a verdict and judgment for $2,000.

Appellant's motion that the complaint be made more specific, by which were challenged as conclusions the allegations which we have placed in italics, was overruled.

1. The allegation that decedent was in the discharge of the duties of his employment on the west side of the track states a conclusion. It is not alleged that he was performing any of the services specifically outlined by the complaint as constituting his duties. *Robertson* v. *Ford* (1904), 164 Ind. 538, 74 N. E. 1. The allegation of itself, however, is not material, since there is no averment that appellant was guilty of any negligence affecting him while in such position. *Louisville, etc., Traction Co.* v. *Leaf* (1907), 40 Ind. App. 214, 79 N. E. 1066. The allegation becomes material only by reason of other allegations with which it is associated. Thus, if decedent was on the west side of the track for some purpose of his own and independent of his employment, and if the proper discharge of his duties required his presence at the scale house, then while journeying back from serving his own purposes, it could scarcely be said that he was in the discharge of the duties of his employment, and, if injured while outside of the line of his employment,

attending to matters of his own, such fact would be important in determining appellant's liability. *Brown* v. *Shirley Hill Coal Co.* (1910), 47 Ind. App. 354, 94 N. E. 574.

The allegation that decedent was compelled to cross the track in front of the approaching car and pass between the car and the scale house is also in the nature of 2. a conclusion. A partial clarification consists in the facts alleged respecting decedent's situation and the location of the scale house and the door therein, and that there was no other available or practicable means of getting into the scale house in time to weigh the car. Assuming that decedent was on the west side of the track discharging the duties of his employment, then it sufficiently appears that his duties required him to cross the track and enter the scale house, and that in so doing he was discharging the duties of his employment, but the facts alleged do not make clear the necessity of passing in front of the car and attempting to travel the narrow space between it and the scale house. The complaint does not disclose the nature of the compelling force that restrained him from making an earlier start, or that required him to undertake the apparently impossible task of traveling such narrow space.

The complaint was filed after the act of 1913 (Acts 1913 p. 850, §343a Burns 1914) went into force. Prior thereto the sufficiency of a pleading depended on the sub-3. stantive facts alleged and not on the conclusions of the pleader, the latter being disregarded. *Frain* v. *Burgett* (1898), 152 Ind. 55, 50 N. E. 873, 52 N. E. 395; *Robertson* v. *Ford, supra.* By the terms of that act, however, any conclusion stated in any pleading must be considered and held to be equivalent to the allegation of all the facts required to sustain such conclusion if necessary to the sufficiency of the pleading. The only remedy afforded the opposite party by the act as against any such conclusion, and to ascertain the facts upon which the pleader bases it, is by motion to make more specific. In view of the radical change and its nature made by the act in favor of the pleader, it is our judgment that the corresponding remedy should be liberally applied, where recourse is had to it.

We, therefore, hold that the court erred in overrul-
4. ing such motion. Considering the entire record, how-
ever, and the apparent fact thereby disclosed that appellant was not prejudiced or placed at a disadvantage by reason of the ruling, we should hesitate to base a reversal thereon. *Diamond Block Coal Co.* v. *Cuthbertson* (1905), 166 Ind. 290, 296, 76 N. E. 1060; *Illinois Central R. Co.* v. *Cheek* (1899), 152 Ind. 663, 53 N. E. 641.

In support of the assignment that the court erred in over-ruling the demurrer to the complaint, appellant urges two points: First, that facts are not averred in negation of the assumption of risk; secondly, that the complaint affirmatively discloses that decedent was guilty of contributory negligence. While not expressly conceded, we fail to discover from appellee's brief that any effort is made to meet the second point. Directed to the first point, appellee argues that the complaint is predicated on the act of 1911 (Acts 1911 p. 145, §8020a *et seq.* Burns 1914), and that by the terms of that act the defense of assumed risk is eliminated in actions brought under it. Appellant rejoins, in substance, that, conceding that the action is brought under that act, the defense of assumed risk is not entirely abrogated thereby; that §3 (§8020c Burns 1914) of the act, if any part of it, is applicable and that by the express terms of such section the defense of assumed risk is eliminated only where the defect complained of (quoting from the act) "was prior to such injury, known to such employer, or by the exercise of ordinary care, might have been known to him in time to have repaired the same, or to have discontinued the use of such defective working place, tool, implement or appliance," and that the complaint here is insufficient by reason of the absence of an allegation that appellant had such knowledge. Appellant's argument is to the effect that the complaint is not sufficient in its averments to render available the provisions of the act of 1911, *supra,* by which the defense of assumed risk is eliminated, and hence that the complaint in its relation to such question must be measured by the rules of pleading in vogue in this state in common-law actions, and hence that the complaint, to be sufficient, should have negatived the assumption of risk. It will be observed that appellant's argument is based on the assumption that in actions brought under the act the burden rests upon the plaintiff to allege in his complaint the facts necessary to invoke the act to the end that he may be relieved from the consequences of an assumed risk; that is, that the burden rests upon him to allege facts to the effect that the employer had knowledge, actual or constructive, of the existence of the defects in time to have repaired, etc. It is expressly provided by the concluding sentence of §3 of the act that ''the burden of proof that such employer did not know of such defect, or that he was not chargeable with knowledge thereof in time to have repaired the same, or to have discontinued the use of such working place, tool, implement or appliance, shall be on the defendant, but the same may be proved under the general denial.'' The act is also so interpreted. *Deer* v. *Suckow Co.* (1915), 60 Ind. App. 277, 110 N. E. 700; *Vandalia R. Co.* v. *Stillwell* (1913), 181 Ind. 267, 104 N. E. 289, Ann Cas. 1916D 258. The act, however, is silent respecting the burden of averring such knowledge, both in its relation to the question of assumed risk and the issue of negligence. We shall revert to the question of pleading thus suggested, after a partial examination of some provisions of the act. We agree with appellee's contention that this action is predicated on the act of 1911. We had occasion in the recent case of *Standard, etc., Car Co.* v. *Martinecz* (1916), — Ind. App. —, 113 N. E. 244, to examine the act somewhat in detail. We, therefore, abbreviate here. The question here invokes a consideration of two provisions of the act rather than one. That part of §2 (§8020b Burns 1914) to the effect that the fact that dangers or hazards inherent or apparent in the employment contributed to the injury shall not be a defense, also has a bearing. We regard such provision of the second section and the provision of the third section first quoted as interdependent. As stated in the Martinecz case

5. and sustained by the decisions therein cited, the mere fact that hazards inherent or apparent in the employment contributed to the injury involved, or the mere fact of the existence of defects in place, etc., of which the employer had knowledge, actual or constructive, as provided by the third section, and in contact with which defects the employe was injured, does not render the employer liable.

The employer is not liable unless such hazards and

6. defects are chargeable to his negligence. In the absence of a case of negligence against the employer, the question of assumed risk is immaterial. *Terre Haute, etc., Traction Co.* v. *Young* (1913), 56 Ind. App. 25, 35, 104 N. E. 780; *Scheurer* v. *Banner Rubber Co.* (1909), 227 Mo. 347, 126 S. W. 1037, 28 L. R. A. (N. S.) 1207, note

p. 1215. Where a cause of action is predicated upon

7. the existence of defects in place,. etc., the employer's knowledge, actual or constructive, is an essential element of negligence, not only at common law but also under the act of 1911. It follows that the question suggested by appellant—that under the third section of

8. the act the burden rests on plaintiff to eliminate the assumption of risk by alleging in his complaint that the employer did have such knowledge, actual or constructive, in time to have repaired the defects or discontinued the use of the defective equipment by the exercise of reasonable care—involves also the question of the burden of averring such knowledge in its relation to the issue of negligence. In such a case as this, in the absence of the element of knowledge, there is no available negligence, and the negligence

existing, including the element of knowledge, actual or constructive, on the part of the employer, the act is invoked to the elimination of the defense of assumed risk, regardless of the employe's knowledge, actual or constructive, of the defect complained of. However, we do not find it necessary to determine the questions of pleading thus suggested. If the burden rested upon appellee it has been discharged. As indicated, there is an express averment that the facts alleged respecting the defects were well known to the defendant. The defect complained of here was the proximity of the scale house to the switch track. While there is no express averment that appellant knew of the defect in time to have remedied it, yet it is alleged that appellant not only negligently maintained, but also negligently constructed, the scale house in such proximity. The defect then is alleged to have been structural, and, being in no sense latent or concealed, appellant was chargeable with knowledge of the defect from its inception, and an express allegation to that effect was not required. *Standard Oil Co.* v. *Bowker* (1895), 141 Ind. 12, 18, 40 N. E. 128; *Louisville, etc., R. Co.* v. *Miller* (1895), 140 Ind. 685, 40 N. E. 116; *Indiana, etc., R. Co.* v. *Snyder* (1895), 140 Ind. 647, 39 N. E. 912; *Indiana Nat. Gas, etc., Co.* v. *Vauble* (1903), 31 Ind. App. 370, 68 N. E. 195; *Louisville, etc., R. Co.* v. *Hicks* (1894), 11 Ind. App. 588, 37 N. E. 43, 39 N. E. 767; 26 Cyc 1144. It follows that appellant's first point is not well taken. We proceed to the second point, the question of contributory negligence.

Under some circumstances, contributory negligence is a defense in actions brought under the act of 1911. In such an action as this, it is available as a defense. See

9. *Standard, etc., Car Co.* v. *Martinecz, supra,* and cases cited. The burden of proof rests upon the defendant, but it may be proven under the general denial. §8020b Burns 1914, *supra; Vandalia R. Co.* v. *Stillwell, supra.* The plaintiff is not required either to allege or prove that the

person for whose injury or death the action is brought
10. was in the exercise of reasonable care. That he did
not exercise such care is matter of defense and may
be proven under the general denial. §362 Burns 1914,
Acts 1899 p. 58. If, however, the complaint affirma-
11. tively discloses that the person injured or killed was
guilty of contributory negligence which proximately
caused or contributed to such injury or death, it discloses
a defense and is insufficient on demurrer. *Pein* v. *Miznerr*
(1908), 170 Ind. 659, 84 N. E. 981. The inferences
12. on that subject, however, which the complaint reasonably admits of, must be indulged in favor of its sufficiency. *Cleveland, etc., R. Co.* v. *Lynn* (1908), 171
13. Ind. 589, 85 N. E. 999, 86 N. E. 1017. Bearing on the
question now under consideration, the complaint discloses the following facts: The scale house was situated so
close to the switch track that at times an ordinary coal car
scraped its sides in passing. Its west wall was not more
than two feet from the east rail of the switch, and as a consequence (considering the width of a car as compared with
the track), employes were likely to be caught and crushed
between the wall and a passing car. It was decedent's duty
to do all the weighing. A loaded car propelled by gravity
was approaching the scale house from the north. Decedent
was west of the switch and south of the scale house. The
entrance to the latter was on its north side. It was his
duty to weigh the car while in motion, and, as there was no
other practicable means of reaching the scale house and gain-
ing entrance thereto in time to weigh the car, he was thereby
compelled to, and did, attempt the hazardous feat of passing between the car and the scale house. It is not alleged
that any of his fellow employes was guilty of any negligence or misconduct, or that there was anything unusual
in the approach of the car or its speed or control, by reason
of which he was deceived and tricked into attempting the
passage. His conduct is accounted for by affirmative aver-

ments to the effect that by reason of his position and the situation of the scale house and its entrance, and the requirement that the car should be weighed while in motion, he voluntarily placed himself in a position certain to result in serious injury or death, rather than let the car pass unweighed and thereby encounter the extra labor of causing it to be stopped or returned to be weighed. It is not alleged that anything out of the ordinary occurred by reason of which he was caused to misjudge the situation. The allegation is that, driven by an influence, averred to have been compulsion, he went between the passing car and the side of the scale house, and was crushed and killed because there was not room between the car and the scale house for his safe passage. The term "place to work," as used in cases

14. such as this, usually means the premises where the services are performed. *Haskell, etc., Car Co.* v. *Przezdziankowski* (1907), 170 Ind. 1, 83 N. E. 626,

13. 14 L. R. A. (N. S.) 972, 127 Am. St. 352. As involved here, it means the scale house and its environment, including the switch track, and also the temporary but frequently recurring element of a passing car. The defect complained of was the proximity of the scale house to the track, creating an apparent hazard while a car was passing to any one who at the time happened to be between the scale house and the track, but involving no peril to any one remote from the car and the passage. Importance, therefore, attaches to the influences accountable for decedent's presence at the danger point. He was not required to perform any service between the two structures, but it is averred that he was compelled to pass between them in order that he might reach a point where he was required to perform services. Peril attached to his position there only during the fraction of a minute, while the car was passing. No overpowering necessity required his presence at the danger point during such interval, but a matter very trivial in its nature when compared to the value of a human life. Under

such circumstances, he voluntarily and inexcusably assumed a position of danger. He was killed, not by reason of defects in the place, but by reason of the use that he made of his place of work, or his conduct in such place. Knowing of the existence of the defect in the place, as alleged, the fact that he continued in the employment, and thereby continued to be in touch with the defective place, presented a question of assumed risk, all defenses based' on which are eliminated by the act of 1911. As to whether his conduct while in contact with such defective place was characterized by the exercise of reasonable care for his own safety presents a question of contributory negligence, a defense based on which in a case such as this remains available under the act of 1911. In the Martinecz case, *supra,* we sought to draw the distinction between the defense of "assumed risk" eliminated by the act of 1911, and the defense of "contributory negligence" recognized by such act, as those terms are used in the act. As measured by the distinction there drawn, we are impressed that the complaint here discloses affirmatively that decedent's contributory negligence was the proximate cause of his death, and that the court therefore erred in overruling the demurrer. See, also, as having some bearing, the following: *New York, etc., R. Co.* v. *Ostman* (1896), 146 Ind. 452, 45 N. E. 651; *Salem-Bedford Stone Co.* v. *O'Brien* (1894), 12 Ind. App. 217, 40 N. E. 430; *Cincinnati, etc., R. Co.* v. *Long* (1887), 112 Ind. 166, 13 N. E. 659; 26 Cyc 1149.

We have carefully considered the assignment based on the overruling of the motion for judgment on the answers to interrogatories returned with the general verdict. We

15. do not believe the court erred in overruling such motion. Answering certain arguments advanced, there is no averment in the complaint that decedent was killed while endeavoring to cross the track, and the answers to interrogatories do not disclose that he was killed in such an attempt. The averment is that he was killed by being

crushed between the side of the car and the side of the
scale house, presumably after he had crossed the track.
While the answers reveal that it was obviously hazardous
for decedent to attempt to pass between the car and the
scale house, they do not disclose the existence of an obvious
hazard in such a degree as necessarily convicts decedent of
contributory negligence in making the attempt. *Jenney
Electric Mfg. Co.* v. *Flannery* (1912), 53 Ind. App. 397, ·
98 N. E. 424; *Kingan & Co.* v. *Gleason* (1913), 55 Ind.
App. 684, 101 N. E. 1027.

By reason of its frequent recurrence in appeals presented
to this court, one other question demands our attention. The
court refused the following instruction tendered by
16. appellant: ''The law does not prescribe when you
shall consider and answer the interrogatories which
will be submitted to you, and you are at liberty to take
into consideration and answer them either before or after
you have agreed upon a general verdict, according to your
own desire and convenience.'' The refusal of an instruction practically identical with the above was considered by
this court in *Deep Vein Coal Co.* v. *Rainey* (1916), 62 Ind.
App. 608, 112 N. E. 392, resulting in a conclusion, as stated
in substance in the opinion, that the instruction might very
properly have been given, but in view of the state of the
record, the court declined to determine whether its refusal
was error. In the course of the opinion *Southern R. Co.*
v. *Weidenbrenner* (1915), 61 Ind. App. 314, 109 N. E. 926,
and *Wabash R. Co.* v. *Gretzinger* (1914), 182 Ind. 155, 104
N. E. 69, are cited. The instruction involved in the former,
as given by the court, does not differ materially in legal
effect from the one under consideration here. It is, in substance, that the jury might consider first in order of time,
either the general verdict or the answers to the interrogatories, or both at the same time, but that the answers to the
interrogatories should be governed solely by the evidence.
The court held, on authority of the Gretzinger case, that

the giving of the instruction was harmless. In the latter the interrogatories submitted were delivered to the jury sealed in an envelope, with instructions that the envelope should not be opened until the jury had agreed on a general verdict. The Supreme Court, in its opinion in that case, while recognizing that the statute does not require that the interrogatories be answered in the absence of an agreement on the general verdict, condemned the practice of submitting interrogatories sealed, and with instructions as indicated, and stated respecting the interrogatories: "We perceive no good reason why they should not be considered by the jury in deliberating on the general verdict, for it is obvious that such consideration might better enable the jury to make a conscientious general finding." In the Raney case, *supra,* this court outlined some of the reasons why the interrogatories might be helpful, as stated by the Supreme Court in the Gretzinger case. Under these decisions, it is apparent that both the Supreme Court and this court are of the opinion that it is proper procedure for the jury first, in order of time, to consider the case as a whole, with a view of agreeing on the general verdict, or to consider the interrogatories submitted with a view to answering them, or to consider both phases of the cause submitted, at the same time, as the jury may discover in the course of their deliberations that they may best arrive at a just determination of the whole matter submitted. It follows at least that the instruction here refused was a proper one to have been given. Whatever confusion exists respecting the question under consideration, and whatever false impression has gained lodgment, possibly grow out of certain language used in *Summers* v. *Tarney* (1890), 123 Ind. 560, 24 N. E. 678 where the interrogatories were delivered to the jury sealed, and with a like instruction as in the Gretzinger case. The court there says: "This is new practice so far as our information goes; but we are not inclined to hold that it amounts to available error, as the statute provides that the interroga-

tories are only to be answered after a general verdict has
been agreed to." That case was decided while §546 R. S.
1881, §555 Burns 1894, was in force, which was in part as
follows: "In all actions, the jury, unless otherwise directed
by the court, may in their discretion, render a general or
special verdict; but the court  *  *  *  in all cases, when
requested by either party, shall instruct them, if they render
a general verdict, to find specially upon particular questions
of fact, to be stated in writing." It will be observed that
that statute did not provide that "the interrogatories are
only to be answered after a general verdict has been agreed
to," but rather, in substance, that the interrogatories were
to be answered and returned only in case the jury rendered
a general verdict. While it may be argued that even under
the statute of 1881, the answering of interrogatories was
futile until it had first been ascertained that an agreement
could be reached on the general verdict, yet neither that
statute, nor any other that has been in force in this state has
prescribed the order in which interrogatories and the general
verdict should be considered. The statute of 1881 was
amended in 1895 (Acts 1895 p. 248). The present statute
(§572 Burns 1914), which repealed the act of 1895,
17. was enacted in 1897 (Acts 1897 p. 128). It requires
that a general verdict be rendered in all cases tried
by a jury, except cases in equity, and that where requested
by either party, the court shall instruct the jury "when they
render a general verdict to find specially upon particular
questions of fact, to be stated to them in the form of interrogatories," etc. To construe the clause "when they render
a general verdict" to mean, as argued, "after they have
agreed on a general verdict," is to do violence to the language. The word "render" as used means more than an
arrival at an agreement. It includes also the idea of reporting the verdict in due form. Hence to construe the word
"when" as argued, would amount to a holding that the
interrogatories are to be considered and answered only after

the general verdict has been agreed on and returned into court. The word "when" is frequently used in the sense of "provided," "in case," and "if." 40 Cyc 921. It is our judgment that it is so used here, and that the "when" clause of the present statute is identical in meaning with the "if" clause of the statute of 1881. The latter was embodied in the statute of 1881, because by that statute either a general or a special verdict, the one exclusive of the other, might be returned. In case of a special verdict, interrogatories and the answers thereto could serve no useful purpose, and hence the provision for interrogatories and that they be answered "if they rendered a general verdict." As indicated, the present statute requires that a general verdict be rendered in all jury cases. When considered in the light of the preceding legislation on the subject, this requirement means simply that a general, rather than a special, verdict

18. be rendered. The jury, however, may fail to agree on a general verdict, in which case there would be no verdict, even though the interrogatories were answered; or the jury may agree on a general verdict but fail to agree on the answers to the interrogatories or some material part thereof. In such case also there would be no verdict, and the trial court would be required to discharge the jury for failure to agree. *Perry, etc., Stone Co.* v *Wilson* (1902), 160 Ind. 435, 67 N. E. 183. Hence the argu-

17. ment that the jury should not consider the interrogatories until after an agreement on a general verdict, because such answers accomplish nothing in the absence of such agreement, applies with equal force conversely, and the conclusion from the argument in its double aspect would result in neither phase of the case being considered. It is therefore apparent that the statutory direction extends only to the fact that interrogatories be answered, and is silent respecting the particular stage of the deliberations when they should be considered or answered.

In view of certain other instructions given, and the general

state of the record, we might consistently hold, as was done
in the cited cases that the refusal of the instruc-
19. tion, if error, was harmless. The bench and bar of
the state, however, are entitled to the judgment of
this court on the involved question. The refusal of the
instruction presents a question, not of substance, but rather
of regularity of procedure. The instruction contains no
direction as to what should be considered by the jury in
answering interrogatories, or as to what should form the
basis of such answers. Had it been given and followed,
the jury would not thereby have been influenced respecting
the facts included in or excluded from their answers, but
they would have been left entirely free to answer interrogatories under the evidence, as directed by other instructions.
Although the instruction was refused, the interrogatories
were answered, and the general verdict rendered by the
jury proceeding under oath. To hold that the refusal of
the instruction was prejudicial error would force the presumption that the jury did not observe the court's instruction that they be truthfully answered, the evidence being
the sole guide. In the absence of an indication to the contrary, it is our judgment that the opposite presumption
should be indulged. While we believe that such instruction should be given when requested, we do not believe that
in any case, its refusal would constitute reversible error.

Other questions presented are not considered, as they are
not likely to arise in a new trial.

Judgment reversed, with instructions to sustain the demurrer to the complaint, with permission to amend, if
desired, and for other proceedings in harmony with this
opinion.

## ON PETITION FOR REHEARING.

CALDWELL, C. J.—Appellee in support of a petition for a
rehearing argues: First, tha t in actions brought under the
act of 1911 (Acts 1911 p. 145, §8020a *et seq.* Burns 1914)

contributory negligence is in no case a complete defense; and second, that if in any case it is a defense, the question of its existence as a controlling factor is under all circumstances one of fact for the jury, and that under no circumstances is it a question of law for the court.

Appellees' first contention is based on certain provisions of the first section of the act, to the effect that liability against the employer may be established, the other 20. circumstances existing, "when such injury or death resulted in whole or in part from the negligence of such employer, or his, its or their agents, servants, employes or officers," etc. The argument is that, since the statute prescribes liability against the employer where the injury or death results only in part from the negligence of the employer, etc., a case wherein the negligence of the employer concurs proximately with the negligence of the employe to produce an injury to or the death of the latter comes within the act, and hence that the existence of contributory negligence is not a defense, where it concurs with the negligence of the employer to produce the injury or death. The decided cases recognize that contributory negligence is not under all circumstances eliminated as a defense by the act. Where not expressly abolished, it remains available. See *Vivian Collieries Co.* v. *Cahall* (1915), 184 Ind. 473, 110 N. E. 672; *Vandalia R. Co.* v. *Stillwell* (1913), 181 Ind. 267, 104 N. E. 289, Ann. Cas. 1916D 258; *Chicago, etc., R. Co.* v. *Mitchell* (1915), 184 Ind. 383, 110 N. E. 680. The second section of the act recognizes the defense by providing that the burden of proof on that issue rests on the defendant.

Said section provides, also, in substance, that an 21. injured employe shall not be held to have been guilty of contributory negligence, where the injury complained of resulted from the employe's conformity or obedience to any order or direction of the employer, etc. If the injury resulted from a conformity or obedience to the order, the effect of the act is that the employe shall not

be held guilty of contributory negligence, by reason of the
mere fact that he did conform or was obedient to the order.
See *Doan* v. *E. C. Atkins & Co.* (1915), 184 Ind. 678, 111
N. E. 312. His manner of carrying out the order, however,
rather than the fact that he did carry it out, might not
be characterized by due care, and he might be injured by
reason of the manner in which he carried out the order,
rather than from the mere fact that he carried it out. As
applied to such a case, the act does not eliminate the defense
of contributory negligence. *Vivian Collieries Co.* v. *Cahall,*
*supra,* pp. 489, 490. It is true that the effect of the statutory provision to which appellee directs our attention is not
discussed in the decisions holding that contributory negligence is restricted rather than abolished as a defense by
the act of 1911. Respecting such provision, it may be said,
however, that the negligence of an employer may concur
with the negligence of some third person, other than an
agent, servant, employe or officer of the employer to produce the injury or death complained of. In such a case, such
injury or death might be said to result only in part from
the employer's negligence. The employer, however, in such
a case is not relieved from liability in actions ruled by the
common law. *Hoosier Stone Co.* v. *McCain, Admr.* (1892),
133 Ind. 231, 31 N. E. 956; Cooley, Torts (2d ed.) 823;
*Fliege* v. *Railway Co.* (1910), 82 Kan. 147, 107 Pac. 555,
30 L. R. A. (N. S.) 734, and note, 20 Ann. Cas. 276. In
our judgment, the provision under consideration refers to
such a case.

Appellee's second contention is based on the seventh section of the act (§8020g Burns 1914), which is, in part, as
follows: ".All questions of * * * contributory
22. negligence shall be questions of fact for the jury to
decide, unless the cause is being tried without a jury
in which case, such questions shall be questions of fact for
the court." Respecting such section, the Supreme Court,
in *Kingan & Co.* v. *Clements* (1915), 184 Ind. 213, 110 N.

E. 366, says: "We are of the opinion that §7 is simply a restatement of the law in relation to trials by jury, as it existed prior to its enactment."

Other questions are discussed, but we discover no reason why we should not adhere to our original conclusion. Petition for rehearing overruled.

NOTE.—Reported in 113 N. E. 465, 114 N. E. 96. Contributory negligence as defense, statutes affecting, in actions by servants against masters, 5 Ann. Cas. 633; 26 Cyc 1229. Conclusions of law, what constitutes, 31 Cyc 52-65.

---

## EDDY v. HONEY CREEK TOWNSHIP OF WHITE COUNTY.

### [No. 9,165. Filed January 11, 1917.]

1. PLEADING.—*Demurrer to Answer.—Sufficiency.—Statute.*—Under §351 Burns 1914, §346 R. S. 1881, providing that a demurrer may be filed to answers where the facts stated therein "are not sufficient to constitute a cause of defense," a demurrer alleging "that the facts stated in each of said paragraphs of answer are insufficient to avoid the cause of action stated in plaintiff's complaint," does not follow the language of the statute and is insufficient to present any question, especially where each of the paragraphs of answer present only a partial defense. p. 529.

2. ANIMALS.—*Township.—Liability for Swine Killed by Dogs.—Nature of.—Compliance with Statute.*—The right to indemnity from townships for swine killed by dogs is solely statutory, and must be asserted in substantial compliance with the conditions in the law creating it. p. 531.

3. ANIMALS.—*Liability of Township for Stock Killed by Dogs.—Report to Township Trustee.—Statute.*—Under §3269 Burns 1914, Acts 1897 pp. 178, 181, providing that owners of live stock maimed or killed by dogs "shall within ten days from the time thereof," report certain facts under oath to the township trustee in order to obtain compensation for the damage suffered, the report must be made within ten days after the injury, regardless of when the animal died. p. 531.

From White Circuit Court; *Henry H. Vinton*, Special Judge.

Action by Harry C. Eddy against Honey Creek township of White county. From a judgment for defendant, the plaintiff appeals. *Affirmed.*

*Sills & Sills,* for appellant.
*Emory B. Sellers,* for appellee.

BATMAN, J.—This was a suit by appellant against appellee to recover damages under §3269 Burns 1914, Acts 1897 p. 178, 181, on account of the killing, by a dog, of certain swine belonging to appellant. The amended complaint alleges, among other things, that certain of such swine died and were killed on the 10th, 12th, 14th, and 28th days of July, 1910, respectively; that within ten days from the killing of each of said swine, the plaintiff filed with the trustee of said township his claim and report of such killing, stating therein the number of the swine and the age and value of each, in which report and claim he was joined by John N. Bunnell and Levi Reynolds, two disinterested and reputable freeholders and householders of said township.

To this amended complaint the appellee filed a paragraph of answer in general denial, which was subsequently withdrawn, and two affirmative paragraphs, designated as second and third. The second paragraph of answer contains, among other things, the following allegations: "The defendant for further answer to so much of said complaint as seeks to recover for the killing of one brood sow, two years old, being plaintiff's amended complaint herein, says that on the 4th day of July, 1910, the one brood sow, two years old, mentioned in the complaint, was bitten by a dog afflicted by hydrophobia, which dog did not belong to the plaintiff and was not harbored by him. He further says that said dog was killed on or before July 5th, 1910. That said dog did not bite or otherwise injure said hogs later than July 5th, 1910. That said sow died on July 28th, 1910." It then alleges, in substance, that the appellant did not make any report to the trustee of such township of the maiming and killing of the hogs until August 2, 1910, which date was more than ten days after the injury had been inflicted upon said animal by the dog.

The third paragraph is likewise a partial answer, and contains substantially the same allegations as the second, except that it applies to the remaining stock mentioned in the complaint, alleging that the injury was inflicted on or about July 5, 1910, fixing the dates on which the same died as the 10th, 12th, and 14th days of July, 1910, respectively, and further alleging that no report of the injury inflicted on July 4, 1910, was filed with the trustee of the township until July 16, 1910, and that as to one of the hogs, no report was filed until August 2, 1910.

The appellant demurred separately to each of said paragraphs of answer, which demurrer was overruled and the proper exceptions were reserved. The appellant refused to plead further, and judgment was thereupon rendered in favor of the appellee.

The appellant has assigned as the sole error, on which he relies for reversal, the action of the court in overruling his separate demurrer to the second and the third paragraphs of his answer. The appellee advances two theories on which the ruling of the court below was proper: (1) That appellant's demurrer was not in the proper form to raise any question as to the sufficiency of either of such paragraphs of answer; (2) that each of such paragraphs of answer alleges facts which show that the reports of such injuries made by the appellant to the township trustee were not filed within ten days from the time thereof, as required by §3269 Burns 1914, *supra*.

The separate demurrer filed by appellant to the second and third paragraphs of answer contains the following as the ground thereof: ''That the facts stated in

1. each of said paragraphs of answer are insufficient to avoid the cause of action stated in plaintiff's com-

plaint." The Code provides but one form of demurrer to an answer, viz.: that it does not state facts "sufficient to constitute a cause of defense." This provision is found in §351 Burns 1914, §346 R. S. 1881, and must be substantially followed. The courts have held the following alleged grounds of demurrer to an answer to be insufficient to present any question, viz.: " 'It does not state facts sufficient to make a good answer to the complaint.' " *Dawson* v. *Eads* (1895), 140 Ind. 208, 39 N. E. 919; " 'that neither of said paragraphs constitutes any defence to this action.' " *Reed* v. *Higgins, Admr.* (1882), 86 Ind. 143; that it does " 'not state facts sufficient to constitute a bar to the plaintiff's complaint.' " *Hildebrand* v. *McCrum* (1885), 101 Ind. 61; " 'that neither of said paragraphs of answer state facts sufficient to bar the plaintiff's action.' " *Angaletos* v. *The Meridian Nat. Bank, etc.* (1891), 4 Ind. App. 573, 31 N. E. 368. It is quite apparent that if a demurrer to a paragraph of answer, which alleges that it does not state facts "sufficient to bar the plaintiff's action," is insufficient in form to raise any question, one that alleges that the facts stated in a paragraph of answer are "insufficient to avoid a cause of action," likewise does not raise any question. This is especially true in this case, since each paragraph of answer to which the demurrer is addressed is a partial answer only, and might be good as such, without stating facts "sufficient to avoid the cause of action stated in plaintiff's complaint". We, therefore, hold that the demurrer raises no question, as to the sufficiency of either paragraph of the answer.

But even if such demurrer had been in statutory form, there would have been no error in overruling the same, as each paragraph of the answer to which it is addressed states facts sufficient to constitute a cause of defense. This conclusion involves the construction of §3269 Burns 1914, *supra*, which provides, among other things, that: "The owners of sheep, cattle, swine, horses, and other live stock or fowls killed, maimed or damaged by dogs, shall within ten days

from the time thereof, report to the trustee of the township
under oath" certain facts with reference to such injury
and damages. Each of said paragraphs of answer state facts
showing that such hogs were injured, having been bitten by
a dog on a certain date, and that no report was made to the
trustee of such township until more than ten days after
such injury; but that a report thereof was made to the trustee of the township, within ten days from the death of such
animals, following such injury. Appellant claims that it is
a sufficient compliance with the statute where the required
report is made within ten days from the death of the animals
injured; while appellee contends that the report must be
made within ten days from the time of the infliction of such
injury, regardless of the time of the death of such animals.

It does not appear that this particular question has been
decided by this court or the Supreme Court. No such
decision has been cited, and our investigation discloses none.
We must, therefore, determine it from the language of the
statute itself. In determining this question, it would be

2.
well to remember that there is no common-law right
to indemnity from the township for swine killed or
injured by dogs, but that such right is statutory and
must be asserted in substantial compliance with the conditions in the law creating it. The requirement as to
making such report is mandatory, and there can be no
recovery from the township until it has been fulfilled.
*Abell* v. *Prairie Civil Tp.* (1892), 4 Ind. App. 599, 31 N. E.

3.
477. The statute provides that upon such injury
being inflicted, the owner "shall within ten days from
the time thereof, report to the trustee of his township
under oath" certain facts. It is apparent that the words,
"from the time thereof," refer, and can refer, only to the
time of the injury, and have no reference whatever as to
whether the animal so injured dies or recovers. It was evidently the intention of the legislature to fix a definite time in
which the owner should report to the township trustee in

order to receive compensation, so that the matter might be brought to his notice while the facts were fresh, in order that he might investigate and protect the fund in his hands from wrongful and excessive claims. Such provisions would be of little value if no definite time were fixed from which the designated period of ten days should begin to run, so the legislature evidently intended from the language used that such time should begin to run from the infliction of such injury, regardless of the results thereof.

Appellant claims that the statute requires certain facts to be stated under oath, in the report of such injury, that can only be stated after the results thereof are known, and urges this as a reason for the construction of the statute for which he contends. We do not concur in this view. If an owner of stock injured by a dog were not required to make a report until within ten days from the time the result of the injury was known, the value of the provision requiring the report would be largely destroyed. Under such a construction, if the injured animal died, the ten days might begin to run from such death; but if the animal should survive, after lingering between life and death for weeks or months, when would such ten-day period begin to run? Who could say when the recovery was sufficient to set the ten-day period in motion? The statute does not provide one time for the ten-day period to begin to run where the injured animal survives and another time where such animal dies, but one time in either event, viz.: ten days from the infliction of such injury. The legislature might have fixed the time otherwise, but it did not see fit to do so and we are bound by the statute as written.

It may be, as appellant urges, that the extent of the injury inflicted and the amount of damages sustained cannot be accurately ascertained until the final result is known, but this fact would not lead to a different construction of the statute. The same fact might be urged with equal force as to personal injuries, and yet all actions for such injuries must be brought within a period of two years from the time the right accrues, or they are barred; notwithstanding the fact that the result of any such injury may remain more or less uncertain for many years. Resort is had to the common experience of men, the opinions of experts, and like means to determine the permanency of the injury and the amount of damages, rather than deferring a right of action until the results are definitely known.

We therefore conclude that each of said paragraphs of answer alleges facts sufficient to constitute a cause of defense. We find no error in the record, and the judgment is therefore affirmed.

NOTE.—Reported in 114 N. E. 783.

---

## BUTLER *v.* BUTLER.

[No. 9,206. Filed January 11, 1917.]

1. TENANCY IN COMMON.—*Tenant in Possession.—Liability for Rents.*—The possession of one tenant in common is the possession of all, and the tenant in possession is not required to pay rent unless he excludes his cotenant; but if he receives rent from a third person, he must account for it. p. 536.

2. TENANCY IN COMMON.—*Ouster of Cotenant.—Purchase of Land at Tax Sale.*—Where a tenant in possession purchases the land at a tax sale and takes a deed in his name, claiming at the time of the sale and subsequent to the execution of the tax deed that he is the owner, and is holding possession under such claim and deed, he is in legal contemplation claiming under a deed conveying the whole estate and will be deemed to have ousted his cotenant. p. 536.

3. TENANCY IN COMMON.—*Purchase of Property by Cotenant at Tax Sale.—Effect.*—Where one of several tenants in common of an estate purchases the common property at a tax sale, he cannot set up his title thus acquired against the common title, but the tax title enures to the common benefit of himself and his cotenants, although the common property is subject to the charge of the purchaser for the money expended at the tax sale. p. 537.

4. TENANCY IN COMMON.—*Purchase of Property by Cotenant at Tax Sale.—Reimbursement.—Rate of Interest.*—Where one of several tenants in common purchases the common property at a tax

sale, the title thus acquired enures to the common benefit of himself and his cotenants and the purchaser cannot profit by the transaction, so that the charge on the common property to which he is entitled for his purchase is limited to the amount paid at the sale and six per cent. interest thereon, §10393 Burns 1914, Acts 1901 p. 336, relating to principal and interest for tax liens, having no application in such a case. p. 537.

From Miami Circuit Court; *Joseph N. Tillett,* Judge.

Action by Cornelius C. Butler against Harlan H. Butler. From a judgment for plaintiff, the defendant appeals. *Affirmed.*

*Albert Ward,* for appellant.

*Antrim & McClintic,* for appellee.

IBACH, J.—This was an action for partition and for an accounting for rents and profits in which the defendant set up, by way of counter-claim, certain claims for taxes and improvements. Defendant also, by way of cross-complaint, claims title to such property under a tax deed.

The correctness of the conclusions of law stated on the special finding of facts is the only question presented for review. The court finds the following facts: On January 31, 1889, the father of appellant and appellee deeded to them a forty-acre tract of land, for which they paid a cash consideration of $30 and assumed a school-fund mortgage for $350. The father, by a provision in the deed, retained control of the rents and profits of the land during his lifetime and also agreed to pay the taxes during such time. It was agreed between appellant and appellee that the one in possession of the land should make needed and valuable improvements thereon, and that the cost should be considered and allowed to the one making them in the final settlement or division by them of the real estate. The taxes became delinquent for the years 1896 and 1897 and, on February 14, 1898, the land was sold for taxes and purchased by appellant at such tax sale. The land was not redeemed and, on March 5, 1900, appellant received a tax deed for it,

which deed was recorded on the same day. At the time of
the sale and afterward, and after the execution of the tax
deed, appellant claimed and still claims to be the owner of
the real estate by virtue of said sale and deed and holds
possession of the real estate by virtue of such deed and sale.
The father died on July 4, 1904.

The court further finds: Appellant "has received all the
rents and profits from said real estate since March 1, 1904,
which were reasonably worth $160 per annum and which,
with interest at the rate of 6 per cent. per annum from the
date of the receipt of each year's rent aggregated (exclusive
of the year 1913) $1,841.94 * * *." Appellant "made
lasting and valuable improvements on said real estate. Paid
the purchase money at said tax sale. Paid taxes and assessments which were liens on said real estate and on principal
and interest on said mortgage, which amounts so paid, and
the value of the improvements so made, together with
interest at the rate of 6 per cent. per annum from the
respective dates of payments and improvements and for
which he should be reimbursed are as follows: Ditches,
$275.95; Well and Clearing, $187.25; Fencing, $379.50;
Flood gates, $34.24; Taxes, $599.08; Payments on mortgage,
$401.64; and Ditch assessments, $24.28, in an aggregate
amount of $1,899.94. * * *." Appellee "made pay-
ments on said improvements and on the principal and interest
of said mortgage which, with interest at the rate of 6 per
cent. per annum from the respective dates of such payments,
aggregate $798.28 and has never been paid therefor. * *
* Said real estate is not susceptible of division without
damage to the interests of the respective owners of the
same." Other facts are found by the court but they are
not important here, as the above facts present the controlling questions in this appeal.

The court concludes as a matter of law that appellant and
appellee are the owners in fee simple as tenants in common
in equal proportions of said real estate; that said real

estate should be sold and, after the payment of the costs of this action and the costs of such sale, the remainder of the proceeds should be distributed as follows: "To Harlan H. Butler (appellant) * * * $58; to Cornelius C. Butler (appellee) * * * $798.28; the remainder to be divided equally between Harlan H. Butler and Cornelius C. Butler." Judgment followed the conclusions of law.

Appellant contends that, as a cotenant in possession, he was not liable for the rents of the land in the absence of an agreement, unless he had excluded his cotenant or received rent from third persons; that the court did not find, either in substance or otherwise, to the effect that appellee ever demanded possession or that he was ever denied possession, that appellant ever received any rents from third parties, that there was any agreement between the parties as to such possession by appellant; and that there is no finding of adverse possession or ouster of appellee.

The principle seems well established in this state that the possession of one tenant in common is the possession of all, and the tenant in possession is not required to pay 1. rent unless he excludes his cotenant; but if he receives rent from a third person, he must account for it. *Geisendorff* v. *Cobbs* (1910), 47 Ind. App. 573, 94 N. E. 236.

When appellant purchased the land at the tax sale and took a deed in his name, claiming at the time of the sale and since the execution of the tax deed that he was 2. the owner, and at all times since its execution holding possession under such claim and deed, he was under the law claiming under a deed conveying the whole estate and will be deemed to have ousted his cotenant. *Nelson* v. *Davis* (1871), 35 Ind. 474, 483; *King* v. *Carmichael* (1893), 136 Ind. 20, 24, 35 N. E. 509, 43 Am. St. 303; *Wright* v. *Kleyla* (1885), 104 Ind. 223, 4 N. E. 16.

Appellant next insists that, inasmuch as the court found that he was entitled to credit for certain taxes paid, he

should have been allowed interest at the rate of twenty
per cent. per annum instead of six per cent., as decreed by
the court.

'Where one of several tenants in common of an estate
purchases the common property at a tax sale, he cannot
        set up his title' thus acquired against the common
3.   title, but his tax title enures to the common benefit of
        himself and his cotenants; though in such a case the
common property is subject to the charge of the purchaser
at the tax sale for the money expended in such purchase. 38
Cyc 48, 49; *Harrison* v. *Harrison* (1878), 56 Miss. 174. "One
tenant in common cannot, while in possession of the joint
property and enjoying the rents and profits thereof, permit
the same to go delinquent for non-payment of taxes and purchase it in at tax sale and thus acquire his cotenant's title."
*English* v. *Powell* (1889), 119 Ind. 93, 95, 21 N. E. 458;
*Bender* v. *Stewart* (1881), 75 Ind. 88. Appellant, having
        purchased the property at tax sale for the benefit of
4.   his cotenants, could not profit by such transaction.
        Therefore, this case is not controlled by §10393 Burns
1914, Acts 1901 p. 366, and the court did not err in fixing
the rate of interest on the payments for taxes.

No available error having been pointed out, the judgment is affirmed.

NOTE.—Reported in 114 N. E. 760. Tenancy in common: (a)
right of a cotenant to buy common property at a judicial sale,
17 Ann. Cas. 1169, Ann. Cas. 1914A 1031, 38 Cyc 40-48, 116 Am.
St. 367; (b) liability of tenant in possession to account to cotenant
for rent and profits in the absence of express agreement, 18 Ann.
Cas. 1082, 28 L. R. A. 829, 29 L. R. A. (N. S.) 224, 38 Cyc 63, 70.

## FRAZURE v. RUCKLES ET AL.

[No. 9,085.  Filed October 4, 1916.  Rehearing denied December 12,
1916.  Transfer denied January 12, 1917.]

MUNICIPAL CORPORATIONS.—*Holding Illegal Race in Village Street.—
Injury to Spectator.—Recovery as for Illegal Act.*—While the
holding of a horse race in a village street is a violation of §§2664,
2665 Burns 1914, Acts 1905 pp. 584, 745, yet one who goes to
attend such a race as a spectator, thereby consenting to the unlawful act, and, while it is in progress, goes upon the street
where the race is being run and is struck by one of the horses
and injured, cannot recover, regardless of the elements of negligence and contributory negligence, merely because the race was
held in violation of the law.

From Noble Circuit Court; *Samuel M. Hench,* Special
Judge.

Action by Jason A. Frazure against John Ruckles and
others.  From a judgment for defendants, the plaintiff
appeals.  *Affirmed.*

*H. G. Zimmerman* and *F. P. Bothwell,* for appellant.
*McNagny & McNagny* and *Grant & Foote,* for appellees.

IBACH, J.—This is an appeal on reserved questions of law
from a judgment in favor of appellees upon a complaint
by appellant for personal injuries sustained at a horse
race conducted under the direction and management of
appellees, and unlawfully run at a dangerous rate of speed
on a street and highway in and through the village of Wolf
Lake, on the occasion of a public entertainment known as
a "Grand Onion Carnival."

One who allows his horse to run in a race along a public
highway, or who acts as a rider in such race, may be pun-
ished by a fine under §2664 Burns 1914, Acts 1905 p. 584,
745; and under §2665 Burns 1914, *supra,* it is a finable
offense to run horses within the limits of a village.  Appellant's contention is that, since this race was run in violation
of statute, appellees who had charge of the race were liable

to appellant for the commission of a wilful injury, and that the rules of negligence or contributory negligence do not apply. The complaint contains no allegations of negligence, but proceeds on the theory of trespass or wilful injury. Appellant seeks to hold appellees liable merely because the horse race was run in violation of law, and that he was injured by one of the horses running against him.

There are various errors assigned, but the merits of the case will be considered in the discussion of instruction No. 5 given by the court to the jury at appellees' request, and what is said concerning that error will be applicable to all others presented.

Instruction No. 5 is in the following words: "If you find from a fair preponderance of the evidence in this case, that the defendants, or other persons, advertised an onion carnival at the town of Wolf Lake, Indiana, to be held on August 22 and 23, 1912, and as one of the attractions of said carnival advertised a horse race to be run thereat, and that the plaintiff then lived in Albion, Indiana, and saw and read said advertisement, and went from his said residence to said town to visit as a spectator said carnival and said horse race, and if when the plaintiff reached said town of Wolf Lake and before said horse race was run, he learned that said horse race was to be run on which is commonly called the Goshen road, and if he knew that said Goshen road was a public highway, and the principal street in said town; and if you further find that the plaintiff knew that said horse race was to be a contest of speed, and that therefore the horses participating therein would be run at the greatest speed of which they were capable, and if you further find that the plaintiff went to the vicinity of the intersection of Wolf Lake street and said Goshen road expressly to see said horse race, and that the plaintiff paid no admission or fee for the privilege of seeing said horse race, and that the plaintiff saw that there were no ropes or barriers separating the place where he was from that portion of the said Goshen road where said horse race was to be run; and if you further find that the plaintiff then knew that six horses were to run in said horse race, and that said race was to be started in said Goshen road somewhere between 600 and 800 feet north-west of where plaintiff then was, and that said horses were to run southeasterly on said Goshen road and past the point where plaintiff was, and if you find that plaintiff saw one or more of the horses in said horse race pass him, and the plaintiff went a short distance into said Goshen road when said horse race was being run, and was watching the horses in said race which had passed him, and paid no attention to the horses in said race which were still to come from the direction of the starting point; and if you further find that if the plaintiff had looked in the direction of said starting point, he would and could have seen other horses in said horse race which had not yet passed him and were coming toward him from the starting point of said race, and could have avoided any injury to him from said horses by the exercise of such care and caution as a reasonably prudent and cautious man would have exercised under like circumstances, and in the situation that plaintiff was then in, as shown by the evidence; and if you further find that by reason of plaintiff's failure to exercise such care and caution, one of the horses running in said race ran against and struck him, and injured him as shown by the evidence, then I instruct you that the plaintiff cannot recover in this suit, and your verdict ought to be for the defendants, and this is true even if said horse race was run upon a public highway.''

This case is in all essential respects similar to that of *Johnson* v. *City of New York* (1906), 186 N. Y. 139, 116 Am. St. 545, 9 Ann. Cas. 824. That action was brought to recover damages for personal injuries suffered by the plaintiff by being struck by an automobile while witnessing an automobile race in a public highway in a borough of New York City. The plaintiff had come from her residence about five miles to see the races, and at first watched the

race from the highway, then went into an adjacent clump
of woods to get a better view, and while there was struck
by an automobile which was by some mischance deflected
from the road.   The act of the city in authorizing the use
of the road as a race course was illegal, and the act of the
other defendants in holding the race under that permission was equally illegal, and the race held by the defendants was an unlawful use and obstruction of the highway
and *per se* a nuisance.

The court said: "But granting that the action of the
defendants in the use of the highway was illegal, the question remains, Was it illegal against the plaintiff so as to
render the parties participating therein liable to her solely
by reason of the illegality of their acts and regardless of
any element of negligence or other misconduct.   If the
plaintiff had been a traveler on the highway when she met
with injury a very different question would be presented.
Highways are constructed for public travel, and, as already
said, the acts of the defendants were doubtless an illegal
interference with the rights of the traveler.   It may well
be that for an injury to the traveler, or to the occupants
of the lands adjacent to the highway, or even to a person
who visited the scene of the race for the purpose of
getting evidence against the defendants and prosecuting
them for their unlawful acts, the defendants would have
been absolutely liable regardless of the skill or care exercised.   But the plaintiff was in no such situation.   She was
not even a casual spectator whose attention was drawn to
the race while she was traveling in the vicinity.   She went
from her home, a distance of five miles from the scene of
the race, expressly to witness it and to enjoy the pleasure
that the contest offered.   As to the elements which made
the contest illegal she was aware of their existence.   She
knew it was to take place on a highway, and she knew it
was to be a contest for speed, and that, therefore, the automobiles would be driven at the greatest speed of which they

were capable. * * * It is entirely possible that as a
matter of fact the plaintiff did not know that the race on
the highway was illegal, but it was illegal not from any
want of permit, but because there was no statutory power
to grant a permit to use the highway for a private purpose.
The plaintiff, like every other person, is chargeable with
knowledge of law, however ignorant in fact she may have
been of it. * * * We are at a loss, moreover, to see
how the legality or illegality of the race affected a person
in the condition of the plaintiff. The danger she would
encounter in witnessing the race would be exactly the same
had there been a statute of the state which expressly authorized it. It does not lie in the mouth of the plaintiff to assert
as a ground of liability the illegality of an act from which
she sought to draw pleasure and enjoyment. It may be
assumed that her mere presence at the race was not sufficient participation therein to render her liable to prosecution as one of the maintainors or abettors of the nuisance
* * * though in the case of a prize fight, at common law,
all spectators were equally guilty with the combatants of a
breach of the peace. * * * The general maxim *injuria
non fit volenti* applies, and one cannot be heard to complain
of an act in which he has participated, if not so far as to
render him liable as a party to the offense or tort, at least to
the extent of witnessing, encouraging it and seeking pleasure
and enjoyment therefrom. Illustrations of this principle
may readily be found. It is a misdemeanor to conduct a
horse race within a mile of court when the court is in session; also to give a theatrical or operatic exhibition on Sunday. It seems to me absurd that persons obtaining admission and attending the prohibited race or opera and meeting
injury there shall successfully assert the illegality of the
exhibition as a ground of recovery. It might with just as
much force be contended that the presence of the person injured at the illegal exhibition or spectacle precluded him
from recovery against the parties by whose negligence or tort

the injury had been occasioned. Such is the law in some jurisdictions, * * *. Had the defendants broken into and entered without permission upon private property and conducted the race thereon, doubtless they would have been absolutely liable for all injuries occasioned thereby to the owners or occupants of the land. But what bearing would the trespass have on the defendants' liability to spectators? * * * As between the plaintiff and these defendants the legality or illegality of the exhibition given and witnessed, so far as that illegality depends on the obstruction and appropriation of the highway, was not the material factor. It did not create a liability against the defendants if they were at fault in the conduct of the race in no other respect. It does not preclude a recovery by the plaintiff if the injury to her was caused by the misconduct or fault of the defendants.'' This case was also followed in the case of *Bogart* v. *City of New York* (1911), 200 N. Y. 379, 93 N. E. 937, 21 Ann. Cas. 466. The case of *Scanlon* v. *Wedger* (1892), 156 Mass. 462, 31 N. E. 642, 16 L. R. A. 395, is similar.

Appellant has cited several cases from this and other states relating to the liability for injuries caused by an unlawful act, but in none of them was the plaintiff in the position of consenting to the unlawful act, as in the case here. There is no Indiana case which we have found in conflict with the New York opinion above quoted, and the reasoning in that case is so cogent that, without further discussion, the judgment is affirmed.

NOTE.—Reported in 113 N. E. 730. Liability of a municipality for consequences of a sanctioned unlawful use of its streets, 116 Am. St. 552. See also 37 Cyc 289.

## ROHRBAUGH v. LEAS, ADMINISTRATOR.

### [No. 9,566.  Filed January 12, 1917.]

1. APPEAL.—*Assignment of Errors.*—*Parties to Appeal.*—*Adminis-trator.*—*Failure to Properly Designate.*—*Dismissal.*—Where the judgment appealed from was rendered in favor of a party in his representative capacity as administrator of the estate of another, but on the appeal he was designated in the assignment of errors merely as administrator, but for whose estate not being indicated, the appeal will be dismissed for failure to comply with the rules of the Appellate Court requiring that the assignment of errors shall contain the full names of all parties to an appeal. p. 545.

2. APPEAL.—*Term-Time Appeal.*—*Time for Perfecting.*—*Approval of Bond.*—To perfect a term-time appeal under §679 Burns 1914, §683 R. S. 1881, it is necessary that the penalty and surety of the appeal bond should be fixed and approved within the term at which final judgment is rendered and the filing and approving of a bond after the close of such term, though within the time allowed by the trial court, will not cure the omission of the essential requirement. pp. 546, 547.

3. APPEAL.—*Time for Perfecting.*—*Judgment Preceding Ruling on Motion for New Trial.*—Where the entry of the judgment precedes the ruling on the motion for a new trial, the latter action of the court marks the beginning of the time limited for an appeal. p. 547.

4. APPEAL.—*Failure to Perfect.*—*Dismissal.*—Where an appeal, not properly perfected as a term-time appeal, has been on the docket for more than ninety days, and no steps have been taken to give notice so as to perfect it as a vacation appeal under §681 Burns 1914, §640 R. S. 1881, a dismissal is required. p. 548.

From Dekalb Circuit Court; *Emmet A. Bratton,* Special Judge.

Action by Earl D. Leas, administrator of the estate of Sarah A. Rohrbaugh, deceased, against Matilda Rohrbaugh. From a judgment for plaintiff, the defendant appeals, and plaintiff moves to dismiss the appeal. *Motion to dismiss appeal sustained.*

*Edgar W. Atkinson* and *C. M. Brown,* for appellant.
*Hoffman & Shearer* and *William H. Leas,* for appellee.

BATMAN, J.—Appellee, under a special appearance, moves to dismiss this appeal on several grounds, only two of which we find it necessary to consider. The judgment below

1. was rendered in favor of Earl D. Leas, as administrator of the estate of Sarah A. Rohrbaugh, deceased, against Matilda Rohrbaugh. The parties are designated in the assignment of errors: "Matilda Rohrbaugh, appellant, vs. Earl D. Leas, Administrator, appellee." The rules of this court require that the assignment of errors shall contain the full names of the parties, and unless this rule is complied with the appeal will be dismissed. *Whisler* v. *Whisler* (1904), 162 Ind. 136, 67 N. E. 984, 70 N. E. 152, and *Bender* v. *State,* ex rel. (1911), 176 Ind. 70, 95 N. E. 305.

In the case first cited, one of the defendants named in the complaint was Cornelius Lumaree, executor of the estate of John Whisler, deceased, with the will annexed. Another was Lewis Signs, who was trustee under the will of John Whisler, deceased, for five or more beneficiaries. Neither of said parties was so described in the assignment of errors, but their names appear therein as "Cornelius Lumaree, executor, Lewis Signs, trustee." The court said, on page 139: "These two defendants were sued in their representative capacity, and not as individuals. * * * Where persons sue or are sued in a representative capacity the rule that the full names of the parties shall be set out in the assignment of errors requires that they shall be properly described in that pleading as such representatives or fiduciaries. Otherwise the court to which the appeal is taken acquires no jurisdiction over them. The appellee 'Cornelius Lumaree, executor of the estate of John Whisler, deceased, with the will annexed,' could not have been sued and charged in his representative character by the description 'Cornelius Lumaree, executor,' without the addition of a further averment or designation showing his relation to the

546    APPELLATE COURT OF INDIANA.

Rohrbaugh *v.* Leas. Admr.—63 Ind. App. 544.

will or estate of some person. The same thing is true of the appellee Lewis Signs, who is described in the assignment of errors simply as 'trustee'; but how created, or for whom, does not appear. Neither of these persons in his representative capacity is before the court. As two of the parties named in the complaint, and in whose favor judgment was rendered against the appellant, are not properly designated in the assignment of errors, either in its title or body, we are compelled to hold that the assignment does not comply with rule six, and therefore the appeal must be dismissed.''

In this case appellee was a party to the judgment in his representative capacity, and not as an individual. Upon the authority of the cases cited, *supra*, we hold that he is not properly described as such representative in the assignment of errors, and therefore is not before this court in the same capacity in which he recovered judgment. This is ground for dismissal.

Appellant cites the case of *First Nat. Bank* v. *Farmers, etc., Bank* (1908), 171 Ind. 323, 86 N. E. 417, in support of his contention that the assignment of errors is sufficient. It will be observed, however, that the name of the appellant in question in that case is set out as "Charles C. Wheeler, trustee for the First National Bank of Peoria, Illinois'' and therefore the question here presented is not the same as the one decided in that case.

Appellee urges as a further reason for the dismissal of this appeal that appellant has not complied with the statute providing for term-time appeals, and has failed
2.    to give notice as required in case of vacation appeals.

The facts are as follows: Judgment was rendered and entered by the trial court against appellant on March 12, 1915, the same being the eleventh judicial day of the March term, 1915. On the same date appellant filed a motion for a new trial, which was subsequently overruled on January 20, 1916, the same being the twenty-eighth judicial day of

NOVEMBER TERM, 1916. 547

Rohrbaugh v. Leas. Admr.—63 Ind. App. 544.

the December term, 1915, at which time appellant prayed
an appeal to this court, which was granted on condition that
appellant would, on or before the second Monday of the
March term, 1916, file its appeal bond with penalty in the
sum of $1,500. On March 13, 1916, the same being the
seventh judicial day of the March term, 1916, of the trial
court, and within the time given by the court, appellant filed
the bond, with penalty in said sum, and with sureties as in
the bond named, which bond was on said date approved
by the court. The transcript was filed in this court on
April 11, 1916, and the cause was submitted on May 11,
1916.' Where, as here, the entry of the judgment pre-
3. ceded the ruling on the motion for a new trial, the
latter action of the court marked the beginning of the
time limited for an appeal. It will be found that
2. neither at the time of the ruling on the motion for a
new trial, nor at any time within the term at which the
action was had, did the court approve the bond or name or
approve the sureties thereon. Appellant concedes that an
effort has been made to perfect this appeal as a term-time
appeal under provision of §679 Burns 1914, §638 R. S. 1881.
The appeal has not been properly perfected as a term-time
appeal. *Penn, etc., Plate Glass Co.* v. *Poling* (1913), 52
Ind. App. 492, 100 N. E. 83; *Kyger* v. *Stallings* (1913), 55
Ind. App. 196, 103 N. E. 674; *W. C. Hall Milling Co.* v.
*Hewes* (1914), 57 Ind. App. 381, 105 N. E. 241; *Coxe
Bros. & Co.* v. *Foley* (1915), 58 Ind. App. 584, 107 N. E.
85; *Michigan Mut. Life Ins. Co.* v. *Frankel* (1898), 151
Ind. 534, 50 N. E. 304; *Tuttle* v. *Fowler* (1915), 183 Ind.
99, 107 N. E. 674.

Appellant cites the case of *Atkinson* v. *Williams* (1898),
151 Ind. 431, 51 N. E. 721, but this authority does not meet
the question. We recognize the rule, as there stated, that
when judgment is rendered before the motion for a new trial
for cause is filed, the final judgment within the meaning of

the statute governing appeals, is the judgment of the court overruling such motion for a new trial for cause, and we have given it full effect in passing upon the motion in this case to dismiss the appeal. The final judgment in this case, according to the rule just stated, was rendered at the December term, 1915. In order to have a term-time appeal, it was necessary that the penalty and surety of the appeal bond should be fixed and approved at that term, but no surety was named or approved at such term. This was an omission of an essential requirement, and the filing and approving of a bond after the close of such term and, within the time given, would not have the effect of curing such omission.

This appeal has been on the docket of this court for more than ninety days, to wit, since April 11, 1916, and no steps have been taken to give notice, as required 4. by §681 Burns 1914, §640 R. S. 1881, in cases of vacation appeal. Appellee has not joined in error nor otherwise entered a general appearance. The authorities are controlling, and determine the duty of the court under the facts shown in the record. Motion sustained and appeal dismissed.

NOTE.—Reported in 114 N. E. 762.

---

# UNION SANITARY MANUFACTURING COMPANY v. DAVIS.

## [No. 9,661.  Filed January 23, 1917.]

1. MASTER AND SERVANT.—*Workmen's Compensation Act.—Intent of Legislature.*—An examination of the Workmen's Compensation Act (Acts 1915 p. 392) in its entirety shows clearly that the intention of the legislature was to provide compensation and the proper award with a minimum of legal procedure. p. 551.

2. MASTER AND SERVANT.—*Workmen's Compensation Act.—Review of Award.*—The provisions for a review of an award authorized by §60 of the Workmen's Compensation Act (Acts 1915 pp. 392, 410) afford opportunity for presenting to the full board all ques-

Union Sanitary Mfg. Co. v. Davis—63 Ind. App. 548.

tions relied upon by the aggrieved party, and, in the main, serve the same purpose that a motion for a new trial serves in a civil action.  p. 551.

3. MASTER AND SERVANT.—*Workmen's Compensation Act.—Procedure.—Appeals.*—The legislature did not contemplate engrafting on the procedure provided by the Workmen's Compensation Act (Acts 1915 p. 392) all the requirements relating to appeals from judgments in ordinary civil suits, and, in construing §61 authorizing appeals from awards, the phrase "under the same terms and conditions as govern appeals in civil actions" is to be applied only to phases of procedure in appeals under the act not specially provided for therein.  p. 551.

4. MASTER AND SERVANT.—*Workmen's Compensation Act.—Appeal. —Motion for New Trial.*—The intent to make the procedure under the Workmen's Compensation Act (Acts 1915 p. 392) simple and direct and to dispense with a motion for a new trial is apparent from the general tenor of the law and the special provisions thereof, and, where a final award has been made by the industrial board, and appeal therefrom will lie, if otherwise properly perfected, though appellant has made no motion for a new trial.  p. 552.

5. MASTER AND SERVANT.—*Workmen's Compensation Act.—Appeals. —Motion to Modify or Set Aside Award.*—It is not necessary to file a motion to modify or set aside the final award made by the full board under the Workmen's Compensation Act (Acts 1915 p. 392) to entitle the party aggrieved to an appeal under the act.  p. 552.

6. MASTER AND SERVANT.—*Workmen's Compensation Act.—Appeal for Errors of Law.—Record.—Assignment of Errors.*—Where the record shows that appellant has properly excepted to the final award of the full board under the Workmen's Compensation Act (Acts 1915 p. 392), has presented its bill of exceptions containing the evidence and the rulings of the court and exceptions thereto, which bill of exceptions has been properly approved, and has filed a duly certified transcript of copies of all papers and entries in the cause, and appellant, on appeal to the Appellate Court from such final award, assigns as error that the award is not sustained by sufficient evidence, "the award is contrary to law," etc., the assignment of error presents alleged "errors of law" and the party aggrieved is entitled to have them passed upon by the court under §61 of the act, so that a motion to dismiss the appeal will be overruled.  pp. 552, 553.

7. MASTER AND SERVANT.—*Workmen's Compensation Act.—Appeal. —Record.—Exceptions.*—Where the record on an appeal from a final award of the industrial board under the Workmen's Compensation Act (Acts 1915 p. 392) shows proper exceptions to the

original award and also to the award of the full board, contention that the record does not show that the exception was taken "at the time" is not available, when the exceptions shown are sufficient under the provisions of the act and would have been sufficient without showing an exception to the first award. p. 552.

From the Industrial Board of Indiana.

Action by Frank L. Davis under the Workmen's Compensation Act against the Union Sanitary Manufacturing Company. Defendant appeals from an award for plaintiff, and the latter moves to dismiss the appeal. *Motion to dismiss appeal overruled.*

*Kane & Kane,* for appellant.
*Gentry & Campbell,* for appellee.

FELT, C. J.—This is an appeal from an award of the Industrial Board of Indiana. Appellee has moved to dismiss the appeal, and the first reason assigned therefor is that appellant filed no motion for a new trial after the final award was made by the board. The record shows a finding and an award by the board and an application by appellant for a review by the full board of the award, which was granted and the case was heard by all the members of the Industrial Board and the award made and entered from which this appeal was taken. Appellant has assigned as error: (1) The award is not sustained by sufficient evidence; (2) the award is contrary to the evidence; (3) the award is not sustained by the finding of facts stated by the board; (4) the award is contrary to the finding of facts stated by the board; (5) the award is contrary to law; (6) the board erred in its rulings of law upon the facts found; (7) the board erred in its award of compensation upon the facts found.

The Workmen's Compensation Act (Acts 1915 p. 392) provides: "Sec. 59. The board or any of its members shall hear the parties at issue and their representatives and witnesses and shall determine the dispute in any summary manner. The award, together with a statement of the findings of fact, rulings of law and any other matters pertinent to the question at issue shall be filed with the record of proceedings, and a copy of the award shall immediately be sent to the parties in dispute.

"Sec. 60. If an application for review is made to the board within seven days from the date of the award, the full board, if the first hearing was not held before the full board, shall review the evidence, or if deemed advisable, as soon as practicable hear the parties at issue, their representatives and witnesses and shall make an award and file same in like manner as specified in the foregoing section.

"Sec. 61. An award of the board, as provided in section 59, if not reviewed in due time, or an award of the board upon such review as provided in section 60, shall be conclusive and binding as to all questions of fact, but either party to the dispute may within thirty days from the date of the award appeal to the appellate court for errors of law under the same terms and conditions as govern appeals in ordinary civil actions. The board, of its own motion, may certify questions of law to said appellate court for its decision and determination."

An examination of the whole act shows clearly that the intention of the legislature was to provide compensation and the proper award with a minimum of legal procedure.

1. The provisions for a review afford opportunity of presenting to the full board all questions relied upon by the aggrieved party and in the main serve 'the same purpose that a motion for a new trial serves in a

2. civil action. At all events it is evident the legislature did not contemplate engrafting on the procedure provided by the act all the requirements

3. relating to appeals from judgments in ordinary civil suits. This is apparent from the general tenor of the law and by §55 which provides that: "The Board may make rules not inconsistent with this act for carrying out the

provisions of this act. Process and procedure under this act shall be as summary and simple as reasonably may be." As above shown, the section authorizing appeals contains the phrase, "under the same terms and conditions as govern appeals in ordinary civil actions," but it is apparent it was only intended to apply to phases of the procedure in appeals under the act not specially provided for by the act itself.

No motion for a new trial was contemplated by the legislature, but on the contrary the intention to dispense with such motion and to make the procedure simple and direct is apparent both from the general tenor of the law and the special provisions to which reference has already been made. For the reasons already announced it was not necessary to file a motion to modify or set aside the final award made by the full board to entitle the aggrieved party to appeal under the provisions of the law above set out.

The record shows that appellant duly excepted to the original award and also to the award made by the full board on review, and then presented its bill of exceptions containing the evidence and the rulings of the court and exceptions thereto, which bill was duly approved and signed by all the members of the board and thereafter filed with the secretary of said board and made a part of the record in this cause by order of the board. The board also duly certifies that the transcript contains full, true and correct copies of all papers and entries in said cause required by the praecipe of appellant.

The further contention that the record does not show that the exception was taken "at the time" is not available since the exceptions shown are sufficient under the provisions of the act and would have been sufficient without showing an exception to the first award, as the record sets forth the proceedings on review by the full board and appellant's exception to the final award from which this appeal was taken.

On this record the assignment of errors presents
6.  alleged "errors of law" which an aggrieved party is
     entitled to have passed upon by this court under §61,
*supra.*  See, also, *Columbia School Supply Co.* v. *Lewis,
ante* 386, 115 N. E. 103.  We are not called upon to decide, and do not decide, the right of a party to appeal from
the first award without applying for a review under the
statute.

Other alleged omissions and irregularities mentioned in
the motion to dismiss need not be specifically mentioned as
they are in effect disposed of by our discussion and disposition of the other questions presented.  The motion to dismiss the appeal is therefore overruled.

Ibach, P. J., Dausman, Caldwell, Batman and Hottel, JJ.,
concur.

NOTES—Reported in 115 N. E. 676.  Workmen's compensation
acts: (a) what is an accident in meaning of, Ann. Cas. 1913C 4,
1914B 498, 1916B 1293, L. R. A. 1916A 23, 40; (b) review of facts
on appeal under, Ann. Cas. 1916B 475.

---

## DUNN *v.* CHICAGO, INDIANAPOLIS AND LOUISVILLE RAILWAY COMPANY.

### [No. 9,199.  Filed January 23, 1917.]

1.  RAILROADS.—*Construction.—Watercourses.*—Although a railroad
    company is by the statutes (§5195, cl. 5, Burns 1914, §3903 R.
    S. 1881, and §7683 Burns 1914, Acts 1905 pp. 521, 532) authorized
    to construct its road across any stream of water, they are re-
    quired to restore and maintain it substantially in its former
    condition and in such manner as not to unnecessarily impair
    its usefulness, and any such company failing to do so is liable
    in damages to any person injured thereby. . p. 557.
2.  RAILROADS.—*Protection of Right of Way.—Obstruction of Sur-
    face Water.*—A railroad company has the right to employ all
    necessary methods which it deems expedient· to prevent surface
    water from flowing onto and across its right of way without
    being liable for the damage done thereby. p. 557·
3.  RAILROADS.—*Protection of Right of Way.—Obstruction of Nat-
    ural Watercourse.—Liability.*—A railroad company in the con-
    struction and maintenance of its road over a natural water-

course must exercise due care not to obstruct the natural flow thereof, including not only such rises of high water as are usual and ordinary but also floods due to natural causes, such as an ordinarily prudent person should reasonably anticipate, considering the topography of the country, character of the soil, climatic conditions and all other conditions and circumstances apparent to a person of usual foresight and experience. p. 557.

4. WATERS AND WATERCOURSES.—*Natural Watercourse.—Obstruction of Flood Channel.—Liability.*—Where a riparian owner obstructs the flood channel of a stream he is liable to respond in damages to any one injured. p. 558.

5. RAILROADS.—*Obstructing Natural Watercourse.—Flood Waters. —Liability.—Instruction.*—In an action against a railroad for damages caused by the obstruction of flood waters of a natural watercourse, it was error to instruct the jury that it is not the legal duty of a railroad company to make openings through its track large enough to prevent the accumulation of water on the up-stream side, but it is only required to make its opening large enough to take care of the water which will flow within the bed of a watercourse. pp. 558, 560.

6. RAILROADS. — *Crossing Natural Watercourse. — Rights.* — The rights of a railway company crossing the bed of a natural watercourse are not the same as those of a proprietor of land in regard to surface water. p. 559.

7. RAILROADS.—*Obstructing Natural Watercourse.—Flood Waters. —Duty of Railroad.*—A railway company constructing its road across a stream and erecting an embankment and culvert is required to consider conditions manifest at other times of high water, the changes in the surrounding territory and the volume of water which would probably flow through the stream during flood times, and must provide ample accommodations for the free passage of all such waters through its right of way at all seasons of the year. p. 560.

8. RAILROADS. — *Obstruction of Natural Watercourse. — Action. — Pleading and Proof.—Evidence.*—Where, in an action against a railroad company for damages for obstructing a natural watercourse it was not the theory of the complaint that there were any permanent injuries to the property involved although it was alleged that the flood waters impaired plaintiff's store building to the extent of $1,000, it was proper to permit proof of the cost of repairs, but offered testimony tending to prove permanent injuries was properly excluded. p. 560.

9. RAILROADS. — *Obstruction of Natural Watercourse. — Action. — Measure of Damages.*—In an action against a railroad company for damages from overflow of flood waters due to the obstruction of a natural watercourse, plaintiff may show the damage to

his property by proving the loss of its rental value, where the complaint proceeds upon the theory that the nuisance is abatable, since, when the nuisance is abated, the damages recoverable are only such as have accrued prior to the action. p. 560.

From Monroe Circuit Court; *Robert W. Miers,* Judge.

Action by Charles C. Dunn against the Chicago, Indianapolis and Louisville Railway Company. From a judgment for defendant, the plaintiff appeals. *Reversed.*

*Ira C. Batman, Robert G. Miller* and *James W. Blair,* for appellant.

*E. C. Field, C. C. Hine* and *J. E. Henley,* for appellee.

IBACH, P. J.—This was an action for damages on account of the overflow of appellant's property occasioned by the alleged negligence of appellee in obstructing a natural watercourse. There is also a prayer that the alleged nuisance be abated. A trial resulted in a verdict and judgment for appellee. The material facts of the case are not controverted. The questions to be determined therefore are questions of law.

Appellant owns certain lots in the town of Stinesville, upon one of which there is a store building. Appellee's railroad runs north and south through the town along Railroad street, which is 100 feet wide. The railroad occupies about forty feet of the street, and about twenty feet along the east side is used for general travel. Appellant's lots face the west and abut on this portion of Railroad street and lie between Spring street on the south and Main street on the north. A stream of water flows down Spring street from the east; thence into Railroad street, and from there it flows in a northwesterly direction under appellee's tracks and road-bed through a culvert. This stream has its source in a spring about one mile to the east of the town, but before it reaches Railroad street a number of other springs flow into it, draining about 400 acres of rough and broken land and the stream is between 150 and 200 feet higher at its source than it is at Railroad street. After rains the water flows down the stream with a rush. Appellee graded its road-bed along Railroad street between Spring street and Main street to a width of forty feet and a height of thirteen feet. Some time prior to 1874 an open wooden culvert ten or twelve feet wide was washed out and appellee or its predecessor replaced it with the one in question, which is built of stone and is three feet and six inches wide by five feet and one inch deep. About the year 1892 appellee or its predecessors constructed a switch, which appellee has since maintained, from its main line in Railroad street, extending southeast from a point south of the culvert, which switch entirely obstructs two other watercourses that crossed appellee's right of way to a creek beyond, and thereby the waters from these streams were turned down Railroad street to Spring street where they met the other waters which flowed down that street and then passed on through the culvert. After a hard rain of an hour or more, the culvert always failed to carry off the water, and as there was no other means of escape, it backed up over a portion of the town, including appellant's premises, and oftentimes raised as high as appellee's grade. The first overflow testified about occurred in 1875, others in 1896, 1904, 1906, and two in 1912, all of much the same character and causing similar damages to those described in appellant's complaint, which covered the overflow of 1912. On all such occasions the water which was backed up by the grade and insufficient culvert passed off with the other waters of the stream just as rapidly as the size of the culvert would permit. The evidence also shows the nature of appellant's injury to his store building and to the vacant lot. It also shows the amount of money necessary to make the repairs required to restore the building substantially to its former condition. There was evidence also tending to show the depreciation in the rental value of the building occasioned by the flood, as well as the depreciation of the rental value of the lot, not improved, occasioned by the flood water.

It is clear that appellee and its predecessors recognized the stream in question to be a natural watercourse, as that term is used in the law, by first constructing the open wooden culvert and then when that was washed away by erecting another more substantial in character to enable its railway to pass over such stream. It is also apparent from the record that both parties tried the case on that theory, and the uncontradicted evidence supports that theory. The

1. statutes of this state give to railroad companies the right to cross a stream of water, but they are also required by the same statutes to restore and maintain it substantially in its former condition and in such manner as not to unnecessarily impair its usefulness. Any such company which neglects or wilfully fails so to do is liable in damages to any person injured thereby. §5195, cl. 5, Burns 1914, §3903 R. S. 1881; §7683 Burns 1914, Acts 1905 p. 521, 532. *Vandalia R. Co.* v. *Yeager* (1915), 60 Ind. App. 118, 110 N. E. 230.

The right of a railroad company to employ all necessary methods as it deems expedient to prevent surface water

2. from flowing onto and across its right of way, just as an individual has the right to take such necessary measures as he may deem expedient to turn surface water from his premises without being liable for the damage done by such water, the flow of which has been thus obstructed, is too well recognized to require the citation of authority.

The law is also well recognized that a railroad company in the construction and maintenance of its road over a

3. natural watercourse must exercise due care not to obstruct the natural flow of the watercourse and this includes not only such rises of high water as are usual and ordinary but also floods due to natural causes, such as an ordinarily prudent person should reasonably anticipate, considering the topography of the country,

character of the soil, climatic conditions and all other conditions and circumstances apparent to a person of usual foresight and experience. As was said by the Supreme Court of this state: "It was incumbent on appellant, in the construction of its road, * * * to take notice of this character of the country, and provide ample accommodations for the free passage of the waters over its right of way at all seasons of the year." *New York, etc., R. Co.* v. *Hamlet Hay Co.* (1897), 149 Ind. 344, 352, 47 N. E. 1060, 49 N. E. 269. See also 40 Cyc 574. Neither can the flood channel of a stream be obstructed by a proprietor

4. without his being liable to respond in damages to anyone injured thereby. *Clark* v. *Guano Co.* (1907), 144 N. C. 64, 56 S. E. 858, 119 Am. St. 931.

Notwithstanding the evidence in this case and the rules of law applicable thereto, the court gave the following instruction: "In a case of this kind it does not neces-

5. sarily follow that because damage was done on account of overflow that a railroad company is liable therefor. It is not the legal duty of a railroad company to make openings through its tracks large enough to prevent the accumulation of water on the upstream side. A railroad company under such conditions is only required to make its opening large enough to take care of the water which will flow within the bed and banks of a watercourse and when it has done this it has performed its legal duty. So in the case at bar, if you find from the evidence that there was a small watercourse crossing defendant's right of way in Stinesville, which was sufficient to accommodate the water which would flow within the bed and banks of this watercourse and at the time the damage complained of was done, there was a heavy down-pour of rain which caused the water to rush down from the nearby hills in great quantity and overflow the banks of this small watercourse and in that way accumulate on the upstream side of defendant's railroad grade and that the damage to plaintiff's property

was done by this water overflowing said banks, your verdict in this case should be in favor of the defendant.''

This instruction is not in harmony with the evidence
6. and with our view governing this case. Our courts, in the cases heretofore cited have fully discussed and determined what shall constitute surface waters, and we see no reason for disturbing the conclusions already reached. It is sufficient to say that, under these holdings, the rights of appellee are not such as a proprietor may have in surface water.

The parties treated the stream in question as a natural watercourse, and the evidence shows without contradiction that the waters which caused the injury to appellant's property was the overflow of such watercourse at a time of ordinary flood. It was not water which had become separated from the main stream so as to prevent its return. It was overflow water, it is true, which had passed over the low-water banks of the stream; yet it, at all times, was inseparably united with the water which remained within such banks but was simply held back until it, like the other water of the stream, might escape through the culvert; and the evidence shows that it did pass through with the remaining water of the stream as rapidly as the size of the culvert would permit. It is apparent that a larger culvert would have rendered the embankment harmless to appellant's lots, and the failure to make it of sufficient size enabled the embankment to force flood waters to flow back over and upon appellant's lots until such time as all the waters of the stream might flow through the opening provided for that purpose. It is also clear that the facts surrounding the rise in question were similar to the facts attending many other floods of the same stream after heavy rains.

Appellee was required when erecting the embankment and culvert complained of to take into account the conditions manifest at other times of high water. They were required to take note of the changes in the surrounding

territory and of the volume of water which would
7. probably flow through this stream during flood times,
in view of all the conditions of which it was required
to take notice, and then to provide ample accommodations for
the free passage of all such waters through its right of way
at all seasons of the year. The undisputed evidence is
5. that the accumulated water which damaged appellant's property was on the up-stream side of the embankment, and, as the jury was compelled to follow the
instructions of the court, it was therefore, in view of this
record, error to instruct that: "It is not the legal duty of a
railroad company to make openings through its track large
enough to prevent the accumulation of water on the up-
stream side."

It becomes unnecessary for us to discuss at length other
errors assigned. It is sufficient to say that we are of the
opinion that the complaint does not proceed upon
8. the theory that there were any permanent injuries to
the real estate through the effect of the flood waters.
although this averment is used in the complaint: "It permanently impaired the said store building to the extent of
$1,000 for repairs." Hence, when appellant was permitted
to make proof of the cost of these repairs he was proving
the apparent theory of his complaint, and the offered testimony tending to prove permanent injuries was properly
excluded. The complaint proceeds also upon the theory
that the nuisance was abatable.

Appellant was permitted to show the damages to his lots
by proving the loss to the rental value thereof. We think
the trial court adopted the proper rule for ascertain-
9. ing appellant's damages. In the consideration of a
similar case this court said: "It is the settled law in
this state as applied to actions of this character that when
the injury is of such a nature as to be abatable, by the
expenditure of either labor or money, the law will not presume its continuance, and that when from the nature of the

case the injury is removed, the injurious consequences will cease the damages recoverable from the wrongdoer are only such as had accrued before action was brought.'' *Southern R. Co.* v. *Poetker* (1910); 46 Ind. App. 295, 91 N. E. 610.

We are also of the opinion that the instruction tendered by appellant and refused was, so far as it had to do with the issues, substantially covered by others given.

Appellant's motion for a new trial should have been sustained. Cause reversed; new trial ordered.

Batman, J., not participating.

NOTE.—Reported in 114 N. E. 888. Waters and watercourses, liability of railroad company, (a) for interference, by construction of road on land acquired for right of way, 19 Ann. Cas. 336; (b) for conducting surface water through embankments onto lands of adjoining owner, 12 L. R. A. (N. S.) 680. As to right to accelerate or diminish flow of water by means of dams, bridges, etc., 85 Am. St. 708; 40 Cyc 571. See under (1) 40 Cyc. 645; (2, 4, 6) 40 Cyc 574; (8) 40 Cyc 581.

---

## STATE OF INDIANA, EX REL. SALT CREEK CIVIL TOWNSHIP OF THE COUNTY OF MONROE ET AL. *v.* STEVENS ET AL.

### [No. 9,578. Filed January 24, 1917.]

1. APPEAL.—*Parties.—Appeal by Township.—Designation of Appellant.—Sufficiency.*—While §9562 Burns 1914, §5990 R. S. 1881, provides that each township is a corporation and shall be designated by the name and style of "........ township of ........ county" according to the name of the township and county in which the same may be organized, and that by such name it may sue and be sued, the name Salt Creek township imports the civil township without the addition of the word "civil" so that an appeal by such township will not be dismissed although it was designated in the proceedings below as "Salt Creek civil township," while in the assignment of errors the word "civil" was omitted.  pp. 563, 564.

2. OFFICERS.—*Official Bonds.—Party in Interest.*—Where actions are brought upon official bonds payable to the state in its name on the relation of the party interested, as provided in §253 Burns

1914, §253 R. S. 1881, the state is but a nominal party, the real party in interest being the relator. p. 564.

3. APPEAL.—*Parties.*—*Presumption.*—Where a political corporation is designated in the assignment of errors as "Salt Creek Township," a conclusive presumption arises that the reference is to the civil township. p. 565.

4. SCHOOLS AND SCHOOL DISTRICTS.—*Townships.*—*Official Bonds.*—*Action.*—*Parties.*—Either the trustee or the civil township, as relator, may prosecute an action on the bond of a preceding trustee to recover funds belonging to or due to the civil township, and likewise the trustee or the school township may, as relator, prosecute a like action to recover funds due or belonging to the school township, or in one action, either the trustee, as relator, or both corporations, as relators, may prosecute such an action to recover funds severally due the two corporations. p. 565.

5. APPEAL.—*Term-Time Appeal.*—*Parties.*—*Statute.*—Under §675 Burns 1914, Acts 1895 p. 179, relating to term-time appeals by part of coparties, where an action was brought to recover on official bonds in behalf of both the civil and school township and the judgment was adverse to each, the school corporation is not a necessary party to a term-time appeal in order that the judgment may be reviewed in behalf of the civil township. p. 566.

6. EVIDENCE.—*Judicial Notice.*—*Civil and School Townships.*—Where it appears that there is in Monroe county a township named Salt Creek township, the court judicially knows that there is also in that county a school corporation known as Salt Creek school township, since §§6404, 6405 Burns 1914, §§4437, 4438 R. S. 1881, declares that each civil township shall also be a distinct school corporation for school purposes to be known by the name and style of the civil township except that the word school should be added thereto, but townships being laid off, bounded, described and named by the board of county comissioners, under the provisions of §9559 Burns 1914, §5987 R. S. 1881, and not by legislative enactment, the court cannot judicially know that a school township designated in the assignment of errors as "Salt School township of Monroe county" is not a body politic separate and distinct from a school corporation known as Salt Creek school township in the same county, so that an appeal by the latter is ineffective where it is designated therein by the name set forth in the assignment of errors. (*Miller* v. *Miller* [1913], 55 Ind. App. 644, disapproved in part.) p. 566.

From Owen Circuit Court; *Robert W. Miers*, Judge.

Action by the State of Indiana, on the relation of Salt Creek civil township and Salt Creek school township of

the County of Monroe. Plaintiffs appeal from a judgment
for defendants, and the latter move to dismiss the appeal.
*Motion to dismiss appeal overruled.*

*Joseph K. Barclay, William M. Louden, Charles B. Wal-
dron* and *Miller, Batman & Blair,* for appellants.

*East & East,* for appellees.

CALDWELL, J.—This action was brought and prosecuted
by the State on the relation of the two corporations indicated to recover on three several official bonds, executed
by appellee, William F. Stevens, as township trustee. The
other appellees were sureties on the bonds. The cause is now
before this court on appellees' motion to dismiss the appeal,
conceded to be a term-time appeal.

The facts as presented by appellees are as follows: In the
complaint and for the most part in the proceedings below,
the relators are named as "Salt Creek civil township"
and "Salt Creek School Township" of Monroe county, Indiana. In the assignment of error, which is several in form,
the relators are named as "Salt Creek township of Monroe county, Indiana" and "Salt school township of Monroe county, Indiana". The judgment appealed from is to
the effect that the plaintiff and relators take nothing by the
complaint and that appellees recover from the relators
their costs, and further that appellee William F. Stevens
recover of Salt Creek township the sum of $67.73 and costs.

It will be observed that in naming the relators in the
assignment of errors, the word "civil" is omitted in one
case, and the word "Creek" in the other case. On
1. such facts, appellees state their position as follows:

"The appeal should be dismissed herein, for the
reason that errors are not assigned by the judgment defendants. On the complaint appellees recovered a judgment
against the relators, Salt Creek civil township and Salt
Creek school township of Monroe county, Indiana. The
assignment of errors does not name either of said relators."

We proceed to determine whether or not such defects in the record necessitates a dismissal. There being in Monroe county a township, the name of which is Salt Creek township, it follows by virtue of statute that there is also in that county another corporation exercising dominion over the same territory as the former, but in a different field of activity, being "Salt Creek school township of Monroe county, Indiana." The first is a civil township and the second, a school township. §§6404, 6405 Burns 1914, §§4437, 4438 R. S. 1881; *Carmichael* v. *Lawrence* (1874), 47 Ind. 554. The trustee of the former is, by virtue of his office, trustee of the latter also. §6405, *supra*. A statute

2.   provides that actions upon official bonds and bonds payable to the State of Indiana shall be brought in the name of the State of Indiana on the relation of the parties interested. §253 Burns 1914, §253 R. S. 1881. In such a case the relator is the real party in interest, the state being but a nominal party. 1 Works' Practice §49 and cases; *State, ex rel.* v. *Wilson* (1888), 113 Ind. 501, 15

1.   N. E. 596. The statute, by virtue of which Salt Creek township involved here exists as a body politic and corporate, prescribes that it may sue and be sued by the name of "Salt Creek township of Monroe county." §9562 Burns 1914, §5990 R. S. 1881. The corporation existing under such name is the civil township rather than the school township. *Baltimore, etc., R. Co.* v. *State, ex rel.* (1902), 159 Ind. 510, 65 N. E. 508. As the word "civil" is not one of the words specified by the statute as constituting the corporate name of a township, it should not be included. However, as the name "Salt Creek township," etc., imports the civil township, the addition of the word "civil" as a qualifying word does not in fact qualify or render either more or less certain the identity of the corporation and body politic to which reference is made. We are able to determine with certainty that Salt Creek civil township named in the proceedings below is the same corpora-

tion as is designated in the assignment of errors as Salt Creek township. Such is practically the holding in the case last cited. There, in a proceeding for a writ of mandate, a township was designated as "Washington civil township," etc. In meeting an objection that there is no such township, the Supreme Court says: "While not necessarily required in this case, nevertheless it was proper for the relator to designate himself as trustee of Washington civil township of Daviess county, Indiana. The word 'civil' might have been omitted without detriment to the petition."

Moreover, a political corporation being designated in
3. the assignment of errors as "Salt Creek township" etc., a conclusive presumption arises that the reference is to the civil township. *Jarvis* v. *Robertson* (1890), 126 Ind. 281, 26 N. E. 182. *Sproat* v. *State, ex rel.* (1914), 182 Ind. 687, 107 N. E. 673. It may be said in addition that the transcript discloses that in the proceedings below, both the terms "Salt Creek civil township" and "Salt Creek township" are used to designate the civil township. Thus, in appellees' application for a change of venue, they designate the civil township as "Salt Creek township," and the judgment in favor of appellee, William F. Stevens, is entered against the civil township under the latter name.

The civil township, as we have said, is a corporation distinct from the school township. Each has its separate duties to perform, and controls and expends its own
4. funds. Either the trustee or the civil township, as relator, may prosecute an action on the bond of a preceding trustee to recover funds belonging to or due the civil township, and likewise the trustee or the school township may, as relator, prosecute a like action to recover funds due or belonging to the school township; or in one action, either the trustee, as relator, or both corporations, as relators, may prosecute such an action to recover funds severally due the two corporations. *State, ex rel.* v. *Wilson, supra; Steinmetz* v. *State* (1874), 47 Ind. 465; *Ross* v. *State, ex rel.*

(1892), 131 Ind. 548, 30 N. E. 702; *Inglis* v. *State, ex rel.* (1878), 61 Ind. 212; *Robinson* v. *State, ex rel.* (1877), 60 Ind. 26.

This action was brought in behalf of both corporations, each seeking to recover funds alleged to be due it. The judgment was adverse to each. ∖ The appeal is a term-time appeal. Such being the case, the school corporation is not a necessary party to the appeal in order that the judgment may be reviewed in behalf of the civil township. The motion to dismiss should therefore be overruled. §675 Burns 1914, Acts 1895 p. 179.

5.

Considering briefly the other phase of the case, this action was brought and prosecuted in the trial court in behalf of Salt Creek school township also, while Salt school township, rather than Salt Creek school township is named as a relator in the assignment of errors. It being conceded or established that there is in Monroe county a township named Salt Creek township, we know judicially that there is also in that county a school corporation named Salt Creek school township. We know that fact judicially because there is a statute to that effect. §§6404, 6405 Burns 1914, *supra.* If we knew judicially that there was not in said county a Salt township also, and consequently a Salt school township, we might perhaps be justified in treating the omission of the word "Creek" in the assignment of errors as a mere clerical error. But townships are laid off, bounded, described and named by the board of county commissioners, rather than by legislative enactment. §9559 Burns 1914, §5987 R. S. 1881. It follows that we do not know judicially that the school township named in the assignment of errors is not an existing corporation and body politic separate and distinct from the school corporation in whose behalf as relator the action was brought in the trial court. We are, therefore, required to hold that the appeal is ineffective as to the school corporation.

6.

It seems that this court erroneously held in *Miller* v. *Mil-*

*ler* (1913), 55 Ind. App. 644, 104 N. E. 588, that the court knows judicially that within a certain county there is a township of a certain name. To the extent indicated, *Miller* v. *Miller, supra,* is disapproved. *See Bragg* v. *Board, etc.* (1870), 34 Ind. 405; *Columbian Oil Co.* v. *Blake* (1895), 13 Ind. App. 680, 42 N. E. 234; *Olive* v. *State* (1888), 86 Ala. 88, 5 South. 653, 4 L. R. A. 33 and note.

The motion to dismiss the appeal is overruled.

Batman, J., not participating.

NOTE.—Reported in 114 N. E. 873.

---

## STIMSON *v.* KRUEGER.

### [No. 9,143. Filed January 25, 1917.]

1. MASTER AND SERVANT. — *Injuries to Servant.* — *Action.* — *Complaint.—Sufficiency.*—On an employe's action for personal injuries, a complaint alleging that plaintiff was ordered to put chains around a log preparatory to moving it, and while he was so doing a fellow servant was directed to start a team hitched to the chain and that he did so negligently and without any warning, thereby causing plaintiff's injury, is not defective as showing that plaintiff gave the order to the driver to start, especially in view of the allegation that the team was started without any warning to plaintiff. pp. 570, 571.

2. MASTER AND SERVANT.—*Employers' Liability Act.—Scope.*—The Employers' Liability Act (§8020a Burns 1914, Acts 1911 p. 145) does not authorize a recovery by the employe for injuries resulting from his own independent orders and directions, whether given negligently or otherwise. p. 570.

3. MASTER AND SERVANT.—*Injuries to Servant.—Employers' Liability Act.—Acts of Fellow Servant.*—The fellow-servant rule is eliminated in cases brought within the provisions of the Employers' Liability Act (§8020a Burns 1914, Acts 1911 p. 145). p. 571.

4. MASTER AND SERVANT.—*Injuries to Servant.—Liability of Master:—Complaint.*—Where, in an employe's action against the master for personal injuries, the complaint alleges that defendant employed more than five persons, that at the time of the injury, plaintiff, in pursuance to the orders of his foreman and in the line of his duty, was putting a chain around a log preparatory to moving it and that while he was so engaged a fellow servant was directed by the foreman to haul the log and that he started a team hitched to the chain negligently and without warning, thereby causing plaintiff's injury, the allegations of the

complaint are sufficient to bring the case within the provisions of the Employers' Liability Act (§8020a Burns 1914, Acts 1911 p. 145). p. 571.

5. APPEAL.—*Review.—Evidence.—Sufficiency.*—The court on appeal can reverse the judgment of the trial court because of insufficient evidence only when there is no evidence to support any element or fact necessary and essential to a recovery. p. 573.

6. APPEAL.—*Review.—Instructions.—Record.—Failure to Show Filing of Instructions.*—In order that instructions given and refused may be brought into the record under §561 Burns 1914, Acts 1903 p. 338, relating to making instructions a part of the record without a bill of exceptions, they must be filed, and there must be an entry so showing. p. 573.

7. APPEAL.—*Review.—Instructions.—Record.—Sufficiency.—Statute.*—Where the record shows that appellant was given time to present a bill of exceptions containing the instructions tendered and those given and refused by the trial court, but discloses no such bill, the instructions are not brought into the record in the manner authorized by §600 Burns 1914, §629 R. S. 1881, providing that when the record does not otherwise show the decision or grounds of objection thereto, the party objecting must, within the time allowed, present a proper bill of exceptions to the judge for signing and that the same shall be filed. p. 573.

From Pike Circuit Court; *John. L. Bretz,* Judge.

Action by Louis Krueger against Jacob V. Stimson. From a judgment for plaintiff, the defendant appeals. *Affirmed.*

*R. W. Armstrong,* for appellant.

*R. M. Milburn, M. A. Sweeney* and *Bomar Traylor,* for appellee.

HOTTEL, J.—This is an appeal from a judgment in appellee's favor, in an action brought by him to recover for personal injuries alleged to have been caused by appellant's negligence. The issues of fact were tendered by a complaint in one paragraph and a general denial. A demurrer to the complaint for want of facts, a motion for judgment on the answers to interrogatories and a motion for new trial, filed by appellant, were each overruled and exceptions properly saved. Each of said rulings is assigned as error in this court and relied on for reversal.

The grounds upon which the sufficiency of the complaint is

challenged, as set out in the memorandum accompanying said demurrer, are, in substance, as follows: (1) It appears on the face of the complaint that the cause of action therein stated is predicated on the act of the legislature, approved March 2, 1911, commonly known as the "Employers' Liability Act," and such act has no application to the cause of action described in appellee's complaint. §8020a *et seq.* Burns 1914, Acts 1911 ·p. 145; (2) the complaint fails to show any duty owed by appellant to appellee which was neglected; (3) the complaint fails to show any order given by appellant to appellee that was negligently given; (4) the complaint shows on its face that the negligence, if any, responsible for the injury was the negligence of a fellow servant.

The averments of the complaint affecting said questions are in substance as follows: Appellant owns and operates a saw mill in Huntingburg, Dubois county, Indiana, and is engaged in the purchase and sale of timber, logs and lumber, and in such mill saws and cuts lumber of all kinds; that in the operation of his said mill and business, he employs more than five persons, to wit, fifty men; that logs purchased and delivered to appellant's mill are brought in on wagons and trains and are unloaded in said mill yard by appellant's employes in the following manner: They are rolled off of the wagons and freight cars on a skidway. A chain is then attached to said logs and a team, hitched to the other end of the chain, pulls and rolls said logs to the place and position desired, piling them one upon another, six or seven logs high. On October 9, 1912, appellee had been employed by appellant for about one year and, on said day, was directed by appellant's foreman and vice principal, Harry Maley, to go into the yard and help one James Collins pile logs that were then being unloaded from cars upon said skidway; *and appellee "was directed by said foreman to put the chains around said logs, and when said chains were around said logs the said * * * Collins was directed to*

*drive up said team and pile said logs upon one another with
said team," and while appellee was thus engaged in putting
a chain around one of said logs upon said skidway, which
chain was attached to a double tree to which two horses of
said defendant were hitched, said Collins carelessly and
negligently started up said team without any warning to
appellee;* that appellee was at said time standing in front
of said logs and between said log and the pile of logs upon
which said log was to be placed, and the team was on the
other side of said pile; that said log to which the chain was
being attached was about five feet from said pile of logs
upon which it was to be placed, and when said team was so
carelessly started by Collins and said log began to move
appellee immediately began to halloo to Collins to stop
the team and at the same time attempted to escape by
jumping and trying to climb over said log, but was in some
way caught and rolled along with said log to said pile when
one arm and leg were caught between said log and said
pile of logs and broken and crushed, etc. *That said injuries
were caused wholly by the carelessness and negligence of
appellant's employe in starting up said team without any
warning to appellee while he, appellee, was in said dangerous
and precarious position;* that when he received his injuries,
appellee was in the line of his duty, obeying the orders
and directions of appellant's said foreman and vice principal,
to whose orders and directions appellee was obliged to conform.

If we correctly interpret appellant's brief, the first three
grounds of his objection to the complaint set out in his memorandum, indicated *supra*, are based upon a contention

1.   that the complaint shows upon its face that the orders
     and directions under which Collins started the team
and caused the log in question to be moved by appellant,
were orders and directions given by appellee himself. Of
     course, the statute under which the action was brought

2.   does not authorize recovery by the employe for in-
     juries resulting from his own independent orders and

directions whether given negligently or otherwise, and if the complaint in fact shows that appellee gave the order and direction to Collins to start the team, and that such order and direction was the proximate cause of his injury, the demurrer thereto should have been sustained.

1. However, we do not so interpret such averments, nor do we think them fairly susceptible of such interpretation. While the language of the first part of the italicized averments, *supra,* is somewhat vague and uncertain as to who directed and gave the order to Collins to start the team, it clearly appears from the other averments, which follow, that, at the time of his injury, appellee did not give any order or signal to start the team, but that *the team was started by Collins without any warning to appellee,* and at a time when he was still doing the work and carrying out the order of his superior, which placed him in a position of peril and danger if the log were moved before he had performed his work and gone to a place of safety.

As to the fourth ground of objection, *supra,* it is sufficient to say that the fellow-servant rule is eliminated in cases brought within the provisions of the act of 1911,

3. *supra. Vandalia R. Co.* v. *Stillwell* (1913), 181 Ind. 267, 104 N. E. 289, Ann. Cas. 1916D 258; *Chicago, etc., R. Co.* v. *Mitchell* (1915), 184 Ind. 383, 110 N. E. 680; *Central Ind. R. Co.* v. *Clark* (1916), 63 Ind. App. 49, 112 N. E. 892. For interpretation and construction of other provisions of said act, see *S. W. Little Coal Co.* v. *O'Brien* (1916), *ante* 504, 113 N. E. 465; *Standard Steel Car Co.* v. *Martinecz* (1916), — Ind. App. —, 113 N. E. 244. The averments of the complaint above indicated

4. are, we think, clearly sufficient to bring the case within said statute, as construed and interpreted in said cases, and sufficient to meet all the objections of appellant above indicated.

No material or essential fact is found by the answers to interrogatories that is in irreconcilable conflict with the general verdict. Indeed, such answers are in harmony with, and tend to support, rather than contradict, such verdict. It follows that no error resulted from the ruling on appellant's motion for judgment on such answers. *Lake Erie, etc., R. Co.* v. *McConkey* (1916), 62 Ind. App. 447, 113 N. E. 24, and cases there cited.

In support of his contention that error resulted from the ruling on his motion for new trial, it is insisted by appellant that there is no evidence that Collins was directed by anybody other than appellee to start the team at the time he, appellee, was injured, and that the team was in fact started pursuant to appellee's signal and direction. There is evidence which might have justified the trial court or jury in reaching such a conclusion, but the appellee himself testified, in substance, that on the morning of his injury he had been ordered and directed by appellant's foreman, Mr. Maley, to help Collins "double-deck" logs; that Maley instructed him in said matter and directed him to attach the chain to the log to be moved, etc.; that they had moved about two dozen logs before they attempted to move the one by which appellee was injured; that in moving the other logs, he, appellee, attached the chain to the log and went out from between it and the pile on which it was to be placed, where he could be seen by Collins, and would then give him the signal or tell him to go ahead; that this course was pursued at the direction of Collins; that while attaching the chain to the log which injured him, it began to move just as he was starting to get up after attaching the chain before any signal or direction had been given by him to Collins; that while he was still in front of the log and before he could escape and get from between it and the pile on which it was to be placed, he called to Collins to stop the team and tried to jump and climb over the log, but was caught, etc.; that he gave Collins no signal or directions to move the log and that Collins gave him no knowledge or warning that he was going to move it.

The jury, both by their general verdict and by their answers to interrogatories, found the facts upon this branch of the case to be as testified to by appellee. It is only

5. in those cases where there is no evidence to support one or more of the facts or elements necessary and essential to recovery that this court can reverse the judgment below because of insufficient evidence. *H. A. McCowen & Co.* v. *Gorman* (1912), 51 Ind. App. 523, 530, 100 N. E. 31, and cases cited.

The action of the trial court in giving and refusing to give certain instructions is challenged by appellant's motion for new trial and urged here as error. It is claimed by

6. appellee that this alleged error is not presented by the record because there is no entry showing the filing of said instructions. We have examined the record and find that it supports appellee's contention. In order that the instructions may be brought into the record under §561 Burns 1914, Acts 1903 p. 338, an entry showing their filing is essential. *Morgan Construction Co.* v. *Dulin* (1915), 184 Ind. 652, 109 N. E. 960; *Suloj* v. *Retlaw Mines Co.* (1914), 57 Ind. App. 302, 107 N. E. 18; *Peterson* v. *Liddington* (1915), 60 Ind. App. 41, 108 N. E. 977. The record shows that appellant asked and was given time in which to

7. prepare and present a special bill of exceptions containing the instructions tendered and those given and those refused by the court, but the record fails to disclose any such bill; and hence there is a failure to bring the instructions in the record in the manner authorized by §660 Burns 1914, §629 R. S. 1881. The instructions are not brought into the record in any way recognized by law; and hence cannot be considered.

Finding no available error in the record, the judgment below is affirmed.

NOTE.—Reported in 114 N. E. 885. Employers' liability act: "injury arising out of and in course of employment," what is, Ann. Cas. 1914D 1284; validity of, as exempting certain employments, Ann. Cas. 1914D 404.

## NATIONAL EXCHANGE BANK v. SMITH.

### [No. 9,150.   Filed January 26, 1917.]

1. MUNICIPAL CORPORATIONS.—*Street Improvements.*—*Foreclosure of Lien.*—*Findings.*—*Review.*—Where, in an action to foreclose the statutory lien securing a street improvement bond, defendant contended that plaintiff had at no time been in possession of the bond and that it was held by the paving contractor, defendant's predecessor in title, at the time he procured a conveyance of the lot involved in payment of the bond and assessment, a finding for defendant is a finding in his favor on the issue of possession of the bond; and, there being some evidence to support such finding, it is conclusive on appeal.   p. 578.

2. MUNICIPAL CORPORATIONS.—*Street Improvements.*—*Foreclosure of Lien.*—*Evidence.*—*Sufficiency.*—In an action to foreclose the statutory lien securing a street improvement bond, the evidence is held sufficient to warrant a finding that neither the assignment of the bond nor a copy thereof was left at the office of the town clerk.   p. 578.

3. VENDOR AND PURCHASER.—*Street Improvements.*—*Proceedings.*—*Record.*—*Notice.*—The proceedings of municipal corporations in street improvements are required by law to be duly recorded and they are open to public inspection, and persons who acquire real estate encumbered by assessments evidenced by such records are bound by the constructive notice given thereby when duly kept; but only records which the law requires to be kept and which have actually been so kept as to impart notice to those who examine them are binding.   p. 580.

4. MUNICIPAL CORPORATIONS. — *Street Improvements.* — *Bonds.*—*Lien.*—*Merger.*—*Discharge of Lien.*—Where a paving contractor, after assigning street improvement bonds, falsely represented that he was still the owner thereof and thereby induced the owner of real estate assessed for the improvement to convey the real estate to him in consideration of the satisfaction of the improvement lien against the property, the lien was not merged in the contractor's title and it could be foreclosed against his grantee, since the lien of the total bond issue covered the property of all the owners who signed waivers and the lien of the assessment for which the bonds were issued is by statute (§4296 Burns 1901, Acts 1899 p. 237) declared to be equal upon the property assessed without priority of one of such bonds over any other, and to discharge an improvement lien against any particular tract or lot there must have been payment in full of the

assessment against it to the person lawfully entitled to receive the same. p. 582.

5. MUNICIPAL CORPORATIONS.—*Street Improvements.—Bonds.—Record.—Notice.*—Where bonds are payable to a person named or bearer, the record of the improvement proceeding is notice to all that such obligation may rightfully be owned and in the possession of some person other than the one named without any assignment or record of transfer. p. 583.

6. MUNICIPAL CORPORATIONS.—*Street Improvements.—Bonds.—Notice.*—The law charges the owner of property assessed for a street improvement with the knowledge that a particular bond is not issued to cover the assessment of any one tract of realty affected by the improvement except as the amount of such assessment is a part of the aggregate sum for which the bonds are issued. p. 583.

7. VENDOR AND PURCHASER.—*Street Improvements.—Record of Proceedings.—Notice.*—Where it appeared in an action to foreclose the statutory lien securing a street improvement bond, that the record kept by the municipal corporation showed the proceedings for the improvement of the street, the making of the assessment, the waiver filed by the owner of the realty involved in the action, the issuance of the bonds payable to the contractor or bearer, and that as to the lot in suit such assessment was unsatisfied, a purchaser of the lot is charged with constructive notice of such facts, and with such other facts as an ordinarily diligent search would have disclosed, since the facts shown by the record are sufficient to put him on inquiry. p. 584.

8. MUNICIPAL CORPORATIONS.—*Street Improvements.—Conveyance of Land Assessed.—Deed.—Notice.*—Where a paving contractor after assigning a street improvement bond, falsely represented that he was still the owner thereof and thereby procured the owner of land assessed for the improvement to convey the same to him in consideration of the satisfaction of the lien against the property, the record of such deed did not give the holder of the bond notice of any fact that would defeat its right to foreclose the lien of the assessment if it was otherwise entitled to do so. p. 585.

9. LIMITATION OF ACTIONS.—*Bonds Payable in Installments.—Action to Foreclose Lien.—Computation of Period of Limitation.*—An action brought on October 16, 1913, to foreclose the statutory lien securing a street improvement bond issued in May, 1902, with the last installment to run ten years from date before maturity, is not barred by the five, six, or ten-year statute of limitations. p. 585.

From Grant Circuit Court; *H. J. Paulus,* Judge.

Action by the National Exchange Bank against Robert C. Smith and another. From a judgment for defendants, the plaintiff appeals. *Reversed.*

*Kittinger & Diven* and *Condo & Browne,* for appellant. *Charles T. Parker,* for appellees.

FELT, C. J.—This suit was brought by appellant to foreclose the statutory lien securing a street improvement bond. The court found for the defendants on the complaint, and for appellee, Robert C. Smith, upon his cross-complaint to quiet his title to the real estate on which appellant sought to foreclose the improvement lien. Appellant's motion for a new trial was overruled and judgment rendered in accordance with the finding of the court.

The error assigned is the overruling of appellant's motion for a new trial, which was asked on the grounds: (1) that the decision of the court is not sustained by sufficient evidence; (2) that the decision is contrary to law.

The pleadings were numerous and lengthy and need not be set out in detail to determine the questions presented by the appeal. The complaint sets out at length the proceedings of the board of trustees of the town of Fairmount, Grant county, Indiana, for the improvement of Main street, and alleges that the property in question abutted on that street and was then owned by Sarah A. Gauntt; that the street was duly improved and the owner aforesaid filed her waiver under the statute and bonds were duly issued, including No. 47, for $500, the bond involved in this suit; that the bonds were made payable to the contractor, Patrick T. O'Brien, or bearer; that the plaintiff is the owner thereof and the same is due and unpaid; that said real estate has been duly conveyed and is now owned by Robert C. Smith.

The complaint was answered by general denial and by several paragraphs of affirmative answer and by pleas of the statutes of limitations. Robert C. Smith filed a cross-complaint to quiet his title to the real estate and it was

answered by general denial and by special answers counting on substantially the same facts that are alleged in appellant's complaint.

It appears that O'Brien, the contractor, made an assignment of his contract and moneys due him for improvement
of the street to appellant, as collateral security, for money
loaned to him to be used in paying for labor and material
in making said improvement, and that upon the issuance
of the bonds he turned them over to the bank, unless it
be bond No. 47 involved in this suit.

It is contended by appellee that O'Brien, the contractor,
on November 10, 1902, was the holder and owner of bond
No. 47 aforesaid, and that on that date Sarah A. Gauntt,
the then owner of the real estate in question, paid to him
the full amount of the assessment against said real estate, by
conveying the same to him by warranty deed in which her
husband joined, in consideration of the satisfaction of the
lien against the property and the payment to her by him
of $27.50; that O'Brien accepted the conveyance in full pay-
ment and satisfaction of the assessment and lien on the
real estate, and the deed was duly recorded; that the owner
made the conveyance in good faith, without any actual
knowledge of any claim to or upon the property by appellant.

Many of the facts were undisputed and upon the trial
the parties made an agreement as to the facts, in substance,
as follows: That the averments of the complaint are true
unless the assessment was paid as alleged in the several
paragraphs of answer, but the parties do not agree as to who
owned bond No. 47; that the contractor, Patrick O'Brien,
represented to Sarah A. Gauntt, the owner of the lot, that
he was the holder and owner of said bond and assessment
on her lot, and in reliance on such representation, and without any knowledge to the contrary, Sarah A. Gauntt and her
husband executed to O'Brien, in payment of said bond and

assessment, a deed for said lot; that appellee, Robert C. Smith, purchased the real estate with knowledge of the aforesaid facts and with no information to the contrary, except such as was shown by the records of the town clerk of Fairmount; that appellant had no knowledge of such transactions other than that available from the records of the town and the office of the county recorder of Grant county, Indiana.

The evidence shows that all the bonds issued for the improvement of said street were paid before the institution of this suit, unless it be the one in dispute; that in 1905, on verified representations of O'Brien and an officer of appellant, bond No. 47 was lost; the town board issued a duplicate of that bond, which is the one offered in evidence in this case.

There is evidence tending to show that all the bonds issued, including No. 47, were turned over to the bank when issued, but there is also evidence tending to show that the bank did not at any time obtain possession of the original bond No. 47; that it was held by O'Brien at the time he procured the conveyance of the lot from Mrs. Gauntt in payment and satisfaction of the bond and the assessment, but the evidence does not disclose what, if anything, was done with the bond at that time. The trial court made a general

1.  finding for appellee, which is a finding in his favor on the issuable fact of the possession of bond No. 47. There being some evidence to support such finding it is conclusive in this court.

It is also contended on behalf of appellant that appellee and his predecessors in title were bound by the notice of the record of the town board and were thereby in-

2.  formed of appellant's ownership of the bonds and assessment in favor of the contractor, O'Brien.

It was shown by the town clerk that he had made a search of the office and examined the records from 1901 to 1905 and found no notice or assignment relating to O'Brien's assign-

ment to appellant. There was other testimony to show that
a notice of such assignment had been left in the office of the
town clerk in January, 1902; and it was shown that on
April 26, 1909, Jacob Briles, town clerk, had furnished an
officer of appellant with a copy of a notice, which copy was
admitted in evidence and is in substance as follows:

> "To the Board of Trustees, Clerk & Treasurer
> of the Town of Fairmount:
> "Patrick T. O'Brien has assigned and transferred to
> the undersigned all money due and coming to him from
> said town in payment for improvements, (which were
> duly identified) and all payments therefor are due the
> undersigned as evidenced by the written assignment of
> said O'Brien executed and delivered to said bank, March
> 4, 1901. The notice was dated January 23, 1902, and
> was signed by
> "The National Exchange Bank of Anderson, Indiana
> by John L. Forkner, Cashier."

There was no evidence that the same was filed as a paper
in the proceedings, but on the contrary the evidence of the
clerk shows that no notice or assignment was ever filed or
made a part of the record or papers in the proceedings for
the improvement of the street and the issuance of the bonds
in controversy. We find no evidence that indicates that the
written assignment of O'Brien to appellant, or a copy
thereof was ever left at the office of the clerk or town board.
But if, as appellant contends, there is evidence tending to
prove such fact, it is by no means conclusive and the finding of the court to the contrary is supported by sufficient
evidence and is binding on this court. Indeed the undisputed evidence seems to show that no such instrument was
ever filed as a paper in the proceedings, or in any way
made a matter of record, in such a way as to be notice to
a purchaser of the real estate at the time of the several
conveyances of the lot subsequent to the making of the assessment. It therefore appears that the court was warranted
in finding that neither the assignment nor a copy thereof
was left at the office of the town clerk. The proceedings

of municipal corporations in street improvements are required by law to be duly recorded and they are public
records open to inspection. Persons who acquire
3. real estate encumbered by assessments evidenced by
such records are bound by the constructive notice
given by such records when duly kept. But it is only
records which the law requires to be kept and which in
fact have been so kept as to impart notice to those who
examine them that are binding. Whatever constructive
notice is imparted by such records must be given effect,
even though, in particular instances, hardships result therefrom. §3324 R. S. 1881; §4346 Burns 1901, Acts 1901 p.
57; §9001 Burns 1914; Acts 1907 p. 52; *Byer* v. *Town of
Newcastle* (1890), 124 Ind. 86, 88, 24 N. E. 578; *State,
ex rel.* v. *Curry* (1893), 134 Ind. 133, 137, 33 N. E. 685;
21 Am. and Eng. Ency. Law (2d ed.) 8.

But accepting the findings of the court as to the possession of the bond, the notice of the assignment and the assignment itself, as above indicated, we must still determine the
legal effect of the undisputed portions of the record of the
town board in this case. Appellant contends that the record
of the proceedings for the improvement of the street, the
report of the assessments, the waiver of appellee's predecessor in title, the issuance of the bonds and the absence of a
record showing payment or satisfaction of the assessment,
affords sufficient constructive notice to appellees to be binding upon them and to warrant the foreclosure of the lien
upon the real estate in controversy.

The proceedings for the improvement of the street were
under the act of 1889, being §4288 *et seq.* Burns 1901, Acts
1889 p. 237. Section 4294 Burns 1901, Acts 1899 p. 63,
provides, among other things, for a lien upon all property
assessed for the improvement, and that if the owner of any
lot so assessed shall "promise and agree, in writing, to be
filed with the clerk of such city or town and to be spread
of record by him in consideration of the right to pay his

or their assessment * * * in installments, that he will
not make any objections * . * * and will pay the same
* * * he shall have the benefit of paying said assessment in ten annual installments." Also that the proceeds
from such assessments shall constitute a special fund for
the payment of the costs of such street improvement "and
the bonds and certificate hereinafter mentioned."

Section 4296 Burns 1901, *supra,* provides for the issuance
of bonds to cover the assessments for which waivers have
been filed as above indicated and that "all such bonds shall
be an equal lien upon the property so assessed without
priority of one over another." Also that the bonds shall
bear the name of the street for the improvement of which
they are issued "and shall be payable, in equal installments,
out of the special fund * * * in one, two, three, four,
five, six, seven, eight, nine, and ten years from date * * *
and such bonds, when issued, shall transfer to the owner
thereof all the right and interest of such city or incorporated town in and to such assessments and the liens thereby
created, with full power to enforce the collection thereof by
foreclosure or otherwise." It is also provided by §4294 of
the statute, *supra,* that when payment is made upon any such
assessment it is the "duty of the treasurer, contractor, or
owner of the assessments or bonds or certificates or installments of assessments, receiving such payment to enter upon
the proper record the receipt of such money, and such receipt shall be a discharge of the lien of such assessment
and that upon the payment of any bonds or certificates"
so issued under the provisions of the statute the same "shall
be surrendered to and cancelled by, the treasurer" of the
municipality which issued such bonds. The same section
provides also that the assessments for which bonds have been
issued shall be collected in the same way taxes are collected,
or in such way as the common council or board of trustees
may provide by ordinance. Where bonds have been issued
they may be and frequently are in the hands of different

persons. By authority of the statute or of an ordinance passed as therein provided, assessments are usually and properly paid to the treasurer from whom the bondholder receives payment on surrender of the bond held by him.

The question of merger of the lien in the title of O'Brien is urged to support the judgment. It appears without dispute that bond No. 47 was the last of the series and 4. that all other bonds issued had been paid and satisfied. If it also appeared that O'Brien, when he obtained the deed from Mrs. Gauntt, was the actual owner of bond No. 47, had the same in his possession, and agreed to receipt the record and surrender the bond for cancellation as required by the statute, all the other assessments being satisfied and the other bonds paid, it would be reasonable to contend that the lien on the lot in suit was merged in the title acquired by O'Brien, and that appellant could not now foreclose the lien against the owners of the real estate who acquired title from Mrs. Gauntt. *Swatts* v. *Bowen* (1895), 141 Ind. 322, 325, 40 N. E. 1057; *Chase* v. *Van Meter* (1895), 140 Ind. 321, 333, 39 N. E. 455; *Coburn* v. *Stephens* (1894), 137 Ind. 683, 687, 36 N. E. 132, 45 Am. St. 218; *Artz* v. *Yeager* (1902), 30 Ind. App. 677, 681, 66 N. E. 917; *Lagrange* v. *Greer-Wilkinson Lumber Co.* (1915), 59 Ind. App. 488, 108 N. E. 373. But it appears from the record that O'Brien was not in fact the owner of either the assessment or the bond in suit, and that Mrs. Gauntt relied solely upon his representations as to the ownership of the assessment and bond, and that his representations were untrue.

The lien for the total bond issue covered the property of all the owners who signed waivers, and the lien of the assessments for which such bonds were issued is by the statute declared equal upon the property assessed without priority of one of such bonds over any other of such issue. To discharge such lien against any particular tract or lot there must be payment in full of the assessment against the same to the party lawfully entitled to receive the same as pro-

vided in §4294, *supra.* Where bonds are payable to a
5.  named person or bearer, the record is notice to every
    one that such obligation may rightfully be owned and
in the possession of some person other than the one so named
without any assignment or record of transfer. *Melton* v.
*Gibson* (1884), 97 Ind. 158, 160; *Paulman* v. *Claycomb*
(1881), 75 Ind. 64, 67.

It is not shown that O'Brien delivered the original of the
bond in suit to Mrs. Gauntt, when he obtained the deed for
the lot, or that it was then or at any time surrendered to
the treasurer of the town board, or what in fact became of
the bond at or prior to the time of that transaction, though
long afterwards there was a showing made that the bond was
lost. There is evidence tending to show that O'Brien assigned the entire assessment roll and his right to, and
ownership of, any bonds issued upon such assessment to the
bank on March 11, 1901, and that the bank served a notice
on the town board on January 23, 1902, showing that such
assignment had been executed. The undisputed record
shows that the assessments were approved in March, 1902;
that the bonds were ordered issued in April, and were issued
in May, 1902. The deed to O'Brien was not executed until
November 10, 1902, and was recorded the next day. It
shows a consideration of $27.50 and recites that the grantors
guaranteed that they had placed no encumbrance on the lot
and that there was none on the same except taxes.

The particular bond in controversy bore the same relation
to the real estate involved in this suit that it bore to all the
other real estate against which assessments had been levied
and which assessments were the basis of the bond issue of
which the one in controversy happened to be the last of the
series. The aggregate amount of the issue was $5,904.95 and
bond No. 47 was for $500. The assessment against appel-
lee's property amounted to $350.28. The law com-
6.  pelled Mrs. Gauntt and appellees to know that the
    particular bond was not issued to cover the assess-

ment on the real estate conveyed except as the amount of such assessment was a part of the aggregate sum for which the bonds were issued.

The owner of any lot or tract could free the same from the lien of the assessment by paying the full amount of the assessment against the same with interest. The property of appellees was not bound primarily for the payment of this particular bond and the basis of the suit was the unsatisfied assessment. The bond was only incidentally involved. It represented the outstanding unpaid portion of the assessments for which the series of bonds had been issued. The measure of liability was primarily the unsatisfied assessment against the lot in suit.

The record showed the proceedings for the improvement of the street, the making of the assessment, the waiver of Mrs.
Gauntt, the issuance of the bonds payable to O'Brien
7.  or bearer, and that as to the lot in suit such assessment was unsatisfied.

Appellees are charged with constructive notice of all the facts shown by such record. Those facts were sufficient to put appellees on inquiry and thereby they became chargeable with such facts as an ordinarily diligent search and investigation would have disclosed. *Hollenbeck* v. *Woodford* (1895), 13 Ind. App. 113, 41 N. E. 348; *Oglebay* v. *Todd* (1905), 166 Ind. 250, 255, 76 N. E. 238; *Reagan* v. *First Nat. Bank* (1901), 157 Ind. 623, 667, 61 N. E. 575, 62 N. E. 701; *Martin* v. *Cauble* (1880), 72 Ind. 67, 73, *Mettart* v. *Allen* (1894), 139 Ind. 645, 649, 39 N. E. 239. From this it follows that as against appellant appellees hold the lot in controversy subject to the lien of the unsatisfied assessment thereon.

However plausible it may have seemed, Mrs. Gauntt was not in law justified in accepting the statements of O'Brien in the face of the records aforesaid. She and her successors in title were informed by such record of the unsatisfied assessment and that the bonds payable to bearer were enforcible against the property to the extent of the assessment against the same by the bona fide owner of such assessment and the rightful holder of any unpaid bond. Appellant's assignment of the assessment preceded the issuance of the bonds and the execution of the deed to O'Brien. The record of the deed did not give to appellant notice

8. of any fact that would defeat its right to foreclose the lien of the assessment if it was otherwise entitled so to do.

This suit was begun on October 16, 1913, and the bonds were issued in May, 1902, with the last installment to run ten years from date before maturity. There is no

9. provision in the statutes applicable to this case by which all the installments become due on default in payment of any one or more of such installments. Appellees have pleaded the five, six and ten-year statute of limitations as a complete defense to the whole cause of action. The dates above given show that neither of such statutes is a bar to the cause of action stated in the complaint.

For reasons already announced the decision of the court is not sustained by sufficient evidence and is also contrary to law. The motion for a new trial should therefore have been sustained. The judgment is reversed, with instructions to sustain appellant's motion for a new trial and for further proceedings not inconsistent with this opinion. Judgment reversed.

Ibach, P. J., Dausman, Caldwell, Batman and Hottel, JJ., concur.

NOTE.—Reported in 114 N. E. 881. Effectiveness as notice of recorded instruments not entitled to record, Ann. Cas. 1913B 1070. See under (9) 25 Cyc 1107.

# CHICAGO, LAKE SHORE AND SOUTH BEND RAILWAY COMPANY *v.* SANDERS.

### [No. 9,693. Filed January 31, 1917.]

1. APPEAL.—*Motion to Dismiss.—Rules of Court.—Substantial Compliance.*—Under Rule 7 of the Appellate Court requiring ten days' notice of a motion to dismiss an appeal and under Rule 14 providing that motions, except such general motions as are made in court upon the call of the docket, shall be filed with the clerk, accompanied by such affidavits and briefs as are necessary to support them, where appellee, on December 30, 1916, served notice on appellant that on January 16, 1917, he would file a motion to dismiss the appeal for insufficiency of the service of appellant's notice thereof, appellant being furnished a copy of the motion, and such motion and briefs thereon were filed on January 15, 1917, appellee substantially complied with the rules of court and the question of the sufficiency of the service of the notice of appeal was presented for determination. p. 588.

2. APPEAL.—*Notice of Appeal.—Service.—Proof.—Statutes.*—Under §681 Burns 1914, §640 R. S. 1881, providing that an appeal may be taken by the service of a notice in writing on the adverse party, or his attorney and also on the clerk of the court, and §504 Burns 1914, §481 R. S. 1881, providing that proof of service of any notice required to be served upon any party, when made by a person other than the sheriff, shall be by affidavit or by the written admission of the party served and requires such proof to show the time and place of service of notice, service of notice of an appeal cannot be made by depositing such notice in the mail, registered and addressed to appellee's attorney, since service of notice, unless otherwise provided by law, means personal service of the individual in such a way that the party who makes the service may be in a position to make proof thereof in court. p. 588.

3. APPEAL.—*Failure to Perfect Appeal.—Dismissal.—Rules of Court.*—Where a case has been on the docket of the Appellate Court more than ninety days and no steps have been taken to perfect the appeal, except to make an insufficient service of notice thereof, the appeal will be dismissed under Rule 36 of the Appellate Court relating to dismissal of causes. p. 589.

From Porter Circuit Court; *H. H. Loring,* Judge.

Action by Wilfred H. Sanders against The Chicago, Lake Shore and South Bend Railway Company. From a judgment for plaintiff, the defendant appeals, and plaintiff moves to dismiss the appeal. *Appeal dismissed.*

*F. J. Lewis Meyer* and *B. F. Parks,* for appellant.
*George E. Hershman,* for appellee.

FELT, C. J.—Appellee by his attorney has entered a special appearance and moved to dismiss this appeal for the alleged reason that the court has not acquired jurisdiction over him.

In his motion it is alleged that appellant did not serve appellee or his attorney with notice of the appeal as provided by §681 Burns 1914, §640 R. S. 1881; that the only information of the proposed appeal obtained by him prior to the filing of the transcript on July 21, 1916, was from a registered letter which appellant's attorney sent to George E. Hershman, appellee's attorney, containing a "purported notice of appeal"; that said letter came to Crown Point, Indiana, the home of said Hershman, on July 19, 1916, when he was absent from the town, and was taken from the post office by his stenographer, who signed the usual receipt for a registered letter. The motion to dismiss contains a copy of the letter and of the notice of appeal enclosed with the letter. It is not contended that the notice is insufficient in form or substance, but that it was not served as contemplated by the statute and is insufficient to give the court jurisdiction over appellee or to authorize a consideration of the appeal on its merits.

Appellant contends that appellee has not complied with the rules of the court in presenting his briefs on the motion, and that inasmuch as it appears that appellee's attorney actually obtained possession of the notice of appeal in due time, the manner of the service is immaterial and the notice is sufficient.

On December 30, 1916, appellant was duly served with notice that on January 16, 1917, appellee would file a motion

to dismiss this appeal and was furnished a copy of
1. the motion. Appellee's motion and briefs thereon
were filed on January 15, 1917. Rule No. 7 requires
ten days' notice unless otherwise provided, and Rule No.
14 provides that: "Motions, except such general motions as
are made in court upon the call of the docket, shall be filed
with the clerk, accompanied by such affidavits and briefs as
are necessary to support them." Appellee has substantially
complied with the rules and the question of the sufficiency
of the service of the notice of appeal is duly presented for
our determination.

Section 681 Burns 1914, *supra*, provides that: "An appeal
may be taken by the service of a notice in writing on the
adverse party or his attorney, and also on the clerk
2. of the court." Section 504 Burns 1914, §481 R. S.
1881, provides that proof of the service of any notice
required to be served upon any party, when made by a person other than the sheriff, shall be by affidavit, or by the
written admission of the party served, and requires such
proof to show the time and place of service.

These statutes contemplate that the person, making the
service of notice, whether an official or a nonofficial, shall
be in a position to definitely inform the court, either by
official certificate or by affidavit, that the party was actually served with notice, in compliance with the rule, order
or statute in pursuance of which the notice was issued. Service of notice has a definite meaning and unless otherwise
provided by law means personal service of the individual
in such way that the party who makes the service may be in
a position to make due proof thereof to the court, and in this
state the statute, *supra*, seems clear and explicit as to the
proof that is sufficient. "Service" has been defined as "the
delivery or communication of a pleading, notice or other
paper in a suit, to the opposite party, so as to charge him
with the receipt of it, and subject him to its legal effect."
Burrill, Law Dictionary; 35 Cyc 1432. Unless provided

by statute service of notice of an appeal, or similar process, cannot be made by depositing such notice in the mail duly addressed to the party upon whom service of the notice is sought to be made. Some states have statutes which authorize certain notices to be given by mail, but even in such states parties relying upon the mails have been held to a strict compliance with the statute to make such service of notice sufficient. We have no such statute. The exact question presented by this motion does not seem to have been decided in this state, but the decisions in other jurisdictions and our statutes as far as applicable clearly indi- cate that the service of the notice of appeal relied upon in this case is unwarranted and insufficient to invoke the jurisdiction of the court further than to determine its want of jurisdiction. As supporting our conclusion see the following: 35 Cyc 1432; 7 Words and Phrases 6432; *Rhode Island, etc., Co.* v. *Keeney* (1891), 1 N. D. 411, 48 N. W. 341; *Rathbun* v. *Acker* (1854), 18 Barb. 393, 395; *McDermott* v. *Board, etc.* (1857), 25 Barb. 635, 647; *Thompson* v. *Brannan* (1888), 76 Cal. 618, 18 Pac. 783; *Marcele* v. *Saltzmàn* (1884), 66 How. Prac. (N. Y.) 205; *Goggs* v. *Huntingtower* (1844), 12 Meeson & Welsby's 502; *Griffin* v. *Board, etc.* (1905), 20 S. D. 142, 104 N. W. 1117.

The case has been upon the docket of this court since July 21, 1916, and no steps have been taken to perfect
3. the appeal except as above indicated. More than ninety days have elapsed and, under Rule 36, the appeal should be dismissed. Appeal dismissed.

NOTE.—Reported in 114 N. E. 986. Notice of appeal, what parties entitled to, 13 Ann. Cas. 181; 21 Ann. Cas. 1277. See under (1) 3 Cyc 193; 4 C. J. 593, 594; (2) 2 Cyc 871; 3 C. J. 1235.

## MORGAN ET AL. *v*. ARNT.

### [No. 9,221.  Filed February 1, 1917.]

APPEAL.—*Questions Presented.—Objections to Instructions.—Ruling on Motion for New Trial.*—Where the sole error assigned on appeal was the overruling of the motion for a new trial and under such assignment the appellant presents only the question of alleged error in an instruction, but the brief fails to disclose that any exception was taken or reserved to the trial court's ruling on the motion, no question is presented for review.

From LaPorte Circuit Court; *James F. Gallaher,* Judge.

Action by Josephine Arnt against Bennett B. Morgan. From a judgment for plaintiff, the defendants appeal. *Affirmed.*

*D. E. Kelly, T. C. Mullen* and *Doran & Conboy,* for appellants.

*F. R. Marine, W. H. Worden* and *E. E. Weir,* for appellee.

CALDWELL, J.—On July 5, 1912, appellee, a young married woman of Polish nativity, while driving a horse and buggy northward along the pike leading from Valparaiso to Chesterton, met a motor truck operated by appellants. Appellee's horse became frightened at the motor truck and the manner of its operation and ran away, and as a consequence appellee was thrown from the buggy, and suffered a compound fracture of a leg and other serious injuries. As a result, she was confined in a hospital for a number of months, receiving treatment for her injuries. Such treatment has not resulted in a complete recovery or restoration of her former physical condition, in that by reason of her injuries she is to an extent permanently crippled. She brought this action to recover damages suffered on account of her injuries, charging appellants with negligence in operating the truck. A trial resulted in a verdict in her favor for $1,400, on which judgment was rendered.

Appellants assign as the sole error complained of the overruling of their motion for a new trial, and under such assignment present the single question of alleged error in giving a certain instruction. The instruction complained of is fairly open to criticism, in that it contained certain assumptions respecting the subject-matter of which the evidence was somewhat contradictory, and as a consequence we cannot approve the instruction. However, an examination of the entire case convinces us that a correct result was reached, and that the assumption contained in the instruction did not materially influence the jury. Moreover, appellant's brief fails to disclose that any exception was taken or reserved to the court's ruling on the motion for a new trial. For such reason, no question is presented. *Chicago, etc., R. Co.* v. *Ader* (1915), 184 Ind. 235, 110 N. E. 67; *Robinson* v. *State* (1916), 185 Ind. 119, 113 N. E. 306; *German Fire Ins. Co.* v. *Zonker* (1914), 57 Ind. App. 696, 108 N. E. 160. Judgment affirmed.

NOTE.—Reported in 114 N. E. 986.

---

## BALTIMORE AND OHIO SOUTHWESTERN RAILROAD COMPANY *v.* POSTON.

[No. 9,184.  Filed February 1, 1917.]

RAILROADS.—*Relief Associations.—Contracts.—Validity.—Waiver of Liability.*—A contract entered into by a railroad with an employe requiring him, as one of the conditions of employment, to become a member of a relief association maintained by the company and to receive benefits from such association in full payment of damages for personal injuries is held to be in violation of §5308 Burns 1914, Acts 1907 p. 46, prohibiting railroad companies from maintaining relief associations when the rules thereof require a waiver by the employe of claims against the company for personal injuries, and such contract is therefore void.

From Lawrence Circuit Court; *Oren O. Swails,* Judge.

Action by Charles M. Poston against the Baltimore and Ohio Southwestern Railroad Company. From a judgment for plaintiff, the defendant appeals. *Affirmed.*

*W. R. Gardiner, C. K. Tharp, C. G. Gardiner* and *R. N. Palmer*, for appellant.

*Giles & Doman,* for appellee.

IBACH, J.—This is a suit by appellee to recover certain dues paid to appellant's relief department. The theory of the complaint is that the contract under which such dues were paid is in violation of the act of 1907. Acts 1907 p. 46, §5308 Burns 1914.

Appellant, to sustain the errors assigned, contends that the by-laws of its relief department contains no provisions obnoxious to the act of 1907, *supra*; that appellee voluntarily became a member of its relief department and paid his dues and at different times accepted benefits from such department; that the contract set out in the complaint in nowise seeks to prevent or restrain appellee from maintaining an action for injury or death predicated on the negligence or wrongful conduct of the company. Other contentions are made but those indicated are sufficient to present the controlling question.

The application by which appellee became a member of such relief department, the form of which is provided by regulation No. 17 of such department, reads in part as follows:

"I, Charles M. Poston, of Seymour, in the county of Jackson and state of Indiana, employed in the service of the Baltimore & Ohio Railroad as engineman in the conducting transportation Department, Indiana Division, do hereby, as one of the conditions of such employment, apply for membership in the Relief Feature, and consent and agree to be bound by all the regulations of the relief department now in force, and by any other regulations of said department hereafter. * * * I further agree that in consideration of the contributions of said company to the relief department, and of the guarantee by it of the payments of the benefits aforesaid, the acceptance of benefits from the said relief department for injury or death, shall operate as a release of all claims against said company or any company owning or operating its branches or division, or any company over whose railroad right of way or property the said The Baltimore and Ohio Railroad Co. shall have the right to run or operate its engines or cars or send its employes in the performance of their duty, for damages by reason of such injury or death, which could be made by or through me; and that the superintendent may require, as a condition precedent to the payment of such benefits, that all acts by him deemed appropriate or necessary to effect the full release and discharge of the said companies from all such claims, be done by those who might bring suit for damages by reason of such injury or death; and also, that the bringing of such a suit by me, my beneficiary or legal representative, or for the use of my beneficiary alone or with others, or the payment of any of the companies aforesaid of damages for such injury or death recovered in any suit or determined by compromise, or of any costs incurred therein, shall operate as a release in full to the relief department of all claims by reason of my membership therein.''

Under the construction placed on said act the contract, under which the dues that appellee paid and now seeks to recover, was in direct violation of its terms and therefore void. *Wells* v. *Vandalia R. Co.* (1913), 56 Ind. App. 211, 103 N. E. 360; *Boes* v. *Grand Rapids, etc., R. Co.* (1915), 59 Ind. App. 271, 108 N. E. 174, 109 N. E. 411; *Acton* v. *Baltimore, etc., R. Co.* (1915), 59 Ind. App. 280, 108 N. E. 535. Upon the authority of these cases, the judgment is affirmed.

NOTE.—Reported in 114 N. E. 981. Contracts: validity of provision of railroad relief department for forfeiture of benefits in case of suit against company for damages, 10 L. R. A. (N. S.) 198; relieving master from liability for future negligence, validity, 3 Am. St. 255; 26 Cyc 1094.

# HOOSIER CONSTRUCTION COMPANY v. SEIBERT.

## [No. 9,336.   Filed February 2, 1917.]

1. JUDGMENT.—*Conclusiveness.*—*Res Judicata.*—The decision of
the Supreme Court, in an injunction suit to prevent the construction of a public improvement, holding the proceedings therefor
void is controlling on the invalidity of the proceedings where
that question is raised in a subsequent action by the paving contractor to enforce a lien for work done and the facts therein
relating to the validity of the proceedings in the latter action are
identical with those involved in the case determined by the Supreme Court.   p. 602.

2. MUNICIPAL CORPORATIONS.—*Public Improvements.*—*Procedure.*—
*Competitive Bidding.*—Competitive bidding in the letting of contracts for the construction of a street improvement is mandatory
and jurisdictional and where it is omitted the proceedings are invalid and void.   p. 602.

3. MUNICIPAL CORPORATIONS.—*Public Improvements.*—*Procedure.*—
*Omission of Competitive Bidding.*—*Collateral Attack.*—The proceedings had in the construction of a street improvement are
subject to collateral attack where it appears that competitive
bidding has been omitted in the letting of the contract.   p. 602.

4. MUNICIPAL CORPORATIONS.—*Public Improvements.*—*Failure to
Object.*—*Assessments.*—*Estoppel to Question.*—It is the general
rule that where the owner of property subject to assessment for
public improvements stands by and makes no objection to improvements which benefit his property, he may not deny the authority by which the improvements are made, nor defeat the assessment made against his property for the benefits derived, and
the rule applies both where the proceedings are attacked for
irregularity and where their validity is denied but color of law
exists for the proceedings.   p. 602.

5. MUNICIPAL CORPORATIONS.—*Public Improvements.*—*Enforcement
of Lien.*—*Estoppel to Question Assessment.*—*Burden of Proof.*—
In a paving contractor's action against a property owner to enforce a lien for work done in the construction of a street pavement, where the invalidity of the proceedings for the improvement appears, plaintiff has the burden of alleging facts estopping
the property owner from questioning the assessment for the improvement.   p. 603.

6. ESTOPPEL.—*Pleading.*—*Sufficiency.*—No intendments are made in
favor of a plea of estoppel, and it is incumbent on the pleader
to plead fully the facts essential to it.   p. 603.

7. **MUNICIPAL CORPORATIONS.**— *Public Improvements.*— *Action to Enforce Lien.*— *Answer.*— *Sufficiency.*—In a contractor's action against a property owner to enforce a street improvement assessment lien, an answer fully pleading the invalidity of the proceedings for the improvement and showing that the property owner brought and prosecuted an injunction proceeding to restrain the city from entering into the contract for the work and appealed to a higher court from an adverse decision, and that the contractor, before entering into the contract, knew of the injunction suit and that the property owner was therein questioning the validity of the improvement proceedings, is sufficient as against demurrer. p. 603.

8. **MUNICIPAL CORPORATIONS.**— *Public Improvements.*— *Assessments. Liability.*— *Estoppel to Question.*—Where the owner of property liable to assessment for a street pavement brought suit to enjoin the city from entering into the contract for the improvement, attacking in such suit the validity of the improvement proceedings, and the paving contractor, with full knowledge of such action and chargeable with the knowledge that the plaintiff therein had the right to appeal from the adverse decision of the lower court, entered into a contract with the city to do the work and constructed the pavement, the property owner was not estopped, after a reversal of the trial court's decision in the injunction suit, to question the improvement assessment, since an estoppel can arise in such a case only where it appears that the complaining party stands by and without objection permits the work to be commenced and continued. p. 604.

9. **LIS PENDENS.**— *Presumptions.*— *Notice.*—An appeal is a right granted by statute, and one having knowledge of a pending appealable cause is conclusively presumed to know that a judgment entered therein may be appealed from within a limited time. p. 605.

10. **NEW TRIAL.**— *Laches.*— *Statutory Period.*—A party who makes his motion for a new trial within the statutory time is not guilty of laches. p. 606.

From Marion Superior Court (74,997); *V. G. Clifford,* Judge.

Action by Hoosier Construction Company against George Seibert. From a judgment for defendant, the plaintiff appeals. *Affirmed.*

*William F. Elliott* and *Clarence A. Kenyon,* for appellant. *Joseph B. Kealing* and *Martin M. Hugg,* for appellee.

CALDWELL, J.—This appeal presents for examination the

same public work as is involved in *Seibert* v. *City of Indianapolis* (1907), 40 Ind. App. 296, 81 N. E. 99. Appellant was contractor in the construction of such work—the improvement of a designated portion of State avenue in the city of Indianapolis. Appellee is the owner of certain real estate abutting on the work, which real estate was liable to assessment for the improvement of the avenue. Appellant brought this action to foreclose a street improvement assessment lien based on said work. The complaint contains, in addition to the usual averments of a complaint of this kind, allegations to the effect that appellee stood by without objection and with knowledge permitted and induced appellant to perform labor and expend large sums of money in prosecuting and completing the work under the contract.

Appellant's demurrer to appellee's answer was overruled, and appellee's demurrer to appellant's reply was sustained, whereupon judgment was rendered against appellant that it take nothing, for failure and refusal to plead further. Appellant assigns error on the ruling on the two demurrers.

The material part of the answer is, in substance, as follows: On June 28, 1905, the board of public works of said city adopted a preliminary resolution for the improvement of the roadway of State avenue. The resolution was subsequently modified so as to specify for the work "Warren's patent bitulithic" pavement, and as modified it was adopted as a final resolution. Certain portions of the specifications are set out in the answer. They are identical with those copied into the opinion in *Seibert* v. *City, supra,* and it is therefore unnecessary to repeat them or to state their substance here. It will be observed from an examination of the opinion in that case that such specifications required in the process of performing the work that Warren's No. 24 Puritan brand hard bituminous cement, Warren's No. 21 Puritan brand bituminous waterproof cement, and Warren's quick-drying bituminous flush coat composition should be used. The answer includes, also, with appropriate averments in aid thereof, a written agreement entered into between the board of public works and the Warren Brothers' Company, prior to the adoption of the specifications. This agreement also is copied into the opinion in *Seibert* v. *City, supra*. It will be observed that by its terms the Warren Brothers' Company released to the city the right to use the patents held by the former, covering the process of constructing and laying said bitulithic pavement during 1905 and 1906, and that the company agreed also to furnish and deliver to the contractor in any contract for the construction of Warren's bitulithic pavement let in either of said years the required amounts of the specified grades of cement, and also of said flush coat composition, in consideration of which the city agreed to cause any such contractor "to pay to Warren Brothers' Company for the use of the patents so transferred and the materials so delivered a sum equal to 90 cents per square yard, for each and every yard of said bitulithic pavement so laid."

The board of public works, by notice duly given, called for sealed bids to be submitted December 29, 1905, for performing the work. On December 28, 1905, appellee commenced an action in the superior court of Marion county against the city and the members of its board of public works, alleging facts to the effect that the proceedings for the improvement of State avenue were invalid, by reason of the contemplated use as specified of said patented process and of said materials manufactured and supplied only by Warren Brothers' Company, and seeking to enjoin the city and its board of public works from proceeding in the matter further than to receive and open bids for the work. On application a restraining order was issued on December 28, 1905, against defendants to the proceedings as prayed. On. December 29, 1905, the board received and opened bids for the construction of the work. Appellant's bid was found to be the lowest and best bid. By reason of the restraining order, the contract was not awarded at that time. Appellant knew, when it submitted its bid, and when the bids were opened, that said action was pending and that the city and its board were restrained from proceeding further with the work. Facts are averred to the effect that appellant, though not a party to the cause, employed counsel, procured the attendance of witnesses, and participated actively in the defense of said action; that it was present by its president throughout the trial of the injunction proceeding, and that its president testified as a witness for the defense therein. On May 10, 1906, the court found for the defendants in the injunction proceeding, and rendered judgment against this appellee, plaintiff therein, dissolving the restraining order, and for costs. On June 1, 1906, appellee filed his motion for a new trial, which was on that day overruled, and appellee prayed and was granted an appeal to the Appellate Court. On June 11th, he filed his bill of exceptions containing the evidence, and thereafter filed the transcript on appeal to this court. Appellant in this proceeding employed counsel, who briefed said cause on appeal in behalf of appellees therein. On June 24, 1907, the Appellate Court reversed the judgment in the injunction proceeding, and held that the specifications and proceedings for the improvement of State avenue were against public policy and void. This court remanded the cause with instructions to the trial court to sustain the motion for a new trial. Said cause on appeal is *Seibert v. City of Indianapolis, supra.*

A petition for a rehearing in said cause was overruled May 28, 1907, and a petition to transfer to the Supreme Court was denied June 28, 1907, and on or about that day a certified copy of the opinion and mandate of the Appellate Court was filed in the office of the clerk of the trial court and thereafter, November 29, 1907, the cause was redocketed in said court on this appellee's motion, as a cause pending therein. Facts are averred to the effect that appellee diligently prosecuted his appeal in said cause.

On May 21, 1906, the contract for the improvement of State avenue was awarded to appellant, and appellant thereupon formally entered into a contract with the board of public works, by which the former agreed to do the work according to specifications. On August 24, 1906, the board of public works adopted and approved the final assessment roll on the work, showing the assessments sought to be enforced in this action. The answer contains a number of specifications respecting the invalidity and illegality of the proceeding which bring it within the decision in *Seibert* v. *City, supra.* The answer closes with the following: "The defendant further says he did not stand by with full knowledge and without objection permit the plaintiff to expend large sums of money, time and labor in making said improvement as set out in plaintiff's complaint, but that he, by his said action and by the diligent prosecution of his said appeal, claimed and does now claim that said contract and the proceedings under and pursuant to which the same was executed were and are illegal and void; that at no time did he acquiesce in plaintiff's claim, but plaintiff knew and had knowledge and notice before the execution of its contract with said Board of Public Works that he was claiming said proceedings to be void and wrong and had been so claiming all the time from the time it made its bid as aforesaid until after the final decision of said appeal and that during all of said time the plaintiff had knowledge and notice that the defendant herein was contesting with said city and said Board of Public Works the legality of said proceedings and the right of said Board to order said State Avenue to be laid with said Warren's bitulithic pavement under said proceedings, and the plaintiff herein appeared in said cause as aforesaid, and that said contract was let to the plaintiff, and said work was done by it after said action was begun, and after it was thereby notified that he, this defendant, claimed that said proceedings were void, but notwithstanding the plaintiff proceeded to execute said contract and do said work, and is now claiming the alleged liens by virtue thereof as set out in its complaint herein."

The material part of the reply is, in substance, as follows: The board of public works modified the preliminary resolution so as to provide for Warren's patent bitulithic pavement, pursuant to the petition of the majority of the property owners affected. Appellant, under a requirement of the board, filed with its bid a certified check, with a condition that it would enter into a contract to perform the work if its bid should be accepted. Appellant had no knowledge of the injunction proceedings when it filed its bid and check. Appellant's bid was accepted May 18, 1906, eight days after the dissolution of the restraining order; on May 25, 1906, it entered into a contract in writing with the city for the performance of the work, and executed a bond with a $10,000 penalty to complete it according to the specifications by September 15, 1906. Appellee knew at all times from December 29, 1905, to May 25, 1906, that appellant was the lowest bidder, and that said check had been filed, but he took no steps to make appellant a party to the action, or to notify it that the action was pending. When appellant entered into the contract on May 25, 1906, to perform the work as aforesaid, appellee had not filed his motion for a new trial in the injunction proceeding, and had given appellant no notice of his intention to prosecute said cause further. Appellee, with full knowledge of the responsibility of appellant under its bid and deposit, stood by without notice to appellant until the latter had executed the contract and bond aforesaid. The reply specifically denies that appellant participated in the defense of the injunction proceeding, either in the trial court or on appeal, or that it employed counsel or procured the attendance of witnesses to that end. Appellant's president was present and testified as a witness in the injunction proceeding, but he did so, not as appellant's representative, but in his individual capacity, and at the request of Warren Brothers' Company. Appellant did request counsel for defendants in the injunction proceedings to take certain steps and file certain answers therein, but the request was ignored. Appellant did not know that a motion for a new trial had been filed in said proceeding, or that it had been appealed, until after the work had been entirely completed according to contract. Appellee stood by day by day and saw appellant spending its money improving said street in front of his property, and receiving the benefit of the same, without verbal or written notice of any kind to appellant showing his intention to prevent appellant from receiving pay for such work.

Immediately after the work was completed, the board of public works made out a primary assessment roll, disclosing the assessments against appellee's property, and gave notice as required by the statute, fixing a time when property owners affected might appear and remonstrate against or object to the same. Appellee took no steps in opposition to such assessment roll, as affecting him, and the same was confirmed. Appellee did not prosecute an appeal from said assessment roll to the circuit or superior court. The reply concludes as follows: "The plaintiff denies that it had any knowledge of the defendant's intention to proceed further in said cause. No notice was given to this plaintiff nor was it made party to the said proceedings, nor did plaintiff know or have any cause to know that defendant would contest the validity or legality of any lien or liens against his said property for the letting of the contract and doing the work thereunder, and the defendant did not even have said cause redocketed nor in court until more than four months after it was decided on appeal and after this plaintiff had instituted this suit and employed counsel herein, and said cause had apparently been abandoned by the defendant."

In determining the sufficiency of the answer and also of the reply, and whether the court erred in overruling the

demurrer to the former or in sustaining the demurrer
1. filed to the latter, it is well to observe that the
facts here bearing on the validity of the proceedings
for the improvement of State avenue are identical with those
involved in *Seibert* v. *City, supra.* The court there considered these identical proceedings from the inception of the
enterprise to the advertising for bids. It is held there
that the fact that the specifications required the use of a
certain particular brand of material to the exclusion of all
others, which material was manufactured and could be supplied by but one company, in effect destroyed competition
in bidding; that as a consequence, one step required by the
statute in proceedings such as are involved here—competitive bidding—was in effect omitted, and hence that such proceeding came within the condemnation of the public policy
of the state as declared by the legislature, and hence that
such proceedings were void and could not support a valid
contract. We regard that case as controlling authority that
the proceedings here were invalid. As we have said, that
decision received the approval of the Supreme Court by the
denial of a transfer. It has since been recognized as sound.
*Tousey* v. *City of Indianapolis* (1910), 175 Ind. 295, 94 N.
E. 225. Competitive bidding' in the letting of such
2. a contract as that for the improvement of State
avenue is mandatory and jurisdictional. It having
in effect been omitted here, the proceedings were invalid and
void. *Edwards* v. *Cooper* (1906), 168 Ind. 54, 79 N. E.
1047; *Zorn* v. *Warren-Scharf, etc., Paving Co.* (1908), 42
Ind. App. 213, 84 N. E. 509. The infirmity here
3. appearing on the face of the proceedings is susceptible
to collateral attack. *Brownell, etc., Co.* v. *Nixon*
(1911), 48 Ind. App. 195, 92 N. E. 693, 95 N. E. 585.
There are left for our consideration only the elements
of estoppel and laches. "It is a general rule, now
4. fully accepted in this State, that where the owner
of property subject to assessment for public improve-

ments stands by and makes no objection to such improvements which benefit his property, he may not deny the authority by which the improvements are made, nor defeat the assessment made against his property for the benefits derived.    And this is true, both where the proceedings for the improvement are attacked for irregularity, and where their validity is denied, but color of law exists for the proceedings.''  *Board, etc.* v. *Plotner* (1897), 149 Ind. 116, 48 N. E. 635, and cases; *Taylor* v. *Patton* (1902), 160 Ind. 4, 66 N. E. 91; *Edwards* v. *Cooper, supra; Phillips* v. *Kankakee Reclamation Co.* (1912), 178 Ind. 31, 98 N. E. 804, Ann. Cas. 1915C 56.    The invalidity of the proceedings

5. appearing, the burden rested on appellant to allege the facts constituting the estoppel.  *Taylor* v. *Patton, supra;* 1 Works' Practice §606.    No intendments are

6. made in favor of a plea of estoppel, and it is incumbent on the pleader to plead fully all the facts essential to the existence of an estoppel.  *Troyer* v. *Dyar* (1885), 102 Ind. 396, 1 N. E. 728; 16 Cyc 809.

With these principles in mind, we proceed to determine the sufficiency of the answer and the reply.    The invalidity of the proceedings did not appear on the face of the

7. complaint in this action.  The pleader, apparently in anticipation of an answer that the proceedings were invalid, alleged in the complaint that appellee with full knowledge and without objection permitted appellant to expend large sums of money, etc.    By the answer the facts showing the invalidity of the proceedings are fully pleaded. It contains in addition other averments meeting the allegations of the complaint that appellant stood by without objection, etc.    These other averments are to the effect that appellee brought and prosecuted the injunction proceeding, and meeting with an adverse decision, he promptly appealed to a higher court.    There are general allegations and facts are specifically alleged. to the effect that before appellant contracted with the city and at all times from and after the

time when it made its bid, it had full knowledge that appellee was claiming that said proceedings were void, and that he was contesting that question with the city. In our judgment the answer successfully met all the averments of the complaint, and that the court did not err in overruling the demurrer filed to it.

Turning our attention to the reply, the parties apparently regard that some importance attaches to the following dates and events disclosed by the answer and the reply:

8. On December 28, 1905, appellee commenced the injunction suit and the restraining order was issued; on December 29, appellant submitted its bid; on May 10, 1906, the injunction proceeding was decided against appellee by the trial court, and the restraining order was dissolved; on May 18, the contract for the improvement of State avenue was awarded to appellant; on May 25, appellant entered into a contract to do the work, and filed its bond, and immediately commenced the work; on June 1, appellee filed and presented his motion for a new trial, which was overruled, and an appeal prayed and granted; on June 11, appellee filed his bill of exceptions containing the evidence and perfected the appeal; on August 24, the work of the improvement was completed; on April 24, 1907, the injunction proceeding was reversed on appeal. The reply contains an averment that appellant when it submitted its bid had no knowledge that the injunction proceeding had been commenced; that it had such knowledge prior to entering into the contract, however, is not denied. The fact of such knowledge affirmatively appears from the reply in that it contains a general averment that all allegations of the answer not specifically denied by the reply are admitted, and also in that it appears from the reply that appellant made certain suggestions relative to conducting the defense of the injunction suit. There is an averment also that appellee, after meeting with an adverse decision in the injunction suit, did not inform appellant that he

intended to move for a new trial or proceed further with such action, and that appellant did not know such fact. There is, however, no averment that appellee deceived appellant in these respects. The situation then was as follows: Appellee, knowing that appellant had knowledge of his objection to the improvement as manifested by the injunction proceeding, proceeded to prosecute his appeal, and said nothing to appellant respecting his intention. Appellant, with knowledge aforesaid, proceeded with the work and made no inquiry whether appellee was continuing his objections as indicated by his attitude in that case. In order that estoppel may be effective here, it must appear that appellee did stand by and without objection permit the work to be commenced and continued. "No estoppel can arise, of course, where the property owner does not acquiesce in the construction of the improvement, but, on the contrary, enters his protest thereto." 25 Am. and Eng. Ency. Law (2d ed.) 1206; *Edwards* v. *Cooper, supra.*

It would seem that no more emphatic protest could be entered than as manifested by the prosecution of a cause to enjoin the proceedings as invalid and void. An appeal is a continuation of an action, rather than the commencement of a new one. Appellant having knowledge of the action in the trial court should be chargeable with knowledge of its continuance on appeal. *Farmers Bank* v. *First Nat. Bank* (1902), 30 Ind. App. 520, 66 N. E. 503. An appeal is a right granted by statute. A person having knowledge of a pending appealable cause is conclusively presumed to know that a judgment entered in such cause may be appealed from within a limited time. *Dunnington* v. *Elston* (1885), 101 Ind. 373; *Smith* v. *Cottrell* (1884), 94 Ind. 379; *Griswold* v. *Ward* (1891), 128 Ind. 389, 27 N. E. 751.

We conclude that it does not appear from the reply, considered in its relation to the answer, that appellee stood by, and without objection or protest permitted appellant to prosecute the work; that, on the contrary, it appears that appellee, without in any manner deceiving or misleading appellant, manifested his nonacquiescence in an effective manner and that appellant was chargeable with notice of the fact.

The reply does not disclose that appellee was guilty of laches in the matter of moving for a new trial. "A party who makes his motion for a new trial within the

10. statutory time is not guilty of laches." *Smith* v. *Cottrell, supra.*

The court did not err in sustaining the demurrer to the reply. The judgment is affirmed.

NOTE.—Reported in 114 N. E. 981. Validity of contract for material patented or held in monopoly where a letting to the lowest bidder is required, 18 L. R. A. 45; 5 L. R. A. (N. S.) 680; 46 L. R. A. (N. S.) 990. See under (1) 23 Cyc 1116; (2) 28 Cyc 1025; (3) 28 Cyc 1022; (4) 28 Cyc 1173; (5) 28 Cyc 1238; (6) 16 Cyc 809; (7) 28 Cyc 1236.

---

BINGHAM, RECEIVER, *v.* NEWTOWN BANK ET AL.

[No. 9,454. Filed June 2, 1916. Opinion modified and rehearing denied November 29, 1916. Transfer denied Februry 2, 1917.]

1. APPEAL.—*Briefs.—Amendment.*—Within the time allowed by the court for the filing of briefs an appellant will be permitted to file amended briefs, or to make any reasonable amendment to those which he may have filed before the expiration of the time allowed, upon notice to the opposite party and leave of court, and, after such time, appellant may in certain contingencies obtain leave of court to amend his briefs; and, if the briefs filed show substantial compliance with the rules of court and duly present some question, on proper showing and after notice to the opposite party, the court will permit any reasonable amendment of the briefs necessary to fully present the merits of the appeal, subject to such orders as to the payment of the costs as the court may deem just and equitable, but, if the briefs filed by appellant, when fairly and liberally construed, under the rules of the court, fail to present any question relating to the merits of the appeal, he will not be permitted to amend after the time for filing briefs and taking an appeal, except in cases where the necessity for the amendment resulted from the acts or conduct

of the appellee, or from some cause for which appellant was in no way to blame. p. 609.

2. APPEAL.—*Briefs.*—*Failure to Comply with Rules of Court.*—*Amendment.*—*Time.*—*Dismissal.*—Where the time for perfecting an appeal has expired, and it appears from the record and the briefs filed by appellant that he has presented no question for review under the rules of the court he will not be permitted to amend, and appellee's timely motion for a dismissal of the appeal will be sustained. p. 610.

3. APPEAL.—*Rules of Court.*—*Effect.*—The rules of the court have the force and effect of law, binding alike upon litigants and the court. p. 610.

From Fountain Circuit Court; *Isaac E. Schoonover,* Judge.

Action by James Bingham, receiver of the Columbia Casualty Company, against the Newtown Bank and others. From the judgment rendered, the receiver appeals. *Appeal dismissed.*

*Bingham & Bingham,* for appellant.

*C. W. Dice, John E. Gavin* and *Adams, Follansbee, Hawley & Shorey,* for appellee.

FELT, J.—Appellee Rudolph C. Keller has moved to dismiss this appeal. The record shows that the judgment overruling appellant's motion for a new trial was rendered September 7, 1915. The appeal was submitted in this court on December 6, 1915. Appellant by procuring an extension of time had until April 10, 1916, in which to file his briefs. The briefs were filed on that day, which was thirty-six days beyond the time allowed for taking an appeal. On April 14, appellee The Newtown Bank filed a confession of error, and on May 1, 1916, appellee Keller filed his motion to dismiss the appeal. On May 4, 1916, appellant, by written motion, asked leave to amend his original briefs, apparently to obviate the grounds of the motion to dismiss. The motion to dismiss alleges that: (1) No question is presented by the record and briefs of appellant; and (2) that appellant has recognized the validity of the judgment from which the appeal is prosecuted.

The suit was brought by appellant, as receiver of the Columbia Casualty Company, to replevin two certificates of bank deposits from appellee The Newtown Bank, each calling for $245, and numbered respectively 840 and 841. By intervening petitions appellee Keller and one W. E. Richards were admitted as parties to the suit and each set up his claim to ownership of one of the certificates. The bank made no claim of ownership but asserted a right of set-off against the Columbia Casualty Company.

Various issues were joined on the complaint, and on a cross-complaint by appellee Keller. On trial of the issues the court found that appellee Keller was the owner and entitled to possession of certificate No. 841; that Richards had no right, title or interest in or to either of the certificates; that appellee The Newtown Bank was entitled to certificate No. 840; that appellee Keller should have return of his certificate and judgment against the bank for the amount thereof and accrued interest. The judgment was in accord with the findings.

The errors assigned are: (1) The overruling of appellant's demurrer to the second paragraph of the reply of appellee Keller; and (2) the overruling of appellant's motion for a new trial. Other attempted assignments are shown but they consist simply of statements in different form of the second alleged error and of grounds for a new trial which cannot be assigned as independent error.

Appellee in his motion to dismiss alleges: (1) That no questions are presented because of failure to comply with the fifth clause of Rule 22 of this court, in this—that appellant has not set out in his briefs the demurrer or the memorandum accompanying the same on which he seeks to predicate error; also that in his points and authorities, under the second assignment of error, appellant has only stated general abstract propositions of law and has in no way indicated their relation or application to any question arising on the motion for a new trial; (2) that the evidence has not been brought up on appeal and no question relating to or depending upon the evidence can be considered; (3) appellant has settled the controversy between himself and appellee The Newtown Bank by paying the judgment and thereby acknowledging its validity.

Appellant in his application to amend his briefs says the demurrer, memorandum, ruling of the court, and exceptions thereto were inadvertently omitted in the preparation of his briefs; that he was not aware of their omission until his attention was called thereto by appellee's motion and briefs to dismiss the appeal; that the omitted matter is shown by the record, is material and necessary to the presentation of the error in overruling the demurrer, and he asks that he now be permitted to supply it by so amending his briefs as to include the same.

Within the time allowed or granted by the court for the filing of briefs an appellant will be permitted to file amended briefs, or to make any reasonable amendments to those which he may have placed on file before the expiration of such time, but in either instance he should give notice to the opposite party and obtain leave of the court. If the time allowed or granted for the filing of briefs has expired, and the appellant thereafter seeks to amend his briefs, he may in certain contingencies obtain leave of court to do so. If the briefs he has filed show substantial compliance with the rules and duly present some question or questions, on proper showing, after notice to the opposite party, the court will permit any reasonable amendment of the briefs necessary to fully present the merits of the appeal, subject to such orders as to the payment of costs as the court may deem just and equitable, and the court usually taxes the costs occasioned by such amendment to the party making the same. If the briefs filed by the appellant, when fairly and liberally construed, under the rules of the court, fail to duly present any question relating to the merits of

1.

the appeal, he will not be permitted to amend the same after the time for filing his briefs and also the time for taking an appeal has expired, "except in cases where the excuse or reason for the necessity for the amendment resulted from the acts or conduct of the appellee, or from some cause for which appellant was in no way to blame." Our examination of appellant's briefs and the motion convinces us that appellant has wholly failed to present any question under the rules promulgated and enforced by our Supreme Court and by this court.

Appellee has made a timely presentation of his motion to dismiss and is asserting his right to an enforcement of the rules by a dismissal of the appeal or an affirmance of
2. the judgment. The record and the briefs support appellee in his contentions. The rules of the court have the force and effect of law, binding alike upon
3. litigants and the court. When a party duly asserts a right under the rules and shows himself clearly entitled thereto, it becomes the duty of the court to grant him the relief to which he is entitled. We therefore conclude that no question is duly presented and that
2. appellant on the showing made in the case should not now be permitted to amend his briefs as prayed. For this reason it is not necessary to consider the question of the effect of the alleged settlement with appellee The Newtown Bank. As supporting our conclusion on the several points involved we cite the following: *Steel* v. *Yoder* (1914), 58 Ind. App. 633, 635, 108 N. E. 783; *German Fire Ins. Co.* v. *Zonker* (1914), 57 Ind. App. 696, 701, 703, 108 N. E. 160; *Palmer* v. *Beall* (1915), 60 Ind. App. 208, 110 N. E. 218; *Harrold* v. *Whistler* (1915), 60 Ind. App. 504, 111 N. E. 79; *Kaufman* v. *Alexander* (1913), 180 Ind. 670, 672, 103 N. E. 481; *Chicago, etc., R. Co.* v. *Dinius* (1913), 180 Ind. 596, 626, 103 N. E. 652; *Hinton* v. *Falls City, etc., Loan Assn.* (1915), 60 Ind. App. 470, 111 N. E. 20; *Continental Nat. Bank* v. *McClure* (1915), 60 Ind. App. 553, 111 N. E.

191; *Goodman* v. *Bauer* (1915), 60 Ind. App. 671, 111 N. E.
315; *Beard* v. *Hosier* (1914), 58 Ind. App. 14, 107 N. E. 558.
Appeal dismissed.

NOTE.—Reported in 114 N. E. 97.

---

## KRISKY v. BRYAN.

### [No. 9,210. Filed February 13, 1917.]

VENDOR AND PURCHASER.—*Contract for Sale of Realty.*—*Forfeiture
for Nonpayment of Installments.*—Where a contract for the sale
of land stipulated that the purchaser should pay the purchase
price in monthly installments and expressly made time in the
payment of deferred installments material and of the essence of
the contract, and it contained a forfeiture clause requiring the
purchaser to make his payments at the times specified to prevent a forfeiture of the money paid, his failure to make payments for more than a year without any fault of the vendor
entitled the latter to treat such failure as an abandonment and
to forfeit the contract, so that the purchaser, in an action for
money had and received, could not recover the money paid on
the contract, even though he made a belated tender of the unpaid
portion of the purchase price and demanded a deed.

From Lake Superior Court; *John M. Stinson,* Special
Judge.

Action by Louis A. Bryan against Joseph Krisky. From
a judgment for defendant, the plaintiff appeals. *Affirmed.*

*Sheehan & Lyddick,* for appellant.

*Otto J. Bruce, William H. Matthew* and *W. Vincent
Youkey,* for appellee.

IBACH, J.—On May 18, 1907, appellee entered into an
agreement with appellant for the sale of a lot in the city
of Gary, Indiana. The agreement is in the following language:

"This agreement made and entered into this 18th day
of May, 1907 between Louis A. Bryan of Gary, Indiana,
hereinafter referred to as Bryan of the first part and
Joseph Krisky of Bridgeport in the county of ————

in the state of Ohio, witnesseth: That the said Bryan agrees to sell and the said party of the second part agrees to purchase one full town lot (here follows description), for $700 with interest at 6 per cent. from date until paid, upon the following conditions: That said Bryan agrees to deliver a warranty deed when the said party of the second part shall have paid the above named sum in manner as follows, to-wit: $250.00 cash, the receipt of which is hereby acknowledged, and also make 18 monthly payments of $25.00 each with interest, to the duly authorized agent of said Bryan, and the said party of the second part agrees to pay without notice the said above named sum in the manner and at the times aforesaid; that should the payments aforesaid be and remain unpaid as herein provided for two consecutive months, then this contract shall at once cease and determine and all moneys paid theretofore by the said party of the second part to the said Bryan shall be forfeited to the use of the said Bryan as ascertained and liquidated damages. And it is hereby stipulated and agreed that time shall be of the essence of this contract and of all the conditions thereof.''

Appellant defaulted in the payments, and he brings this action to recover the money paid by him on the contract. The complaint was in two paragraphs and both were for money had and received. In the second paragraph appellant has set out in full the written contract and has further alleged: ''That he had failed to make any payment on the contract after March 31, 1908, until May, 1909, when he offered to pay and tendered to appellee the amount due on the contract; that Bryan refused to accept the money and cancelled and attempted to forfeit said contract and the money paid in thereon and kept said money and refused to give appellant a deed to said lot and refused to return the money paid in although demanded so to do.'' Following these averments is a demand for judgment for a sum equal to the payments made. Issues were joined by answer in general denial. A trial by the court resulted in judgment for appellee. The overruling of appellant's motion for a new trial is assigned as error and relied on for reversal.

Under this assignment appellant has challenged the sufficiency of the evidence to support the judgment.

"As a general rule where there has been no rescission, and no cause for the rescission of the contract exists, there can be no recovery by the vendee of partial payments made thereunder. The cases in which the vendee is allowed to recover back money paid on a contract for the purchase of real estate, where it has been rescinded, may be generally classified, as where the rescission is by mutual consent; where the vendor fails to perform; where there is fraud in the contract; where by the terms of the contract the purchaser may rescind, and where both parties are in default in performance. If the vendor is in no default, and the vendee is, no recovery may be had." 29 Am. and Eng. Ency. Law (2d ed.) 727.

Appellant contends, in effect, that the act of appellee in forfeiting the contract was wholly unauthorized and without any justification whatever and, therefore, the payments made by appellant were unlawfully withheld by appellee.

By the express terms of the contract, time in the payment of deferred payments of the purchase price is made material and of the essence of the contract. The contract also contains a forfeiture clause which requires appellant to make his several payments at the times specified to prevent a forfeiture. It is admitted by appellant in his brief, and the evidence shows conclusively that he failed to make any of his deferred payments for more than a year, when he tendered the balance of the purchase price and demanded a deed of appellee. It is also apparent from the evidence that the failure to pay according to the terms of the contract was not due to any fault or conduct of appellee. In *Glock* v. *Howard, etc., Co.* (1898), 123 Cal. 1, 55 Pac. 713, 69 Am. St. 17, 43 L. R. A. 199, the status of a defaulting purchaser under a contract for the sale of real estate is fully discussed, and the rule declared that such a purchaser, who, without excuse, failed to make payment of installments as they fell due cannot by a belated tender put the seller in default and thus establish a right to recover the sums paid under the contract.

Under the evidence in this case appellee had the right to treat appellant's failure to meet his payments at the stated times as an abandonment, and when he forfeited the contract he was acting entirely within its terms and wholly within his legal rights, and therefore appellant could not recover the money paid. Warvelle, Vendors (2d ed.), 835, 836; *Glock* v. *Howard, etc., Co., supra; Maloy* v. *Muir* (1901), 62 Neb. 80, 83, 86 N. W. 916; *Satterlee* v. *Cronkhite* (1897), 114 Mich. 634, 72 N. W. 616; *Wheeler* v. *Mather* (1870), 56 Ill. 241, 8 Am. Rep. 683; *Rounds* v. *Baxter* (1827), 4 Me. (4 Greenl.) *454, *457; *Coughran* v. *Bigelow* (1893), 9 Utah 260, 34 Pac. 51; *Dana* v. *St. Paul Investment Co.* (1889), 42 Minn. 194, 44 N. W. 55; *Whiteman* v. *Perkins* (1898), 56 Neb. 181, 76 N. W. 547.

As before indicated this is an action for money had and received. We do not hold, nor mean to be understood, that the rules stated cover the entire subject-matter. There may be cases where the principles of equity are invoked that would entitle the vendee to other relief, but the vendee must always show equitable grounds for relief before equity will interpose. Pomeroy, Eq. Jurisp. (2d ed.), §455; *Glock* v. *Howard, etc., Co., supra.*

In the case last cited the facts were very similar to the case at bar, and in conclusion the court said: "The payment of the final amount under the contract, at the time and in the manner agreed upon, was a condition precedent to the right of the vendee to demand a conveyance. Upon his failure to make payment the vendee committed a breach, and no affirmative act upon the part of the vendor was necessary to bring about this result. Months after, and without any equitable showing to relieve the default, the vendee makes tender, and because of its refusal claims the right of recovery. But the vendor, in refusing to accept the tender and to repay the money, is neither violating his contract nor rescinding it, nor treating it as at an end. He is standing squarely upon its terms."

Judgment affirmed.

NOTE.—Reported in 115 N. E. 70. Vendor and purchaser, sale of realty, default by purchaser, vendor's right to possession, 107 Am. St. 722; 39 Cyc 2025.

## WILSON ET AL. v. JINKS.

[No. 9,239. Filed February 14, 1917.]

1. DEEDS.— *Delivery.*— *Validity.*— *Recording.*— Where there is a valid and effective delivery of a warranty deed to the grantee by the grantor the title passes regardless of whether the purchase money is paid or secured, and such deed may be recorded without the further express consent of the grantor. p. 618.

2. DEEDS.—*Delivery.*—*Conditions.*—*Validity.*—Where a grantor delivered a deed to his grantee conditioned only on its return if a loan was not secured on the land, and the condition was satisfied by the grantee, he was in rightful possession of the deed with no authority in the grantor to recall it. p. 618.

3. DEEDS.—*Delivery.*—*Intent of Grantor.*—The intention of the grantor to give effect to a deed is essential to a valid delivery, and if such intention is clearly shown the means by which it is established and made effective are not of controlling importance. p. 618.

4. DEEDS.—*Delivery in Escrow.*—*Effect.*—Where a deed or written obligation is placed in escrow with the grantee, payee or obligee thereof, the conditions imposed become inoperative and invalid and the delivery is thereby made absolute and unconditional. p. 619.

5. EJECTMENT.—*Findings.*—*Right of Possession.*—In an action in ejectment, a conclusion of law that plaintiff is entitled to immediate possession, cannot stand where there was no finding of fact that plaintiffs were entitled to possession of the realty in controversy when the suit was begun, and the omission is not cured by a finding that plaintiff was the owner of the real estate in fee simple, since ownership does not necessarily include the right to immediate possession. p. 619.

From Decatur Circuit Court; *Hugh Wickens*, Judge.

Action by James Jinks against Irene Wilson and another. From a judgment for plaintiff, the defendants appeal. *Reversed.*

*Lou Conner* and *M. E. Forkner*, for appellants.
*I. N. McCarty* and *George R. Foster*, for appellee.

FELT, C. J.—This is an action in ejectment to recover possession of seventy-eight and one-half acres of real estate in Franklin county, Indiana. The complaint is in the usual form and was answered by a general denial. The case was tried by the court, and upon request a special finding of facts was made, on which conclusions of law were stated in favor of appellee, plaintiff below, for possession of the real estate described in the complaint and for $250 damages for its unlawful detention. The judgment follows the conclusions of law. The only errors assigned challenge the correctness of the conclusions of law.

The finding of facts, in substance, states that on September 27, 1913, appellant Irene Wilson was the owner of the real estate in controversy and on that day made a parol agreement to sell the same to appellee for a consideration of $2,500, part of which was to be paid by appellee assuming or paying a mortgage on the real estate for $500; that on the date aforesaid appellants, husband and wife, duly signed and acknowledged a warranty deed conveying said real estate to appellee; that appellant Irene Wilson then delivered said deed to appellee to be taken by him and used to procure a loan to him, the proceeds of which were to be used to pay off the existing mortgage on said real estate; that appellee took the deed to Rushville, Indiana, and procured a loan through one Ben Miller, who was the agent of the Rush County Mortgage and Loan Association, and appellee left said deed with said loan agent to be duly recorded which was accordingly done; "that said deed was delivered to said plaintiff under an agreement, and if he should be unable to secure a loan from said Miller as such agent, said

deed should be returned to defendant, Irene Wilson''; that
the proceeds of the loan so obtained were used by appellee
to pay said mortgage indebtedness and he did pay the same
in full to the Farmers' Bank of Franklin county, Indiana,
the owner and holder thereof; that appellants accepted from
appellee as part payment for said real estate a wagon at the
agreed price of $85; that on October 14, 1913, appellee paid
to said Irene Wilson $515 on the purchase price of said
land and on October 15, 1913, executed to said Irene Wilson
his promissory note for $900, due in one year from date,
which note she received and retained in her possession until
November 21, 1913, when through her attorneys she returned
the note to appellee; that appellee claimed that the total
purchase price of said land was $2,000 and he sent the
note aforesaid as payment of the balance in full of the purchase price of the land but the same was not so accepted;
that on November 21, 1913, appellant Irene Wilson began
suit against appellee and the Rush County Mortgage and
Loan Association and alleged in her complaint her ownership
of the land and that on September 27, 1913, ''she sold and
conveyed said real estate to'' appellee at and for the price
of $2,500; that he had paid thereon the sum of $1,100 and
she demanded payment of the balance of $1,400 which appel-
lee had refused and she asked that the court adjudge in her
favor a vendor's lien against the real estate for the sum
aforesaid with accrued interest thereon; that on and prior
to March 23, 1914, appellee demanded possession of said
real estate from appellants, which was refused and he was
excluded therefrom by appellants who retained and still
retain possession thereof; that the reasonable rental value
of said real estate, for the use thereof from October 1, 1913,
to the time of the trial in January, 1915, was $250.

The judgment was rendered on January 15, 1915. The
substance of the conclusions of law is as follows: (1) That
plaintiff (appellee) is entitled to recover possession of the
real estate; that the defendants (appellants) unlawfully and

without right have kept him out of the possession thereof;
(2) that plaintiff is entitled to recover from defendants
damages for the unlawful detention of the possession of
said real estate in the sum of $250.

Appellants contend that the court erred in its conclusions
of law because the finding of facts shows that the deed was
never delivered to appellee so as to vest title in him and
because there is no finding that appellee was the owner of
the property and entitled to the possession thereof; that
the agreement to pay and the agreement to convey are
dependent covenants and the delivery shown by the finding
is not sufficient to entitle appellee to possession of the land
without full payment of the purchase money.

Where there is a valid and effective delivery of a warranty
deed to the grantee by the grantor the title passes whether
the purchase money is or is not paid or secured, and
1. such deed may be recorded without further or express
consent of the grantor, for such delivery places the
deed entirely beyond the control of the grantor. *Ronan* v.
*Meyer* (1882), 84 Ind. 390, 393.

The finding of facts shows a delivery of the deed to appellee, by appellants, conditioned only on its return if the loan
was not secured on the land. The facts show con-
2. clusively that the loan was so obtained and the money
applied in strict compliance with the agreement of the
parties, so that the only condition imposed by the grantors
was satisfied in every particular, as contemplated by appellants, and the deed was therefore in the rightful possession
of appellee with no right or authority in appellants, or
either of them, to claim or recall it. The intention of
the grantor to give effect to the deed is essential to
3. a valid delivery, and where such intention is clearly
shown, the means by which it is established and made
effective are not of controlling importance. In the case at
bar the facts found show an actual delivery which became
effective in strict accordance with the expressed intention

of the grantors. *Townsend* v. *Millican* (1912), 53 Ind. App. 11, 15, 101 N. E. 112; *Merritt* v. *Temple* (1900), 155 Ind. 497, 500, 58 N. E. 699; *Schaefer* v. *Purviance* (1902), 160 Ind. 63, 69, 66 N. E. 154; *Franklin Ins. Co.* v. *Feist* (1903), 31 Ind. App. 390, 395, 396, 68 N. E. 188; *Vaughan* v. *Godman* (1884), 94 Ind. 191, and cases cited.

While not essential to the sufficiency of the finding of delivery in the case at bar, the ultimate conclusion reached is sustained by another line of decisions which hold

4. that where a deed or written obligation is placed in escrow with the grantee, payee or obligee thereof, the conditions imposed become inoperative and invalid and the delivery is thereby made absolute and unconditional. *Deardorff* v. *Foresman* (1865), 24 Ind. 481, 484; *Madison, etc., Co.* v. *Stevens* (1857), 10 Ind.' 1; *State, ex rel.* v. *Chrisman* (1850), 2 Ind. 127, 131; *Foley* v. *Cowgill* (1838), 5 Blackf. 18, 20, 32 Am. Dec. 49. Furthermore the primary facts found admit of but a single inference on the subject of the delivery of the deed which is that the deed was delivered to appellee, and passed beyond the control of appellants and became effective in strict accordance with the expressed intention of the grantors at the time of the delivery.

The finding of facts therefore sufficiently shows the ultimate fact of delivery to warrant the court in considering it, though such fact may be imperfectly stated. *Harris* v. *Riggs* (1916), *ante* 201, 112 N. E. 36, 38, and cases cited; *Shedd* v. *American Maize, etc., Co.* (1915), 60 Ind. App. 146, 163, 108 N E. 610, and cases cited; *Knight* v. *Kerfoot* (1915), 184 Ind. 31, 110 N. E. 206, 209; *Mount* v. *Board, etc.* (1907), 168 Ind. 661, 665, 666, 80 N. E. 629, 14 L. R. A. (N. S.) 483.

Appellants further contend that there is no express finding that appellee is the owner of the real estate and was entitled to the possession thereof when this suit was

5. begun. Section 1100 Burns 1914, §1054 R. S. 1881, provides that: "The plaintiff in his complaint shall

state that he is entitled to the possession of the premises, particularly describing them, the interest he claims therein, and that the defendant unlawfully keeps him out of possession."

Our discussion of the execution and delivery of the deed is conclusive upon the proposition that the findings show appellee to be the owner in fee simple of the real estate, but there is no express finding of the fact that he was entitled to the possession thereof when this suit was begun. This is a possessory action, and to entitle the plaintiff to judgment the court properly stated as a conclusion of law that he was entitled to recover the possession of the real estate.

Appellee contends that this is all that is necessary and that the facts found fully warranted the trial court in drawing such conclusion of law; that no other inference can be drawn from the facts found, other than that appellee was and is entitled to the possession of the real estate; that the essential conclusion of law is identical with the fact of appellee's right to possession and that its statement as a conclusion of law is supported by the decisions, and among them are the following: *Crawfordsville Trust Co.* v. *Ramsey* (1913), 55 Ind. App. 40, 73, 74, 100 N. E. 1049, 102 N. E. 282; *DePauw Plate Glass Co.* v. *City* (1898), 152 Ind. 443, 453, 52 N. E. 608; *Indiana Trust Co.* v. *Byram* (1905), 36 Ind. App. 6, 10, 72 N. E. 670, 73 N. E. 1094.

The contention has merit and has been applied in cases bearing some analogy to the one under consideration. Furthermore, it is quite apparent that the principal controversy at the trial was over the delivery of the deed, which question we have decided adversely to appellant's contention. But the decisions do not recognize the delivery of an unconditional warranty deed or the ownership of the fee-simple title, in suits of this kind, as necessarily entitling the holder of such deed or title to the immediate possession of the real estate, and under the statute, *supra*, have held the statement of the fact of the right of possession to be essential to the sufficiency of a complaint, or of a finding of facts warranting the conclusion of law that the plaintiff is entitled to recover the possession of the real estate in controversy. The decisions seem so conclusive upon the point as to give this court no choice other than that of following them. *Pittsburg, etc., R. Co.* v. *O'Brien* (1895), 142 Ind. 218, 222, 21 N. E. 528; *Miller* v. *Shriner* (1882), 87 Ind. 141, 143; *Levi* v. *Engle* (1883), 91 Ind. 330, 331; *Simmons* v. *Lindley* (1886), 108 Ind. 297, 299, 9 N. E. 360; *Vance* v. *Schroyer* (1881), 77 Ind. 501, 503; *Jose* v. *Hunter* (1915), 60 Ind. App. 569, 103 N. E. 392, 398.

For the want of a finding of the fact that appellee was entitled to the possession of the real estate when this suit was begun, we are compelled by the foregoing authorities to hold the conclusions of law unwarranted and therefore erroneous; but the facts of the case are such as to convince the court that the ends of justice will be subserved by ordering a new trial rather than by directing a restatement of the conclusions of law. *McCord* v. *Bright* (1909), 44 Ind. App. 275, 291, 87 N. E. 654.

The judgment is therefore reversed and a new trial ordered.

NOTE.—Reported in 115 N. E. 67. Deeds: delivery to grantee. subject to future extrinsic condition, 16 L. R. A. (N. S.) 941; what constitutes delivery, 53 Am. St. 537. See under (1, 2) 13 Cyc 564; (5) 15 Cyc 169.

---

## CRUMPACKER v. JEFFREY ET AL.

[No. 9,099. Filed February 14, 1917.]

1. APPEAL.—*Review.*—*Evidence.*—*Sufficiency.*—In determining the sufficiency of the evidence to support the verdict, the court on appeal must group that part of it in which there is no conflict with that part of it tending to support the verdict where there is conflict. p. 624.

2. BROKERS.—*Realty Broker.*—*Authority to Find Purchaser.*—*Letter.*—A letter from a landowner to a real estate agent stating, "I

do not care to sell it even at $350, but will let it go at that price in order to clean up things. If you sell it for $350 per acre, I will allow you two and one-half per cent commission," conferred authority merely to find a, purchaser for the land at the price specified, and did not authorize the broker to execute a binding contract of sale in the name of the owner, or to specify in detail the terms of sale. p. 629.

3. BROKERS.—*Real Estate Broker.—Ratification of Acts.*—Where a real estate broker, without authority from the landowner, made a contract to sell through letters to prospective purchasers, specifying therein definite terms, and the owner, without knowledge of the letters, verbally expressed his entire satisfaction with the terms as reported by the agent, he thereby ratified the act of the broker in specifying and agreeing to such terms. p. 630.

4. PRINCIPAL AND AGENT.—*Unauthorized Acts of Agent.—Ratification.—Effect.*—Where the principal ratifies his agent's unauthorized act in specifying and agreeing to terms of sale, the situation is the same in legal effect as though the principal personally, rather than the agent, had agreed to such terms. p. 631.

5. FRAUDS, STATUTE OF.—*Oral Agreement for Sale of Lands.—Action for Breach of Contract.*—Where a landowner and prospective purchasers have agreed verbally to terms for the sale of land, an action by such prospective purchasers for damages for the owner's breach of contract is barred by the statute of frauds (§7462 Burns 1914, §4904 R. S. 1881). p. 631.

6. BROKERS.—*Unauthorized Acts.—Ratification.—Knowledge.*—The nature of a ratification of an agent's unauthorized acts by the principal is such that knowledge of the material facts is a necessary element of its existence, and without such knowledge there cannot be an effectual ratification. p. 631.

7. BROKERS.—*Real Estate Broker.—Ratification of Acts.—Burden of Proof.—Action on Contract for Sale of Lands.*—Where, in an action for damages for breach of contract for the sale of lands, plaintiffs relied on a ratification by defendant of the act of his agent in entering into the contract, the burden was on them to prove the fact of ratification, and evidence to that end would not be effective unless it established that defendant had knowledge of the material facts. p. 632.

8. BROKERS.—*Ratification of Unauthorized Act.—Evidence.—Sufficiency.*—In an action for damages for breach of contract for the sale of land, where plaintiffs relied on defendant's ratification of his agent's unauthorized act in executing the contract, embodying specific terms, the evidence is held insufficient to establish a ratification. p. 632.

9. BROKERS.—*Ratification of Unauthorized Act.—Agent's Letter.—Principal's Liability.*—Where a landowner, whose agent had with-

out authority made a contract, by letter, to sell land, knew that the agent had written a letter to the prospecive purchasers, presumably relating to the sale, such owner is not chargeable with knowledge of the contents of the letter, so as to constitute a ratification of the agent's unauthorized act, where it appears that the owner, after being informed by the agent that he had not executed a written contract but had written a letter, asked to see a copy of it but it could not be found and the agent then agreed to obtain a copy and deliver it to the owner, who thereafter did not receive any information respecting the letter's contents until a copy was delivered to him shortly before an action was commenced for a breach of the purported contract, since such facts show that the owner did not wilfully remain ignorant respecting the existence of a written contract, or that he had purposely failed to prosecute an inquiry. p. 633.

10. BROKERS.—*Realty Brokers.—Authority.—Duty of Buyer to Ascertain.*—Where parties negotiate with a real estate broker for the purchase of lands, with knowledge that he is acting as the owner's agent, it is their duty to ascertain the nature and extent of the broker's authority and whether he has been empowered to contract in writing for the sale of the lands. p. 634.

From LaPorte Circuit Court; *James F. Gallaher,* Judge.

Action by Charles L. Jeffrey and another against Edgar D. Crumpacker. From a judgment for plaintiffs, the defendant appeals. *Reversed.*

*Grant Crumpacker, O. L. Crumpacker* and *Osborn, McVey & Osborn,* for appellant.

*Hickey & Wolfe, F. L. Welshcimer* and *Samuel Parker,* for appellees.

CALDWELL, J.—Appellees brought this action against appellant in the Porter Circuit Court to recover damages for the breach of a contract alleged to have been executed between the parties by which appellant sold and agreed to convey to appellees a twenty-acre tract of land situate in Lake county. The cause was venued to the Laporte Circuit Court, where a trial resulted in a verdict against appellant for $4,000, on which judgment was rendered. Error is assigned on the overruling of appellant's motion for a new trial.

The trial involved issues formed on a complaint in two paragraphs, numbered first and third. The negotiations had respecting the purchase and sale of the land were conducted by appellees on their own account and by A. R. Hardesty, as agent representing appellant. Whatever contract was made consisted of correspondence, and involved also a contested element of ratification by appellant. Appellant construes the first paragraph of the complaint as proceeding on the theory that Hardesty, as such agent, and with full power and authority to do so, entered into a written contract with appellees and in appellant's name, by which he sold the land and bound appellant to convey it. The theory of the third paragraph as construed by appellant is that Hardesty as agent exceeded his authority in entering into the contract, but that appellant, with knowledge of the facts, subsequently ratified Hardesty's action. Appellees, however, insist that the two paragraphs of the complaint are alike in theory, that Hardesty exceeded his authority as agent in entering into the contract in writing, but that appellant, with knowledge of all of the material facts, ratified Hardesty's action. As we regard appellees' theory of the complaint as more favorable to appellant than his own construction of it, we shall adopt appellee's theory, and as a consequence we shall give but little attention to the question of Hardesty's authority. As the sufficiency of the complaint is not challenged, we shall not further state its substance, but proceed to consider the sufficiency of the evidence. There was some conflict in the evidence.

1. Grouping that part of it in which there was no conflict with that part of it that tends to support the verdict where there was conflict, as we are required to do in considering its sufficiency, it was, in substance, as follows: In the fall of 1909 Hardesty, a real estate broker, approached appellant on the subject of selling real estate for him. Appellant stated, in substance, that it was likely that he would acquire a tract of land in Lake county, and if

so, it would be for sale. In the spring of 1910, Hardesty again interviewed appellant, and was informed that he had acquired the land involved in this action. He thereupon authorized Hardesty verbally to sell the land at $350 per acre on the "usual terms". In June, 1910, appellees offered Hardesty $300 per acre for the land, which proposition Hardesty reported to appellant at Washington, D. C., by letter, appellant at that time being a member of Congress. In response appellant wrote the following letter to Hardesty:

"Washington, D. C. June 11, 1910.

Mr. A. R. Hardesty,
Valparaiso, Ind.

My dear Hardesty:

I have your letter of the 8th inst. about the twenty acre tract of land in Tolleston. I would not sell that land for less than $350 an acre. In my judgment within five years it will be worth a thousand dollars an acre. I do not care to sell it even at $350, but will let it go at that price in order to clean up things. If you sell it at $350 an acre I will allow you two and a half per cent commission.

Sincerely Yours,

E. D. Crumpacker."

Soon after Hardesty received the above letter there was a telephone conversation between him and appellees, leading to an exchange of letters as follows:

"Valparaiso, Ind. June 23, 1910.

Jeffrey and Morgan,
Chesterton, Ind.

Gentlemen:

This will confirm my telephone conversation of this date, with Mr. Jeffrey, whereby I sell to you (Charles L. Jeffrey and Ed. L. Morgan) for Hon. E. D. Crumpacker of this city, twenty (20) acres of land in Tolleston, now Gary, Ind., and described as follows: E. ¼ of the N. W. ¼ of the N. E. ¼ of Sec. 18, Town. 36, N. R. 8, W., in Lake County, Ind. The terms of sale are as follows: The consideration is $350.00 per acre, or $7000.00, the receipt of $100.00 of which is hereby acknowledged as earnest money, and to be applied on the purchase price, the balance of one third to be paid on delivery of warranty deed and merchantable abstract of title, one third to be paid on or before one year from that date, and one third on or before two years from the same date, deferred payments to bear int. at six per cent per annum, payable annually, and secured by first mortgage on the land, the deed to have the usual release clause.

Very truly,<br>A. R. Hardesty, Agent."

"Chesterton, Ind., June 23, 1910.

Mr. A. R. Hardesty, Agent for E. D. Crumpacker, Valparaiso, Ind.

Dear sir:

As per conversation with you today over the telephone, I am enclosing you herein Chicago exchange made payable to your order as agent for E. D. Crumpacker for $100.00. This payment is made as earnest money in the purchase from Mr. E. D. Crumpacker by Edward L. Morgan and myself of a twenty acre tract located in section 18, township 36, range 9 west, in the corporate limits of Tolleston, now Gary, Lake County, Indiana.

According to the terms of sale, the price of this twenty acres is three hundred and fifty dollars ($350.00) per acre, one third cash upon Mr. Crumpacker delivering to Mr. Morgan and myself warranty deed and abstract showing merchantable title to the property in question. The remaining two thirds to be payable on or before one and two years time from date of deed, and evidenced by two notes of even date therewith, bearing six per cent interest payable annually and secured by first mortgage on the property. The deed to have the usual release clause contained therein.

As soon as the proper continuation of the abstract has been made, you will deliver the same to us at our office in Gary, Indiana.

Kindly acknowledge receipt of this letter and oblige,

Yours very respectfully,<br>Charles L. Jeffrey,<br>Edward L. Morgan."

CLJ/SA

Enclosed in the letter last set out there was a $100 check drawn by appellees and payable to Hardesty as appellant's agent. Hardesty thereupon wrote and mailed to appellant a letter, enclosing the $100 check, properly endorsed by him as appellant's agent. This letter was received by appellant in due course, but he made no response to it by letter or otherwise in writing. The letter is as follows:

"Valparaiso, Ind., June 24, 1910.
Hon. E. D. Crumpacker,
Washington, D. C.
Dear sir:

As I informed you yesterday, by telegraph, I sold the 20 acres which you own at Tolleston, Ind., described as the E. ¼ of the N. W. ¼ of the N. E. ¼ of Sec. 18, Town. 36, N., R. 8, W.

The sale was made to Charles L. Jeffrey and Edward L. Morgan of Chesterton, Ind., for $7000.00, check for $100.00 of which is enclosed herewith, the balance of one-third to be paid on delivery of warranty deed and merchantable abstract showing good and sufficient title, one-third to be paid on or before one year from that date, and one-third on or before two years from that date, the deferred payments to bear interest at six per cent payable annually and be secured by first mortgage on the land, the deed to contain the usual release clause.

Now, if you will have the abstract brought down to date at once or send it to me for that purpose or tell me where to find it, so I can have it brought down, we can have the deal closed soon.

Awaiting your reply soon, I am,
Very truly,

A. D. Hardesty."

Appellant returned to his home in Valparaiso early in July. There was evidence that on several occasions thereafter he stated to Hardesty, and on one occasion to appellees, that the terms of the sale were satisfactory to him. There were, however, certain complications in the title involving liens, some of which were disputed by appellant. There was evidence that he proceeded as rapidly as possible, considering other matters that demanded his attention, in an effort to clear the title. The effort, however, was not successful as to a lien claimed by Ward and Gill, but disputed by appellant, amounting to $600. On appellant's part there was evidence that he did not approve of

Hardesty's acts in selling the land, especially considering the specific terms of the sale, and that he did not regard the sale as binding on him, and that he merely held the proposition under advisement, to be accepted or rejected as he should finally determine. In the latter part of July, or early in August, 1910, he asked Hardesty whether he had executed any formal contract for the sale of the land. Hardesty said that he had not, but that he had written a letter. Appellant asked to see a copy, but Hardesty was unable to find it. There was evidence that prior to or about the middle of August, Hardesty, by appellant's direction, notified appellees that appellant did not regard the agreement for the sale of the land as binding on him, and that he would not perform it. In the early part of September there was a meeting in Hardesty's office, at which appellant and appellees were present. There was evidence that at such meeting appellees agreed to take care of the Ward and Gill claim, and appellant stated that the terms were otherwise satisfactory to him. This evidence, however, was contradicted. On July 6, 1910, appellant deposited the $100 check for collection. He testified that he did so as a matter of convenience, intending to apply it as a credit on the selling price of the land, in case he determined to consummate the sale; otherwise that he intended to return the amount to appellees.

On a former occasion Hardesty had acted as broker in the sale of a tract of real estate for appellant. In that transaction the former had asked the latter to execute a contract after a purchaser had been found. The latter replied "I will not sign a contract, but get your buyers ready with the money and we will do business." Hardesty testified that, remembering such transaction, he did not ask appellant to sign a contract in the sale involved here. As we have said, appellant on inquiry was informed the last of July or early in August that Hardesty had not executed a formal contract for the sale of the land, but that he had written a letter, a copy of which Hardesty was unable to produce. Appellant was not informed respecting the contents of such letter prior to a few days after October 3, and shortly before this action was commenced, when Hardesty procured and delivered a copy to him. The letter of which a copy was so delivered to appellant is the one written by Hardesty to appellees under date of June 23. The first knowledge that appellant had that appellees had written a letter to Hardesty on the subject of the sale and purporting to make or accept a proposition was after the suit was commenced. He then saw and examined the complaint in this action, which set out a copy of appellees' letter of June 23 written to Hardesty. On September 12, appellant sent a draft for $100 by letter to appellees, informing them that the draft was for the purpose of returning the money they had advanced to Hardesty, and that the negotiations for the sale of the land might be considered at an end. On September 13, appellees, by letter, returned the draft with the statement that they would proceed for specific performance or damages. Appellant, by letter dated September 17, acknowledged receipt of the draft and notified appellees that he held it subject to their order. Appellees tendered performance of the contract. There was evidence that the value of the land was greater than $350 per acre.

We proceed to consider the sufficiency of this evidence to sustain the verdict. Under the averments of the complaint, Hardesty's authority in the matter rested

2. upon appellant's letter to him dated June 11, 1910, and above set out, and especially on the following expression contained in it: "I do not care to sell it even at $350, but will let it go at that price in order to clean up things. If you sell it for $350 per acre, I will allow you two and one half per cent commission." Such language addressed to a real estate broker is very generally construed as conferring authority merely to find a purchaser, rather than as authorizing the broker to go further and execute

in the name of the owner a binding contract of sale. The overwhelming weight of authority seems to be to that effect. *Duffy* v. *Hobson* (1870), 40 Cal. 240, 6 Am. Rep. 617; *Armstrong* v. *Lowe* (1888), 76 Cal. 616, 18 Pac. 758; *Tyrrell* v. *O'Connor* (1897), 56 N. J. Eq. 448, 41 Atl. 674; *York* v. *Nash* (1903), 42 Ore. 321, 71 Pac. 59; *Jones* v. *Howard* (1908), 234 Ill. 404, 84 N. E. 1041; *Watkins, etc., Co.* v. *Campbell* (1907), 100 Tex. 542, 101 S. W. 1078; *Thorne* v. *Jung* (1912), 253 Ill. 584, 97 N. E. 1073; *Furst* v. *Tweed* (1895), 93 Iowa 300, 61 N. W. 857; *Simmons* v. *Kramer* (1891), 88 Va. 411, 13 S. E. 902. See, also, notes 17 L. R. A. (N. S.) 210; and *Jasper* v. *Wilson*, 23 L. R. A. (N. S.) 982, where the cases bearing on the point are grouped. The rule established by the weight of authority has been recognized as sound in this jurisdiction. *Campbell* v. *Galloway* (1897), 148 Ind. 440, 447, 47 N. E. 818; *McFarland* v. *Lillard* (1891), 2 Ind. App. 160, 163, 28 N. E. 229, 50 Am. St. 234; *Lockwood* v. *Rose* (1890), 125 Ind. 588, 25 N. E. 710.

We therefore conclude that Hardesty's authority was limited to procuring a purchaser for the land at $350 per acre. It follows that in attempting as appellant's agent to bind him by entering into the written contract constituted of the two letters dated June 23, 1910, Hardesty exceeded his authority in two respects: First, in specifying in detail the terms of sale as expressed in such letters; and, second, in entering into what purported to be a binding contract in writing. We proceed to the question of ratification.

By the letter dated June 24, 1910, written by Hardesty to appellant, the latter was fully informed respecting the specific terms of the sale as embodied in the letters
3. dated June 23, 1910. But he was not thereby informed of the existence of such letters, or that Hardesty and appellees had committed to writing in any form and duly signed the terms of their agreement respecting the sale of the land. There was evidence that on several occasions, after receiving the letter dated June 24, appellant

verbally expressed his entire satisfaction with the specific terms of sale as reported to him by such letter. It would seem, therefore, that in so far as concerns the mere terms of the sale, if such element considered alone has any importance, appellant should be held to have ratified the act of Hardesty as his agent in specifying and agreeing to such terms. If appellant ratified Hardesty's act to the

4. extent we have indicated, then the situation is the same in legal effect as if appellant personally, rather than through an agent, agreed to such terms. As far as we have thus analyzed the case, there is no question of a written contract involved. Assuming then that in legal effect appellees and appellant agreed verbally to

5. terms of sale identical with those reported to appellant by the letter of June 24, the statute of frauds (§7462 Burns 1914, §4904 R. S. 1881), would stand as a barrier to the maintaining of this action by appellees. We therefore proceed to determine whether Hardesty's act of contracting in writing was ratified by appellant.

The facts and circumstances bearing on the subject of ratification in the respect now under consideration are as follows: Appellant was informed specifically respect-

6. ing the terms of the sale; he expressed himself as satisfied with such terms; he cashed the $100 check, the amount of which was subsequently returned; he took certain steps in the line of clearing the title to the land. If appellant ratified Hardesty's act of contracting in writing for the sale of the land, such ratification was indicated by the foregoing facts and circumstances. The subject-matter of the ratification now under consideration is not the making of a contract, but rather the making of a contract in writing. It is universally held that knowledge of the material facts is essential in order that there may be an effectual ratification. The nature of a ratification is such that knowledge is a necessary element of its existence. It follows that appellant could not be held to

have ratified Hardesty's act in entering into a contract in
writing, unless he knew that Hardesty had entered into such
a contract.   As appellees relied on ratification, it was
7.  incumbent on them to prove the fact of ratification.
Evidence to that end would not be effective, unless
it established also knowledge on the part of appellant, without which there could be no ratification.   There was no
evidence that appellant knew that Hardesty, by the
8.  letters dated June 23, had entered into what purported to be a binding contract for the sale of the
land, until long after he had declared both verbally and in
writing that all negotiations respecting the sale of the land
might be considered as ended.   His first information that
Hardesty had agreed in writing to the sale of the land was
after October 3, 1910, when a copy of Hardesty's letter
of June 23 was delivered to him.   His first information that
appellees had agreed in writing to purchase the land was
obtained after this action had been commenced.   There was
no evidence that appellant, when he cashed the $100 check,
had any information that Hardesty had attempted to bind
him in writing.   His information that a letter had been
written was received several weeks later.   There was evidence that appellant took steps to clear the title to the land
after learning that Hardesty had written a letter, but information merely that a letter had been written was not information that a written contract had been executed.   Moreover, the claims against the land were such that appellant
might reasonably have been expected to proceed to dispose of them, independent of any purpose to convey the
lands to appellees.   We do not regard the evidence as sufficient to establish a ratification by the appellant.   See the
following: *Metzger* v. *Huntington* (1894), 139 Ind. 501, 37
N. E. 1084, 39 N. E. 235; *Strong* v. *Ross* (1904), 33 Ind.
App. 586, 597, 71 N. E. 918; *Wheeler* v. *Northwestern
Sleigh Co.* (1889), 39 Fed. 347; *Combs* v. *Scott* (1866), 12
Allen (Mass.) 493; *Lightfoot* v. *Horst* (1909), (Tex. Civ.

App.) 122 S. W. 606; *Clement* v. *Young, etc., Co.* (1905), 70 N. J. Eq. 677, 67 Atl. 82, 118 Am. St. 747; 1 Mechem, Agency (2d ed.) §393; *Johnson* v. *Ogren* (1907), 102 Minn. 8, 112 N. W. 894; *Adams' Express Co.* v. *Trego* (1871), 35 Md. 47, 68.

It is argued, however, that since appellant knew about August 1, 1910, that Hardesty had written a letter to appellees, presumably on the subject of the sale of
9. the lands, appellant should be chargeable with knowledge of the contents of such letter. It will be remembered that the facts are as follows: Appellant asked Hardesty whether he had executed a contract for the sale of the land. Hardesty replied that he had not, but that he had written a letter. Appellant then asked to see a copy of the letter, but Hardesty, having searched, was unable to find it, and then agreed to get a copy and deliver it to appellant. Neither Hardesty nor any one else at any time gave appellant any information respecting the contents of such letter. The copy was delivered after October 3, as we have stated. These facts do not indicate that appellant wilfully remained ignorant respecting the existence of a written contract, or that he purposely shut his eyes to means of information. No duty rested on him to ratify the unauthorized acts of his agent, nor was he bound to inquire if there had been such unauthorized acts. He should not be chargeable with knowledge of the contents of such letter, unless he wilfully or purposely failed to prosecute an inquiry.

"Ratification is a voluntary act upon the part of the principal, and he is under no legal obligation to make inquiries about the unauthorized acts of his agent, and knowledge will not be presumed because of the opportunity to acquire it." *Lightfoot* v. *Horst, supra.* "The principal, before a ratification (of unauthorized acts of an agent) becomes effectual against him, must be shown to have had previous knowledge of all the facts and circumstances in the case; and if he assented to or confirmed the act of his agent while in ignorance of all the circumstances, he can afterwards, when informed thereof, disaffirm it. * * * And the principal's want of such knowledge, even if it arises from his own carelessness in inquiring, or neglect in ascertaining the facts, or from other causes, will render such ratification invalid. His knowledge is an essential element." Story, Agency (9th ed.) §239, note 1. "So if a principal ratify a sale made by his agent without knowledge of a warranty given by the agent, though it would seem clear that the duty of inquiry as to warranty was upon the principal, he is not bound by such ratification." *Brown* v. *Bamberger, etc., Co.* (1895), 110 Ala. 342, 20 South. 114. See, also, *Smith* v. *Tracy* (1867), 36 N. Y. 79.

"Generally speaking it does not devolve upon the principal to make inquiry as to the facts. He has a right to presume that his agent has followed instructions, and has not exceeded his authority. Whenever he is sought to be held liable on the ground of ratification, either express or implied, it must be shown that he ratified upon full knowledge of all material facts, or that he was willfully ignorant; or purposely refrained from seeking information, or that he intended to adopt the unauthorized act at all events, under whatever circumstances." *Oxford Lake Line, etc.* v. *First Nat. Bank* (1898), 40 Fla. 349, 24 South. 480. "It is a well-settled rule that knowledge of the terms and conditions of an unauthorized contract, entered into by an agent, is not to be presumed from the fact that the principal had a reasonable opportunity to acquire such knowledge." *Haswell* v. *Standring* (1911), 152 Iowa 291, 132 N. W. 417, Ann. Cas. 1913B 1326. See, also, *Heinzerling* v. *Agen* (1907), 46 Wash. 390, 90 Pac. 262; 1 Mechem, Agency (2d ed.) §403.

Appellees were fully informed of the existence of the written contract, and that it was made by Hardesty 10. as agent, rather than by appellant personally. It was therefore appellee's duty to ascertain the nature and extent of Hardesty's authority, and whether he had been empowered to contract in writing for the sale of the lands. Although opportunities were presented to appellees to do so, they made no inquiry of appellant at any time respecting the scope of Hardesty's authority. *Metzger* v. *Huntington, supra; Strong* v. *Ross, supra; Davis* v. *Talbot* (1894), 137 Ind. 235, 36 N. E. 1098; 1 Mechem, Agency (2d ed.) §743. "Whoever, therefore, seeks to procure and rely on a ratification is bound to show that it was made under such circumstances as in law to be binding on the principal, especially to see to it that all material facts were made known to him. The burden of making inquiries and of ascertaining the truth is not cast on him who is under no legal obligation to assume a responsibility, but rests on the party who is endeavoring to obtain a benefit or advantage for himself. This is not only just, but it is practicable. The needful information or knowledge is always within the reach of him who is either party or privy to a transaction which he seeks to have ratified, rather than of him who did not authorize it, and to the details of which he may be a stranger." *Combs* v. *Scott, supra.*

We conclude that the evidence is insufficient to sustain the verdict. Other questions presented are not considered or decided. The judgment is reversed, with instructions to sustain the motion for a new trial.

Note.—Reported in 115 N. E. 62. Brokers: real estate, power to make contracts of sale, Ann. Cas. 1917A 522; what constitutes a contract for the sale of land within the statute of frauds, 102 Am. St. 232. See under (2) 19 Cyc 294; 9 C. J. 668; (3) 19 Cyc. 206; 9 C. J. 582; (4) 19 Cyc 290; 9 C. J. 534; (5) 20 Cyc 226; (6) 19 Cyc 296; (7) 19 Cyc 306; (10) 19 Cyc 294.

## Aubain v. United Brotherhood ·of Carpenters and Joiners of America.

[No. 9,149.   Filed February 15, 1917.]

1. APPEAL.—*Assignments of Error.—Question Presented.—Exceptions.*—Assignments of error that are not based on exceptions shown in the record cannot be considered on appeal. p. 637.

2. APPEAL.—*Agreed Case.—Presenting Questions for Review.—Exceptions.*—A motion for a new trial is not contemplated in an agreed case, there being no question for decision except the law arising upon the agreed facts, and a question of law in such a case, to be presented on appeal, must be saved by an exception to the decision of the trial court taken at the proper time. p. 637.

3. APPEAL.—*Agreed Statement of Facts.—Presenting Question for Review.—Motion for a New Trial.—Bill of Exceptions.*—Where issues are joined upon an agreed statement of facts, a motion for a new trial is required to raise any question on appeal involving the evidence, and the agreed statement of facts must be made a part of the record by a bill of exceptions, and the record must affirmatively show that it contains all the evidence that was adduced at the trial. p. 637.

From Marion Circuit Court (23,904); *Charles Remster,* Judge.

Action by Eva Dufresne Aubain against United Brotherhood of Carpenters and Joiners of America. From a judgment for defendant, the plaintiff appeals. *Affirmed.*

*Frank G. West* and *Wetzel Swartz,* for appellant.

*Joseph O. Carson,* for appellee.

BATMAN, J.—This is an agreed case under §579 Burns 1914, §553 R. S. 1881, involving the construction of certain sections of the constitution of appellee with reference to the payment of a funeral donation to appellant, as the widow of a deceased member. The court below made a general finding in favor of appellee, who was the defendant in the action, and rendered judgment that appellant take nothing and that appellee recover its costs. Appellant filed a motion for a new trial, which motion was overruled, and an exception was reserved to such ruling. This was the only exception reserved in the court below as appears from the record. Appellant, who was plaintiff below, appealed and assigned errors as follows: The court erred in finding for the defendant; in rendering judgment on the agreed case in favor of the defendant; and in overruling the motion for a new trial.

If it should be conceded that the first two assignments of error are sufficient to raise any question on appeal,

1. they could not be considered in this case, as they are not based on any exception shown in the record.

This leaves for consideration only the ruling of the court on appellant's motion for a new trial. It is well settled in this state that a motion for a new trial

2. is not contemplated in an agreed case, as the facts would necessarily be the same on a second trial, and there would be nothing gained thereby; that, the facts being agreed upon, there is no question for decision, except the law arising upon such facts, as in a demurrer to the evidence or on a special finding of facts by the court; that a question of law in such case is saved by an exception to the decision of the trial court upon the agreed case, and unless the record shows that such an exception was taken to the decision at the proper time, no question will be presented on appeal. 2 Woolen, Trial Procedure §4363; *Fisher* v. *Purdue* (1874), 48 Ind. 323; *State, ex. rel.* v. *Board, etc.* (1879), 66 Ind. 216; *Thatcher* v. *Ireland* (1881), 77 Ind. 486; *Lofton* v. *Moore* (1882), 83 Ind. 112; *Hall, Executor,* v. *Pennsylvania Co.* (1883), 90 Ind. 459; *North* v. *Barringer* (1896), 147 Ind. 224, 46 N. E. 531; *City of Shelbyville* v. *Phillips* (1897), 149 Ind. 552, 48 N. E. 626; *Geisen* v. *Reder* (1898), 151 Ind. 529, 51 N. E. 353, 1060.

The record indicates that the trial court may have treated the agreed case as an agreed statement of facts in its finding and judgment. However, if we should so con-

3. sider it here, still there would be no question for our determination, as the evidence would not be in the

record on that theory. There is a marked difference between an "agreed case" and an "agreed statement of facts," although some confusion has arisen from an evident inadvertent misuse of terms. The courts hold that where issues are joined in a case submitted for trial, either to a court or jury, upon an agreed statement of facts, a motion for a new trial is required to raise any question on appeal involving the evidence, and the agreed statement of facts must be made a part of the record by a bill of exceptions, and such record must affirmatively show that it contains all the evidence that was adduced on the trial of the cause. *Pennsylvania Co.* v. *Niblack* (1884), 99 Ind. 149; *Citizens Ins. Co.* v. *Harris* (1886), 108 Ind. 392, 9 N. E. 299; *Reddick* v. *Board, etc.* (1895), 14 Ind. App. 598, 41 N. E. 834, 43 N. E. 238; *Wright* v. *Shelt* (1897), 19 Ind. App. 1, 48 N. E. 26; *Morrison* v. *Morrison* (1896), 144 Ind. 379, 43 N. E. 437.

There is no bill of exceptions in the record in this case, and it therefore follows from the authorities cited that the action of the court in overruling appellant's motion for a new trial raises no question in this court in either event; and since an exception to the action of a trial court is essential in order to make the same available on appeal, and the record discloses no exception, save the one relating to the ruling on the motion for a new trial, we conclude that there is no question presented for our determination. *Butler* v. *Thornburgh, Admr.* (1895), 141 Ind. 152, 40 N. E. 514; *Hedrick* v. *Whitehorn* (1896), 145 Ind. 642, 43 N. E. 942; *State* v. *Friedley* (1898), 151 Ind. 404, 51 N. E. 473.

Judgment affirmed.

NOTE.—Reported in 115 N. E. 78.

## A. KIEFER DRUG COMPANY *v.* DeLAY ET AL.

[No. 9,241. Filed February 15, 1917.]

1. PARTITION.—*Commissioner for Sale of Land.—Duties.—Liability on Bond.*—The duties of a commissioner appointed to make the sale of land in a partition proceeding are determined by the statutes and the orders of the court, and he is an instrument of the court primarily answerable thereto, and only becomes liable on his bond when he fails to faithfully discharge the duties of his trust. p. 642.

2. PARTITION.—*Parties.—Lienholders.—Distribution of Proceeds.*— In partition suits it is proper to make those who hold liens on undivided interests in the land parties to the action, and the court has power to protect their interests and, in case of sale, to provide for the payment or satisfaction of such liens out of funds derived from the sale of such interests to the extent that the net proceeds from the sale thereof shall be sufficient so to do. p. 642.

3. PARTITION.—*Commissioner for Sale of Land.—Duties.—Liability to Lienholder.*—A commissioner for the sale of land in partition who follows the order of sale and distributes the funds according thereto has discharged the obligation of his trust in that respect, and he is not liable to one who acquired a lien on the real estate subsequent to the order of sale and the appointment of the commissioner, unless such lienholder before the funds were distributed duly petitioned the court and obtained an order which entitled him to receive payment out of the funds derived from the sale. p. 643.

4. JUDGMENT.—*Money Judgment.—Enforcement.—Duty of Owner.*—Money judgments are not self-executing, and in the collection thereof the duty rests upon the owner of the judgment to take the necessary steps provided by law for their enforcement, and if he fails to do so he cannot place the responsibility for such failure upon others who have no legal duty resting upon them in respect thereto. p. 644.

5. PARTITION.—*Sale of Land.—Proceeds.—Distribution.—Commissioner's Bond.—Liability.*—Where, in a partition proceeding, an order is made for the sale of land and it is sold in accordance with the order, one holding a judgment against one of the parties in partition who was not himself a party and who did not file a transcript with the clerk until after the entry of the order of sale cannot recover on the commissioner's bond because the commissioner, even though notified of the judgment creditor's claim, did not pay him the amount thereof. p. 644.

6. PARTITION.—*Judgment against Party.—Presumptions.*—The mere

fact that a judgment is of record and appears unsatisfied is not conclusive evidence that it is unpaid or that there is not some valid reason why funds in the hands of the commissioner in a partition proceeding should not be applied to such a judgment against an heir to the lands sold. p. 645.

7. JUDGMENT.—*Money Judgment.*—*Lien.*—The lien of a money judgment is general and not specific. p. 645.

From Knox Circuit Court; *Benjamin M. Willoughby*, Judge.

Action by the A. Kiefer Drug Company against Judson DeLay and another. From a judgment for defendants, the plaintiff appeals. *Affirmed.*

*Louis Newberger, Milton N. Simon, Lawrence B. Davis, Clarence B. Kessinger* and *Elmer F. Williams,* for appellant.
*D. Frank Culbertson* and *W. S. Hoover,* for appellee.

FELT, C. J.—This suit was brought by appellant to recover on the bond executed by appellee Judson A. DeLay, as commissioner for the sale of real estate, and appellee Corbin, his surety. The complaint was in two paragraphs, to each of which a demurrer for insufficiency of facts to state a cause of action was sustained.

Appellant duly excepted to the ruling of the court, refused to plead further and judgment was rendered against it for costs and that it take nothing by its complaint. From this judgment appellant appealed and has assigned as error the ruling on the demurrer to each paragraph of its complaint.

The complaint is long and many of the details are not essential to a determination of the questions presented. It is averred that on May 5, 1913, appellant recovered judgment against one William M. DeLay for $715 in the Sullivan Circuit Court and on May 20, 1913, filed transcripts thereof in the clerk's office in the counties of Greene and Knox; that the father of said DeLay died intestate in 1912, the owner of certain real estate in both Knox and Greene counties, leaving surviving him six children; that a suit was instituted in the Knox Circuit Court for the partition of said real estate and, on November 18, 1912, appellee Judson A. DeLay was duly appointed commissioner to make sale of said real estate, and gave bond in the sum of $25,000 with appellee Corbin as surety thereon, which bond is made a part of the complaint as "Exhibit A"; that thereafter said real estate in Greene county, Indiana, was sold by the commissioner for $8,500 in cash and at the time of such sale the aforesaid judgment against William M. DeLay was a lien upon the real estate in Greene county and became a lien upon that part of the funds, in appellee DeLay's hands, which were derived from the sale of the interest of William M. DeLay in the real estate so sold; that said commissioner in disregard of the rights of appellant paid to said William M. DeLay his share of the proceeds and ignored the aforesaid transcript of the judgment in favor of appellant and failed and refused to pay the aforesaid judgment to appellant out of the funds aforesaid; that it was the duty of said commissioner to pay to appellant from the funds in his hands derived from the sale of the interest of said William M. DeLay in said real estate, the amount due on said judgment in its favor.   The prayer asks judgment for $1,000.

The second paragraph is the same as the first, except it contains the additional averments that while the funds were in the hands of the commissioner, appellant notified him in writing of said judgment and that it was unpaid; that when be paid the proceeds of the sale to William M. DeLay he knew that said judgement had been taken against said William M. DeLay and that it was unpaid.

The substance of appellant's memorandum and of the points and propositions presented is that the averments show that appellant's judgment was a lien on the interest of William M. DeLay in the real estate sold, at the time the sale was made by the commissioner; that the lien followed the funds and that, without further action on appellant's part other than filing the transcript of its judgment, it became the duty of the commissioner to pay appellant's judgment out of the funds in his hands derived from the sale of that part of the real estate belonging to William M. DeLay.

The averments do not show that appellant was a party to the partition suit or that the attention of the court was in any way brought to the fact that it held a lien on the land sold, either when the order of sale was made or subsequent thereto, or that the order of the court directed payment of any of the funds derived from the sale to appellant, but the averments do clearly show that the transcript of the judgment was not filed until May 20, 1913, and that the real estate was ordered sold and the commissioner appointed in November, 1912.

When the court decides that land which is the subject of a partition suit shall be sold, the statute provided that "Such sale shall be made by a commissioner to be appointed by the court." §1258 Burns 1914, §1201 R. S. 1881. The statute further provides that "the moneys arising from such sale, after payment of just costs and expenses, shall be paid by such commissioner to the persons entitled thereto, according to their respective shares in the land sold by him "under the direction of the court," and he receives such compensation for his services as the court deems reasonable.

1. His duties are determined by the statutes of the state and the orders of the court. He is an instrument or arm of the court for the discharge of certain designated duties and is primarily answerable to the court, and only becomes liable on his bond when he fails to faithfully discharge the duties of his trust. *Huffman* v. *Darling* (1899), 153 Ind. 22, 24, 53 N. E. 939.

2. In partition suits it is proper to make those who hold liens on undivided interests in the land parties to the action, and the court has power to protect their interests and in case of sale to provide for the payment or satisfaction of such liens out of the funds derived from

the sale of such interests to the extent that the net proceeds from the sale thereof shall be sufficient so to do. *Milligan* v. *Poole* (1871), 35 Ind. 64; *Clark* v. *Stephenson* (1881), 73 Ind. 489, 490; *Arnold* v. *Butterbaugh* (1884), 92 Ind. 403, 405. In *Arnold* v. *Butterbaugh, supra,* it is said: "If partition is made the liens follow the tracts of land to which they properly belong when set off in severalty. If the land is sold the liens are transferred to the fund which is the proceeds of the sale, and satisfied therefrom. But the rule as to making lien holders parties applies only to persons having liens at the commencement of the action for partition. The action is an action *in rem,* and when it results in the sale of the real estate, the purchaser acquires all the right, title and interest held by the parties to the action at the time of its commencement. Where, after · the action is begun, a party conveys his interest, or a lien is acquired against it, this does not affect the rights of a purchaser at a sale ordered in the partition action. Such subsequent vendee of one of the parties or lien holder may, perhaps, by petition to the court acquire an ·interest in the proceeds of the sale, but the sale divests his title or lien." In the case from which the above language is quoted a commissioner was appointed to sell the property and, subsequent thereto and before the sale, transcripts of judgments were filed which became liens on an undivided interest in the real estate sold. After the confirmation of the sale executions were issued on the judgments, and such undivided interest was sold by the sheriff. The purchaser at the commissioner's sale brought suit to set aside the sheriff's sale and to quiet his title against the purchaser at the sheriff's sale. He obtained a judgment quieting his title, which was

3.  affirmed by the Supreme Court. The statement in the opinion that "the rule as to making lien holders parties applies only to persons having liens at the commencement of the action" clearly indicates that a commissioner who follows the order of sale and distributes the funds ac-

cording thereto has discharged the obligation of his trust
in that respect, and is not liable to one who acquired a lien
on the real estate subsequent to the order of sale and appointment of the commissioner, unless such lienholder before the
funds were distributed duly petitioned the court and obtained an order which entitled him to receive payment out
of the funds derived from the sale. *Huffman* v. *Darling,
supra,* 25. In the case above cited the court says: "Neither
a judgment nor mortgage lienor holds the land as land. He
only holds the right to have the land appropriated for the
payment of his debt."

Money judgments are not self-executing. To enforce the
collection thereof the duty rests upon the owner of the judgment to take the necessary and appropriate steps pro-
4. vided by law for their enforcement, and if he fails so
to do he cannot shift responsibility for such failure to
others who have no legal duty resting upon them in respect
thereto. §§716, 717, 721, 859 *et seq.* Burns 1914, §§674, 675,
679 R. S. 1881; 23 Cyc 1350; 17 Am. and Eng. Ency. Law
770.

From the foregoing we think it is clear that the court did
not err in sustaining the demurrer to the first paragraph
of the complaint. Since there was no legal duty im-
5. posed on the commissioner to institute proceedings
to apply funds in his hands to the payment of appellant's judgment, a mere notice of the existence of such judgment and that it was unpaid would not be sufficient to charge
the commissioner with legal responsibility for failure to
so apply the funds in his hands. He might very well have
set up the facts in his report to the court. If this had
been done and the proper parties had been duly joined
thereon and the court had made an order in respect thereto,
it would have served the same purpose as a petition by
appellant followed by an order of the court. *Huffman* v.
*Darling, supra.*

To place the responsibility on the commissioner, in such

instances, of ascertaining the existence of liens placed upon the real estate subsequent to his appointment and to require him to assume responsibility for the discharge thereof would lead to many complications and require him to keep his information fresh up to the very time of the sale. Furthermore the mere fact that a judgment is of record and

6. appears unsatisfied is not conclusive evidence that it is unpaid or that the owner of the real estate does not have some valid reason why the funds in the hands of the commissioner should not be applied to its payment. 23 Cyc 1402, 1404, 1405. We therefore conclude that the court did not err in sustaining the demurrer to the second paragraph of the complaint. Other questions are sug-

7. gested by the pleadings though not presented by the briefs. It is a well-known fact that the lien of an ordinary money-judgment is general and not specific. 23 Cyc 1350.

Query—waiving the point of the lack of a legal duty on the part of the commissioner to pay appellant the amount of its judgment, whether the allegations are sufficient on the question of appellant's damages and its right to receive payment out of the particular fund in the commissioner's hands? *King* v. *Easton* (1893), 135 Ind. 353, 35 N. E. 181.

The trial court did not err in its rulings. Judgment affirmed.

NOTE.—Reported in 114 N. E. 35. Duties and powers of commissioners in partition proceedings, 41 Am. St. 146, 147. See under (2, 3) 30 Cyc 294; (4, 6) 23 Cyc 1351, 1352.

---

# RUCKER *v.* KELLEY.

[No. 9,089. Filed October 13, 1916. Rehearing denied December 19. 1916. Transfer denied February 15, 1917.]

1. GUARDIAN AND WARD.—*Final Settlements.—Vacating.*—Applications to set aside final settlements of guardians must show that the person seeking to set it aside were not notified to appear and did not appear at the hearing of the final settlement report. p. 647.

2. GUARDIAN AND WARD.—*Successive Guardianships.—Attack on First Guardian's Accounts after Final Settlement.*—Where a guardian resigned and was succeeded by another, who made a final settlement of the estate, an heir to the ward could not, after such final settlement, recover compensation allowed the first guardian at the time of making her last report and penalties for alleged failure to comply with the statutes in making current reports, it not appearing from the heirs' complaint that she was not notified to appear and was not present at the hearing of the final report, at which time error in partial reports should be presented, since the attack on the last report of the first guardian, which was not a final report, was, under the allegations of the complaint, an attempt to question the final settlement indirectly and a final report which has been approved cannot be questioned on a collateral proceeding. p. 647.

From Benton Circuit Court; *Burton B. Berry,* Judge.

Action by Nettie Rucker against Elizabeth Kelley. From a judgment for defendant, the plaintiff appeals. *Affirmed.*

*Charles R. Milford,* for appellant.

*Edmon G. Hall,* for appellee.

IBACH, J.—This is an action by appellant on a complaint of which the following are the substantial allegations: Appellee was appointed guardian of Mary E. Kelley on January 10, 1908, and qualified as such. She filed her final report as such guardian on January 14, 1913. Her first current report was filed on April 12, 1910. An amended first current report was filed on June 13, 1910. On October 7, 1912, she filed a second current report, and no other reports have been filed by her. In filing said reports on the dates above mentioned, she failed, neglected and refused to comply with the statutes of Indiana to render on oath an account of her receipts and expenditures as guardian, at least once in every two years. She was allowed by the court the sum of $150 for her services as guardian. Because of her failure to file reports as required by law, she was not entitled to any compensation as guardian whatsoever; that there was due from her to the ward an amount equal to ten per cent. in damages of the whole estate in her hands. The said final report by appellee as guardian was duly approved, and she and her bondsmen were discharged on the — day of January, 1913. After the approval of the final report and discharge of the guardian, Mary E. Kelley died in July, 1913, leaving plaintiff as her sole heir at law. The report filed by appellee was not the final settlement of the estate of Mary E. Kelley, and another guardian was appointed to succeed appellee. Mary E. Kelley died intestate, and all of her debts have been paid and satisfied, and her estate has been settled out of court without administration. The money due from the guardian to Mary E. Kelley is due plaintiff as her sole heir. The allowance by the court to said guardian was unlawful and unauthorized, and her discharge as guardian was premature, since there was due by the guardian to the ward the amount of $182.36 as penalty for failure to make the reports required by law. The prayer is that the order approving said final report and discharging the appellee as guardian should be set aside, and rendered null and void, and the guardian should be compelled to pay into court the amount allowed her for services, and $32.36 as penalty for failure to comply with her duties as guardian. The only error assigned is the sustaining of appellee's demurrer to the complaint.

It is the rule that applications to set aside final settlements of guardians must show that the persons seeking to set it aside were not notified to appear and did

1. not appear at the hearing of the final settlement report. *Euler* v. *Euler* (1913), 55 Ind. App. 547, 102 N. E. 856; *Dillman* v. *Barber* (1888), 114 Ind. 403, 16 N. E. 825.

But appellant contends that the final settlement of the guardian who resigns or is discharged and a new guardian appointed, and the trust continued, is not a final

2. settlement within the meaning of the statute, which precludes objections being made to final settlement reports, when the person interested is present at that time

or has received notice to appear and file objections, if any, and cites *State* v. *Parsons* (1896), 147 Ind. 579, 47 N. E. 17, 62 Am. St. 430, and *State* v. *Peckham* (1894), 136 Ind. 198, 36 N. E. 28. These cases hold that such a final report of an outgoing guardian, resigning his trust before settlement of the estate, is not a bar to an action on the bond of such guardian, but such settlement is binding on all persons interested in the estate as to matters properly embraced in the report and its approval by the court.

Although the report which is here sought to be set aside is not a final report of the guardianship, but merely the last report filed by a guardian that resigned, yet it seems apparent to us from the allegations of the complaint that there is an attempt to go behind the final report of the entire guardianship in a collateral attack, without directly attacking it. It is averred that the estate of the ward has been settled. This being the case, there must have been a final report of the guardian who succeeded appellee and this report must have been approved. There could have been no settlement of the estate without such procedure. The time to present error in partial reports is at the time of the final settlement of the guardianship. There are no averments in the complaint of any fraud or concealment, or of any matter that would not be fully adjudicated by the final report of the entire guardianship, and embraced in the final settlement. The complaint does not seek to set aside the final settlement, and would be insufficient for that purpose, since it does not aver that appellant was not notified to appear and was not present at the time of the hearing of the final report. A final report which has been approved cannot be questioned in a collateral proceeding. *Campbell* v. *Smith* (1911), 49 Ind. App. 639, 97 N. E. 954, and cases cited.

There was no error in sustaining the demurrer to the complaint. Judgment affirmed.

NOTE.—Reported in 113 N. E. 759. See under (2) 21 Cyc 178, 179.

# TOWN OF FRENCH LICK *v.* ALLEN.

### [No. 9,587. Filed February 16, 1917.]

1. **MUNICIPAL CORPORATIONS.**—*Personal Injuries.*—*Defective Streets.*—*Notice.*—Failure to give a town notice in writing containing a brief general description of the time, place, cause and nature of the injury, as required by §8962 Burns 1914, Acts 1907 p. 383, 408, precludes the right to maintain an action for personal injuries resulting from any defect in the condition of a street or alley. p. 650.

2. **MUNICIPAL CORPORATIONS.**—*Personal Injuries.*—*Notice to City or Town.*—*Construction.*—*Sufficiency.*—In determining whether the time, the place and the nature of the injury, etc., are disclosed with sufficient clearness in a notice served on a city pursuant to §8962 Burns 1914, Acts 1907 p. 383, 408, a liberal construction will be applied, and relief will not be denied when by any fair and reasonable construction it can be said that it substantially complies with the statute, but the notice must be sufficiently definite and accurate as to the place of injury that the officers of the municipality will be able to locate it without the aid of any extraneous information, so that they may ascertain the facts and determine the question of liability before suit is brought. p. 651.

3. **MUNICIPAL CORPORATIONS.**—*Personal Injuries.*—*Notice.*—*Sufficiency.*—*Description of Place.*—A notice to a town that plaintiff had been injured by a fall on a street leading from the town to a certain highway, on the hill south of the street car barn where the street was being improved, and that her fall was caused by the uneven surface of the street and sidewalks, is insufficient to comply with the requirements of §8962 Burns 1914, Acts 1907 p. 383, 408, since no unusual place in the street is designated, and the only defect indicated is not even definitely located at any particular place in the street described. p. 652.

From Washington Circuit Court; *Emmett C. Mitchell,* Special Judge.

Action by Lillie Allen, by her next friend, Nathan Allen, against the Town of French Lick. From a judgment for plaintiff, the defendant appeals. *Reversed.*

*Talbott & Roland* and *Wilbur W. Hottel,* for appellant.

*Perry McCart, Arthur McCart* and *Elliott & Houston,* for appellee.

IBACH, P. J.—This case again comes to us on a petition for rehearing and a majority of the court have concluded that appellant's brief is sufficient in form to present some of the errors assigned for review. The action is to recover damages for injuries alleged to have been sustained by appellee from falling on one of appellant's streets. There was a trial by a jury, with verdict and judgment for appellee for $2,000.

It is appellant's contention that the trial court erred in overruling appellant's demurrer to the complaint because the notice given to appellant was insufficient in that it did not state the place where the injury was received, nor did it state the nature of the plaintiff's injury, nor was the cause of plaintiff's injury clearly set forth in the notice.

It is well settled that the failure to give the notice required by §8962 Burns 1914, Acts 1907 p. 383, 408, pre-

1.  cludes the right to maintain the action. The notice required by this statute must be in writing and must "contain a brief general description of the time, place, cause and nature of the injury." *Touhey* v. *City of Decatur* (1910), 175 Ind. 98, 93 N. E. 540, 32 L. R. A. (N. S.) 350; *City of East Chicago* v. *Gilbert* (1915), 59 Ind. App. 613, 108 N. E. 29, 109 N. E. 404.

The notice, which is annexed to and made part of the complaint, so far as it relates to the place where appellee received her injuries, is as follows: "Lillie Allen fell on a street in your town leading from said town to the French Lick and Hillman public highway on the hill south of the street car barn where said street is being improved. As a result of the fall she was cut and bruised on and over her face and on her body and limbs. That said fall was caused by the uneven surface of the street and sidewalk and said street and by failure to have such defective place guarded or lighted."

The law is also well settled that in determining whether the time, the place and the nature of the injury, etc., are

disclosed in the notice with sufficient clearness and
2.   definiteness so as to meet the requirements of the section of the statute, *supra*, the rules of liberal construction will be applied and relief will not be denied when by
any fair and reasonable construction it can be said that the
notice substantially complies with the statute. *City of East
Chicago* v. *Gilbert, supra*, and cases cited.

In cases where this rule has been applied, however, it has
been held that "to be legally sufficient, a notice must contain a description of the place of the accident so definite as
to enable the interested parties to identify it from the notice.
* * * The notice must be sufficiently definite in itself to
enable a person of ordinary capacity, with knowledge of the
physical condition of the streets, in the exercise of reasonable diligence, to locate the place of injury." *Sollenbarger*
v. *Town of Lineville* (1909), 141 Iowa 203, 119 N. W. 618,
18 Ann. Cas. 991, and cases cited.

Many other cases wherein the same question has been considered and like language used have been collated in the
recent case of *City of East Chicago* v. *Gilbert, supra*, so
that it will serve no good purpose to repeat them here. It
is sufficient to say that the courts of all the states having
similar statutes universally hold in effect that, while the
notice is not required to point out the precise spot where the
accident occurred, it is necessary, to be sufficient, that it be
so definite and accurate as to the place of injury that the
officers of the municipality will be able to locate it without
the aid of any extraneous information.

It seems to be the conclusion of all the courts that the
real purpose of the notice is to furnish to the city or town
such information, within a reasonable time after the accident, from which it may know the time, the exact location,
the circumstances and the nature of the injury so that the
authorities may determine the question of its liability; that
they may have an opportunity to investigate before any suit
can be brought and also the opportunity to obtain and pre-

serve testimony as to the condition of the street and the circumstances attending the injury. The city receiving the notice intended for this purpose is not required to examine places not mentioned in the notice nor to respond in damages for injuries not mentioned.

The question now presented is whether the statement of the place and the cause of appellee's injury in her notice is a sufficient compliance with the statute. The only

3. statement of the place is somewhere on the street leading from said town to the French Lick and Hillman public highway, on the hill south of the street-car barn where said street is being improved, and that her fall was caused by the uneven surface of the street and sidewalks on said street and by failure to have such defective place guarded or lighted. There is no unusual place in the street designated in the notice. The only defect indicated is an uneven surface somewhere; it is not even limited to the sidewalks, nor that portion of the street not included within the sidewalks, but somewhere, either at the center or on either side of the street, within the limits of the street on the hill south of the street-car barn where the street is being improved.

If there had been but one defect in the street of the character described where plaintiff might have fallen and become injured and that place could be located by the exercise of reasonable diligence on the part of the town officers, and the complaint had averred such fact, it might possibly be said that the notice was reasonably clear and definite and the purpose of the statute had been accomplished, but no such condition is presented here; rather the contrary appears. The record discloses the fact that the street was being improved by grading the hill down from the top to the bottom and the hill was between a quarter and a half mile in length; that the street-car barn was near the top of the hill; and that the entire street was torn up by reason of the improvement and there were a number of *uneven* places and depressions where a person might have fallen.

In view of this record we do not believe that the notice contained sufficient information to lead the town officers, using reasonable diligence, to the place of the alleged injury; consequently plaintiff has failed to comply with a cardinal and definite requirement of the statute preliminary to her right to maintain her suit. Our reference to the record here is not for the purpose of aiding the complaint, but to show the uncertainty of the notice, when applied to the particular facts of this case.

There are many cases in the books, and this may be another, where the application of the foregoing rules would tend to make the statute here involved appear to be a harsh one, and it is for this reason that the courts have applied to it the rule of liberal construction; but to go so far in the present case as to hold that the notice was a sufficient compliance with the statute would in effect entirely disregard the statute and destroy the very purpose for which it was enacted.

The demurrer to the complaint should have been sustained. Judgment reversed.

NOTE.—Reported In 115 N. E. 79. See under (1) 28 Cyc 1447 (2, 3) 28 Cyc 1453, 1455, 1461.

---

## PERRY v. STATE OF INDIANA, EX REL. SNYDER.

[No. 9,153. Filed February 16, 1917.]

1. BASTARDS.—*Parentage of Child.—Evidence.—Sufficiency.*—In a bastardy proceeding, evidence by the relatrix that the only occasion upon which she ever had intercourse was with the defendant on a certain date, which was corroborated by the testimony of other witnesses that the defendant had admitted the act of intercourse, and by the attending physician that relatrix had given birth to a fully developed child after the usual period of gestation had elapsed, was sufficient to warrant In finding that

the defendant was the father of relatrix's child, even though the evidence adduced at the trial was conflicting. p. 656.

2. BASTARDS.—*Bastardy Proceeding.*—*Presence of Child in Court.* —The mere fact that during the trial of a paternity suit the mother was permitted by the court, over the objection of the defendant, to have her child with her in the court room where the jury might see it affords no cause for a reversal. p. 657.

3. APPEAL.—*Review.*—*Harmless Error.*—*Presence of Child in Court.*—*Instruction.*—Any possible harm which might have resulted to the defendant in a bastardy proceeding by the court's action in permitting the relatrix to bring her child into the courtroom during the trial was cured by an instruction that in passing upon the question whether the defendant was the father of the child, the jury should not take into consideration the appearance of the child's countenance or draw any conclusion whatever from the child's appearance, but should consider only the oral testimony. pp. 658, 659.

4. APPEAL.—*Question Reviewable.*—*Misconduct of State.*—*Record.* —Alleged misconduct on the part of the State, in a trial of a bastardy proceeding, in permitting the relatrix to exhibit her child to the jury contrary to the direction of the court is not available for reversal of the judgment, where the record shows no order of the court directing relatrix not to bring her child into the presence of the jury and that defendant's motion for such an order was overruled. p. 658.

5. APPEAL.—*Bill of Exceptions.*—*Authentication.*—Matters set out in a bill of exceptions not authenticated by the signature of the court cannot be considered on appeal, even though such bill is brought into the record by being incorporated in another bill. p. 659.

6. APPEAL.—*Harmless Error.*—*Misconduct of Counsel.*—*Cure by Instruction.*—In a bastardy proceeding, alleged misconduct of relatrix' attorney during the argument to the jury in pointing at the child and saying that there could be no question that a child was conceived, "because there's the evidence," even if constituting reversible error when properly presented on appeal, was harmless where the jury was instructed not to consider the appearance of the child, but to decide the case on the oral testimony alone. p. 660.

7. APPEAL.—*Question Reviewable.*—*Misconduct of Counsel.*—*Bill of Exceptions.*—*Record.*—Where, in a paternity suit, misconduct of the attorney for the State in the presence of the court and jury were relied on for a reversal of the judgment of the trial court, mere affidavits as to the facts, accompanying the motion for a new trial, cannot take the place or serve the purpose of an unsigned bill of exception, by which appellant attempted to pre-

sent such facts, and unless the acts complained of are brought into the record by a proper bill of exceptions no question relating thereto is presented. p. 660.

8. APPEAL.—*Questions Reviewable.—Misconduct of Counsel.—Objections.*—In an appeal in a bastardy proceeding, alleged misconduct of opposing counsel during the trial of the cause is not available to the defendant where it does not appear from the record that he at the time objected, or called the court's attention, to the acts complained of. p. 661.

9. APPEAL.—*Assignment of Error.—Grounds.*—That "the judgment appealed from is not fairly supported by the evidence" and that it "is clearly against the weight of the evidence," are not grounds for independent assignment of error. p. 661.

10. APPEAL.—*Assignment of Error.—Grounds.—Refusal of Court to Sign a Bill of Exceptions.*—No question is presented for review on appeal by an assignment of error which attempts to present an exception to the refusal of the trial court to sign a bill of exceptions. p. 662.

11. APPEAL.—*Review.—Harmless Error.—Refusal of Judge to Sign Bill of Exceptions.*—The refusal of the trial judge to sign a bill of exceptions was harmless error, where the questions attempted to be presented by the bill would in no event afford any ground for a reversal of the judgment. p. 662.

From St. Joseph Circuit Court; *Thomas W. Slick*, Judge *pro tem.*

Action by the State of Indiana, on the relation of Mary Mandy Snyder, against Donald Perry. From a judgment for plaintiff, the defendant appeals. *Affirmed.*

*Charles Weidler, Orie Parker* and *Samuel Pettengill*, for appellant.

*Chester R. Montgomery, Samuel P. Schwartz* and *DuComb & DuComb*, for appellee.

HOTTEL, J.—This is an appeal from a judgment in a bastardy proceeding instituted before a justice of the peace of St. Joseph county. The justice found that appellant was not the father of the bastard child. There was an appeal to the circuit court of said county, where the case was tried by a jury before the Hon. T. W. Slick, who, on account of the "serious illness" of the regular judge of such court was, by such regular judge, appointed "to try all cases and transact all business of said Court * * * from the 5th day of October 1914 until further order."

The jury found that appellant was the father of the child, and judgment was rendered ordering appellant to pay to the relatrix $500 for the education and maintenance of said child. Appellant's motion for a new trial was overruled. From said judgment appellant appeals and assigns the following alleged errors: "1. The court erred in overruling appellant's motion for a new trial. 2. The judgment appealed from is not fairly supported by the evidence. 3. The judgment appealed from is clearly against the weight of the evidence. 4. The court erred in refusing to sign, appellant's bill of exceptions No. 2."

Under his first assigned error, appellant first urges that the verdict of the jury is not sustained by sufficient evidence, and insists that, where it appears from the record that substantial justice has not been done, this court should and will disregard a mere scintilla of evidence, citing *McClellan* v. *State* (1913), 54 Ind. App. 144, 101 N. E. 387. The case cited, while recognizing the rule contended for by appellant, holds, in effect, that it has no application in a case where, like the one under consideration, the relatrix herself testifies to all the facts necessary to justify the conclusion reached by the jury.

In the instant case, the relatrix testified that, on April 8, 1913, her thirteenth birthday, the appellant had intercourse with her in a bedroom at the home of appel-

1. lant's father; that she never had intercourse with any other person before or since; that her bastard child was born January 11, 1914. The uncontradicted evidence shows that relatrix stayed all night at the home of appellant's father the night of April 8, 1913; that appellant's father and mother were away that evening until ten o'clock; that appellant, relatrix and four other children were left together during their absence. The attending

physician testified to the birth of the child on January 11, 1914, and that it was fully developed; that the usual period of gestation is nine calendar months. Other witnesses testified to statements made by appellant in which he told them that he had had intercourse with the relatrix.

Appellant denied ever having had intercourse with relatrix, and denied the admissions testified to by other witnesses. Other witnesses contradicted some of the facts testified to by the relatrix. There was opinion evidence to the effect that conception, under the facts and circumstances testified to by relatrix, was unusual, but there was no evidence that it was impossible. It is apparent, we think, that the evidence in appellee's favor which we have indicated, *supra,* is more than a scintilla upon each of the facts essential to the verdict of the jury, and that on appeal it must be held as sufficient to warrant the jury in concluding, not only that appellant had intercourse with the relatrix as testified to by her, but that her conception resulted therefrom, and hence that appellant is the father of her bastard child. *Michael* v. *State, ex rel.* (1914), 57 Ind. App. 520, 108 N. E. 173; *Evans* v. *State, ex rel.* (1905), 165 Ind. 369, 74 N. E. 244, 75 N. E. 651, 2 L. R. A. (N. S.) 619, 6 Ann. Cas. 813.

Before the trial appellant filed a motion to exclude the child of relatrix from the court during the examination of the jurors and the trial. This motion was overruled and appellant excepted. This action of the court was made a ground for appellant's motion for new trial, and is here urged as reversible error. This was not error. The mere fact that the mother was permitted by the court to have her child with her in court at the trial where the jury might see it affords no cause for reversal. *State* v. *Stark* (1911), 149 Iowa 749, 129 N. W. 331, Ann. Cas. 1912D 362; *State* v. *Clemons* (1889), 78 Iowa 123, 42 N. W. 562; *Hutchinson* v. *State* (1886), 19 Neb. 262, 27 N. W. 113; *Benes* v. *People* (1905), 121 Ill. App. 103; *Rose* v. *People* (1898), 81 Ill. App. 128; *Esche* v. *Graue* (1904), 72

Neb. 719, 101 N. W. 978; *Johnson* v. *State* (1907), 133 Wis. 453, 113 N. W. 674; 7 C. J. 994, §125.

And, in any event, any *possible harm* which might have resulted to appellant by such action of the court was carefully guarded against and cured by the following

3.   instruction given by the trial court: "No. 3. In passing upon the question as to whether or not the defendant is the father of the child of Mary Mandy Snyder, *you should not take into consideration the appearance of the countenance of the child; nor should you draw any conclusion whatever from the appearance* of the child. And in considering and determining this case, you should look only to and consider the oral testimony given at the trial." *La-Matt* v. *State, ex rel.* (1891), 128 Ind. 123, 27 N. E. 346; *Reitz* v. *State, ex rel.* (1870), 33 Ind. 187.

Appellant, in his motion for new trial, as ground No. 9 thereof, set out alleged misconduct on the part of the State

·   as follows, viz.: "It permitted the relatrix to *exhibit*

4.   her child to the jury during the trial of said cause *contrary to the direction of the court,* all of which facts more fully appear by the affidavits of Charles Weidler, Samuel Pettengill, Bert Perry and defendant, Donald Perry." The affidavits referred to were nothing more than sworn statements made by each of such affiants to the effect that he was present in court during the trial of said cause, and that the matters and facts set out in grounds Nos. 9 and 10 of said motion for new trial are true.

Such alleged misconduct is not available for a reversal of the judgment below for either of two reasons: (1) No such misconduct is shown by the record. The misconduct relied on is an alleged violation of an order or *"direction"* of the court. The only action taken by the trial court in reference to such matter, disclosed by the record, was the overruling of appellant's motion above indicated, and the overruling of a second motion made by appellant, at the conclusion of appellee's evidence, in which he asked the court to make the

record show that the relatrix, on several occasions during
the progress of the trial, brought her child into the court
and sat with it in her arms near the table of her counsel
in full view of the jury. The record before us shows no
order or direction of the trial court directing relatrix not
to bring her child into the presence of the jury.

It should be stated in this connection, however, that it
appears from a third bill of exceptions set out in the record
that a second bill of exceptions was tendered by
5. appellant to the regular judge for his signature,
in which said motion and the action of the trial
court thereon were set out in full, and it appears from
such second bill that the court, at the time it overruled appellant's first motion, *supra*, made the following
statement: "While the court overruled this motion the court
does not think that it would be fair to the defendant to allow
the child to be brought up to the counsel tables and held
there in full view of the jury. I therefore direct that the
child be kept back in the audience where the jury will not
see it or know whose child it is."

This second bill further states, in substance, that after this
direction was given by the court, the relatrix, on several occasions, during the progress of the trial, brought her child
in her arms to the table of her counsel in full view of the
jury. Such second bill, however, was not signed by the
court, and it gets into the record by being incorporated into
the third bill, which expressly shows the court's refusal to
sign it, the purpose of the latter bill being an attempt to save
and present the exceptions taken to such refusal. It follows
that the matters set out in said second bill are not authenticated by the court's signature, and hence cannot be considered.

(2) If, however, all that is contained in such bill could be
considered by the court, the mere fact that it shows
3. that the relatrix brought her child into the court
room and sat with it at the table of her counsel in

full view of the jury, in the absence of some further showing, would not show reversible error under the authorities above cited, and any possible harm that might have resulted from such conduct because of an exhibition of such child to the jury (if there were such exhibition) and an observance or inspection of its appearance or features by the jury with the idea that such appearance and features could be considered by it in determining whether appellant was its father, was guarded against and cured by the instruction, *supra*.

In his motion for new trial, appellant assigned as one of the grounds thereof, misconduct of appellee's counsel, in that, during the argument of the cause to the jury, such counsel said to the jury: "There can be no question that a child was conceived about that time because there's the evidence." (at the time pointing to the child of relatrix.) The misconduct relied on in this ground of said motion is also set out in said unauthenticated bill of exceptions No. 2, as incorporated in said third bill of exceptions.

Assuming, without deciding, that said conduct was misconduct which, if properly presented, would constitute reversible error, what we have said in our discussion of the previous ground of said motion with reference to that error being cured by the instruction indicated, is applicable alike to this ground. However, the exact nature and character of the latter misconduct is fully set out in said motion and such motion being supported by the affidavits above indicated, this court knows what the misconduct relied on is and that the appellee's counsel was guilty thereof, provided that such affidavits can have the effect of taking the place of a bill of exceptions presenting such facts.

The misconduct relied on occurred in the presence of the trial court, and hence the affidavits in support thereof were not conclusive on such court as to the facts therein stated. The trial court may have refused to sign such bill because it knew that the facts therein set out were not true. Such court alone has the right to determine and say what occurred in its presence, and give authority to the record intended to present such a question to this court. The affidavits accompanying said motion cannot take the place or serve the purpose of said unsigned bill of exceptions. Such misconduct, not being brought into the record in the manner provided by law, this court has no way of knowing whether it occurred. *Hood* v. *Tyner* (1891), 3 Ind. App. 51, 28 N. E. 1033; *Manion* v. *Lake Erie, etc., R. Co.* (1907), 40 Ind. App. 569, 572, 80 N. E. 166; *Michael* v. *State, ex rel., supra,* 522.

There is another reason why this ground of said motion is not available on appeal. It does not appear from the record that appellant at the time objected to or called the court's attention to said alleged misconduct. If he thought that his rights had been prejudiced by such conduct, he at the time should have objected thereto, and by proper motion or request should have given the trial court an opportunity to take such steps as the law authorizes to be taken in such cases to cure or provide against any possible harm that might have resulted from such conduct. *Hasper* v. *Weitcamp* (1906), 167 Ind. 371, 374, 79 N. E. 191; *Southern Ind. R. Co.* v. *Fine* (1904), 163 Ind. 617, 72 N. E. 589; *Cleveland, etc., R. Co.* v. *Dixon* (1912), 51 Ind. App. 658, 660, 96 N. E. 815, and cases there cited.

8.

The second and third assigned errors, *supra*, are not causes for independent assignment of error. *Walters* v. *Walters* (1906), 168 Ind. 45, 48, 79 N. E. 1037; *State, ex rel.* v. *Davisson* (1910), 174 Ind. 705, 93 N. E. 6; *Bradford* v. *Wegg* (1913), 56 Ind. App. 39, 40, 102 N. E. 845. The questions which such assigned errors attempt to present are in any event fully considered and disposed of in our discussion of that ground of the motion for new trial which challenges the sufficiency of the evidence.

9.

It is insisted by appellee, in effect, that the fourth assigned error presents no question because the record shows that such second bill of exceptions was presented to the regular judge

of said court for his signature when the same should have
been presented to the special judge who tried the case.    The
following cases will throw light on the question whether, in
a particular case, a special judge, who tried the case or the
regular judge should sign a bill of exceptions. *Aetna Indemnity Co.* v. *Wassall Clay Co.* (1911), 49 Ind. App. 438,
442, 97 N. E. 562; *Shugart* v. *Miles* (1890), 125 Ind. 445,
25 N. E. 551; *Staser* v. *Hogan* (1889), 120 Ind. 207, 21 N.
E. 911, 22 N. E. 990; *Stewart* v. *Adam, etc., Co.* (1899), (Ind.
Sup.) 55 N. E. 760; *Lee* v. *Hills* (1879), 66 Ind. 474; *Wilson*
v. *Piper* (1881), 77 Ind. 437; *Smith* v. *Baugh* (1869), 32
Ind. 163; *Hedrick* v. *Hedrick* (1867), 28 Ind. 291; *McKeen*
v. *Boord* (1878), 60 Ind. 280; *Reed* v. *Worland* (1878),
64 Ind. 216; *Lerch* v. *Emmett* (1873), 44 Ind. 331; *Toledo,
etc., R. Co.* v. *Rogers* (1874), 48 Ind. 427.

For the purposes of the question under consideration, the
question to whom said bill should have been presented for
signature is wholly unimportant for either of two reasons,
        viz.: (1) No question is presented by an assignment
10. of error which attempts to present an exception to
        the refusal of the trial court to sign a bill of excep-
tions.    *Hartford Life Ins. Co.* v. *Rossiter* (1902), 196
Ill. 277, 63 N. E. 680; *Hulett* v. *Ames* (1874), 74 Ill. 253;
*Garibadli* v. *Carroll* (1878), 33 Ark. 568; *Whipple* v. *Hop-
kins* (1897), 119 Cal. 349, 51 Pac. 535; *Brode* v. *Goslin*
(1910), 158 Cal. 699, 112 Pac. 280; *Green* v. *Bulkley* (1879),
23 Kan. 130; *State* v. *Ford* (1885), 37 La. Ann. 443; *Carey*
v. *Merryman* (1876), 46 Md. 89; *Richardson* v. *Rogers*
(1887), 37 Minn. 461, 35 N. W. 270; *Priddy* v. *Hayes*
(1907), 204 Mo. 358, 102 S. W. 976; *Wilson* v. *Moore* (1842),
19 N. J. Law 186; *Budd* v. *Crea* (1821), 6 N. J. Law 450;
*Mallon* v. *Tucker Mfg. Co.* (1881), 7 Lea (Tenn.) 62;
*Messenger* v. *Broom* (1846), 1 Pin. (Wis.) 630; *Martin*
        v. *Ihmsen* (1859), 21 How. 394, 16 L. Ed. 134.    (2)
11. The only questions attempted to be presented by
        said bill of exceptions were the questions of miscon-

NOVEMBER TERM, 1916.     **663**

Croly *v.* Indianapolis Traction, etc., Co.—63 Ind. App. 663.

duct of appellee and her counsel, indicated *supra;* and for
the reasons stated, they would in no event afford any ground
for reversal of the judgment below, and hence no harm could
have resulted from a refusal to sign such bill by either or
both judges. Judgment affirmed.

NOTE.—Reported in 115 N. E. 59. Bastardy proceeding, right to
exhibit child to jury, rule, 6 Ann. Cas. 560; 19 Ann. Cas. 536; 5
Cyc 663. Necessity and sufficiency of objection and exception to
improper argument of counsel, Ann. Cas. 1916A 551· See under (7)
2 Cyc 1090.

---

## CROLY *v.* INDIANAPOLIS TRACTION AND TERMINAL COMPANY.

### [No. 9,238. Filed February 20, 1917.]

1. TRIAL.—*Order of Receiving Evidence.—Discretion of Court.—*
The trial court has discretionary power as to the time or order
of receiving testimony, and a judgment will not be reversed for
any irregularity in regard thereto unless it clearly appears that
such discretion has been abused. p. 665.

2. APPEAL.— *Review.— Order of Receiving Evidence.— Recalling
Witness.—Discretion of Court.—*In an action for personal injuries, the action of the trial court in permitting defendant to
recall a witness for plaintiff after defendant's motion for a peremptory instruction had been overruled, was not an abuse of the
court's discretionary power as to the order of receiving evidence.
p. 665.

3. APPEAL.—*Subsequent Appeals.—Law of the Case.—Evidence.—*
As the opinion in a former appeal is the law of the case on all
questions presented and decided therein, where the evidence was
held sufficient on such appeal to sustain a verdict for plaintiff
for personal injuries, it was error for the court to peremptorily
instruct the jury to find for the defendant upon a retrial of the
cause in which the evidence was substantially the same as at the
former trial, since, where a proposition decided on appeal depends upon a state of facts shown by the evidence, it is controlling until the termination of the litigation unless the testimony
relating thereto upon a subsequent trial differs in some material
respect from that upon which the opinion of the appellate tribunal was based. p. 666, 670.

4. APPEAL.— *Review.— Evidence.—*The court on appeal cannot
weigh conflicting evidence. p. 670.

5. STREET RAILROADS.—*Injuries to Person on Track.*—*Evidence.*— *Last Clear Chance.*—*Jury Questions.*—In an action against a street railroad company for personal injuries sustained when plaintiff was struck by a car, the right of recovery being predicated on the last clear chance doctrine, whether the motorman, who saw plaintiff running backward across the street toward the track, knew, or should have known, of her peril in time to have avoided the accident, and whether after discovering her peril he used reasonable and ordinary care under the circumstances to avoid injuring plaintiff, were questions for the jury. p. 670.

From Morgan Circuit Court; *Nathan A. Whitaker,* Judge.

Action by Alpha C. Croly, by her next friend Joseph Croly, against the Indianapolis Traction and Terminal Company. From a judgment for defendant, the plaintiff appeals. *Reversed.*

*Grubbs & Grubbs, George W. Galvin* and *Joseph W. Williams,* for appellant.

*S. C. Kivett, D. E. Watson* and *W. H. Latta,* for appellee.

FELT, C. J.—This is a suit for damages for personal injuries and is the second appeal to this court. *Croly v. Indianapolis Traction, etc., Co.,* 54 Ind. App. 566, 96 N. E. 973, 98 N. E. 1091. The complaint in one paragraph is the same as it was at the first trial and sufficiently appears in the former opinion. The answer was a general denial. At the close of appellant's testimony, the defendant, appellee, moved the court to instruct the jury to return a verdict for the defendant, which motion was overruled. Thereupon, at the request of appellee, the court permitted it to recall one of appellant's witnesses, the motorman who operated the car which struck appellant, and to further examine him, all of which was done over the objection and exception of appellant. At the close of such examination appellee renewed its motion for a peremptory instruction in its favor, and the same was sustained by the court, who in ruling on the motion said: "It strikes me that under the first decision of this case I will have to sustain this motion.

Under the evidence in this case there is no showing that the motorman was guilty of any negligence after discovering the dangerous position' of the plaintiff. I believe it will be my duty to sustain the motion.''

Thereupon the court ordered the jurors to be brought in and instructed them to return a verdict for the defendant, and in so doing stated in substance that there was no evidence tending to prove that the motorman operating the car saw appellant, and saw that she was in a dangerous position or about to come into a dangerous position, and was unconscious of her danger, in time to have stopped the car, or to have given such warning, as would have prevented the injury complained of.

Appellant has assigned as error that: (1) The court erred in sustaining appellee's motion to recall the witness Hough, after the court had overruled appellee's motion for a peremptory instruction; (2) overruling appellant's motion to set aside the verdict; (3) overruling her motion for a new trial. The first assigned error is also one of the grounds for a new trial. The motion for a new trial alleges: (1) that the verdict of the jury is contrary to law, and (2) it is not sustained· by sufficient evidence; (3) error in instructing the jury as above shown; and (4) error in the admission of certain evidence.

. The trial court has discretionary power as to the time or order of receiving testimony and a judgment will not
1. be reversed for any irregularity in regard thereto unless it clearly appears that such discretion was abused.

In the case at bar we cannot say that the court abused its discretionary power, or that appellant was prejudiced in any substantial right by permitting the witness
2. Hough to be recalled and further examined after appellee had presented and the court had overruled a motion for a peremptory instruction. *Miller* v. *Dill* **(1897), 149** Ind. 326, 335, 49 N. E. 272; *Roush* v. *Roush*

(1899), 154 Ind. 562, 572, 55 N. E. 1017; *Stewart* v. *Stewart* (1901), 28 Ind. App. 378, 383, 62 N. E. 1023.

The overruling of appellant's motion for a new trial presents the question whether there was any evidence tending to show negligence on the part of appellee's motorman, in charge of the car which injured appellant, after he saw appellant and knew or should have known of her peril, and whether such negligence, if any, was the proximate cause of appellant's injury. Both parties rely upon the opinion of this court on the former appeal. Appellee contends that it fully warranted the peremptory instruction given 3. by the trial court, and appellant insists that in the light of the evidence introduced, the former opinion clearly shows that it was error for the court to declare as a matter of law that there was a total failure of evidence tending to show a liability under the doctrine of the last clear chance as therein announced. The former opinion is the law of the case on all questions presented and therein decided. Where the proposition decided depends upon a state of facts shown by the evidence, it is controlling to the end of the litigation unless the evidence relating thereto upon a subsequent trial differs in some material respect from that upon which such opinion was based. *Alerding* v. *Allison* (1907), 170 Ind. 252, 260, 83 N. E. 1006, 127 Am. St. 363; *Fifer* v. *Rachels* (1905), 37 Ind. App. 275, 277, 76 N. E. 186.

As we interpret the briefs, appellant contends that appellee's liability arises under the last clear chance doctrine, and the ruling of the trial court and the instruction of the jury indicate that such was the theory upon which the case was presented and decided below.

After reviewing the evidence, this court in the former opinion, by Lairy, J., said: "In our judgment, the undisputed evidence shows that the plaintiff failed to use due care in view of her age and experience. * * * We have held in this case that the undisputed evidence shows that the

NOVEMBER TERM, 1916.    667

Croly *v.* Indianapolis Traction, etc., Co.—63 Ind. App. 663.

plaintiff failed to use due care for her own safety in approaching and entering upon the tracks of defendant; * * * but this does not amount to a finding that she was guilty of contributory negligence. Before it can be held as a matter of law that she was guilty of contributory negligence, it must further appear that the second essential element of contributory negligence was present, namely, the causal connection between the want of due care on the part of the plaintiff and her injury."

Judge Lairy then takes up the last clear chance doctrine, and after an extended and able discussion thereof, applies it to the case at bar, and in so doing, among other things, says:

"If there is some evidence in the record tending to prove that the motorman actually saw the plaintiff approaching the track and that her conduct and appearance at that time was such as to indicate that she did not observe the approach of the car and was oblivious of her danger, then the verdict can be sustained, even though her want of care in failing to see the car, continued up to the time of her injury, provided that there is also evidence tending to prove that after the motorman knew of her perilous situation, he had time to have avoided the injury by the exercise of due care. The evidence upon this question is conflicting. * * * In deciding whether the motorman saw plaintiff and observed the danger to which her conduct was about to expose her, in time to have prevented the injury, the jury had a right to consider the speed at which the car was moving and also the speed at which plaintiff was walking as well as the distance that each was required to move to reach the point of collision. From a consideration of the evidence, we cannot say that the jury could not have properly found that the motorman knew of the danger to which plaintiff was about to expose herself in time to have prevented the injury. The evidence is sufficient to sustain the verdict."

The opinion then takes up the instructions to the jury and

the judgment was reversed because of an erroneous instruction on the subject of the last clear chance doctrine. From the foregoing it clearly appears that the court erred in peremptorily instructing the jury to find for the defendant, unless the evidence was materially different from that considered and passed upon in the former opinion.

We have carefully reviewed the former opinion and the statement of the evidence which it contains (*Croly* v. *Indianapolis Traction, etc., Co., supra*, pp. 573-586) and also the evidence in the record on this appeal, and find it to be substantially the same as it was upon the former trial, with some exceptions which seem to strengthen rather than weaken the evidence which the former opinion held sufficient to sustain a verdict in appellant's favor on the question of the last clear chance, as shown by the following language: "We cannot say that the jury could not have properly found that the motorman knew of the danger to which plaintiff was about to expose herself in time to have prevented the injury. The evidence is sufficient to sustain the verdict." As the question comes to us, we are only required to consider the evidence, if any, tending to sustain appellant's contention that appellee is liable under the last clear chance doctrine. The evidence of Mrs. Nellie Swan, a sister of appellant, is to the effect that she was on the opposite side of the street at a window in her house, and saw the car which struck appellant, when it was twenty or thirty feet or more away from the place where it struck her; that it was running twenty or thirty miles an hour and did not stop until after it ran over appellant, and that she heard no gong or bell or anything of the kind sounded; that when she first saw the car appellant was just leaving the sidewalk and starting to cross the street, moving rapidly; that she hallooed to her and just then a freight train came along on the elevated tracks and she did not hear her and was struck by the street car; that appellant looked up and down the street after she left the sidewalk to cross the street.

Roosevelt avenue runs in a northeasterly and southwesterly direction and is intersected by Lewis street which runs north and south. Appellant was injured when she was about five feet east of the curve at the corner of Roosevelt avenue and Lewis street while crossing Roosevelt avenue, going in a northwesterly direction toward her home on the north side of the street.

Her mother testified, in substance, that the car which struck appellant was going rapidly and did not stop after it ran over her until it ran down to the elevated tracks, about a square around on the curve, and then backed up near the place of the accident; that a Brightwood car came off of Lewis street and stopped opposite appellant on the street.

Appellant testified that she was on the south side of the street and waited at the curb for a car to pass going toward Brightwood; that she did not leave the curb until it passed; that she looked both ways after she left the curb and saw no other car and did not see the car that struck her; that she was walking across the street, heard no one halloo to her, and would have stopped if the motorman had sounded the gong or rung the bell.

The motorman testified that he was running a Columbia avenue car; that he first saw appellant on the south side of Roosevelt avenue on the sidewalk, shortly after he passed an outgoing car and when his car was probably 150 feet from the place of the accident; that shortly thereafter, when his car, thirty feet long, had proceeded probably one or two lengths, he saw appellant leave the curb, which was about twelve feet from the tracks; that he saw her when she first started across the street, before his car came up to her and saw that she was running backwards toward the tracks and had her face turned from the car and seemed to be looking back toward the south; that as soon as he saw her start to run across the street he "hollered" and commenced to apply his brakes; that appellant was ten or

670	APPELLATE COURT OF INDIANA,

Croly *v.* Indianapolis Traction, etc., Co.—63 Ind. App. 663.

fifteen feet from the tracks when he called to her and began
to set his brakes and he believed she was unconscious of the
approach of the car; that he did not think he could stop the
car and avoid the accident and did not know why he tried to
stop the car; that when he put both hands on the brake, the
child was some ten feet in front of the car and he knew
there would be an accident; that the car was equipped with
a gong which could be sounded by using either foot. There
is other evidence in the record which contradicts
4. and some which corroborates the foregoing testimony,
but we cannot weigh the evidence.

In harmony with, and following, the first opinion in this
case we hold that it was error to direct the jury to return a
verdict for the defendant, and that on the evidence
3. submitted it was a question of fact for the jury to
determine whether appellee's motorman saw appellant
and knew or should have known of her peril in time to
5. have avoided the accident, and whether under the
facts of the case, after discovering her peril, if he did
so discover it as aforesaid, he used reasonable and ordinary
care under the circumstances to avoid injuring her. *Croly
v. Indianapolis Traction, etc., Co., supra,* pp. 586-590.

The judgment is reversed, with instructions to sustain
appellant's motion for a new trial and for further proceedings not inconsistent with this opinion.

Note.—Reported in 115 N. E. 105. Applicability of doctrine of
last clear chance where danger is not actually discovered, 55 L.
R. A. 418; 36 L. R. A. (N. S.) 957. Last clear chance doctrine,
applicability, 29 Cyc 531; 36 Cyc 1517, 1565, 1567. Subsequent appeals, "law of the case," conclusiveness of prior decisions, 34 L. R.
A. 321; 3 Cyc 493; 4 C. J. 1217. See under (1) 3 Cyc 337; (2) 38
Cyc 1366; (5) 36 Cyc 1631.

# PARKER *v.* STATE OF INDIANA.

[No. 9,467. Filed October 10, 1916. Rehearing denied December 13, 1916. Transfer denied February 23, 1917.]

1. APPEAL.—*Appeal from Juvenile Court.—Assignment of Error.—Error Assignable.—Statute.*—Under §1635 Burns 1914, Acts 1907 p. 221, relating to appeals from the juvenile to the Appellate Court, the only assignment of error allowed on appeal is, "that the decision of the court is contrary to law"; and such assignment is sufficient to present both the sufficiency of the facts found to sustain the judgment and the sufficiency of the evidence to sustain the findings. p. 672.

2. APPEAL.—*Appeal from Juvenile Court.—Consideration of Evidence.—Bill of Exceptions.—Statute.*—Where the appellant from the juvenile to the Appellate Court fails to incorporate the evidence in a bill of exceptions filed in the juvenile court and to have it made a part of the record, as required by §1635 Burns 1914, Acts 1907 p. 221, no question concerning the evidence can be considered on the appeal. p. 673.

3. APPEAL.—*Review.—Criminal Prosecution.—Findings.—Sufficiency.*—Where, in a prosecution for contributing to the delinquency of a girl under the age of sixteen years, the juvenile court found "that the defendant did cause and encourage ...... to commit an act of delinquency at or about August 14, 1915, at or about 2 p. m. of that day and again on or about Saturday, August 21, 1915, at about 2 o'clock p. m.," the last date being the one mentioned in the affidavit filed in the cause on September 8, 1915, such finding was not insufficient as failing to show that the alleged offense was committed prior to the time of the filing of the affidavit, or because the use of the words "on or about" is not sufficiently certain. p. 673.

4. WORDS AND PHRASES.—*"On or About."*—The common understanding of the words "on or about," when used in connection with a definite point of time, is that they do not put the time at large but indicate that it is stated with approximate certainty. p. 673.

5. APPEAL.—*Criminal Prosecution.—Failure to Incorporate Evidence in Record.—Findings.*—Where, in an appeal from the judgment of the juvenile court in a criminal prosecution, the evidence is not before the court, the facts found by the juvenile court must be taken as correctly found. p. 674.

From Marion Juvenile Court (10,481a); *Frank J. Lahr,* Judge.

Action by the State of Indiana against Cecil Parker. From a judgment of conviction, the defendant appeals. *Affirmed.*

*Donald S. Morris,* for appellant.

*Evan B. Stotsenburg* and *Ele Stansbury,* Attorneys-General, *U. S. Lesh, Elmer E. Hastings, Edward M. White. John G. McCord, Wilbur T. Gruber* and *Omer S. Jackson,* for the State.

IBACH, J.—Appellant was convicted in the juvenile court of Marion county for contributing to the delinquency of a girl under the age of sixteen years. An appeal having been prayed to this court the judge of the juvenile court, as directed by §1635 Burns 1914, Acts 1907 p. 221, certified the facts of the case in the form of a special finding.

For the purposes of this appeal it is unnecessary to set out these findings in full. It is sufficient to say that they show the grossest misconduct on the part of appellant. They show that by the most deceptive and basest practices he induced and persuaded ————, a girl then under the age of sixteen years, on different days during the month of August, 1915, to accompany him to the Elite Hotel in the city of Indianapolis and there committed acts of the most revolting nature with the girl and persuaded her to have illicit sexual intercourse with him, all of which of necessity contributed to her delinquency.

Appellant's assignment of errors contains a number of specifications, but we are precluded from considering any except the first because the only assignment of error

1. allowed by the statute regulating such appeals is, "that the decision of the court is contrary to law." §1635 Burns 1914, *supra.* This statute provides "an assignment of error that the decision of the juvenile court is contrary to law" shall be sufficient to present both the sufficiency of the facts found to sustain the judgment and the sufficiency of the evidence to sustain the findings. See, also, *Murphy* v. *State* (1915), 61 Ind. App. 226, 111 N. E. 806.

This statute also provides: "In case the party appealing questions the sufficiency of the evidence to warrant the findings thus made by the court, such evidence shall
2. be incorporated in a bill of exceptions filed in said juvenile court and made a part of the record." This the appellant has failed to do and since the evidence is not in the record no question concerning the same can be considered on appeal. §1635 Burns 1914, *supra*; *Beard* v. *State* (1876), 54 Ind. 413; *Enners* v. *State* (1874), 47 Ind. 126; *Walbert* v. *State* (1896), 17 Ind. App. 350, 353, 46 N. E. 827.

The court found by specifications Nos. 8 and 9 of his special findings, "that the defendant did cause and encourage ————— to commit an act of delinquency on or
3. about August 14, 1915, at or about 2 p. m. of that day and again on or about Saturday, August 21, 1915, at about 2 o'clock p. m." The last date is the one mentioned in the affidavit filed in the cause on September 8, 1915.

Appellant now claims that the finding is insufficient because it fails to show that the alleged offense was committed prior to the time of filing the affidavit, and that the use of the words "on or about" a particular day is not certain enough.

Time here was not of the essence of the offense. The language of the affidavit and the finding of the court are sufficiently certain. §2046 Burns 1914, Acts 1905 p. 584, 622; .*Shell* v. *State* (1896), 148 Ind. 50, 47 N. E. 144. The common understanding of the words "on or about"
4. when used in connection with a definite point of time is that they do not put the time at large but indicate that it is stated with approximate certainty. *Rinker* v. *United States* (1907), 151 Fed. 755, 757, 81 C. C. A. 379.

So in this case the finding of the court that the offense
3. of which appellant was charged was committed "on or about" a definite time is a statement of the date

with approximate accuracy and is sufficiently definite and certain to show that the offense charged was committed before the filing of the affidavit and before it became barred by the statute of limitations. *Cotner* v. *State* (1909), 173 Ind. 168, 89 N. E. 847.

Since the evidence is not before us, the facts found by the juvenile court must be taken as correctly found and as

5. before stated they conclusively show that appellant was guilty of contributing to the offense charged within the meaning of the statute. Judgment affirmed.

NOTE.—Reported in 113 N. E. 763. Appeals from judgments of juvenile courts, procedure, Ann. Cas. 1916E 1017. Meaning of "on or about," 17 Ann. Cas. 742; 29 Cyc 1492.

---

## WELTY v. TAYLOR.

[No. 9,234. Filed February 23, 1917.]

1. LANDLORD AND TENANT.—*Contract.*—*Action for Breach.*—*Pleading.*—*Sufficiency of Complaint.*—In an action to recover money alleged to be due on a parol contract, a complaint containing allegations showing that plaintiff, who was under contract with defendant to manage and cultivate his farm, orally agreed with defendant to remain on the land after it was found to be unproductive and apply fertilizers, etc., to be furnished by defendant, and was to receive as compensation for his services, if the plan of fertilization proved successful, such an amount in excess of a stipulated figure as the land would bring in the market, such complaint is held to sufficiently state the issuable facts constituting the cause of action and to show a breach of the alleged contract and it is not objectionable as being a statement of evidence. p. 679.

2. CONTRACTS.—*Construction.*—*Commission for Sale of Land.*—Where a complaint predicates the right of recovery on an alleged parol contract providing that plaintiff should receive as compensation for his services in fertilizing an unproductive farm any excess of the market value of the land over a stipulated figure, such complaint did not seek to recover a commission for procuring a purchaser for the real estate, and the cause of action did not therefore come within the prohibition of §7463 Burns

1914, Acts 1913 p. 638, providing that contracts for commissions for the sale of land must be in writing. p. 679.

3. CONTRACTS.—*Parol Contract.—Construction.*—Where the question of the construction of a parol contract arises on the complaint, the intention of the parties at the time they entered into the alleged contract must be determined from a consideration of all the averments which set forth the agreement. p. 680.

4. LANDLORD AND TENANT.—*Parol Contract.—Construction.—Complaint.*—Where, in an action to recover money due on a parol contract, the averments of the complaint show· that a lessee's compensation for services rendered in pursuance to a contract to make farm lands· productive by the application of fertilizers, etc., depend upon the land becoming more productive and of greater value than a stipulated sum, a subsequent statement in the complaint that the lessee should receive as compensation the amount over such stipulated sum that the land would bring in the market did not require the lessee, as a condition precedent to his right of recovery, to obtain a purchaser, but was a statement that the lessee's recovery was limited to the actual market value of the land in excess of the amount stipulated in the agreement, and the lessee, upon proof that he had performed the labor contemplated by the contract, that the farm had been made productive and had a market value in excess of the stipulated sum, established his right of action. p. 680, 681.

5. CONTRACT.—*Construction.—"Fair Market Value of Land."*—The fair market value of land is the price it would probably bring after fair and reasonable negotiations where the owner is willing to sell but not compelled to do so, and the buyer desires to purchase but is under no necessity of obtaining the property. p. 680.

6. LANDLORD AND TENANT.—*Contracts.—Independent Oral Agreement between Lessor and Lessee.*—Where a leased farm was conceded by the lessor to be unproductive after the lessee had unsuccessfully attempted to cultivate the land, and the parties thereupon mutually entered into an independent parol agreement to carry out a plan of fertilization and improvement by means not previously contemplated, compensation being provided for the lessee for the extra labor to be performed, such agreement was not a modification of the original lease, but was independent thereof and rested upon an entirely new consideration. p. 681.

7. LANDLORD AND TENANT.—*Contracts.—Action for Breach.—Evidence.—Sufficiency.*—In action by the lessee of a farm, admitted by defendant lessors to be unproductive, to recover money alleged to be due on an oral agreement providing that if the lessee would remain on the land and apply fertilizers to be furnished by the lessors in consideration of the amount the market value of the

farm should exceed a stipulated sum, where there was evidence tending to show the original value of the farm and that it was less productive than the owners believed it to be, that the tenant was about to abandon the premises because of the poor yield of crops, whereupon the parol agreement to increase the fertility of the soil was entered into, the lessor being required thereby to furnish the necessary materials and the lessee to do the work, that both parties performed their respective parts of the agreement and, as a result, the land became productive and reached a market value in excess of the amount stipulated in the parol contract, such evidence is sufficient to support every material issuable fact essential to a recovery. p. 681.

8. CONTRACT.—*Action for Breach.—Burden of Proof.*—In an action based on a parol contract recovery must be under the terms of the contract, and the burden is on the plaintiff to prove every material part thereof substantially as alleged in the complaint. p. 682.

9. CONTRACTS.—*Action for Breach.—Refusal of Interrogatories.*—In an action for a breach of a parol contract, it was proper for the court to refuse to submit interrogatories requested by defendant, where they did not relate to issuable facts, and the answers thereto could not have aided the defendant, but would necessarily have been treated as surplusage relating to immaterial questions. p. 683.

10. DAMAGES.—*Contracts.—Action for Breach.—Excessive Damages.*—Where plaintiff, in an action for money due on a parol contract, contended that he was to receive, as compensation for certain services in the development of a farm, the market value of the land in excess of $70,000, a verdict for plaintiff for $3,500 is not excessive where the evidence sustains the jury's finding that the market value of the land was $73,500 and also the general verdict. p. 683.

From LaPorte Circuit Court; *James F. Gallaher*, Judge.

Action by Albert S. Taylor against Sam Welty. From a judgment for plaintiff, the defendant appeals. *Affirmed.*

*Frank E. Osborn, W. A. McVey, Lee L. Osborn* and *John Sterling*, for appellant.

*M. R. Sutherland* and *R. N. Smith*, for appellee.

FELT, C. J.—This is a suit to recover money alleged to be due on a parol contract entered into by appellant and appellee. The case was tried on the amended second paragraph of complaint and an answer of general denial. The jury returned a verdict for $3,500 in appellee's favor and with it answers to certain interrogatories. Appellant's motion for judgment on the answers of the jury to the interrogatories and for a new trial were overruled and judgment was rendered on the general verdict, from which this appeal was taken.

Appellant has assigned as error: (1) That the court erred in overruling his demurrer to the second paragraph of amended complaint; (2) the overruling of his motion for judgment on the answers of the jury to the interrogatories; and (3) the motion for a new trial.

The amended second paragraph of complaint, in substance, charges that in November, 1907, appellee entered into a written contract with appellant and his wife whereby they became partners in the cultivation and management of a farm of 735 acres in LaPorte county, Indiana, owned by appellant and his wife; that by the terms of the contract appellee was to move upon and cultivate the farm and the owners were to furnish certain live stock and other things necessary to the operation of the farm, and appellee and said owners were each to receive one-half of the proceeds therefrom; that by the terms of said contract it was to run until March 1, 1913; that in compliance therewith appellee moved upon and operated said farm for the period of two years and thereby discovered that the soil was cold, sour and deficient in certain elements requisite to the production of crops; that the land was nonproductive and would not grow grains or other crops of any kind or description; that he was a farmer of experience and tilled and managed the farm in a husbandmanlike manner but the crops were entire failures; that on account of the nonproductiveness of the land he lost time and money in trying to raise crops thereon and at the expiration of the second year of his lease he informed appellant that it was impossible to raise crops on the farm because of the nonproductiveness of the soil and that it was impossible for him to continue longer under their contract, and that, if he continued to work and farm the land, they would have to make some different arrangement; that thereupon appellant said he himself had been deceived in the quality of the land and was convinced that crops could not be raised on the land in its present condition and informed appellee that he desired him to continue on the farm, and if he would do so he, appellant, would furnish such materials as were necessary to cause the soil to produce crops, and would purchase lime, fertilizers and all things necessary to be placed on the land to make it productive, if appellee would superintend the work and perform or cause to be performed the labor of placing the same on the land; that if he would agree to the foregoing proposition as compensation for the extra labor required to carry out such plan, if they were successful and the farm was made productive and of the value of $70,000, appellee "should receive an amount over $70,000 that the land would bring in the market"; that the plaintiff then and there accepted the said proposition and thereafter the said plaintiff and defendant proceeded to carry out said contract. It is also averred that appellant furnished the necessary materials to improve the fences and buildings, and bought lime and manure from the stockyards of Chicago to be used on the farm; that appellee caused the same to be hauled to the farm and spread upon the land and continued to carry out said contract for two years, at the end of which time the farm was in "a good, productive condition and was worth in the market upwards of $70,000, to wit, the sum of $84,525.00. That plaintiff has performed all and singular every part of said contract entered into" by the parties aforesaid; that he demanded from appellant the sum of $14,525, the value of the farm above $70,000, and appellant refused to pay the same to him; that by reason of the aforesaid premises appellant is indebted to appellee in the sum of $14,525 with six per cent. interest from September 9, 1913, for which he demands judgment.

The demurrer was for insufficiency of the facts alleged to state a cause of action. The substance of the memorandum accompanying the same is as follows: (1) The pleading is a statement of evidence and not of issuable facts; (2) the allegations do not show a breach of the alleged contract; (3) the alleged contract is void under §7463 Burns 1914.

Under the rules that now control the construction of pleadings, the allegations are sufficient to state the issuable facts constituting the cause of action and to show a

1. breach of the alleged contract. *Domestic Block Coal Co.* v. *DeArmey* (1913), 179 Ind. 592, 601, 100 N. E. 675, 102 N. E. 99; *Waters* v. *Delagrange* (1915), 183 Ind. 497, 499, 109 N. E. 758; *Toledo, etc., R. Co.* v. *Levy* (1891), 127 Ind. 168, 26 N. E. 773; *Robinson* v *Horner* (1911), 176 Ind. 226, 233, 95 N. E. 561.

The complaint does not seek to recover a commission or reward for procuring a purchaser of real estate, and

2. the cause of action stated does not, therefore, come within the prohibition of §7463 Burns 1914, Acts 1913 p. 638, because the contract relied upon is not in writing.

The answers to the interrogatories show that in the winter of 1908 and 1909 appellant began to ship manure and lime to the farm and continued until he had shipped about fifty-two carloads of manure and twenty or more carloads of lime; that appellee hauled and spread upon the land of appellant all of the material so furnished; that after the same was applied to the land it became more productive; that said fertilizers were furnished and applied as aforesaid under an agreement between appellant and appellee that the same should be so furnished and applied; that in September, 1913, the said farm of 735 acres belonged to appellant and his wife and was of the market value of $73,500, and had not been sold.

Appellant contends that the averments of the complaint which show that appellee had performed all the conditions of the contract by him to be performed required of him proof that the farm had been sold; that the finding by the jury that the farm had not been sold is in irreconcilable conflict with the general verdict, because under the complaint the sale of the land for more than $70,000 is a condition precedent to appellee's right of recovery.

The averments show that the parties agreed that, if their efforts to make the farm productive were successful, "and the farm was made productive and of the value of $70,000" appellee "should receive an amount over $70,000 that the land would bring in the market." In construing the contract and determining whether appellee, as a condition precedent to his right to recover, was required to furnish a purchaser who would pay more than $70,000 for the

3. farm, we must ascertain the intention of the parties at the time they entered into the alleged contract, and where it rests in parol, and the question arises upon the complaint, then from a consideration of all the averments which set forth the alleged agreement of the parties. *Phillbrook* v. *Emswiler* (1884), 92 Ind. 590, 593.

In this instance the averments clearly show the extra labor appellee agreed to perform and that his compensation depended upon the farm becoming productive

4. and of the value of $70,000. The subsequent statement that appellee should receive as compensation the amount over $70,000 "that the land would bring in the market," did not compel appellee to furnish a purchaser nor require appellant to sell if he furnished a purchaser willing and able to pay for the farm something more than $70,000, but it was a statement that appellee's recovery was limited to the actual market value of the land in excess of $70,000.

The fair market value of land is the price it would probably bring after fair and reasonable negotiations where the owner is willing to sell but not compelled to do so, and

5. the buyer desires to purchase, but is under no necessity of obtaining the property. 5 Words and Phrases

4383; *Ligare* v. *Chicago, etc., R. Co.* (1897), 166 Ill. 249, 46
N. E. 803, 808; *Stewart* v. *Ohio River R. Co.* (1893), 38 W.
Va. 438, 18 S. E. 604, 608; *Boom Co.* v. *Patterson* (1878), 98
U. S. 403, 25 L. Ed. 206, 208.

If appellee proved that he performed the labor contemplated by the alleged agreement; that the farm had been
made productive and had a market value of more than

4. $70,000, his right of action was established without
showing an actual sale or furnishing a purchaser as
above stated. *Watson* v. *Deeds* (1891), 3 Ind. App. 75, 77,
29 N. E. 151; *Claypool* v. *German Fire Ins. Co.* (1903), 32
Ind. App. 540, 544, 70 N. E. 281; *Halstead* v. *Jessup* (1897),
150 Ind. 85, 87, 49 N. E. 821; *National Surety Co.* v.
*Schneidermann* (1911), 49 Ind. App. 139, 141, 96 N. E.
955.

Appellant contends that the verdict is not sustained by
sufficient evidence and that the amount of damages awarded
is excessive. The complaint proceeds on the theory

6. that appellee and appellant agreed that the farm
was not productive and could not by usual cultivation
be made to yield crops of value, and that thereupon they
mutually entered into an independent parol agreement to
carry out a plan to fertilize and improve the farm on a scale
and by means not previously contemplated by them. Such
an agreement was not a modification of the original lease but
entirely independent of the same and rested upon an entirely
new consideration. The evidence tends to show that

7. the farm cost appellant about $41,000 and that it had
proven to be less productive than he believed it to be;
that his tenant was about to abandon the farm because it
could not be made to yield crops of any value; that under
these conditions the parol contract was entered into for the
improvement of the fertility of the soil; that appellant
was to furnish the necessary material and fertilizers and
appellee was to do the work; that both parties performed
their respective parts of the agreement; that as a result

thereof the land became productive and reached a value in the market above $70,000; that by the terms of the independent parol agreement such result entitled appellee to the market value of the land in excess of $70,000. There is evidence tending to support every material issuable fact essential to appellee's recovery.

Complaint is also made of the refusal of the court to give certain instructions tendered by appellant and of certain instructions given by the court. The principal objections are based upon appellant's contention that the actual sale of the farm for more than $70,000 was a condition precedent to appellee's recovery. We have decided the proposition adversely to such contention and need not specifically consider the several instructions upon which that question arises.

The court adopted the theory of the complaint above indicated and told the jury that the action was based on the alleged parol agreement and that "the recovery, if 8. any, must be under the terms of the contract"; that the burden was on appellee to prove every material part thereof substantially as alleged and that if they found for the plaintiff he "would be entitled to recover from the defendant such amount as you shall find the market value of the farm exceeded the sum of $70,000." The court also informed the jury that appellee could not recover unless he proved he was to receive as compensation for his extra labor under the parol contract the market value of the land in excess of $70,000, and that if they believed from the evidence that appellant was to furnish and appellee was to distribute the fertilizer, and that the one was to offset the other, there could be no recovery. The court also informed the jury that the rights and obligations of the parties under the lease were not involved in the suit; that the lease was not the contract sued upon, but the action was based upon the alleged parol agreement and appellee must recover thereon, or not at all. These instructions correctly state the law applicable to the issues and evidence in the case. The instructions, when considered as a whole, fairly and accurately state the law. Those refused which state correct propositions of law applicable to the case were fully covered by those given.

Complaint is made of the refusal of the court to submit certain interrogatories relating to the sale of the land. On the theory of the case above indicated, the interroga-

9. tories did not relate to issuable facts and the answers thereto could not have aided appellant in his defense and would necessarily have been treated as surplusage relating to immaterial questions. By answer to an inter-

10. rogatory the jury found the market value of the land to be $73,500. The evidence sustains the answer and likewise the general verdict. The amount of the recovery cannot, on such showing, be held to be excessive.

Some other questions are suggested, which are purely technical and do not bear upon the merits of the controversy. The case seems to have been fairly tried and a correct result reached. No intervening errors are pointed out which deprived appellant of any substantial right. No reversible error is shown. §700 Burns 1914, §658 R. S. 1881; *Inland Steel Co.* v. *Ilko* (1913), 181 Ind. 72, 80, 103 N. E. 7; *Hall* v. *Grand Lodge, etc.* (1913), 55 Ind. App. 324, 331, 103 N. E. 854. Judgment affirmed.

NOTE.—Reported in 115 N. E. 257. See under (1) 31 Cyc 49; (3) 9 Cyc 577; (8) 9 Cyc 757; (10) 13 Cyc 125. Sale of real estate, commission, when earned, 139 Am. St. 225.

---

## NATIONAL LIVE STOCK INSURANCE COMPANY
### *v.* WOLFE.

[No. 9,226.  Filed March 7, 1917.]

APPEAL.—*Record.—Including Separate Causes.—Dismissal.*—Where the record on appeal embodies the proceedings in several separate actions, the appeal will be dismissed, since but one cause may be appealed in one record.

From Daviess Circuit Court; *James W. Ogdon*, Judge.

Action by the National Live Stock Insurance Company against Harry M. Wolfe. From a judgment for defendant, the plaintiff appeals. *Appeal dismissed.*

*Mitchel S. Meyberg*, for appellant.

*Gardiner, Tharp & Gardiner* and *Padgett & Padgett*, for appellee.

IBACH, P. J.—On June 5, 1914, appellant filed in the court below a petition for the review of a proceeding and judgment in favor of appellee for $500 on a live-stock insurance contract. On September 12, 1914, appellee filed what purports to be an answer to such petition, in which he sets out, among other averments, in substance, that appellant has appealed from the original judgment, which it now asks to have reviewed, upon questions of law and fact, and that such appeal is still pending and undetermined and asks that the action be dismissed. On the same day appellant was ruled to reply to such purported answer. On September 17, 1914, and after the day ruled for reply, appellee filed a motion to dismiss said cause for failure of appellant to file reply. On September 25, 1914, among the proceedings had in said cause, the record discloses the following: "Comes now the defendant by his attorneys, and the plaintiff being called in open court to file reply to defendant's answer heretofore filed herein, and failing to appear in person or by attorney, it is now ordered by the court that the motion of said defendant heretofore filed to dismiss this cause, be, and the same hereby is sustained. It is therefore ordered and adjudged by the court that this cause be, and the same is hereby dismissed, and that said plaintiff pay all costs accrued herein."

On December 5, 1914, and at a succeeding term of said court, appellant by leave of court withdrew its complaint from the files. It appears from other pleadings that this same petition or complaint was again filed on December

5, 1914, and new summons issued thereon; the record, however, discloses no entry of filing. On December 10, 1914,
appellee filed a motion to dismiss the complaint filed on
December 5, 1914. The motion discloses, among other
things, that on December 5, 1914, appellant withdrew its
complaint from the files, and on the same day without leave
of court and without changing any allegation or word of
said complaint refiled said instrument as another complaint
herein. Further facts are set out which are substantially
the same as those set out in the former answer.

Among the records of the proceedings had in said cause
on December 17, 1914, appears the following: "Comes again
the parties by their respective attorneys, and now the court
being sufficiently advised, sustains defendant's motion heretofore made to dismiss plaintiff's complaint filed Dec. 5th,
1914, and it is ordered by the court that the said complaint
be restored to and remain as a part of the files of this cause.
It is further ordered and adjudged by the court that the
plaintiff pay the costs accrued herein by its said action, and
to all of which orders and rulings of the court the plaintiff
excepts." On February 9, 1915, upon motion of appellant,
it was ordered by the court that the cause be redocketed
as a pending cause. On the same date appellant requested
and was granted permission to file a motion to set aside the
"order heretofore entered dismissing said cause." On
February 10, 1915, appellee filed a motion to strike out the
motion of appellant heretofore filed to reinstate said cause
on the docket, as a pending cause. Each of said motions
were accompanied by affidavits.

Among the proceedings had in said cause on February
16, 1915, the record discloses the following: "Comes again
the parties by their respective attorneys, and the motion of
the said defendant heretofore filed to strike from the files,
motion of said plaintiff to reinstate said cause, is now by the
court sustained, to which ruling of the court the plaintiff
at the time excepts. It is ordered by the court that the

plaintiff's motion to reinstate said cause on the docket be, and the same is hereby stricken from the files, to which order of the court the plaintiff at the time excepts. Now comes said plaintiff and prays an appeal of said cause to the appellate court of the state of Indiana, and now the court fixes the appeal bond,'' etc.

Appellant filed an appeal bond from which it appears that it is appealing from a judgment rendered on the — day of September, 1914. The term-time appeal was afterwards abandoned and the appeal sought to be perfected as a vacation appeal. The sufficiency of the notice issued below is not questioned and will not be discussed here.

The errors assigned in this court are as follows: 1. The court erred in sustaining defendant's motion to dismiss plaintiff's cause of action. 2. The court erred in sustaining defendant's motion filed December 10,.1914, to dismiss plaintiff's complaint that was filed December 5, 1914. 3. The court erred in dismissing plaintiff's complaint that was filed December 5, 1914. 4. The court erred in overruling plaintiff's motion to set aside the court's order of dismissal of plaintiff's cause of action. 5. The court erred in sustaining defendant's motion to strike from the file the plaintiff's motion to reinstate the said cause and striking the said motion from the file. 6. The court erred in striking from the files plaintiff's motion to reinstate plaintiff's complaint.

Much confusion and uncertainty characterize this appeal. The record apparently embodies the proceedings in three separate actions, and is authenticated by one certificate of the clerk of the trial court.

A question quite analogous was presented to our Supreme Court in an early case (*Rich* v. *Starbuck* [1873], 45 Ind. 310), and the court there said: ''The transcript contains a complete record of two distinct and separate actions. * * * The statute allows appeals from judgments in the circuit and common pleas courts, but it does not contemplate that several judgments shall be included in one transcript, and brought to this court in one appeal, simply because they are between the same parties, and relate to the same subject-matter. * * * We are not willing to sanction the practice of appealing two causes in one record, and thus uniting them in one appeal." See, also, *Roach* v. *Baker* (1896), 145 Ind. 330, 332, 43 N. E. 932, 44 N. E. 303; *Glassburn* v. *Deer* (1895), 143 Ind. 174, 182, 41 N. E. 376; Elliott, App. Proc. §197.

This court cannot give its approval to such method of appeal. Appeal dismissed.

Note.—Reported in 115 N. E. 338.

---

## Chaney, Administrator, v. Wood.

[No. 9,712.   Filed March 7, 1917.]

1. EXECUTORS AND ADMINISTRATORS.—*Sales of Realty.—Report.—Petition by Purchaser for Disapproval.—Sufficiency.*—Where an administrator filed a report of a sale of real estate, a petition by the purchaser seeking a disapproval of the report, a cancellation of the contract of sale and a return of money paid on the purchase price is not demurrable on the ground that a recovery of the money paid could only be obtained by filing a claim against the decedent's estate as provided by §2828 Burns 1914, Acts 1883 p. 153, as the principal object of the petition was to have the contract cancelled and the report disapproved, the recovery of the money paid being only an incident to the proceedings. p. 691.

2. EXECUTORS AND ADMINISTRATORS.—*Sales of Realty.—Report.—Petition by Purchaser for Disapproval.—Sufficiency.*—On a report of a sale of realty by an administrator, a petition by the purchaser to have the report disapproved and the contract cancelled because of false representations concerning the land is not insufficient because it did not show that the alleged false warranties or promises arose prior to the death of the decedent where the petitioner specifically based his right of action on facts occurring subsequent thereto. p. 692.

3. EXECUTORS AND ADMINISTRATORS.—*Sales of Realty.—False Warranties by Administrator.—Liability of Estate.—Recovery of Purchase Price.*—While it is generally true that an estate will not be rendered liable for any damages resulting from any false statements, representations or warranties made by the administrator,

the rule does not apply to an action against an estate wherein it is sought, merely as an incident to the principal purpose of the proceeding, to recover money paid on a contract to purchase a decedent's land by one who was induced to purchase by the fraudulent representations made by the administrator concerning the realty. p. 692.

4. EXECUTORS AND ADMINISTRATORS.—*Sales of Realty.—Fraud.*— False representations knowingly made by an administrator to a buyer of real estate that only one boulder other than one in sight was on the farm, whereas there were twelve acres upon which there actually were thousands of boulders of various sizes which were concealed by growing crops, thereby preventing personal inspection, are sufficient, when relied on by the purchaser, to constitute actionable fraud and to authorize a cancellation of the contract for the sale of the land and a return of money paid thereunder. p. 693.

5. APPEAL.—*Review.—Findings.—Evidence.—Sufficiency.*—Where, in an action against an estate to cancel a contract of sale of realty for fraud, the evidence was conflicting as to the alleged fraudulent representations by the administrator, the finding of the trial court will not be disturbed on appeal for insufficiency of the evidence. p. 693.

6 APPEAL.—*Briefs.—Specification of Errors.—Exceptions in Trial Court.*—Alleged error in the admission of evidence will not be reviewed on appeal where appellant's brief fails to show what specific objections, if any, were made, or that any exceptions were reserved to the rulings of the court. p. 694.

7. APPEAL.—*Briefs.—Specification of Errors.—Exceptions in Trial Court.*—No question is presented for review on appeal as to alleged error in excluding evidence and refusing to strike out an answer of a witness where appellant's brief does not show that any exceptions were reserved to the ruling of the court. p. 694.

8. APPEALS.—*Briefs.—Requirements.—Rules of Court.*—The rules of the Appellate Court require that appellant's brief be so prepared that all questions presented by the assignment of errors can be determined by an examination of the brief without looking to the record, and only to the extent the rules have been complied with will the errors assigned be determined, and the others will be considered waived. p. 694.

From Huntington Circuit Court; *Samuel E. Cook,* Judge.

Action by Walter C. Wood against Elias A. D. Chaney, administrator of the estate of Martha E. Bell, deceased. From a judgment for plaintiff, the defendant appeals. *Affirmed.*

*John Q. Cline* and *Claude Cline*, for appellant.
*W. A. Branyan* and *Wilbur E. Branyan*, for appellee.

BATMAN, J.—The record in this case shows that appellant filed his petition in the court below, and obtained an order for the private sale of certain real estate to make assets for the payment of the debts of his decedent. After certain negotiations, he entered into a contract for the sale of the real estate to the appellee and, on July 8, 1916, issued to him a certificate evidencing the same. Subsequently some difference arose between appellant and appellee with reference to the presence of certain boulders on the real estate and the representations of appellant concerning the same during the negotiations leading up to such contract. The appellant filed a petition and procured an order to expend not to exceed $100 in the removal of such stone, and afterwards filed his report of the sale, setting forth his version of the controversy with reference to such stone, asking that such sale be approved, his acts confirmed, and that he be authorized to take such steps as might be necessary to compel a performance of such contract by appellee.

Appellee filed a petition asking that such contract be cancelled, the sale disapproved, and that the administrator be ordered to return to him the $500 paid by him on such contract, which contained, among others, the following averments in substance: That on the — day of July, 1915, the appellant attempted to sell to appellee the real estate in question; that when he went to look at the same, to ascertain its quality and determine its value, he came upon a large boulder on the land, and asked the appellant, who was present at the time, if there were any other stones of like character on the farm; that appellant answered that there was one other stone upon the farm of like character, and only one other; that appellant made such representations falsely and fraudulently for the purpose of misleading the appellee

and inducing him thereby to purchase said farm, and to pay
a higher price for the same than it was worth.

The petition further avers that there are about twelve
acres of such land, in the central part of such farm, which is
badly encumbered with boulders of various sizes, ranging
from six inches to three feet in diameter; that there are
thousands of them, many being just beneath the surface of
the soil, and many slightly protruding therefrom; that at
the time of such inquiry, there was growing over that part
of the farm encumbered by such boulders a crop of oats,
headed out and uncut, which was wet from dew, rain, and
other moisture, which facts prevented a personal inspection
of such part of the farm; that he had no reason to doubt
the truthfulness of the representations made to him by
appellant and, relying upon his representations and believing them to be true, he made no further investigations; that
at the time appellant made such representations he knew
they were false and fraudulent, and he knew that appellee
did not know they were false and was relying upon the same
being true; that had he not been thus misled he would not
have entered into such contract of purchase at the price
agreed upon and would not have parted with his money in
making the cash payment thereon; that he entered into a
contract with appellant to purchase such farm for the sum
of $7,000 and he paid thereon the sum of $500 cash, but soon
afterwards, when the oats crop growing thereon was har-
vested, he discovered said boulders on said farm; that he at
once called appellant's attention to such stone and to the
representations made by him and asked that he rescind such
contract and pay back to him the $500 paid thereon, which
request appellant refused and still refuses to do; that if said
farm were free from boulders, its actual value would be
$7,000, but when encumbered with boulders as alleged, its
actual value is only $5,500; that if the court would approve
and confirm such sale it would result in defrauding him
of the sum of $1,500; that such sale ought not to be approved

and confirmed, as the estate of said decedent will suffer no loss thereby, since it is still in possession of the land and the crops thereon, and will be left in *statu quo* if such sale is rejected. The prayer asks for the cancellation of such contract, the disapproval of such sale, and an order directing the appellant to return to him his $500 paid on such contract. To this petition appellant filed his demurrer for want of facts, which was overruled and the proper exception was reserved. Appellant then filed an answer in general denial, and a trial was had on the issue thus formed, resulting in a judgment that the report of the sale of real estate to appellee be not approved and that the appellant return to appellee within ten days, $250 of the $500 paid by him on said real estate and that the cost be paid by the estate. Appellant filed a motion for a new trial, prior to the rendition of judgment, which was overruled and the proper exception reserved.

Appellant has presented two questions for the determination of this court arising from the action of the court below in overruling his demurrer to appellee's petition, and in overruling his motion for a new trial.

A number of specifications of insufficiency are set out in the memorandum filed with appellant's demurrer, but only four questions are presented thereby, the first question being, as to the right of appellee to recover the $500 paid by him in the manner attempted. Appellant insists that this could only be done by filing a claim against the estate of decedent with the clerk, as provided by §2828 Burns 1914, Acts 1883 p. 153. We do not concur in this contention. The primary object of appellee's petition was to have the contract of sale cancelled and appellant's report thereof disapproved. If this were done, the return of the money paid would follow as a natural result, and hence its recovery was only an incident to the main object of the proceedings and was not governed by §2828 Burns 1914, *supra.*

The next question raised by the demurrer and memorandum challenges the right of appellee to any relief under his petition, because it does not show that the considera-
2. tion for the alleged promises or warranties arose prior to the date of the death of decedent. Such a showing was not necessary to accomplish the purpose for which the petition was evidently filed. Any such allegations would have been foreign to the theory upon which it proceeds, as appellee specifically grounds his rights on facts occurring subsequent to decedent's death.

Appellant also claims in his specification of insufficiency that the appellee by his petition is seeking to recover damages from the decedent's estate for the tort of appel-
3. lant, as administrator thereof, and that under the law this cannot be done. As said in the case of *Bright Nat. Bank* v. *Hanson* (1916), —— Ind. App. ——, 113 N. E. 434, on page 437: "It is no doubt true, as appellant contends, that generally speaking an estate will not be rendered liable for any damages resulting from any false statements, representations, or warranties made by the administrator. *Riley* v. *Kepler*, 94 Ind. 308; *Huffman* v. *Hendry*, 9 Ind. App. 324, 36 N. E. 727, 53 Am. St. Rep. 351, and cases cited. This is so because an administrator as such has no authority to make such statements, representations, or warranties for or on behalf of his estate, and hence, if liable at all, he is individually liable." However, this is not a case coming within that rule, as the appellee is not seeking by his petition to recover damages from any one on any account, but solely to have his own money returned to him, as an incident to the primary object of the petition. While we concede that the administrator of an estate cannot bind the estate by his warranty or render it responsible in damages for frauds or torts committed by him, yet in his dealings with third persons in respect to the estate he is not, by his representative character, absolved from the universal obligation to observe the dictates of natural justice

and common honesty, which require that he shall act fairly
and not fraudulently. Nor can the estate which he represents be permitted to derive an unjust and unconscientious
advantage to the injury to those with whom its legal representative contracts, by means of his unauthorized fraudulent
conduct. *Able* v. *Chandler* (1854), 12 Tex. 88, 62 Am. Dec.
518.

The final objection urged to the sufficiency of the petition is that it does not state facts sufficient to constitute
actionable fraud. We do not consider such objection
well taken. The representations alleged to have been
made by appellant to appellee, with reference to the
presence of boulders on the land, while appellee was looking over the same with a view of becoming a purchaser, were
of such a nature as to mislead and deceive appellee with
reference thereto. They concerned matters which evidently
materially affected the value of the land. Facts are alleged
which afforded appellee a reasonable excuse for not making further investigation on his own part. If such representations were relied on and were false and fraudulently made,
as alleged, for the purpose of deceiving him as to the character of the land and the value thereof, they are sufficient on
which to base a petition for the relief asked.

The questions raised on overruling appellant's motion for
a new trial are based upon the alleged insufficiency
of the evidence to support the decision of the trial
court, and the action of the court in the admission
and rejection of certain evidence. Appellant has
failed to show in his brief that he reserved any exception to
such ruling of the court, and under the rules we would be
justified in refusing to consider such question on that
account. However, we have given the evidence, which is
largely oral, due consideration. We find that there is a
conflict in the evidence as to what was actually said between
the parties at the time it is claimed that the fraudulent
representations were made, and also as to the terms of the

alleged agreement with reference to the removal of the stone and what had actually been done in pursuance thereof. The court, after hearing the evidence, found in favor of appellee, and with the presumption in favor of the decision of the trial court, we are unable to say that it is not sustained by the evidence. We cannot therefore disturb the decision of the trial court on account of the alleged insufficiency of the evidence. *McKeen* v. *A. T. Bowen & Co.* (1914), 182 Ind. 333, 106 N. E. 529; *Wheatcraft* v. *Myers* (1914), 57 Ind. App. 371, 107 N. E. 81.

It is insisted by appellant that the court erred in admitting certain evidence during the trial. Appellant has not stated or shown in his brief what specific objections, 6. if any, were made in the court below to the admission of such evidence, nor is it stated or shown that any exceptions were reserved to the ruling of the court in admitting such evidence, as required by the rules of this court. Appellant under his statement of points and authorities assigns reasons for his present contention that the court erred in admitting such evidence, but it is not stated or shown that such reasons were given in the court below on the trial of said cause as a reason for its rejection. *American Fidelity Co.* v. *Indianapolis, etc., Fuel Co.* (1912), 178 Ind. 133, 98 N. E. 709.

Appellant also complains of the ruling of the court in refusing to strike out a certain answer, and in sustaining appellee's objections to a certain question, but it is 7. not stated or shown in his brief that any exception was reserved to the ruling of the court in either instance and hence no question is presented for determination. It has been held uniformly that the rules require that appellant's brief be so prepared that all questions presented by the assignment of errors can be determined by an examination of the brief, without looking to the record, and that, to the extent that said rules have been complied with, the errors assigned will be determined and the others will be considered waived. Ewbank's Manual (2d ed.) §181; *Lake Erie, etc., R. Co.* v. *Shelley* (1904), 163 Ind. 36, 71 N. E. 151; *American Fidelity Co.* v. *Indianapolis, etc., Fuel Co., supra.*

We find no error in the record. Judgment affirmed.

NOTE.—Reported in 115 N. E. 333. Executors and administrators, fraudulent representation of, resulting in advantage to estate, recovery against estate, 18 Cyc 296, 297.

---

## TRAYLOR *v.* McCORMICK ET AL.

### [No. 9,235. Filed March 7, 1917.]

1. APPEAL.—*Review.—Harmless Error.—Withdrawal of Interrogatory.*—Where, in an action on a note, the jury answered affirmatively an interrogatory as to whether defendant A signed the note in suit as surety for two of the defendants and by their verdict found that the note was given for a partnership debt of such defendants and was executed by A as surety for them, the withdrawal of an interrogatory, asking whether A agreed with one of the partners that he would stand for the other partner and make good one-half of the partnership business, was harmless, especially as even an affirmative answer to such question would not have been in irreconcilable conflict with the general verdict. p. 697.

2. TRIAL.—*Verdict.—Conflicting Answers to Interrogatories.*—Answers to interrogatories which are contradictory neutralize each other and the general verdict prevails. p. 698.

3. APPEAL.—*Briefs.—Questions Presented.—Rules of Court.*—No question is presented for review as to alleged error in the giving of instructions where appellant fails to set them out in his brief or to show that any exceptions were reserved to those complained of and no specific point or proposition is directed to the alleged error as required by the fifth clause of Rule 22 of the Appellate Court. p. 699.

From Pike Circuit Court; *John L. Bretz,* Judge.

Action by Ebb McCormick against Manford Traylor and others. From the judgment rendered, Traylor appeals. *Affirmed.*

*J. W. Wilson,* for appellant.

*E. P. Richardson* and *A. H. Taylor*, for appellees.

FELT, C. J.—This is a suit on a promissory note brought by appellee, Ebb McCormick, against appellant and appellees, Chelsea Gray, Oliver H. Gray, George W. Traylor and William T. Sherman. The complaint alleges in substance that appellees, Chelsea Gray, Oliver H. Gray and appellant, Manford Traylor, executed their promissory note to appellee George W. Traylor for $200; that the payee indorsed the note to William T. Sherman, who likewise indorsed and transferred it to the plaintiff, Ebb McCormick.

Appellant, Manford Traylor, filed a cross-complaint in which he sought to show that he and Chelsea Gray were partners in business; that Oliver H. Gray is the father of Chelsea Gray, who was and is the son-in-law of appellant; that by an arrangement between said parties appellant agreed to sign the notes of said firm to make good the liability thereon of Chelsea Gray only, who was insolvent; that appellant and said Oliver H. Gray were and are solvent; that he signed the note in suit under said agreement and not otherwise, and is only liable for one-half of the amount thereof and should have judgment accordingly against said Oliver H. and Chelsea Gray. Oliver H. Gray also filed a cross-complaint in which he set up facts seeking to show that appellant and Chelsea Gray were partners in business and that he was surety for them on the note in suit, as such partners, and that he received no part of the consideration therefor; that judgment should be rendered against him only as such surety.

Issues were joined on the complaint by general denial of the parties thereto other than George W. Traylor, Chelsea Gray and William T. Sherman, who were defaulted. All the defendants to the cross-complaints answered the same by general denials.

The case was tried by a jury which returned a verdict as follows: "We the jury find for the plaintiff and that he recover of and from defendants Manford Traylor, Chelsea A. Gray, and Oliver H. Gray, the sum of $223.60 principal and interest on the note sued on herein and the further sum of $30.00 attorney fees. We further find that the note sued on was given for the partnership debt of Manford Traylor, and Chelsea A. Gray and that Oliver H. Gray, executed said note as the surety of Manford Traylor and Chelsea A. Gray." Judgment was rendered in accordance with the verdict.

The only error assigned and relied on for reversal is that the court erred in overruling appellant's motion for a new trial.

Appellee, Oliver H. Gray, by his attorneys earnestly insists that no questions are presented by the briefs under the rules of the court and that the appeal should be dismissed or the judgment affirmed by reason of such failure to duly present any question for decision. The briefs are justly subject to criticism and only by the most liberal interpretation permissible can we hold that they present any question to this court. To the extent that we can ascertain from the briefs the questions appellant seeks to present they will be considered.

An interrogatory was submitted to the jury as follows: "Did Oliver H. Gray agree with Manford Traylor at the beginning of the business of Gray and Traylor, that

1. he would stand for Chelsea Gray and make good one-half of the partnership business?" The jury failed to answer the question. The record shows that the court directed the jury to return to their room and answer the question, and is immediately followed by an entry which shows that the court of its own motion withdrew the interrogatory from the consideration of the jury over the objection and exception of appellant. This action of the court is assigned as one of the grounds for a new trial. Assuming that the interrogatory was a proper one to submit to the jury, and that there was some evidence from which the

jury could have answered it, the error, if any, in withdrawing it was harmless to appellant. The jury were asked,
"Did the defendant, Oliver H. Gray, sign the note in suit
as surety for the firm of Gray and Traylor?" and they
answered, "Yes." In addition to this, by the peculiar form
of their general verdict, the jury state that the note in suit
was given for the partnership debt of appellant and Chelsea
Gray, and that Oliver H. Gray executed the note as surety
for both of such partners. Had the jury given an affirmative answer to the question which was withdrawn by the
court, and this would have been the most favorable answer
for appellant that could have been made, it would not have
been in irreconcilable conflict with the general verdict, for
such an arrangement as is indicated by the question might
have been made, and still it would not conclusively show
that Oliver H. Gray was not surety on the note in suit for
both appellant and Chelsea Gray.

Furthermore, proof was clearly admissible under the issues
to show that appellant executed the note in suit as surety
for both the partners. *American Steel, etc., Co.* v. *Carbone*
(1915), 60 Ind. App. 484, 491, 109 N. E. 220, 1095. We
do not think the interrogatory or any answer that might have
been made to it could have been influential in the decision
of the case, but in any event, if the question had remained
before the jury and an affirmative answer had been made to
it, such answer would have done no more than suggest some
slight inconsistency with the answer above set out, which
shows that Oliver H. Gray was surety for both appellant
and Chelsea Gray. Answers which are contradict-

2.    ory neutralize each other and the general verdict prevails. *Baltimore, etc., R. Co.* v. *Keiser* (1912), 51
Ind. App. 58, 70, 94 N. E. 330; *Southern R. Co.* v. *Utz*
(1912), 52 Ind. App. 270, 279, 98 N. E. 375.

Some suggestion is made of error in the giving of the
instructions, but the instructions are not set out in the

briefs; it is not shown that any exceptions were duly
3. reserved to the ones of which complaint is made and
no specific point or proposition is directed to the
alleged error as required by the fifth clause of Rule 22 of
the court. *Hart* v. *State* (1913), 181 Ind. 23, 27, 103 N. E.
846; *Chicago, etc., R. Co.* v. *Dinius* (1913), 180 Ind. 596,
626, 103 N. E. 652.

The case seems to have been fairly tried. The controverted questions were plainly submitted to, and definitely
decided by the jury adversely to appellant. No error has
been pointed out which deprived appellant of any substantial right or in any way prejudiced him in his defense to
the suit. Judgment affirmed.

Note.—Reported in 115 N. E. 346. See under (1) 38 Cyc 1928;
(2) 38 Cyc 1927.

---

# DICKINSON TRUST COMPANY, GUARDIAN, *v.* STUDY, GUARDIAN, ET AL.

[No. 9,018. Filed April 28, 1916. Rehearing denied December 13, 1916.]

From Wayne Circuit Court; *Daniel W. Comstock*, Special Judge.

Action between the Dickinson Trust Company, guardian of Mabelle M. Howard and Ruth M. Howard, and Thomas J. Study,
guardian *ad litem* of Herbert Myers, and others. From the judgment rendered, the former appeals. *Reversed.*

*Shively & Shively*, for appellant.
*John F. Robbins, Byram C. Robbins* and *Phillip H. Robbins*, for
appellee.

Hottel, J.—The questions involved in this appeal are presented
by the ruling on a demurrer to a cross-complaint filed by appellant in a suit to quiet title. They involve the construction of the
will of Moses Myers, deceased, the grandfather of Mabelle M. and
Ruth M. Howard, and particularly item three thereof. Said questions are the same in all essential particulars as those involved
and decided by this court at this term in the case of *Paul, Guardian, etc.,* v. *Dickinson Trust Co., ante* 230, wherein item four of the
same will was construed. Upon the authority of that case and the

cases there cited the judgment in this case is reversed with instructions to the lower court to overrule the demurrers to appellant's cross-complaint, and for further proceedings not inconsistent with this opinion.

---

### TOWNSHIP BOARD OF FINANCE OF LEXINGTON TOWNSHIP v. SMITH ET AL.

[No. 9,440. Filed December 21, 1916.]

From Jefferson Circuit Court; *John McGregor*, Judge.

*Noble Hays*, for appellant.
*Perry E. Bear, Bernard Korbly* and *Willard New*, for appellees.

PER CURIAM.—From a judgment in favor of appellee, "The Lexington Bank," appellant appeals. Judgment affirmed.

---

### THE CLEVELAND, CINCINNATI, CHICAGO AND ST. LOUIS RAILWAY COMPANY v. WISE, ADMINISTRATOR.

[No. 9,704. Filed December 29, 1916.]

From the Marion Superior Court (80,406); *John J. Rochford*, Judge.

Action between The Cleveland, Cincinnati and St. Louis Railway Company and Thomas Wise, administrator of the estate of Thomas F. Wise, deceased. From a judgment for the latter, the former appeals. *Transferred to Supreme Court.*

*Isaac Carter*, for appellant.
*George W. Galvin*, for appellee.

PER CURIAM.—This cause being submitted to the entire court and four judges not concurring in the result, the case is hereby transferred to the Supreme Court under §15 of the act approved March 12, 1901, Acts 1901 p. 565, §1399 Burns 1914.

## STANDARD STEEL CAR COMPANY *v.* FREDERICH, ADMINISTRATOR.

[No. 9,218. Filed February 2, 1917.]

From Porter Superior Court; *Harry L. Crumpacker*, Judge.

Action between the Standard Steel Car Company and Charles H. Frederich, administrator. From a judgment for the latter, the former appeals. *Transferred to Supreme Court.*

*Crumpacker & Crumpacker*, for appellant.
*McAleer & McAleer, D. J. Moran* and *D. E. Kelly*, for appellee.

DAUSMAN, J.—It appearing that the constitutionality of a statute is involved in this appeal, this cause is now hereby transferred to the Supreme Court, this 1st day of February, 1917.

---

## FLETCHER *v.* FLETCHER ET AL.

[No. 9,584. Filed February 13, 1917.]

From Marion Circuit Court (25,056); *Louis B. Ewbank*, Judge.

Action between Emily Fletcher and Nellie W. Fletcher and others. From a judgment for the latter, the former appeals. *Transferred to Supreme Court.*

*Fred E. Barrett* and *William L. Taylor*, for appellant.
*H. N. Spaan* and *Jackson Carter*, for appellees.

CALDWELL, J.—This cause is transferred to the Supreme Court under the provisions of §1420 Burns 1914, Acts 1893 p. 29, jurisdiction being in the Supreme Court rather than in the Appellate Court.

---

## HARTER *v.* BOARD OF COMMISSIONERS OF BOONE COUNTY.

[No. 9,511. Cause transferred to Supreme Court November 28, 1916.]

From Boone Circuit Court; *Willett H. Parr*, Judge.

Action by Samuel W. Harter against the Board of Commissioners of Boone county. *Transferred to Supreme Court.*

Harter *v.* Board, etc.—63 Ind. App. 701.

*L. Ert Slack, Willis C. Nusbaum* and *Miller & Dowling*, for appellants.

*Roy Ardney,* for appellee.

[REPORTER'S NOTE.—This cause was transferred to the Supreme Court by the Appellate Court under the provisions of §1694 Burns 1914, Acts 1901 p. 565, with recommendations by Felt, J. The opinion of the Supreme Court on the questions involved is reported in *Harter* v. *Board, etc.,* 186 Ind. ——, 116 N. E. 304.]

# INDEX

**ADOPTION—**

Of child, inheritance, effect on rights of illegitimate child, statute, see BASTARDS 3.

*Power of Legislature.*—The legislature has the power to declare the legal status of an adopted child and invest him with the capacity of inheriting from his adopting parent the same as if he were the adopting parent's child born in wedlock.
                                  *Cooley* v. *Powers*, 59, 61 (1).

**AGENCY—**

See PRINCIPAL AND AGENT; BROKERS.

**AGREED CASE—**

Presenting questions for review, exceptions, see APPEAL 62, 63.

**ALIENATION—**

Of affections, see HUSBAND AND WIFE; EVIDENCE 5.

**"ALLOWED"—**

Use of in contract, meaning, see INSURANCE 3.

**AMBIGUITIES—**

See CONTRACTS 6, 8.

**AMENDMENT—**

See PLEADING.
Of briefs, when permitted, see APPEAL 36, 37.
When presumed to have been made, see APPEAL 69.

**ANIMALS—**

1. *Liability of Township for Stock Killed by Dogs.—Report to Township Trustee.—Statute.*—Under §3269 Burns 1914, Acts 1897 pp. 178, 181, providing that owners of live stock maimed or killed by dogs "shall within ten days from the time thereof," report certain facts under oath to the township trustee in order to obtain compensation for the damage suffered, the report must be made within ten days after the injury, regardless of when the animal died.        *Eddy* v. *Honey Creek Tp.*, 527, 531 (3).

2. *Township.—Liability for Swine Killed by Dogs.—Nature of.—Compliance with Statute.*—The right to indemnity from townships for swine killed by dogs is solely statutory, and must be asserted in substantial compliance with the conditions in the law creating it.        *Eddy* v. *Honey Creek Tp.*, 527, 531 (2).

**ANSWER—**

See PLEADING.
Demurrer to bad answer, presumption, see APPEAL 91, 136.

# APPEAL.

See COURTS; JUVENILE COURTS; EXCEPTIONS, BILL OF; TRIAL.
From Industrial Board under Workmen's Compensation Act, see MASTER AND SERVANT.

## I. NATURE AND FORM OF REMEDY.

1. *Right.—Statute.*—Independent of statute, the right of appeal does not exist. *Kurtz* v. *Phillips*, 79, 81 (1).
2. *Right.—Power of Legislature.*—There is no vested right of appeal, and such right is the subject of legislative discretion, to be given or withheld as the general assembly sees fit. *Crittenberger* v. *State, etc., Trust Co.*, 151, 153 (1).

## II. DECISIONS REVIEWABLE.

3. *Ruling on Motion to Set Aside Default.*—Where judgment was taken against defendant by default, and, after the expiration of the term, she filed a motion, under §405 Burns 1914, §396 R. S. 1881, to set aside the default and judgment on the ground of inadvertence, mistake and excusable neglect, and such motion was overruled, but no final judgment was rendered against defendant, the ruling of the court on the motion did not constitute a final judgment from which an appeal would lie under §671 Burns 1914, §632 R. S. 1881, relating to appeals from final judgments. *Kurtz* v. *Phillips*, 79, 81 (2).

4. *Sustaining Demurrer.*—A ruling sustaining a demurrer to a complaint seeking to set aside a judgment under §405 Burns 1914, §396 R. S. 1881, is not appealable, in the absence of a judgment against the party against whom the ruling is made, since it is not a final judgment within the meaning of §671 Burns 1914, §632 R. S. 1881, relating to appeals from final judgments. *Kurtz* v. *Phillips*, 79, 83 (4).

## III. PARTIES.

See APPEAL 52, 57-59.

5. *Vacation.—Statute.—Coparties.*—The word "coparties," as used in §674 Burns 1914, Acts 1899 p. 5, relating to vacation appeals, which provides that a part of several coparties may appeal but must serve notice on all the other parties, means coparties to the judgment appealed from. *Phillips* v. *Ball*, 224, 227 (1).

6. *Vacation.—Assignment of Errors.*—In a vacation appeal all parties to, and those affected by, the judgment must be named

in the assignment of error, and there should be named therein as appellees all parties in whose favor the judgment appealed from was rendered, and those who are interested in having it maintained. *Antioch Baptist Church* v. *Morton*, 117, 118, (1).

7. *Defect.—Waiver.*—Where, in a vacation appeal, a defendant to whom the judgment appealed from was adverse was not made a coappellant in the assignment of errors, the defect in parties was not waived by the principal defendant, who moved to dismiss the appeal, joining in an agreement for immediate submission of the cause, since the defect in parties was jurisdictional, and could be waived only by the party affected by the judgment. *Phillips* v. *Ball*, 224, 229 (4).

8. *Appeal by Township.—Designation of Appellant.—Sufficiency.*—While §9562 Burns 1914, §5990 R. S. 1881, provides that each township is a corporation and shall be designated by the name and style of "........ township of ........ county" according to the name of the township and county in which the same may be organized, and that by such name it may sue and be sued, the name Salt Creek township imports the civil township without the addition of the word "civil" so that an appeal by such township will not be dismissed although it was designated in the proceedings below as "Salt Creek civil township," while in the assignment of errors the word "civil" was omitted. *State, ex rel.* v. *Stevens*, 561, 563, 564 (1).

9. *Term-Time Appeal.—Statute.*—Under §675 Burns 1914, Acts 1895 p. 179, relating to term-time appeals by part of coparties, where an action was brought to recover on official bonds in behalf of both the civil and school township and the judgment was adverse to each, the school corporation is not a necessary party to a term-time appeal in order that the judgment may be reviewed in behalf of the civil township. *State, ex rel.* v. *Stevens*, 561, 566 (5).

IV. Requisites and Proceedings for Transfer of Cause.

10. *Appeal Without Bond.—Inheritance Tax Determination.—Statute.*—Where the auditor of state instituted an action for the rehearing and redetermination of an inheritance tax assessment, although the suit was not brought by the State, or in its name on the relation of the Attorney-General, yet the trial court and the parties treated it as an action so brought, and it was, in fact, prosecuted by the Attorney-General, an appeal by the auditor may be taken from the judgment rendered without bond under §9270 Burns 1914, Acts 1899 p. 219, providing that in civil actions brought in the name of the state, or in its name on the relation of the Attorney-General or on the relation of any state board, any relief to which the state is entitled therein may be obtained without filing any bond either for costs or damages. *Crittenberger* v. *State, etc., Trust Co.*, 151, 155 (3).

11. *Notice.—Service.—Proof.—Statutes.*—Under §681 Burns 1914, §640 R. S. 1881, providing that an appeal may be taken by the service of a notice in writing on the adverse party, or his attorney and also on the clerk of the court, and §504 Burns 1914, §481 R. S. 1881, providing that proof of service of any notice required to be served upon any party, when made by a person other than the sheriff, shall be by affidavit or by the written admission of the party served and requires such proof to show the time and place of service of notice, service of notice of an

**APPEAL—Continued.**

appeal cannot be made by depositing such notice in the mail, registered and addressed to appellee's attorney, since service of notice, unless otherwise provided by law, means personal service of the individual in such a way that the party who makes the service may be in a position to make proof thereof in court.
*Chicago, etc., R. Co.* v. *Sanders,* 586, 588 (2).

12. *Perfecting when no Bond is Required.—Time.*—When no bond is required to be given by a party appealing under §2977 Burns 1914, §2454 R. S. 1881, relating to appeals from decisions growing out of any matter connected with a decedent's estate, the appellant has 120 days from the date of the decision complained of within which to perfect his appeal.
*Crittenberger* v. *State, etc., Trust Co.,* 151, 156 (4).

13. *Term-Time.—Time · for Perfecting.—Approval of Board.*—To perfect a term-time appeal under §679 Burns 1914, §683 R. S. 1881, it is necessary that the penalty and surety of the appeal bond should be fixed and approved within the term at which final judgment is rendered and the filing and approving of a bond after the close of such term, though within the time allowed by the trial court, will not cure the omission of the essential requirement.
*Rohrbaugh* v. *Leas, Admr.,* 544, 546, 547 (2).

14. *Time for Perfecting.—Judgment Preceding Ruling on Motion for New Trial.*—Where the entry of the judgment precedes the ruling on the motion for a new trial, the latter action of the court marks the beginning of the time limited for an appeal.
*Rohrbaugh* v. *Leas, Admr.,* 544, 547 (3).

### V. RECORD—PREPARATION AND CONTENTS.

15. *Review.—Instructions.—Failure to Show Filing of Instructions.*—In order that instructions given and refused may be brought into the record under §561 Burns 1914, Acts 1903 p. 338, relating to making instructions a part of the record without a bill of exceptions, they must be filed, and there must be an entry so showing. *Stimson* v. *Krueger,* 567, 573 (6).

16. *Review.—Instructions.—Sufficiency.—Statute.* — Where the record shows that appellant was given time to present a bill of exceptions containing the instructions tendered and those given and refused ´ by the trial court, but discloses no such bill, the instructions are not brought into the record in the manner authorized by §660 Burns 1914, §629 R. S. 1881, providing that when the record does not otherwise show the decision or grounds of objection thereto, the party objecting must, within the time allowed, present a proper bill of exceptions to the judge for signing and that the same. shall be filed.
*Stimson* v. *Krueger,* 567, 573 (7).

17. *Appeal from Juvenile Court.—Consideration of Evidence.— Bill of Exceptions.—Statute.*—Where the appellant from the juvenile to the Appellate Court fails to incorporate the evidence in a bill of exceptions filed in the juvenile court and to have it made a part of the record, as required by §1635 Burns 1914, Acts 1907 p. 221, no question concerning the evidence can be considered on the appeal. *Parker* v. *State,* 671, 673 (2).

18. *Question Reviewable.—Misconduct of Counsel.—Bill of Exceptions.*—Where, in a paternity suit, misconduct of the attorney for the State in the presence of the court and jury were

**APPEAL—Continued.**

relied on for a reversal of the judgment of the trial court, mere affidavits as to the facts, accompanying the motion for a new trial, cannot take the place or serve the purpose of an unsigned bill of exception, by which appellant attempted to present such facts, and unless the acts complained of are brought into the record by a proper bill of exceptions no question relating thereto is presented.                          *Perry* v. *State*, 653, 660 (7).

19. *Transcript.—Motion for a New Trial.*—No question is presented for review on appeal by an assignment of error that the trial court erred in overruling defendant's motion for a new trial, where such motion was not made part of the record by setting it out in the transcript.                 *Scott* v. *Baird*, 16, 17 (2).

20. *Transcript.—Supplemental.—Certiorari.*—Where appellants, after the filing of the original transcript, procured a *nunc pro tunc* entry correcting the finding and the judgment rendered by the trial court, and a record of all proceedings concerning such action was embodied in a document which was certified to by the clerk of the court and filed in the Appellate Court under the title of "additional transcript," such document is no part of the record and will be stricken from the files, since it was the duty of appellants to bring the *nunc pro tunc* entry, and the proceedings related thereto, before the appellate tribunal by means of a writ of *certiorari*.
                *Brownstown Water, etc., Co.* v. *Hewitt*, 6.

21. *Bill of Exceptions.—Authentication.*—Matters set out in a bill of exceptions not authenticated by the signature of the court cannot be considered on appeal, even though such bill is brought into the record by being incorporated in another bill.
                          *Perry* v. *State*, 653, 659 (5).

22. *Bill of Exceptions.—Certificate of Judge.—Sufficiency.*— The evidence is properly in the record even though the certificate of the trial judge to the bill of exceptions fails to show that he examined the bill before allowing and signing it, since the presumption is that he did so, and the sufficiency of the certificate is not affected by the failure to recite the fact therein.
                          *Dammeyer* v. *Vorhis*, 427, 434 (6).

23. *Presenting Questions for Review.—Bill of Exceptions.—Time for Signing and Settlement.*—The bill of exceptions containing the evidence must be presented to the trial judge for his signature within the time fixed for filing the bill in order to present for determination on appeal any questions requiring a consideration of the evidence.      *Haehnel* v. *Seidentopf*, 218, 222 (5).

24. *Review.—Failure to Include Evidence.*—In an action to set aside a judgment under §405 Burns 1914, §396 R. S. 1881, where it appeared from the record that the motion was not denied until after the court had heard the evidence, which was not made part of the record on appeal by a bill of exceptions or otherwise, no question on the order of the court is presented for review on appeal, even though appellant, who made the motion, asserted that the facts set up in her motion were not denied, and that the case was submitted on such verified motion alone.                          *Kurtz* v. *Phillips*, 79, 85 (5).

25. *Ruling on Demurrers.—Several Exceptions.*—A single exception to the ruling of the court sustaining demurrers to several paragraphs of answer is separate and several and

**APPEAL—Continued.**

presents the question of the sufficiency of each of such answers, where the demurrers were separate and several and the ruling was on each of them.

*National Live Stock Ins. Co.* v. *Owens*, 70, 73 (2).

26. *Questions Reviewable.—Sufficiency of Complaint.—Waiver of Defects.—Statute.*—Since the enactment of §3481 Burns 1914, Acts 1911 p. 415, an assignment of error challenging the complaint for not stating facts sufficient to constitute a cause of action is no longer available.

*Haehnel* v. *Seidentopf*, 218, 222 (6).

27. *Presentation of Error.—Motion for New Trial.—Assignment of Error.*—A specification in a motion for a new trial, alleging that the trial court erred in not requiring a bond for costs to be filed by plaintiff, who became a nonresident of the state subsequent to the commencement of his action, does not present any question for review as to the court's ruling permitting plaintiff, after the motion for a cost bond, to prosecute his action as a poor person, since such ruling must be challenged by an independent assignment of error.

*Haehnel* v. *Seidentopf*, 218, 221 (2).

28. *Matters Not in Record.—Bill of Exceptions.—Failure to File in Time.*—Under §657 Burns 1914, Acts 1897 p. 244, concerning the use of original bills of exception on appeal, a bill of exception containing the evidence which is not presented to the trial judge for settlement and signing within the time allowed by the court is not a part of the record on appeal, and presents no question for consideration.

*National Live Stock Ins. Co.* v. *Owens*, 70, 72 (1).

VI. ASSIGNMENT OF ERRORS.

See APPEAL 19, 26, 27.

29. *Grounds.*—Alleged error of the trial court in directing a verdict is not ground for an independent assignment of error.

*Cobe* v. *Darrow*, 169, 170 (1).

30. *Grounds.*—That "the judgment appealed from is not fairly supported by the evidence" and that it "is clearly against the weight of the evidence," are not grounds for independent assignment of error.

*Perry* v. *State*, 653, 661 (9).

31. *Grounds.—Refusal of Court to Sign a Bill of Exceptions.*—No question is presented for review on appeal by an assignment of error which attempts to present an exception to the refusal of the trial court to sign a bill of exceptions.

*Perry* v. *State*, 653, 662 (10).

32. *Appeal from Juvenile Court.—Error Assignable.—Statute.*—Under §1635 Burns 1914, Acts 1907 p. 221, relating to appeals from the juvenile to the Appellate Court, the only assignment of error allowed on appeal is, "that the decision of the court is contrary to law"; and such assignment is sufficient to present both the sufficiency of the facts found to sustain the judgment and the sufficiency of the evidence to sustain the findings.

*Parker* v. *State*, 671, 672 (1).

33. *Question Presented.—Exceptions.*—Assignments of error that are not based on exceptions shown in the record cannot be considered on appeal.

*Aubain* v. *United Brotherhood, etc.*, 636, 637 (1).

**APPEAL—Continued.**

34. *Sufficiency.*—Assignments of error that the decision of the court is contrary to the evidence and that the decision of the court is contrary to the law and the evidence present no cause for a new trial, as they are not in the form provided by statute, and, since the alleged errors relate to matters which are required to be brought into the record by a motion for a new trial, they cannot be made the subject of independent assignments of error on appeal. *Fox,* v. *Close,* 66, 68 (1).

35. *Parties.—Administrator.—Failure to Properly Designate.—Dismissal.*—Where the judgment appealed from was rendered in favor of a party in his representative capacity as administrator of the estate of another, but on the appeal he was designated in the assignment of errors merely as administrator, but for whose estate not being indicated, the appeal will be dismissed for failure to comply with the rules of the Appellate Court requiring that the assignment of errors shall contain the full names of all parties to an appeal.
*Rohrbaugh* v. *Leas, Admr.,* 544, 545 (1).

### VII. Briefs.

See APPEAL 60, 73, 129-133.

36. *Amendment.*—Within the·time allowed by the court for the filing of briefs an appellant will be permitted to file amended briefs, or to make any reasonable amendment to those which he may have filed before the expiration of the time allowed, upon notice to the opposite party and leave of court, and, after such time, appellant may in certain contingencies obtain leave of court to amend his briefs; and, if the briefs filed show substantial compliance with the rules of court and duly present some question, on proper showing and after notice to the opposite party, the court will permit any reasonable amendment of the briefs necessary to fully present the merits of the appeal, subject to such orders as to the payment of the costs as the court may deem just and equitable, but, if the briefs filed by appellant, when fairly and liberally construed, under the rules of the court, fail to present any question relating to the merits of the appeal, he will not be permitted to amend after the time for filing briefs and taking an appeal, except in cases where the necessity for the amendment resulted from the acts or conduct of the appellee, or from some cause for which appellant was in no way to blame.
*Bingham, Rec.,* v. *Newtown Bank,* 606, 609 (1).

37. *Failure to Comply with Rules of Court.—Amendment.—Time.—Dismissal.*—Where the time for perfecting an appeal has expired, and it appears from the record and the briefs filed by appellant that he has presented no question for review under the rules of the court he will not be permitted to amend, and appellee's timely motion for a dismissal of the appeal will be sustained. *Bingham, Rec.,* v. *Newtown Bank,* 606, 610 (2).

38. *Omissions.—Supplied by Adverse Party.—Rules of Court.—* Although the points and authorities in appellant's brief are not applied to any specific ruling of the trial court relied on for reversal, yet where appellee has, by the statements in his brief, supplied the omissions of appellant, the questions sought to be presented may be considered without disregarding the rules for the preparation of briefs. *Royer* v. *State, ex rel.* 123, 126 (1).

**APPEAL—Continued.**

**39.** *Omissions by Appellant.—Supply by Appellee.—Sufficiency.* —Where appellant's brief, in seeking to question the sufficiency of the complaint, fails, in its statement of the record, to set out enough of the complaint to properly present the objections thereto, it is subject to criticism as not complying with the rules of the Appellate Court, but when the omissions from the record are supplied by appellee, such brief is sufficient to present the objections urged against the complaint.
*Vandalia Coal Co.* v. *Ringo, Admr.,* 323, 324, (1).

**40.** *Presenting Grounds for Review.—Instructions.*—No question is presented for review by criticism of certain instructions made in the argument in appellant's brief, where the rule of the Appellate Court relating to the presentation of alleged error under the heading of points and authorities has not been complied with. *Chicago, etc., R. Co.* v. *Biddinger,* 30, 47 (21).

**41.** *Points and Authorities.—Abstract Statements.—Instructions.* —Where appellant's brief, under its points and authorities, makes general statements concerning what is proper and required in giving the instructions, but under such heading makes no application of any of these statements nor reference to any particular instruction, the brief does not comply with the rules of the Appellate Court, and no question on the instructions is presented for review.
*Chicago, etc., R. Co.* v. *Biddinger,* 30, 46 (20).

**42.** *Questions Presented.—Rules of Court.*—No question is presented for review as to alleged error in the giving of instructions where appellant fails to set them out in his brief or to show that any exceptions were reserved to those complained of and no specific point or proposition is directed to the alleged error as required by the fifth clause of Rule 22 of the Appellate Court. *Traylor* v. *McCormick,* 695, 699 (3).

**43.** *Requirements.—Rules of Court.*—The rules of the Appellate Court require that appellant's brief be so prepared that all questions presented by the assignment of errors can be determined by an examination of the brief without looking to the record, and only to the extent the rules have been complied with will the errors assigned be determined, and the others will be considered waived. *Chaney, Admr.,* v. *Wood,* 687, 694 (8).

**44.** *Rules of Court.—Substantial Compliance.*—Although the rules for the preparation of appellant's brief have not been strictly followed, the errors presented will be considered where there has been a substantial compliance therewith.
*Cleveland, etc., R. Co.* v. *Gannon,* 289, 293 (1).

**45.** *Specification of Errors.—Rules of Court.*—Where appellant assigns as error the overruling of its motion for a new trial, and its brief under such assignment contains four points, each general in its nature, to the effect that it is error to admit evidence of a certain nature, and such points are not directed to any particular ruling complained of, there is a failure to comply with the rules of the Appellate Court and no question is presented for review on appeal.
*Town of Carlisle* v. *Pirtle,* 475, 481 (6).

**46.** *Specification of Errors.—Exceptions in Trial Court.*—No question is presented for review on appeal as to alleged error in excluding evidence and refusing to strike out an answer of a

**APPEAL—Continued.**

witness where appellant's brief does not show that any exceptions were reserved to the ruling of the court.

*Chaney, Admr.,* v. *Wood,* 687, 694 (7).

47. *Specification of Errors.—Exceptions in Trial Court.*—Alleged error in the admission of evidence will not be reviewed on appeal where appellant's brief fails to show what specific objections, if any, were made, or that any exceptions were reserved to the rulings of the court.

*Chaney, Admr.,* v. *Wood,* 687, 694 (6).

48. *Sufficiency.—Questions Presented for Review.*—An assignment of error based on the overruling of a demurrer to an answer presents no question for review where appellant's brief sets out neither the complaint nor the answer, nor the substance of either, and fails to show that such answer was filed.

*New Albany Nat. Bank* v. *Brown,* 391, 404 (10).

49. *Sufficiency.*—Where the only proposition or point mentioned in appellant's brief applying to questions arising under the motion for a new trial is a general statement that instructions must be confined to the issues made by the pleadings, and must be based on the evidence, and neither the pleadings nor the evidence is set out, no question is presented for review as to the instructions or motion for a new trial based on error therein.

*Vandalia Coal Co.* v. *Ringo, Admr.,* 323, 326 (3).

50. *Sufficiency.*—Where appellant's brief fails to show that a motion for a new trial was filed or ruled on, and it is impossible to determine, without a search of the record, what questions were sought to be presented by the motion, the brief fails to comply with the fifth clause of Rule 22 of the Appellate Court, relating to the preparation of appellant's briefs, and no question is presented for review by an assignment of error based on the overruling of the motion for a new trial.

*York* v. *Cooper,* 119, 120 (2).

51. *Waiver of Error.*—A ground for a motion for a new trial not referred to under the heading of points and authorities in appellant's brief is waived.

*Chicago, etc., R. Co.* v. *Biddinger,* 30, 47, (22).

## VIII. DISMISSAL.

See APPEAL 37.

52. *Determination.—Defect of Parties.*—In passing on a motion to dismiss an appeal for defect of parties the court can only consider the question whether all the parties were properly before the court on the day of submission, even though it appears from the record that the party whom it is claimed should have been made a coappellant could not have appealed because more than 180 days had elapsed between the time of overruling the motion for a new trial and the filing of the motion to dismiss the appeal.

*Phillips* v. *Ball,* 224, 228 (3).

53. *Failure to Perfect.*—Where an appeal, not properly perfected as a term-time appeal, has been on the docket for more than ninety days, and no steps have been taken to give notice so as to perfect it as a vacation appeal under §681 Burns 1914, §640 R. S. 1881, a dismissal is required.

*Rohrbaugh* v. *Leas, Admr.,* 544, 548 (4).

54. *Failure to Perfect Appeal.—Rules of Court.*—Where a case has been on the docket of the Appellate Court more than ninety

APPEAL—Continued.

days and no steps have been taken to perfect the appeal, except to make an insufficient service of notice thereof, the appeal will be dismissed under Rule 36 of the Appellate Court relating to dismissal of causes. *Chicago, etc., R. Co.* v. *Sanders*, 586, 589 (3).

55. *Motion to Dismiss.—Rules of Court.—Substantial Compliance.*—Under Rule 7 of the Appellate Court requiring ten days' notice of a motion to dismiss an appeal and under Rule 14 providing that motions, except such general motions as are made in court upon the call of the docket, shall be filed with the clerk, accompanied by such affidavits and briefs as are necessary to support them, where appellee, on December 30, 1916, served notice on appellant that on January 16, 1917, he would file a motion to dismiss the appeal for insufficiency of the service of appellant's notice thereof, appellant being furnished a copy of the motion, and such motion and briefs thereon were filed on January 15, 1917, appellee substantially complied with the rules of court and the question of the sufficiency of the service of the notice of appeal was presented for determination.
*Chicago, etc., R. Co.* v. *Sanders*, 586, 588 (1).

56. *Record.—Including Separate Causes.*—Where the record on appeal embodies the proceedings in several separate actions, the appeal will be dismissed, since but one cause may be appealed in one record. *National, etc., Ins. Co.* v. *Wolfe*, 683.

57. *Vacation.—Parties.—Coappellants.*—On a vacation appeal all parties against whom judgment was rendered must be made coappellants or the appeal will be dismissed.
*Phillips* v. *Ball*, 224, 227 (2).

58. *Vacation.—Parties.*—Where it affirmatively appears from the record of a vacation appeal that the judgment appealed from was rendered in favor of persons who are not named as appellees in the assignment of error, and that such persons are interested in maintaining the judgment, the appeal will be dismissed. *Antioch Baptist Church* v. *Morton*, 117, 118 (2).

59. *Vacation.—Parties.—Defect.—Jurisdiction.*—Where, in an action against several defendants to foreclose a real-estate mortgage, the judgment, from which a vacation appeal was taken, decreed that one of the defendants had no interest in the land in controversy, such defendant had a right to appeal, and should have been made a coappellant in the assignment of errors, and notified, as provided in §674 Burns 1914, Acts 1899 p. 5, relating to vacation appeals, and where the appeal was taken without making him a coappellant, it must be dismissed for want of jurisdiction. (*Rooker* v. *Fidelity Trust Company* [1915], 185 Ind. 172, distinguished.)
*Phillips* v. *Ball*, 224, 229 (5).

IX. HEARING AND REHEARING.

60. *Petition for Rehearing.—Scope of Review.—Briefs.*—On a petition for a rehearing appellants may not present questions not presented by their original briefs.
*Royer* v. *State, ex rel.* 123, 134 (10).

61. *Rehearing.—New Question.*—Where appellant on rehearing seeks for the first time to challenge the complaint as being insufficient under the statute relating to the creation of trusts in real estate, such question cannot be considered.
*Trook* v. *Trook*, 272, 281 (6).

**APPEAL—Continued.**

### X. Review.

(A)  Scope and Extent in General.

62.  *Agreed Case.—Presenting Questions.—Exceptions.*—A motion for a new trial is not contemplated in an agreed case, there being no question for decision except the law arising upon the agreed facts, and a question of law in such a case, to be presented on appeal, must be saved by an exception to the decision of the trial court taken at the proper time.
*Aubain* v. *United Brotherhood, etc.,* 636, 637 (2).

63.  *Agreed Statement of Facts.—Presenting Question.—Motion for a New Trial.—Bill of Exceptions.*—Where issues are joined upon an agreed statement of facts, a motion for a new trial is required to raise any question on appeal involving the evidence, and the agreed statement of facts must be made a part of the record by a bill of exceptions, and the record must affirmatively show that it contains all the evidence that was adduced at the trial.     *Aubain* v. *United Brotherhood, etc.,* 636, 637 (3).

64.  *Errors Assignable on Review.—When Waived.—Statute.*— Under §344 Burns 1914, Acts 1911 p. 415, providing that where a demurrer to a complaint is filed for want of facts, a memorandum shall be filed therewith stating wherein such pleading is insufficient and that defects not questioned in such memorandum shall be deemed waived, and under §348 Burns 1914, Acts 1911 p. 415, providing that when objection is not taken by answer or demurrer to any of the matters enumerated as grounds for demurrer, except joinder of causes, which do not appear on the face of the complaint, such objection shall be deemed waived, an assignment of error that "the complaint  *  *  * does not state facts sufficient to constitute a cause of action against appellant" presents no question for review on appeal.
*American Car, etc., Co.* v. *Williams,* 1, 5 (4).

65.  *Excessive Damages.—Presenting Questions.*—In order to present for review on appeal an objection that an instruction states an erroreous measure of damages, there must have been an assignment, as a ground for a new trial, that the damages recovered were excessive.
*Cleveland, etc., R. Co.* v. *Gannon,* 289, 295 (5).

66.  *Invited Error.—Instructions.*—In an action by the wife for alienation of her husband's affections, defendants cannot complain of an instruction directing a finding for plaintiff if either of them maliciously alienated the husband's affections, where the error, if any, in such instruction was invited by an instruction of the same nature requested by defendants.
`Daywitt* v. *Daywitt,* 444, 449 (2).

67.  *Incomplete Instructions.*—Where the instructions given, although incomplete, were correct as far as they went, appellant, having failed to present more complete instructions on the subject, cannot on appeal object for that reason.
*National Life Ins. Co.* v. *Headrick,* 54, 59 (8).

68.  *Instructions.—Refusal.*—In an action for the unlawful appropriation of a tract of real estate and damages, the refusal of defendant's requested instructions on the question of the burden of proof as to the title of the land in controversy and the different elements to be considered in arriving at the measure of damages was proper, where the court informed the jury, in an instruction on the subject of ownership, that plaintiff, to

## APPEAL—Continued.

recover, must show by a fair preponderance of the evidence that he was the legal owner of the real estate in controversy at the time of its appropriation, and where the instructions given as to the measure of damages were more favorable to defendant than it was entitled to.

*Cleveland, etc., R. Co.* v. *Gannon*, 289, 296 (6).

69. *Issues.—Amendments Deemed Made.*—In an action against a railroad for injuries sustained by plaintiff when struck by a train at a street crossing, even though the averments of the second paragraph of complaint were insufficient to show that the crossing was within the corporate limits of the city of Rochester, and that the railroad was, therefore, subject to its ordinances, where the issue as to the location of such crossing was fully tried and proof thereon made under the first paragraph of complaint, the second paragraph, being in all other respects sufficient as against demurrer will be treated on appeal as having been amended in respect to such defect to conform to the proof. *Chicago, etc., R. Co.* v. *Biddinger*, 30, 42 (11).

70. *Instructions.—Applicability to Pleading.*—In an action for personal injuries received when plaintiff was struck by defendant's automobile, defendant cannot on appeal complain of an instruction that does not follow the averments of the complaint as to plaintiff's location at the time of the accident, where the facts referred to in such instruction are supported by uncontradicted evidence which was received without objection.

*Gardner* v. *Vance*, 27, 28 (1).

71. *Motion for a New Trial.—Grounds.—Form of Assignment.*—Under §585 Burns 1914, §559 R. S. 1881, authorizing the granting of a new trial for the reason "that the * * * decision is not sustained by sufficient evidence, or is contrary to law," no question is presented for review on appeal, where trial was had without a jury, by an assignment of error predicated on the overruling of a motion for a new trial based on the grounds that the judgment and order rendered by the court were contrary to the law and the evidence and that they were not sustained by sufficient evidence, since the word "decision," as used in the statute, has reference to the finding where the trial is by the court, and neither assigned cause for a new trial challenges the decision or finding of the court.

*Indianapolis Electric Supply Co.* v. *Trapschuh*, 120.

72. *New Trial.—Effect.—Errors Prior Thereto.*—Where defendant procured the court below to grant it a new trial, it waived any error in that court's ruling, made prior to the order for the new trial, on its motion for judgment on the interrogatories. *Evansville R. Co.* v. *Cooksey, Admx.*, 482, 488 (4).

73. *Questions Presented.—Ruling on Demurrer.—Scope of Review.*—Where appellant assigns as error the overruling of its demurrer to the complaint but in its brief, under "Points and Authorities," the complaint is challenged as being insufficient in only one respect, the appellate tribunal is not required to determine the sufficiency of the pleading on any other point than the one attacked.

*Evansville R. Co.* v. *Cooksey, Admx.*, 482, 486 (1).

74. *Questions Presented.—Record.—Refusal of Instructions.*—Error cannot be predicated on the trial court's refusal to give requested instructions, unless it appears affirmatively from the

record that they were offered at the proper time and in the appropriate mode.

*Herald Publishing Co. v. State, ex rel, 465, 469 (5).*

75. *Question Reviewable.—Misconduct of State.—Record.*—Alleged misconduct on the part of the State, in a trial of a bastardy proceeding, in permitting the relatrix to exhibit her child to the jury contrary to the direction of the court is not available for reversal of the judgment, where the record shows no order of the court directing relatrix not to bring her child into the presence of the jury and that defendant's motion for such an order was overruled. *Perry v. State, 653, 658 (4).*

76. *Questions Reviewable.—Misconduct of Counsel.—Objections.*—In an appeal in a bastardy proceeding, alleged misconduct of opposing counsel during the trial of the cause is not available to the defendant where it does not appear from the record that he at the time objected, or called the court's attention, to the acts complained of. *Perry v. State, 653, 661 (8).*

77. *Questions Presented.—Objections to Instructions.—Ruling on Motion for New Trial.*—Where the sole error assigned on appeal was the overruling of the motion for a new trial and under such assignment the appellant presents only the question of alleged error in an instruction, but the brief fails to disclose that any exception was taken or reserved to the trial court's ruling on the motion, no question is presented for review.

*Morgan v. Arnt, 590.*

78. *Questions Presented.—Motions.*—An assignment of error predicated on the trial court's refusal of a motion to modify its finding of facts by striking out certain special findings presents no question for review on appeal, since motions to modify, strike out or add to the special findings are not recognized by the code of procedure, the proper remedy being by a motion for a new trial. *York v. Cooper, 119, 120 (1).*

79. *Record.—Matters Not in Record.—Scope of Review.*—Where the evidence is not in the record, it is not available to determine appellee's argument that error, if any, in sustaining demurrers to several paragraphs of answer was harmless because evidence in support of such answers was introduced at the trial.

*National Live Stock Ins. Co. v. Owens, 70, 73 (3).*

80. *Refusal of Instructions.*—It is not error to refuse requested instructions where the subject-matter thereof is fully covered by the instructions given. *Daywitt v. Daywitt, 444, 450 (5).*

81. *Rulings on Demurrers.—Memorandum of Defects.—Scope of Review.*—Although the court on appeal, in reviewing the overruling of a demurrer to a complaint, can consider only the defects pointed out in the memorandum required by §344, cl. 6, Burns 1914, its review is not so limited where a demurrer to a complaint is sustained for insufficiency of facts alleged, and it will uphold such a ruling if the complaint is insufficient for any reason. *Barnum v. Rallihan, 349, 356 (1).*

82. *Searching the Record.*—The court on appeal will search the record to affirm a cause, but not to reverse it.

*Vandalia Coal Co. v. Ringo, Admr., 323, 326 (4).*

83. *Vendor's Lien.—Action to Enforce.—Conclusions of Law.—Failure to Except.—Effect on Appeal.*—Where, in an action to enforce a vendor's lien, the trial court found that land in the hands of a grantee was subject to a vendor's lien in favor of a

**APPEAL—Continued.**

remote grantor to the extent of the unpaid money due from such grantee, who neither excepted to the conclusions of law nor made any motion to modify the judgment rendered thereon, it is unnecessary for the court on appeal to consider whether the grantee, who gave his note to his grantor for the unpaid portion of the purchase price, was an innocent purchaser as to the entire purchase price, as any error in the conclusions of law in this respect would not be prejudicial to his immediate grantor who is a coappellant.　　*Essig* v. *Porter*, 318, 322 (6).

84. *Waiver of Objections.—Instructions.*—Where, in an action by the wife for alienation of her husband's affections, ample opportunity was afforded two defendants to submit a form of verdict to find against one only if found liable, in addition to the two forms submitted, one to find for plaintiff and the other for defendants, but they made no request therefor at the proper time, they cannot complain of an instruction directing a verdict against both, if either of them maliciously did the acts charged.　　*Daywitt* v. *Daywitt*, 444, 449, (3).

85. *Witnesses.—Objection to Competency.—Sufficiency.—Presumption.*—An objection to the competency of a party as a witness presents no question for review on appeal where the party objecting failed to point out any reason for the alleged incompetency, since the presumption is that all parties to an action are competent to testify in their own behalf.
　　*New Albany Nat. Bank* v. *Brown*, 391, 404 (11).

86. *Witnesses.—Credibility.—Jury Question.*—It is for the jury to determine the credibility of witnesses, and not for the court on appeal.　　*Daywitt* v. *Daywitt*, 444, 455 (12).

(B) PRESUMPTIONS.

Absence of assignment of error, ruling of trial court, see COSTS 2.

87. *Action of Trial Court.*—Presumptions should be indulged in favor of the action of the trial court until it is made to appear that the court erred therein.
　　*Doak, etc., Co.* v. *Raabe*, 250, 257 (6).

88. *Instructions Refused.—Absence of Evidence.*—Where the evidence is not in the record, it will be presumed on appeal that requested instructions were not applicable to the evidence and were properly refused for that reason.
　　*Herald Publishing Co.* v. *State, ex rel.*, 465, 469 (6).

89. *Master Commissioner's Findings.—Adoption by Court.*—In an action by an insurance company against its agent to recover money alleged to be due under an agency contract, the court on appeal cannot presume, even though certain provisions of the contract made it defendant's duty to collect premiums on insurance written by him, that the agent collected the premiums in controversy, where the master commissioner's report adopted by the court found that the agent did not collect such premiums.
　　*Doak, etc., Co.* v. *Raabe*, 250, 254 (2).

90. *Parties.*—Where a political corporation is designated in the assignment of errors as "Salt Creek Township," a conclusive presumption arises that the reference is to the civil township.
　　*State, ex rel.* v. *Stevens*, 561, 565 (3).

91. *Prejudicial Error.—Overruling Demurrer to Bad Answer.*—Error in overruling a demurrer to a bad answer is presumed to be harmful and will constitute reversible error, unless it is

**APPEAL—Continued.**

affirmatively shown by the record that the ruling was not prejudicial, and the duty of making such showing rests upon the party who contends that the error was harmless.

*Denney v. Reber*, 192, 200 (7).

92. *Receivers.—Discharge of Duties.—Presumption.*—It will be assumed on appeal, in the absence of a showing to the contrary, that a receiver has or will discharge his duties as such, and that the court under whose directions such receiver is acting will make all orders necessary upon the receiver to the full protection of the corporation and the interests of its shareholders. *Marcovich v. O'Brien, Auditor,* 101, 116 (15).

93. *Review.—Erroneous Instruction.*—In an action to recover benefits on an accident insurance policy, an instruction that, if a person was so disabled that he was disqualified and rendered unable to perform substantially and in a reasonable way his usual and ordinary work and vocation, he was totally disabled, was, in view of the stipulations in the policy, incorrect, and will be presumed to have been harmful.

*Workingmen's Mutual, etc., Assn. v. Roos,* 18, 25 (3).

94. *Review.—Master Commissioner's Report.—Evidence Not in Record.*—Where the evidence is not in the record, the master commissioner's report of the facts, having been adopted by trial court, must be presumed to be correct.

*Doak, etc., v. Raabe,* 250, 256 (4).

(C) DISCRETION OF TRIAL COURT.

See PLEADING 1.

95. *Review.—Order of Receiving Evidence.—Recalling Witness.* —In an action for personal injuries, the action of the trial court in permitting defendant to recall a witness for plaintiff after defendant's motion for a peremptory instruction had been overruled, was not an abuse of the court's discretionary power as to the order of receiving evidence.

*Croly v. Indianapolis Traction, etc., Co.,* 663, 665 (2).

(D) QUESTIONS OF FACT, VERDICTS AND FINDINGS.

A conclusion of law showing right of possession is of no force in the absence of a finding supporting it, see EJECTMENT.

96. *Action on Insurance Policy.—Judgment.—Error in Favor of Appellant.*—A defendant appealing from an adverse judgment cannot object that the judgment is for a smaller amount than should have been allowed under the findings of fact.

*Nat. Live Stock Ins. Co. v. Cramer,* 211, 217 (6).

97. *Criminal Prosecution.—Failure to Incorporate Evidence in Record.—Findings.*—Where, in an appeal from the judgment of the juvenile court in a criminal prosecution, the evidence is not before the court, the facts found by the juvenile court must be taken as correctly found. *Parker v. State,* 671, 674 (5).

98. *Criminal Prosecution.—Findings.—Sufficiency.*—Where, in a prosecution for contributing to the delinquency of a girl under the age of sixteen years, the juvenile court found "that the defendant did cause and encourage ...... to commit an act of delinquency at or about August 14, 1915, at or about 2 p. m. of that day and again on or about Saturday, August 21, 1915, at about 2 o'clock p. m.," the last date being the one mentioned in the affidavit filed in the cause on September 8, 1915, such finding was not insufficient as failing to show that the alleged

APPEAL—Continued.

offense was committed prior to the time of the filing of the affidavit, or because the use of the words "on or about" is not sufficiently certain. *Parker* v. *State*, 671, 673 (3).

99. *Evidence.—Sufficiency.—Scope.*—In determining the sufficiency of the evidence on appeal the court will not weigh the evidence, but will determine whether there is any evidence to support the finding in appellee's favor, and will consider only the evidence which tends to support such finding.
*New Albany Nat. Bank* v. *Brown*, 391, 405 (12).

100. *Evidence.—Sufficiency.*—The court on appeal can reverse the judgment of the trial court because of insufficient evidence only when there is no evidence to support any element or fact necessary and essential to a recovery.
*Stimson* v. *Krueger*, 567, 573 (5).

101. *Evidence.—Sufficiency.*—Where there is some competent evidence to support a verdict for plaintiff, it must be sustained on appeal, even though the weight of the evidence was favorable to the defendant. *Christie* v. *Walton*, 234, 237 (2).

102. *Evidence.—Sufficiency.—Conflicting Evidence.*—If there is some evidence to sustain the verdict, it is neither the right nor duty of the court on appeal to weigh conflicting evidence.
*Smith* v. *Weston*, 268, 271 (2)

103. *Evidence.—Sufficiency.*—Where there is evidence from which the facts found by a verdict that are essential to a recovery may have been reasonably inferred by the jury, the evidence is sufficient on appeal, even though other and contrary inferences may be reasonably drawn therefrom.
*National Life Ins. Co.* v. *Headrick*, 54, 58 (2).

104. *Evidence.—Sufficiency.*—In determining the sufficiency of the evidence to support the verdict, the court on appeal must group that part of it in which there is no conflict with that part of it tending to support the verdict where there is conflict.
*Crumpacker* v. *Jeffrey*, 621, 624 (1).

105. *Evidence.*—The court on appeal cannot weigh conflicting evidence. *Croly* v. *Indianapolis Traction, etc., Co.*, 663, 670 (4).

106. *Evidence.—Verdict.*—Where there is some evidence to sustain the verdict, that is sufficient on appeal.
*Bosson* v. *Brash*, 86, 89 (3).

107. *Evidence.—Public Records.—Deeds.—Certification.—Admissibility.—Statute.*—In an action for the unlawful appropriation of land, where plaintiff relied on certified copies of certain deeds to establish his title, it was not error for the trial court to admit in evidence certified copies of deeds upon which appeared, above the recorder's certificates attached thereto, the words "Decatur County Recorder's Seal, Indiana," since this was a substantial compliance with §478 Burns 1914, §462 R. S. 1881, which requires that copies of deeds and other instruments required by law to be recorded in public offices, to be admissible in evidence, must be duly certified by the officer having the custody thereof, and authenticated by the officer's seal, which should be attached to the certificate of the officer to the instrument exemplified.
*Cleveland, etc., R. Co.* v. *Gannon*, 289, 297 (9).

108. *Jury Question.*—In an action for the unlawful appropriation of realty, the weight to be given the evidence relied on by

**APPEAL—Continued.**

plaintiff to establish ownership was, if such evidence were competent, for the jury, and, as the general verdict necessarily found for plaintiff upon such issue, the court on appeal is precluded from further inquiry.
*Cleveland, etc., R. Co.* v. *Gannon*, 289, 296 (7).

109. *Master Commissioner's Report.—Conclusions.*—Mere conclusions in the report of a master commissioner, in a case referred to him for a finding of facts, must be excluded.
*Doak, etc., Co.* v. *Raabe*, 250, 256 (5).

110. *Findings.—Evidence.—Sufficiency.*—Where, in an action against an estate to cancel a contract of sale of realty for fraud, the evidence was conflicting as to the alleged fraudulent representations by the administrator, the finding of the trial court will not be disturbed on appeal for insufficiency of the evidence. *Chaney, Admr.,* v. *Wood*, 687, 693 (5).

111. *Findings of Fact.—Contradictions in Evidence.*—Where findings of facts are supported by substantial evidence, they cannot be disturbed on appeal because there are contradictions in the evidence given at the trial. *Bueter* v. *Aulbach*, 91, 94 (2).

112. *Presumptions.—Verdict.—Answers to Interrogatories.*—In an action for personal injuries in a railroad crossing accident where the general verdict was for the plaintiff, it will be assumed on appeal, on consideration of the refusal of a motion for judgment on the answers to interrogatories, that the evidence showed that there was something to prevent the plaintiff from hearing the approach of the train at the time inquired about in the interrogatories, in the absence of a contrary finding. *Chicago, etc., R. Co.* v. *Biddinger*, 30, 46 (19).

113. *Excessive Verdict.—Erroneous Instruction.—Cure by Remittitur.*—Where, in an action on an accident insurance policy, defendant made no contention that plaintiff was not partially disabled so as to bring him within the stipulation of the policy in respect thereto, an instruction, which erroneously defined the insurer's liability under the total disability provision contained in the policy, could not have been prejudicial to defendant's rights except to the extent that the verdict exceeded what it would have been had the recovery been for partial disability and will be cured by a remittitur of such amount.
*Workingmen's Mutual, etc., Assn.* v. *Roos*, 18, 26 (4).

114. *Verdict.—Conclusiveness.—Conflicting Evidence.* — Where there is a conflict in the evidence, the decision of the trial court is conclusive. *Hartzell* v. *Pranger*, 380, 383 (1).

115. *Verdict.—Answers to Interrogatories.—Presumptions.*—A general verdict for the plaintiff is a finding that every averment of the complaint essential to his cause of action is true, and to support the verdict against a motion for judgment on the answers to interrogatories, the court on appeal must assume as proven every fact provable under any supposable evidence admissible under the issues which in any way tends to support the general verdict, or which tends to reconcile it with the answers to interrogatories. *Chicago, etc., R. Co.* v. *Biddinger*, 30, 44 (15).

(E) HARMLESS ERROR.

116. *Admission of Incompetent Evidence.—Cure by Instruction.* —In an action for injuries sustained by plaintiff falling over a guy wire, error, if any, in permitting witnesses to testify that

**APPEAL—Continued.**

they had, since plaintiff's accident, tripped over the wire in question was cured by an instruction informing the jury that they should not consider such testimony in making up their verdict. *Lafayette Telephone Co.* v. *Cunningham*, 136, 149 (15).

117. *Instruction.*—In an employe's action for personal injuries sustained by the breaking of a drift pin used in the repair of a boiler, a statement in an instruction that the master was bound to furnish safe tools and appliances for his employes to work with, which was a too broad statement of the law as tending to impute that the master was the insurer of the safety of his servants, was harmless where the jury found by answers to interrogatories that the pin provided was not made of proper material and that it was not suitable for the purpose for which it was being used at the time of the accident.
*Central, etc., R. Co.* v. *Clark*, 49, 52 (4).

118. *Misconduct of Counsel.*—Cure by Instruction.—In a bastardy proceeding, alleged misconduct of relatrix' attorney during the argument to the jury in pointing at the child and saying that there could be no question that a child was conceived, "because there's the evidence," even if constituting reversible error when properly presented on appeal, was harmless where the jury was instructed not to consider the appearance of the child, but to decide the case on the oral testimony alone.
*Perry* v. *State*, 653, 660 (6).

119. *Refusal of Requested Instruction.*—Although a requested instruction that the jury could consider and answer the special interrogatories submitted either before or after agreeing upon the general verdict might properly have been given, its refusal was harmless error, where the interrogatories were answered.
*S. W. Little Coal Co.* v. *O'Brien*, 504, 524 (19).

120. *Review.*—Presence of Child in Court.—Instruction.—Any possible harm which might have resulted to the defendant in a bastardy proceeding by the court's action in permitting the relatrix to bring her child into the court room during the trial was cured by an instruction that in passing upon the question whether the defendant was the father of the child, the jury should not take into consideration the appearance of the child's countenance or draw any conclusion whatever from the child's appearance, but should consider only the oral testimony.
*Perry* v. *State*, 653, 658, 659 (3).

121. *Review.*—Refusal of Judge to Sign Bill of Exceptions.—The refusal of the trial judge to sign a bill of exceptions was harmless error, where the questions attempted to be presented by the bill would in no event afford any ground for a reversal of the judgment. *Perry* v. *State*, 653, 662 (11).

122. *Review.*—Withdrawal of Interrogatory.—Where, in an action on a note, the jury answered affirmatively an interrogatory as to whether defendant A signed the note in suit as surety for two of the defendants and by their verdict found that the note was given for a partnership debt of such defendants and was executed by A as surety for them, the withdrawal of an interrogatory, asking whether A agreed with one of the partners that he would stand for the other partner and make

**APPEAL—Continued.**

good one-half of the partnership business, was harmless, especially as even an affirmative answer to such question would not have been in irreconcilable conflict with the general verdict.
*Traylor* v. *McCormick*, 695, 697 (1).

123. *Review.—Instructions.—Consideration.—Misleading Instruction.*—In an action for unlawful appropriation of a tract of real estate and for damages, an instruction that the burden was on defendant to prove by a fair preponderance of the evidence that the material allegations of its several paragraphs of answer which pleaded the different statutes of limitations, while misleading, if standing alone, was not prejudicial to defendant when read in connection with other instructions given by the court on its own motion which covered specifically each paragraph of answer, except that pleading the ten-year statute of limitations.        *Cleveland, etc., R. Co.* v. *Gannon*, 289, 293 (2).

124. *Review.—Instructions.—Burden of Proof.—Preponderance of the Evidence.*—In an action for unlawful appropriation of real estate and for damages, an instruction which informed the jury that the "burden of proof" and the "fair preponderance of the evidence" did not mean that either party must prove any particular fact by a greater number of witnesses than the opposing party, but meant the facts testified to by the witnesses that carried the greater weight, was not prejudicial to defendant as confusing the burden of proof with the preponderance of the evidence, or as excluding documentary evidence from the consideration of the jury, when read in connection with other instructions that "if you find from a fair preponderance of the evidence," and that, in determining whether defendant had been in possession of the real estate in controversy, the jury should consider all the evidence and be governed by a fair preponderance thereof, and to consider, among facts shown by all the evidence, defendant's use of the realty.
*Clevealnd, etc., R. Co.* v. *Gannon*, 289, 294 (3).

125. *Review.—Instructions.—Appropriation of Lands.—Measure of Damages.*—In an action for possession of lands unlawfully appropriated and for damages, an instruction that, if it should be found that defendant unlawfully appropriated the real estate in controversy, the measure of damages would be the value of the land appropriated, while not a correct statement of law, was more favorable to defendant than one could have been embodying the general rule that the measure of damages was the difference in the value of the whole tract of real estate before the alleged appropriation and thereafter, as the defendant was not required by the instruction complained of to answer for any damages that might have resulted to the residue of the land by reason of the taking of a part thereof.
*Cleveland, etc., R. Co.* v. *Gannon*, 289, 295 (4).

126. *Admission of Evidence.—Submission of Issues.—Verdict.—Scope and Effect.*—In an action by a shipper for damages to a shipment of live stock, where the carrier claimed that the shipment was made under a special contract restricting its liability, but the shipper contended that he was allowed to exercise no option as to rates or other conditions of transportation, but was compelled to ship under the special contract or not at all, the general verdict for plaintiff was a finding in his favor on such issue, so that any error by the trial court in the in-

**APPEAL—Continued.**

structions or admissions of evidence relating to such special contract was harmless.

*Chesapeake, etc., R. Co.* v. *Jordan,* 365, 380 (12).

127. *Review.—Admission of Evidence.*—In an action for damages to a shipment of live stock, where the verdict and the jury's answers to the interrogatories showed that the jury found adversely to defendant's contention that the shipment was made under a special contract restricting carrier's liability and that the shipper was bound thereby, the defendant could not have been harmed by the ruling of the trial court, even though erroneous, on certain instructions, the admission of evidence, etc., relating to the provisions of such special contracts.

*Chesapeake, etc., R. Co.* v. *Jordan,* 365, 379 (11).

128. *Ruling on Demurrer.—Want of Memorandum of Defects.*—While it is error for the trial court to sustain a demurrer not accompanied by the memorandum required by statute, yet such ruling is not prejudicial where the pleading attacked is defective in many respects, and in such case the court on appeal will look beyond the mere form of the demurrer to uphold the ruling of the trial court.

*Herald Publishing Co.* v. *State, ex rel.,* 465, 468 (4).

(F) ERROR WAIVED IN APPELLATE COURT.

See APPEAL 72.

129. *Briefs.*—Alleged error in overruling the demurrer to the complaint is waived where appellant's brief fails to address any point or proposition thereto.

*Workingmen's Mutual, etc., Assn.* v. *Roos,* 18, 19 (1).

130. *Briefs.*—Alleged error in the ruling of the trial court on the demurrer to the complaint is waived on appeal by appellant's failure to state any point or proposition relating thereto, or to mention or discuss the same in his brief under the heading of "Points and Authorities," as required by the fifth clause of Rule 22 of the Appellate Court.          *Scott* v. *Baird,* 16, 17 (1).

131. *Briefs.*—An assignment of error predicated on the overruling of the motion for judgment on the interrogatories is waived by failure of appellant to present any point or proposition relating thereto in its brief.

*Chesapeake, etc., R. Co.* v. *Jordan,* 365, 371 (3).

132. *Briefs.*—An assignment of error predicated on the overruling of the demurrer to the complaint is waived by failure to present it in appellant's briefs.     *Smith* v. *Weston,* 268, 269 (1).

133. *Briefs.—Failure to Set Out Proposition in Points and Authorities.*—Alleged error is waived on appeal by failure to set out the proposiiton in appellant's brief under the points and authorities.          *American Car, etc., Co.* v. *Williams,* 1, 4 (1).

(G) SUBSEQUENT APPEALS.

134. *Law of the Case.—Evidence.*—As the opinion in a former appeal is the law of the case on all questions presented and decided therein, where the evidence was held sufficient on such appeal to sustain a verdict for plaintiff for personal injuries, it was error for the court to peremptorily instruct the jury to find for the defendant upon a retrial of the cause in which the evidence was substantially the same as at the former trial, since, where a proposition decided on appeal depends upon a state of facts shown by the evidence, it is controlling until the

**APPEAL—Continued.**

termination of the litigation unless the testimony relating thereto upon a subsequent trial differs in some material respect from that upon which the opinion of the appellate tribunal was based. *Croly* v. *Indianapolis Traction, etc., Co.* 663, 666, 670(3).

### XI. DETERMINATION AND DISPOSITION OF CAUSE.

135. *Joint Exceptions.*—Where the exceptions to conclusions of law are joint, the judgment must be affirmed if any one of such conclusions is correct. *Hypes* v. *Nelson,* 304, 305 (1).

136. *Review.—Overruling Demurrer to Bad Answer.—Reversible Error.*—Overruling a demurrer to a bad answer is reversible error, even though the evidence admissible thereunder might have been presented under a general denial.
*Excel Furniture Co.* v. *Brock,* 494, 498 (1).

**ASSESSMENT—**

See TAXATION.

For public improvements, see MUNICIPAL CORPORATIONS.

**ATTORNEY AND CLIENT—**

*Compensation.—Action.—Jury Question.*—In an action by a client against an attorney for money collected, where the defendant contended that the money sought to be recovered was retained by him, with plaintiff's consent, as a reasonable attorney fee, it was for the jury to determine the amount, if any, due planitiff. *Bosson* v. *Brash,* 86, 89 (2).

**AUDITOR—**

County, certificate of, as to quality of goods, statute, see COUNTIES 2.

**AUTOMOBILES—**

See APPEAL 70.

**BALLOTS—**

Recount, petition, see ELECTIONS.

**BANKRUPTCY—**

1. *Action Against Bankrupt.—Parties.—Substitution of Trustee.*—Where, in an action in replevin, the defendant, a bankrupt, counterclaimed for a breach of warranty originating prior to his bankruptcy, it was proper for the trial court to substitute defendant's trustee in bankruptcy as a party to prosecute such claim, since it passed to the trustee by reason of the bankruptcy proceedings and he was, therefore, the real party in interest. *Crouch* v. *Fahl,* 257, 268 (6).

2. *Sale of Mortgaged Property.—Purchase by Mortgagor.—Lien of Mortgages.*—Where a buyer of personal property secured the purchase price by a chattel mortgage authorizing the mortgagee to take possession in case of default, and upon the mortgagor becoming bankrupt, the mortgaged property was scheduled as a part of his assets, the purchase by the mortgagor of the mortgaged chattel at the sale in bankruptcy did not defeat the mortgagee's right to recover the property, since the sale could only be made subject to the lien of the mortgage.
*Crouch* v. *Fahl,* 257, 267 (5).

## BASTARDS—

See APPEAL 18.

1. *Proceeding.—Presence of Child in Court.*—The mere fact that during the trial of a paternity suit the mother was permitted by the court, over the objection of the defendant, to have her child with her in the court room where the jury might see it affords no cause for a reversal.
*Perry* v. *State,* 653, 657 (2).

2. *Parentage of Child.—Evidence.—Sufficiency.*—In a bastardy proceeding, evidence by the relatrix that the only occasion upon which she ever had intercourse was with the defendant on a certain date, which was corroborated by the testimony of other witnesses that the defendant had admitted the act of intercourse, and by the attending physician that relatrix had given birth to a fully developed child after the usual period of gestation had elapsed, was sufficient to warrant a finding that the defendant was the father of relatrix's child, even though the evidence adduced at the trial was conflicting.
*Perry* v. *State,* 653, 656 (1).

3. *Inheritance.—Adoption.—Legitimate Child.—Statutes.*—Under §§870, 871 Burns 1914, §§825, 826 R. S. 1881, providing that an adopted child shall be entitled to receive the same rights and interest in the estate of the adopting parent by descent or otherwise that it would if the natural heir, and that the adopting parent shall occupy the same position toward such child as a natural father or mother, an adopted child, by virtue of the statute, stands in the same relation to the estate of the adopting parent as a legitimate child, and must be regarded as such, and, when such child survives, the right of an illegitimate child to inherit the estate of the father under §3000 Burns 1914, Acts 1901 p. 288, providing that where any man acknowledges an illegitimate child as his own, such child shall inherit from his estate, unless a legitimate child or descendants of legitimate children survive, is barred. *Cooley* v. *Powers,* 59, 61 (2).

4. *Inheritance.—Statute.—Construction.*—Section 3000 Burns 1914, Acts 1901 p. 288, provides only for a contingent right of inheritance in some instances in the illegitimate child, and cannot be construed to include the children or descendants of such illegitimate child. *Cooley* v. *Powers,* 59, 63 (3).

## BENEFITS—

As constituting ratification, see PRINCIPAL AND AGENT.

Insurance, action to recover, instruction, presumption, see APPEAL 93.

Loss of prospective, see DEATH.

## BILLS AND NOTES—

*Promissory Note—Construction.—Negotiablity.*—An instrument promising to pay, for value received, a specified sum of money and containing the expression "negotiable and payable" at a bank named, is a negotiable note, even though it does not contain the words "or order," "or bearer," or other like words of negotiabliity, since the wording of the note clearly shows that it was intended to be negotiable. *Essig* v. *Porter,* 318, 320 (2).

**BONDS—**

See APPEAL 10-14; COSTS; OFFICERS; PARTITION 5; PRINCIPAL AND SURETY; SCHOOLS AND SCHOOL DISTRICTS.

Premium, taxation as part of costs, see COSTS 3.

Of contractors, must be in writing, see FRAUDS, STATUTE OF.

Payable in installmetns, action to foreclose lien, period of limitation, see LIMITATION OF ACTIONS.

**BREACH—**

Of contract, see CONTRACTS; INSURANCE; LANDLORD AND TENANT; SALES.

**BRIEFS—**

See APPEAL 36-51.

**BROKERS—**

See CONTRACTS 4.

1. *Realty Brokers.—Authority.—Duty of Buyer to Ascertain.—* Where parties negotiate with a real estate broker for the purchase of lands, with knowledge that he is acting as the owner's agent, it is their duty to ascertain the nature and extent of the broker's authority and whether he has been empowered to contract in writing for the sale of the lands.
*Crumpacker* v. *Jeffrey*, 621, 634 (10).

2. *Realty Broker.—Authority to Find Purchaser.—Letter.—* A letter from a landowner to a real estate agent stating, "I do not care to sell it even at $350, but will let it go at that price in order to clean up things. If you sell it for $350 per acre, I will allow you two and one-half per cent commission," conferred authority merely to find a purchaser for the land at the price specified, and did not authorize the broker to execute a binding contract of sale in the name of the owner, or to specify in detail the terms of sale. *Crumpacker* v. *Jeffrey*, 621, 629 (2).

3. *Real Estate Broker.—Ratification of Acts.—* Where a real estate broker, without authority from the landowner, made a contract to sell through letters to prospective purchasers, specifying therein definite terms, and the owner, without knowledge of the letters, verbally expressed his entire satisfaction with the terms as reported by the agent, he thereby ratified the act of the broker in specifying and agreeing to such terms.
*Crumpacker* v. *Jeffrey*, 621, 630 (3).

4. *Real Estate Broker.—Ratification of Acts.—Burden of Proof. —Action on Contract for Sale of Lands.—* Where, in an action for damages for breach of contract for the sale of lands, plaintiffs relied on a ratification by defendant of the act of his agent in entering into the contract, the burden was on them to prove the fact of ratification, and evidence to that end would not be effective unless it established that defendant had knowledge of the material facts. *Crumpacker* v. *Jeffrey*, 621, 632 (7).

5. *Unauthorized Acts.—Ratification.—Knowledge.—* The nature of a ratification of an agent's unauthorized acts by the principal is such that knowledge of the material facts is a necessary element of its existence, and without such knowledge there cannot be an effectual ratification. *Crumpacker* v. *Jeffrey*, 621, 631 (6).

**BROKERS—Continued.**

6. *Ratification of Unauthorized Act.—Evidence.—Sufficiency.—* In an action for damages for breach of contract for the sale of land, where plaintiffs relied on defendant's ratification of his agent's unauthorized act in executing the contract, embodying specific terms, the evidence is held insufficient to establish a ratification. *Crumpacker* v. *Jeffrey*, 621, 632 (8).

7. *Ratification of Unauthorized Act.—Agent's Letter.—Principal's Liability.—*Where a landowner, whose agent had without authority made a contract, by letter, to sell land, knew that the agent had written a letter to the prospective purchasers, presumably relating to the sale, such owner is not chargeable with knowledge of the contents of the letter, so as to constitute a ratification of the agent's unauthorized act, where it appears that the owner, after being informed by the agent that he had not executed a written contract but had written a letter, asked to see a copy of it but it could not be found and the agent then agreed to obtain a copy and deliver it to the owner, who thereafter did not receive any information respecting the letter's contents until a copy was delivered to him shortly before an action was commenced for a breach of the purported contract, since such facts show that the owner did not wilfully remain ignorant respecting the existence of a written contract, or that he had purposely failed to prosecute an inquiry. *Crumpacker* v. *Jeffrey*, 621, 633 (9).

**BURDEN OF PROOF—**

See APPEAL 124; BROKERS 4; CONTRACTS 1; EMINENT DOMAIN; MASTER AND SERVANT 16; MINES AND MINERALS 1; MUNICIPAL CORPORATIONS 9; PRINCIPAL AND AGENT 2; TAXATION 6.

**CANCELLATION OF INSTRUMENTS—**

See ESTOPPEL 2; EXECUTORS AND ADMINISTRATORS 7-10; INSURANCE 25.

*Deeds.— Action.— Complaint.— Sufficiency.— Duress.— Consideration.—*In an action to cancel and set aside a deed alleged to have been executed by plaintiff under duress, a complaint averring that plaintiff conveyed certain lots to defendant to prevent his carrying out threats to prosecute her husband for a criminal offense, "and for no other purpose or consideration whatever," and that by the threats and promises of defendant she was coerced, put in fear and induced to convey her property, and not otherwise, sufficiently shows, under the rules of pleading, that no consideration was paid for the property, although there was no specific allegation to that effect, and that through fear plaintiff was deprived of her free agency in making the conveyance. *Denney* v. *Reber*, 192, 198 (3).

**CARRIERS—**

See APPEAL 126; COURTS 4; SALES 9-11.

1. *Carriage of Passengers.—Action for Wrongful Ejectment.— Evidence.—Admissibility.—Res Gestae.—*In an action against an interurban railroad for wrongful ejectment, the statement made to plaintiff by the conductor on the occasion of the occurrence involved, concerning fares charged by defendant, was admissible as part of the res gestae. *Brown* v. *Terre Haute, etc., Traction Co.*, 327, 337 (3).

## CARRIERS—Continued.

2. *Carriage of Passengers.—Action for Wrongful Ejectment.—
Passenger Fares.—Splitting up Journey.—Instructions.—Statutes.*—Section 1 of the act of 1911 (Acts 1911 p. 545), §§3,
cl. g, 7, 13 and 14, cls. a, b, of the act of 1907 (Acts 1907 p.
454) only make it unlawful for a carrier to charge or collect
any rate or tariff different from that fixed in the tariff schedule
or by the use of any special rate, rebate, etc., to demand or receive from any person a greater or less fare than it charges any
other person for like transporation, and forbids the acceptance
by any person or firm of a rebate, but such statutes do not prohibit a passenger from making his journey by stages, regardless of his motive for so doing, and when a carrier offers the
traveling public both a local and a through tariff in the duly
published schedules, and the sum of the local fares between any
two points on the carrier's line is less than the through rate, a
passenger, although he cannot elect at the commencement of
his journey to pay the sum of the local fares for a through
passage, may make his journey by stages in order to get the
benefit of the local tariffs, and it is the duty of the carrier to
accept a fare to any regular stopping point that a passenger
may indicate; hence, in an action against an interurban railroad for wrongful ejectment instructions stating that one becoming a passenger is obligated to pay the through fare to the
final destination intended when boarding a car is erroneous as
making the passenger's original intention controlling, and depriving him of the right to change his destination.
   *Brown* v. *Terre Haute, etc., Traction Co.,* 327, 337, 346 (4).

3. *Carriage of Passengers.—Passenger Fares.—Local and
Through Fares.—Duty of Carrier.*—Where a passenger on an
interurban railroad when first approached by the conductor indicated a desire to contract for a through passage to a certain
station on the carrier's line, but upon learning the amount of
the through fare expressed his intention to contract for transportation to an intermediate stop and tendered the fare to such
point, the conductor should have received the same and carried
him to such intermediate stop, even though the passenger's purpose was to obtain the benefit of the scheduled local fares,
which aggregated less than the through fare to the destination
originally named by him.
   *Brown* v. *Terre Haute, etc., Traction Co.,* 327, 345 (5).

4. *Carriage of Passengers.—Action for Wrongful Ejectment.—
Splitting of Journey.—Evidence.*—Where a passenger on an
interurban railroad has the right to make his journey by stages
and to pay the local fares between the various stops, evidence,
in an action for wrongful ejectment, that the passenger alighted at the point to which the first local fare covered his transportation is of no controlling importance, except as part of
plaintiff's conduct tending to show that he stood on his right
to take advantage of the local fares, which aggregated less than
the through fare to his destination.
   *Brown* v. *Terre Haute, etc., Traction Co.,* 327, 345 (6).

5. *Carriage of Passengers.—Action for Wrongful Ejectment.—
Trial.—Instructions.—Retention of Fare.*—A conductor on an
interurban car is not authorized to eject a passenger for failure
to pay the proper fare while retaining the fare tendered by the
passenger, so that, in an action for wrongful ejectment, instructions purporting to state facts which would justify defendant

**CARRIERS—Continued.**

in ejecting plaintiff from its car, but ignoring evidence tending to prove that the conductor had received and retained the fare tendered by plaintiff, are erroneous.

*Brown* v. *Terre Haute, etc., Traction Co.,* 327, 346 (7).

6. *Carriage of Passengers.—Local and Through Fares.—Election by Passenger.—Discrimination.—*Where a railroad's published schedule of fares offers to the traveling public two different fares, one a local and the other a through fare, each having the same legal sanction and authority, a passenger may elect which fare he will take, and, where the carrier permits one passenger to contract for a through passage at the through rate, and another for local passage at the local rate, it is not guilty of discrimination, although the aggregate of the local fares between two points on the carrier's line may be less than the through fare for the same journey.

*Brown* v. *Terre Haute, etc., Traction Co.,* 327, 348 (8).

7. *Carriage of Passengers.—Action for Wrongful Ejectment.—Fares.—Evidence.—*Where a carrier's published schedules of fares, as filed with the Railroad Commission, fixed the fare from A to B at ten cents, from A to C at twenty cents, and from B to C at five cents, the schedules not mentioning two stops between B and C, known as stops Nos. 8 and 9, and when passengers boarded trains at other than established fare points, authorized the collection of five cents to the first fare point plus the fare from the first fare point to the destination, while a supplementary schedule fixed the fare at fifteen cents between A and stop No. 8, but fixed no fare between such stop and any other station, such schedule did not definitely or certainly establish the fare between stops No. 9 and B, so that, in an action against the carrier for wrongful ejectment, evidence was admissible to show the fare actually charged by defendant between such points on the day in question for the purpose of ascertaining the interpretation and construction placed on the schedules by the carrier.

*Brown* v. *Terre Haute, etc., Traction Co.,* 327, 335, 336 (1).

8. *Carriage of Goods.—Interstate Shipment.—Action for Damages.—Common-law Liability.—*There may be a cause of action under the common law against a common carrier for its negligence or wrongful acts resulting in damages to an interstate shipper, although there is a federal statute governing interstate shipments. *Chesapeake, etc., R. Co.* v. *Jordan,* 365, 370 (1).

9. *Carriage of Goods.—Action for Damages.—Defenses.—*Under §8592, cl. 11, U. S. Comp. St. 1913, 34 Stat. at Large p. 595, providing that every common carrier receiving property for transportation from one state to another shall issue a receipt or bill of lading therefor and shall be liable to the lawful holder thereof for any loss or damage to such shipment, the duty is imposed on the carrier of issuing a receipt or bill of lading for an interstate shipment of freight, and, in an action for damages thereto, it cannot predicate a defense on its failure to issue the receipt required by the statute.

*Chesapeake, etc., R. Co.* v. *Jordan,* 365, 371 (2).

10. *Carriage of Goods.—Limiting Liability.—Special Contracts.*—Notwithstanding the federal statute governing interstate shipments common carriers may make contracts whereby they limit and define the extent of their liability for interstate shipments under specified conditions, but such carriers cannot, by

## CARRIERS—Continued.

contract, relieve themselves from liability for damages caused by their negligence or that of their employes.

*Chesapeake, etc., R. Co. v. Jordan,* 365, 375 (4).

11. *Carriage of Goods.—Shipping Under Oral Agreement.*—If a bill of lading is not furnished a shipper until after the goods are fully accepted by the carrier under an oral agreement, the bill of lading constitutes no part of the contract and the oral agreement controls.

*Chesapeake, etc., R. Co. v. Jordan,* 365, 379 (10).

12. *Carriage of Live Stock.—Action for Damages.—Evidence.*— In an action against a common carrier for damages to a shipment of live stock, evidence that on a few occasions prior to the transaction in controversy plaintiff had shipped live stock under a special contract limiting the carrier's liability, but that the contracts were procured at the time of the shipment and that in some instances bills of lading had been obtained after shipments were made, was insufficient to show the establishment of a custom, as claimed by defendant, permitting the carrier, where a shipment of live stock was made under an oral agreement, to issue to the shipper several months thereafter a special contract restricting its liability as to such shipment.

*Chesapeake, etc., R. Co. v. Jordan,* 365, 377 (9).

13. *Carriage of Live Stock.—Damages.—Liability.—Limiting by Special Contract.*—Where, in an action against a common carrier for damages to an interstate shipment of live stock, the defendant answered that its liability was limited by a special contract issued and accepted by the shipper several months after the shipment and payment of the freight charges, no receipt or bill of lading having been issued at the time of the shipment, the acceptance of the special contract under such circumstances was without consideration unless it was in accordance with a custom, as claimed by defendant, established by prior similar transactions between the parties.

*Chesapeake, etc., R. Co. v. Jordan,* 365, 376 (7).

## CASES—

For cases cited in this volume, see p. vi.

Distinguished, see STATUTES 1; APPEAL 59.

Disapproved, see EVIDENCE 2.

## CERTIORARI—

Writ of, when necessary, see APPEAL 20.

## CHATTEL MORTGAGES—

*Remedies of Mortgagee.—Replevin.—Sale of Property.—Application of Proceeds.*—Where a buyer of personal property gives notes for the purchase price secured by a chattel mortgage authorizing the mortgagee to take possession on default, the mortgagee may, upon failure to pay the notes, maintain an action in replevin to regain possession of the mortgaged chattel and, having thus acquired possession, could cause the property to be sold, purchase the same at the sale, and apply the proceeds to the discharge of the notes.     *Crouch v. Fahl,* 257, 267 (4).

## CHILD—

See ADOPTION; BASTARDS.

**COLLATERAL ATTACK—**

On settlement in decedent's estate, effect, see EXECUTORS AND ADMINISTRATORS 1; GUARDIAN AND WARD 2.

**COLLATERAL SECURITY—**

See INSURANCE 13-15.

**COLLUSION—**

In bidding for public contracts, statute, see DRAINS.
Relief from, where legal remedy is inefficient, see INJUNCTION.

**COMMERCE—**

*Interstate Shipments.—Federal Legislation.*—Where shipments of freight are interstate, the state law is superseded by the federal statutes relating to interstate commerce as to all questions of liability or defense covered by such statutes.
*Chesapeake, etc., R. Co.* v. *Jordan,* 365, 375 (5).

**COMMISSION—**

See INSURANCE 3.
For sale of land, see CONTRACTS 4.

**COMMISSIONERS—**

Board of, see COUNTIES.

**COMMON LAW—**

See CARRIERS 8.

**COMPENSATION—**

Money collected by attorney, action by client to recover, jury question, see ATTORNEY AND CLIENT.

**COMPETITION—**

Unfair, see TRADE-MARKS AND TRADE-NAMES.

**COMPLAINT—**

See PLEADING.
Challenge of, for first time on petition for rehearing, effect, see APPEAL 61.
Challenge of, demurrer, scope of review, see APPEAL 73.

**CONCLUSIONS—**

Of law, see APPEAL; TRIAL; PLEADING 3, 4.
Of law, in master commissioner's report, effect, see APPEAL 109.

**CONDITIONS—**

See DEEDS; PRINCIPAL AND SURETY 3; SALES 8.

Precedent, to suit by stockholder on behalf of corporation, see CORPORATIONS 5-7.

**CONSIDERATION—**

See CANCELLATION OF INSTRUMENTS; CONTRACTS; EXECUTORS AND ADMINISTRATORS; INSURANCE 15, 18.

**CONSTRUCTION—**

See CONTRACTS; COURTS; DRAINS 2; EXECUTION; EXECUTORS AND ADMINISTRATORS; INSURANCE 3, 11, 12; LANDLORD AND TENANT.

**CONSTRUCTIVE FRAUD—**

See EXECUTORS AND ADMINISTRATORS 6.

**CONTRACTORS—**

See PRINCIPAL AND SURETY.

Bonds of, must be in writing, see FRAUDS, STATUTE OF.

Independent, see MASTER AND SERVANT.

**CONTRACTS—**

See BROKERS; CARRIERS; CANCELLATION OF INSTRUMENTS; CHATTEL MORTGAGE; DAMAGES; DRAINS; FRAUDS, STATUTE OF; INSURANCE; LANDLORD AND TENANT; MECHANIC'S LIENS; MORTGAGES; MUNICIPAL CORPORATIONS; PATENTS; PLEDGES; PRINCIPAL AND AGENT; PRINCIPAL AND SURETY; SALES; VENDOR AND PURCHASER.

1. *Action for Breach.—Burden of Proof.*—In an action based on a parol contract recovery must be under the terms of the contract, and the burden is on the plaintiff to prove every material part thereof substantially as alleged in the complaint.
*Welty* v. *Taylor,* 674, 682 (8).

2. *Action for Breach.—Refusal of Interrogatories.*—In an action for a breach of a parol contract, it was proper for the court to refuse to submit interrogatories requested by defendant, where they did not relate to issuable facts, and the answers thereto could not have aided the defendant, but would necessarily have been treated as surplusage relating to immaterial questions.
*Welty* v. *Taylor,* 674, 683 (9).

8. *Construction.*—When a contract is to be interpreted or when the effect of some separate provision thereof is involved, separate clauses and provisions will not be considered apart from the genearl context or apart from connected clauses, but the meaning of the entire contract and of each of its clauses will be determined from all the language used, and the parties will be held to have intended that meaning to each clause which makes the whole contract consistent, and which is reasonable in view of all the terms employed.
*Nat. Fire Proofing Co.* v. *Imperishable Silo Co.* 183, 189 (3).

4. *Construction.—Commission for Sale of Land.*—Where a complaint predicates the right of recovery on an alleged parol contract providing that plaintiff should receive as compensation for his services in fertilizing an unproductive farm any excess of the market value of the land over a stipulated figure, such complaint did not seek to recover a commission for procuring a purchaser for the real estate, and the cause of action did not therefore come within the prohibition of §7463 Burns 1914, Acts 1913 p. 638, providing that contracts for commissions for the sale of land must be in writing.
*Welty* v. *Taylor,* 674, 679 (2).

## CONTRACTS—Continued.

5. *Construction.—"Fair Market Value of Land."*—The fair market value of land is the price it would probably bring after fair and reasonable negotiations where the owner is willing to sell but not compelled to do so, and the buyer desires to purchase but is under no necessity of obtaining the property.
*Welty* v. *Taylor*, 674, 680 (5).

6. *Contracts in Writing.—Ambiguities.—Intention.—Parol Evidence.*—If the language, or any portion thereof, used in a written contract is ambiguous or of uncertain meaning or application, parol evidence may be heard not to vary or contradict the writings, but to ascertain the sense in which the language was used and its application to the subject-matter of the contract, to determine the true intention of the parties at the time the contract was entered into, and, in ascertaining such intention, the court will, if necessary, consider the relation and situation of the parties, the character of the transaction and all the surroundings and conditions attending the execution of the contract. *Robbins* v. *Brazil Syndicate, etc., Co.*, 455, 463 (6).

7. *Contracts in Writing.—Construction.—Intention.*—Where a contract is in writing and the language employed is unambiguous, it must be so interpreted as to carry into effect the intention of the parties as expressed by the writings.
*Robbins* v. *Brazil Syndicate, etc., Co.*, 455, 463 (5).

8. *Construction.—Parol Evidence.—Ambiguity.*—Unless the court can say from a consideration of the entire contract that a clause contained therein is ambiguous, resort cannot be had to extrinsic facts to determine its meaning.
*Nat. Fire Proofing Co.* v. *Imperishable Silo Co.*, 183, 189 (1).

9. *Parol Contract.—Construction.*—Where the question of the construction of a parol contract arises on the complaint, the intention of the parties at the time they entered into the alleged contract must be determined from a consideration of all the averments which set forth the agreement.
*Welty* v. *Taylor*, 674, 680 (3).

10. *Validity.—Duress.—Evidence.*—In determining the question of duress courts consider the age, sex, capacity, situation and relation of the parties and all the attending circumstances which throw any light upon the particular transaction under investigation. *Denney* v. *Reber*, 192, 199 (5).

11. *Validity.—Execution.—Duress.*—Duress is a species of fraud in which compulsion in some form takes the place of deception in accomplishing the injury, and where a deed, mortage, or note is obtained from the wife upon a threat to prosecute, arrest or imprison her husband, the instrument so procured is voidable by the wife. *Denney* v. *Reber*, 192, 198 (4).

## CONTRIBUTORY NEGLIGENCE—
See MASTER AND SERVANT; NEGLIGENCE.

## COPARTIES—
Appeal by, notice, construction of statute, see APPEAL 5.

## CORPORATIONS—
See CARRIERS; INSURANCE; MUNICIPAL CORPORATIONS; RAILROADS; RECEIVERS; STREET RAILROADS; TELEGRAPHS AND TELEPHONES.
Acts of officers, ratification, see PRINCIPAL AND AGENT.

## CORPORATIONS—Continued.

## CORPORATIONS—Continued.

relations of the corporation with third persons only in cases in which appear one or more of the following conditions: (a) some action, or threatened action, by the board of directors or trustees, beyond their power; (b) a fraudulent transaction, contemplated or completed by the acting managers, in connection with some other party or among themselves causing injury to the corporation or stockholders; (c) action by the board of directors or a majority of them in their own interest, and in a manner destructive of the corporation or the rights of other stockholders; (d) where a majority of the stockholders are illegally or oppressively pursuing a course in the name of the corporation which is in violation of the right of other stockholders, and can be restrained only by a court of equity.
*Marcovich v. O'Brien, Auditor*, 101, 111 (2).

8. *Stockholders.—Suing or Defending Action in Behalf of Corporation.*—As a general rule, the stockholders of a corporation, for the purposes of all litigation growing out of the relations of the corporation and a third person, surrender their personal or individual entity to the corporation, and when it is properly in court, the stockholders are also in court so far as is necessary for the purpose of adjudicating all matters incident to the issues between such corporation and other parties litigant, and it is only in exceptional cases that stockholders will be permitted to sue or defend a suit for and on behalf of themselves as stockholders of such corporation.
*Marcovich v. O'Brien, Auditor*, 101, 111 (1).

9. *Stockholders.—Suing or Defending Actions in Behalf of Corporation.—Corporation in Receiver's Hands.*—The rules governing stockholders of a corporation in bringing actions originally, for and in behalf of themselves, apply where the corporation is insolvent and its affairs are being managed and settled through a receiver appointed by, and acting under, the direction and orders of the court.
*Marcovich v. O'Brien, Auditor*, 101, 112 (5).

## COSTS—

1. *Bond.—Permission to Sue as a Poor Person.—Nonresidence of Plaintiff.*—A party granted the right to prosecute an action as a poor person under §261 Burns 1914, §260 R. S. 1881, relating to the appointment of attorneys for persons without means to prosecute or defend actions, cannot be required to give a bond for costs because he thereafter becomes a nonresident of the state. *Haehnel v. Seidentopf*, 218, 220 (1).

2. *Bond.—Permission to Sue as a Poor Person.—Nonresidence of Plaintiff.—Ruling of Trial Court.—Presumption.*—In the absence of an assignment of error challenging the action of the trial court in permitting plaintiff, after a motion had been filed to require him to furnish a cost bond because he was a resident of another state, to prosecute his suit as a poor person, it will be assumed on appeal that the ruling of the trial court was proper, and it was not, therefore, error to overrule the motion for a bond for costs. *Haehnel v. Seidentopf*, 218, 221 (3).

3. *Bond.—Premiums.—Taxation.—Statutes.*—Section 7 of the act of 1897 (§5728 et seq. Burns 1914, Acts 1897 p. 192, 196), which, after authorizing a receiver, etc., to include as part of the expense of executing his trust, money paid to a corporate surety company for becoming surety on his bond, provides that

## COSTS—Continued.

in all actions or proceedings the party entitled to recover costs may include such reasonable sum as may have been paid a surety company by such party for executing any bond therein, allows all litigants who are entitled to recover costs to have taxed as a part thereof premiums paid to surety companies for the execution of bonds or undertakings required in the action.
*Jose* v. *Hunter*, 298, 303 (3).

## COUNSEL—

See ATTORNEY AND CLIENT.

Misconduct of, bill of exceptions, review, see APPEAL 18, 75, 76.

## COUNTIES—

1. *Claims.—Partial Allowance.—Acceptance.—Effect.*—Where a bill against a county is allowed in part by the board of county commissioners and the part so allowed is accepted and receipted for by the claimant, the acceptance is a settlement or determination of the claim.
*Herald Publishing Co.* v. *State, ex rel.*, 465, 468 (3).

2. *Illegal Payments.—Recovery.—Auditor's Certificate.—Statutes.*—Under §§5955, 5962 Burns 1914, Acts 1899 pp. 343, 357, 362, a claim against a county must be accompanied by a certificate from the auditor showing that the quality of the goods furnished and the price corresponded with the provisions of the contract under which they were purchased, and money paid by a county on claims not so certified to may be recovered by it.
*Herald Publishing Co.* v. *State, ex rel.*, 465, 467 (2).

## COURTS—

See JUDGES; JUSTICES OF THE PEACE; TRIAL.

Rules, on appeal, see APPEAL 36-51, 55.

Action of trial courts, presumptions on appeal, see APPEAL 87-94.

Discretion of, see APPEAL 95.

Juvenile courts, see APPEAL 17, 32, 97, 98; INFANTS.

1. *Rules of Court.—Effect.*—The rules of the court have the force and effect of law, binding alike upon litigants and the court.
*Bingham, Rec.,* v. *Newtown Bank,* 606, 610 (3).

2. *Appellate Jurisdiction. — Statutes. — Construction. —* Under §1389 Burns 1914, Acts 1903, p. 280, providing that appeals shall not be taken to the Supreme or Appellate Courts in any civil case where the amount in controversy, exclusive of interest and costs, does not exceed $50, except as provided in §1391 Burns 1914, Acts 1901 p. 565, declaring that in every case where the question of the validity or proper construction of a statute is presented, and which case would be otherwise unappealable under §1389 Burns 1914, shall be appealable directly to the Supreme Court, and the Appellate Court has no jurisdiction in a case where the judgment appealed from is less than $50, and such case is appealable to the Supreme Court for the sole and express purpose of procuring the construction of a statute.
*Greer* v. *Lake,* 470.

3. *Superior.—Jurisdiction.—Setting Aside Order for New Trial Made by Circuit Court.*—Where an order for a new trial as a matter of right was made by the Grant Circuit Court and the cause was thereafter transferred to the Grant Superior Court on change of venue, the latter had authority to inquire into the

**COURTS—Continued.**

correctness of the order for a new trial and to vacate the same if improperly granted. *Trook* v. *Trook*, 272, 278, 279 (4).

4. *Jurisdiction of State Courts.—Interstate Commerce.—Carriage of Goods.—Action for Damages.*—Although there are federal statutes governing the liability of common carriers for interstate shipments of freight, the state courts are not thereby deprived of jurisdiction in actions for damages to such shipments, for the federal law is a part of the law of the state and, in such actions, may be applied by the state courts and the relief warranted given.
*Chesapeake, etc., R. Co.* v. *Jordan*, 365, 375 (6).

**CREDITORS—**

Allowances to by receiver, remedies of stockholders, see CORPORATIONS 3.

**CRIMINAL LAW—**

Appeal from juvenile court, procedure and rules, see APPEAL 17, 32, 97, 98; INFANTS.

**CROSS-COMPLAINT—**

See PLEADING.

**CROSSINGS—**

See RAILROADS.

**DAMAGES—**

See CARRIERS; COURTS 4; DEATH.

Measure of, in alienation action, see HUSBAND AND WIFE 1.

Measure of, for wrongful cutting of timber, see TRESPASS.

Excessive, presenting question, see APPEAL 65.

1. *Contracts.—Action for Breach.—Excessive Damages.*—Where plaintiff, in an action for money due on a parol contract, contended that he was to receive, as compensation for certain services in the development of a farm, the market value of the land in excess of $70,000, a verdict for plaintiff for $3,500 is not excessive where the evidence sustains the jury's finding that the market value of the land was $73,500 and also the general verdict. *Welty* v. *Taylor*, 674, 683 (10).

2. *Medical Expenses of Minor.—Liability of Father.*—While a father is liable for necessaries furnished to a minor child, such as a physician's services, yet such obligation is also the debt of the minor, and he may recover for his medical expenses in an action for personal injuries.
*Central, etc., R. Co.* v. *Clark*, 49, 53 (10).

3. *Personal Injuries.—Medical Expenses of Minor.*—In an action by an infant for personal injuries, where there was testimony that the physician attending plaintiff had made a certain charge for his services, but it was not in evidence to whom the charge was made, it was not improper to allow plaintiff to recover for medical expenses.
*Central, etc., R. Co.* v. *Clark*, 49, 53 (9).

4. *Personal Injuries.—Diminished Earning Capacity.—Instruction.*—In an action for personal injuries, an instruction that

**DAMAGES—Continued.**

the jury should consider, in assessing damages, plaintiff's diminished earning capacity, due to his injuries, was proper.
*Central, etc., R. Co. v. Clark*, 49, 53 (8).

**DEATH—**

*Action for Wrongful Death.—Damages.—Loss of Prospective Benefits.*—Damages, in case of wrongful death, may be the loss by the beneficiary of any pecuniary benefit which he might reasonably have expected to receive by gift during the lifetime of the deceased, so that it is competent, in an action for the death by negligence for the benefit of the parents and brothers and sisters, to show decedent's earnings and that he gave a large part thereof to his parents and their children for their maintenance and support.
*Vandalia Coal Co. v. Ringo, Admr.*, 323, 326 (2).

**DECEDENTS—**

See EXECUTORS AND ADMINISTRATORS; WILLS.

Estates of, appeal, perfection of, see APPEAL 12.

**DECISION—**

Meaning of, as used in statute, see APPEAL 71.

**DEEDS—**

See CANCELLATION OF INSTRUMENTS; ESTOPPEL 2; MUNICIPAL CORPORATIONS 10.

Copies as evidence, certification, see APPEAL 107.

Tax deeds, *prima facie* evidence, see TAXATION 6.

Tax deed, execution to cotenant, effect, see TENANCY IN COMMON.

1. *Delivery.—Conditions.—Validity.*—Where a grantor delivered a deed to his grantee conditioned only on its return if a loan was not secured on the land, and the condition was satisfied by the grantee, he was in rightful possession of the deed with no authority in the grantor to recall it.
*Wilson v. Jinks*, 615, 618 (2).

2. *Delivery.—Validity.—Recording.*—Where there is a valid and effective delivery of a warranty deed to the grantee by the grantor the title passes regardless of whether the purchase money is paid or secured, and such deed may be recorded without the further express consent of the grantor.
*Wilson v. Jinks*, 615, 618 (1).

3. *Delivery in Escrow.—Effect.*—Where a deed or written obligation is placed in escrow with the grantee, payee or obligee thereof, the conditions imposed become inoperative and invalid and the delivery is thereby made absolute and unconditional.
*Wilson v. Jinks*, 615, 619 (4).

4. *Delivery.—Intent of Grantor.*—The intention of the grantor to give effect to a deed is essential to a valid delivery, and if such intention is clearly shown the means by which it is established and made effective are not of controlling importance.
*Wilson v. Jinks*, 615, 618 (3).

5. *Validity.—Presumption.*—A deed fair and valid upon its face is evidence of an honest transaction, and until it is assailed by evidence, effective as proof, that it was obtained by the fraud of the grantee, he is not required to adduce any evidence in its support.
*Greathouse v. Harrison*, 295, 100 (2).

DEFAULT—

Motion to set aside, appeal, effect, see APPEAL 3.

DELINQUENT CHILDREN—

See INFANTS; JUVENILE COURTS.

DELIVERY—

Of deed on condition, fulfillment of condition, effect, see DEEDS.

DEMURRER—

See PLEADING.

Sustaining, when appealable, see APPEAL 4.

To complaint, failure of memorandum to state grounds of insufficiency, effect on appeal, see APPEAL 64, 128.

Overruling, waiver of error, see APPEAL 129, 130.

Overruling of, to bad answer, reversible error, see APPEAL 91, 136.

DISCRETION OF COURT—

See PLEADING 1; TRIAL.

Order of receiving evidence, see APPEAL 95.

DISCRIMINATION—

See CARRIERS 6.

DOGS—

Live stock killed by, liability of township, procedure, see ANIMALS.

DRAINS—

1. *Cleaning Ditch.—Expenses.—Action to Enjoin Collection.—Complaint.—Sufficiency.*—In an action to enjoin a county treasurer from collecting, under §6152 *et seq.* Burns 1914, Acts 1907 pp. 527, 600, relating to the repair and cleaning of ditches, the expenses of cleaning out a landowner's allotment of a public ditch, where the complaint alleges that the landowner had been notified by the township trustee to clean and repair according to the original specifications certain sections of a ditch which had been regularly alloted to him, that within the time specified in the notice the work alloted was completed in conformity with the specifications, and that the trustee, after notice of the performance of the work, accepted it as completed in accordance with the specifications, such complaint is sufficient as against objections that it does not sufficiently allege the acceptance of the work by the trustee as completed by the landowner, or when the work was done by him, or that he completed the work according to the requirements of the notice given bv the trustee, and that the contents of the notice were not disclosed.

*Bueter* v. *Aulbach,* 91, 92 (1).

2. *Construction.—Contract.—Action to Annul.—Necessary Parties.*—In an action under the act of 1907, Acts 1907 p. 490, §§3866-3877 Burns 1914, by the State, on the relation of a taxpayer, to have a contract for the construction of a public drain declared void and to enjoin the parties to the contract from the performance thereof, the persons assessed for the improvement were not necessary party defendants, under §269 Burns

**DRAINS—Continued.**

1914, §262 R. S. 1881, providing that any person may be made
a defendant who has, or claims, any interest in the controversy
adverse to the plaintiff, or who is a necessary party to the
complete determination or settlement of the questions involved,
since the persons so assessed were not parties to the contract,
and could not have prevented the relator obtaining the relief
sought, if he had brought himself within the provisions of the
statute, and as they neither had nor claimed any interest adverse to the right asserted by the relator they were not necessary parties to the determination of the questions involved in
the suit.                              *Royer* v. *State, ex rel.* 123, 135 (11).

3. *Construction.—Objection to Contract.—Collusion and Fraud.
—Legislative Power.*—It was the province of the legislature
to designate who may institute and maintain the actions contemplated by the act of 1907 (Acts 1907 p. 490, §§3866-3877
Burns 1914), prohibiting fraud and collusion in the bidding for
public work, and a taxpayer and property owner whose property is assessable for a drainage improvement is within the
purview of the statute.               *Royer* v. *State, ex rel.* 123, 130 (2).

4. *Establishment.—Injunction.—Laches.—Public Interest.—Statute.*—In an action by the State, on the relation of a taxpayer,
to annul the contract for the construction of a public drain, to
enjoin the collection of assessments for the improvement and
the payment of money by the drainage commissioner to the
contractor, the remedy invoked under the statutes, §§3866-3877
Burns 1914, Acts 1907 p. 490, directed to the prevention of
collusion and fraud in bidding for public contracts, was not intended to be limited to the private rights or interests of the
taxpayer, but to reach all concerned in, or affected by, any particular contract or transaction tainted with fraud or collusion,
and to secure or protect the interests of the public, so that those
violating the statute cannot avoid the provisions thereof by
showing that a party authorized to invoke the remedies afforded by such statute has not acted promptly.
                                       *Royer* v. *State, ex rel.* 123, 133 (9).

5. *Establishment.—Bidding for Contract.—Collusion or Fraud.
—Statute.*—Under the act of 1907 (Acts 1907 p. 490, §§3866-
3877 Burns 1914), directed to the prevention of fraud and collusion in the bidding for contracts for public work, if the successful bidder is a party directly or indirectly to collusion or
fraud, no liability arises against the parties who would otherwise be liable for the work contracted for, as a contract procured in violation of the act is void and unenforcible by the
party who participated in the fraud or collusion by which the
contract was procured, and anything remaining unperformed
under the contract, or the awarding thereof, may be restrained
if suit be instituted for that purpose by any of the persons
designated by the statute, it being clear that the legislature
intended to prevent a person who obtains a contract by fraud
and collusion to derive any benefit therefrom directly or indirectly.                             *Royer* v. *State, ex rel.* 123, 131 (4).

6. *Establishment.—Bidding for Contract.—Collusion or Fraud.
—Remedies.—Statute.*—The purpose of the act of 1907 (Acts
1907 p. 490, §§3866-3877 Burns 1914), relating to combinations
to restrain trade, is to prevent fraud and collusion in the bidding for contracts for public work, and to that end the legislature authorized not only that suits may be maintained by the

**DRAINS—Continued.**

proper persons to restrain violations of the act, but money paid under any contract procured in violation of the statute, before notice of fraud or collusion, may be recovered and that any person who has been injured by the doing of anything prohibited by the act may recover a penalty.

*Royer* v. *State, ex rel.* 123, 131 (3).

7. *Injunction.—Laches.—Public Interest.*—Where fraud and collusion have been employed to procure a contract for the construction of a public drain, the rule as to the effect of laches in dealings between individuals does not apply where public rights are involved. *Royer* v. *State, ex rel.* 123, 132 (8).

**DURESS—**

See CANCELLATION OF INSTRUMENTS; CONTRACTS 10; ESTOPPEL 2.

**EARNING CAPACITY—**

Diminished, as element of damages, see DAMAGES 4.

**EJECTMENT—**

*Findings.—Right of Possession.*—In an action in ejectment, a conclusion of law that plaintiff is entitled to immediate possession, cannot stand where there was no finding of fact that plaintiffs were entitled to possession of the realty in controversy when the suit was begun, and the omission is not cured by a finding that plaintiff was the owner of the real estate in fee simple, since ownership does not necessarily include the right to immediate possession. *Wilson* v. *Jinks*, 615, 619 (5).

**EASEMENTS—**

A fee may exist in an easement.

*Meyer* v. *Pittsburgh, etc., R. Co.*, 156, 162 (1).

**ELECTIONS—**

1. *Petition for Recount.—Dismissal.—Right of Appeal.*—An order dismissing a petition based on §6991 Burns 1914, §4739 R. S. 1881, for a recount of ballots cast for township trustee is not appealable, since the proceedings for a recount is under a special statute (§§6990-6994 Burns 1914, §§4738-4742 R. S. 1881) containing no provision for an appeal.

*Layman* v. *Dixon*, 501, 503 (1).

2. *Recount. — Petition. — Sufficiency. — Statute.* — Under §6990 Burns 1914, §4738 R. S. 1881, relating to proceedings to obtain a recount of ballots cast at an election, where the petition provided for fails to show that the candidate desires to contest the election it is insufficient to invoke the action of the court in the matter, since one seeking the benefit of a statute must bring himself within its terms. *Layman* v. *Dixon*, 501, 504 (2).

**EMINENT DOMAIN—**

*Appropriation of Land.—Action by Owner.—Burden of Proof.—Title.*—In an action for possession of land alleged to have been unlawfully appropriated and for damages, where plaintiff was not in possession of the realty in controversy at the time the action was commenced and had not been for a long time prior thereto, the burden was on him to establish title as alleged.

*Cleveland, etc., R. Co.* v. *Gannon*, 289, 297 (8).

**EMPLOYERS' LIABILITY ACT—**

See MASTER AND SERVANT.

**EQUITY—**

See CANCELLATION OF INSTRUMENTS; FRAUD; INJUNCTION.

*Jurisdiction.—Prevention of Fraud.—*Independent of statute, equity may be invoked to prevent fraud or to deprive a wrong-doer of the benefit of a fraudulent deal or transaction.

*Royer* v. *State, ex rel.* 123, 132 (7).

**ESCROW—**

Delivery in, effect, see DEEDS 3.

**ESTATES—**

See DEEDS; EASEMENTS; EXECUTORS AND ADMINISTRATORS; LANDLORD AND TENANT; TENANCY IN COMMON; WILLS.

**ESTOPPEL—**

See MUNICIPAL CORPORATIONS.

1. *Pleading.—Sufficiency.—*No intendments are made in favor of a plea of estoppel, and it is incumbent on the pleader to plead fully the facts essential to it.

*Hoosier Construction Co.* v. *Seibert,* 594, 603 (6).

2. *Action to Cancel Deed.—Payment of Rent.—*The fact that one claiming to have conveyed property under duress paid her grantee rent to occupy the premises for a time after an agreed judgment, which was not appealed from, for possession of the real estate in controversy had been rendered against her by a justice of the peace, did not estop her from subsequently prosecuting an action against her grantee to have the deed set aside for duress, where both parties had equal knowledge of all the facts in the transaction, and the grantee had not been induced to change his position to his damage by any act of the plaintiff.

*Denney* v. *Reber,* 192, 197 (2).

**EVIDENCE—**

See BURDEN OF PROOF; PRESUMPTION.

For review of ruling on, see APPEAL.

For evidence as to particular facts or issues or in particular actions or proceedings, see also the various specific topics.

Reception of, at trial, see TRIAL.

Statement of account, receipt of as evidence of amount due, see ACCOUNT STATED 1.

1. *Best and Secondary.—Railroad Fares.—Schedules Filed With Railroad Commission.—*A carrier's published schedules of fares as filed with, and approved by, the Railroad Commission, such body being invested with control thereof, are the best and, therefore, the proper evidence by which to prove the established fares between stopping places on the carrier's line.

*Brown* v. *Terre Haute, etc., Traction Co.,* 327, 336 (2).

2. *Judicial Notice.—Civil and School Townships.—*Where it appears that there is in Monroe county a township named Salt Creek township, the court judicially knows that there is also in that county a school corporation known as Salt Creek school township, since §§6404, 6405 Burns 1914, §§4437, 4438 R. S. 1881, declare that each civil township shall also be a distinct school corporation for school purposes to be known by the name

**EVIDENCE—Continued.**

and style of the civil township except that the word school should be added thereto, but townships being laid off, bounded, described and named by the board of county commissioners, under the provisions of §9559 Burns 1914, §5987 R. S. 1881, and not by legislative enactment, the court cannot judicially know that a school township. designated in the assignment of errors as "Salt School township of Monroe county" is not a body politic separate and distinct from a school corporation known as Salt Creek school township in the same county, so that an appeal by the latter is ineffective where it is designated therein by the name set forth in the assignment of errors. (*Miller v. Miller* [1913], 55 Ind. App. 644, disapproved in part.)
*State, ex rel.* v. *Stevens,* 561, 566 (6).

3. *Public Officers.—Performance of Official Duties.—Presumption.*—In considering the sufficiency of a pleading, it is presumed that public officials have done and will do their duty unless the contrary appears from the allegations.
*Barnum* v. *Rallihan,* 349, 362 (13).

4. *Res Gestae.*—The term *res gestae* includes the surrounding facts of a transaction and also the accompanying declarations to explain the act done, or for showing motive for acting, although such declarations aside from this doctrine may be in the nature of hearsay evidence.
*Daywitt* v. *Daywitt,* 444, 454 (11).

5. *Res Gastae.—Alienation of Affections.—Malice.*—Where, in an action by a wife against her husband's parents for alienation, plaintiff contended that defendants permitted their daughter to move into a house provided by them for the purpose of driving her out, defendants should have been permitted to show, as a part of the *res gestae,* the arrangement made concerning the occupancy of the house.
*Daywitt* v. *Daywitt,* 444, 454 (9).

6. *Res Gestae.—Alienation of Affections.—Malice.*—In an action by a wife against her husband's parents for alienation, defendants should have been permitted to show as part of the *res gestae* that they allowed the son at the time of his marriage to bring his wife to the parental home to reside, and furnished him money for medical expenses during her illness, and that when informed by the doctor that an operation on plaintiff was necessary, they instructed the doctor to perform such operation, for which the evidence showed they subsequently paid.
*Daywitt* v. *Daywitt,* 444, 452 (8).

7. *Self-Serving Declarations.—Physician's Examination.—Personal Injury.*—In an action for personal injuries, the testimony of a physician that he found, when examining the plaintiff to ascertain his injuries, a "slight soreness in the intercostal region," was not objectionable as being a self-serving declaration, where such statement did not purport to be what the plaintiff told the witness, but was based on what the witness found in his examination. *Chicago, etc., R. Co.* v. *Biddinger,* 30, 48 (24).

8. *Testimony of Physician.—Personal Injuries.—Examinnation.* —In an action for personal injuries, a physician, called to examine plaintiff to ascertain the extent of his injuries, but not to treat him, could testify as to what he saw and found in such examination. *Chicago, etc., R. Co.* v. *Biddinger,* 30, 48 (23).

**EXCEPTIONS, BILL OF—**

See APPEAL.

Refusal of court to sign, presenting question, see APPEAL 31.

*Time of Presenting for Signing.—Recitals in Bill.*—The recital in a bill of exceptions of the day it was presented to the judge for signing, which was after the time given to file the bill, will be taken as correct, regardless of a recital that it was presented within the time allowed for filing.
*Haehnel* v. *Seidentopf,* 218, 221 (4).

**EXCESSIVE DAMAGES—**

Presenting questions for review as to, see APPEAL 65.

**EXECUTION—**

Money judgment, enforcement, see JUDGMENT 3.

1. *Proceedings Supplementary.—Complaint.—Sufficiency.*—In a proceeding supplementary to execution based on §§859, 860 Burns 1914, §§816, 817 R. S. 1881, where the complaint does not in direct terms aver that execution had been returned unsatisfied and that defendant did not have property, other than that alleged to be concealed, on which execution might be satisfied, is insufficient, when properly attacked, to warrant the issuance of an execution against the body of a judgment debtor alleged to be about to leave the state. *Fox* v. *Close,* 66, 69 (3).

2. *Proceedings Supplementary.—Statutes.—Construction.*—Section 859 Burns 1914, §816 R. S. 1881, providing that if, after issuing an execution against property, the execution plaintiff, or other person in his behalf, shall file an affidavit with the clerk of any court of record that the judgment debtor has property which he unjustly refuses to apply toward the satisfaction of the judgment, the court shall make an order requiring the judgment debtor to appear to answer the affidavit, and such proceeding may thereafter be had for the application of the property of the judgment debtor toward the satisfaction of the judgment, as provided upon the return of an execution, and §860 Burns 1914, §817 R. S. 1881, providing that when the plaintiff, his agent or attorney, shall at the time of applying for the order, or at any time afterward, file an affidavit that there is danger of the debtor leaving the state or concealing himself, and that there is reason to believe he has property, etc., which he unjustly refuses to apply to the judgment, with intent to defraud the creditor, an order for arrest and bail shall issue, must be considered together, and, when so construed, an execution against the body of a judgment debtor cannot issue, under the provisions of such sections, while an execution against his property is unreturned. *Fox* v. *Close,* 66, 68 (2).

**EXECUTORS AND ADMINISTRATORS—**

Appeal by, failure to properly designate, effect, see APPEAL 35.

Taxes on realty, death of owner, liability of estate, see TAXATION 16.

1. *Accounting and Settlement.—Collateral Attack.*—The settlement of a decedent's estate, although irregular or invalid, can not be attacked collaterally. *Barnum* v. *Rallihan,* 349, 363 (14).

2. *Accounting.—Technicalities.*—In determining questions arising out of the administraion of decedent's estates, courts will

## EXECUTORS AND ADMINISTRATORS—Continued.

not permit an injustice to be sustained upon mere technical questions of practice. *Hancock* v. *Hancock*, 173, 182 (5).

3. *Claim Against Estate.—Failure to File.—Liability of Devisees.*—Where the taxes on a testator's real estate should have been paid by his executrix out of the funds of the estate, but she permitted the same to become delinquent, and one purchasing such realty from testator's devisees paid the tax to protect his property, such purchaser, on failure to enforce his claim against the estate for the money so paid, cannot recover such money from the devisees after the settlement of the estate, at least in the absence of a showing that they still have the property received by them in their possession at the time the action was instituted. *Barnum* v. *Rallihan*, 349, 364 (18).

4. *Filing Claims Against Estate.—Taxes.—Collection.*—While ordinary claims against an estate can only be collected through administration as provided by statute, claims for taxes need not be filed by the county treasurer and may be collected from the administrator out of funds in his hands, or the treasurer may seize and sell property assessed to liquidate the amount due. *Barnum* v. *Rallihan*, 349, 364 (17).

5. *Contracts.—Construction.—Fiduciary Relations.*—Where an administrator, an heir to the estate, voluntarily assumed the management of the business affairs of, and established his residence with, decedent's widow, who was uneducated, aged and without business experience, he sustained toward her a fiduciary relation which cast upon him the burden of showing good faith and fair dealing in the management of the trust property in his care, particularly where the result of his action enures to his own benefit and to the injury of the party whose interest he should protect, and, unless good faith is shown, any contract entered into by such administrator with decedent's widow concerning her trust property would be unenforcible as constructively fraudulent. *Hancock* v. *Hancock*, 173, 179 (2).

6. *Contract with Widow.—Constructive Fraud.—Fiduciary Relations.*—Where an administrator, an heir to the estate, voluntarily assumed the management of the business affairs of decedent's widow, who was aged, in feeble health, uneducated and wholly without business experience, he sustained toward her a fiduciary relation which charged him with acting in the utmost good faith respecting the management of the trust property in his care; and a contract between himself as administrator, and the widow, which she signed, under his persuasion and veiled threats, without proper advice as to the effect of its terms, and by its stipulations surrendered to the administrator, to her injury, her interest in the personalty to be administered in the estate, in which was included certain certificates of deposit which were her personal property, is void as being constructively fraudulent, on the failure of the administrator to show the good faith required of him in his fiduciary capacity. *Hancock* v. *Hancock*, 173, 178, 180, 182 (1).

7. *Sales of Realty.—Report.—Petition by Purchaser for Disapproval.—Sufficiency.*—Where an administrator filed a report of a sale of real estate, a petition by the purchaser seeking a disapproval of the report, a cancellation of the contract of sale and a return of money paid on the purchase price is not demurrable on the ground that a recovery of the money paid could only be obtained by filing a claim against the decedent's

## FIDUCIARY RELATIONS—

Contracts of person acting in, construction, see EXECUTORS AND ADMINISTRATORS 5, 6.

## FINDINGS—

See TRIAL.

Omission of, effect on conclusion, see EJECTMENT.

Special, review of questions as to, see APPEAL.

Of master commissioner, adoption by court, presumption, see APPEAL 89.

## FIRE INSURANCE—

See INSURANCE.

## FORFEITURES—

See INSURANCE 12, 18, 23, 24; VENDOR AND PURCHASER.

## FRAUD—

See EQUITY; EXECUTORS AND ADMINISTRATORS; LIMITATION OF ACTIONS; PAYMENT.

Duress constituting, see CONTRACTS 11.

In establishment of drains, public interest, injunction, see DRAINS 4-7.

Relief from, where legal remedy is not efficient, see INJUNCTION.

## FRAUDS, STATUTE OF—

1. *Contractor's Bond.—Waiver of Condition by Parol.*—An oral waiver by a surety of a provision in a contractor's bond relative to the time within which suit must be brought is not binding, since the bond itself is required to be in writing by the statute of frauds (§7462 Burns 1914, §4904 R. S. 1881), and cannot be varied by parol.
   *Wainright Trust Co.* v. *U. S. Fidelity, etc., Co.*, 309, 315 (2).

2. *Contractor's Bond.*—Under the statute of frauds (§7462 Burns 1914, §4904 R. S. 1881), a contractor's bond indemnifying the obligee against loss resulting from a breach of the contract must be in writing, since its purpose is to charge one person upon a special promise to answer for the default of another.
   *Wainright Trust Co.* v. *U. S. Fidelity, etc., Co.*, 309, 314 (1).

3. *Oral Agreement for Sale of Lands.—Action for Breach of Contract.*—Where a landowner and prospective purchasers have agreed verbally to terms for the sale of land, an action by such prospective purchasers for damages for the owner's breach of contract is barred by the statute of frauds (§7462 Burns 1914, §4904 R. S. 1881). *Crumpacker* v. *Jeffrey*, 621, 631 (5).

## FREIGHT—

See CARRIERS; COMMERCE.

## GAS—

See MINES AND MINERALS.

**GIFTS—**

Prospective, as element of damages, see DEATH.

Of personalty, delivery, effect, see HUSBAND AND WIFE 4.

**GOOD FAITH—**

Contracts, fiduciary relations, construction, see EXECUTORS AND ADMINISTRATORS.

Parent and child, advice, presumption, see HUSBAND AND WIFE 3.

**GUARDIAN AND WARD—**

1. *Final Settlements.—Vacating.*—Applications to set aside final settlement of guardians must show that the person seeking to set it aside were not notified to appear and did not appear at the hearing of the final settlement report.

*Rucker* v. *Kelley*, 645, 647 (1).

2. *Successive Guardianships.—Attack on First Guardian's Accounts after Final Settlement.*—Where a guardian resigned and was succeeded by another, who made a final settlement of the estate, an heir to the ward could not, after such final settlement, recover compensation allowed the first guardian at the time of making her last report and penalties for alleged failure to comply with the statutes in making current reports, it not appearing from the heirs' complaint that she was not notified to appear and was not present at the hearing of the final report, at which time error in partial reports should be presented, since the attack on the last report of the first guardian, which was not a final report, was, under the allegations of the complaint, an attempt to question the final settlement indirectly and a final report which has been approved cannot be questioned on a collateral proceeding.

*Rucker* v. *Kelley*, 645, 647 (2).

**HARMLESS ERROR—**

See APPEAL 116-128.

**HEIRS—**

See WILLS.

**HIGHWAYS—**

See STREETS.

Use of, by licensee, liability for injuries to pedestrian, see TELEGRAPHS AND TELEPHONES.

**HUSBAND AND WIFE—**

See APPEAL 66; EVIDENCE 5.

Liability of wife for improvements, see MECHANICS' LIENS.

1. *Alienation of Affections.—Measure of Damages.*—The services, conjugal affection and society of a husband are valuable property, and, in a suit by the wife for the alienation of her husband's affections, the measure of damages is the value of the husband of whom she has been deprived.

*Daywitt* v. *Daywitt*, 444, 446 (1).

2. *Alienation of Affections.—Action.—Evidence.—Admissibility.* —In an action by a wife against her husband's parents for alienation of affections, testimony of the wife as to certain acts of

## HUSBAND AND WIFE—Continued.

her husband and sister-in-law just prior to plaintiff's separation from her husband is inadmissible in the absence of other evidence connecting defendants with such acts.

*Daywitt v. Daywitt*, 444, 450 (6).

3. *Alienation of Affections.—Parent and Child.—Advice.—Presumptions.*—A parent may always in good faith and for the best interest of his child advise and counsel with him, and, where advice is given, the presumption is that it was induced by feelings of the highest parental affections and only for the child's good. *Daywitt v. Daywitt*, 444, 452 (7).

4. *Gifts of Personalty.—Delivery by Husband to Wife.*—Where a husband delivered to his wife certificates of deposit and stated at the time that she should care for them as they were her property, he made a complete unconditional gift by delivery which passed title to her. *Hancock v. Hancock*, 173, 182 (4).

## IMPLICATION—

Repeal of statutes by, see STATUTES.

## INDUSTRIAL BOARD—

Action of, under Workmen's Compensation Act, see MASTER AND SERVANT.

## INFANTS—

Appeals from juvenile courts, evidence, bill of exceptions, see APPEAL 17; assignment of error, see APPEAL 32.

In an appeal from a criminal prosecution in a juvenile court, where the evidence is not before the appellate court, the facts found by the trial court must be taken as correctly found, see APPEAL 97, 98.

Medical expenses, liability, see DAMAGES 2, 3.

## INHERITANCE—

Tax on, see TAXATION 3.

Of adopted child, legislative power, see ADOPTION.

Of illegitimate child, see BASTARDS.

## INHERITANCE TAX—

Determination, appeal without bond, statute, see APPEAL 10.

## INJUNCTION—

See DRAINS 4, 7.

To prevent collection of taxes, pleading and proof, see TAXATION.

Unfair competition, use of name, injunctive relief, see TRADE-MARKS AND TRADE-NAMES.

1. *Grounds.—Multiplicity of Suits.*—Where there is a legal remedy, equity will frequently grant injunctive relief to prevent a multiplicity of suits.

*Royer v. State, ex rel.* 123, 132 (6).

2. *Right to Relief.—Remedy at Law.*—Even in the absence of the statute giving the right to restrain the performance of a contract procured by collusion or fraud, the existence of a remedy at law would not necessarily deprive a party of injunc-

**INJUNCTION—Continued.**

tive relief, for, if the legal remedy is not as prompt, practical, efficient and adequate as that afforded by equity, an injunction will issue if the case is otherwise established.

*Royer* v. *State, ex rel.* 123, 182 (5).

**INSOLVENCY—**

See CORPORATIONS; RECEIVERS.

**INSTRUCTIONS—**

See TRIAL.

Review of instructions on appeal, see APPEAL.

Cure of error by, see APPEAL 116.

**INSURANCE—**

1. *Agent.—Contract.—Unpaid Premiums.—Liability of Agent.—* Under a contract between an insurance company and its agent whereby he was required to collect first premiums on applications taken by him and was prohibited from extending the time for the payment thereof, the agent is not chargeable with premiums unpaid by applicants on insurance written by him, in the absence of any provision in the contract evidencing an intention to make him liable therefor.

*Doak, etc., Co.* v. *Raabe*, 250, 254, 255 (1).

2. *Contracts of Insurance.—Power of Agents.—Restrictions in Policy.—*Provisions in policies of insurance limiting the powers of agents have reference to that policy only, and have no application to preliminary agreements to insure or to renew existing insurance.

*Nat. Live Stock Ins. Co.* v. *Cramer,* 211, 217 (5).

3. *Contract with Agent.—Commissions.—Accounting for Premiums.—Master's Report.—Construction.—*Where in an action by an insurance company against an agent to recover money alleged to be due under an agency contract, a master commissioner found certain "commissions due or allowed defendant from plaintiff," such commissions being on uncollected premiums, the word "or" was used, not in its alternative sense, but as a connective, and the world "allowed" as meaning "to concede, consent to, or to grant," so that the report of the master could be construed as meaning that the company consented to allow such commissions to defendant, though unpaid, notwithstanding a provision in the contract that commissions should be payable only on premiums collected in cash on policies issued on applications procured by the agent and accounted for by him. *Doak, etc., Co.* v. *Raabe*, 250, 255 (3).

4. *Parol Contracts.—Validity.—*Parol contracts of insurance may be valid and of binding force.

*Nat. Live Stock Ins. Co.* v. *Cramer,* 211, 215 (1).

5. *Parol Contracts.—Validity.—*An insurance company can, by a preliminary oral contract, bind itself to issue or renew a policy of insurance in the future.

*Nat. Live Stock Ins. Co.* v. *Cramer,* 211, 216 (2).

6. *Authority of Agent.—Oral Contract.—*Where an agent for an insurance company has apparent power to solicit insurance, collect premiums, deliver policies, and do all things necessary to transact the company's business intrusted to his care, and no

**INSURANCE—Continued.**

tion therefor, did not change his position in any way to his injury, and could not, in interpleader to determine the ownership of the proceeds of the policy, rely on the alleged laches of a prior assignee, who had been induced by the false representations of the assignor to return the policy to him.
*New Albany Nat. Bank* v. *Brown*, 391, 410 (15).

16. *Action on Policy.—Pleading.—General Denial.—Evidence Admissible.*—In an action on an insurance policy, where it was unnecessary to make plaintiff's application a part of the complaint, and for plaintiffs to allege or prove, in the first instance, that the answers made in such application were true to entitle them to a recovery, evidence in support of a paragraph of answer interposing a defense that false answers in the application constituted a warranty upon which defendant relied, and that, when it learned that such answers were untrue the premiums paid were tendered to the assured, was inadmissible under an answer of general denial, since §361 Burns 1914, §356 R. S. 1881, provides that "all defenses, except the mere denial of the facts alleged by the plaintiff, shall be pleaded specially," the scope of the general denial being merely to put in issue such of the averments of the complaint as the plaintiff is bound to prove to maintain his action.
*National Live Stock Ins. Co.* v. *Owens*, 70, 74 (4).

17. *Action on Policy.—Application.—Warranties.*—In an action on a live stock insurance policy, it was error for the trial court to sustain demurrers to paragraphs of answer interposing as a defense alleged false answers in an application for insurance on a horse that the assured had not lost live stock by death, accident, disease or theft within two years and that the horse insured would be cared for by the assured, where such answers were made warranties by the terms of the application, since a breach of such warranties, as pleaded, constituted a defense to the action.
*National Live Stock Ins. Co.* v. *Owens*, 70, 78 (12).

18. *Policy.—Breach.—Avoidance of Contract.—Return of Premiums.*—Where an insurance company's defense to an action on a policy is based upon a breach thereof that renders the contract ineffectual from its inception, so that, the risk never having attached, there was no consideration for the premium received, the insurer, upon learning of the breach, must seasonably offer to return the premium, or it cannot insist upon a forfeiture of the policy.
*Ohio, etc., Ins. Co.* v. *Williams*, 435, 439 (3).

19. *Policy.—Breach—Avoidance of Contract.—Return of Premium.*—Where an insurer's liability attaches upon the execution of the policy, the return of the premium by the insurer is not necessary to avoid the contract for a breach of its stipulations by the insured. *Ohio, etc., Ins. Co.* v. *Williams*, 435, 439 (4).

20. *Accident Insurance.—Total Disability.*—Where an accident insurance policy provided for the payment of total disability benefits in case the assured should suffer injury which should, from the date of the accident, disable him and prevent him from performing every duty pertaining to any and every kind of business or occupation, and if such injuries wholly and continuously from date of accident should disable and prevent the assured from performing one or more important duties pertaining to his occupation, or in event of like disability immediately following total loss of time, partial disability benefits should be

## INSURANCE—Continued.

paid, the words "total loss of time" in the provision concerning partial disability, when read in connection with the stipulation in reference to total disability, make it clear that the assured would not be entitled to recover for total disability except in event of total loss of time, during which he was prevented from performing every duty pertaining to any and every kind of business. *Workingmen's Mutual, etc., Assn.* v. *Roos,* 18, 20 (2).

21. *Fire Insurance Policy.—Stipulation Against Other Insurance.—Validity.*—Stipulations in a fire insurance policy to the effect that the policy shall be void if the insured has or procures any other contract of insurance on the property covered are valid and reasonable, and when they are violated, the insurer may defend against loss on the ground of breach of the contract. *Ohio, etc., Ins. Co.* v. *Williams,* 435, 438 (1).

22. *Fire Insurance Policy.—Stipulation Against Other Insurance.—Use of Word "Void."—Effect.*—Where a stipulation in a fire insurance policy provides that the policy shall be void if the insured shall procure additional insurance on the property covered, a breach of such stipulation does not render the policy void, but only voidable at the election of the insurer.
*Ohio, etc., Ins. Co.* v. *Williams,* 435, 438 (2).

23. *Fire Insurance.—Action on Policy.—Pleading.*—Where, in an action on a fire insurance policy, the defense of forfeiture because of a breach of the stipulations in the contract, interposed by answer, was waived by the insurer, a reply setting up such waiver properly presents the same.
*Ohio, etc., Ins. Co.* v. *Williams,* 435, 443 (7).

24. *Fire Insurance Policy.—Construction.*—Fire insurance contracts are strictly construed as against the insurer, so as to prevent a forfeiture, and liberally construed in favor of the insured to the end that the contract may serve its purpose of furnishing indemnity in case of loss.
*Ohio, etc., Ins. Co.* v. *Williams,* 435, 442 (6).

25. *Fire Insurance Policy.—Breach of Insured.—Return of Premium.—Cancellation.*—An insurer's denial of liability on a policy because of a breach of its stipulations by the insured does not amount to a cancellation of the policy requiring the return of the *pro rata* share of the premium, under a provision of the contract stating that upon cancellation of the policy by the company, it shall only retain a *pro rata* share of the premium for the time elapsed. *Ohio, etc., Ins. Co.* v. *Williams,* 435, 442 (5).

## INTERPLEADER—

See INSURANCE 15.

1. *Answer.—Sufficiency.—Interest in Action.*—Where, in interpleader, the cross-complaint of a claimant to the proceeds of a life insurance policy merely alleged that another wrongfully asserted an adverse interest therein, the other claimant's answer, pleading the statute of limitations, but failing to show that he had interest in the fund, was insufficient.
*New Albany Nat. Bank* v. *Brown,* 391, 402 (6).

2. *Cross Complaint. — Demurrer. — Laches. —* In interpleader, where one party claims a first lien on the fund in controversy by a cross-complaint alleging that another is wrongfully as-

**INTERPLEADER—Continued.**

serting an adverse interest therein, the other claimant cannot
raise the question of laches by demurrer, but only by answer
showing an interest in the fund.

> *New Albany Nat. Bank* v. *Brown*, 391, 401 (4).

3. *Cross-Complaint.—Nature of Proceedings.*—In interpleader,
the cross-complaint of a claimant asserting a first lien on the
fund is a proceeding *in rem*, and where such pleading alleges
that another claims an adverse interest in the fund it is sufficient to require the other claimant to answer.

> *New Albany Nat. Bank* v. *Brown*, 391, 401 (3).

**INTERROGATORIES—**

See CONTRACTS 2; MASTER AND SERVANT 9, 19; RAILROADS 7-9;
TRIAL.

Review as to, on appeal, see APPEAL.

**INTERSTATE COMMERCE—**

See CARRIERS 8; COMMERCE; COURTS 4.

**INVENTION—**

See TRADE-MARKS AND TRADE-NAMES.

**INVITED ERROR—**

See APPEAL 66.

**JOINDER—**

See NEW TRIAL.

**JUDGES—**

Certificate of, to bill of exceptions, presumption, see APPEAL 22.

Refusal of, to sign bill of exceptions, when harmless, see APPEAL
121.

**JUDICIAL NOTICE—**

See EVIDENCE 2.

**JUDGMENT—**

Default, motion to set aside, appeal, effect, see APPEAL 3.

Final, appeal from, statute, see APPEAL 4.

Parties to, coappellants, see APPEAL 57, 58.

That the judgment appealed from is not supported by the evidence and is against the weight of the evidence, is not grounds
for an independent assignment of error, see APPEAL 30, 34.

Error in amount of, in favor of appellant, effect, see APPEAL 96.

Of justice of the peace, matters adjudicated, see JUSTICES OF THE
PEACE.

1. *Conclusiveness.—Res Judicata.*—The decision of the Supreme
Court, in an injunction suit to prevent the construction of a
public improvement, holding the proceedings therefor void is
controlling on the invalidity of the proceedings where that
question is raised in a subsequent action by the paving contractor to enforce a lien for work done and the facts therein

## JUDGMENT—Continued.

relating to the validity of the proceedings in the latter action are identical with those involved in the case determined by the Supreme Court.

*Hoosier Construction Co.* v. *Seibert*, 594, 602 (1).

2. *Money Judgment.—Lien.*—The lien of a money judgment is general and not specific. *Kiefer Drug Co.* v. *DeLay*, 639, 645 (7).

8. *Money Judgment.—Enforcement.—Duty of Owner.*—Money judgments are not self-executing, and in the collection thereof the duty rests upon the owner of the judgment to take the necessary steps provided by law for their enforcement, and if he fails to do so he cannot place the responsibility for such failure upon others who have no legal duty resting upon them in respect thereto. *Kiefer Drug Co.* v. *DeLay*, 639, 644 (4).

4. *Motion to Set Aside Default.—Pleadings.—Complaint.—Demurrer.*—While an action seeking to set aside a judgment by default on the ground of inadvertence, mistake and excusable neglect should be determined in a summary manner and no pleadings are contemplated other than the complaint or motion, yet such complaint or motion may be tested by demurrer.

*Kurtz v. Phillips*, 79, 83 (3).

5. *Satisfaction.—Vacating.*—An entry of satisfaction of a judgment does not necessarily bar its collection, since the entry might be vacated for sufficient cause or otherwise be shown to be ineffectual against parties claiming to own the judgment.

*Chicago, etc., R. Co.* v. *Dunnahoo*, 237, 248 (7).

## JURISDICTION—

See APPEAL; COURTS; EQUITY.

Defect of parties, effect on appeal, see APPEAL 7, 59.

Competitive bidding, public contracts, jurisdictional question, see MUNICIPAL CORPORATIONS 4.

## JURY—

See TRIAL; VERDICT.

Question for, see ATTORNEY AND CLIENT.

Question for, contributory negligence, see MASTER AND SERVANT 22.

Credibility of witness, question for jury, see APPEAL 86.

Inferences drawn by, sufficiency of evidence, see APPEAL 103.

Weight of evidence, jury question, see APPEAL 108.

## JUSTICES OF THE PEACE—

*Judgment.—Matters Adjudicated.—Title to Real Property.*—A judgment of a justice of the peace, rendered by agreement of the parties, awarding possession of certain lots did not adjudicate the title thereto; and an answer, in a subsequent action between the same parties to cancel and set aside a deed for such real estate as having been executed under duress, reciting the rendition of the judgment, is insufficient as a plea of former adjudication of title, since such question could not have been adjudicated by the justice of the peace.

*Denney* v. *Reber*, 192, 196 (1).

JUVENILE COURTS—

See INFANTS.

Appeal from, procedure, see APPEAL 17, 32.

KNOWLEDGE—

As essential element of ratification, see BROKERS; PRINCIPAL AND AGENT.

Of obstruction in street, jury question in action for injuries, see TELEGRAPHS AND TELEPHONES 5, 6.

LACHES—

See DRAINS 4, 7; INTERPLEADER 2; INSURANCE 15; NEW TRIAL 5; PLEADING 19.

LANDLORD AND TENANT—

1. *Contracts.—Independent Oral Agreement between Lessor and Lessee.*—Where a leased farm was conceded by the lessor to be unproductive after the lessee had unsuccessfully attempted to cultivate the land, and the parties thereupon mutually entered into an independent parol agreement to carry out a plan of fertilization and improvement by means not previously contemplated, compensation being provided for the lessee for the extra labor to be performed, such agreement was not a modification of the original lease, but was independent thereof and rested upon an entirely new consideration.
*Welty* v. *Taylor*, 674, 681 (6).

2. *Contract.—Action for Breach.—Pleading.—Sufficiency of Complaint.*—In an action to recover money alleged to be due on a parol contract, a complaint containing allegations showing that plaintiff, who was under contract with defendant to manage and cultivate his farm, orally agreed with defendant to remain on the land after it was found to be unproductive, and apply fertilizers, etc., to be furnished by defendant, and was to receive as compensation for his services, if the plan of fertilization proved successful, such an amount in excess of a stipulated figure as the land would bring in the market, such complaint is held to sufficiently state the issuable facts constituting the cause of action and to show a breach of the alleged contract and it is not objectionable as being a statement of evidence.
*Welty* v. *Taylor*, 674, 679 (1).

3. *Contracts.—Action for Breach.—Evidence.—Sufficiency.*—In action by the lessee of a farm, admitted by defendant lessors to be unproductive, to recover money alleged to be due on an oral agreement providing that if the lessee would remain on the land and apply fertilizers to be furnished by the lessors in consideration of the amount the market value of the farm should exceed a stipulated sum, where there was evidence tending to show the original value of the farm and that it was less productive than the owners believed it to be, that the tenant was about to abandon the premises because of the poor yield of crops, whereupon the parol agreement to increase the fertility of the soil was entered into, the lessor being required thereby to furnish the necessary materials and the lessee to do the work, that both parties performed their respective parts of the agreement and, as a result, the land became productive and reached a market value in excess of the amount stipulated in the parol

**LANDLORD AND TENANT—Continued.**

of a leased building are raised, it is the duty of the tenant in possession to guard the opening.

*Dammeyer* v. *Vorhis*, 427, 431 (4).

9. *Repairs to Premises.*—It is not the duty of the landlord to keep the leased premises in repair, in the absence of an agreement with the tenant to that effect.

*Dammeyer* v. *Vorhis*, 427, 431 (2).

**LANDS—**

See EASEMENTS; EMINENT DOMAIN; PARTITION; PUBLIC LANDS.

Unlawful appropriation, measure of damages, see APPEAL 125.

Sale of by agents, see BROKERS; DEEDS.

Wrongful cutting of timber, measure of damages, see TRESPASS.

Vendor's lien, see VENDOR AND PURCHASER.

**LAST CLEAR CHANCE—**

See STREET RAILROADS.

**LAW OF THE CASE—**

See APPEAL 134.

**LAWYERS—**

See ATTORNEY AND CLIENT.

**LEGISLATIVE POWER—**

See ADOPTION.

Right of appeal, see APPEAL 1, 2.

**LETTERS—**

See BROKERS 2; INSURANCE 7.

**LIENS—**

See TAXATION; VENDOR AND PURCHASER.

Of vendor, action, conclusions of law, failure to except, effect, see APPEAL 83.

Of mortgages, see BANKRUPTCY.

Improvement, action, see MUNICIPAL CORPORATIONS.

Surrender of possession of collateral, effect, see INSURANCE 14.

Payment of, by purchaser of property, rights, see SUBROGATION.

**LIMITATION OF ACTIONS—**

1. *Pledge.—Right to Foreclose Lien.*—The right to foreclose the lien of a pledge given to secure notes is not barred until the expiration of the ten-year period fixed by the statute of limitations (§295 Burns 1914, §293 R. S. 1881) in which action may be brought to recover on the notes.

*New Albany Nat. Bank* v. *Brown*, 391, 403 (8).

2. *Action to Foreclose Lien on Pledge.—Fraud.—Possession of Pledge.*—Where in interpleader, a claimant to the proceeds of a policy of life insurance assigned to her as security for notes alleged that possession of the policy was obtained by the assignor through fraudulent representations, fraud was not the

## LIMITATION OF ACTIONS—Continued.

basis of the action, so that claimant's right to recover is not barred within six years by §294, cls. 3, 4, Burns 1914, §292 R. S. 1881. *New Albany Nat. Bank* v. *Brown*, 391, 403 (9).

3. *Bonds Payable in Installments.—Actions to Foreclose Lien.— Computation of Period of Limitation.*—An action brought on October 16, 1913, to foreclose the statutory lien securing a street improvement bond issued in May, 1902, with the last installment to run ten years from date before maturity, is not barred by the five, six, or ten-year statute of limitations.
*Nat. Exchange Bank* v. *Smith*, 574, 585 (9).

## LIS PENDENS—

*Presumptions.—Notice.*—An appeal is a right granted by statute, and one having knowledge of a pending appealable cause is conclusively presumed to know that a judgment entered therein may be appealed from within a limited time.
*Hoosier Construction Co.* v. *Seibert*, 594, 605 (9).

## LIVE STOCK—

See CARRIERS.

Liability of township for stock killed by dogs, see ANIMALS.

Shipment of, contract, review of evidence, see APPEAL 126, 127.

## MALPRACTICE—

See PHYSICIANS.

## MARKET VALUE—

See CONTRACTS 5.

## MASTER AND SERVANT—

See APPEAL; PLEADING; TRIAL.

1. *Independent Contractor.—Determination.—Questions of Law and of Fact.*—The question of what constitutes an independent contractor is ordinarily one of mixed law and fact. Where the evidence with respect to the relation is oral, and is sufficient to establish the existence of some relation, and if it be uncontradicted and reasonably susceptible of but a single inference, the question of what relation is thereby shown to exist is a law question, but if the evidence is conflicting, or is such that different deductions may reasonably be drawn therefrom leading to different conclusions as to what relation is establshed, it is a question of fact, in the sense that the triers of the facts must determine the facts and draw the inferences and make the deductions, but even in such a case certain legal standards and principles must be applied to the facts after they are ascertained and a question of law is thereby involved, so that the ultimate question of whether a person is an employe or an independent contractor under certain facts involves a law question. *Columbia School Supply Co.* v. *Lewis*, 386, 389 (2).

2. A contract entered into by a railroad company with an employe requiring him to become a member of a relief association maintained by the company and to receive benefits from the association in full payment for damages for personal injuries is void. *Baltimore, etc., R. Co.* v. *Poston*, 591.

3. *Injuries to Servant.—Independent Acts of Negligence.—Liability.—Instruction.*—In an action for personal injuries, a state-.

**MASTER AND SERVANT—Continued.**

ment in an instruction that the jury should find for the plaintiff, if any of the acts of negligence charged in the complaint were established and such negligent act was the proximate cause of the injury, as it was not incumbent upon the plaintiff to prove all the acts of negligence alleged, was not erroneous, when considered in connection with other instructions given, where several distinct acts of negligence were charged in the complaint, any one of which might have been sufficient to make the defendant liable. *Central, etc., R. Co.* v. *Clark*, 49, 52 (6).

4. *Injuries to Servant.—Duty to Furnish Safe Tools.—Instruction.*—In an action for personal injuries, an instruction that it was the employer's duty to furnish safe tools and appliances for its servants to work with was too broad a statement of the law. *Central, etc., R. Co.* v. *Clark*, 49, 52 (3).

5. *Injuries to Servant.—Liability of Master.*—In an action by a boiler-shop employe for personal injuries sustained by the breaking of a defective drift pin, the act of defendant's boiler maker who had charge of the boiler repair work, in getting the drift pin from the blacksmith shop rather than from the tool room, where tools and supplies were provided for use in the shops, was the act of the defendant and he was responsible therefor. *Central, etc., R. Co.* v. *Clark*, 49, 51 (2).

6. *Injuries to Servant.—Employers' Liability Act.—Fellow-Servant Doctrine.—Instruction.*—In an action for injuries to plaintiff caused by the breaking of a drift pin, an instruction that defendant was not liable, if the boilermaker with whom plaintiff was working at the time of the injury procured the defective drift pin from the blacksmith shop instead of from the tool room where defendant kept the supply of drift pins for use in the shop, was properly refused, since it is based on the fellow-servant doctrine which was abolished by §1 of the act of 1911 (Acts 1911 p. 145, §8020a *et seq.* Burns 1914).
*Central, etc., R. Co.* v. *Clark*, 49, 51 (1).

7. *Injuries to Servant.—Action.—Complaint.—Negligence.—Proximate Cause.*—Where, in an action for wrongful death, the complaint avers that the injury to the decedent and his death was caused by the negligence of the defendant in operating its freight car on a defective track, which was laid in violation of a city ordinance, and that all the wrongs and grievances set out, particularly the death of decedent, were entirely due to the negligence of the defendant as set out in the pleading, such complaint sufficiently charges that the negligence alleged was the proximate cause of the injury suffered.
*Evansville R. Co.* v. *Cooksey, Admx.*, 482, 486 (2).

8. *Injuries to Servant.—Action.—Complaint.—Negligence.—General and Specific Allegations.*—Where in an action against a street railway company for wrongful death, the complaint contains a general averment directly charging that defendant's negligence in unlawfully constructing its tracks in too close proximity to its poles was the proximate cause of the injury suffered, such general averment is not overcome by a specific allegation that decedent received his injury because the swaying of the car threw him through the door thereof and against a pole, and the complaint is sufficient as against demurrer, since the swaying of the car was but an incident in its operation which extended the negligence charged so as to result in the death. *Evansville R. Co.* v. *Cooksey, Admx.*, 482, 487 (3).

## MASTER AND SERVANT—Continued.

9. *Injuries to Servant.—Contributory Negligence.—Answers to Interrogatories.*—Where, in an action against a street railway company for the wrongful death of a conductor who was injured when struck by a trolley pole, negligence is predicated on the alleged construction of the tracks too close to the trolley poles, the jury's answers to interrogatories showing that decedent knew that in passing the particular pole causing the injury it was dangerous to put one's head outside the car door, a motion for judgment on the interrogatories as showing decedent guilty of contributory negligence was properly denied, where the answers do not show that decedent voluntarily, unnecessarily or negligently extended any part of his person beyond the car, or that he was negligent in occupying a position near the door, as it must be assumed, in the absence of answers to the contrary, that decedent occupied such position in the discharge of his duties, and that while so engaged he was thrown through the door and against the pole by the swaying of the car, as alleged in the complaint.
*Evansville R. Co.* v. *Cooksey, Admx.*, 482, 488, 490 (5).

10. *Injuries to Servant.—Assumption of Risk.—Violation of Ordinance.*—Where, in an action against a street railway company for the wrongful death of a conductor who was struck by a trolley pole, the negligence charged consisted in the violation of a city ordinance, the doctrine of assumption of risk is not applicable notwithstanding decedent's knowledge of the risk.
*Evansville R. Co.* v. *Cooksey, Admx.*, 482, 490 (6).

11. *Injuries to Servant.—Duty of Master.—Safe Place to Work. —Delegation of Duty.*—A street railway company using the tracks of another company is not relieved of liability for injury to its employes due to defective or negligent construction of the tracks because they are maintained by the other company, since the duty to provide a safe working place for employes is nondelegable.
*Evansville R. Co.* v. *Cooksey, Admx.*, 482, 493 (10).

12. *Injuries to Servant.—Master's Negligence.—Violation of Municipal Ordinance.*—The violation by a street car company of a city ordinance requiring that double tracks be laid an equal distance from the center of the street, resulting in the death of an employe, constitutes negligence.
*Evansville R. Co.* v. *Cooksey, Admx.*, 482, 492 (9).

13. *Injuries to Servant.—Action.—Master's Negligence.—Violation of City Ordinance.—Proximate Cause.—Evidence.*—In an action against a street-car company for the wrongful death of an employe, defendant's negligence, as established, in maintaining its tracks in violation of a city ordinance was actionable only if the proximate cause of decedent's injury, so that it was proper to permit an expert witness to testify that the manner in which the tracks were maintained at the place of the accident was improper construction, such evidence being pertinent to the question of proximate cause.
*Evansville R. Co.* v. *Cooksey, Admx.*, 482, 492 (8).

14. *Injuries to Servant.—Action.—Jury Questions.—Contributory Negligence.—Weighing Evidence.*—In an action against an electric line for the death of a conductor who was killed when struck by a trolley pole, where several witnesses testified that at the time of the accident decedent had his head out of the car door, and a single witness testified that while he was stand-

## MASTER AND SERVANT—Continued.

ing in the doorway, but wholly within the car, the swaying of
the car threw him out of the door and against the pole, the
weighing of the evidence and the credibility of the witness was
for the jury to determine, and the court on appeal cannot disregard the evidence of the single witness and say as a matter
of law that decedent was guilty of contributory negligence.
*Evansville R. Co.* v. *Cooksey, Admx.*, 482, 490 (7).

15.  *Injuries to Servant.—Action.—Complaint.—Sufficiency.*—On
an employe's action for personal injuries, a complaint alleging
that plaintiff was ordered to put chains around a log preparatory to moving it, and while he was so doing a fellow servant
was directed to start a team hitched to the chain and that he
did so negligently and without any warning, thereby causing
plaintiff's injury, is not defective as showing that plaintiff gave
the order to the driver to start, especially in view of the allegation that the team was started without any warning to plaintiff.
*Stimson* v. *Krueger*, 567, 570, 571 (1).

16.  *Injuries to Servant.—Action.—Complaint.—Allegations.—
Defenses.—Contributory Negligence.—Burden of Proof.—Statute.*—In an action for personal injury, under §362 Burns 1914,
Acts 1899 p. 58, the plaintiff is not required either to allege
or prove that he was in the exercise of reasonable care at the
time of the injury, and that he did not exercise such care is
matter of defense and may be made under the general denial.
*S. W. Little Coal Co.* v. *O'Brien*, 504, 517 (10).

17.  *Injuries to Servant.—Action.—Defenses.—Contributory Negligence.—Statute.*—The defense of contributory negligence is
not abolished in all cases by the act of 1911 (Acts 1911 p. 145,
§8020a *et seq.* Burns 1914), relating to employers' liability for
injuries to servants, and it is available in an action for wrongful death where the facts show that decedent, who was crushed
and killed between a moving car on a switch track and defendant's scale house which he was attempting to enter to
weigh the car in pursuance of his duty, voluntarily and under
no requirement of his employment placed himself in the perilous position occupied when killed so that death resulted not
from the alleged defect in the working place due to the proximity of the scale house to the track, but rather from the use
decedent made of the place to work.
*S. W. Little Coal Co.* v. *O'Brien*, 504, 516 (9).

18.  *Injuries to Servant.—Action.—Complaint.—Allegations of
Knowledge of Defect.—Sufficiency.*—Where, in an action for
wrongful death caused by decedent being crushed, owing to insufficient clearance between a scale house constructed by defendant and a car on a switch track, the complaint alleges that
all the facts concerning the defect complained of, which was the
proximity of the scale house to the switch track, were known
to defendant, sufficiently charges the employer with notice to
bring the case within §8020c Burns 1914, Acts 1911 pp. 145,
146, relating to actions for injuries to employes, although the
complaint contains no express averment that defendant knew
of the defect in time to have remedied it, since, the defect
alleged being structural in nature and neither latent nor concealed, defendant was chargeable with knowledge thereof from
its inception.        *S. W. Little Coal Co.* v. *O'Brien*, 504, 515 (8).

19.  *Injuries to Servant.—Verdict.—Answers to Interrogatories.*
—In an action for the wrongful death of an employe, a general

**MASTER AND SERVANT—Continued.**

is not characterized by due care, rather than because he did obey the order, such section does not eliminate the defense of contributory negligence.
> *S. W. Little Coal Co.* v. *O'Brien*, 504, 525 (21).

25. *Injuries to Servant.—Action under Statute.—Complaint.— Sufficiency.*—Where the complaint in an employe's action for personal injury alleged facts to show that the defendant was a corporation employing more than five men; that at the time of the injury plaintiff was acting in the line of his employment and was, in obedience to his foreman's order, to which order he was bound to conform, about to remove certain timbers from a building to another part of defendant's yard, when he was struck by a timber which was pushed out of a window by other of defendant's employes across an alley through which plaintiff was required to pass in carrying out the foreman's order, and that at the time such order was given the foreman knew that timbers were being frequently shoved across the alley, so that it was dangerous to pass through the same, such complaint states a cause of action within the provisions of the Employers' Liability Act of 1911 (Acts 1911 p. 145, §8020 *et seq.* Burns 1914). *American Car, etc., Co.* v. *Williams*, 1, 4 (3).

26. *Injuries to Servant.—Negligence of Master.—Elements.— Notice of Defects.*—Where a cause of action for injury or death is predicated upon the existence of defects in the working place, tools, etc., the employer's knowledge of such defects, actual or constructive, is an essential element of negligence, both under the Employers' Liability Act of 1911 (Acts 1911 p. 145, §8020a *et seq.* Burns 1914) and at common law.
> *S. W. Little Coal Co.* v. *O'Brien*, 504, 515 (7).

27. *Injuries to Servant.—Action.—Complaint.—Disclosure of Contributory Negligence.—Sufficiency.*—Where the complaint in an action brought under the Employers' Liability Act of 1911 (Acts 1911 p. 145, §8020 *et seq.* Burns 1914) affirmatively shows that the person injured or killed was guilty of contributory negligence which proximately caused or contributed to such injury or death, it discloses a defense and is insufficient on demurrer.
> *S. W. Little Coal Co.* v. *O'Brien*, 504, 517 (11).

28. *Injuries to Servant.—Verdict.—Answers to Interrogatories.* —In an employe's action for personal injuries under a complaint stating a cause of action within the provisions of the Employers' Liability Act of 1911 (Acts 1911 p. 145, §8020a *et seq.* Burns 1914) answers to interrogatories supporting the averments of the complaint are not in irreconcilable conflict with a general verdict for plaintiff, even though such answers tend to establish plaintiff's assumption of risk and contributory negligence while obeying his superior's command, since the Employers' Liability Act eliminates the defenses of contributory negligence where the injury complained of resulted from the employe's obedience to his superior's command, and that the inherent dangers of the employment contributed to the injury.
> *American Car, etc., Co.* v. *Williams*, 1, 5 (5).

29. *Injuries to Servant.—Defective Appliance.—Knowledge of Employer.—Burden of Proof.—Statute.*—Under §3 of the Employers' Liability Act of 1911 (Acts 1911 p. 145, §8020a *et seq.* Burns 1914), when an appliance furnished the complaining

## MASTER AND SERVANT—Continued.

servant has been proved defective, the burden is on the employer to prove that it did not know of the defect.

*Central, etc., R. Co. v. Clark,* 49, 52 (5).

30. *Injuries to Servant.—Liability of Master.—Complaint.—*
Where, in an employe's action against the master for personal injuries, the complaint alleges that defendant employed more than five persons, that at the time of the injury, plaintiff, in pursuance to the orders of his foreman and in the line of his duty, was putting a chain around a log preparatory to moving it and that while he was so engaged a fellow servant was directed by the foreman to haul the log and that he started a team hitched to the chain negligently and without warning, thereby causing plaintiff's injury, the allegations of the complaint are sufficient to bring the case within the provisions of the Employers' Liability Act (§8020a Burns 1914, Acts 1911 p. 145). *Stimson v. Krueger,* 567, 571 (4).

31. *Injuries to Servant.—Negligence of Master.—Liability.—Assumed Risk.—Statute.—*Under the Employers' Liability Act of 1911 (Acts 1911 p. 145, §8020a *et seq.* Burns 1914) the employer is not liable unless the hazards of the employment and the defects in the working place, tools, etc., are chargeable to his negligence, and in the absence of negligence of the employer, the question of assumed risk is immaterial.

*S. W. Little Coal Co. v. O'Brien,* 504, 515 (6).

32. *Injuries to Servant.—Contributory Negligence.—Negligence of Master.—Liability.—Burden of Proof.—*The mere fact that hazards inherent or apparent in the employment contributed to the injury involved, or the mere fact of the existence of defects in the working place, etc., of which the employer had knowledge, actual or constructive, and because of which defects the employe was injured, does not render the employer liable under §§2 and 3 of the Employers' Liability Act of 1911 (Acts 1911 pp. 145, 146, §§8020b, 8020c Burns 1914), providing that dangers or hazards inherent or apparent in the employment shall not be a defense for the employer in an employe's action for injuries, and that the employer has the burden of proving that he did not know of the defect causing the injury, either actually or constructively, in time to have remedied the same.

*S. W. Little Coal Co. v. O'Brien,* 504, 515 (5).

33. *Employers' Liability Act.—Constitutionality.—*The Employers' Liability Act of 1911 (Acts 1911 p. 145, §8020 *et seq.* Burns 1914) is constitutional.

*American Car, etc., Co. v. Williams,* 1, 4 (2).

34. *Injuries to Servant.—Employers' Liability Act.—Acts of Fellow Servant.—*The fellow-servant rule is eliminated in cases brought within the provisions of the Employers' Liability Act (§8020a Burns 1914, Acts 1911 p. 145).

*Stimson v. Krueger,* 567, 571 (3).

35. *Employers' Liability Act.—Scope.—*The Employers' Liability Act (§8020a Burns 1914, Acts 1911 p. 145) does not authorize a recovery by the employe for injuries resulting from his own independent orders and directions, whether given negligently or otherwise. *Stimson v. Krueger,* 567, 570 (2).

36. *Employers' Liability Act.—Contributory Negligence of Servant.—Compliance with Command.—*In an employe's action for personal injuries, the foreman's order to plaintiff to carry

**MASTER AND SERVANT—Continued.**

timbers from the defendant's building to the yard, obedience to such order necessitating plaintiff's passing through an alley where he was injured, was a sufficiently specific direction to bring the case within the purview of the Employers' Liability Act of 1911 (Acts 1911 p. 145, §8020 *et seq.* Burns 1914), abolishing the defense of contributory negligence where the injury complained of results from the employe's obedience to the command of a superior.

*American Car, etc., Co.* v. *Williams,* 1, 6 (6).

37. *Workmen's Compensation Act.—Scope.—Employe.*—Under §76 of the Workmen's Compensation Act (Acts 1915 p. 392), which defines an employe as every person in the service of another under any contract of hire or apprenticeship written or implied, except casual laborers, etc., one who is an independent contractor is not included within the protection of the act. *Columbia School Supply Co.* v. *Lewis,* 386, 388 (1).

38. *Workmen's Compensation Act.—Injury in Course of Employment.—Question of Law.*—Where the facts, including all reasonable inferences to be drawn therefrom, are ascertained, the ultimate question from such facts of whether an injury under consideration was an injury by accident arising out of and in the course of the employment within the meaning of the Workmen's Compensation Act involves a law question.

*Columbia School Supply Co.* v. *Lewis,* 386, 390 (3).

39. *Workmen's Compensation Act.—Award for Injury.—Appeal.* —If, in an action for an award under the Workmen's Compensation Act (Acts 1915 p. 392) the uncontradicted evidence, when measured by legal standards that must be applied, established the relation of contractee and independent contractor rather than that of employer and employe, as those terms are used in the act, or if such uncontradicted evidence established that the injury complained of was not an injury arising out of and in the course of employment, an award involves errors of law, and the cause is appealable under §61 of such act, providing that appeals may be taken from awards of the industrial board to the Appellate Court for errors of law.

*Columbia School Supply Co.* v. *Lewis,* 386, 390 (4).

40. *Workmen's Compensation Act.—Intent of Legislature.*—An examination of the Workmen's Compensation Act (Acts 1915 p. 392) in its entirety shows clearly that the intention of the legislature was to provide compensation and the proper award with a minimum of legal procedure.

*Union Sanitary Mfg. Co.* v. *Davis,* 548, 551 (1).

41. *Workmen's Compensation Act.—Review of Award.*—The provisions for a review of an award authorized by §60 of the Workmen's Compensation Act (Acts 1915 pp. 392, 410) afford opportunity for presenting to the full board all questions relied upon by the aggrieved party, and, in the main, serve the same purpose that a motion for a new trial serves in a civil action.

*Union Sanitary Mfg. Co.* v. *Davis,* 548, 551 (2).

42. *Workmen's Compensation Act.—Procedure.—Appeals.*—The legislature did not contemplate engrafting on the procedure provided by the Workmen's Compensation Act (Acts 1915 p. 392) all the requirements relating to appeals from judgments in ordinary civil suits, and, in construing §61 authorizing appeals from awards, the phrase "under the same terms and

## MASTER AND SERVANT—Continued.

conditions as govern appeals in civil actions" is to be applied only to phases of procedure in appeals under the act not specially provided for therein.

*Union Sanitary Mfg. Co.* v. *Davis*, 548, 551 (3).

43. *Workmen's Compensation Act.—Appeal.—Motion for New Trial.*—The intent to make the procedure under the Workmen's Compensation Act (Acts 1915 p. 392) simple and direct and to dispense with a motion for a new trial is apparent from the general tenor of the law and the special provisions thereof, and, where a final award has been made by the industrial board, an appeal therefrom will lie, if otherwise properly perfected, though appellant has made no motion for a new trial.

*Union Sanitary Mfg. Co.* v. *Davis*, 548, 552 (4).

44. *Workmen's Compensation Act.—Appeal.—Motion to Modify or Set Aside Award.*—It is not necessary to file a motion to modify or set aside the final award made by the full board under the Workmen's Compensation Act (Acts 1915 p. 392) to entitle the party aggrieved to an appeal under the act.

*Union Sanitary Mfg. Co.* v. *Davis*, 549, 552 (5).

45. *Workmen's Compensation Act.—Appeal for Errors of Law.—Record.—Assignment of Errors.*—Where the record shows that appellant has properly excepted to the final award of the full board under the Workmen's Compensation Act (Acts 1915 p. 392), has presented its bill of exceptions containing the evidence and the rulings of the court and exceptions thereto, which bill of exceptions has been properly approved, and has filed a duly certified transcript of copies of all papers and entries in the cause, and appellant, on appeal to the Appellate Court from such final award, assigns as error that the award is not sustained by sufficient evidence, "the award is contrary to law," etc., the assignment of error presents alleged "errors of law" and the party aggrieved is entitled to have them passed upon by the court under §61 of the act, so that a motion to dismiss the appeal will be overruled.

*Union Sanitary Mfg. Co.* v. *Davis*, 549, 552, 553 (6).

46. *Workmen's Compensation Act.—Appeal.—Record.—Exceptions.*—Where the record on an appeal from a final award of the industrial board under the Workmen's Compensation Act (Acts 1915 p. 392) shows proper exception to the original award and also to the award of the full board, contention that the record does not show that the exception was taken "at the time" is not available, when the exceptions shown are sufficient under the provisions of the act and would have been sufficient without showing an exception to the first award.

*Union Sanitary Mfg. Co.* v. *Davis*, 549, 552 (7).

## MECHANIC'S LIEN—

1. *Filing.—Last Work Done.*—Where plaintiff, under a contract fixing no time for the completion of the work, installed a heating plant in a residence, and several months thereafter, under the direction and with the consent of the owner, removed a section of the boiler for the purpose of remedying defects in the plant, a notice of an intention to hold a mechanic's lien, filed within the statutory time after the completion of such additional work, was within the proper time and plaintiff was entitled to a foreclosure of the lien.

*Hartzell* v. *Pranger*, 380, 384 (2).

**MECHANIC'S LIEN—Continued.**

2. *Husband and Wife.—Tenancy by Entireties.—Liability of Wife for Improvements.—Statute.—*Section 7860 Burns 1914, §5123 R. S. 1881, which requires the written consent of the wife in order to charge her personally and alone with repairs or improvements made on her separate real estate by order of the husband, has no application to real estate which the wife and husband own as tenants by the entireties.
*Haehnel* v. *Seidentopf,* 218, 223 (8).

**MEMORANDUM—**

See Demurrer; PLEADING.

Of defects, demurrer, scope of review, see APPEAL 64, 81, 128.

**MEMORIAL—**

James B. Black, see p. xxxiv.

Daniel W. Comstock, see p. xxxvi.

**MERGER—**

Improvement lien, conveyance of property to contractor, false representations of contractor, effect, see MUNICIPAL CORPORATIONS 13.

**MINES AND MINERALS—**

1. *Oil and Gas Leases.—Actions.—Burden of Proof.—*In an action on an oil and gas lease, the burden of proof is on the plaintiffs to show their right to the relief sought, and they cannot base a recovery on the weakness of defendant's position.
*Harris* v. *Riggs,* 201, 210 (11).

2. *Oil and Gas Leases.—Actions.—Failure to Find Essential Facts.—*In an action to quiet title based on an oil and gas lease, the failure of the trial court in its findings of fact to find any material fact essential to plaintiff's recovery is a finding against them as to such fact.
*Harris* v. *Riggs,* 201, 210 (12).

3. *Oil and Gas Lease.—Abandonment.—New Lease.—Effect.—*Where, after the abandonment of an oil and gas lease, the lessor, who had never been out of possession of the leased premises, so that he could not re-enter upon himself, again leased the premises, such new lease sufficiently showed the lessor's intention to treat the first lease as annulled.
*Harris* v. *Riggs,* 201, 211 (13).

4. *Oil and Gas Leases.—Abandonment.—*Because of the nature of the subject-matter, abandonment of oil and gas leases may be more readily found than in most cases and, as the rights granted thereunder are for exploration and development, the lessee will not be permitted to fail in development and hold the lease for speculative or other purposes, except in strict compliance with his contract for a valuable and sufficient consideration other than such development.
*Harris* v. *Riggs,* 201, 210 (10).

5. *Oil and Gas Leases.—Abandonment.—*A lease, giving the lessee the right to drill the leased premises for oil and gas for a fixed period of time and providing that, if a well shall not have been completed prior to a certain date, the lessee is obligated to pay the lessors a stipulated rental until the completion of a well, may be abandoned by the lessee, and, if it is abandoned, he cannot thereafter enforce any right thereunder without first securing the consent of the lessor or a renewal of the lease.
*Harris* v. *Riggs,* 201, 209 (9).

**MINORS—**

See INFANTS.

**MISCONDUCT—**

Of party or counsel, review, see APPEAL 18, 75, 76, 118.

**MORTGAGES—**

See CHATTEL MORTGAGES.

Sale of property, purchase by mortgagor, lien, see BANKRUPTCY.

*Action to Foreclose.—Release by Mistake.—Evidence.—Bona Fide Purchaser.*—In an action to foreclose a mortgage which plaintiff claimed he had released of record by mistake, where the complaint averred that one of the defendants, who had obtained title to the real estate involved subsequent to such release, paid no consideration for the transfer of the property, and that he held the title as a volunteer for the benefit of the mortgagor and for the fraudulent purpose of preventing plaintiff from enforcing his lien against the real estate, plaintiff, in order to defeat such title, was required to show either that such defendant held as a mere volunteer, or fraudulently, or that no consideration was paid by him.

*Greathouse v. Harrison*, 95, 99 (1).

**MOTIONS—**

See APPEAL; NEW TRIAL; PLEADING.

**MUNICIPAL CORPORATIONS—**

See NUISANCE; SCHOOLS AND SCHOOL DISTRICTS; STREET RAILROADS; TELEGRAPHS AND TELEPHONES; VENDOR AND PURCHASER.

1. *Personal Injuries.—Defective Streets.—Notice.*—Failure to give a town notice in writing containing a brief general description of the time, place, cause and nature of the injury, as required by §8962 Burns 1914, Acts 1907 p. 383, 408, precludes the right to maintain an action for personal injuries resulting from any defect in the condition of a street or alley.

*Town of French Lick v. Allen*, 649, 650 (1).

2. *Personal Injuries.—Notice to City or Town.—Construction.—Sufficiency.*—In determining whether the time, the place and the nature of the injury, etc., are disclosed with sufficient clearness in a notice served on a city pursuant to §8962 Burns 1914, Acts 1907 p. 383, 408, a liberal construction will be applied, and relief will not be denied when by any fair and reasonable construction it can be said that it substantially complies with the statute, but the notice must be sufficiently definite and accurate as to the place of injury that the officers of the municipality will be able to locate it without the aid of any extraneous information, so that they may ascertain the facts and determine the question of liability before suit is brought.

*Town of French Lick v. Allen*, 649, 651 (2).

3. *Personal Injuries. — Notice. — Sufficiency. — Description of Place.*—A notice to a town that plaintiff had been injured by a fall on a street leading from the town to a certain highway, on the hill south of the street-car barn where the street was being improved, and that her fall was caused by the uneven surface of the street and sidewalks, is insufficient to comply with the requirements of §8962 Burns 1914, Acts 1907 p. 383, 408, since no unusual place in the street is designated, and the only defect indicated is not even definitely located at any particular place in the street described.

*Town of French Lick v. Allen*, 649, 652 (3).

MUNICIPAL CORPORATIONS—Continued.

4. *Public Improvements.—Procedure.—Competitive Bidding.—*
Competitive bidding in the letting of contracts for the construction of a street improvement is mandatory and jurisdictional and where it is omitted the proceedings are invalid and void.
*Hoosier Construction Co.* v. *Seibert,* 594, 602 (2).

5. *Public Improvements.—Procedure.—Omission of Competitive Bidding.—Collateral Attack.—*The proceedings had in the construction of a street improvement are subject to collateral attack where it appears that competitive bidding has been omitted in the letting of the contract.
*Hoosier Construction Co.* v. *Seibert,* 594, 602 (3).

6. *Public Improvements.—Action to Enforce Lien.—Answer.—Sufficiency.—*In a contractor's action against a property owner to enforce a street improvement assessment lien, an answer fully pleading the invalidity of the proceedings for the improvement and showing that the property owner brought and prosecuted an injunction proceeding to restrain the city from entering into the contract for the work and appealed to a higher court from an adverse decision, and that the contractor, before entering into the contract, knew of the injunction suit and that the property owner was therein questioning the validity of the improvement proceedings, is sufficient as against demurrer.
*Hoosier Construction Co.* v. *Seibert,* 594, 603 (7).

7. *Public Improvements.—Assessments.—Liability.—Estoppel to Question.—*Where the owner of property liable to assessment for a street pavement brought suit to enjoin the city from entering into the contract for the improvement, attacking in such suit the validity of the improvement proceedings, and the paving contractor, with full knowledge of such action and chargeable with the knowledge that the plaintiff therein had the right to appeal from the adverse decision of the lower court, entered into a contract with the city to do the work and constructed the pavement, the property owner was not estopped, after a reversal of the trial court's decision in the injunction suit, to question the improvement assessment, since an estoppel can arise in such a case only where it appears that the complaining party stands by and without objection permits the work to be commenced and continued.
*Hoosier Construction Co.* v. *Seibert,* 594, 604 (8).

8. *Public Improvements.—Failure to Object.—Assessments.—Estoppel to Question.—*It is the general rule that where the owner of property subject to assessment for public improvements stands by and makes no objection to improvements which benefit his property, he may not deny the authority by which the improvements are made, nor defeat the assessment made against his property for the benefits derived, and the rule applies both where the proceedings are attacked for irregularity and where their validity is denied but color of law exists for the proceedings.
*Hoosier Construction Co.* v. *Seibert,* 594, 602 (4).

9. *Public Improvements.—Enforcement of Lien.—Estoppel to Question Assessment.—Burden of Proof.—*In a paving contractor's action against a property owner to enforce a lien for work done in the construction of a street pavement, where the invalidity of the proceedings for the improvement appears, plaintiff has the burden of alleging facts estopping the prop-

## MUNICIPAL CORPORATIONS—Continued.

erty owner from questioning the assessment for the improvement. *Hoosier Construction Co.* v. *Seibert*, 594, 603 (5).

10. *Street Improvements.—Conveyance of Land Assessed.—Deed. —Notice.*—Where a paving contractor after assigning a street improvement bond, falsely represented that he was still the owner thereof and thereby procured the owner of land assessed for the improvement to convey the same to him in consideration of the satisfaction of the lien against the property, the record of such deed did not give the holder of the bond notice of any fact that would defeat its right to foreclose the lien of the assessment if it was otherwise entitled to do so.
*Nat. Exchange Bank* v. *Smith*, 574, 585 (8).

11. *Street Improvements.—Foreclosure of Lien.—Findings.—Review.*—Where, in an action to foreclose the statutory lien securing a street improvement bond, defendant contended that plaintiff had at no time been in possession of the bond and that it was held by the paving contractor, defendant's predecessor in title, at the time he procured a conveyance of the lot involved in payment of the bond and assessment, a finding for defendant is a finding in his favor on the issue of possession of the bond; and, there being some evidence to support such finding, it is conclusive on appeal.
*Nat. Exchange Bank* v. *Smith*, 574, 578 (1).

12. *Street Improvements.—Foreclosure of Lien.—Evidence.— Sufficiency.*—In an action to foreclose the statutory lien securing a street improvement bond, the evidence is held sufficient to warrant a finding that neither the assignment of the bond nor a copy thereof was left at the office of the town clerk.
*Nat. Exchange Bank* v. *Smith*, 574, 578 (2).

13. *Street Improvements.—Bonds.—Lien.—Merger.—Discharge of Lien.*—Where a paving contractor, after assigning street improvement bonds, falsely represented that he was still the owner thereof and thereby induced the owner of real estate assessed for the improvement to convey the real estate to him in consideration of the satisfaction of the improvement lien against the property, the lien was not merged in the contractor's title and it could be foreclosed against his grantee, since the lien of the total bond issue covered the property of all the owners who signed waivers and the lien of the assessment for which the bonds were issued is by statute (§4296 Burns 1901, Acts 1899 p. 237) declared to be equal upon the property assessed without priority of one of such bonds over any other, and to discharge an improvement lien against any particular tract or lot there must have been payment in full of the assessment against it to the person lawfully entitled to receive the same. *Nat. Exchange Bank* v. *Smith*, 574, 582 (4).

14. *Street Improvements.— Bonds.— Record.— Notice.—* Where bonds are payable to a person named or bearer, the record of the improvement proceeding is notice to all that such obligation may rightfully be owned and in the possession of some person other than the one named without any assignment or record of transfer. *Nat. Exchange Bank* v. *Smith*, 574, 583 (5).

15. *Street Improvements.—Bonds.—Notice.*—The law charges the owner of property assessed for a street improvement with the knowledge that a particular bond is not issued to cover the assessment of any one tract of realty affected by the im-

## MUNICIPAL CORPORATIONS—Continued.

provement except as the amount of such assessment is a part of the aggregate sum for which the bonds are issued.

*Nat. Exchange Bank* v. *Smith*, 574, 583 (6).

16. *Streets.—Use by Public.—Control by Municipality.*—While the public is entitled to the free use of any portion of a public street, yet the municipal corporation may devote portions of the sidewalk to other purposes useful and convenient to the public.

*Lafayette Telephone Co.* v. *Cunningham*, 136, 144 (6).

17. *Holding Illegal Race in Village Street.—Injury to Spectator. —Recovery as for Illegal Act.*—While the holding of a horse race in a village street is a violation of §§2664, 2665 Burns 1914, Acts 1905 pp. 584, 745, yet one who goes to attend such a race as a spectator, thereby consenting to the unlawful act, and, while it is in progress, goes upon the street where the race is being run and is struck by one of the horses and injured, cannot recover, regardless of the elements of negligence and contributory negligence, merely because the race was held in violation of the law.                         *Frazure* v. *Ruckles*, 538.

18. *Public Nuisance.—Obstruction in Street.—Abatement.*—An unauthorized and unlawful obstruction of a public street in a town or city is a public nuisance, and as such may be abated.

*Town of Carlisle* v. *Pirtle*, 475, 480 (3).

19. *Public Nuisance.—Obstruction in Street.—Abatement by Incorporated Town.—Burden of Proof.*—Where an incorporated town resorted to the courts to have declared a nuisance and abated as such a cement sidewalk which was built on a higher grade than the walks adjoining at either end, the town assumed the burden of establishing that the walk, by reason of its comparative elevation, was a public nuisance, in that its use was perilous to pedestrians.   *Town of Carlisle* v. *Pirtle*, 475, 481 (5).

20. *Public Nuisance.—Power of Incorporated Towns to Declare and Abate.—Statute.*—Under §9005, cl. 4, Burns 1914, Acts 1909 pp. 359, 363, incorporated towns are authorized to declare, by general ordinance, what shall constitute a nuisance and to prevent, abate or remove it, and they may also at their election resort to the courts to abate a public nuisance.

*Town of Carlisle* v. *Pirtle*, 475, 481 (4).

## NAMES—

See TRADE-NAMES.

## NEGLIGENCE—

See CARRIERS; DEATH; LANDLORD AND TENANT 5; MASTER AND SERVANT; RAILROADS; TELEGRAPHS AND TELEPHONES.

1. *Complaint.—Disclosure of Defense.—Contributory Negligence.* —Contributory negligence is a defense, and, while it may appear from the complaint, when it does, it is the duty of the court to hold the complaint insufficient as against a demurrer predicated on such ground, yet the court can do this only when it can say, as a matter of law, that under the facts pleaded, honest and reasonable men could draw but one inference therefrom—that the plaintiff's conduct was not that of a man of ordinary care and prudence.

*Chicago, etc., R. Co.* v. *Biddinger*, 30, 42 (13).

2. *Complaint.—Necessary Averments.—Sufficiency.*—Where the duty to use ordinary care is shown by the complaint, the gen-

## NEGLIGENCE—Continued.

eral averment therein that defendant carelessly and negligently did, or omitted to do, the acts necessary to the discharge of such duty, and that such negligent acts were the proximate cause of the injury complained of, renders the complaint sufficient as against a demurrer, unless the specific acts pleaded are of a character to destroy the force and effect of such general charge of negligence.

*Chicago, etc., R. Co. v. Biddinger*, 30, 40 (7).

3. *Contributory Negligence.—Crossing Street Between Street Crossings.*—Where a police officer in response to a call from another officer, attempted to cross a street at a place where there was no intersection of a street or alley, and at a place not provided for crossing and in so doing tripped over a telephone guy wire and was injured, it cannot be said, as a matter of law, that the officer was guilty of contributory negligence in crossing the street where no street crossing was provided.

*Lafayette Telephone Co. v. Cunningham*, 136, 143 (4).

4. *Driving Automobile.—Collision on Highway.—Verdict.—Evidence.—Sufficiency.—Violation of Statute.*—In an action for personal injuries, where it appeared from the evidence that defendant was proceeding along a public highway in his automobile at a speed of twenty-five miles per hour, and, although he was signalled to stop his car or slacken its speed, failed to do so, but, in attempting to pass plaintiff's wagon and team, struck and injured plaintiff who was walking on the road beside his horses so as to better control them, such evidence was sufficient to sustain a verdict for plaintiff, since it showed defendant guilty of actionable negligence, especially as he was so operating his motor car at the time of the accident as to violate one of the penal laws of the state.

*Gardner v. Vance*, 27, 29, 30 (2).

5. *Use of Highway.—Presumption.*—In an action for personal injuries sustained in a collision with a motor car, plaintiff was without fault in walking on the road beside his horses so as to better control them, since one lawfully using a public highway has the right to assume that others using the highway in common with him will take notice of his presence and exercise a proper degree of care not to harm him.

*Gardner v. Vance*, 27, 30 (4).

## NEGOTIABLE INSTRUMENTS—

See BILLS AND NOTES.

## NEW TRIAL—

See APPEAL 19, 34, 50, 68, 71.

Change of venue after order for, jurisdiction of court to which change is taken to review order, see COURTS 3.

Where a party procured the court to grant a new trial, he waived any error in the court's ruling, made prior to the order for new trial, on a motion for judgment on interrogatories, see APPEAL 72.

1. *As of Right.—When Granted.*—In an action seeking to have a trust in land declared and an accounting by defendant for rents and profits, wherein defendant by cross-complaint asked to have his title quieted to the land involved, but the decree rendered did not grant such relief, defendant was not entitled to a new trial as of right.          *Trook v. Trook*, 272, 276 (1).

NEW TRIAL—Continued.

2. *As of Right.—Joinder of Several Causes of Action.*—A complaint seeking to have a trust declared in land and asking also for an accounting by the defendant for rents and profits states two substantive causes of action and if the first mentioned cause so involves the questions of title and possession that, if standing alone, defendant would be entitled to a new trial as of right, such right is properly denied where, as in this case, both causes have proceeded to judgment; since a new trial as of right is not permissible in a suit for an accounting.

Trook v. Trook, 272, 280 (5).

3. *As of Right.—Vacating Order for.*—Where a motion for a new trial as a matter of right is improperly sustained, the same court may thereafter vacate the order.

Trook v. Trook, 272, 278 (3).

4. *As of Right.—Joinder of Causes in Same Case.*—Where two causes of action are joined and proceed to judgment in the same case, in one of which a new trial as of right is allowable, and in the other it is not, the statute is not applicable, and a new trial as of right will not be granted.

Trook v. Trook, 272, 277 (2).

5. *Laches.—Statutory Period.*—A party who makes his motion for new trial within the statutory time is not guilty of laches.

Hoosier Construction Co. v. Seibert, 594, 606 (10).

NOTICE—

See LIS PENDENS; MUNICIPAL CORPORATIONS; PRINCIPAL AND SURETY.

Failure to serve, vacating final settlement, see GUARDIAN AND WARD.

Of defects, employe's action, see MASTER AND SERVANT 26.

Of appeal, service on coparties, construction of statute, see APPEAL 5.

Service of, on appeal, sufficiency, see APPEAL 11.

Failure to serve, dismissal, see APPEAL 53, 54.

Street improvements, record, see VENDOR AND PURCHASER.

NUISANCE—

See LANDLORD AND TENANT 5; MUNICIPAL CORPORATIONS 18-20.

*Public Nuisance.—Private Nuisance.—Distinction.*—The distinction between a public and a private nuisance does not necessarily consist in the nature of the thing done or of the character of the structure maintained, either of which may constitute a public nuisance if prejudical to the general public, and also a private nuisance as to some particular person if he suffers an injury not common to the general public.

Town of Carlisle v. Pirtle, 475, 480 (2).

NUNC PRO TUNC—

Entry, presenting question on appeal, *certiorari*, see APPEAL 20.

OBJECTIONS—

See APPEAL.

## OFFICERS—

Acts of, ratification by corporation, see PRINCIPAL AND AGENT 4.

Performance of duties, presumption, see EVIDENCE 3.

*Official Bonds.—Party in Interest.*—Where actions are brought upon official bonds payable to the state in its name on the relation of the party interested, as provided in §253 Burns 1914, §253 R. S. 1881, the state is but a nominal party, the real party in interest being the relator.

*State, ex rel.* v. *Stevens,* 561, 564 (2).

## OIL LEASES—

See MINES AND MINERALS.

## "OR"—

Construed as connective, see INSURANCE 3.

## ORDINANCES—

City, violation, negligence, see MASTER AND SERVANT 10, 12.

## PARENT AND CHILD—

See ADOPTION; BASTARDS; GUARDIAN AND WARD; HUSBAND AND WIFE.

## PAROL AGREEMENTS—

See CARRIERS 11; CONTRACTS; DAMAGES 1; INSURANCE 4-6; LANDLORD AND TENANT.

## PARTIES—

On appeal, see APPEAL 5-9, 35, 52, 57-59; BANKRUPTCY; CORPORATIONS 1, 2; DRAINS 2; PARTITION 4; SCHOOLS AND SCHOOL DISTRICTS.

*Joining.—Mode of.—Cross-Complaint.—Motion to Strike Out.*—Where, in an action to recover a deposit made to indemnify defendant company against loss or damage by reason of its having paid a judgment obtained against it as garnishee in a prior suit, defendant filed a cross-complaint against plaintiff and additional parties containing averments showing the existence of various conflicting claims to the money held as a deposit, that defendant could not safely go to trial unless the additional parties were joined, so that the proper claimant to the money involved might be determined, and that it might be compelled to litigate the several claims in separate suits unless all claimants were joined in the present action, the cross-complaint, since the facts alleged therein tended to state a cause of action against some of the defendants thereto and were germane to the subject-matter of the transaction in controversy, should have been allowed to prevent multiplicity of suits, and it was error for the trial court to strike out the pleading.

*Chicago etc., R. Co.* v. *Dunnahoo,* 237, 246, 249 (6).

## PARTITION—

1. *Commissioner for Sale of Land.—Duties.—Liability on Bond.*—The duties of a commissioner appointed to make the sale of land in a partition proceeding are determined by the statutes and the orders of the court, and he is an instrument of the court primarily answerable thereto, and only becomes liable on his bond when he fails to faithfully discharge the duties of his trust. *Kiefer Drug Co.* v. *DeLay,* 639, 642 (1).

## PARTITION—Continued.

2. *Commissioner for Sale of Land.—Duties.—Liability to Lien-holder.*—A commissioner for the sale of land in partition who follows the order of sale and distributes the funds according thereto has discharged the obligation of his trust in that respect, and he is not liable to one who acquired a lien on the real estate subsequent to the order of sale and the appointment of the commissioner, unless such lienholder before the funds were distributed duly petitioned the court and obtained an order which entitled him to receive payment out of the funds derived from the sale.        *Keifer Drug Co.* v. *DeLay,* 639, 643 (3).

3. *Judgment against Party.—Presumptions.*—The mere fact that a judgment is of record and appears unsatisfied is not conclusive evidence that it is unpaid or that there is not some valid reason why funds in the hands of the commissioner in a partition proceeding should not be applied to such a judgment against an heir to the lands sold.
        *Keifer Drug Co.* v. *DeLay,* 639, 645 (6).

4. *Parties.—Lienholders.—Distribution of Proceeds.*—In partition suits it is proper to make those who hold liens on undivided interests in the land parties to the action, and the court has power to protect their interests and, in case of sale, to provide for the payment or satisfaction of such liens out of funds derived from the sale of such interests to the extent that the net proceeds from the sale thereof shall be sufficient so to do.
        *Kiefer Drug Co.* v. *DeLay,* 639, 642 (2).

5. *Sale of Land. — Proceeds. — Distribution. — Commissioner's Bond.—Liability.*—Where, in a partition proceedings, an order is made for the sale of land and it is sold in accordance with the order, one holding a judgment against one of the parties in partition who was not himself a party and who did not file a transcript with the clerk until after the entry of the order of sale cannot recover on the commissioner's bond because the commissioner, even though notified of the judgment creditor's claim, did not pay him the amount thereof.
        *Kiefer Drug Co.* v. *DeLay,* 639, 644 (5).

## PASSENGERS—

See CARRIERS.

## PATENTS—

See TRADE-MARKS AND TRADE-NAMES.

*License Contract.—Construction.*—A contract licensing the defendant to manufacture and sell patented silos and silo blocks in accordance with the stipulations therein set forth and providing for the payment to plaintiff of a royalty of five per cent on the gross sales of silos by the licensee, is held to mean, when the contract is construed as an entirety, that there could be a recovery of five per cent of the proceeds of the sales of patented silos only, even though a clause of the contract provided that defendant was obligated to pay the stipulated royalty on the sales of "all vitrified block silos," since the general subject-matter of the contract, and of the recitals therein, was the patented silo blocks alone.
*Nat. Fire Proofing Co.* v. *Imperishable Silo Co.,* 183, 189, 190 (2).

**PATERNITY PROCEEDINGS—**

See BASTARDS.

Misconduct of counsel, presenting question, see APPEAL 18, 118, 120.

**PAYMENT—**

*Recovery of Payments.—Mutual Mistake.—Fraudulent Claim.—Demand.*—The rule that, where there has been a mutual mistake in the payment of money, the party receiving it must first be given an opportunity to return it before an action will lie for its recovery applies only in cases in which there has been neither a breach of a contract nor a duty, and not where money has been paid on items which the defendant knowingly and fraudulently included in bills rendered to plaintiff.
*Herald Publishing Co.* v. *State, ex rel.,* 465, 467 (1).

**PEDESTRIAN—**

Injury, unguarded cellarway, liability, see LANDLORD AND TENANT 5-9.

Injury of, by wire, action, see TELEGRAPHS AND TELEPHONES.

**PERSONAL INJURIES—**

See DAMAGES; MASTER AND SERVANT; MUNICIPAL CORPORATIONS; TELEGRAPHS AND TELEPHONES.

**PERSONAL PROPERTY—**

See PLEDGES.

Purchase by mortgagor, lien, see BANKRUPTCY.

Gifts of, delivery, effect, see HUSBAND AND WIFE 4.

As primary source for collection of taxes, see TAXATION.

**PHYSICIANS AND SURGEONS—**

See EVIDENCE 7, 8.

*Malpractice.—Complaint.—Sufficiency.*—In an action against a physician for malpractice in treating a burn on plaintiff's foot, a complaint containing allegations showing the nature and extent of the injury, that the only cure was a certain treatment which the defendant unskilfully and negligently failed to employ, that he negligently used, and continued to use, an insufficient remedy and failed to observe that it was not healing the wound, and that as a result of defendant's negligence and unskilfulness plaintiff suffered great pain, etc., and the foot was amputated, sufficiently states a cause of action for improper diagnosis, from want of skill or care, for use of an improper remedy and the continuance thereof after it should have been observed to be ineffectual. *Christie* v. *Walton,* 234, 235 (1).

**PLEADING—**

See ANSWER; DEMURRER; COMPLAINT; COURTS; INTERPLEADER.

For pleadings in particular actions or proceedings, see also the specific topics.

For review of rulings on pleadings, see APPEAL.

Nature of, to set aside default, demurrer, see JUDGMENT 4.

1. *Amendment.—Withdrawal of Submission.—Discretion of Court.—Failure to Show Harm.*—Where the trial court, after

**PLEADING—Continued.**

the hearing of the evidence, permitted plaintiff to withdraw the submission of the cause and file an additional paragraph of complaint, the accrued costs having been assessed against plaintiff, the withdrawal was not a dismissal of the action, and the procedure was fully within the discretion of the court, under §403 Burns 1914, §394 R. S. 1881, relating to amendments to pleadings, especially when the complaining party fails to show that he was harmed by the action of the court, and where the judgment rendered was favorable to him.

*Denney* v. *Reber*, 192, 200 (6).

2. *Complaint.—Facts.—Conclusions.*—In an action for wrongful death, an allegation in the complaint that decedent, at the time of his injury, was in the discharge of the duties of employment, but not averring that he was performing any of the services set forth in the complaint as such states a conclusion.

*S. W. Little Coal Co.* v. *O'Brien*, 504, 511 (1).

3. *Complaint.—Facts.—Conclusions.*—In an action for death by negligence, an allegation that decedent, who was crushed between a car and a scale house, was compelled to cross a railroad track in front of a moving car and to pass between it and a scale house, but no facts are pleaded showing the necessity which compelled decedent to so do, states a conclusion.

*S. W. Little Coal Co.* v. *O'Brien*, 504, 512 (2).

4. *Complaint.—Motion to Make More Specific.—Pleading Conclusions.*—Where, in an action for wrongful death, the complaint pleads conclusions to the effect that decedent, at the time he was killed, was on the farther side of a railroad track "in the discharge of the duties of his employment" and that he was "compelled" to cross such track in front of an approaching car and to pass between it and defendant's scale house, but no facts are alleged showing the necessity which compelled deceased to so do, it was error for the trial court to overrule a motion to make the complaint more specific.

*S. W. Little Coal Co.* v. *O'Brien*, 504, 513 (4).

5. *Complaint.—Relief Granted.—Prayer.*—The relief to which a party is entitled is determined by the facts averred and not by the prayer of the pleading.    *Barnum* v. *Rallihan*, 349, 361 (11).

6. *Complaint.—Exhibits.*—Where, in an action to recover a deposit made to indemnify defendant, the complaint alleged that plaintiff had, in another suit, obtained judgment against defendant company as garnishee, that the judgment had been paid by check and the money immediately placed in the keeping of the company by plaintiff to indemnify it against loss by reason of having satisfied such judgment, and that the purpose of the indemnity had been accomplished and payment thereof had been refused plaintiff on his demand, such complaint was not based on the judgment, since it was shown by the averments therein to have been satisfied, nor was it necessary to set forth a copy of the check, as a recovery was not sought thereon.

*Chicago, etc., R. Co.* v. *Dunnahoo*, 237, 242 (1).

7. *Complaint.—Motion to Make More Specific.—Knowledge.*—Where, in an action to foreclose a mechanic's lien, the complaint alleged that the property on which the lien was taken was owned by the defendants, husband and wife, as tenants by entireties, that the buildings erected on the premises were constructed under a contract with the husband with the full knowl-

## PLEADING—Continued.

edge, consent and acquiescence of the wife, and that in all things relating to the contract the husband acted as her agent, a motion to make the complaint more specific as to what knowledge, if any, the plaintiff had given to the wife concerning the contract for the erection of the buildings was properly overruled, since the averments of the complaint, in effect, charge the wife with having all knowledge possessed by the husband.

*Haehnel* v. *Seidentopf*, 218, 222 (7).

8. *Complaint.—Attack by Motion for a New Trial.*—Where, in a proceeding supplemental to execution, the defect in the complaint consists of omissions of essential averments and its sufficency is attacked on appeal by a motion for a new trial, such defect will be deemed cured by the verdict, the statute of amendments, or waived by failure to demur.

*Fox* v. *Close*, 66, 69 (4).

9. *Complaint.—Omission of Material Averments.—Cure by Evidence.*—Since the amendment of §348 Burns 1908, §343 R. S. 1881, by the Act of 1911 (Acts 1911 p. 415, §348 Burns 1914), it will be assumed on appeal that any omission of a material averment from the pleading was cured by the evidence, if from the affirmative facts pleaded it might have been so cured.

*Fox* v. *Close*, 66, 69 (5).

10. *Cross-Complaint.—Insufficient Allegations.—Motion to Strike Out.*—Insufficiency of a cross-complaint to state a cause of action is not a ground for striking it out, since such question can only be raised and presented by a demurrer for want of facts alleged. *Chicago, etc., R. Co.* v. *Dunnahoo*, 237, 246 (2).

11. *Cross-Complaint Not Germane to Action.—Motion to Strike Out.*—If the facts averred in a pleading are so palpably irrelevant to the matter in controversy that the pleading could not, by amendment, be made germane thereto, it would not he error to strike it out.

*Chicago, etc., R. Co.* v. *Dunnahoo*, 237, 246 (4).

12. *Demurrer.—Complaint.—Sufficiency.—Inferences.*—Where, in an action for wrongful death, the complaint is demurred to as affirmatively disclosing that decedent was guilty of contributory negligence, all inferences reasonably permissible under the allegations of the complaint must be indulged in favor of the sufficiency of the pleading.

*S. W. Little Coal Co.* v. *O'Brien*, 504, 517 (12).

13. *Demurrer to Answer.—Memorandum of Defects.—Failure to File.—Waiver.*—The right to question an answer for insufficiency of facts is waived by failure to file with a demurrer thereto the memorandum of defects required by statute, and no question is presented for review on appeal by an assignment of error challenging the action of the trial court in overruling such demurrer. *Town of Carlisle* v. *Pirtle*, 475, 477 (1).

14. *Demurrer to Answer.—Sufficiency.—Statute.*—Under §351 Burns 1914, §346 R. S. 1881, providing that a demurrer may be filed to answers where the facts stated therein "are not sufficient to constitute a cause of defense," a demurrer alleging "that the facts stated in each of said paragraphs of answer are insufficient to avoid the cause of action stated in plaintiff's complaint," does not follow the language of the statute and is insufficient to present any question, especially where each of the paragraphs of answer present only a partial defense.

*Eddy* v. *Honey Creek Tp.*, 527, 529 (1).

**PLEADING—Continued.**

15. *Theory.—Determination.*—In determining the theory of a pleading, the relief demanded may be considered in connection with the averments.　　　　*Barnum* v. *Rallihan,* 349, 361 (12).

16. *Theory.—Determination.—Theory on Appeal.*—The theory of a pleading must be determined by a consideration of its general scope and tenor, and the theory adopted by the trial court will be adhered to on appeal where such pleading, from its plain terms, is susceptible of such construction and theory, particularly where it appears from the record that the parties themselves proceeded on such theory.
*Bosson* v. *Brash,* 86, 88 (1).

17. *Answer.—Pleading Conclusions.—Rights of Plaintiff.—Statute.*—Under §343a Burns 1914, Acts 1913 p. 850, relating to the construction of allegations in pleadings, the pleading of conclusions in a paragraph of answer is permissible, and, if plaintiff desires the facts pleaded which are required to sustain the conclusions, he may obtain relief by the filing of a proper motion, as provided in such statute.
*National Live Stock Ins. Co.* v. *Owens,* 70, 77 (7).

18. *General Denial.—Defenses Admissible.*—Defenses admissible under the general denial are those which deny that there ever was a cause of action.
*National Live Stock Ins.* v. *Owens,* 70, 76 (6).

19. *General Denial.—Scope.—Laches.*—Under §361 Burns 1914, §356 R. S. 1881, providing that all defenses, except the mere denial of the facts alleged by plaintiff, shall be pleaded specially, the defense of laches is not provable under the general denial, but must be specially pleaded.
*New Albany Nat. Bank* v. *Brown,* 391, 402 (5).

20. *Motion to Strike Out.*—A motion to strike out a pleading ordinarily reaches formal defects only, and where the pleading tends to state a cause of action or defense, though insufficient when tested by demurrer, it should not be stricken out, thereby barring the right to amend.
*Chicago, etc., R. Co.* v. *Dunnahoo,* 237, 246 (3).

21. *Pleading Conclusions.—Motion to Make More Specific.*—Since the enactment of §343a Burns 1914, Acts 1913 p. 580, providing that any conclusion stated in any pleading must be considered and held to be equivalent to the allegation of all the facts required to sustain such conclusion if necessary to the sufficiency of the pleading, but that a motion may be made to require the party filing such pleading to state the facts necessary to sustain the conclusion alleged, motions to make more specific in such cases should be liberally granted.
*S. W. Little Coal Co.* v. *O'Brien,* 504, 512 (3).

22. *Sham.—Motion to Strike Out.*—It is proper to strike out a sham pleading.　　*Chicago, etc., R. Co.* v. *Dunnahoo,* 237, 246 (5).

**PLEDGES—**

1. *Elements.—Possession.*—Possession of a chattel is the essence of a pledge, and without it no privilege can exist against third persons.　　　　*New Albany Nat. Bank* v. *Brown,* 391, 400 (1).

2. *Renewal of Notes.—Effect.*—Where notes secured by a pledge are renewed, the pledge remains as security for the new notes,

**PLEDGES—Continued.**

in the absence of anything showing that the parties intended that the original debt should be regarded as paid.
*New Albany Nat. Bank* v. *Brown*, 391, 402 (7).

3. *Surrender of Possession for Special Purpose.—Possession Wrongfully Obtained.—Effect.*—Possession and control of pledged property acquired without the assent of the pledgee, or by deception and false pretenses, will not create a forfeiture of his lien, nor will the delivery of the pledged chattel to the pledgor for merely a temporary or special purpose divest the pledgee's lien as against the pledgor or attaching creditors, although it would have that effect as against bona fide purchasers from the pledgor while in such temporary possession.
*New Albany Nat. Bank* v. *Brown*, 391, 400 (2).

**POOR PERSON—**

Action by, nonresidence of plaintiff, bond, see COSTS.

**POSSESSION—**

See EJECTMENT; JUSTICES OF THE PEACE.

**PREPONDERANCE—**

Of evidence, see APPEAL 124.

**POSTPONEMENT—**

Words of, vesting of estates, see WILLS.

**PRESCRIPTION—**

Title by, see RAILROADS 24.

**PRESUMPTIONS—**

See ACCOUNT STATED 1; COSTS 2; DEEDS 5; TRIAL.

On appeal, see APPEAL 87-94, 112, 115; EVIDENCE 3; HUSBAND AND WIFE 3; PRINCIPAL AND AGENT 1.

**PRINCIPAL AND AGENT—**

See BROKERS; INSURANCE; PATENTS.

Action against agent, findings by commissioner, adoption by court, presumption, see APPEAL 89.

1 *Authority of Agent.—Presumption.*—There is no presumption that a special agent selling the goods of his principal has authority to pay his personal debts with the goods he sells.
*Excel Furniture Co.* v. *Brock*, 494, 500 (4).

2. *Authority of Agent.—Burden of Proof.*—Where, in an action for the price of goods sold, the buyer relies on the agent's authority to sell the principal's goods in payment of his personal obligations, the burden is on the buyer to show that the agent had the right to so sell the goods, or that such sale was acquiesced in, or ratified by, the principal.
*Excel Furniture Co.* v. *Brock*, 494, 500 (5).

3. *Ratification.—Knowledge.—Evidence.*—Where it is sought to show ratification of an unauthorized act, transaction, or contract by the fact that benefits have been knowingly accepted, knowledge, like other facts, need not be proven by a particular kind or class of evidence, and may be inferred from facts and circumstances. *National Life Ins. Co.* v. *Headrick* 54, 58 (7).

**PRINCIPAL AND AGENT—Continued.**

4. *Ratification.—Corporations.—Acts of Officers.*—Ratification by a corporation, which can act only through its officers and agents, may be shown by conduct without any formal action by its board of directors, and may be inferred from affirmation, from passive acquiescence, or from the recept of benefits with knowledge.      *National Life Ins. Co. v. Headrick, 54, 58 (6).*

5. *Ratification.—Acceptance of Benefits.—Estoppel.*—Knowingly accepting benefits of an unauthorized employment amounts to a ratification of such contract of employment, and is in the nature of an estoppel to deny the authority to make such contract.
      *National Life Ins. Co. v. Headrick, 54, 58 (5).*

6 *Ratification.—Evidence.*—Ratification is a question of fact which may ordinarily be inferred from the conduct of the parties, and the acts, words, silence, dealings and knowledge of the principal, as well as many other facts and circumstances, may be shown as evidence tending to warrant the inference or finding of the ultimate fact of ratification.
      *National Life Ins. Co. v. Headrick 54, 58 (4).*

7. *Ratification.*—Ratification means the adoption of that which was done for and in the name of another without authority, and, when ratification takes place, the act stands as an authorized one and makes the whole act, transaction, or contract good from the beginning.
      *National Life Ins. Co. v. Headrick, 54, 58 (3).*

8. *Unauthorized Acts of Agent.—Ratification.—Effect.*—Where the principal ratifies his agent's unauthorized act in specifying and agreeing to terms of sale, the situation is the same in legal effect as though the principal personally, rather than the agent, had agreed to such terms. *Crumpacker v. Jeffrey, 621, 631 (4).*

**PRINCIPAL AND SURETY—**

See Appeal 122.

Surety companies, organization, statute, see Statutes 1.

1. *Bonds.—Construction.*—Where a bond is ambiguous or open to two constructions, the interpretation most favorable to the obligee should be adopted, but this rule does not apply to bonds, the terms of which are certain, definite and unambiguous.
      *Wainright Trust Co. v. U. S. Fidelity, etc., Co., 309, 315 (3).*

2. *Contractor's Bond.—Notice of Default.—Acceptance of Premium.—Effect.*—The acceptance and retention by a surety company of a renewal premium on a contractor's bond was not a waiver of the company's right to a notice of the contractor's default, as provided in the bond, where the alleged default did not occur until several months after the payment of the premium.
      *Wainright Trust Co. v. U. S. Fidelity, etc., Co. 309, 316 (6).*

3. *Contractor's Bond.—Conditions.—Notice of Default.*—Where, in an action against a surety company on a road contractor's bond, the complaint contained allegations showing that on May 13, the board of county commissioners notified the obligee that work under the contract should begin within ten days in order to complete it by August 1, to which date the board had extended the time limit fixed in the contract, and that immediately upon receipt of such notice the obligee had written notice of the contractor's alleged default to the surety company and informed it of the board's order, such allegations do not show a compliance

## PRINCIPAL AND SURETY—Continued.

with a condition in the bond requiring, in order that liability should attach to the surety, that notice of the principal's default be given to the guarantor by the obligee not later than thirty days after knowledge of default, as the alleged notice of default was given more than two and one-half months before the expiration of the time limit fixed for the completion of the work.

*Wainright Trust Co.* v. *U. S. Fidelity, etc., Co.,* 309, 316 (5).

4. *Contractor's Bond.—Notice of Breach.—Failure to Give.—* Where a contractor's bond provided that no liability should attach to the surety unless, in the event of the principal's default, notice thereof should be given the surety not later than thirty days after knowledge of such default such condition was valid.

*Wainright Trust Co.* v. *U. S. Fidelity, etc., Co.,* 309, 315, (4).

## PRIORITIES—

See INSURANCE 13.

## PROMISSORY NOTES—

See BILLS AND NOTES.

## PROXIMATE CAUSE—

See MASTER AND SERVANT.

## PUBLIC IMPROVEMENTS—

See DRAINS; MUNICIPAL CORPORATIONS.

## PUBLIC LANDS—

*Swamp Lands.—Patents.—*A state patent conveying title to a certain described section of land, together with all rights, privileges, immunities and appurtenances of whatever nature thereto belonging, such patent having been made according to the act of 1852 regulating the sale by the state of swamp lands donated by the United States to the State of Indiana, is held, on the authority of the *State* v. *Tuesburg Land Company* (1915), 61 Ind. App. 555, not to convey title to the thread of a stream forming a boundary line of the section, even though the stream is a nonnavigable river. *Cobe* v. *Darrow,* 169, 172 (2).

## RAILROADS—

See CARRIERS; EASEMENTS; MASTER AND SERVANT; NEGLIGENCE; STREET RAILROADS.

1. *Crossing Accidents.—Complaint.—Construction.—*In an action for injuries sustained in a railroad crossing accident, an averment in the complaint as to the frequency of travel at the crossing strengthens the averment that defendant negligently and carelessly failed to maintain a watchman at such crossing.

*Chicago, etc., R. Co.* v. *Biddinger,* 30, 41 (9).

2. *Crossing Accidents.—Complaint.—Construction.—*In an action for personal injuries sustained in a railroad crossing accident, the specific averment in the complaint that the train which injured plaintiff was running at the high and dangerous speed of fifty miles an hour, when considered in the light of averments showing that the crossing where the accident occurred was in a city where vehicles were passing over it every two

**RAILROADS—Continued.**

minutes, did not tend to destroy the effect of a general charge of negligent speed. *Chicago, etc., R. Co.* v. *Biddinger*, 30, 40 (8).

3. *Crossing Accidents.—Complaint.—Construction.—*Averments in a complaint alleging that defendant railroad was operating a line of railway through a county named and was doing business therein; that Main street, or the Michigan road, which is crossed, is the principal street of the city of Rochester, and very much used by the public at the point where it crosses defendant's railway, are sufficient to show, aided by reasonable inference permitted in favor of a pleading, that the crossing referred to was located within the city of Rochester, and that the railroad was therefore subject to its ordinances.
*Chicago, etc., R. Co.* v. *Biddinger*, 30, 41 (10).

4. *Crossing Accidents.—Complaint.—Construction.—*In an action for personal injuries sustained in a railroad crossing accident, while averments in the complaint charging that plaintiff's view of the crossing was obstructed by buildings, etc., as he approached riding in a top buggy with the side curtains down, and that on account of obstructions he could not see or hear any train approaching, may tend to show, when standing alone, that plaintiff was guilty of contributory negligence in going upon the crossing, yet such averments, read in connection with others in the complaint alleging that when he approached the crossing he proceeded carefully and exercised all due care and caution to see and hear any train, may be fairly interpreted as meaning that plaintiff used all care and caution usually exercised by a man of ordinary care and prudence to see and hear an approaching train, and that he could not, and did not, see the train. *Chicago, etc., R. Co.* v. *Biddinger*, 30, 42, 43 (12.)

5. *Contracts.—Relief Associations.—Validity.—Waiver of Liability.—*A contract entered into by a railroad with an employe requiring him, as one of the conditions of employment, to become a member of a relief association maintained by the company and to receive benefits from such association in full payment of damages for personal injuries is held to be in violation of §5308 Burns 1914, Acts 1907 p. 46, prohibiting railroad companies from maintaining relief associations when the rules thereof require a waiver by the employe of claims against the company for personal injuries, and such contract is therefore void. *Baltimore, etc., R. Co.* v. *Poston*, 591.

6. *Crossing Accidents.—Complaint.—Allegations.—Inferences.—Sufficiency.—*In an action for personal injuries sustained in a railroad crossing accident, allegations in the complaint that defendant negligently ran its train against plaintiff while running at the high and dangerous speed of fifty miles per hour, and that the engine crew carelessly and negligently failed to sound the whistle or ring the bell of the locomotive on approaching the crossing when within 100 rods thereof, until about 150 feet therefrom, sufficiently showed, aided by reasonable inference permitted in favor of a pleading, that the train which injured plaintiff approached from a point not less than 100 rods from the crossing, and that from such point the whistle was not blown until the train was about 150 feet from the crossing, and such averments were sufficient to charge defendant with negligence in failing to give the signals required of trains by statute when approaching highway crossings.
*Chicago, etc., R. Co.* v. *Biddinger*, 30, 38 (2).

**RAILROADS—Continued.**

7. *Crossing Accidents.—Answers to Interrogatories.—Construction.*—In an action for injuries in a railroad crossing accident, the jury's finding, in answer to interrogatories, that with a box car standing east of the crossing on the elevator track, which was about 21 feet south of defendant's main track, plaintiff could have heard the approach of the train which struck him without stopping his horse, and could have heard the approach of the train before he crossed such elevator track if he had stopped and listened, is not in irreconcilable conflict with the general verdict, which is a finding that plaintiff used ordinary care and that he did not hear the train, since the answer of the jury, under the interpretation most favorable to defendant, will be construed as meaning that plaintiff could have heard the approaching train either by stopping his horse and listening, or without stopping his horse, which is not the equivalent of a finding that he did hear such train, or that by the use of ordinary care he could have heard it.

*Chicago, etc., R. Co. v. Biddinger*, 30, 45 (17).

8. *Crossing Accidents.—Answers to Interrogatories.—Construction.*—In an action against a railroad for injuries sustained in a collision at a street crossing, a finding by the jury, in answer to an interrogatory, that obstructions along and immediately east of the street, the side curtains on plaintiff's buggy and the noise from the steel tires on the buggy did not prevent him from hearing the train approaching as he traveled from a distance 200 feet south of defendant's main track toward the crossing, is not in irreconcilable conflict with a general verdict for plaintiff, since it does not mean that he heard, or could have heard, the train within the distance mentioned, but means, fairly interpreted, that the things mentioned in the interrogatory did not prevent plaintiff from hearing the train, and not that he may not have been prevented from hearing it by something else, or that he in fact heard it.

*Chicago, etc., R. Co. v. Biddinger*, 30, 44 (16).

9. *Crossing Accidents.—Review.—Answers to Interrogatories.*—In an action for personal injuries sustained in a collision with defendant's train at a crossing, where the facts elicited by the jury's answers to interrogatories do not show that plaintiff failed to use ordinary care to ascertain the approach of the train before proceeding upon the crossing, or that obstructions or noises other than those mentioned in the interrogatories may not have made it difficult or impossible to hear the approach of the train except by the use of extraordinary care, such facts will not invoke the application of the principle that the law will presume, generally, that a person actually saw what he could have seen if he had looked, and heard what he could have heard if he had listened, such presumption being indulged only in cases where one fails to look or listen, or where the physical surroundings and conditions are such as to force conviction that one did see or hear, notwithstanding a statement or finding that he did not. *Chicago, etc., R. Co. v. Biddinger*, 30, 45 (18).

10. *Crossing Accidents.—Negligence.—Failure to Give Statutory Signals.*—The failure of a railroad company to ring the bell on the engine continuously as a train approaches a street crossing, being in itself a violation of the statute, consitutes negligence.

*Chicago, etc., R. Co. v. Biddinger*, 30, 39 (3).

**RAILROADS—Continued.**

11. *Crossing Accidents.—Failure to Give Signals.*—Independent of statute, it is the duty of those in charge of a railroad train to give reasonable and timely warning of its approach to a highway crossing, and failure to do so constitutes negligence.
*Chicago, etc., R. Co.* v. *Biddinger,* 30, 39 (4).

12. *Crossing Accidents.—Speed.—Negligence.—Care Required.*— The rule permitting a train to be run in the country at a high rate of speed without the imputation of negligence does not obtain as to trains when operated through populous cities and over the much traveled crossings therein, but the railroad owes to those traveling over such crossings the duty of ordinary care.
*Chicago, etc., R. Co.* v. *Biddinger,* 30, 39 (6).

13. *Crossing Accidents.—Duty of Traveler Approaching Crossing.—Pleading.*—The law requires persons traveling on the streets of a city in a vehicle, and approaching a railroad crossing, to stop before passing over a crossing only in those cases where ordinary prudence would dictate such a course, and it is only in exceptional cases that the court can say that the facts pleaded affirmatively show the necessity for such action.
*Chicago, etc., R. Co.* v. *Biddinger,* 30, 43 (14).

14. *Crossing Watchman.— Operation.— Speed.— Negligence.*— While running a train over a crossing at a high rate of speed, or failure to have a flagman or watchman stationed at the crossing, is not negligence *per se,* in the absence of a statute making it so, yet such operation of a train may, in fact, constitute negligence depending upon all the facts and circumstances surrounding the particular case under consideration .
*Chicago, etc., R. Co.* v. *Biddinger,* 30, 39 (5).

15. *Crossing Natural Watercourse.—Rights.*—The rights of a railway company crossing the bed of a natural watercourse are not the same as those of a proprietor of land in regard to surface water.        *Dunn* v. *Chicago, etc., R. Co.,* 553, 559 (6).

16. *Construction.—Watercourses.*—Although a railroad company is by the statutes (§5195, cl. 5, Burns 1914, §3903 R. S. 1881, and §7683 Burns 1914, Acts 1905 pp. 521, 532) authorized to construct its road across any stream of water, they are required to restore and maintain it substantially in its former condition and in such manner as not to unnecessarily impair its usefulness, and any such company failing to do so is liable in damages to any person injured thereby.
*Dunn* v. *Chicago, etc., R. Co.* 553, 557 (1).

17. *Obstruction of Natural Watercourse.—Action.—Measure of Damages.*—In an action against a railroad company for damages from overflow of flood waters due to the obstruction of a natural watercourse, plaintiff may show the damage to his property by proving the loss of its rental value, where the complaint proceeds upon the theory that the nuisance is abatable, since, when the nuisance is abated, the damages recoverable are only such as have accrued prior to the action.
*Dunn* v. *Chicago, etc., R. Co.,* 553, 560 (9).

18. *Obstruction of Natural Watercourse.—Action.—Pleading and Proof.—Evidence.*—Where, in an action against a railroad company for damages for obstructing a natural watercourse it was not the theory of the complaint that there were any permanent injuries to the property involved although it was alleged that the flood waters impaired plaintiff's store building

**RAILROADS—Continued.**

to the extent of $1,000, it was proper to permit proof of the cost of repairs, but offered testimony tending to prove permanent injuries was properly excluded.

*Dunn* v. *Chicago, etc., R. Co.,* 553, 560 (8).

19. *Obstructing Natural Watercourse.—Flood Waters.—Duty of Railroad.—*A railway company constructing its road across a stream and erecting an embankment and culvert is required to consider conditions manifest at other times of high water, the changes in the surrounding territory and the volume of water which would probably flow through the stream during flood times, and must provide ample accommodations for the free passage of all such waters through its right of way at all seasons of the year. *Dunn* v. *Chicago, etc., R. Co.,* 553, 560 (7).

20. *Obstructing Natural Watercourse.—Flood Waters.—Liability.—Instruction.—*In an action against a railroad for damages caused by the obstruction of flood waters of a natural watercourse, it was error to instruct the jury that it is not the legal duty of a railroad company to make openings through its track large enough to prevent the accumulation of water on the up-stream side, but it is only required to make its opening large enough to take care of the water which will flow within the bed of a watercourse.

*Dunn* v. *Chicago, etc., R. Co.,* 553, 558, 560 (5).

21. *Protection of Right of Way.—Obstruction of Surface Water.* —A railroad company has the right to employ all necessary methods which it deems expedient to prevent surface water from flowing onto and across its right of way without being liable for the damage done thereby.

*Dunn* v. *Chicago, etc., R. Co.,* 553, 557 (2).

22. *Protection of Right of Way.—Obstruction of Natural Watercourse.—Liability.—*A railroad company in the construction and maintenance of its road over a natural watercourse must exercise due care not to obstruct the natural flow thereof, including not only such rises of high water as are usual and ordinary, but also floods due to natural causes, such as an ordinarily prudent person should reasonably anticipate, considering the topography of the country, character of the soil, climatic conditions and all other conditions and circumstances apparent to a person of usual foresight and experience.

*Dunn* v. *Chicago, etc., R. Co.,* 553, 557 (3).

23. *Right of Way.—Title by Prescription.—Extent of Title.—* It is the general rule that where a railroad right of way is acquired by prescription, the company takes only an easement.

*Meyer* v. *Pittsburgh, etc., R. Co.,* 156, 165 (2).

24. *Right of Way.—Title by Prescription.—Interest Acquired.— Grant Presumed.—*The charter of a railway company authorizing it to acquire lands in fee for right of way purposes and providing that when the right of way should be procured the company "shall be seized in fee simple of the right to such lands" did not prohibit the railroad and its successors in interest from acquiring a less interest or smaller estate in the lands desired, and where the company, claiming title by prescription, has been in possession and occupataion of lands used in the operation of its railroad for tracks and embankments for more than twenty years, such user of the lands being continuous and adverse to the claim or interest of any owner thereof, the grant presumed, and the prescriptive title acquired, from such use

**RAILROADS—Continued.**

and occupancy is not that of an estate in fee simple, but is only
a fee in an easement sufficiently comprehensive to protect the
railroad's use of the land as exercised during such occupancy.
                    *Meyer* v. *Pittsburgh, etc., R. Co.*, 156, 165 (3).

**RATIFICATION—**

See BROKERS 3-7; PRINCIPAL AND AGENT.

**REAL ACTIONS—**

See EJECTMENT; JUSTICES OF THE PEACE; PARTITION.

**REAL-ESTATE AGENTS—**

See BROKERS; CONTRACTS.

**REAL PARTY IN INTEREST—**

See BANKRUPTCY; OFFICERS.

**RECEIVERS—**

See CORPORATIONS; COSTS 3.

Discharge of duties, presumption, see APPEAL 92.

1. *Action by or Against Insolvent Corporation.—Rights of Receiver.*—The receiver of an insolvent corporation is the proper
party to bring any action which the corporation might have
brought, and, as trustee for the creditors, can maintain and
defend actions which the corporation could not.
                    *Marcovich* v. *O'Brien, Auditor*, 101, 113 (9).

2. *Application for Appointment for Insolvent Bank.—Notice to
Stockholders.—Statute.*—Under §3346 Burns 1914, Acts 1895 p.
202, relating to the examination of banks, a notice by publication to the stockholders of a bank, alleged to be insolvent, is a
necessary prerequisite to the appointment of a receiver therefor.
                    *Marcovich* v. *O'Brien, Auditor*, 101, 115 (12).

3. *Insolvent Corporation.—Property as Trust Fund.*—Where a
court has taken possession of the property of an insolvent corporation for administration, and appointed a receiver, the
property of the corporation is a trust fund for the payment of
its debts.              *Marcovich* v. *O'Brien, Auditor*, 101, 112 (6).

4. *Officers of Court.—Functions and Duties.*—The receiver of an
insolvent corporation is not the agent of either party to the
action, but is regarded as an officer of the court, exercising his
functions for the common benefit of all parties in interest.
                    *Marcovich* v. *O'Brien, Auditor*, 101, 113 (7).

5. *Represents Both Stockholders and Creditors.—Duties.*—While
for the purposes of determining the nature and extent of his
title, a receiver represents the insolvent corporation itself, yet
he represents both stockholders and creditors and is to be regarded as their trustee, charged with the duty of collecting,
assembling, protecting and preserving the assets of such corporation for the benefit of those entitled thereto, subject to
the orders and directions of the court whose officer he is.
                    *Marcovich* v. *O'Brien, Auditor*, 101, 113 (8).

**RECORDS—**

On appeal, see APPEAL 15-28.

Public, evidence, certification, statute, see APPEAL 107.

**REMAINDERS—**
See WILLS.

**REMEDIES—**
Exclusive or optional, distinction, see SALES 5.
Vendor's lien, enforcement, see VENDOR AND PURCHASER 8.

**REMEDY AT LAW—**
See EQUITY.
Inefficiency of, injunctive relief, see INJUNCTION.

**REMITTITUR—**
Cure of verdict by, see APPEAL 113.

**REPRESENTATIONS—**
See INSURANCE 8, 15.

**RES GESTAE—**
See CARRIERS 1; EVIDENCE.

**RES JUDICATA—**
See JUDGMENT; JUSTICES OF THE PEACE.

**REVIEW—**
Of judgments on appeal, see APPEAL.

**REHEARING—**
Petition for, scope of review, see APPEAL 60.

**REPLEVIN—**
See BANKRUPTCY; CHATTEL MORTGAGES.

**RISKS—**
Assumption of, see MASTER AND SERVANT.

**RULES OF COURTS—**
See APPEAL; COURTS.

**SALES—**
See BROKERS; CONTRACTS 4; EXECUTORS AND ADMINISTRATORS.
For taxes, see TAXATION.

1. *Action for Price.—Answer.—Sufficiency.—*In an action on account to collect the price of goods sold, defendant's answer that the goods were purchased from the seller's agent under an agreement that they were to be charged to him, and not to defendant, and that such stipulation was embodied in the written order for the goods received and accepted by the seller, is sufficient as against demurrer.
                    *Excel Furniture Co. v. Brock,* 494, 501 (6).

2. *Action for Price.—Answer.—Sufficiency.—*In an action on account to collect for goods sold, the averments of the answer are held sufficient to show that plaintiff's agent, who was indebted

**SALES—Continued.**

to defendant, assumed to have authority to sell the goods and have the price charged to his account with defendant, and that the written order, which advised plaintiff of such assumption of authority, was the only order given for the goods and that they were delivered thereunder.

*Excel Furniture Co. v. Brock,* 494, 499 (2).

3. *Contract.—Construction.—Action for Purchase Price.—* Where, in an action to recover the purchase price of goods sold, plaintiff relies on a contract made up of letters and telegrams, effect must be given to all parts of the contract alleged, if it can be done without doing violence to the evident intention of the parties, as ascertained from a consideration of all portions of the writings. *Robbins v. Brazil Syndicate, etc., Co.,* 455, 463 (4).

4. *Contracts.—Breach of Warranty.—Remedies.—Return of Property.—*A written contract of warranty of a stallion, providing that in case of a breach thereof the vendor will take the stallion back and that the buyer will accept another stallion of equal value and return the former to the seller in as sound condition as at the time of delivery, provides an exclusive remedy for a breach of the warranty, which is available to ·the purchaser, under the contract, only in case he returns or offers to return the stallion. *Crouch v. Fahl,* 257, 263, 265 (1).

5. *Contracts.— Breach of Warranty.— Remedies.— Exclusive Remedy.—Return of Property.—*Where a warranty confers on the purchaser of personal property the mere right or privileg? of returning the property in case it does not comply with the warranty and making settlement on specified terms, but does not require him to do so to avail himself of a breach, it is the general rule that such stipulation confers merely an optional or cumulative remedy, so that the purchaser may retain the property and maintain an action for damages based on the breach of the warranty; but where the stipulation for the return of the property, if not as warranted, is mandatory, the remedy afforded thereby is exclusive. *Crouch v. Fahl,* 257, 264 (2).

6. *Contracts.—Warranty.—Remedy for Breach.—Extension.—* Where a contract of warranty provided that the purchaser should return the property before a specified date if found not to be as warránted, a subsequent agreement between the parties that the purchaser should try the property another year extended the warranty for that length of time and required a return of the property at the expiration thereof to make available an action for a breach of the warranty; and, in the absence of proof that the buyer returned or offered to return the property within the time stipulated, the evidence is insufficient to sustain a verdict in favor of the purchaser for damages for breach of the warranty. *Crouch v. Fahl,* 257, 266 (3).

7. *Contract.—Construction.—Certainty.—Action to Recover Purchase Price.—Answer.—Sufficiency.—*Where, in an action to recover the purchase price of goods sold, plaintiff alleged a contract consisting of letters and telegrams, wherein defendant wrote "Quote us 25-50's Santos 4's same as last," and plaintiff wired "Santos fours sixteen and half subject to return confirmation," and defendant then replied by telegram, "Ship twenty-five fifties Santos fours at quotation," such contract is so ambiguous, especially the meaning of the phrase "same as last" that parol evidence must be resorted to in order to ascertain the interpretation to be placed on the contract; hence an answer

SALES—Continued.

averring that the words "same as last" had a special meaning established by prior dealings between the parties and was understood as signifying delivery at the city where defendants resided, with the right to inspect the goods, and that delivery was not so made, is sufficient as against demurrer.

*Robbins* v. *Brazil Syndicate, etc., Co.*, 455, 464 (7).

8. *Conditions in Written Order Accepted by Seller.—Effect.—* Where a seller receives a written order for goods showing that the price was to be charged to his agent and not to the buyer, the seller cannot accept the order and deliver the goods thereunder without being bound by such conditions.

*Excel Furniture Co.* v. *Brock*, 494, 500 (3).

9. *Delivery to Carrier.—Effect.—*Where goods are bought at one place to be consigned and transported to the purchaser at another place, it is the general rule, in the absence of a contrary arrangement, that delivery by the seller to a common carrier is a delivery to the purchaser, since the carrier thereby becomes the agent of the purchaser and title to the property passes to him at the time of such delivery.

*Robbins* v. *Brazil Syndicate, etc., Co.*, 455, 460 (1).

10. *Delivery to Carrier.—Effect.—Right of Inspection.—*The right of inspection, in the absence of any established custom or agreement to the contrary, does not prevent the title from passing to the purchaser on delivery to the carrier of goods duly consigned to the purchaser, but if, on inspection the goods are not found to be such as were purchased, that fact may authorize a rescission of the contract of sale.

*Robbins* v. *Brazil Syndicate, etc., Co.*, 455, 461 (2).

11. *Delivery to Carrier.—Effect.—Recovery of Purchase Price.* If goods are sold to be delivered by the seller at the residence or place of business of the purchaser, a delivery to the carrier is not a delivery to the purchaser, since in such case the carrier is the agent of the seller, and failure to deliver the goods to the purchaser according to the terms of the sale will defeat recovery of the purchase price of the goods.

*Robbins* v. *Brazil Syndicate, etc., Co.*, 455, 461 (3).

SATISFACTION—

Entry of, as to judgment, vacating, see JUDGMENT 5.

SCHOOLS AND SCHOOL DISTRICTS—

1. *Official Bonds.—Action.—Parties.—*Either the trustee or the civil township, as relator, may prosecute an action on the bond of a preceding trustee to recover funds belonging to or due to the civil township, and likewise the trustee or the school township may, as relator, prosecute a like action to recover funds due or belonging to the school township, or in one action, either the trustee, as relator, or both corporations, as relators, may prosecute such an action to recover funds severally due the two corporations.          *State, ex rel.* v. *Stevens*, 561, 565 (4).

2. *Joint Elementary and High School.—Relocation.—Township Trustee.—Powers.—Statute.—*It is within the discretionary power of a township trustee to change the site of a joint elementary and high-school building by constructing another elsewhere, and injunction will not issue to restrain him from so doing where it does not appear that the trustee has exceeded

## SCHOOLS AND SCHOOL DISTRICTS—Continued.

the scope of his discretionary authority and there is no charge of bad faith or fraud, §6417 *et seq.* Burns 1914, Acts 1893 p. 17, which provides that a petition for the relocation of a school building shall be signed by a majority of the patrons of the school, applying only to the relocation of district schools, and it is not necessary for a majority of the patrons of a high school to join with a trustee in a petition for its relocation.

*Parker* v. *Humfleet*, 281.

## SELF-SERVING DECLARATIONS—

See EVIDENCE 7.

## SPECIAL FINDINGS—

See TRIAL.

## SPECIFICATION OF ERRORS—

See APPEAL 27, 45-47.

## STATES—

Civil action by, appeal without bond, statute, see APPEAL 10.

## STATUTE OF LIMITATIONS—

See LIMITATION OF ACTIONS.

## STATUTES—

Action on, rule, see ACTION.

Appeal, right of, power of legislature, see APPEAL 1, 2.

For statutes cited and construed in this volume, see p. xxv.

Federal, supersede state, as to interstate shipment, see COMMERCE.

1. *Repeal by Implication.—Recovery of Costs.—Premiums on Bonds Executed by Corporate Sureties.*—The repeal of a statute by implication is not favored, and, in the absence of a repealing clause, the act of 1901, Acts 1901 p. 63, §5737 *et seq.* Burns 1914, concerning the incorporation and regulation of bonding and surety companies, did not repeal the act of 1897, Acts 1897 p. 192, §5728 *et seq.* Burns 1914, relating in part to the charging by litigants, as costs, the expense of procuring sureties on bonds or undertakings required in any action; and, although §7 of the latter act, concerning the recovery, as costs, of money paid as premiums on bonds executed by surety companies, was declared invalid, when embodied in the act of 1901, as not being embraced within the scope of the title of such act, it is still in full force and effect as part of the act of 1897. (*Indianapolis, etc., Traction Co.* v. *Brennan* [1909], 174 Ind. 1, distinguished.)

*Jose* v. *Hunter*, 298, 300, 302 (1).

2. *Validity.—Title.*—The title of the act of 1897 (§5728 *et seq.* Burns 1914, Acts 1897 p. 192, 196), is sufficiently comprehensive to embrace the subject-matter of §7 thereof, which relates to the taxing, as costs of premiums paid by litigants to corporate surety-companies for the execution of bonds or other undertakings.

*Jose* v. *Hunter*, 298, 302 (2).

## STOCKHOLDERS—

See CORPORATIONS.

**STREAMS—**

See WATERS AND WATERCOURSES.

**STREET RAILROADS—**

See CARRIERS; NEGLIGENCE; RAILROADS.

*Injuries to Person on Track.—Evidence.—Last Clear Chance.— Jury Questions.*—In an action against a street railroad company for personal injuries sustained when plaintiff was struck by a car, the right of recovery being predicated on the last clear chance doctrine, whether the motorman, who saw plaintiff running backward across the street toward the track, knew, or should have known, of her peril in time to have avoided the accident, and whether after discovering her peril he used reasonable and ordinary care under the circumstances to avoid injuring plaintiff, were questions for the jury.

*Croly* v. *Indianapolis Traction, etc., Co.,* 663, 670 (5).

**STREETS—**

See MUNICIPAL CORPORATIONS.

Opening in sidewalk, guarding, liability for injuries to pedestrians, see LANDLORD AND TENANT 5-9.

Use of, by licensee, liability, see TELEGRAPHS AND TELEPHONES.

**SUBROGATION—**

*Payment of Taxes.—Liability.—Rights of Payor.*—Where an executrix was obligated to pay the taxes on her decedent's realty, but permitted them to become delinquent, and the purchaser of the real estate paid such taxes after final settlement of the estate to prevent the loss of part of his lands, he is entitled to recover the money so paid, on the principle of subrogation, from those who should have paid it.

*Barnum* v. *Rallihan,* 349, 363 (16).

**SUBSEQUENT APPEALS—**

See APPEAL 134.

**SUBSTITUTION—**

Of party, see BANKRUPTCY.

**SUPPLEMENTARY PROCEEDINGS—**

See EXECUTION.

**SURETYSHIP—**

See PRINCIPAL AND SURETY.

**SURPLUSAGE—**

Answers to interrogatories as, see CONTRACTS 2.

**SURVIVORSHIP—**

Words of, see WILLS.

**SWAMP LANDS—**

See PUBLIC LANDS.

## TAXATION—

Payment of taxes by purchaser of land, rights, see SUBROGATION.
Tax sale, purchase of land by cotenant, effect, see TENANCY IN COMMON.

1. *Collection of Taxes.—Injunction.—Pleading and Proof.*—One seeking to enjoin the collection of taxes must show by averment and proof either that the property upon which the taxes are assessed is not subject to taxation or that such taxes have been paid. *Barnum* v. *Rallihan*, 349, 358 (3).

2. *Collection of Taxes.—Resort to Personalty.*—Under §10324 Burns 1914, Acts 1903 p. 49, relating to the sale of property for nonpayment of taxes, personalty is the primary source of funds out of which to pay all taxes, and, if the person liable for taxes has personal property in the county, it is the duty of the officials charged with the collection of taxes to exhaust it before selling the assessed realty. *Barnum* v. *Rallihan*, 349, 358 (4).

3. *Inheritance Tax.—Appeal from Determination of Tax.—Statute.*—As the provisions of the inheritance tax law of 1913 (Acts 1913 p. 79 *et seq.*, §10143a *et seq.* Burns 1914), indicate that the legislature intended to make the ascertainment and collection of inheritance taxes a part of our probate law, and since the act contains no express denial of the right of appeal from judgments rendered thereunder, an appeal from a judgment of a probate court on the rehearing and redetermination of an inheritance tax may be taken under §2977 Burns 1914, §2454, R. S. 1881, providing that any person considering himself aggrieved by any decision of a circuit court growing out of any matter connected with a decedent's estate, may prosecute an appeal to the Supreme Court; and §15, clause 3, of the inheritance tax law, providing for a rehearing of the determination of an inheritance tax, refers only to the procedure in the trial court and does not bar an appeal. *Crittenberger* v. *State, etc., Trust Co.*, 151, 153 (2).

4. *Lien for Taxes.—Date of Attachment.*—The lien for taxes attaches to the property assessed upon the date that the taxes accrue. *Barnum* v. *Rallihan*, 349, 359 (6).

5. *Payment of Taxes.—Conditions.—Effect.—Recovery.*—Where the owner of lands sold to satisfy delinquent taxes tendered to the county treasurer the full amount of money necessary to redeem the land from the tax sale and it was received by him, an attempted imposition of certain conditions in the tender as to a refund of part of the money was of no effect, and on failure to comply with the conditions there could be no recovery of the money so paid. *Barnum* v. *Rallihan*, 349, 360 (8).

6. *Tax Deeds.—Validity.—Burden of Proof.*—Under §10380 Burns 1914, Acts 1891 p. 199, 275, making tax deeds *prima facie* evidence of the regularity of the sale of the land and all prior proceedings, and *prima facie* evidence of a valid title in fee in the grantee, a party assailing the validity of a tax deed has the burden of proof. *Hypes* v. *Nelson*, 304, 307 (3).

7. *Tax Sales.—Failure to Exhaust Personalty.—Sale of Realty.—Injunction.*—Where one liable for taxes has personal property in the county out of which his taxes may be collected, he may enjoin the sale of his real estate for the payment of such taxes. *Barnum* v. *Rallihan*, 349, 358 (2).

## TAXATION—Continued.

8. *Tax Sales.—Validity.*—Where an owner of land dies leaving ample funds in his estate with which to pay delinquent taxes assessed against his realty in his lifetime, but his executrix fails to pay the same and the county treasurer sells the land to satisfy such taxes but fails in various ways to comply with the law relating to the collection of delinquent taxes and the sale of land therefor, the purchaser could not acquire title to the real estate by virtue of such sale, since there was a failure to follow the law governing the collection of delinquent taxes.
*Barnum* v. *Rallihan*, 849, 359 (7).

9. *Tax Sales.—Invalid Sales.—Rights of Purchaser.*—Where a sale of land for taxes is invalid and ineffectual to convey title because the law for the collection of delinquent taxes was not followed, although the tax was valid and constituted a lien on the realty sold, the lien of the State is transferred to the purchaser at the sale.
*Barnum* v. *Rallihan*, 349, 360 (9).

10. *Tax Sales.—Invalid Sales.—Payment of Redemption Money to County Treasurer.—Effect.*—The payment to the county treasurer of the amount necessary to redeem land sold for taxes at an irregular sale inures to the benefit of the purchaser at such sale, and satisfies the lien acquired by him.
*Barnum* v. *Rallihan*, 349, 361 (10).

11. *Tax Sales.—Action to Redeem.—Complaint.—Sufficiency.*—A complaint, in an action to set aside a sale of land for taxes, is insufficient so far as seeking redemption from the tax sale, where it appears from the averments that the redemption is in legal contemplation already consummated, since there is no need of invoking the power of the court.
*Barnum* v. *Rallihan*, 349, 363 (15).

12. *Tax Sales.—Conduct of Sale.—Vadility.—Statute.*—Under §10356 Burns 1914, Acts 1891 p. 199, 269, providing that on the day fixed in the notice the county treasurer shall commence the sale for delinquent taxes and continue the same until so much of each parcel assessed shall be sold as will pay the taxes, a sale was valid where made by an auctioneer in the presence and under the direction of the county treasurer, even though such auctioneer had no written appointment and did not take any oath as deputy treasurer. *Hypes* v. *Nelson*, 304, 308 (7).

13. *Tax Sales.—Place of Holding.—Validity.—Statute.*—Under §10355 Burns 1914, Acts 1891 p. 199, 269, providing that tax sales shall be at public auction at the door of the county courthouse, a sale is valid, although conducted inside the courthouse near the door, which was closed at the time on account of cold weather. *Hypes* v. *Nelson*, 304, 308 (6).

14. *Tax Sales.—Search for Personal Property.—Demand.—Statute.*—Where a county treasurer, prior to making a sale of realty for delinquent taxes, not knowing that one in possession of the property involved was the real owner or claimed any interest therein, searched the tax duplicates for personal property belonging to the owner of record, but found none listed in her name for taxation, and made no further search or demand for property to pay the delinquent taxes, this was sufficient under §10324 Burns 1914, Acts 1903 p. 49, 60, making it the duty of the county treasurer to make demand and a search for personal property out of which to pay delinquent

## TAXATION—Continued.

taxes of each resident delinquent, since the statute refers tc
delinquents whose names appear on the tax duplicate.
　　　　　　　　　　　　　*Hypes* v. *Nelson*, 304, 308 (5).

15. *Tax Sales.—Validity.*—To convey title, a tax sale must be
conducted in accordance with the statute,' and if any material
act required has been omitted, or has been improperly done, the
sale is ineffectual and insufficient to convey title to the purchaser.　　　　　　　　　　　*Hypes* v. *Nelson*, 304, 307 (4).

16. *Taxes on Realty.—Death of Owner.—Liability of Estate.*—
Taxes accruing on realty before the owner's death but not those
accruing thereafter, become a charge against him, as well as
a lien upon all his property, and should be paid by his executor
out of the decedent's personal estate.
　　　　　　　　　*Barnum* v. *Rallihan*, 349, 358, 359, 363 (5).

## TELEGRAPHS AND TELEPHONES—

1. *Guy Wires.—Care Required by Telephone Company.*—The
primary and general use of a highway is for travel, and, although a telephone company may have the right to occupy a
highway with its poles, yet, if it secures them with guy wires,
its duty is to use reasonable care to so erect and maintain such
wires as not to endanger the public travel, or the safety of individuals in the reasonable and ordinary use of the highway.
　　　　　　*Lafayette Telephone Co.* v. *Cunningham*, 136, 142 (1).

2. *Injuries from Guy Wire.—Complaint.—Averments.—Duty to
Use Care.—Negligent Violation of Duty.*—In an action by a
police officer against a telephone company for injuries incurred
when plaintiff tripped over a guy wire, averments in the complaint that plaintiff, at the time of the injury, was walking
along a city street in the performance of his duties and that
defendant had erected its poles and wires in such street show
that defendant was charged with the duty to use reasonable
care to so maintain its guy wire that it would not endanger
the use of the street by the public, including plaintiff, so that,
such duty being shown, allegations that the guy wire was
"carelessly, negligently and unlawfully constructed and built in
said highway * * * and has been carelessly, negligently
and unlawfully maintained" by defendant, sufficiently charge a
negligent violation of its duty to plaintiff, there being nothing
shown by the complaint which would destroy the effect of such
general allegations of negligence.
　　　　　　*Lafayette Telephone Co.* v. *Cunningham*, 136, 142 (2).

3. *Maintenance of Guy Wire.—Care Required.—Crossing Street
Between Street Intersections.*—In an action against a telephone
company for personal injuries, the fact that the plaintiff, when
injured by falling over a guy wire, was attempting to cross a
public street at a place where there was no intersection of a
street or alley, and at a place not provided for crossing, while
pertinent to the question of whether plaintiff was guilty of
contributory negligence, did not discharge the defendant from
its duty to use reasonable care in maintaining its guy wire so
as not to endanger the public in the use of the street.
　　　　　　*Lafayette Telephone Co.* v. *Cunningham*, 136, 143 (3).

4. *Injuries to Pedestrian from Guy Wire.—Crossing Street in
Absence of Street Crossing.*—In an action against a telephone
company for injuries incurred by plaintiff falling over a tele-

## TELEGRAPHS AND TELEPHONES—Continued.

phone guy wire, the fact, as established by the jury's answers
to interrogatories, that plaintiff went upon a grassplot for the
purpose of crossing the street at a point where there was no
cross-walk, did not relieve the defendant of its responsibility to
him, since a pedestrian is not restricted to cross-walks or street
intersections in crossing a street, but he may cross at any place,
and he is not necessarily guilty of contributory negligence in
so doing. *Lafayette Telephone Co.* v. *Cunningham*, 136, 146 (8).

5. *Injuries to Pedestrian from Guy Wire.—Knowledge of Obstruction.—Contributory Negligence.—Question for Jury.*—In
an action by a police officer for injuries received in falling over
a guy wire, evidence that plaintiff had previous knowledge of
the presence of the wire and that he momentarily forgot it
when summoned across the street by his superior officer were
facts for the consideration of the jury in determining whether
the injured party was exercising reasonable care.
*Lafayette Telephone Co.* v. *Cunningham*, 136, 149 (14).

6. *Injuries to Pedestrian from Guy Wire.—Contributory Negligence.—Evidence.—Knowledge of Obstruction.*—In an action
against a telephone company by a police officer, who was injured by falling over a guy wire when attempting to cross a
street, the fact that the plaintiff had previous knowledge of the
obstruction does not, *per se*, establish his contributory negligence. *Lafayette Telephone Co.* v. *Cunningham*, 136, 149 (13).

7. *Injuries to Pedestrian from Guy Wire.—Negligence.—Evidence.—Sufficiency.*—In an action against a telephone company
for injuries incurred by plaintiff, a night police officer, tripping
over a guy wire when attempting to cross a street in the performance of his duties, where there was evidence that the guy
wire, which was located in a grassplot between the sidewalk
and curb and could not be seen easily at night, was strung
from the top of a telephone pole to an anchor which protruded
about five inches above the ground, that the wire was not properly constructed for use in a street, and that it would have been
practicable either to have fastened such a guy wire to a stub-
pole several feet above the ground or to have so trussed the
telephone pole so that no guy wire would have been needed,
such evidence was sufficient to warrant the jury finding that
the defendant was negligent in using the particular construction of guying its pole, rather than some construction which
would have dispensed with the guy wire or which would have
made it more conspicuous or elevated it so as to place it where
it could not trip travelers on the street.
*Lafayette Telephone Co.* v. *Cunningham*, 136, 147 (12).

8. *License to Place Poles and Wires in Street.—Care Required
by Licensee.*—The proper municipal officers may devote a portion of a city's sidewalks to the use of telephone poles, lines
and guy wires, but such portions of the sidewalks are, in the
absence of an ordinance showing the contrary, a part of
the street which the pedestrian may use for travel, and any
authority or license to use such part of the street for telephone
poles and wires must be exercised with reference to the possible
uses thereof by pedestrians, which must be anticipated by the
licensee, and his license will not absolve him from the duty
of using ordinary care not to expose pedestrians to unnecessary
danger in using such portion of the street.
*Lafayette Telephone Co.* v. *Cunningham*, 136, 145 (7).

## TELEGRAPHS AND TELEPHONES—Continued.

2. *Use of Highway.—Care Required.—License to Locate Poles and Wires in Highway.*—A telegraph or telephone company using a highway is under a duty to exercise care to prevent injury to persons using the highway, and a license from a municipal corporation to use the way does not relieve the company from that duty; but, on the contrary, the acceptance of the license implies a duty on the part of the electric company to exercise care and diligence to prevent injury to persons using the highway.

*Lafayette Telephone Co. v. Cunningham, 136, 144 (5).*

## TENANCY IN COMMON—

1. *Ouster of Cotenant.—Purchase of Land at Tax Sale.*—Where a tenant in possession purchases the land at a tax sale and takes a deed in his name, claiming at the time of the sale and subsequent to the execution of the tax deed that he is the owner, and is holding possession under such claim and deed, he is in legal contemplation claiming under a deed conveying the whole estate and will be deemed to have ousted his cotenant.

*Butler v. Butler, 533, 536 (2).*

2. *Purchase of Property by Cotenant at Tax Sale.—Effect.*—Where one of several tenants in common of an estate purchases the common property at a tax sale, he cannot set up his title thus acquired against the common title, but the tax title enures to the common benefit of himself and his cotenants, although the common property is subject to the charge of the purchaser for the money expended at the tax sale.

*Butler v. Butler, 533, 537 (3).*

3. *Purchase of Property by Cotenant at Tax Sale.—Reimbursement.—Rate of Interest.*—Where one of several tenants in common purchases the common property at a tax sale, the title thus acquired enures to the common benefit of himself and his cotenants and the purchaser cannot profit by the transaction, so that the charge on the common property to which he is entitled for his purchase is limited to the amount paid at the sale and six per cent interest thereon, §10393 Burns 1914, Acts 1901 p. 336, relating to principal and interest for tax liens, having no application in such a case.

*Butler v. Butler, 533, 537 (4).*

4. *Tenant in Possession.—Liability for Rents.*—The possession of one tenant in common is the possession of all, and the tenant in possession is not required to pay rent unless he excludes his cotenant; but if he receives rent from a third person, he must account for it.                          *Butler v. Butler, 533, 536 (1).*

## TEXT-BOOKS—

Cited in this volume, see p. xxx.

## THEORY—

See PLEADING.

## THREATS—

Execution of contract under, effect, see CONTRACTS 11.

## TIMBER—

Cutting and removing, measure of damages, see TRESPASS

TITLE—

See DEEDS; EASEMENTS; EMINENT DOMAIN; JUSTICES OF THE PEACE.

Proof of a fee simple, does not show right of possession, see EJECTMENT.

Tax deed, title acquired by cotenant, see TENANCY IN COMMON.

TOWNS—

See MUNICIPAL CORPORATIONS.

TOWNSHIPS—

See DRAINS; EVIDENCE 2; SCHOOLS AND SCHOOL DISTRICTS.
Liability for live stock killed by dogs, see ANIMALS.
Appeal by, designation of appellant, see APPEAL 8, 9, 90.

TRADE-MARKS AND TRADE-NAMES—

1. *Name of Inventor.—Use by Rival Companies.*—Where one Deister, an inventor of certain mining machinery called a concentrator, after organizing a company known as the Deister Concentrator Company and assigning to it his patents and giving it the right to manufacture and sell machinery made thereunder, disposed of his interest in such concern but was not by contract or otherwise precluded thereafter from the use of his name in connection with another business, injunction will not issue at the instance of such company to restrain the mere use of the name "Deister" by a new corporation, known as the Deister Machine Company, subsequently organized by the inventor to fabricate and dispose of his improved patented concentrator.
    *Deister Concentrator Co. v. Deister Mach. Co.*, 412, 419 (2).

2. *Unfair Competition.—Use of Surname in Business Enterprises.*—A person may make a fair and reasonable use of his own name in commercial pursuits, and in so doing he cannot be held liable for incidental damages to a competitor in business using the same name, but he must be honest in such use and not injure the good will of a rival by palming off his goods as that of such rival; nor can he employ his name fraudulently so as to appropriate the good will of an established business of his competitor.
    *Deister Concentrator Co. v. Deister Mach. Co.*, 412, 418 (1).

3. *Unfair Competition.*—Nothing less than conduct tending to pass off one man's merchandise or business as that of another will constitute unfair competition, the essence of the wrong being the sale of goods of one manufacturer for those of a competitor.
    *Deister Concentrator Co. v. Deister Mach. Co.*, 412, 419 (3).

4. *Unfair Competition.—Intent.*—In order to constitute unfair competition by conduct tending to pass off the goods of one person for that of another, it is not necessary that one should take some affirmative action in that respect, or that he should intend to sell his goods for those of his rival, as actual deception is not necessary; for, if the name under which he disposes of his products, together with the method of disposing of the same, is manifestly liable to deceive purchasers, the result would be accomplished.
    *Deister Concentrator Co. v. Deister Mach. Co.*, 412, 420 (4).

**TRADE-MARKS AND TRADE-NAMES—Continued.**

5. *Unfair Competition.—Deception.—Knowledge of Purchasers.*
—The class of persons who buy the particular kind of articles
manufactured, such as servants or children, upon the one hand,
or persons skilled in the particular trade, upon the other, must
be considered in determining the question of probable deception.
   *Deister Concentrator Co.* v. *Deister Mach. Co.*, 412, 421 (5).

6. *Unfair Competition.—Use of Name.—Injunctive Relief.—
When Granted.*—Where one Deister, an inventor and patentee
of certain mining machinery called a concentrator, organized a
company known as the Deister Concentrator Company, to manufacture and sell such machinery, and assigned his patents to it,
retaining the right to manufacture the concentrators for sale
in foreign countries, and thereafter disposed of his interest in
the company, with no restrictions as to his right to again engage in the manufacture and sale of mining machinery under
the name "Deister" or the use of that name in connection therewith, injunction for unfair competition will not issue at the
instance of such company to restrain a corporation, known as
the Deister Machine Company, subsequently organized by the
inventor to manufacture his concentrators under new patents
in this country and under the old patents for the foreign market, from using the name "Deister" in the title of the corporation or upon its manufactured product, where the machines
made under the new patents were easily distinguished from the
type made under the old patents, and the concentrators were
sold to those familiar with mining machinery, thereby diminishing the likelihood of purchasers being deceived, and in view
of the fact that the new company's advertisements contained the
words, "Note carefully the new name," and its catalogues were
of a different color from those circulated by the older company.
   *Deister Concentrator Co.* v. *Deister Mach. Co.*, 412, 421 (6).

7. *Unfair Competition.—Resemblance Between Devices.—Use of
Name.—Questions of Fact.*—No inflexible rule can be formulated as to what conduct will constitute unfair competition, and
as the degree of resemblance between the names of articles
made and sold, as well as the precaution taken to differentiate
one article from another, or the name, is not capable of exact
definition, it becomes, from the nature of the case, a question of
fact to be determined by the circumstances as they are brought
before the court in each particular case.
   *Deister Concentrator Co.* v. *Deister Mach. Co.*, 412, 424 (7).

**TRANSCRIPTS—**

See APPEAL 15-28.

Additional, how made part of record, see APPEAL 20.

**TRESPASS—**

1. *Actions.—Cutting and Removal of Timber.—Measure of Damages.*—In an action to recover damages for the wrongful removal of timber under a complaint seeking recovery for injury
to the land caused thereby, the diminution in the value of the
land occasioned by cutting and removing the timber for the
most part immature, rather than the value of the timber as a
severed product, was the proper measure of recovery, particularly as much young and growing timber was destroyed in felling and hauling the trees which were removed.
   *Lewis* v. *Guthrie*, 8, 13 (2).

**TRESPASS—Continued.**

2. *Evidence.—Sufficiency.*—In an action against joint tort-feasors to recover damages for trespass to timber lands and the wrongful removal of timber therefrom, evidence as to the removal and sale of timber from plaintiff's land owing to a mistake as to boundary lines and the acquiescence by two of the defendants in an estimate of the amount of timber taken is held sufficient to sustain a verdict against such defendants, but insufficient to justify a verdict against one of the defendants where it appeared that he neither participated in, directed, nor ratified the trespass complained of.
*Lewis* v. *Guthrie*, 8, 10 (1).

**TRIAL—**

See COSTS; COURTS; EVIDENCE; JURY; NEW TRIAL.

For review of instructions on appeal, see APPEAL.

For review of rulings at, see APPEAL.

For trial of particular actions or proceedings, see the various specific subjects.

1. *Conclusions of Law.—Sufficiency.*—In an action to enforce an oil and gas lease, a conclusion of law that on and prior to a certain date the lease had been forfeited and was null and void is not subject to criticism as containing a finding of facts.
*Harris* v. *Riggs*, 201, 209 (6).

2. *Conclusions of Law.—Sufficiency.*—In an action to quiet title based on an oil and gas lease, conclusions of law that plaintiffs had no right, title, or interest in the leased premises in controversy, are entitled to no relief in the action and should pay the costs of the suit are supported by the finding of the ultimate fact that the lease was abandoned.
*Harris* v. *Riggs*, 201, 209 (7).

3. *Findings of Fact.—Failure to Find.—Effect.*—The absence of a finding on any material issuable fact is by presumption a finding against the party having the burden on that issue.
*Hypes* v. *Nelson*, 304, 307 (2).

4. *Findings of Fact.—Ultimate and Evidentiary Facts.*—Ultimate and not evidentiary facts should be stated in a finding of fact, and facts contained in conclusions of law must be disregarded.
*Harris* v. *Riggs*, 201, 208 (1).

5. *Findings of Fact.—How Considered.—Presumptions.*—A finding of fact should be considered as a whole, and all intendments and presumptions are in its favor rather than against it, and if, by considering one part in connection with other parts, relative to the same matter, the finding can be said to be sufficient, it will be upheld.
*Harris* v. *Riggs*, 201, 208 (2).

6. *Findings of Fact.—Evidentiary Facts.*—While evidentiary facts should not be included in a finding of facts, yet their presence therein does not necessarily render the finding insufficient to support conclusions of law. *Harris* v. *Riggs*, 201, 208 (3).

7. *Findings of Fact.—Sufficiency.*—Where the primary facts contained in a finding of facts are of such a character that they necessitate the inference of an ultimate fact, such ultimate fact will be treated as found and as sufficient on appeal, even though there may be a technical defect of statement in the finding.
*Harris* v. *Riggs*, 201, 208 (4).

**TRIAL—Continued.**

8. *Findings of Fact.—Ultimate Facts.—Sufficiency.—*If a finding of facts contains sufficient ultimate facts to support the judgment, it will be sufficient, though it may not find all the issuable facts and may contain primary or evidentiary facts.

*Harris* v. *Riggs,* 201, 208 (5).

9. *Findings of Fact.—Ultimate Facts.—Evidentiary Facts.—*Where, in an action on an oil and gas lease, the trial court in its findings of facts found as an ultimate fact that the lease had been abandoned by the lessees prior to a certain date, such finding is not invalidated by the court's statement of evidentiary facts which authorized the inference of the ultimate facts that the lease had been abandoned and forfeited under a construction thereof mutually agreed and acted upon by the parties.

*Harris* v. *Riggs,* 201, 209 (8).

10. *Evidence, Order of Receiving.—Discretion of Court.—*The trial court has discretionary power as to the time or order of receiving testimony, and a judgment will not be reversed for any irregularity in regard thereto unless it clearly appears that such discretion has been abused.

*Croly* v. *Indianapolis Traction, etc., Co.,* 663, 665 (1).

11. *Instruction.—Malice.—Invading Province of Jury.—*In an action for alienation of the husband's affections, an instruction defining malice and informing the jury that, if it found that defendants did the acts charged in the complaint and thereby caused the alienation of the husband's affections, and if it found that such acts were done purposely without just or probable cause, it could infer that such acts were done maliciously, but that in case it should so find, whether such inference should be drawn from the acts of the defendants was for the jury to determine from all the evidence, was not objectionable as invading the province of the jury to determine whether it should infer that the acts charged were malicious.

*Daywitt* v. *Daywitt,* 444, 449 (4).

12. *Instructions.—Special Interrogatories.—When Answered.—*Where interrogatories are submitted to the jury under the provisions of §572 Burns 1914, Acts 1897 p. 128, it is proper, when requested, to instruct the jury that "the law does not prescribe when you shall consider and answer the interrogatories which will be submitted to you, and you are at liberty to take into consideration and answer them either before or after you have agreed upon a general verdict, according to your own desire and convenience."

*S. W. Little Coal Co.* v. *O'Brien,* 504, 520 (16).

13. *Instructions.—Special Interrogatories.—When Answered.—Statute.* —Section 572 Burns 1914, Acts 1897 p. 128, requiring that a general verdict be rendered in all cases tried by a jury, except cases in equity, and that where requested by either party, the court shall instruct the jury "when they render a general verdict to find specially upon particular questions of fact to be stated to them in the form of interrogatories," requires only that the interrogatories be answered and is not directory as to when, during the jury's deliberation, this shall be done, since the clause, "when they render a general verdict," is not to be interpreted as meaning after the jury has agreed on a general verdict, as the word "render" as used in the statute means not only the arrival at an agreement, but also re-

**TRIAL—Continued.**

22. *Verdict.—Answers to Interrogatories.—Failure of Jury to Agree.—Discharge.*—Under §572 Burns 1914, Acts 1897 p. 128, requiring the rendition of a general verdict and providing for the submission of interrogatories in cases tried by jury, where interrogatories are submitted, and the jury fails to agree on either the· general verdict or the answers to interrogatories, there is no verdict and the jury should be discharged for failure to agree.     *S. W. Little Coal Co.* v. *O'Brien*, 504, 523 (18).

23. *Verdict.—Scope and Effect.*—A general verdict for plaintiff is a finding in his favor of every issuable fact and is conclusive on all questions where there is any evidence tending to support the verdict.     *Chesapeake, etc., R. Co.* v. *Jordan*, 365, 377 (8).

24. *Verdict.—Construction.*—The verdict of a jury for the plaintiff is a finding for plaintiff of every fact essential to a recovery.     *National Life Ins. Co.* v. *Headrick*, 54, 58 (1).

25. *Verdict.—Conflicting Answers to Interrogatories.*—Answers to interrogatories which are contradictory neutralize each other and the general verdict prevails.
     *Taylor* v. *McCormick*, 695, 698 (2).

26. *Witnesses.—Credibility.—Jury Question.*—In action for alienation, declarations which are part of the *res gestae* are admissible in evidence, and it is for the jury to determine whether they were made in good faith by the party offering them or were merely manufactured evidence for use at the trial, it being no objection to such declarations that they were self-serving.     *Daywitt* v. *Daywitt*, 444, 454 (10).

**TRUSTS—**

See EXECUTORS AND ADMINISTRATORS; GUARDIAN AND WARD; RECEIVERS.

Bonds of trustees, taxation of premium as part of costs, see COSTS 3.

**UNFAIR COMPETITION—**

See TRADE-MARKS AND TRADE-NAMES.

**VACATION—**

Appeal, coparties, construction of statute, see APPEAL 5, 6.
Parties to, appeal, see APPEAL 57.

**VENDOR AND PURCHASER—**

See APPEAL 83; BROKERS; CONTRACTS; PRINCIPAL AND AGENT; SALES.

1. *Contract for Sale of Realty.—Forfeiture for Nonpayment of Installments.*—Where a contract for the sale of land stipulated that the purchaser should pay the purchase price in monthly installments and expressly made time in the payment of deferred installments material and of the essence of the contract, and it contained a forfeiture clause requiring the purchaser to make his payments at the times specified to prevent a forfeiture of the money paid, his failure to make payments for more than a year without any fault of the vendor entitled the latter to treat such failure as an abandonment and to forfeit the contract, so that the purchaser, in an action for money had and

## VENDOR AND PURCHASER—Continued.

received, could not recover the money paid on the contract, even though he made a belated tender of the unpaid portion of the purchase price and demanded a deed.  *Krisky* v. *Bryan*, 611.

2. *Remedies of Vendor.—Lien.—Waiver.*—Where one holding a vendor's lien accepted the vendee's note for the unpaid portion of the purchase price of land, he did not thereby waive his lien.
*Essig* v. *Porter*, 318, 321 (3).

3. *Remedies of Vendor.—Vendor's Lien.—Purchase Price of Realty.*—Where plaintiff, in an action to enforce a vendor's lien, after having purchased and paid for a tract of land and entered into possession, caused a deed of conveyance to be made directly from his vendor to his purchaser, he was entitled to a vendor's lien for the purchase price, for when the actual vendor of realty holds only a title in equity and the conveyance is made directly from the party holding the legal title in trust, a vendor's lien arises in favor of the actual vendor.
*Essig* v. *Porter*, 318, 319 (1).

4. *Street Improvements.—Proceedings.—Record.—Notice.*—The proceedings of municipal corporations in street improvements are required by law to be duly recorded and they are open to public inspection, and persons who acquire real estate encumbered by assessments evidenced by such records are bound by the constructive notice given thereby when duly kept; but only records which the law requires to be kept and which have actually been so kept as to impart notice ι those who examine them are binding.  *Nat. Exchange Bank* v. *Smith*, 574, 580 (3).

5. *Street Improvements.—Record of Proceedings.—Notice.*—Where it appeared in an action to foreclose the statutory lien securing a street improvement bond, that the record kept by the municipal corporation showed the proceedings for the improvement of the street, the making of the assessment, the waiver filed by the owner of the realty involved in the action; the issuance of the bonds payable to the contractor or bearer, and that as to the lot in suit such assessment was unsatisfied, a purchaser of the lot is charged with constructive notice of such facts, and with such other facts as an ordinarily diligent search would have disclosed, since the facts shown by the record are sufficient to put him on inquiry.
*Nat. Exchange Bank* v. *Smith*, 574, 584 (7).

6. *Vendor's Lien.—Notice to Purchaser.*—Where a grantee of land, the defendant in an action to enforce a vendor's lien, was present when her grantor gave her note, and knew of its execution and that it was for unpaid purchase money for the land involved, and that the note was unpaid at the time such land was conveyed to her, such grantee took the land with notice that it was subject to a vendor's lien in favor of the payee of the note.  *Essig* v. *Porter*, 318, 321 (4).

7. *Vendor's Lien.—Purchaser Without Notice.—Rights of Parties.*—A remote grantor may enforce his vendor's lien against a subsequent purchaser without notice, who is afterwards notified of the lien, to the extent of the purchase price unpaid by him at the time he receives notice.  *Essig* v. *Porter*, 318, 322 (5).

8. *Vendor's Lien.—Enforcement.—Remedies of Vendor.—Judgment.*—Where, in an action to enforce a vendor's lien, it was found by the trial court that the grantor of the land involved knew at the time of the conveyance that it was subject to a

**VENDOR AND PURCHASER—Continued.**

vendor's lien, a judgment decreeing that the grantor pay into court a sufficient amount to satisfy the lien out of money in her possession derived from the sale of the land, and providing that she should be subject to citation and punishment for disobedience of the decree, was proper, since, in such a case equity will transfer the lien to the funds received from the sale of the land.
*Essig* v. *Porter*, 318, 322 (7).

**VERDICT—**

See APPEAL 96-115; MASTER AND SERVANT 28; TRIAL.

Direction of, is not grounds for independent assignment of error, see APPEAL 29.

Direction of, waiver of error, see APPEAL 84.

Contract, breach, damages, excessiveness, see DAMAGES 1.

**VESTED REMAINDERS—**

See WILLS.

**"VOID"—**

Construction, see INSURANCE 22.

**VOLUNTEERS—**

See MORTGAGES.

**WAIVER—**

See PLEADING 13.

Of error on appeal, see APPEAL 129-133.

Contracts, waiver of liability, validity, see RAILROADS 5.

Vendor's lien, acceptance of note, see VENDOR AND PURCHASER.

**WARRANTY—**

See CONTRACTS; SALES.

False, by administrator, in sale of realty, liability of estate, see EXECUTORS AND ADMINISTRATORS 7-10.

Represenation distinguished, see INSURANCE 8.

Promissory, construction, see INSURANCE 10, 11.

Breach of, defense, see INSURANCE 17.

**WATERS AND WATERCOURSES—**

See DRAINS; RAILROADS.

Natural watercourse, crossing of, by railroad, duties, see RAILROADS.

*Natural Watercourse.—Obstruction of Flood Channel.—Liability.* —Where a riparian owner obstructs the flood channel of a stream he is liable to respond in damages to any one injured.
*Dunn* v. *Chicago, etc., R. Co.*, 553, 558 (4).

**WIFE—**

See HUSBAND AND WIFE.

**WILLS—**

1. *Construction.— Remainders.— Estates Created.*— Where a testator devised to his daughter for life certain lands which, at her death, were to go to her children, should any survive, and, if not, to her grandchildren in fee simple, the child of the devisee, born subsequent to the execution of the will but prior to the death of the testator, is vested at the death of the testator with the fee, subject only to the life estate and to the one-third interest therein taken by the testator's widow under the laws of descent. *Paul, Gdn.*, v. *Dickinson Trust Co.*, 230, 233 (4).

2. *Construction.—Vesting of Estates.*—The law favors the vesting of remainders absolutely, rather than contingently or conditionally. *Paul, Gdn.*, v. *Dickinson Trust Co.*, 230, 233 (2).

3. *Construction.—Words of Postponement.—Vesting of Estates.* —The law looks with disfavor on postponing the vesting of estates, and the intent to do so must be clear and not depend upon inference or construction, the presumption being that words in a will postponing the estate relate to the beginning of the enjoyment of the remainder and not to the vesting of the estate, unless the contrary clearly appears. *Paul, Gdn.*, v. *Dickinson Trust Co.*, 230, 233 (1).

4. *Construction.—Words of Survivorship.*—Words of survivorship in a will generally refer to the death of the testator where the first taker is given a life estate and the remainder over is devised to another. *Paul, Gdn.*, v. *Dickinson Trust Co.*, 230, 233 (3).

**WIRES—**

See TELEGRAPHS AND TELEPHONES.

**WITNESSES—**

See APPEAL 85, 86; TRIAL 26.

Recalling of, after ruling on motion for peremptory instruction, review, see APPEAL 95.

**WORDS AND PHRASES—**

"Allowed," meaning of, see INSURANCE 3.

"Decision," meaning as used in statute, see APPEAL 71.

"Fair market value," meaning, see CONTRACTS 5.

"Negotiable and payable," construed as words of negotiability, see BILLS AND NOTES.

"Or," construed as connective, see INSURANCE 3.

"Place to work," meaning, see MASTER AND SERVANT 20.

"Render," use in statute, meaning, see TRIAL 13.

"Void," construction, INSURANCE 22.

"When," use in statute, meaning, see TRIAL 13.

"On or About."—The common understanding of the words "on or about," when used in connection with a definite point of time, is that they do not put the time at large but indicate that it is stated with approximate certainty. *Parker* v. *State*, 671, 673 (4).

**WORKMEN'S COMPENSATION ACT—**

See MASTER AND SERVANT.

Lightning Source UK Ltd.
Milton Keynes UK
UKHW031959020219
336576UK00009BA/228/P